109.

ANDRÉ GIDE
Homosexual Moralist

Frontispiece   *André Gide, aged twenty-four, in his travelling costume.*

——————— ANDRÉ GIDE ———————

Homosexual Moralist

Patrick Pollard

YALE UNIVERSITY PRESS
NEW HAVEN AND LONDON 1991

Set in Goudy Old Style by Excel Typesetters Co., Hong Kong
Printed and bound in Great Britain by The Bath Press, Avon

Library of Congress Cataloging-in-Publication Data

Pollard, Patrick
    André Gide: Homosexual Moralist/Patrick Pollard.
      p.   cm.
    Includes bibliographical references and index.
    ISBN 0-300-04998-6
      1. Gide, André, 1869-1951—Criticism and interpretation.
    2. Homosexuality and literature—France.   3. Ethics in literature.
    I. Title.
    PQ2613.I2Z6637   1991
    848'.91209—dc20   90-27047
                                                                        CIP

I know, and am persuaded by the Lord Jesus, that *there is* nothing unclean of itself: but to him that esteemeth any thing to be unclean, to him *it is* unclean.

Romans 14:14
(cited in 'Numquid et tu . . . ?'
Journal, I p. 592)

trahit sua quemque voluptas.

Vergil, *Eclogue* II 65

Contents

CONTENTS

List of Illustrations

Frontispiece *André Gide, aged twenty-four, in his travelling costume.* Photo private collection.

Note: The illustrations listed below are between pages 408 and 409.

Plate 1 *Portrait bust of Elagabalus.* Capitoline Museum, Rome.

Plate 2 *Mercury Inventing his Wand.* Idrac. Louvre, Paris. © Photo R.M.N.

Plate 3 *Doryphorus.* Polyclitus. From an illustration in Collignon, *Histoire de la sculpture grecque.*

Plate 4 *The Spinario.* Capitoline Museum, Rome.

Plate 5 *The Barberini Faun.* Glyptothek, Munich.

Plate 6 *David.* Donatello. Bargello, Florence.

Plate 7 *David.* Pollaiuolo. State Museum, Berlin.

Plate 8 *Pastoral Concert* (detail). Giorgione. Louvre, Paris.

Plate 9 *The Council of Trent.* 'Titian'. Louvre, Paris. © Photo R.M.N.

Plate 9a *The Council of Trent.* Bystanders (detail).

Plate 9b *The Council of Trent.* Bystanders (detail).

Plate 10 *Love Disarmed.* Bouguereau. Photo private collection.

Plate 11 *Breton Boy.* Gauguin. Wallraf-Richartz Museum, Cologne.

Preface

Shortly after the First World War André Gide (1869–1951) considered that the time had come to put his cards on the table. He published two books, and in so doing he established a place for himself in the history of twentieth-century sexual politics. The first work, *Corydon*, is polemical and sets out in dialogue form the case for tolerating pederasty – specifically the love of adolescent boys. The second book, *Si le grain ne meurt*,[1] is autobiographical.

André Gide: Homosexual Moralist takes *Corydon* as its starting point for the very good reason that Gide considered it the most important of his books; and follows this in Part Two with an account of the material on homosexuality which Gide consulted. However, as my object is not to write biography, I have used details from his life sparingly, choosing instead to concentrate on the history and nature of his ideas. Nor have I felt it appropriate to investigate the subsequent fate of *Corydon* and the reactions which it provoked among his contemporaries, which would demand a separate book to itself. The third part of my study, the analysis of homosexual themes in Gide's creative fiction and drama, is not intended as a comprehensive interpretation of all the works which I discuss, but provides another window on to the author's private world, justified by his own statement that to view his books otherwise would be to gain only a partial understanding of what he was trying to say.

But *Si le grain ne meurt* is also an important book. In it Gide covers the years from his childhood and adolescence, through his first steps in Parisian literary circles and his travels in North Africa, to the death of his mother and his engagement to his cousin Madeleine Rondeaux. These episodes describe a journey from innocence to knowledge. At the outset, however, there is something which should arrest our attention. In talking about his adolescent friendships with his older cousin Albert Démarest, with Paul Laurens, who accompanied him on the Algerian trip, and with Pierre Louÿs, his close friend at school, Gide does not state that sexual contact occurred between himself and these people of his own age and standing. Disinterested friendship, he says, sprang from a deep need in his being (p. 525). Descriptions of sensual arousal and homosexual experiences are reserved for the second portion of *Si le grain ne meurt*, which describes the children in Algeria. Here are Mohammed (p. 566), the dark-skinned 'Amyntas' and the healthy youths who make another appearance in *L'Immoraliste* (pp. 563, 565), and Athman, who, at fourteen, had become Gide's servant (p. 562). Here is Ali, who seduces Gide in the dunes with ecstatic results, and who is evidently none other than the demon who tempts the King to his downfall in Gide's play *Saül*. In a curious way, *Si le grain ne meurt* may be seen as the more problematic of the two works centring on homosexuality. 'Memoirs,' Gide wrote, 'are only ever half sincere, however great one's care for truth: everything is always more complicated than one thinks' (p. 547). He added for our greater confusion: 'Perhaps one gets nearer to the truth in novels.' Despite the carefully contrived artifice of the book's discourse, the Devil (who is conspicuously absent from *Corydon*) is shown here as a force to be reckoned with. Gide's innocence at the age of ten is portrayed as the fruit of ignorance (p. 386), and when he masturbated he did so, he says – perhaps playing down the traumas of his adolescent sexuality – unaware that anyone could think it harmful (pp. 349, 390).

His memoirs start on a note of purity – and shame: 'At the age when most people wish to find a soul that is clear, tender and pure, I see only darkness, ugliness and slyness in myself' (pp. 349–50). There is deliberate honesty in this description of his childhood vices, but a complementary religious feeling carries through into his conclusion when he emphasises that his marriage was destined to unite his wife's 'pure heaven' with his 'insatiable hell' (p. 613). His frank disclosures were chosen, no doubt, to throw his conflict into shocking relief: Oscar Wilde laughing with demonic delight at having tempted him into admitting his desire for the youthful flute player Mohammed (p. 591); 'Daniel', like a vulture, covering a boy without even bothering to take off his own overcoat (pp. 595–6). The fifty-year-old Gide concludes from these examples that it is always hard to understand (and hence to come to terms with) the ways in which others practise love.

If *Corydon* shows us an aspect of the world as Gide would like it to become, then *Si le grain ne meurt* provides the statement of his dilemma: 'I began to see that duty was perhaps not identical for everyone, and that God Himself might well hate that uniformity against which Nature protested, but towards which – it seemed to me – the Christian ideal tended, by seeking to conquer Nature' (p. 542). The problem which he saw as he was about to set out for North Africa shortly before his twenty-fourth birthday was similar: 'In the name of what God, what ideal, do you forbid me to live according to my nature?

And where would this nature lead me if I were simply to follow it?' (p. 550). He would have us believe that the exact object of his quest was still unknown to him before he discovered the sexual delights of North Africa. But we shall see that his reading lists reveal a knowledge of homosexuality far wider than *Si le grain ne meurt* suggests.

Gide was a French Protestant, an individualist, a sexual noncon-formist, and, in his own mind at least, an outsider. He was both puritan and libertine. He took pride in being a creature of contradictions, and in never being willing overtly to conclude an argument. He styled himself a man of dialogue. His role he conceived as being one of educator – in the widest sense – and, when his words were especially addressed to a youthful audience, he taught that one should break the mould. He was a cultured European, widely read in history, sociology, the natural sciences and literature. Like many of his contemporaries he believed that an intimate link existed between morals and aesthetics,[2] and that science could explain behaviour – though unlike most of them his viewpoint was unrepentantly homosexual. But when he viewed society and the individual in a positivist or Darwinian perspective, he still had his own moral commentary to add. Paradoxically, although the law in France was less oppressive than the law in England and Germany, there were no French homosexual apologists like the English socialist Edward Carpenter, the art historian and man of letters John Addington Symonds and the sexologist Havelock Ellis. Nor were there Frenchmen who, like the German Magnus Hirschfeld, argued vigorously for sexual reform. Gide called for witnesses to stand up, not for more victims to be paraded: he had his own understanding of the phenomenon of homosexuality, and of pederasty in particular. He certainly did not neglect contemporary controversy, and we shall see how he crossed swords with Rémy de Gourmont, the notable rival theoretician on love, and welcomed the arguments of the American sociologist Lester Ward. But inevitably the ideas with which he was familiar are strongly in contrast with the political liberationist ideologies of the late twentieth century. However, by advocating the individual's right to live an authentic life in accordance with his own desires, Gide can be seen as the pioneer of significant modern trends which go beyond the realm of sexual behaviour.

The present investigation is not so much concerned with what Gide *did* as with what he *read* and *thought*. To study the books with which he was familiar is to enter directly into his mind and the world of his ideas. We can also learn something from the way in which he chose what to read: his eclecticism indicates a voracious rather than a disorderly appetite for knowledge. He began gathering material in a rather haphazard manner from an early date, and until he focused on the idea of writing *Corydon* there was no definite pattern in his activity.

Curiosity and a need to know spurred him on. He gathered together in his files a wealth of information of varying value from different sources, ranging from the academic to the anecdotal, from the comic to the sordid, from the ancient world to modern newspapers. His close friends collaborated by pointing items out to him: Jean Schlumberger, Arnold Naville, Henri Ghéon, André Ruyters, Valery Larbaud, and even his brother-in-law Marcel Drouin (although he disapproved of the publication of *Corydon*) helped him in this way. The Sternheims and Franz Blei in Germany, Dorothy Bussy (the sister of Lytton Strachey) and others from England, gave him their assistance and suggestions. Many more names could be added to the list. Such a collection could only incidentally provide Gide with a coherent history of sexual attitudes, but it was not his intention to use the material for that purpose. What he wanted to do was to illustrate his thesis that pederasty was normal, as a preliminary to deciding whether it was desirable.

His files became very bulky, fed by his wide reading and by his many conversations. But it is clear that what survives in the archive is only a small part of the original collection. The rest must be reassembled – as the ensuing pages attempt to do – by using direct references and quotations in Gide's manuscripts, letters and printed works, by taking casual remarks as a hint to look more closely at what he read, and by paying attention to what was being published in the literary periodicals of the time. Gide was an avid reader of these magazines, particularly the *Revue Blanche*, *L'Ermitage* and, above all, the *Mercure de France*.[3] His connections with them were extensive. Together with a group of friends, he first set up his own *Nouvelle Revue Française* in 1908.

The results of Gide's explorations – and the present exposition of them – add up to something which at first sight may seem dauntingly encyclopaedic. Even so, what is offered here is not a comprehensive history of homosexuality, but rather a detailed account of *one individual* Frenchman's view of that history. It is of course also true that since Gide was necessarily a child of his time he had access to knowledge which was shared by others who, like Marcel Proust or Jean Cocteau, were giving voice to similar (but not identical) ideas.

There is a paradox in Gide's attitudes: he was a person who wished simultaneously to make self-revelation a cornerstone of his ethical system and to retain modesty (*la pudeur*) as a cardinal virtue. What follows, therefore, is an attempt to set Gide's pederasty in its ideological context and to help to explain what has until now remained veiled by the hostility or reticence of critics.

Patrick Pollard
London, August 1989

Acknowledgements

My first and most pleasant duty is to thank my friends for their support and assistance. Without their kind help the present book would not have been completed. Foremost among them is William Poole, to whom this study is dedicated and whose invaluable suggestions have enriched the text and enabled me to avoid many errors. Guy Dickenson has greatly eased my labours by reading the typescript at various stages. I should like to thank Monsieur Claude Courouve for his many kind-nesses and for the interest which he has shown in this project. I owe a particular debt of gratitude to Madame Catherine Gide for permission to consult Gide's papers, to Monsieur François Chapon of the Bibliothèque littéraire Jacques Doucet for his considerate assistance, and to members of the staff of the Bibliothèque nationale and the British Library. My thanks are finally due to the British Academy for a travel grant which assisted my research in Paris, and to Birkbeck College London for generous financial support towards the preparation of this book.

Note

Except where otherwise indicated, all translations into English are my own. The majority have been made from the French texts and translations used by Gide, but in some instances they are from languages other than French. All page references to *Corydon* are to the 1947 edition (the last to be reset in his lifetime), unless the contrary is explicitly stated.

Part One

CORYDON

CHAPTER ONE

The Chronology of *Corydon*

Our earliest testimony that Gide was actively constituting a 'dossier' entitled 'Pédérastie' dates from 1895,[1] but we may well suppose that he had become concerned with the topic long before that date. In the absence of firm evidence, however, we do not know whether he had already formulated the notion that his task was to lead a crusade in defence of his sexual preferences.

It is not easy to separate a chronological account of the writing of *Corydon* from an analysis of Gide's method of working. As we shall see, although the main periods of activity may be determined without too much difficulty, the number of revisions and rewritings which the text underwent complicates our investigation. It is also evident that much of the material Gide collected for his book was stored in his files and not used when he first had an opportunity of doing so.

It was in 1908, the editors of the Gide–Ghéon *Correspondance* remind us in their interesting and informative preface, that Gide undertook a journey to Bagnols and to England in company with friends who had similar inclinations. It was while he was with Ghéon, Copeau and Schlumberger – or shortly afterwards – that he wrote, in part or in whole, the first two Dialogues. We must be careful, however, for this statement may yet be no more than a reasonable inference from a remark added in manuscript to the 1911 edition of *Corydon* to the effect that 'almost all this dialogue [that is, Dialogue II] was written in the summer of 1908'. We will return to this point later when we discuss the 'layers' of composition.

On 13 August 1909 Alibert wrote to Gide and referred to a reading of *Corydon* which had taken place.[2] This was the same year in which Gide was striving to finish writing *La Porte étroite*. On 5 July of the following year, Gide wrote to Ghéon about the progress he had been making with his project:

I have started my terrible book all over again. I have rewritten whole sections, made the tone of the dialogue more definite, and I have completely refashioned certain arguments whose logic now seems to me to be unshakeable. I think I can now rebut people who criticise the form *and* the content – and listen all the more readily only to criticisms of detail. And I'm more and more decided about publishing it. But I haven't yet got any further than where I was last year – indeed I haven't even reached that point.

At this date, Gide was presumably not only encouraged by the active support and interest of Ghéon, the 'franc camarade' of the dedication of *L'Immoraliste*, but he was also stimulated by the contact he was beginning to make with the liberated and exciting world of Nijinsky, Diaghilev and the Russian Ballet. He was, however, to wait for two or three years before he properly entered their charmed circle.

On 12 July 1910 Gide wrote the following entry in his *Journal*: 'A feeling of the indispensable. Since writing *André Walter* I have never had it as strongly as I do now when I am writing *Corydon*. The fear that someone else will overtake me. I have the impression that the subject is "in the air".' In the air it may well have been, for Gide was becoming more aware of the assertiveness of organised and articulate groups of homosexual men. At the end of July 1910 he wrote to his faithful Ghéon that he was 'fairly satisfied with the second part of *Corydon*'. We do not know to what extent this 'second part' corresponds with what we know as the 'second Dialogue'. Perhaps it focused sharply on the second theme of the book, namely the argument from natural science. In the event, the 'new' version of the second part pleased A. Ruyters.[3] A few months later, Gide was making good progress on *Isabelle*, and if he finished that task, he promised Ghéon on 1 October 1910, he would perhaps take up *Corydon* once more.

We must assume that Gide soon succumbed to his urgent feeling that he should publish his book, for on 22 May 1911 an extremely small anonymous limited edition entitled *C.R.D.N.* was published in Bruges.[4] This text breaks off somewhat arbitrarily in the third Dialogue in the middle of an ironic exchange concerning Darwin. It does, however, generally seem well prepared for the press, and we know that Gide went to the printers and collected his proofs personally.[5]

If we can accept the date attributed by Claude Martin to a letter from Gide to Alibert, it was later in the same year that Gide told this particular correspondent that 'The book [*Corydon* (editor's note)] which I spoke to you about is three quarters finished. But I don't know what to think about it, nor what to do with it.'[6] His doubts were probably resolved by a conversation with Paul Albert Laurens which took place later and was noted in the *Journal* for 14 January 1912. Laurens had given Gide a glimpse of how he might write *Corydon* in a completely different fashion, by making it as serious (*grave*) as the *Enfant prodigue*. Gide reflected on this advice at length. Two years later, he wrote again to Alibert, reaffirming his intention to complete *Corydon*.[7] But on 28 March 1914 the *Journal* tells us that still nothing was ready; and again a note of apprehension is sounded on 15 June of the same year: 'the importance of what I have to say . . . *Corydon* [. . .]. I tell myself that I am mad to delay and play for time in the way I do. If I died today I would leave behind a one-eyed or totally blind image of myself.' War was declared on 3 August, and for some time Gide was caught up in the charitable work of helping refugees in the Foyer Franco-Belge. It is obvious that this experience influenced him deeply and made him more aware than he had been hitherto of the quality and nature of human suffering.

By 15 December 1917 Gide was free from these commitments and he noted in his *Journal* that he had now written the 'preamble' to *Corydon* with ease. This section is presumably the new beginning to the first Dialogue in which the narrator sets the scene and introduces his representative homosexual. The following day he noted more difficulties and we see him coming to grips once again with the quotations and extracts he had been collecting over the years: 'Struggled with *Corydon* today and yesterday. I keep on losing my way among the heaps of notes, sketches and abandoned drafts which I had left more or less in a muddle.' He is additionally annoyed that his friends and relatives are concerned that he should not publish material they consider compromising. He was still working on *Corydon* on 22 December, and with some degree of success. On 14 January 1918 it was virtually finished: what remained to be done could only be achieved when he could distance himself a little from the book. On 8 June 1918 it was almost ready for the press: 'Doubtless I shall still have various small touches to put to the proofs, and many additions to include in the Appendix, but I could give it to the press in its present state.' He intended to have only thirteen copies printed. At this date a curious arrangement was being prepared whereby the expense of publishing a limited edition of *Corydon* and *Si le grain ne meurt* would be undertaken by Jacques Doucet, an avid bibliophile, and by Lady Rothermere, sister-in-law of Lord Northcliffe of *The Times*.[8] However, on 11 November 1918, Gide, Lady Rothermere, Doucet and Paul Méral met to sign an agreement. They came to no firm decision. Several months later, Doucet discovered that he still might not obtain the coveted volumes. He therefore agreed to underwrite the printing on the express condition that he would have one of the copies, and that Gide would not reissue the work, or cause it to be reissued, without altering the text. Doucet called for further clarification, and met Gide towards the end of January or the beginning of February 1919. By now Lady Rothermere had withdrawn: Doucet and Gide agreed to share the contract between themselves. On 8 February 1919 Gide sent a copy of the manuscript to Doucet, as a token of his good faith. The letters between Gide and Doucet which F. Chapon reproduces in his informative article,[9] further chronicle the delays in printing which occurred during 1919. The printer was slow, but there were also strikes to be contended with and he had other, more urgent, work connected with the *Nouvelle Revue Française*. The result was that Mme Mayrisch was also informed by Gide on 18 November 1919: 'I have all sorts of problems with Verbecke [sic: the printer] who is still keeping me waiting for CRDN.'[10] On 30 January 1920 it was to Dorothy Bussy that Gide also wrote about publishing *Corydon* and his memoirs, *Si le grain ne meurt*. *Corydon* was eventually published on 5 March 1920, in a limited edition of twenty-one copies. It was not until August that Gide appears to have been able to give Doucet his copy,[11] although he had previously written of its imminent appearance on 3 March. At some point between 25 December and 1 January Gide had been in Bruges himself to put pressure on the printer. He had been successful, and he had given the 'bon à tirer' (authorisation to print) halfway through January. However, when we look at the 1920 edition it appears to have been printed from a manuscript that was evidently less carefully prepared for the press than had been the case in 1911.

On 13 August 1922 Gide wrote in his *Journal* the reasons why he had delayed the publication of the book for so long. No doubt referring back to 16 December 1917 he repeated a quotation from Ibsen concerning friends: they are dangerous in so far as they *prevent* one from doing things. Now he revealed that what some people had taken as a sign of timidity was in fact a concern not to cause sorrow to someone he held dear. Gide presumably means his wife from whom he had now become to some degree estranged. This was partly the result of her learning the truth about her husband's conduct at some time towards the end of the war. It was also partly the result of Gide's continued insistence on having a life apart. He did not, however, regret the delays which had occurred, for many works of art, he said, gain by being slowly matured. He wanted to be sure that he would not soon deny the ideas he was advancing in *Corydon*. He knew himself to be a creature of contradictions. Since the time of writing, however, he had become more sure of himself, and if anything could be criticised he felt it was his earlier prudence and timidity. In ten years, he states, new arguments had been put forward which confirmed his theories. The book was necessary: but it had its shortcomings, and, if it had to be rewritten, its message would be presented differently. Perhaps Gide is now concerned with his own relationship to the book and with the conclusions a reader might feel himself entitled to draw about the author's integrity: 'The precautions I felt I had to take when I gave the best arguments to the opposite side now seem to me a cowardly way of dealing with the matter. It is unskilful, too, for no one will be taken in by the device, and some will be tempted to think that I wanted to deceive my audience.'[12] In November 1922 Gide was reworking *Corydon* and had written the 'Préface'.[13] But quite extensive alterations were to be made to the 1920 text. On 27 April 1923 Gide wrote to Martin du Gard mentioning that he was correcting the book. The *Journal* tells us that he was still working on it on 2 May. What happened then to prevent publication we do not know. Perhaps the printer had too much work in hand; perhaps Gide was still undecided about the advisability of a public 'confession'. All we can be certain of is that Jacques Maritain, a Catholic apologist, came to visit him on 21 December 1923 to ask for publication to be suspended.[14] Gide explained patiently and politely why this was not possible. Ten years previously he had read the first two Dialogues to Marcel Drouin, he states, and had then decided to do nothing more about them in deference to the wishes of that close relative. He was now unwilling even to accede to Maritain's parting wish that he should pray to Christ for guidance, not being accustomed, as he termed it, to ring up God on the telephone for advice.

An edition of *Corydon* appeared soon after, with an *achevé d'imprimer* of 7 January 1924 (fine paper copies; copyright 1923). Another 'edition' appeared, dated 9 January 1924 (ordinary paper copies; copyright 1924). The book was put on general sale in May 1924,[15] and contained, in addition to the 'Préface de la seconde édition (1920)', a preface dated 'November 1922'. This edition was reissued on 14 August 1924 (8e mille). A new, augmented, edition appeared in 1929[16] which included an appendix consisting of a letter from Gide to François Porché (dated 'January 1928' but published in the *NRF* XXXII January 1929, pp. 59–65),[17] a reply from Porché ('2 January 1928'), a brief comment by Gide on some remarks by Benjamin Crémieux and a letter from Léon Kochnitzky (18 January 1929). Thereafter there were republications of this latest text at irregular intervals (December 1932, 27e mille).

A new edition in which the text was reset was published on 4 July 1947 (37e édition; copyright 1925), and formed the basis of several subsequent reprints. Naville also records a limited edition, published by Gallimard in 1948 (No. CCXXXIX bis). The book has since been reset again. In March 1949, not long before the end of his life, Gide composed the preface which was to appear with the American translation: 'I am convinced that *Corydon* remains the most important of my books'.

If now for a moment we return to the published text and analyse the source material which Gide used we confront a standard methodological problem. How can we know what distance in time separates the date of a work's publication and the date at which it was read by Gide? There is the further problem of ascertaining the date when such information was incorporated into *Corydon*. We may, however, notice, as we progress from Dialogue to Dialogue, that there is not a marked difference in date of the works consulted, setting to one side those books written before 1890 and which could clearly have been available to Gide for most of his adult life.

In Dialogue I we note that the first edition of Bazalgette's *Whitman* is dated 1908, although among the manuscript fragments are many extracts concerning the poet dating from the years 1913–14. In June 1907 Gide composed his brief article on Rimbaud containing more references to Bazalgette: this remains in manuscript. However, Wilde (1895), Krupp (1902), Macdonald (1903) and Eulenburg (1907) all appear in a single list.

In Dialogue II the following occur: E. Charles in *La Grande Revue* 25 July 1910; R. de Gourmont (1903), Havelock Ellis (1909), L. Ward (1906), Perrier (*Discours*, 1905; also a press cutting among the ms. material – *Le Temps* 26 October 1905 taken up in the first section of Dialogue III), Darwin (noted in the *Journal* as read on 3 February and in May 1906). An article by Perrier dated 1 August 1912 was added in the 1920 edition.

In the part of Dialogue III which was printed in 1911 we notice more references to Ward, Perrier (*Discours*, 1905) and Darwin. A note on Haeckel quoted from Carpenter's *Ioläus* (1906) appears only in 1920. After this section, the text continues in our public edition with references to Rémy de Gourmont and Michelangelo. This last name is worthy of notice because a long extract concerning him from *Le Temps* 25 June 1912 is to be found among the press cuttings. Since we know that the text published in 1911 stops short soon after the start of the third Dialogue (p. 129) it is also interesting to observe the large number of press cuttings left unused in the files.[18]

When we turn to the fourth Dialogue, however, there are indications that although parts were indubitably composed after 1911 some of the groundwork derives from an earlier period. Thus Blum's *Du mariage*, published in 1907, was very much to the forefront of Gide's mind in that same year,[19] and the criticisms Gide made then are essentially the ones we find in *Corydon*. A citation from the *Mémorial* of Napoleon (*Corydon*, p. 155) derives from Ward (1906), who was extensively used in the earlier dialogues. Halévy's *Vie de Nietzsche* appeared in 1909; Carpenter's *Ioläus* (with references to Symonds) was published in 1906, as we have seen, but there is no indication that Gide was acquainted with it before 1911:[20] all the material derived from it first appears in 1920. Ruskin, *Sésame et les lys*, translated by Proust in 1906, likewise occurs first in 1920. The *Livre d'amour des anciens* from which some 1920 material is also derived was published in 1912. Remarks about the imminent threat of the German war machine (*Corydon*, p. 175) must have been made before 1914.

Three fragments, one in the text (p. 178: *Le Matin* 7 August 1909) and the others in the files (*Le Journal* and *Le Temps* 9 February 1909) concern the Affaire Renard and the so-called homosexual 'crime de la rue de la Pépinière' (γ 885.44).

In discussing the source books in turn, we will see the significance of certain dates. Thus, for example, the *Journal* reveals that Collignon, Pascal, Mme d'Épinay and Lautréamont were all read towards the end of 1905. Darwin and the *Apologie de Raymond de Sebonde* appear in 1906. On 19 June 1910 there are reflections on Darwin, Fabre and de Vries. Fielding's *Tom Jones* belongs to 3 July 1911, as does Thomson's *Evolution of Sex*. Marlowe's *Hero and Leander* was read on 13 November 1912, preceded three days earlier by Spenser's *Faerie Queene*. Marlowe was taken up again on 15 July 1918, shortly after a reading of Fielding's *Amelia* on the 9th. This list is by no means exhaustive.

Evidence of a different sort may also be adduced. Corydon's confession of his love is based on events mentioned in the early exchanges of letters between Gide and Ghéon, as the editors of that correspondence have noted. We can also see without too much difficulty the similarities between the description of Corydon's outcast state (1911 version) and the position of Ménalque described in *L'Immoraliste* (Part II, ii). In the first case the incidents occurred in Ghéon's unpublished novel *L'Adolescent* which Gide had read in 1907, and again in 1908, and these could have been written up at any subsequent date. In the second case, material which was in fact published in 1902 was, quite simply, reused later.

What may be deduced from this brief analysis is the following. In the period from 1905 to 1908 Gide began seriously to collect material for his project. He then wrote a version of Dialogues I and II which he subsequently altered, probably quite fundamentally. In or shortly after 1909 he continued to work at his project. The time before 1908 is marked by the influence of Ward, whereas the period after 1909 shows his indebtedness to Havelock Ellis. Next, after 1911, the first published version was altered and expanded. The result of this revision appeared in 1920, but it is reasonable to assume that not all the newly printed material was composed after 1911. Work continued during the years 1909–14.

The evidence shows that Gide applied himself seriously to *Corydon* in late 1917 and early 1918. The 1924 text is in many respects an 'alternative' and 'tidier' version of what was published in 1920, for this earlier edition left many footnotes in a rough state and did not even include the promised 'Appendix'. Bearing in mind the negotiations over publication in 1918/20 and the state of the manuscript submitted to Doucet, it would probably be correct to assign a reasonably early date to both 1920 and 1924 texts and assume that the one was a preliminary draft of the other.

CHAPTER TWO

Corydon: A Summary

Mais en effet les lois de la nature permettent ce qu'interdisent les lois des hommes et de Dieu.

The Minister in *La Symphonie pastorale* (conceived 1893; published 1919)

Corydon is a hybrid production in that it stands midway between a work of imagination and one of documentary fact. What is more, the author is absent from the stage and the dialogues are conducted by two persons with neither of whom he can be totally identified. The outline of the book seems to have been decided fairly early on. We can nevertheless notice some important changes which Gide gradually introduced, especially in regard to the irony he deployed. The first three Dialogues develop coherently along a predetermined path; the fourth Dialogue stands apart. We shall base our summary on the final 1924 text. We will deal with the prefatory matter and the appendices afterwards, since strictly speaking they lie outside the scheme of 'Four Socratic Dialogues'.

Dialogue I

Dialogue I comprises three sections together with an introduction which presents to the reader Corydon and his interlocutor, the first-person narrator. (The 1911 version of the Introduction differs significantly.) In the first section Corydon expounds the key concepts of the health and naturalness of homosexuality. Whitman is his example; Bazalgette his enemy. In detailing the current situation (that is, *circa* 1908) he briefly describes social pressures and the hypocrisy and cowardice to which these give rise. There is a need, he says, for people to stand up and be counted.

11

The second section is Corydon's own confession. For him 'volupté' is separate from 'désir'; his experience with the boy Alexis has taught him about his own pederasty; he knows that he has no inherited weakness. Thence the argument develops firstly again to the notion of natural-ness, and secondly to an awareness of the necessary distinction between physiology (what is natural) and morality (what is permissible conduct). In the third section Corydon tells how in his book he will treat the question of pederasty from several aspects, dealing with the disciplines of medicine, natural history, morality, sociology and history. (Corydon does not adhere strictly to this programme.) Making a number of other introductory remarks he stresses the normality of homosexual conduct. However, among the range of homosexual types, he will not concern himself with effeminates. Furthermore, the lover, he says, is in love with beauty – and his own beauty is of no account in the argument. He returns to Nature: a work of art is the only truly unnatural thing, and so homosexuality, when not being scrutinised by a moralist, should be considered by the natural historian into whose domain it falls. This points forward to the next Dialogue, but, before we get there, more remarks have to be made on the distinction between what is 'normal' and what is 'permissible'. That sexual acts have a moral aspect is beyond dispute: self-restraint and chastity are not unknown among homosexuals; many perversions are practised by married couples. Corydon perceives this paradox – that fecundation is one of the least 'natural' things in Nature, being as it were an accidental in her infinite sexual bounty. The act of procreation is rare: it is 'sufficient' for it to occur once in ten months.[1]

Dialogue II

A brief introduction sketches the future course of these discussions: today, natural history; tomorrow, history, literature and the fine arts; on the third day, sociology and morality.

Section I returns to the distinction between Nature and Culture (citing Pascal and Montaigne), and making two further points: we generally confuse these categories; uniformity does not exist in Nature. As for Culture, the pressures of society vary in different countries. An inherited disposition (goût inné) is natural – but may still be classified according to whether it is social or anti-social. It may be both described scientifically (as an instinct) and judged as to its morality (in its social context). The old theory of love where homosexuality was labelled 'contrary to nature' has falsified our view of Nature.

CORYDON: A SUMMARY

Section II is largely an attack on Gourmont, who was too ready, asserts Corydon, to equate mankind with the lower animals and to neglect the moral question. The argument derived from natural history properly begins here. Love is a human invention which does not exist in Nature; for mankind the so-called sexual instinct does not exist. When this 'instinct' appears at different levels of animal life it is not consistent: fecundation is not necessarily linked to enjoyment – and this is especially true of the higher animals. It is enjoyment which is sought, and fecundation is incidental. There is a brief reference to Plato and Schopenhauer, and Corydon acknowledges his debt for this part of his discourse to L. Ward.

Section III is largely based on Ward's theories of andro- and gynaecocentrism. The female is indispensable, the guardian of heredity; the male is dispensable and material for variation. Males are thus a luxury and epitomise Nature's disinterestedness. With examples from Darwin Corydon displays the hermaphroditism of the lower orders, and ponders the consequences of there being too many males.

Section IV continues with a consideration of the key provided by sexual dimorphism: since castration does not occur in Nature, variations will happen. Nature's lack of interest is as uncontrolled as the act of a gambler. Following Bergson, another, similar, distinction between male and female must be made: the former manifests catagenesis (gratuitous expenditure; the production of variants; chastity is a desirable consequence). The female manifests anagenesis (assimilation. Here chastity is unnecessary). Nature says to the male: 'Fertilise!'; to the female: 'Choose!'; and to both: 'Enjoy!' What he has developed in Section IV, says Corydon, is a summary view of the consequences of over-production of the male element.

Section V. Corydon next turns to the causes of what he described in Section III. He is not a finalist. Prodigality in the production of eggs is to be explained by a lack of precision in the sexual element. Populations of males and females are governed by the available food. Both evolutionist and finalist arguments agree that an overpopulation of males is necessary because of insufficient precision in the sexual instinct. Males are necessary to fecundate the female; females are not necessary for males to obtain pleasure. If the sexual act depends on pleasure this arrangement is precarious. There is no intention in Nature, concludes Corydon (intention belongs to God); there is no intention in pleasure.

Section VI is a continuation of the argument. Dogs and other animals are stimulated by the odour of the female on heat. Even cows are stimulated by cows. For a female 'love' occurs at certain seasons; a male is always able to perform. Corydon then applies these observations to examples of homosexual behaviour between animals (dogs, pigeons

13

and so on). A suggestion by the interlocutor that impregnation with the female odour gives rise to this is rejected by Corydon. Dogs mount other dogs when no bitches are on heat: this is because their desires continue to be present. More evidence should be collected, says Corydon, as he deploys what he has already observed and learned about the behaviour of animals kept in close confinement. The interlocutor accuses him of partiality in choosing his evidence. Corydon's final point is that when mating domestic animals the sexual instinct often needs a helping hand.

Section VII draws conclusions from the preceding section: for males and females the sexual instinct is indeterminate and both groups seek pleasure. Homosexual behaviour is to be found in most animals – but probably not in those cases where the sexual act is 'complicated', as is the case with butterflies or when the male is devoured. When the lover is sacrificed to his wife, explains Corydon, desire for coition has to be *precise*, and therefore an excess of males is not needed. [The critic may well notice the introduction here of an intentionalist argument.] Corydon repeats his conclusions drawn from his examination of natural history.

Dialogue III

An introduction serves as a bridge passage. We are now to consider the question from a human point of view. New theories must be put forward in order to push back the frontiers, even if those theories are eventually discredited.

Section I recalls that a female is identified by her odour: but this is true of animals, not of mankind. Similarly, male animals are splendidly arrayed in their diversity. Men are not. Therefore, concludes Corydon, love, for humans, has become a game (*un jeu*).

Section II continues: among humans, attractiveness and the role of the chooser have been reversed. But when women adorn themselves, it is a case of Art hastening to help Nature. Their beauty is insufficient. Women must be clothed, but men appear to better advantage naked. Modesty and the veil are necessary for women. [The 1911 printed text terminates here.] Beauty is an abstract notion belonging to the race: it is for this that men strive.

Section III carries the argument forward into the realm of Art. Greek statues showed women veiled and adolescents naked. Homosexuality is noticeable at times of artistic renaissance, but not at times of decadence. A sign of decadent times is the glorification of woman.

There follow the examples of paintings by Giorgione and 'Titian' – and raising, incidentally, a new definition of vice ('amusement exceptionnel de débauchés').

Section IV considers the evidence provided by art, literature and history. It is brief and necessarily concentrates on a few main propositions. Homosexuality is 'natural', 'spontaneous', 'unsophisticated' (*naïf*). Heterosexuality is none of these. There follow quotations from Goethe (the male body is more beautiful and more perfect than the female; pederasty (*pédérastie, Knabenliebe*) is natural) and from Greek and Latin historians, philosophers and poets, somewhat indiscriminately collected together. From these instances Corydon deduces that primitive man sought caresses rather than coition, and that heterosexuality had to be learned. Artists are against the denigration of masculine beauty. With examples from the Orient Corydon reminds us that not all societies have the same customs.

Section V provides a summary of the argument and conclusions. For an adolescent, who is 'naïf' and unformed in his sexual preferences, it is *pleasure* which predominates. His desire has no precise object. The Dialogue ends with a reference to Goethe's distinction between Nature and Culture. The adolescent is being natural when he seeks his delight.

Dialogue IV

Dialogue IV differs from the preceding ones in that it is not divided into separate sections. In addition, although its thrust is historical, it deals with modern society and concludes on a note of idealism. Some of the ground covered here was also discussed in the earlier Dialogues.

The Dialogue begins with an attack on Blum. Chastity is an important element in our social attitudes. The problem therefore arises as to how we should deal with an excess of the 'male element' and how we should protect our women. The consequences of Blum's programme are prostitution and adultery. Corydon's answer is pederasty. He cites ancient Greece: the harmony of its civilisation is reflected in its art, literature and philosophy. The harmony of Art is to be identified with the harmony of morals. A hypocritical attitude is displayed by modern educationalists who praise Greek art without mentioning its moral premises. Corydon cites the example of Epaminondas. He also refers to Marlowe, and bases his argument on material from Carpenter. This leads to a conclusion regarding the position of women: the pure images we have of them in Greek tragedy (and elsewhere) are due to pederasty, he asserts. Whereas modern French literature is full of adultery (which,

15

he says, reflects our debased moral standards), Greek homosexuality entailed respect for womanhood. Corydon returns to the Greek example: Sparta was a society which through selection cultivated the ideal of physical perfection. There were no artists there because 'deviants' were eliminated. This leads to an account (derived from Plutarch) of Spartan pederasty and the Sacred Band. Corydon concludes that this type of love strove to attain self-denial and chastity.

Heterosexuality is linked with misogyny in art; pederasty (again) is profoundly connected with respect for women. 'Uranian' periods are not decadent (Pericles, Augustus, Shakespeare) – and without homosexuality there is practically no worthwhile art. Homosexuality has always existed: there are some periods when it is *affirmed*. There is, perhaps, a recrudescence of pederasty in times of war, as under Napoleon and in modern (pre-1914) Germany. This leads to comments on modern society. People commonly call the Germans decadent: on the contrary, homosexuality is a sign of strength. In France, on the other hand, the birthrate is declining, debauchery is widespread, and women are turned aside from their duty. *All* covetousness should be controlled, homosexual and heterosexual alike. Pederasty does not undermine the state. Degenerates exist among both homosexuals and heterosexuals. People become evasive and hypocritical when they are oppressed. Thus Corydon launches into a general incrimination of lax moral attitudes.

A return to Greek customs would make society more honest. Corydon is in favour of marriage and chastity. He repeats that he dislikes 'covetousness'. Then he turns to his concept of the Friend (the lover of youths). Like the Greek, this Friend will be of good counsel for the adolescent (modern heterosexual education, he says, often leads to debauchery). Corydon opens a parenthesis to show with some literary examples how chastity and respect may be attained within marriage if there is opportunity for sexual expression 'on the side' [so much for the earlier hostility to Blum]. Pederasts are as capable of chastity as heterosexuals. To return to the Friend: his role is idealised; he understands the youth's position intimately through having experienced it himself (women are thus excluded from a full understanding); he can mitigate the bad effects of masturbation. The adolescent will be between the ages of thirteen and twenty-two,[2] though Corydon admits to a preferred upper limit of eighteen. [In all this section it is clear, though never made exactly explicit, that the youth is an *object* of the man's love ('plus désirable et désiré que désirant').] The Friend is a pure, radiant, exalted lover: it is bad if a youth should fall into the hands of a woman – but, fortunately, it is not natural (*sic*) for a woman to be attracted to adolescents, who are only mediocre lovers. Marriage, following the Greek model, will occur after the attainment of manhood at the age of twenty-two. [The 1920 printed text ends here.]

16

There is a brief conclusion to this Dialogue and to the book as a whole. The interlocutor judges that silence is the best commentary on what has been said.

However, *Corydon* is not complete without its prefaces and appendices. These, conceived as separate from the somewhat artificial Dialogues, provide a frame within which the 'invented' material may be set.

There are two prefaces in the current edition. The first, in order of date, is the one issued with the limited edition of 1920. In it Gide tells how his friends had urged him not to complete the book, but he had felt these matters were important. He was ready to withhold anything which might 'trouble public order'. It was this consideration (if we can accept his sincerity here) rather than personal reasons that had ensured his previous silence. He had recently come to believe that his book attacked not morality but lies, and the latter are deleterious to individuals and to society. He was therefore publishing the book, and, conscious of the difference between the phrases 'exists' and 'ought to exist', tried to examine if 'these things' are really as deplorable as people commonly believe.[3] The tone of the preface is somewhat defensive and apologetic. It must be remembered that this is the first full publication. Since Gide was issuing only a very few copies, he was not so much making a public gesture as ensuring that the work should survive his death. In the proof copy of the 1920 edition[4] there is also another version of the 1920 preface, entitled 'Avertissement', which was deleted in order to be replaced by the foregoing. Here Gide pretended that a friend of his named 'D' (doubtless an ironic gesture towards Marcel Drouin) had had 'this strange little book' privately printed and, shortly before he was killed at the Front, had asked him to supervise its republication. Gide makes several points: his friend considered it essential to publicise his ideas, but he was equally concerned not to upset the social order. This was why the book had been hidden away: 'D's' motive had not been simply to protect himself. Further elements which later appear in the 1920 preface are attributed here to the friend, notably the distinction between what *is* and what *should be*. Gide then comments that he found several of the book's arguments persuasive, but that he could not judge the zoological evidence. He tries to give the impression that he is a sceptical but disinterested third party. However, he also says that he is irritated by the way in which the adversary of accepted morality is always given the better arguments; he dislikes the way in which 'D' lines himself up with foolish opinions. To these criticisms of the form of the book he adds his disapproval of 'D's' equivocal attitude. 'D's' reply is that he had written the work some time ago, and that he cannot rewrite it now. Were he to do so, he is reported to say, he would probably change it. Gide therefore receives the material which will 'complete' the book, and adds to the incomplete 1911 version all that we can now read. Resolved to cut down on the ironic mocking tone which characterises the opening of *C.R.D.N.* he launches into the text. The tone of the 'Avertissement' is disingenuous, and the unwieldy stratagem of having yet another person between the reader and the author's message must have persuaded Gide (at least in his prefatory material) to be more straightforward.

The second preface, dated 'November 1922', is prefixed to the current (1924) public edition. Gide again repeats the advice of his friends that the work will do him harm. But he can dispense with public honours; he wants the esteem of the happy few. He is even willing to sacrifice that esteem as the price for fighting against untruth. He develops some personal reasons for reticence, but if he has waited a long time for publication it is, he declares, so that he could be sure the work was 'ripe'. Not for him is the ill-considered rushing into print of some modern writers. He criticises his book: it is too timid and too reserved. Of the need to speak out he is more than ever convinced. However, he does not believe that everything one thinks should be said – nor that it can be said at just any time. This is amplified in a footnote. The public are now more aware, Gide says. Proust and Hirschfeld may have misled them – but it is also possible that what these writers say is true. They, however, deal with inversion, effeminacy and sodomy – which are not Gide's province. This, he says, shows up another defect in his book because he should have dealt with these topics. Nevertheless he does not believe that the theory of a 'third sex' explains 'Greek' pederasty.

Gide's friends say that in *Corydon* the extent of the material on natural history will put off a number of readers. But he rejoins that he does not write to entertain: his book is 'the simplest expression of a serious thought'. This austerity finds a complement in his closing words: wisdom does not consist in yielding to natural impulses – but we have to understand them before we can control them.

The Appendices help to complement the ideas expressed in the text by Corydon. The first item is an open letter to François Porché whose recently published book *L'Amour qui n'ose pas dire son nom* contained a portrait of Gide. Gide's letter praises Porché's decency and honesty, for here, he says, was one of the few reactions to him which were not hostile. Gide makes three points: he had decided to declare his position earlier than Porché's suggested date of 1902; Dante's treatment of homosexuals is tolerant; writers should not camouflage themselves (Gide probably has Proust in mind), for this misleads public opinion. Furthermore, Gide is not convinced (a) that homosexuality is easily acquired; nor (b) that these morals are prejudicial to the individual, the state or society.

The second item is Porché's reply. He argues that there is an important difference between deciding to publish and acting on that decision: Gide's *Saül* is not a confessional book; *L'Immoraliste* is. He discusses Dante and Balzac. As for Proust, he admires the creation of Charlus (it is truthful), but he can only regret the alleged sexual transpositions in the case of Albertine ('dishonest' and therefore unconvincing art). One should distinguish between a work of art and propaganda (*Corydon* is a tract). He disagrees with Gide on whether homosexuality is acquired and on its anti-social nature.

The third item refers briefly to two letters, one from Benjamin Crémieux arguing that Dante was not lenient towards homosexuals, and another from an unknown Italian, arguing that Dante was favourable towards them.

The fourth item is a long detailed letter from another correspondent, Léon Kochnitzky, dated 18 January 1929. This is an erudite analysis of Dante's treatment of the sodomites. The conclusion it offers is that Dante showed no particular leniency (or severity) towards them.

A further item was published with *Corydon* in Volume IX of Gide's *Œuvres complètes* (1935). It is a letter, dated Paris, 2 May 1934 from a young man aged twenty-one, in which the writer reveals how his homosexuality sets him apart from his friends and family. He asks for Gide's help and advice. *Corydon* has shown him, he says, that his case is not rare. He finds that the hypocritical lifestyle society forces him to adopt is profoundly distressing. This letter is only one among many similar ones which Gide received after the publication of *Corydon*.

The silence at the end of the main text commits nobody – and this is one device which enables Gide to avoid giving voice to an identifiable moral conclusion. Theoretically, at least, we are still free to choose. And we have two persons to listen to, Corydon and his interlocutor. We ought nevertheless to add a third, the author, who is present in the prefaces, appendices and footnotes. Our next task, therefore, is to turn to an analysis of the characterisation and the narrative levels of the text. After doing that, we will consider Gide's use of irony in *Corydon*.

CHAPTER THREE

Characterisation and Irony

The interlocutor's role is to act as an objective reporter and to give voice to standard prejudices. This is in itself a difficult task for Gide to handle since it might be expected that a person with such prejudices could not honestly record Corydon's views. But the interlocutor's attitude changes as the dialogues proceed.

He is first presented as a reasonable man, for 'tired of hearing the theories of uninformed fools' he decides not to let his feelings dictate his judgement. Knowing Corydon's 'deplorable reputation' he has ceased to see him: but is this cowardice or distaste? We are not told. From his reaction when he does go to Corydon's flat we understand that he is prejudiced and entertains the widespread idea that all homosexuals are degenerate effeminates. (The 1911 text[1] presented a much sharper picture: the interlocutor is sometimes regretful that he has had to break with Corydon – but in view of Corydon's vicious habits he had no choice. He is broadminded enough to frequent gangsters, but he draws the line at pederasts – they are unworthy and incapable of friendship. He is proud of his sense of virtue. The alert reader will have noticed that his virtue is being exercised at the expense of previous friendship, and that the interlocutor is nothing more than the creature of society. His cowardice and lack of true virtue are underlined by the fact that he waits until he no longer runs the risk of being seen before he goes to Corydon. This is hypocrisy. He adds a word on his objectivity: if he does not criticise what he reports, he says, this is because he wants the reader to enjoy doing so. This comment, by referring obliquely to the prejudice of the average member of the public, is an example of authorial irony. We are surely meant to take the interlocutor at his word – and think the less of him for his unreflecting stupidity. As in 1920 and 1924, the expectations of this 1911 interlocutor are disappointed when he at last meets Corydon.)

In the first Dialogue the interlocutor shows himself to be impertinent, provocative and insolent.[2] In supporting Bazalgette's syllogism (homosexuality is unnatural; Whitman was healthy; therefore Whitman was not a homosexual) he shows he is not really interested in the truth; in following the standard medical views he does not have an open mind. He is morally squeamish (silence is preferable, on grounds of taste, p. 21), and he also thinks that to discuss the matter will encourage layabouts. [But is this what Gide had in mind when he said in his preface that he did not wish to 'undermine' society? The difference surely is that Gide came to the conclusion that his book would not have that effect.] In saying that homosexuals should keep a low profile the interlocutor shows once more his unfeeling hostility.

As well as being sarcastic, the interlocutor gives voice to many ironic jibes. For the moment, he is won over by Corydon's gravity. He has been speaking flippantly of homosexuality, but now he pays serious attention to what is said. This does not mean that he is sympathetic to the arguments, but that he is in effect better behaved. When he makes a lubricious remark, he is self-conscious enough to apologise. He has responsible ideas on how to protect the young, and is sensitive enough to be a little upset by Corydon's story of Alexis' love. His hostility and irony reassert themselves, until, after a rapid heated exchange, the Dialogue concludes with his impatience and disgust at Corydon's quite objective remarks on marriage.

The second Dialogue opens with the interlocutor's remark that he 'nearly didn't show up'. This is the sign of a prejudiced person who is annoyed at finding his moral position challenged. But of course he *did* come, and this may well reflect his curiosity. He continues to be scornful and ironic. His anti-pederastic assertions are nationalistic – and this means laughably irrational (an added footnote draws our attention to the existence of these ideas in the press. There are of course as many pederasts in France as elsewhere).[3]

At this point he is not intimidated, but grudgingly comments on Corydon's deftness (p. 52). He nevertheless accuses Corydon of playing on words, and takes a pro-Gourmont stance. As Corydon begins to expound the theories of Ward, the interlocutor's behaviour becomes more reasonable and, one might almost say, co-operative. Realising that on two occasions he has unwittingly furnished arguments in favour of Corydon's theories, he begins to understand, but still has misgivings. His altered character allows a more sustained development of the arguments.

The third Dialogue reveals a man who 'has been thinking things over' (p. 115). He is still ironic, but will admit that Corydon shows common sense (p. 122). He participates in banter (pp. 126–7), and is now unsympathetic to some things said by Gourmont (p. 120). He still declares himself hostile to pederasty, but becomes excited about corruption (pp. 132, 134). Scorn and impatience dominate a section of his remarks as he exclaims once again chauvinistically about pederasty in France and Germany.

The final Dialogue shows him scandalised in concert with Corydon: neither of them cares for the implications of Blum's book on marriage. But, in addition, the interlocutor is very openly anti-Jewish. This is probably meant to be another sign of prejudice: he is unreasonable (p. 153). He is shocked and also inconsistent (p. 157): he believes, with Corydon, that chastity is a virtue. [They will of course differ on how to promote it.] Although he admires the Theban Band, he will have to add that 'these heroes were not debauched'. But does he listen properly to Corydon's deployment of the evidence? He still voices the prejudice which says that virtue cannot include pederasty, and that all homosexuals are vicious. He is in favour of Christianity (Catholicism), family and chastity. Corydon, it may be noted, favours only the last two. Finally, our interlocutor slips away with only an 'Adieu', since, he says, silence is the best commentary. This may be held to indicate stubborn prejudice and reluctance to admit publicly that he has seen some point in Corydon's view, or – and this is more probable – it may be just an authorial pirouette. Has the interlocutor's sting been drawn?

Corydon is our hero, although he appears at something of a disadvantage. Unlike the interlocutor, he is cultured and intelligent. Rather than consider him prejudiced, it would be more appropriate to speak of self-interest in his case. He is austere, and not at all effeminate. He is healthy, of sound constitution and without inherited weakness. With a sensitive appreciation of art, he is a lover of truth. Slow to blame others, he does not want to be provocative. His book is styled a 'Defence' not a 'Praise' of pederasty. He is not pusillanimous, and if he refrains from publishing, it is not because he is a coward. He thinks of others and the effect scandal might have on them. [We remember the reasons for Gide's reticence given in the preface.] He needs the good opinion of good men (les honnêtes gens). If he does occasionally seem to be provoked by the behaviour of the interlocutor, he remains patient. He will shrug, not with indifference, but with stoic resignation. A man of good faith himself, he has progressed from disquiet to severe gravity through an analysis of his own personality. He is a profoundly moral person. And although he is a doctor he is more a humanist than a clinician.

The second Dialogue reveals his occasional excitement and a tone which the interlocutor labels 'peremptory'. He is critical of Gourmont (pp. 55; and 129, 132), and does not believe that his own theory is subversive (p. 62). Here, a sign of his good taste is his sensitivity to bad style (pp. 65 and 125). When he is ironic, it is gentle irony at the expense of the interlocutor (pp. 88, 93, 95; and 145). He is on occasion diffident ('oserai-je', p. 96, and elsewhere), but this does not prevent him from being scornful of Deville's pusillanimity (p. 100). He is too human not to smile with satisfaction when his opponent gives away a point (pp. 101; and 87 'un air narquois [bantering]').

The third Dialogue shows more examples of these qualities as Corydon continues intelligently and articulately to deploy his case. Towards the end, his silence, when faced by the interlocutor's truculence, is followed not by anger but by reasonableness.

In the discussion on Blum which opens the fourth Dialogue Corydon is scandalised, but emphasises again the need for reasoned argument. Where perhaps his equanimity deserts him is in the curious sentence: 'In fact I think that many Catholics would hesitate to marry a girl whose sexual apprenticeship has already been undertaken by a Jew.' If this is not an irony directed at the interlocutor, and it is quite difficult to take it in this way, then either Corydon is stepping out of character and giving vent to an unexpected prejudice – or Gide is intruding his own ironic voice into the text (p. 156).

Later (p. 165) Corydon will yield a point when he has, for once, seemingly overstated the case for the supremacy of Spartan beauty. But he retains his gravity as he narrates the virtues of ancient Sparta and Thebes. It is of modern moral attitudes that he is scornful: his comments on the birthrate and the position of women show him to be puritanical. Here we have the enthusiasm of the moral crusader, and this may seem at variance with his previous claim to intellectual urbanity. He is not sympathetic to effeminate inverts. [We remember that Gide's claim in his preface was that they were merely outside the scope of the discussion.] He repeats his hostility to hypocrisy. He declares his concern for chastity and the family. His enthusiasm increases as he makes his final statement of belief in the benefits of pederasty as a social institution. But he is not an enthusiast who is deafened by his own words: he expects to be contradicted.

Here at last we may think that we have an answer: if the interlocutor does not speak, then we assume he tacitly agrees. But might it not alternatively be the case that Corydon is still to be seen as a 'victim', constant in adversity, and an object of scornful silence?

Our third character is the author. We have already seen what he has said in the prefaces and appendices. What may be added here will give extra weight to his partisanship in Corydon's cause. His presence also detracts seriously from the dramatic independence of the dialogues. For let us simply ask the following question: if the narrator–interlocutor is responsible for reporting the conversations, who added the footnotes? Had Gide kept to the plan set out in the 1920 'Avertissement' in which he pretended that he was preparing the manuscript of 'D's' book for the press, the answer would clearly have been the 'Editor'. By far the greatest number of these footnotes in the 1924 edition are appended to remarks by Corydon. This was also the case in the earlier versions. For the most part they contain amplifications of what has been said, and references. In two cases, however, the line between Corydon and the author is barely discernible: Corydon was 'preparing an article on Whitman' – of course, but so was Gide, as the manuscripts bear witness (p. 19). But perhaps this material was originally intended to find its place in the dialogues. On another page (p. 109) 'Corydon' promises that he will perhaps 'publish some *more* remarks on male and female insects' (my italics). Is this dramatic realism? or is it not rather Gide speaking in his own person? More obviously, an example from the second Dialogue (where Gide tells when he wrote this part of his text) stands well outside the fictional structure (p. 58). The note belongs to a remark of Corydon's, but the addition, in the first person, would have to be made by the narrator–interlocutor, which is impossible.

Is there any difference between notes by the interlocutor and those by Corydon? On page 49 a citation from the *Grande Revue* reinforces the interlocutor's prejudice and is well found: it represents just the sort of thing he has been saying. On page 58 he has added a reference to the book from which he is quoting. But this and the three remaining notes attached to his speeches adopt the same manner and tone as the parallels adduced by Corydon. There is no perceptible difference between the characters in this regard. What we must conclude is that the formal apparatus of notes turns the work more definitely into a tract and derogates from the autonomy of the characters.

It remains to be seen to what extent irony enhances this effect. On 19 October 1942, Gide wrote in his *Journal* that he had probably been quite wrong (*mal avisé*) 'to treat such serious questions ironically'. He evidently meant more than simply that he should have composed an open and straightforward book.

The irony displayed by the interlocutor could easily undermine our sympathy for Corydon: certainly Corydon finds it destructive (p. 25). 'I did not know you were so able,' the interlocutor says when Corydon proposes his grandiose plan to write as doctor, naturalist, moralist, sociologist and historian (p. 35). From several remarks, the interlocutor draws what seems to him (and to the average reader) an obvious but unsympathetic conclusion. Thus in the space of two pages he reminds Corydon that lesbianism is greatly in vogue, that handsome men are 'desirable from every point of view' – and that 'normal pederasty' is the matter at issue (pp. 36–7). The technique is well known. When the irony is not correctly appreciated, it can also misfire.

In the second Dialogue the interlocutor points out the apparent indelicacy of using Pascal to support an argument the philosopher would have found abhorrent (p. 48). He questions whether Corydon is really so dissatisfied with what has already been said on love that he thinks he can create a new system (p. 54). There are occasions when the interlocutor scorns insights made from a homosexual standpoint (for example, the idea that animals seek pleasure, not fertilisation, p. 61); and a particular view of the superior charms of women ('prééminente vénusté' – the mocking mannered style is important: p. 124). For stating the obvious Corydon is ironically complimented (nature cannot do without the male, p. 63). On several occasions Corydon's theories are ridiculed directly (pp. 86, 100, 106 and elsewhere). The interlocutor comments ironically on the apparent absurdity of Corydon's position by drawing the conclusions that sexual connection between men and women is artificial (p. 147), and that adolescents are 'naturally' homosexual (p. 150). And so on: there are examples where a degree of levity is introduced into the book by the tone of some of the comments. Irony is not of course only levelled at Corydon. As we have seen he uses it himself, and Gourmont is several times a target. It is almost as if Gide cannot resist using this means to enliven his debate, but in so doing he introduces light relief rather indiscriminately among the more serious attacks on substantial issues. The force of irony must be judged with reference to the source from which it comes and, unfortunately, the interlocutor is not a sympathetic character. The problem becomes acute when we consider the attitude of society: people probably would expect that of the two persons Corydon would be criticised because he is the one who is commonly supposed to have stepped out of line. If Gide wanted a hostile reader to identify with the interlocutor and to be led *in consequence* to reconsider the question of homosexuality, then he was running a risk. The ironic tone of the 1911 version might well have confirmed some readers in their ignorance and strengthened the prejudices of others. If the irony had been misunderstood it would quickly have led to a misinterpretation of the book. To avoid this is perhaps the advice Gide took from Laurens when he conceived his subject 'more seriously'.[4] At all events, he later felt that he should have gone much further in this direction and not clouded his message.

CHAPTER FOUR

Language and Ideology:
A Lexis for *Corydon*

'Je n'aimerai jamais d'amour qu'une seule femme' (il pensait à Madeleine),
'et je ne puis avoir de vrais désirs que pour les jeunes garçons.'

Gide, November 1916, reported in *Les Cahiers de la Petite Dame* I p. 150
(30 August 1922)

When due allowance has been made for the ironic elements within *Corydon*, we can focus on the debate more clearly. Furthermore, an analysis of Gide's vocabulary is an essential preliminary. This will allow us to progress to an examination of the major themes in the dialogues.

Current French usage at the turn of the century was roughly this: pederasty (*pédérastie*) had been the common (and generally uninformed) term for 'le vice contre nature'. If sodomy (*sodomie*) was not used to refer specifically to the act of anal intercourse, its meaning would often overlap with that of pederasty. Both these words of long standing could be used to signify what we now call 'homosexual orientation' and 'homosexual practices'. The word 'homosexual' was coined by a Swiss writer, Karoly Maria Benkert, in 1869, and gained acceptance in France in the early 1890s following the publication of Krafft-Ebing's *Psychopathia sexualis*.[1] It occurs frequently in translations into French from the German and English. 'Uranian' (*uranien*) is a term invented by Karl Heinrich Ulrichs in the 1860s and signifies 'having a woman's soul in a man's body'. A logical extension of this concept is Magnus Hirschfeld's theory of a 'third sex'. Such persons were also called 'urnings'. 'Uranism' is used in a rather more generalised sense in Raffalovich's book of 1896.

In the undated 'feuillets' belonging to the *Journal* of 1918[2] Gide wrote:

> I call the person who falls in love with young boys [*jeunes garçons*] a *pederast* [*pédéraste*], which is what the word means. I call the person whose desire is turned towards grown men [*hommes faits*] a *sodomite*. . . . I call the person

who in love making adopts the role of a woman and wants to be possessed an *invert* [*inverti*]. These three types of *homosexual* are not always clearly differentiated; there are possible movements from one sort to another; but in most cases the difference between them is such that they experience a deep mutual disgust – and this disgust is accompanied by a disapproval which is sometimes every bit as severe as you (heterosexuals) harshly show towards all three.

Pederasts, of whom I am one (why can't I say that quite simply without your immediately claiming to see a boast in my confession?), are much more rare, and sodomites much more numerous, than I at first believed. I'm speaking on the basis of confessions people have made to me, and I'm willing to believe that at another time or in another country it would have been different. As for inverts, with whom I have seldom mixed, it has always seemed to me that they, and they alone, merited the reproach [*sic*] of being morally or intellectually deformed, and were the target of certain accusations commonly levelled at all homosexuals.

In addition, this may seem specious, but I believe it to be perfectly true, many heterosexual men, either because they're afraid or semi-impotent, behave like women towards the opposite sex, and in an apparently 'normal' union assume the role of real inverts. One is tempted to call them *male lesbians* [*lesbiens*]. Dare I say that I think they're very numerous.

This extract occurs, together with several other remarks on *Corydon*, in the *Journal*. One might reasonably assume that it was an early draft of an assertion by Corydon. The case of material being deployed in this way would not be unprecedented: the drifting of items between auto-biographical and imaginative works is plainly evidenced in *Les Faux-Monnayeurs* and the *Journal des Faux-Monnayeurs*, as well as in *Corydon* itself in the discussion of Blum's *Du Mariage*.

With the naturalness and health of our hero in mind, the 1922 preface declares that inversion, effeminacy and sodomy will not be discussed, nor will the theory of a being of intermediate sex ('l'homme–femme', 'le troisième sexe'). Pederasty is our subject, and this is characterised as 'having not the slightest element of effeminacy on either side'. It is on this basis that Corydon inveighs against inverts. He groups them, for example, in the phrases 'uranistes honteux' (shameful), 'invertis malades' (sick). They are 'chétifs' (puny, sickly), 'plaintifs' (complaining, self-pitying) – and are the ones most readily found in public hospitals. They are at one end of a continuous spectrum (p. 36). When the interlocutor also finds inverts distasteful ('les invertis, les dégénérés ou les malades': p. 51), disagreement will centre on whether any *healthy* homosexuals exist. After all, the interlocutor was surprised that Corydon was not an effeminate invert. Corydon, too, puts inverts to one side (p. 177): 'Their defect is too evident' (1920 text) and 'poorly informed people confuse normal homosexuals with them'. We infer that they are 'degenerates', like 'maniacs, or diseased persons' who also complete the range of heterosexual disorders. (Virtually the same remark is made in the first Dialogue, p. 38).

Effeminacy is not the mark of a 'normal' homosexual: Corydon first called Alexis' natural affection effeminacy – but this was the mistake which led to tragedy (p. 31). The common assumption that homosexuals are effeminate is wrong (p. 37). Corydon's bias disappears, however, when he speaks against the common prejudice associating pederasty and homosexuality with effeminacy ('the sad prerogative of effeminate races', p. 172). After all, he approves highly of the 'masculine' state of Sparta.

There is a further moral difference when we come to sodomy. Corydon equates it with vice and debauchery (p. 135). The act is seen to be deliberate and therefore perverse. (Inversion, it could be assumed, was, for Corydon, inborn.) Corydon refers to his own position perhaps rather coyly as his 'anomaly' – but this is early in Dialogue I, and perhaps Gide wanted to suggest a certain tentativeness. We are not to suppose that he is being mealy-mouthed – simply that a neutral word which had a certain currency at the time is being used. Most of the remaining derogatory terms which occur in *Corydon* are used by the interlocutor ('dénaturé', 'perversion', 'contre nature', 'passion coupable', 'déviation'). The words 'homosexual' and 'homosexuality' are used in a general sense and are often contrasted with 'heterosexual'. They are not to be understood as synonymous with 'pederasty'/'pederast'. But heterosexuality is also contrasted with uranism (p. 53), and this brings us to a fuller consideration of the two most important word groups: uranism/uranist, and pederasty/pederast.

Although the word 'homosexual' was fairly well established at the time at which Gide was writing, 'uranism' was older and had at least as much currency. The way in which Corydon uses 'uranism' is instructive. On several occasions he gives it the general meaning of homosexual. Thus there is a manuscript note added to the 1911 text (a translation of Calderón where Gide substitutes 'uranist' for the translator's 'sodomite').[3] It is used generally on pages 35, 38, 129, 180 and is contrasted with heterosexuality on pages 53 and 172. On the other hand we are not surprised to see the word take on the meaning of pederasty when it is specifically applied to adolescents (pp. 133, 136), and to Greek boy-love (pp. 177 and 181). It is to be understood as boy-love when Plato and Schopenhauer are referred to (p. 61), and again in the historical examples of periods when boy-love flourished (p. 173). In translating Goethe, Gide (or should we say Corydon?) uses the words 'uranism' and 'pederasty' synonymously (pp. 137–8). The interlocutor, perhaps reflecting common usage, employs 'uranism' in a general sense (pp. 15, 51, 124).

The case with 'pederasty'/'pederast' is slightly different. Although the words are sometimes misused in the mouth of the interlocutor (pp. 18, 49; exceptions on pp. 132, 135) they quickly reveal their precise meaning. They constitute Corydon's 'anomaly' (p. 26), the subject of his 'Defence' (pp. 21, 53), and Greek love (pp. 162, 166, 172, 173 (with Oriental and other examples)).

They are contrasted with sodomy (p. 135). One problem does however arise: Corydon remarks that Napoleon framed no law against pederasty (p. 174). We would naturally take this to mean 'against boy-love', although it in fact signifies that no law was framed against adult homosexual love. The interlocutor takes the latter sense, and contrasts the situation in Germany. Without seeming to notice, Corydon carries on the argument, talking now about adult love. Similarly, the word 'pederasty' when used in the translation of Goethe on p. 138 (already seen to make uranism and pederasty synonymous) is certainly capable of having adult connotations, even though the German is 'Knabenliebe'.

We must probably conclude that the only distinction which it is essential for us to make is between invert and pederast. These are the two poles which represent the extremes of the 'bad' and the 'good' homosexual, and we have to bear in mind the possibility that Gide was not always consistent in using words notwithstanding his avowed principles.

From Corydon's words we learn something about the type of youth with whom the pederast will fall in love. He will be (as La Bruyère describes him, p. 186), between the ages of thirteen (or fifteen in the 1920 edition) and twenty-two. Alexis, we remember, was no longer a child (*enfant*) although he did retain some attractive childish characteristics (p. 31). He was an *adolescent*. Despite his young age, it could truly be said that what he felt towards Corydon was love (*amour*) (p. 32). Corydon also recognises that such affection may quite understandably arise between young boys (*jeunes garçons*) and 'friends of the same age' (pp. 183, 184). The examples he quotes are in their teens.

Adolescents, Corydon argues, do not possess desire for a precisely fixed sexual object (p. 149). And this he finds an attractive quality. He did however argue earlier that those adolescents not affected by the social pressures to conform to heterosexual practices must thereby be showing an innate disposition towards homosexuality (p. 50. On p. 145 this applies to 'le jeune garçon').

If an adolescent is handsome we are put in mind of Greek statues (pp. 131–2, 134) and paintings in the Sistine Chapel (p. 132: an ironic context – they *do* awaken our desires, contrary to the intended effect). Again, when talking of beauty, Corydon makes little distinction between the terms 'adolescent' and 'jeune garçon' (pp. 145–7). The idealism represented by the figure of the adolescent is manifest: not only is it revealed by the great achievement of Greek art, but, Corydon asserts, it is present on the stage in the form of boy-players. Women actors are a sign of a decadent culture (p. 134). There are many men who fall in love with boys (garçons) (p. 149), and they are better able to help 'adolescents' (p. 184) for they understand their beloved's nature as fully as they do their own. However, the exact form which this ideal may take in Greek sculpture is left imprecise, and we have perhaps to bear in mind some of Gide's personal comments. Corydon admires the soft grace of one type of figure, the nudity of another, and, had Gide incorporated material left in manuscript, the long hair (not a sign of effeminacy) of the Spartan youths.

What is the nature of the relationship envisaged by Corydon? He realises that the beloved has a need for caresses (pp. 31, 142), and these he views as an alternative to coition (le coït), for they still include sensual enjoyment (plaisir, volupté, jouissance). This argument is however delicate, for Corydon has to move from the animal world to the human in pursuing it. Since a large part of his line of reasoning is based on the examples offered by Nature, we start by observing that animals are limited to the sole pleasure provided by contact (p. 86). (The reader might not at first see how this differs from the adolescent's caress.) Nature urges all animals to enjoy themselves (p. 76), but in both sexes this pleasure is automatic and is not directly linked to the procreative act (pp. 60, 84–5, 104). Corydon in fact calls on a quotation from Spinoza to lend weight to the distinction between animals and mankind which he wishes to make: since their natures are different, their 'volupté' will be different, too (pp. 121–2).[4] It does not however follow that for a youth the urge to seek sexual pleasure will be any more precise than it is in the case of many animals. A boy, indeed, can obtain delight in several ways (p. 144), and he will address himself indiscriminately (as we have seen) to members of either sex (p. 149). On one occasion, however, a remark by Corydon seems to imply that a society which erects pleasure as its goal panders too much to vice (p. 136: Renaissance Venice).

But how does desire manifest itself? The adolescent is 'more desirable and desired than desiring' (p. 185). Does this mean that the relationship is not a reciprocal one, and that there is little distinction to be made between 'amour' and 'désir'? On the contrary, Corydon, when talking of his experience with his fiancée, finds it quite natural to separate amour and désir (pp. 27 and 29). Volupté and désir are also to be kept distinct (p. 28). In fact the more amorous an individual becomes (in a homo- or heterosexual context), the more careful he is to respect and protect the beloved from harm. Harm is clearly to be understood to include a sexual dimension (p. 143).

If love differs from desire, Corydon may indeed be right in maintaining that it is a human invention (p. 56). It is none the less valuable for that, since this dichotomy serves to establish more firmly the line which divides animals from humanity. Among animals desire is instinctual, but is not linked necessarily with procreation; in this sense it can easily operate in homosexual encounters (pp. 100–1), since it is never truly fixed (p. 104). We may only apply this lesson superficially to the imprecise and floating desires of an adolescent (pp. 149, 185). For, although sexual desire is a powerful imperative for both men and animals, the moral sense of mankind is an additional factor. Thus the object of desire has to be beautiful (p. 37), although the beauty of the desirer is not important. Desire, to vary the cliché, is in the eye of the beholder (p. 123). Corydon argues that men desire specific objects, and in this they differ importantly from animals (p. 121). A woman provokes our respect and adoration (this is a definition of 'amour') more particularly when she is veiled (pp. 128, 130, 132).[5] A boy will do so by revealing his naked beauty (p. 132). If women resort to embellishments, it is in order to enhance their beauty, which may well be insufficient to stimulate desire (p. 145). Making allowances for cultural differences, the Oriental youth who dresses finely makes himself yet more beautiful, Corydon avers.

Love for a boy is in important respects identical with love for a woman. Corydon's pederasty does not prevent him from developing his own theory of love, the keywords in which are 'pudeur', 'abnégation' and 'chasteté': all three exhibit a puritanical attitude towards sensuality.

There is one major respect in which Corydon considers that homosexuality and heterosexuality are alike. With an austere ethic himself (p. 16) he believes that in both cases virtue consists in controlling 'la convoitise' (p. 176). This could be roughly translated as 'lust'. The whole range of behaviour from 'Platonic virtue' to 'salacious vice' is present among both groups (p. 36). Homosexuals are as capable as heterosexuals of acting in a chaste manner and of denying themselves mere pleasure (pp. 39, 170, 182). This is because chastity will always be the result of a deep love (p. 182), although it must be admitted that for the Greeks this was not necessarily the *aim* of the lover of boys when he embarked on an affair (p. 171). There is in this connection an interesting alteration made in the 1924 text. As printed in 1920, the text read (Dialogue IV, pp. 176–7): 'Without going as far as Lycurgus . . . and saying that a citizen can only really be honest and useful to the State if he has a friend with whom he sleeps, I maintain that in itself uranism is not anti-social.' In 1924 the phrase 'with whom he sleeps' was deleted, and a footnote citing Plutarch's *Life of Lycurgus*[6] was added, amplifying the notion of lovers striving to instil virtue in the beloved. On the other hand, in a further correction, the 1920 text 'if someone older than him falls in love with him . . . nothing can be better' was enlarged in 1924 to read: 'nothing can be better, nothing more to be preferred than a lover [un amant]'. In the following sentence, 'ami' (friend) in the 1920 text was strengthened in 1924 to 'amant' (lover) (p. 185).

For the modern homosexual, chastity may be attained if desire is controlled (p. 184). This reflection at least recognises that the homo-sexual is confronted by a temptation. If, like St Augustine, he can sublimate it, so much the better (p. 181). However, Corydon has had the experience of thinking he was in love with his fiancée. In one sense he was, but while with her he remained chaste (p. 27). This was, not particularly meritorious. He describes his abstinence as 'deceptive' (trompeuse): what he thought was virtue was only indifference (p. 27), a thing of no positive moral worth.[7]

Corydon does not regard uranism as incompatible with chastity. An ancient Greek who had had an older male lover, he contends, was probably more often better suited for marriage than the boy's modern heterosexual counterpart. For Corydon is in favour of marriage, and of chastity within that institution (p. 181). He is not in favour of free heterosexual love. This is the sense of his quotation from Malthus (p. 155) and the epigraph to the same effect Gide chose for the 1911 edition.[8] It is clear that idealisation of this sort brings about in Corydon's mind an association between abstinence from heterosexual intercourse and adoration of Woman. Thus he believes that the pure images of women which he sees in Greek tragedy are the result of homosexual mores (p. 162). It is for this reason, too, that he is able to link to the notion of chastity the idea of feminine nobility (p. 149). In this case, a woman's natural and essential 'pudeur' (modesty) is yet further enhanced by her veil (p. 130). Proof is at hand: the Greek statues of women which Corydon has in mind are veiled. They may therefore be thought of as representing the highest moral ideal.

Among the ancient Greeks young girls were reared so that they would become mothers, Corydon asserts (p. 163). This is seen as noble and honourable in direct contrast with modern degenerate society where the promotion of cheap pornography has corrupted many women and turned them away from the moral path (p. 176). French literature is full of adultery and women of loose morals. Is there any doubt that we have sunk very low, asks Corydon (p. 163)? It is, in short, corruption which he abominates, especially when vice, sheltered by the conjugal bed, is whitened over and given an acceptable face (p. 40). It is with the ringing sound of the word 'marriage' that Corydon closes his final sentence, a state in which his ideally educated youth will revere his maiden wife (p. 186).

It would not be correct to leave this topic without remarking two examples concerning chastity from the section on natural history. Firstly, although it is well established that 'chastity' does not exist in Nature, Corydon adduces it in support of his idea of 'variation' in the male. His argument amounts to saying that overabundance of unspent sperm is the determining factor in the production of male beauty among animals (p. 72). Secondly, Corydon asserts that castration does not occur in Nature, for, according to him, this would make the male who was subject to it virtually undifferentiated from the female (p. 72). In the animal kingdom females are not, however, chaste (p. 73) (and one wonders, irreverently perhaps, if this is why Gide believes they remain dowdy).

We have noticed in talking about women the emphasis Corydon places on maternity. This touches on a political and demographic question which Gide researched but did not include in the finished dialogues. Although Corydon's animal and insect specimens had been multiplying at a satisfactory rate, the same could not be said of French citizens at the turn of the century. There is an allusion to this in Dialogue IV (p. 175) where the interlocutor becomes agitated at the thought that Corydon's solution will depress the birthrate still further. Corydon incriminates current heterosexual immorality. What Gide has noticed was the numerical superiority of males in the younger age groups. He clearly had in mind a way of integrating this into Corydon's argument: he has a recipe for ensuring the sexual health of adolescent males.

Because of the time at which it was conceived, and because of the implications of some of the Spartan arguments, Corydon manifests certain nationalistic traits. It is also for this reason perhaps that the population question was raised in Gide's mind. Sparta, a pre-eminently warrior society, is the common model for virtue and manly beauty. It was also an austere society (pp. 164, 166). Warrior societies are particularly noteworthy for encouraging homosexuality, Corydon says (p. 174), and, therefore, Germany should be feared by the French (p. 175). Corydon's argument is confused because he does not distinguish between those societies (like Sparta and Thebes) where homosexuality was praised as a martial virtue, and those (like modern Germany and Republican Rome)[9] where such behaviour was prosecuted and punished with severity.

The debate about Custom and Nature is as old as the Greeks. However, as a consequence of mechanistic and determinist views which were widely held in the nineteenth century, Corydon has had to reopen the question, for despite their claims to scientific objectivity many persons still identified what was 'good' with what was 'natural', and they were inclined to reverse this proposition: 'What we call bad must be by definition unnatural.' Unnatural meant aberrant. On this confusion of moral judgement and objective observation *Corydon* seeks to throw some light. Gide's 1920 preface clarifies the author's intention: 'I try to explain what is . . . and try to examine . . . whether it *should be* allowed' (p. 12). As we shall see, Goethe and Pascal are called upon in the text to establish that there is a difference between what occurs in Nature (however antipathetic we consider it to be) and the judgements we form concerning its practice. We should not confuse the so-called laws of Nature (which are mechanical) with the laws of men (which deal with moral imperatives) (pp. 47, 48, 53, 138, 150). Indeed, this proposition is neatly illustrated by Corydon's comment on perversions within marriage, which are legitimate. It is the rules of society which allow these particular heterosexuals to do what they do. The laws are rules which may permit (or prohibit) actions, regardless of the 'normality' of such behaviour (p. 40). Thus what the interlocutor describes as Alexis' 'deviation' or 'perversion' is pointedly placed by Corydon within the ambit of Nature (p. 34). Corydon perceives that many games are played 'outside the rules'. Man is in fact unfettered by the mechanical constraints which animals obey. In his love making he has become in Nature's eyes a free agent (p. 121). These are not, need we say, the eyes of Society. Corydon does not wish to be an outlaw in 'natural' terms. However, if forced to, he can accept that Society condemns him (pp. 61–2). 'Unfortunately,' noted Gide in his manuscripts, 'it is partly true: nothing so greatly encourages the individual to step outside the law [as Society's condemnation].'[10] With two firmly established separate lines of enquiry into what is 'normal' and what is 'allowed', we can more clearly appreciate Corydon's dictum that when we cease to examine morals we must turn to the natural physical world (p. 38). This time the reverse proposition is also true: 'When the physiological problem has been solved, the moral problem demands our attention' (p. 34). It might seem to follow from this that for Corydon 'vice' would be no more than a relativistic moral label attached to certain naturally recurring phenomena. But we have seen that Corydon has his own moral standards. Thus 'convoitise' (lust) was a vice. So is hypocrisy. So is sodomy.

Corydon itself was composed with these standards very much in mind. As the 1920 preface says: 'I persuaded myself that this little book, however apparently subversive, was after all only fighting untruth, and that on the contrary nothing is more unhealthy for the individual and society than a lie which has gained credence' (p. 12). Because of the constraints which it imposes on a homosexual, our society requires him to be hypocritical (p. 178), for, as Corydon says, quoting Balzac,

'Morals are a Nation's hypocrisy' (p. 179).[11] The evil goes deeply. Thus it is that homosexuals hide from society (p. 180), and even hide from themselves. For this reason even Corydon is forced to play the hypocrite with Alexis (pp. 33–4). He has also behaved similarly, let us not forget, towards his fiancée when he pretended to be a heterosexual (p. 28). There is an important sense here in which health is seen not only as the wholesome operation of the body but also as the moral rectitude of the spirit. To me the phrase 'an authentic mind in a healthy body' would not miss the mark. 'The important thing is not to be cured but to live with one's misfortunes (*maux*),' says Corydon, citing the Abbé Galiani. But, when he is taken up on this by the interlocutor, he paradoxically replies that a cure *is* possible – for the very reason that pederasty is *not* a disease (p. 34). Was not the glory of Greece and the Renaissance the health, both moral and natural, embodied in their art (p. 133)? There is a possibility that Corydon's physical rejection of women stems in some degree from his commitment to truth. He does not, however, say so explicitly, and we should be very careful in analysing the psychology of a fictional character. A woman's beauty needs veils and adornments, not only to make her more appealing in her modesty, but to enhance her insufficient ability to attract the male. Corydon calls this 'l'attrait postiche' ('artificial attraction'), thereby drawing our attention to the way in which she contrasts with the honesty of the naked adolescent (p. 145).

The point towards which the moral aspect of the dialogues leads is truthful and honest education. The irresponsibility and gratuitous 'jeu' (game) adduced in animal behaviour (pp. 68, 72, 106, 110) are now forgotten. The lover must stand as an example to the beloved and guide him with his knowledge and experience. If he has good principles, these will be instilled in the youth. If he is truly in love with the beloved, then his advice will be chastely disinterested. He will set the boy on the path of virtue, for the adolescent is as yet unformed. Open to many influences, the youth will listen to his lover, and together they will choose the best. The lover is 'exalted and purified by this love' and will 'guide the beloved towards the radiant summits where only love can lead' (p. 185). Adulthood and marriage lie beyond.

This is undoubtedly a romantic conclusion, and one which shows that Corydon has passed from natural history through morality to sentimentalism. But such an attitude is surely not objectionable in a lover. What in fact the reader also notices is that there is no word about the evanescent quality of the love inspired by boys. A paedophile is somewhat like Sisyphus, and his love has to be eternally repeated as each youth passes into maturity. By the time Gide wrote *Les Faux-Monnayeurs* he was willing to address himself to this question.

Part Two

HISTORY, SCIENCE AND SOCIOLOGY

At the heart of Gide's polemic lies the relationship between science and morals. He considered that it was not sufficient for him simply to assert the naturalness of homosexuality, but that he should seek to understand it before justifying it in terms which would, he hoped, persuade his contemporaries. The account of his childhood and adolescent sexuality in *Si le grain ne meurt* highlights his masturbation and his pederasty, but the reading of the scientific, philosophical and sociological books which contributed to his understanding of his situation belongs to the period which extends from his late teens until the end of his life.

The fact that Corydon's own projected book was to have started out with an enquiry into natural history amply illustrates the importance which Gide accorded to this discipline. But the observed behaviour of insects is not enough, even when the argument ranges from sexual dimorphism to the relative frequency of male and female births and the superabundance of sperm in certain creatures. To these facts Gide added the remarks of social theoreticians and the conceptual framework provided by philosophers and historians.

The material in the following chapters therefore represents the observations and opinions (most of them hostile) which were available to Gide and of which he made use. They clearly demonstrate the complexity of attitudes expressed towards homosexuality at the time, and show how Gide selected from them in order to construct his own case. To understand the context of this part of Gide's argument there is no better place to begin than with a medical dictionary, and no more sobering a chapter with which to conclude than one on society's victimisation of the homosexual.

CHAPTER FIVE

Ideologies

Panckoucke's Medical Dictionary

At a time well before he began seriously to collect material for *Corydon* Gide noted in his private reading list for 1890 several works of medical or medico-legal interest.[1] He had nearly reached his twenty-first birthday. Among the most interesting of these was a medical dictionary 'in 60 volumes' in the Bibliothèque Cardinal (*sic*) which can be identified as the *Dictionnaire des sciences médicales par une société de médecins et de chirurgiens*, published in Paris by C.L.F. Panckoucke in 1812–22.[2] It will serve as our starting point, for it doubtless offered the young Gide the first answers to his questions about sexuality. We have to hazard a guess at which articles attracted his attention, for he tells us only that he read many 'medical articles, and especially medico-legal ones'. We then have to imagine how he might have come to terms with what he discovered. But here in the 'Subjectif' already we seize the moral tone of his comments:

> How lamentable it is to see how few resources Man has available in crime! How limited is the field of depravations! Beyond a certain degree of perversity conscience is so blunted that a man is not accountable. He is a maniac, he is mad or ill. The whole horror of evil is in a grey area, in remorse, in the fear of the evil that one is about to commit,[3] in blasphemy – which makes one tremble for oneself when reading certain things, as the Athenians used to shudder when naming the Erinyes [Avenging Furies]. . . . The individual must remain perfectly conscious of his acts.

What could these 'certain things' have been? The dictionary ranges widely over the areas of physiology and pathology. It deals with parts of the body (including the sexual organs) and diseases (including venereal diseases). There are long articles on madness, drunkenness, chastity and other subjects which are described clinically while at the same time they are viewed with either moral favour or disapproval. The contributors describe medical 'conditions' from 'Abstinence' to 'Viol' (rape). Of especial interest are the entries: 'Pédérastie', 'Sodomie', 'Masturbation' and 'Libertinage'.

Pédérastie

The tone of the article is extremely harsh, but the writer hopes that although it is his duty to 'unmask this vice' he has observed the laws of modesty. In fact his essay falls into three sections. Firstly he is concerned to discredit the Greeks 'who far outstripped us in this immorality'; few Greeks did not practise it, and even the 'virtuous Socrates' was accused of being over-familiar with Alcibiades; and, similarly, many great modern men have also been suspected. 'We feel that a people whose tastes had taken such a vicious turn could not have been very strong admirers of women.' But, he adds, there are the examples of the philosophers who condemned this ignominy: Plato, Plutarch, Achilles Tatius, Clement of Alexandria, Maximus of Tyre and Lucian. (This is a misrepresentation, especially in the case of the last named, and even the writer of the article is puzzled by the contradictions he has found.) If the Greeks showed moral turpitude and impudence, how much more vicious were their pupils the Romans: 'Formosum pastor Corydon ardebat Alexin'?

The second section concerns morality in a modern state. 'This criminal penchant is an infamous vice condemned by morality, nature and reason.' It demonstrates 'the depths to which a man may be dragged when controlled by vile, overwhelming appetites – those common fruits of the deepest depravity'. The Bible tells us of God's vengeance for this sin; in France it used to be punished by burning (a case of two executions, 5 June 1750, is referred to). But now public horror has to express its outrage, for indifference undermines the nation's moral strength. Whatever the degree of infamy associated with this vice, the evil is far worse when innocent young persons are taken advantage of and led in consequence into a life of depravity. Ecclesiastics and religious persons should be severely punished for abusing their position of trust when educating the young; seduction practised beneath the veil of friendship should give us cause for great alarm. This vice, the writer says, has not been completely eradicated from our society.

The third section deals with causes: hot climates foster pederasty, for they inflame desire – and women are often kept separate by law in hot countries. (This is a popular notion one may trace back to the eighteenth century and beyond.) Both lack of women (as in the case of sailors) and excess of intercourse with women will give rise to pederasty. The fourth aspect is medical, but here the writer briefly concludes 'there are no important remarks to make'. Pederasts seen in hospitals manifest the symptoms of venereal diseases, deformities and other disorders of the rectum, 'those cruel and often incurable ills which are the suitable punishment for such immorality' (*démoralisation*).

The hostile tone is obvious and an attempt to understand homo-sexuality is absent. The author does not clearly distinguish between pederasty (sexual attraction towards children and adolescents) and homosexuality (a more general same-sex attraction covering all age groups), for popular linguistic usage confused the two terms at this date and continued to do so for some time to come.

Sodomie

The writer of this article is again at pains to disclaim any sympathy with his subject. This crime, he says, is called pederasty when perpetrated between a man and a child or between two men. Sodomy may be practised between two adult men or by a man with a woman. He spends most time on a historical and geographical description of its occurrence and gives details of the Biblical accounts in Genesis 19 and Judges 19. In India, according to him, the Brahmins established a regular form of male prostitution of which he gives details. Sodomy is widespread in North Africa where Christian prisoners are often abused in this manner. The Turks also practise it widely. Ecclesiastics in the past have been accused, although happily contemporary churchmen are innocent of this vice. In modern France sailors are 'said to be' sodomists – but one can be more definite in the case of prisoners, for they are deeply corrupted and 'contract the vilest marriages'.[4] If modern laws punish sodomy more leniently than in the past they are at least more equitable, the writer avers. As for the medical effects of these practices on the passive victims, he notes the same results as we have seen in the article on pederasty. 'Often a painful death is the cruel punishment meted out by Nature to those who have so odiously broken her laws.'

Masturbation

It is in *Si le grain ne meurt*[5] that Gide narrates how he was caught in class 'alternating pleasure with pralines' at the age of eight. He was taken to the doctor, who tried to frighten him into abandoning his 'bad habits'. In the event he felt more responsive to his mother's feelings than to the doctor's threats.

This article in the *Dictionnaire* depends largely on previous work, notably Tissot's famous book on onanism which had by 1821 run through many editions. Both girls and boys are said to be addicted to this vice. 'The patient, encouraged by a delusive pleasure, yields himself with fury to a vice which will soon be his ruin or call down upon him evils more terrible than death itself.' It is particularly prevalent, the writer says, in public institutions for either sex. He gives examples and details of the articles and methods used to obtain orgasms. The stories are cautionary, for the most part decidedly unalluring, but occasionally unconsciously amusing. In countering some of the more extravagant claims concerning the effects of too much masturbation, he denies that it will lead automatically to paralysis, blindness and fever. But even if indulged in with moderation it will affect digestion and hence the patient's health, and may well lead to general debility, epilepsy and, in some cases, madness. The frequency of abuse is linked with the climate, but onanism, the writer states, is nevertheless extremely widespread in France. A cure is possible: for younger persons special trousers, hands tied up at night and a particular diet are recommended. For older youths, one should not say that it is against the laws of God and man. It is sufficient to show them the awful effects of such behaviour and encourage them to indulge in exercise, cold baths, a rigorous country life and marriage. A lengthy bibliography concludes the article.

Libertinage

Among more general examples of licentiousness the author of this article feels that he too must dwell on 'pederasty' and on the depravity of the Greeks and Romans. It is true that one may observe curious examples of hermaphroditism among animals and insects, he writes, but the inhabitants of Sodom, the Bedouins, Orpheus, the Thebans, Jupiter and Ganymede, Apollo and Hyacinthus, Hercules and Hylas, not to mention Sophocles, Aeschylus and several other ancient writers also pass beneath his scrutinising pen. He records that the Persians learned this vicious practice from the Greeks,[6] and that some philosophers, including Socrates, were reported to be pederasts. Some authors, he comments, referring to Winckelmann and d'Hancarville, even wonder whether this type of love was not responsible for the sublimity achieved by certain ancient sculptors.

The picture of 'disgusting licentiousness' under the Romans mainly comprises a list of the activities of statesmen and emperors, from Julius Caesar to Elagabalus, drawn uncritically from the Roman historians, although there is a list (without translation) of the principal relevant Latin and Greek vocabulary. There are also some paragraphs on the early Christian period. The dissolute clergy at Avignon in the fourteenth century, licentiousness in Venice, and the stories related by Brantôme, are only briefly alluded to, such is the distaste of the writer for his subject. Finally, he considers the causes of 'libertinage' and its effects on health. Believing climate to be the determining factor, he considers that the most undesirable consequences are the transmission of venereal diseases and the bad influence on character, which results in effeminacy and degeneracy. He adds to these, as might be expected at this date, other general warnings about the unwholesome effects of masturbation. Certain conclusions must be drawn from these observations, he says. Measures to improve and protect public health must be instituted and properly policed. We must pay attention to the fact that Zoroaster, Confucius and Mahomet made laws against celibacy – our Christian state should perhaps encourage marriage more than it does at present. Mankind, he says with a final flourish, is especially inclined to debauchery, and it is this which has brought about the downfall of nations and empires.[7]

If Gide was already preoccupied at this date with customs related to modesty he would have found some interesting observations in the articles on 'Pudeur' and 'Pudicité'. He would have been told that there were many variations from society to society. Had he consulted the entries on 'Génération', 'Hermaphrodite' or 'Sexe' he would have encountered a great deal of material derived from a study of natural history, which again showed that a wide range of possibilities exists in Nature. This complemented his own interest in the study of insects and flowers.

But one article above all would have provided him with a wealth of strange case histories, 'Cas rares' (vol. 4, pp. 135–256), in which are recounted all sorts of stories which often strain the modern reader's credulity. The other articles we have mentioned contain relatively few case histories. The oddities, the monsters, the self-incinerating alcoholics, the hermaphrodites and the deviants of many sorts are all collected here.

*

Ribot

It is difficult to know with precision the extent to which Gide read about so-called deviant behaviour in this early period. One more work is however mentioned in the 'Subjectif' for January 1893. This is T. Ribot, Les Maladies de la personnalité,[8] and, although it is somewhat superficial, it merits a moment or two of our consideration. It is divided into four main sections, dealing in turn with organic disturbances (double personality; monsters; twins), affective troubles (depression; exaltation; sexuality), intellectual troubles (hallucinations; hypnosis;

mysticism) and the dissolution of personality (madness). Ribot's thesis is that all these phenomena are directly linked to physical factors. This is particularly true of sexuality: 'desires, feelings and passions which give the character its basic tone are rooted in the physical organism and are predetermined by it' (p. 59). What then of the exceptions and morbid cases? Ribot is brief: if it may be said that hermaphrodites possess the physical characteristics of both sexes, the same is not true of 'transsexuals' (by which he means transvestites or 'cross-dressers') for in their case the cause will be found in the 'cerebro-spinal organ'. Naming Westphal, Krafft-Ebing and a few other authorities with footnote references to articles which Gide may have followed up (Gley, Charcot and others), Ribot briefly considers 'contrary sexuality'. This he defines as 'a normal physical constitution together with an instinctive and violent attraction towards a member of the same sex with a noticeable revulsion for members of the opposite sex'. However, he concludes, 'these facts are in complete disagreement with the lessons of logic and experience'. Such 'psychological monstrosities' are few, and when they do occur derive most probably from inherited degeneracy. But Gide did not consult most of the material dealing with these aspects of sexuality until later, when he was composing *Corydon*. It will therefore be convenient to pause for a moment in order to look at books which exercised a formative influence on his thought before returning to a more extended consideration of the works of Krafft-Ebing and other scientists.

Theoreticians of Love: Schopenhauer, Spinoza, Nietzsche

> Corydon: 'On a beaucoup écrit sur l'amour; mais les théoriciens de l'amour sont rares. En vérité, depuis Platon et les convives de son *Banquet*, je n'en reconnais point d'autre que Schopenhauer.'
>
> *Corydon*, p. 55

Schopenhauer

While admitting that Plato and Schopenhauer realised the necessity of taking homosexuality into account in their respective theories, Corydon is more cautious when speaking about the German philosopher (p. 61). In fact he does not keep his promise to return to the topic and explain his strictures, but merely says: 'Schopenhauer, whose theory is dominant, only considers homosexuality as a sort of exception to his rule – and he explains this exception plausibly but incorrectly.' Gide, or rather Corydon, may well have felt uneasy about expounding a philosophy which praised chastity but explained homosexuality in terms of madness (*égarement*).

Schopenhauer's argument is that desire is normally implanted by Nature as a way of fulfilling the need for the continuance of the race. In the main part of his book, homosexuality is briefly alluded to and classified as an aberration. For example, the second volume of the translation which Gide read[9] (Chapter XLIV) contains in the *Metaphysics of Love* the remark that the great dominance of the mind explains why man has fewer instincts than animals, and why even the ones which he does possess can easily go astray. Thus it is that the feeling for the Beautiful, which guides him in the choice of objects destined to satisfy his sexual instinct, wanders from the true path when it degenerates into pederasty ('pédérastie'). In a similar way, he writes, the meat fly *musca vomitoria* may be misled by the smell of the *arum dracunculus*, which is like that of decomposing meat, and will mistakenly lay its eggs there. The analogy reveals the author's distaste. In an 'annexe' at the end of the second volume[10] to which the main text refers, Schopenhauer takes up the problem with which he is confronted. Why does pederasty still exist despite fierce social and legal pressures? The answer is that at those ages when from the procreative act there would result the birth of a substandard being Nature has ensured (*sic*) that the sexual drive is channelled elsewhere. Thus very young boys and very old men are tempted to act in this way. The appendix continues with references to ancient writers and cites anecdotes from their works. First there is Vergil's *Eclogue* II, followed by the story of Orpheus, who was dismembered by the Maenads for allegedly preferring boys to women. Mention is also made of Xenophon as reporting in his *Memorabilia* that Socrates said pederasty was praiseworthy;[11] of Aristotle (*Politica* II 9: the Celts publicly honoured pederasty, and the Cretans favoured it by laws, as a means of limiting the growth of the population); of Cicero; and of the *Gulistan* of Sa'di, and the Bible, among a general but superficial account of the phenomenon in other societies. Reference is also made to the same argument as Schopenhauer's in Aristotle, *Politica* VII 16, and in Plutarch, *Amatorius* 5.

If we are to seek the truth behind Gide's statement concerning the value of Schopenhauer's views, we must surely look towards Schopenhauer's more general theorising on love, rather than to his particular examples of pederasty. Schopenhauer states that when the sexual instinct cools towards the end of his life an old man enters another childhood where his will is also cooler. This 'euthanasia of the will' is like the goal for which the Brahmins prepare themselves when, after the best years of their life, they abandon both family and worldly goods and lead the life of anchorites.[12] Gide has a similar symbol, notably in the character of Ménalque, without however referring the notion specifically to sexuality or the act of love. Again – and here we remember the effort of the soul in, for example, *La Porte étroite* – this way is a 'sentier étroit' (II p. 968). The effort, however, is twofold, for, on the one hand: 'We are only will-to-live, and what we understand by the notion of happiness is precisely the successive satisfaction of the will [*volonté*]' (II p. 961). On the other hand we read shortly thereafter: 'suffering is, in fact, a means of purification' (II p. 964). We may therefore glimpse here a common ground between the attitudes of Gide, Plato and Schopenhauer, consisting in the praise of self-control and in struggling to attain an Ideal Beauty, sometimes synonymous with happiness (*bonheur*), lying for ever beyond the frontier of our desire but towards which we strive.

In the 'Subjectif' 15 July–1 August 1891 (p. 89) Gide also records reading T. Ribot's *La Philosophie de Schopenhauer*. One chapter in this work focuses on *La Morale* (pp. 118–49) and suggests many points of contact with Gide's statements about Schopenhauer. Thus the solipsism of which much is made in *Le Traité du Narcisse* is defined here as 'at the lowest level that egotism which is the burning affirmation of the will-to-live, the source of all wickedness and every vice' (p. 120). But pity – 'the true basis of morality' for Schopenhauer – can only be obtained by complete renunciation of the will-to-live, through a type of asceticism such as was practised by the saints (p. 121). This definition of vice is special because, as Ribot represents the matter, Schopenhauer's concept of love is based on a notion of mutual attraction of opposites. Thus women are not attracted to effeminate men (*l'homme–femme*) because they can find nothing there with which to compensate their own natures. (Gide refers to this system of compensations, though not in a sexual context, in his *Journal*.)[13] Furthermore Ribot alludes to Aristophanes' speech in Plato's *Symposium*, indicating that the myth of the hermaphrodite as the origin of mankind symbolises the way in which we seek our 'complementary heterosexual' companions (p. 136). This is reflected in *Le Traité du Narcisse*. Ribot also reminds his reader that Schopenhauer quotes part of a maxim of Chamfort: 'Women are like grown-up children. . . . They are constructed to complement our weaknesses and our madness [*folie*], not our reason. Between women and men there exist sympathies which are skin deep and few sympathies of soul and character' (p. 130). We will do well to remember that the hero of *André Walter* strives unsuccessfully for a 'sympathetic' union, and his effort ends in madness.

Finally Ribot deals with Schopenhauer's view of unnatural love (p. 134). He summarises his views, remarking that instinct has its errors and that Nature knows no moral imperative. This is another place from which Gide could have learned that Schopenhauer believed that the purity of the race was maintained by the removal of the generative act from the very old and the very young. In suggesting that the myth of Plato's Aristophanic hermaphrodites could be interpreted anew, Ribot was perhaps offering to Gide an idea he was to incorporate into *Le Traité du Narcisse*. In Schopenhauer's pessimism, he concludes, 'only suffering is positive' (p. 138). These words are to be read in the context of Schopenhauer's remarks cited at the opening of this chapter on 'La Morale': 'Virtue can be acquired no more readily than genius; abstract notions are as useless for it as they are for art. It would be as foolish to believe that our systems of morals and good behaviour will produce saints and virtuous citizens, as it would be to think that our systems of aesthetics will give birth to poets, musicians and artists.'

Importance has to be attached to the period in the early 1890s during which Gide read *Le Monde comme volonté* with assiduity.[14] It is also the period in which, significantly, the ideal of the 'héros malade' (the diseased hero) makes its appearance in Gide's writings.

A quotation from Clement of Alexandria occurs on a small scrap of Gide's notepaper and may be confidently dated to the time when he was composing *Le Traité du Narcisse*.[15] The interest of the citation lies primarily in the idea of renunciation, which, in this particular case, is neither specifically Schopenhauerean, nor puritanically Christian. Gide has only noted part of the sentence which he read in Book IV of *Die Welt als Wille und Vorstellung* where Schopenhauer presents his analysis of instinct and the genital act.

> In Greek mythology we find another allegory which also expresses sexual satisfaction considered as a will-to-live affirmed beyond the individual life, as a condemnation to live pronounced by the act itself, or as a renewing of the title giving a right to life. . . . It is strange that Clement of Alexandria (Strom. III c. 15), when discussing this topic, uses the same image and the same expression . . . (Qui se castrarunt ab omni peccato, propter regnum coelorum, ii sunt beati, *a mundo jejunantes*).
>
> The sexual instinct shows that it is the most positive and most energetic affirmation of the will-to-live, by the fact that it constitutes for man in the natural state, as it does for animals, the final purpose and the supreme result of life.

We are thus introduced to the notion of the positive and absolute value of the sexual drive. Despite this, however, we read at the beginning of the *Traité du Narcisse* that Narcisse was perfectly handsome – and that is why he was chaste. In Gide, beauty *precedes* chastity, and a deliberate

47

act of castration is not at issue (*pace* Clement's most distinguished pupil Origen).[16] The point of real contact is in the following passage: 'This woman who in the blind effort of recreating through self the perfect being, and thus putting an end to the generation of the species, will cause the unknown member of a new race to move within her body, and soon another being will enter Time: he will still be incomplete and insufficient in himself,'[17] which may be directly compared with Schopenhauer: 'Our own conscience and the quickness of our instinct teach us that the genital act makes the most positive affirmation of the will-to-live; it is pure and unadulterated. . . . as a result of this act a new existence springs forth in Time and in the series of causes, that is to say in Nature.' It may be seen that Gide has elaborated at two points: first the woman's effort is 'blind' because in hoping to conquer Time she does not foresee her lack of success in only giving birth to yet another finite creature; second, the offspring is not only 'incomplete' but 'insufficient in himself' – he is not only a symbol of sublunary non-perfection, but also needs (and hence desires) a companion. Schopenhauer's pessimism seems to have taken on a quite different form in the *Traité*. It is surely obvious that the key to the change is to be found in the concept of renunciation of the phenomenal world, for this is the sense which has artificially been emphasised by Gide's truncated quotation from Clement. It is moreover possible to reconcile this apparent discrepancy by reading further and seeing Schopenhauer's conclusion: 'This affirmation which goes beyond the individual's own body and attains the procreation of a new organism, simultaneously affirms both suffering and death, integral parts of the phenomenon of life; and thus any redemption is now declared to be vain which might have been brought about by intelligence at its most perfect state' (p. 525). Thus Gide in his turn talks of the sin of knowledge and intelligence ('to know – one gesture . . . and the now withered tree Yggdrasill begins to fall'), and of the necessity of striving for redemption ('le Paradis') through a constant and repeated effort to replace each imperfect being by another. Suffering and death are thus the necessary condition of life ('numberless Masses each day to recrucify Christ'). In this form, abnegation is glossed by its contrary: 'To prefer oneself – that is the fault'; in another form, it is a reformulation of the Gidean 'Si le grain ne meurt'; in another , it is the attitude of the contemplative poet who has withdrawn from the world; in another, it is the contrary of Adam's sin when he sought for certain knowledge.

We can therefore see the relevance of two other complementary Gidean themes which are implicit in Le Traité du Narcisse: desire (*le désir*) and happiness (*le bonheur*). Whether understood in a purely sexual or in an aesthetic context, the source of the image is clear: 'désir' is the constant effort of the will we have seen in Schopenhauer, 'bonheur' (or its analogue) is the goal towards which that desire will tend. Thus Gide could say elsewhere: 'The blinded nightingale sings better, not from regret but from enthusiasm.'[18]

As for Gide's use of the image of the hero who has a disease ('le héros malade'): 'Illness sets before a man a new disquiet which he has to legitimate.'[19] Nothing, he writes, may be obtained from persons who are 'satisfied' (*satisfaits*). This motif demands a short but important digression. Gide names as great men who were ill ('les grands malades') 'Mohammed, St Paul, St John, Rousseau, Nietzsche, Dostoievsky, Flaubert, etc.'; as ancient heroes who manifested an immense morbid disquiet ('une grande inquiétude maladive') 'Prometheus, Orestes, Ajax, Phaedra, Pentheus and Oedipus' (noting the last named as the antithesis of Macbeth); and as great men about whose state of health we are under an illusion 'Molière, Racine, etc.'.[20] No reasonable person, one might add, could believe that the nature of the 'illness' was identical in all the cases cited. We cannot but compare this list with another, written probably on 10 July 1891:[21] 'The extraordinary vibrations of true artists ... who all manifested some deviation of the genetic impulse: Dante, Shakespeare [deleted], Pascal, Vigny, Schumann, Michelet, Gustave Moreau, the Preraphaelites, and, finally, the great legendary types like.' Here, unfortunately, the bottom half of the page has been torn away, and we will never know whether the list was meant to continue with the names of heroes like Oedipus and Philoctetes. It is not at all clear what sexual deviation (or irregularity) Gide had in mind, for the acquisition of syphilis seems to be the only criterion for the inclusion of some of the names, and it is curious to say the least that Shakespeare was crossed through. However, it is obvious from what remains that the subject of Gide's reflections was debauchery. On the recto of the leaf in question, he had written: 'As for debauchery, I expect it to be extraordinary – or if this is impossible I prefer to do without, –' It is after this point that the rest of the line and the remainder of the page have been carefully torn and removed. On the verso, the text begins again at the top of the leaf: 'reflection of their manliness [*virilité*]; how they practised debauchery. That is an essential feature – and, for myself, I know that everywhere what'. This sentence is left unfinished, and Gide continues: 'That must be said, but better.' It is possible that his 'improved' version is the one we can read in the published *Journal* (p. 98). He then contrasts 'the sickening bourgeoisie' of Victor Hugo with the vibrant 'true artists' we have already mentioned. He seems at first glance to be saying something here very much at odds with the asceticism of his other remarks. We do not know what was torn out, nor why he suppressed the passage, but we can surmise that the words revealed the darker side of his sexual being. His assertion that 'absolute debauchery' was acceptable may seem a reckless exaggeration on his part, but so imperious a desire may still find its validation in the act of artistic creation. By bearing this in mind, we can perceive an extra resonance in the phrase 'a new disquiet' ('une nouvelle inquiétude'). Furthermore, in these words we see another echo of Schopenhauer, and of a morality which is closely derived from the philosopher's particular analysis of the role of sexuality and the will. Other connections are permissible, for what is non-conformist is, by definition, anomaly and dissonance: 'The substance and the real aim of love being procreation and the qualities of the child, it can happen that between two young persons of opposite sexes and good education there only exists a friendship based on a similarity in feelings, character and turn of mind, with no thought [arrière pensée] of physical love. . . . The reason for this is that the child they would engender would lack harmony in his physical or intellectual aspects . . . a marriage agreed upon in these conditions would be extremely unhappy' (II p. 813). Harmony, Schopenhauer notes elsewhere (I p. 682), is 'the image of the satisfied will'; whereas Dissonance is 'the image of that which contradicts our will'. This provides Gide with yet another way of expressing the notion of truth towards which he strove. Here the example is musical. For Narcisse, Proserpine and other models the ideal is one of selfhood; for Corydon the analogy will cease to hold firm. For the heroes whose willpower drives them on, a fitting epitaph will be 'Therefore, in most cases, very satisfied Theseus will surely abandon his Ariadne.'[22] Gide took up this image, but a consideration of it here would, unfortunately, lead us too far from our present subject.

As a footnote to the foregoing remarks, it may be added that Gide probably knew of an article by Etienne Rey, *Métaphysique de l'amour*, published in the *Mercure de France* at the time of the Rémy scandal.[23] Rey attacks Schopenhauer's idea that Man is not a free agent. On the contrary, he writes, although Man is dependent on Nature he can choose to act freely; and Man's conquest of Nature is virtually synonymous with love. Rey asserts that love is unknown to Nature, for, in the non-human sphere, only sexual instinct may be perceived. In *Corydon* Gide also deals with the proposition that the animal world differs from the human in this respect.

Spinoza

'You know how to choose your authorities,' scoffs Corydon's inter-locutor, when Spinoza's name is mentioned. But it is even more true in this case than it was for Schopenhauer and Plato, that Corydon is plucking out a quotation to save his immediate argument, and ignoring the main body of the philosopher's writings. The quotation is taken from *Ethica* III (On the origin and nature of the passions), Proposition

57, Scholia. Proposition 57 states that the affection of one individual differs as greatly from that of another as the essence of one differs from the essence of the other.[24]

Corydon's reason for citing Spinoza is to add weight to his assertion that the animal world is different from the human, and that therefore one may not argue that what is true for animals is necessarily true for human beings. The sensuality (*volupté*) of mankind, as Gide reports Spinoza, is as different from the *volupté* of animals as are their natures. Spinoza, on the other hand, is not specifically concerned with the question of one particular passion – love. 'Irrational beasts differ from mankind in their affections as greatly as their nature differs from human nature . . . for example a horse and a man have the same passion to engender, but the former has an equine passion and the latter a human one.' Similarly, adds Spinoza, fishes, insects and birds are all different from each other. His conclusion shows how superficial is the contact between this proposition and Corydon's allusion to it, for he continues: 'Although each individual is happy and rejoices in his own nature, this life . . . and this joy are none other than the idea or the soul of that individual. Therefore the joy of one individual only differs from the joy of another in so far as the essence of the one differs from the essence of the other. Furthermore, it follows from the preceding proposition [no. 56] that there is a great difference between the joy of a drunkard and the joy of a philosopher. . . .' Corydon does not pursue this thought in order to explore the difference between varieties of homosexuals.[25]

In Part 3 it is to be observed that Spinoza expresses a view very close to one Gide undoubtedly read in Peladan's collection of Leonardo da Vinci's aphorisms:[26] '120. Whosoever does not control desire [*volupté*] becomes like the beasts.' Although Gide does not seem to have noted either occurrence, he would clearly have welcomed the maxim for use in his argument.

Nietzsche

The relevance of Nietzsche's appearance here is determined by a quotation in the 1911 version of *Corydon*. As a note on the benefits of restricting the expenditure of semen (*Corydon*, p. 73) Gide had added: '"It is one and the same force which is expended in an artistic conception and the sexual act. . . . To yield *in this case*, and to waste himself, is dangerous for the artist: it betrays a lack of instinct, and more generally a lack of will. It may be a sign of decadence, and always depreciates his art to an incalculable degree." Aphorism 367.'[27] Aphorism 366, which he had also read, offers the thought that sexuality and sensual delight (*volupté*) are to be found with the opposing forces of both Dionysus and Apollo – but in different ways. Aphorism 367

51

continues the train of thought: 'Relative chastity, as a principle, and great circumspection in erotic matters (be they only in the realm of thought) can both participate in superior reason, even in the case of abundant and finely gifted temperaments. This is especially true of artists, and is the best wisdom of all.' Nietzsche expresses the opinion that the artist, however sensitive he might be, must necessarily remain sober and even chaste in his will to master his art. This leads to the passage Gide has quoted. Aphorism 368 continues: 'Artists are not men of great passion, whatever they imagine and whatever they tell us. There are two reasons for this: they lack modesty [*pudeur*] towards themselves (they watch themselves living and subject themselves to self-scrutiny), and they also lack modesty when faced with a great passion (as artists they want to use it).'

Gide's *Journal* of 15 June 1910 also contains an extract from Aphorism 324 (*Anti-Darwin*) which is not unconnected with the principal effects of natural selection to which Corydon refers. Nietzsche maintains that Darwin and his school note that natural selection favours the strongest and best-formed beings and contributes to the progress of the species. 'But,' he asserts, 'it is precisely the opposite which strikes us so forcibly: suppression of these fortunate examples [*cas heureux*] . . . the futility of those best-formed beings, and the inevitable domination of all by average types.' Here is a dimension of the debate to which Gide would have subscribed at this date. And presumably he would have been attracted by what followed, although he did not comment on it:

My conception of the world of values shows that in the highest values now placed above humanity, it is not happy chance or types resulting from selection which are most important, but it is types drawn from *decadence*. . . . However strange such a statement might appear, the strong must always be placed higher than the weak, the well-favoured above the misbegotten, the healthy above the degenerates and those who have inherited their illness. If reality is to be reduced to a *moral* formula, then it will be this: the average is worth more than the exception, the decadent more than the average; the will towards nothing has the advantage over the will to believe. . . .

Gide could not have followed Nietzsche, however, in saying 'I *revolt* against this way of formulating reality in order to create a moral code: that is why I detest Christianity with mortal hatred.' What had attracted his attention is to be found at the end of this argument in Aphorism 324:

I find that Nature's cruelty which is so often talked about lies elsewhere: Nature is cruel towards fortune's favourites: she accommodates, protects and loves the *humble*.

In conclusion, the growth of the power of a given species is perhaps less guaranteed by the larger quantity of its well-favoured and strong members than by the preponderance of average and lower than average types. . . . These latter possess great fecundity and longevity [durée]. In the first category, the danger increases, the rapid destruction, the decrease in numbers. [sic]

Gide quotes this in connection with his own observation that in his garden rare varieties disappear whereas the common 'mediocre' ones triumph. Transposed into the realm of human affairs, he will therefore see the reversal of this 'law' as a matter of social policy.

Writing to Ernst Robert Curtius on 28 July 1930 Gide repeated his acknowledgement of this specific debt to Nietzsche. Without believing in the gross theories of Lombroso, he said, he was nevertheless aware of an inner lack of equilibrium which had probably created that anxiety which first drew him towards imaginative literature. 'Nothing had thrown more light on this,' he added, 'than Nietzsche's splendid pages on Greek illness – on illness through the very excess of health. And I firmly believe that a people who are incapable of illness would also lack art and literature. Perhaps that is what those doctors really want. . . .'

The allusion, as the editors of the *Correspondance* point out, is to *Menschliches Allzumenschliches*, Aphorism 214 'On ennobling reality'. It is here that we may perceive the seed of an idea we witness in Gide's writings on more than one occasion. The Aphorism states that since men saw a godhead in the sexual instinct, and felt it working within themselves, they endowed this complex concept with nobility. Thus, by the means of this idealisation, some civilisations used certain illnesses as a powerful support. This is how the Greeks evolved the religious figure of the Bacchant. 'The Greeks,' wrote Nietzsche, 'had a truly well-balanced health. Their secret was to render divine honours to illness – provided it was powerful.'

There is every reason to believe that Gide was acquainted with this work when it was issued in translation by the *Mercure de France* in 1899. Among the other aphorisms, no. 100, 'On modesty', coincides with thoughts he had already expressed in *Le Traité du Narcisse*. For Nietzsche, modesty was the necessary concomitant of mystery and therefore belonged primarily to the religious sphere. However, modesty was transferred by an analogical reasoning to the field of sexual contact. Thus women became 'sanctified', and being divine necessarily evoked feelings of awe and respect. Aphorism 398 on the same subject adds that a woman's modesty increases with her beauty (but this is an argument Corydon will certainly not follow, since beauty is a quality he more readily associates with males).[28]

Our conclusion regarding these matters must be that although they have no direct relevance to homosexuality, for this was not Nietzsche's concern, they do have a more general bearing on Gide's view of the 'exceptional' individual. Their import is not sexual, but they contribute to a moral view which in turn does derive from Gide's presentation of sexuality. They are perhaps more important for the light they shed on a theory of immoralism whereby the Christian principle of Charity is rejected. In this respect, however, they lie outside the scope of the present enquiry. If we are to take them into account, we will do so when noting the change from Gide's portrayal of the egotist Michel in *L'Immoraliste* to the post-First World War humanism of Édouard in *Les Faux-Monnayeurs*.

*

There are other moralists, historians and philosophers who had something to say about homosexuality, but whose attitude to the topic was mainly hostile. Gide consulted the works of several of these writers.

Senancour

It is not unreasonable to assume that in 1911 Gide perused the new edition of Étienne-Pivert de Senancour's *De l'Amour selon les lois primordiales et selon les convenances des sociétés modernes*, edited with a preface by C.A.V. de Boisjolin.[29] When Senancour turns his attention to deviant sexual behaviour he finds that homosexuality (although he does not use this exact term) is even more contrary to the natural order than bestiality, because it is necessarily sterile. One of the primary causes of this 'disruption' among men, he adds, has perhaps been the fact that women have abandoned their natural modesty. Gide argues that the relationship between female modesty and pederasty is very much the reverse of this. Senancour continues that, as soon as Man saw that Woman was not absolutely necessary, 'strange fantasies' took the place of his diminishing appetites. Subsequently Senancour's attitude seems to be one of bewildered hostility: how, he asks, has it come about that such relationships between men have been so splendidly celebrated? If on occasion an individual devoid of taste, delicacy and principles should firmly take hold of another man we would not be absolutely surprised – but how one can find something gracious to say about such an act is beyond his comprehension. On masturbation, as a substitute for heterosexual gratification, he remarks that despite its occurrence in prisons and the army it should always be condemned when practised frequently, for, in excess, it is both hateful and fatal to the constitution. Such ideas, we know, were not novel.

Chamfort

Another writer of the early nineteenth century to whom Gide refers in *Corydon* (p. 84), S.R.N. Chamfort, was perhaps more traditional in his approach to these matters, in as much as he ignored them altogether. In a cynical collection[30] of maxims on love, women, marriage and dalliance he commented on the role of love in society: it is only the exchange of two 'fantaisies' and the contact of two 'épidermes', a point which we see Gide use to distinguish the human from the animal world. This is also reminiscent of a quotation from Balzac's *Les Paysans* which Gide recorded in his *Journal*, probably in 1911:[31] 'If, as Buffon says, love resides in the sense of touch, the softness of this skin should be active and penetrating – like the scent of the datura [a poisonous narcotic plant].'

Mantegazza

It is also reasonable to assume that Gide knew of Mantegazza's popular work on love. The French translation, *L'Amour dans l'humanité*, had been published by E. Chesneau in 1886. Again the writer's attitude to homosexuality is scarcely sympathetic, and the consideration of this form of love is relegated to a short chapter on 'aberrant behaviour'. Chapter V deals with masturbation, tribadism, sodomy, shoe fetishism and bestiality. 'The naturalist psychologist does not shun the filth of humanity,' and the reasons for this filth may easily be determined. The shameful and aberrant practices of physical love, writes Mantegazza, stem from one of two causes – either the 'physiological' union of the opposite sexes is difficult or impossible to achieve, or there is a desire to experience pleasures which are new and different. Here, says Mantegazza, is found the psychological explanation for all genital perversions, from Sodom to Lesbos, and Babylon to Capri. Among the practices involving males, he seems only to consider sodomy. For this he offers the explanation that the nerves responsible for giving us pleasure have been 'redirected' to the rectum. He furthermore distinguishes three classes of this perversion: peripheral sodomy, where the nerves have merely been realigned; luxurious sodomy, defined by a desire for narrowness and constriction; psychic sodomy, 'not a vice, but a passion – reprehensible and revolting'. Victims of all three classes may be pitied, and, Mantegazza hopes, eventually cured. Excess in love, be it homo-

or heterosexual, may sometimes kill: masturbation is more frequently lethal, for even when the body does not die the individual's character and dignity succumb. The least spark of idealism dies with this expenditure of virile energy.

Bourget

Towards the end of February 1891 Gide recorded reading and taking notes from *Physiologie de l'amour moderne. Fragments posthumes d'un ouvrage de Claude Larcher recueillis et publiés par Paul Bourget*. The book is in fact by Bourget, and Gide considered it 'perhaps his best, after his essays'.[32] The 'Fragments' turn out to be a collection of 'Meditations' on love, divided into sections of unequal length, each based on an apophthegm. Their standpoint is heterosexual, and on the whole rather libertine (but not too much so) and tending towards the cynical. In the first 'Meditation' (p. 19) Bourget reflects on the nature of love: 'A dictionary definition: "*Love*: In physiology, the totality of cerebral phenomena which make up the sexual instinct. It becomes the starting point for intellectual initiatives and numerous other actions which vary according to individuals and exterior conditions. . . . *Among most mammals – and even sometimes among mankind – the instinct for destruction is manifest at the same time as sexual love*.' Gide may have noted this, as he may also have noted the contents of 'Meditation II' (pp. 28–44) on the reasons for being excluded from love. Among eight reasons Bourget lists, we find 'timidity' (as with Rousseau), 'beauty' (as with Narcissus), 'scrupulousness' (to obey the Church's rules on chastity) and 'frigidity' (as with Octave in Stendhal's *Armance*).

Michelet

With Jules Michelet we reach the historians and the philosophers of history. Gide recorded reading him in his 'Subjectif' on 23 August 1891, and made an adverse judgement on his book *L'Amour* in a letter to Paul Valéry in August of the same year,[33] adding: 'but I like it – it's sometimes quite apocalyptic'. On the whole, however, he considered the volume 'rather ridiculous'. First published in 1859, the book in fact takes as its starting point the thesis that modern society is corrupt. The nation has become degenerate through the increasing abuse of the solitary pleasures obtained from alcohol and tobacco. The time has now come to reinvigorate the corporate pleasures of the family and to re-erect Woman on the pedestal where she rightly belongs. When French youth becomes serious, Michelet announces, then liberty is safe. The book is permeated by an overbearing, patronising attitude towards women, and examines the nature of love in and through the institution of marriage. Nothing is said of animal sexuality or deviant behaviour, while the reader – who is obviously presumed to be male – is constantly exhorted to protect and embellish his wife, by impregnating her mind as well as her body. He should take care lest too much reading coarsen her mental capacities, and should take full advantage of the conjugal bed to improve her moral education. This activity is called 'l'incubation morale'. For our present purposes the most important point to note is that, despite Gide's disapproval, Michelet does in fact put forward what can be seen as a key element in Corydon's case. The argument turns on the innate purity of Woman and the need for her to be honoured in her community. Even if she is constantly a victim and may on occasion commit adultery with disastrous consequences, her role is noble and her grace should not be debased by prostitution, be it metaphorical or literal. Where Gide departs from this general attitude is obviously in seeking to associate the occurrence of pederasty with the elevated role of Woman.

In the years preceding 1911 Gide read several works on Roman history, among them Michelet's *Histoire romaine* from which he quoted in his *Journal*,[34] and there is an early reference to reading 'the first 130 pages' in late July 1898 in his unpublished *Journal*.[35] The material in question deals with Republican Rome,[36] and, although mention is made of education in Sparta, Michelet is not specifically concerned with pederasty. However, as we shall see, Gide realised that a detailed study of this subject such as he was undertaking in preparation for writing *Corydon* could not ignore the sexual practices of antiquity.

Herder

Herder's *Ideen zur Philosophie der Geschichte der Menschheit* first appeared in 1784–91, and was translated into French with an introduction by E. Quinet in 1827–8. Gide referred to it by its French title in *Corydon*,[37] but he was probably doing no more on that occasion than translate from Carpenter's *Ioläus*, for it is obvious from a note which was deleted from the 1920 proofs that this was his immediate source.[38] Carpenter's brief text, in English, contains Herder's views on how athletic games

57

gave to the youth of Greece their 'good looks, good health and good spirits', and continues: 'The feminine sex, despite the splendid examples of every virtue that it exhibited in Greece, as elsewhere, remained there only a secondary object of manly life. The thoughts of aspiring youths reached towards something higher. The bond of friendship which they knitted among themselves or with grown men, compelled them into a school which Aspasia herself could hardly have introduced them to. . . .' Gide made a note 'to check this against the original German',[39] but we do not know whether he did so. Herder's chapter contains more material: even if we are astonished by what we read in Plato, he writes, and find what he says as exotic as a novel set on another planet, we must note the power and depth of this affection. 'Happy and touching youthful loves! No feeling is so delicious as the love of those who strive with us in our first efforts towards perfection.' If licentious habits did spring from the very institutions which encouraged this noble spirit of emulation, then Herder is ready to deplore these abuses while at the same time remembering the commendable characteristics of the ancients. Such disorders were inevitable, he asserts, given their fiery imagination and their love of beauty, which was the noblest attribute of their gods. Had they been more hidden, these affections would have been vicious and more dangerous. It was, however, fortunate that this type of love developed under the careful scrutiny of the laws, which ensured that it contributed to the public good. That Herder's brief picture is sentimental, romantic and idealistic is perhaps too obvious to deserve mention. No more than a gesture is made to relate this behaviour to the social institutions of the state, but the reader sees here a justification of homosexual behaviour which was often repeated later in the century.

Herder mentions homosexual behaviour only in the chapter devoted to the moral and political institutions of the Greeks from which I have quoted. Other points of a more general nature may well have atrracted Gide's attention, for they seem to have their counterparts in Corydon's general attitudes and elsewhere in Gide's writings. Such are, for example, Herder's pronouncement in Book 4, Chapter 4, that in regard to his instincts Man is organised in a purer form than are animals, and therefore moves towards liberty in his actions. In Book 8, Chapter 1, there is a statement concerning cultural relativisim: the sensitivity of the human race varies with its forms and the climate, but the development of humanity only – and always – occurs in those places where sensuality is indulged in the least gross manner. Again, custom and religion regulate mankind's behaviour, even though Man's appetites are determined by his circumstances and social organisation (Book 8, Chapter 4). It is often interesting to see how past authors have accounted for the decadence of Rome, the more so since it was commonly accepted that 'corrupted morals' were among the major reasons for the Empire's decline. Herder does not ascribe the fall of the state to sexual deviation, but rather seeks to account for it by constitutional reasons, the corruption engendered by too many slaves, too great a taste for luxury, and self-destructive military despotism resulting from the power of the army. Gide did not address himself to this topic directly, but did feel it necessary to consider the questions of slavery, and war, and their relation to the institutionalisation of male friendship. What he used from Herder is to be found in the fourth Dialogue of *Corydon*.

Montesquieu

Another historian to whom Gide often refers is Montesquieu.[40] There is an allusion in *Corydon* to a note by Laboulaye in the Garnier edition of *L'Esprit des lois* concerning Lycurgus, the reformer of Sparta's laws, but despite Laboulaye's evidently hostile attitude towards 'Sparta . . . this convent of soldiers' from which nothing good has issued, he does not discuss the citizens' homosexual customs.

More interesting is a section from Book 12, Chapter 6 (pp. 71–2), 'Du crime contre nature', from which, however, Gide does not quote. Montesquieu has no wish to make light of the horror which he feels for a crime which, he says, religion, morals and politics alike condemn. Nor, he states, will such behaviour make headway in society unless the people are encouraged towards it, as was the case with the Greeks. In the briefest possible way, Montesquieu limits himself to mentioning its ignominy and horror which, he says, may nevertheless be turned to the advantage of tyranny. There is also a quotation from Book 4, Chapter 8 in *Corydon* (p. 166) which faithfully reflects Montesquieu's attitude: pederasty is 'a love which should be proscribed by all the nations of the world'. The historian thinks that we should blush when we learn that such conduct was even enshrined in the laws of the Thebans. Here, however, we come to something of a contradiction. In 1904 Gide also noticed some remarks in Book 8, Chapter 11 ('Effets naturels de la bonté et de la corruption des principes') from *L'Esprit des lois* and copied them out on to a paper which has not found its way into the printed *Journal*.[41] Once the principles of government are corrupted, Montesquieu declares, the best laws are rendered bad and turn to the detriment of the state. He cites the example of athletics among the Greeks which 'were equally dependent upon the principles of government', and reports Plato's opinion that, when the Spartans and the

Cretans had first established 'these [athletic] academies', modesty, which at first prevailed, soon yielded to the fact that these exercises were useful to the state (*Republic* 5). This was because exercise contributed directly to military success (Corydon makes a somewhat similar point about modern Germany).[42] Montesquieu adds, however, that 'When the Greeks ceased to be virtuous [*sic*]' these habits destroyed military art itself, for people no longer went to the palaestra to train their bodies, but to corrupt them, and he adds a citation from Martial IV 55 to this effect. Gide's quotation begins shortly after this point: '"In Plutarch's time, the places where young men fought and wrestled naked made them cowardly, encouraged them to indulge in nameless vice, and only made fops out of them. But in the days of Epaminondas, wrestling enabled them to win," etc. See the rest of the note and B. Constant's remark.' What the Thebans were enabled to win was the battle of Leuctra. Constant's note makes the obvious point which effectively destroys Montesquieu's argument: the army which the Thebans were thus able to defeat was composed of Spartans, who for four hundred years had also been perfecting themselves by means of athletic training.[43] It is not difficult to perceive that Gide also noticed the flawed reasoning, though we shall see that he, too, had an idealised view of Epaminondas.

In *Corydon* (p. 143), Gide also refers to the edition of Montesquieu's *Voyages* which appeared at Bordeaux in 1894–6, but here the historian is recounting his surprise, albeit without puritanical condemnation, at the contemporary Roman practice of dressing castrati as attractive young females. A similar passage from Gérard de Nerval's travels in Egypt is cited at the same point in the text of *Corydon* to much the same effect.[44] In the remainder of the *Voyages* there is much to interest Gide, though little of a distinctly homosexual nature. In Volume 2, while commenting on the statues in the Duke's collection at Florence, for example, Montesquieu makes a passing remark about a bust of Nero with little or no beard:[45] this, he comments, was evidently a sign of this prince's unbridled nature, for he dishonoured his sex and married one of his own freedmen. A statue of Ganymede where the eagle, covering one buttock with a wing, looks lovingly at the boy, is mentioned without distaste.[46] Elsewhere there are a few scattered references to the dissolute Emperor Elagabalus and to Hermaphroditus. The conclusion we may draw is that, although on occasion Montesquieu revealed his hostility towards homosexuality, he was also able to keep silent either out of regard for Art, or from indifference.

Montesquieu's *Correspondance* is also relevant to our enquiry. In it, Gide noticed an opinion which obviously concurs with Corydon's remarks on Rousseau's misfortune at having been schooled by Mme de Warens:[47]

Read in Montesquieu's Corresp. vol. II p. 592: 'There is a fundamental vice in France in this domain [education], because it is . . . provided by women. They interfere in everything, they eventually spoil everything, and destroy everything. A *child* [Gide's ms. italics (*Un enfant*)] is soon corrupted in their hands, from the age of two to six.' See the rest.[48]

The sequel describes how the child is next given into the charge of an unknown man (the tutor) who carries out his duties only through self-interest, and whose actions are not dictated by inclination. Next, the boy spends ten years 'vegetating' within the narrow confines of a school, or among society ladies with their loud and sterile conversation. Women, Montesquieu adds, whose minds never give a moment's thought to serious or useful matters, are the people who appoint the tutors. Men are as weak as children, for they give in to women's whims. Thus no one escapes his criticism, and his correspondent ('Philinte') should therefore not be surprised that France has no great men, for French boys are spoiled from birth. Gide was not concerned with the education of rulers, it is true, but he believed that sound moral principles could seldom, if ever, be imparted by a woman. But he did not share Montesquieu's scepticism about the tutor's motives. Moreover, in an unpublished reply to a questionnaire on education and social hygiene written in 1922, he was sceptical about the ability of the parents themselves to educate children, for, in his opinion, they were prevented from doing so by the very reticence and modesty (*pudeur*) which they had instilled in their offspring: he was firmly convinced that an older lover would prove more successful.[49]

Gibbon

Throughout his life Gide noticed when historians revealed their prejudices or voiced a thought-provoking comment on homosexual behaviour. Thus, in 1943, when he was reading Guizot's edition of Gibbon's *Decline and Fall of the Roman Empire*, he included his latest discovery in his *Journal*: 'I find in a note by Gibbon, Chapter III AD 117: "Of Hadrian" (speaking about Antinous): "We may remark that, of the first fifteen emperors, Claudius was the only one whose taste in love was entirely *correct*."'[50] By italicising the word 'correct' Gide is plainly directing our attention to the flaw he sees in Gibbon's assumption that only heterosexual behaviour can be thought of as proper. He makes no comment on Gibbon's hostile report of homosexual practices among the Taifali, a Gothic tribe, and among the Cretans;[51] nor does he have anything to say about Gibbon's denunciation of homosexuality in the celebrated chapter on Roman law.[52]

Carpenter

In 1906 there appeared, in London, the second, enlarged edition of Edward Carpenter's *Ioläus, an Anthology of Friendship*. Material from this collection was predominantly incorporated into the fourth Dialogue of *Corydon*.[53] In Carpenter's book we have a sympathetic collection of literary extracts from antiquity and more recent times, including some travellers' accounts of their amorous encounters with boys. It is divided into five sections with an appendix: I – Friendship customs in the pagan and early world (pp. 1–38); II – The place of friendship in Greek life and thought (pp. 39–64); III – Poetry of friendship among the Greeks and Romans (pp. 65–94); IV – Friendship in early Christian and mediaeval times (pp. 95–120); V – The Renaissance and modern times (pp. 121–82). The appendix includes material from various periods (for example: Aristotle; Hafiz; Beaumont and Fletcher; Schiller; Frederick of Prussia; Ludwig II and Wagner; Edward Fitzgerald and 'Posh'). In the 1920 edition of *Corydon*, a footnote to the quotation from Darwin in Dialogue III reads:[54] 'Reproduce here the admirable passage by Haeckel, *My Visit to Ceylon*, p. 200, quoted in *Ioläus*.' The discussion in Gide's text is concerned with Darwin's account of the beauty of the male Tahitians and the corresponding disappointment he felt on viewing the women. Haeckel, is simply describing the devotion manifested towards him by his Rodiya (or pariah) serving boy Gamameda, a name calculated to suggest echoes of Ganymede. 'The favourite of Jove himself could not have been more finely made, or have had limbs more beautifully proportioned and moulded.'[55] In a footnote printed in the 1920 edition of *Corydon*, Gide added a reference to stories of deep sentimental male friendships in the East.[56] In one of these, a dervish has left his heart in Baghdad, and the travel writer J.S. Buckingham, in his *Travels in Assyria, Media and Persia*, is shocked when he learns that the object of the dervish's affections is a boy. In another tale, anguished love at first sight is experienced by a dervish who cared for his beloved during his illness and was so affected by his death that he nearly pined away himself with grief. These, Carpenter remarks, are the very signs of the friendship known among the Greeks. Both stories were intended to illustrate Corydon's proposition that homosexual lovers are capable of self-sacrifice (*abnégation*). Another example taken from *Ioläus* was deleted from the 1920 proofs of *Corydon*.[57] It concerns a report of the death of the Khalifa and the devoted band of soldiers who formed his bodyguard during the British expedition to Khartoum in 1899. 'In almost all primitive nations, warfare has given rise to institutions of military comradeship,' wrote Carpenter (p. 11), citing in further support of his argument Tacitus and Ammianus Marcellinus on the primitive Germans.[58] Corydon was to have made the same point, adding that 'uranian customs were not exclusive to the Greeks'. The bulk of Carpenter's texts which Gide quotes in the public edition of *Corydon* come from the section on Greek love and the institutions of the Spartan state. But what Carpenter collected are literary witnesses to the power of love, and not sociological or factual historical documents. Thus Symonds, quoted by Carpenter and repeated by Gide, reminds the reader that 'the chivalry of Hellas found its motive force in friendship rather than in the love of women'.[59]

Carpenter's *Intermediate Types among Primitive Folk. A Study in Social Evolution* appeared in 1914, but we cannot be sure that Gide was familiar with it. From Corydon's point of view, the more interesting chapters would have been those concerned with the Intermediate (that is, homosexual) as warrior, particularly those sections dealing with Dorian military comradeship and its relation to the status of women and to civic life and religion.[60] Much the same arguments are deployed here as in certain later passages in *Corydon*: the Dorian customs of male friendship in Sparta and Crete lead naturally to an identification of homosexual behaviour with valour and a general sense of public duty. Some writers, reports Carpenter, maintain that pederasty (that is, homosexual love) shows a lack of concern for women. Lowes Dickinson in his *Greek View of Life* did in fact put forward this opinion. But in Homer the ideal of military comradeship 'must have been in its inception associated with just such a high standard in the position of women. . . . For the main motive of the Iliad is, as Benecke observes, undoubtedly the dramatic and passionate comradeship between Achilles and Patroclus; yet no one could say that Andromache or Penelope or Nausicaa are negligible or servile characters.'[61] The same point of view was argued by John Addington Symonds: 'It is notorious that in those Dorian states where the love of comrades became an institution, women received *more* public honour and enjoyed fuller liberty and power over property than elsewhere.'[62] After quoting Chapter XIV of Plutarch's *Life of Lycurgus* to the same effect, Carpenter resumes: 'It is the Uranian classes of men, or those at least who are touched with the Uranian temperament, who chiefly support the modern woman's movement.'[63] But at that point occurs a major political difference between Gide and the English socialist.

CHAPTER SIX

Social Theory

Blum

Gide took over the literary reviews in *La Revue Blanche* from Léon Blum in 1900.[1] The latter's work *Du mariage* appeared in 1907 and provoked a hostile reaction from Gide even before its publication. It is evident from the *Journal* of 5 January 1907 that the two writers discussed it together. At the beginning of the fourth Dialogue of *Corydon* both the interlocutor and Corydon are shown in an ironic light when they praise Blum's book. On occasion, they also overtly criticise it. To say, as Corydon does, that Blum's solution to the social problem posed by man's sexual drive is to have recourse to a form of prostitution is to isolate and exaggerate one part of Blum's argument. One also senses an anti-semitic element in the text of *Corydon*, which is not entirely compensated for by the author's evidently ironic tone. The reference to Blum, however, is not a prelude to a close examination of his ideas, but a preparation for Corydon's notion that the purity of women and the moral security of society are more surely safeguarded by the adoption of pederastic customs akin to those accepted in ancient Greece. It was in his *Journal* that Gide gave a more reasoned and detailed account of how he understood the main thrust of *Du mariage*. On 16 June 1907 he wrote of his disgust at the way in which 'happiness' seemed to him to be Blum's only concern. Nor did it seem to him that Blum properly understood the nobility of women's resignation:

> But his constant, his only (and avowed) preoccupation with *happiness* in his book continues to shock me. I am far from being convinced that in the easiest and least costly conjunction of his ways of obtaining satisfaction a man becomes worthy of my love and admiration. And what about women, then!! The finest figures of women I have known are resigned; and I cannot even imagine being pleased (and not being aroused to some hostility) by the contentment of a woman whose happiness does not include a little resignation.

On 29 June 1907 Gide consigned to his *Journal* the text of a letter he had thought it wisest not to send: he considered Blum's book actually harmful in that it did not provide the new light it claimed to reveal. In short it would encourage its readers to find in its pages an authorisation for their actions. After carefully rereading the book Gide focused on the goal of happiness, and Blum's comfortable recipe for obtaining it, which he found unacceptable. The book had some positive merit, he considered, but the major flaw lay in its neglect of the value of restraint and resignation.

Blum did in fact suggest that men should have older mistresses to induct them (and this runs counter to Corydon's views), and he had also noticed how married bliss is frequently haphazard and difficult to achieve: 'Taking it for granted that marriage or legal monogamy is an institution which works badly, I wondered whether we should abandon it totally and rely on our modern forms of polygamy, that is to say on multiple and precarious relationships.' Or was it possible to correct it? It is interesting to see that in Blum's view the stereotypes of faithful woman and questing man can be reversed: 'The true vice in modern marriage is that it unites a man who has reached or almost reached the period of monogamy with a woman who before settling should normally spend and exhaust her instinct for change.' Thereafter happiness and domestic peace would ensue. Corydon is unjust to assert that this view has an 'Oriental or Levantine' flavour. What would Blum's reaction have been to reading Gide's laconic reply to a survey on marriage conducted by the periodical *La Plume* in 1901: 'All the happy households I have known have been happy *despite* marriage, and almost all the unhappy ones *because of it*. But that is no reason why . . .'?[2]

Malthus

When we consider the influence of Malthus we find, perhaps surprisingly, that Gide's hostility to the idea of social and sexual control is by no means total. Although the issue is not the tolerance or otherwise of homosexual conduct, there are points at which the position advocated by Malthus and his followers does connect with certain attitudes adopted by Gide in the course of his argument. For example the 1911 edition of *Corydon* bears on page 5 a revealing epigraph about the primacy of virtue.[3] In the public edition of *Corydon* reference is made to Malthus in the fourth Dialogue where he is appealed to in the course of the argument against Blum. Corydon declares that according to Malthus chastity has its roots in nature and reason, and that this virtue is the only legitimate means of avoiding the vices and misfortunes that the laws of population entail. The epigraph we have noticed eventually found its place later in this same fourth Dialogue, again in the mouth of Corydon (p. 181). It was not greatly to Gide's purpose to take further note of Malthus' theories, although, as we shall observe, Gide correctly saw that the question of homosexual behaviour was not separable from the wider implications of the distribution of male and female births within a given society.

At the beginning of the fourth Dialogue Corydon uses a quotation from Malthus to counter the notion that prostitution is necessary. The extract is taken from the translation[4] of *An Essay on the Principle of Population*, Book IV, Chapter 2: '[These considerations shew that] the virtue of Chastity is not, as some have supposed, a forced product of artificial society;[5] but that it has the most real and solid foundation in nature and reason; being apparently the only virtuous[6] means of avoiding the vice and misery which result so often from the principle of population.'

What precisely are these 'considerations'? Malthus' argument places the concept of chastity in a different perspective. He is arguing that poverty will be avoided when the wages of labour are sufficient to maintain with decency a large family. 'The interval between the age of puberty and the period at which each individual might venture on marriage must, according to the supposition, be passed in strict chastity; because the law of chastity cannot be violated without producing evil.' Promiscuous intercourse degrades the female character.[7] But it immediately becomes clear that Malthus' model is not one where abstinence is praised as the greatest virtue. After the passage cited in *Corydon* he continues: 'In such a society as we have been supposing it might be necessary for some of both sexes to pass many of the early years of life in the single state. . . . If the custom of not marrying early prevailed generally, and if violations of chastity were equally dishonourable in both sexes, a more familiar and friendly intercourse between them might take place without danger'; and, a little further on, 'The earlier years of life would not be spent without love, though without the full gratification of it' – which the translator has expanded and explained: 'The early years would not be strangers to love – to a chaste and pure love which far from being extinguished by satiety would be maintained with constancy.' It is therefore only part of Malthus' argument that Corydon has retained, and, what is more, Corydon has his own special answer for sexual experience before marriage.

There are, however, a number of other sections from the *Essay on Population* which have a bearing on our present investigation and with which it is reasonable to assume Gide was acquainted. He passed over them in silence. The first is connected with the passage already quoted from p. 489 of the translation. The text continues: '[Vices] can rarely or never be committed without producing unhappiness. . . . A large class of women, and many men, I have no doubt, pass a considerable part of their lives consistently with the laws of chastity; but I believe there will be found very few who pass through the ordeal of squalid and hopeless poverty . . . without a great moral degradation of character.' But, unlike Malthus, Corydon is not concerned with the economic aspects of chastity. Malthus goes on to discuss how poverty corrupts a man's financial probity and causes crime. If persons in this situation marry and have offspring, it is in these conditions that every vice will multiply, and in rags and filth they will live in ignorance of all moral duties and obligations. Furthermore, Malthus considers, it may on occasion occur that an individual's chastity is too severely tried and he succumbs; the poor man will be both weaker in this respect and more corrupt. If we are concerned only with the duties of chastity, we will soon see that marriage is far from being a sure means of respecting them. The upper classes offer many examples of this, and even among the lower classes examples are probably not much rarer. This tallies with Corydon's hostile commentary on the virtue of the married state. Malthus concludes the chapter thus: 'abject poverty, particularly when joined with idleness, is a state the most unfavourable to chastity that can well be conceived'. However, female prostitution is only incidentally of interest to Gide, for he can link the role of women to the benefits of pederasty and leave immodest sexual activity to the heterosexuals.

Elsewhere in this work, speaking of chastity, Malthus considers it a rule to be more rigorously applied in the case of women. Women's happiness is increased in civilised society; and celibacy, enjoined on the two sexes and recommended by Plato and Aristotle, has as its chief advantage not a diminution of the population but a decrease in the rate of mortality. These are again utilitarian arguments which Gide would have been slow to espouse. We are under an obligation to practise moral constraint in Malthus' view, because the evils which flow from abuse of the passions are too great for us to think of doing otherwise. Moral constraint can shape society; and there are similarly many advantages in late marriage for women. Here we return to Malthus' capital point: marriage is the only way to improve the lot of the poor. It is a social duty; moral constraint is not in conflict with this idea, nor with the laws of nature, for it is the means by which a healthy and vigorous population is produced, unaffected by vice and misfortune.

The second section concerns marriage more directly, and is again seen to be at a tangent to the views expressed in *Corydon*. The effects of direct encouragement to marry are shown to be pernicious, although the origin of prejudice against marriage can be traced back to St Paul. The upper classes are seldom lacking in prudence where marriage is at issue, for their concern is with property. Malthus proposed no law against marriage (although he is often credited with such a libertarian attitude). He also considered, as he was a man of the world, that marriage was sometimes nothing more than legalised prostitution. It was encouraged in France, he reports, through fear of the military laws requiring an increase in the birthrate.

The third section concerns the incidence of births at different periods. Malthus notices that the annual birthrate increased during the French Revolution, and that the deathrate diminished among the citizens who remained in France. He was also interested in the relationship of the number of soldiers to the remainder of the population. We remember that Corydon raises a similar point, and that Gide refined his investigation in order to ascertain the periodic ratio of male to female births.[8]

We may note that Malthus' doctrine was not favourable to slavery which, he considered, undermined society. Corydon's attitude to slaves is more ambiguous. Furthermore, Malthus refers to the Greek practice of child exposure as a method of controlling numbers, and to Plato's and Aristotle's proposals for preventing an excessive increase in the population, but he does not mention pederasty in this context. However, in an early part of the *Essay* he does touch on 'unnatural passions'.[9] He writes: 'A promiscuous intercourse[10] to such a degree as to prevent the birth of children, seems to lower, in the most marked manner, the dignity of human nature. It cannot be without its effect on men, and nothing can be more obvious than its tendency to degrade the female character.' A little later he continues: 'Promiscuous intercourse,[11] unnatural passions, violations of the marriage bed, and improper arts[12] to conceal the consequences of irregular connections[13] are preventive checks that clearly come under the head of vice.' The French translator adds a note to 'vice': 'We must not forget that this word can be replaced by "misère" [abject poverty] which corresponds to the English word *misery* used by Malthus.' Gide does not seem to have wished to take these last remarks into account at all, any more than he took up Malthus' crediting the Romans and Turks with 'vicious habits' and 'polygamy and other vices' which were held to explain the epidemics and illnesses suffered in those societies.

Gourmont

One book which was widely acclaimed when it was published, and which Gide used the better to define his own position, was *Physique de l'amour. Essai sur l'instinct sexuel* by Rémy de Gourmont, first published in 1903. In 1912 it had achieved an eleventh edition. Ghéon reviewed it briefly in *L'Ermitage* XV March 1904 (p. 224), drawing his readers' attention to the pages on modesty: 'There is no detail so strange, whether it belong to mole, bull or oyster, for him not to draw from it a piquant generalisation applied to us.' Gide first read it in 1905, styling it 'Métaphysique de l'amour' in his list of books to be read.[14]

In the second Dialogue Corydon expresses his surprise that so ingenious a writer has not drawn the conclusions that he himself will shortly draw. Instead, he maintains, Gourmont's book is inspired by an overwhelming desire to bring love among mankind down to the level it occupies in the animal world. In effect Corydon at this point denies that love is merely a matter of sexual appetite, more or less convincingly disguised. That is Gourmont's position, and, as reported by Corydon, Gourmont also maintains that such an instinct calls for ineluctable obedience. Gide's position is more startling: the instinct, he says, is an invention, and does not exist. Edmond Perrier, writing in *Le Temps* 1 August 1912, and cited by Corydon, quotes with approval a remark of Gourmont's on males who cannot fulfil their 'destiny' because of the disparity in the relative distribution of male and female births to the disadvantage of the males. This earns an ironic exclamation mark. On Gourmont's representation of aberrant sexual behaviour Gide is also ironic. Gourmont writes of cows which mount each other, and says that they do so either because they thereby wish to provoke the bull or because the visual sensation of the sexual union that they conjure up in their own minds obliges them to simulate the act. Echoing but twisting the author's words, Gide decides that this is indeed 'more absurd than marvellous'.[15] There are certain physiological details which Gourmont observes correctly: the female, Corydon agrees (p. 93), ceases to emit her odour as soon as she is mounted. But he is again scornful about Gourmont's notion that Woman represents Beauty and that any contrary view is 'necessarily to be considered a paradox or the product of the most unwelcome sexual aberration' (p. 129). In short, Gide represents Gourmont's thesis as objectionably zoomorphic and unacceptably based on a heterosexual model.

A brief analysis of *Physique de l'amour* will illustrate the selective nature of Gide's argument. It will also help us to gain a wider view of a theory against which Gide's polemic stands as a new way to assert the value of certain individuals within the mass of human society. Nevertheless, some willingness to provide zoological illustrations is to be found in *Corydon* as well, and we may wish to reflect on the proposition that *Corydon* is an 'answer' to Gourmont.

Rémy de Gourmont's book is divided into twenty chapters, with a bibliography and index. The first section introduces his subject: a general psychology of love is expounded, taking into consideration the 'natural laws', sexual selection and the place of mankind in Nature, describing the 'animal character' of love, and equating human and animal psychology. The second chapter deals with the imperative character of the sexual act: some animals live only in order to reproduce themselves. There is a struggle for life, as there is a struggle against death. Chapter three deals with asexual reproduction, touching briefly on hermaphroditism at the lower levels of animal life. Chapter four, dealing with invertebrates, considers sexual dimorphism, and notices, inter alia, the purely sexual role of the male in this category, as well as the superiority of the female among the majority of insects. (Corydon also takes these points into account.) Among the vertebrates, considered in the following chapter, examples are adduced to indicate a change in the position of the male who is now favoured by the role-structure of sexual dimorphism. Chapter six, continuing an examination of the vertebrates, brings us to men and women. The effects of civilisation lead to a 'moderate' form of dimorphism, and the human couple becomes a firm social necessity. Indeed the existence of the couple favours the female. But the analysis of her privileged position is one which we would now recognise as dependent upon a male-dominated view. Thus, remarking on sexual aesthetics, Gourmont seeks to account for the superiority of female beauty: there is a unique reason in that the line of her body is not interrupted by a projecting member. This absurdity was taken notice of by Gide.[16] Chapter seven continues the discussion of sexual dimorphism and feminism, and adduces examples of relative inferiority and superiority from the animal kingdom. In a biological sense the male could be eliminated and parthenogenesis become familiar in the human context. Nutrition determines the relative number of male and female births.[17]

Chapter eighteen is one where Gide might well have focused his attention more precisely: 'La question des aberrations'.[18] Aberrations, according to Gourmont, are of two sorts. They may be the result of internal or external impulsion. For example, in the case of sodomy among drakes the cause may be a burning desire, a momentary madness (folie) or a purely muscular need. Similarly, the lesbian activities of cows are described in this chapter. From life at the microscopic level to Man himself we see that aberrations are always present. These include masturbation, according to Gourmont. But at least among animals, he says, a more correct name for this behaviour would be 'impatience'. There would be far fewer deviant men and women if our usual moral code allowed a simple satisfaction of our sexual needs. If people could join with a partner of the opposite sex at the opportune moment the only 'aberrations' we would need to take into account would be 'anatomical' or 'physiological'. Among all the aberrations, the author continues, perhaps the oddest is chastity. This is because asceticism has religious connotations and the impulse towards satisfying it does not in the least derive from a sexual need. Indeed quite the contrary is the case. Is modesty, then, also an aberration? There follow examples of artificiality and variety in sexual modesty. The parts of the body which it is sinful to expose vary from civilisation to civilisation. The chapter concludes with some examples of cruelty, so normal in Nature, so repressed in human society.

The final chapters are concerned with the role of instinct, and the modifying role of intelligence. The conclusion is reached that men and animals are alike subject to the tyranny of the nervous system, and that 'among mankind, especially in the case of the male, all the senses unite in a drive towards [heterosexual] love unless moral prejudices or religious scruples prevent them from so doing'.[19]

We may therefore notice that despite the fact that Gide has on occasion borrowed examples from this book, he has also taken general issue with the author. *Physique de l'amour* adopts a firm and distinct stand on several points relative to our argument:

(1) no distinction is to be made between love and desire;
(2) heterosexuality constitutes a normal pattern for the great majority of humans;
(3) 'aberrations' occur frequently in Nature, but this does not validate such behaviour among humans;
(4) the practice of chastity is an unnatural imposition by society.

Gourmont was a populariser of scientific observations and little in his book was original. The organising of his material into a coherent whole was his achievement. The work is also typical of its time in that it places a great deal of importance on entomological evidence and connects both the behaviour and the physiology of man with what are seen as his 'biological' forebears.

It was in 1927 that André Rouveyre published his book on Gide and Gourmont, *Le Reclus et le retors*, consisting of material which had first appeared in the *Mercure de France* in 1923 and 1924. The work in fact consists of two character sketches and aims to describe the two writers' personalities. Rouveyre discovers the paradox of finding in their search for self-knowledge a common ground between these mutually antagonistic writers. As an appendix, he published some letters from Gide, who commented on remarks made in the original articles. On the whole Gide limited himself to several expressions of polite enthusiasm and a few protests. He rejected the suggestion that he was jealous of Gourmont's importance at the *Mercure* and that he had left it for that reason ('It was so dusty it was stifling').

One has the impression on reading Gide's remarks on other occasions that he was intensely aware of this rival, a few years his senior. They had very probably first met at one of Mallarmé's receptions, and thereafter they frequented the same circles of Parisian symbolist writers in the 1890s. The few letters which have been published[20] date from the years 1902–3. It was then that Rémy de Gourmont was doubtless very surprised to receive a violent letter from Gide in the following terms:

> You are one of the spirits whom I have detested the most. You have too successfully and too often formulated truths which it does not seem to me are good to utter. You write: 'The terrible thing about seeking truth is when one finds it.' What I found terrible in your case was that one found truths *without* seeking them. I would have preferred merely to seek. . . .

They were divided on matters of religion and morality, but despite this it seems that Gourmont had sought Gide's collaboration when, in 1904, he launched a new periodical to bridge the gap between the arts and the sciences, *La Revue des idées*.[21] It was in fact in early 1904 that Gide found himself on an errand to the periodical's office and there he met Gourmont face to face for the first time in several years.[22] For a long period before he actually saw Gourmont again, Gide noted, he knew that he would be awkward and hostile towards him. Although Gourmont had always been very considerate and had shown in his writings that he was intelligent and shrewd, Gide could not control his own feelings. He was all ready to greet him, a smile on his lips: 'but no, I could not. He is too ugly.' Gide did not by this mean to indicate his adversary's physical disfigurement but 'a profound ugliness. I say categorically that I felt he was ugly when I *read* him.' The reasons for this antipathy, Gide wrote, were probably a feeling that Gourmont's way of thinking was not 'involuntary', not a living, sensitive and suffering activity, not raw and liable to 'bleed' as was his own. Thus Gourmont appeared to him to be 'brutal' in his analyses. He was a cold and competent 'operator'.[23]

A curious exchange took place when, although Gourmont had sketched a reasonably sympathetic literary portrait of Gide in his first series of *Masques* in 1896, Gide later (in 1910) printed a hostile article on Gourmont's recently published series of dialogues.[24] The dialogues, as we shall see shortly, were on several moral and aesthetic issues and are, it must be admitted, of variable quality. Gide attacked Gourmont's moral attitudes and the lack of imagination shown in the form of his conversations between M. Desmaisons and M. Delarue. 'M. de Gourmont cannot understand, does not admit and does not wish to admit, that all intelligence is not on the side of free thought, and all stupidity on the side of religion.' Furthermore, Gide maintained that Gourmont was driven by 'two passions, two hatreds: of Christianity and of modesty [*la pudeur*]' – and these have 'thrown him into the arms of science [*sic*]'. Gide accuses him of dishonesty: 'In the most "scientific" of his books *Physique de l'amour* he is obsessed by the notion of reducing human love to the level of animals.'[25] It is easy to find incongruous quotations and Gide does so, hoping thereby to show his adversary a fool. Thus he discovers Gourmont unfortunately comparing a mole to a virgin in distress. (Fabre had used similar comparisons for his insects, but these Gide found charming.) Gide criticises him for arguing by intimidation: '"We are no longer in the naive times of Darwin" [and so on]' – but we may wonder whether Gide's beliefs were not at least as indebted to Darwin as were Gourmont's. Referring to the latest dialogue of 1 March 1910, Gide wrote:

> I place myself in your position – the position of mobile relativity which is your country. I grant for the present that all *truths* are equivalent and that none *matters*; that no conviction is so urgent that it cannot be reduced to some question of physiological suitability and organic adaptation; that nothing matters except pleasure, and I add 'the most urgent one'. Why at that point does it matter to me whether this theory is *true*, seeing that it is ugly, destructive and harmful for works of art!

Thus Gourmont's idea of what appeared to Gide as merely *mechanical* pleasure was criticised on the grounds that it could not inspire the creative act of the imagination.

Clearly one of the domains of greatest disagreement between the two men was that of love. Gourmont had written in 1909[26] that there are many forms of love and hence many different opinions on the matter. He considered it was therefore imprudent to write a book on love: healthy men *do* their loving – they do not read or write about it. (One remarks an irony of fate: Gourmont contracted a disfiguring skin disease in the 1890s, and in consequence lived as a semi-recluse, finding, it was rumoured, his stimulation in books.) All books on love, he said, are to some degree sad or cynical – and they are necessarily egotistical. This is all argued from the heterosexual viewpoint. Gourmont had, however, already turned his attention to the morality of 'aberrant' sexuality in 1900.[27] Here he took issue with those writers who wished to call all extramarital sexual activity a crime (for example, Seved Ribbing, *L'Hygiène sexuelle et ses conséquences morales* and works by Féré and others). His attitude was libertarian: he considered it was absurd to prosecute Moll, since his material was already to be found in Tardieu, Liguori, Martial and the *Priapeia*. He added a few historical remarks on sodomy and sapphism. But quoting La Rochefoucauld he repeated: 'Sobriety consists in the love of good health and the inability to over-eat.' Chastity should be defined in the same terms: if a man takes the vow of chastity he does so *because* he is frigid, for 'one only acts decently in conformity with one's own nature'. This is not in fact, it

73

may be added, a novel definition of sin and the merit of being pure. There follows a long extract from Campanella on the City of the Sun, describing eugenic proposals, and referring in particular to Plato, *Republic* Book 5. The legislator's problem is how to enforce agreement. Castration is undesirable, although perhaps efficacious. Prostitution will not be eradicated, although it may change its form. Love is essentially an *individual* matter. As for sodomy and sapphism, they can easily be induced by shutting up together young people of the same sex. 'It is certain that whoever chooses to spend his life exclusively with persons of the same sex thereby reveals particular tendencies which should be respected' – but the state should not actively encourage this. In the opinion of the Church Fathers, he reports, marriage is a saving grace. And Féré has written that inversion of the sexual instinct is rare among animals in a free state. It is true, he adds, that the presence of syphilis has changed our habits and our moral outlook since its introduction from America. Our attitudes have in consequence been shaped partly by the Church and partly by Medicine. We must beware of legislation: 'Lycurgus' whims cost Sparta her intelligence . . . Athens with her courtesans and freedom in love gave intellectual conscience to the modern world.' We do not have to reflect long to see how far this departs from Gide's praise of Sparta.

In *Epilogues* (1912) Gourmont had written on 'Celibacy and Love', rebutting the modern view that love is the same as marriage. On the contrary, he said, love is temporary, and marriage is permanent. Love is only delicious when it is fresh. He was in fact reviewing O. Uzanne's recent book *Le Célibat et l'amour. Traité de vie passionnelle et de dilection féminine*, published by the Mercure de France in 1912. 'Uzanne,' he wrote, 'does not have a conjugal soul. . . . This is a manual of free love for lovers. . . . All love, including mystical love, has a physical basis.' How stupid it was, Gourmont had written in 1897, for the League for Repopulation to propose a law obliging state employees and officials to father three or four legitimate children.[28] Later, in 1903, Senator Bérenger was to mount another campaign on behalf of State Purity, and to draw criticism from both Gide and Gourmont. Bérenger's bill was to outlaw 'les outrages aux bonnes mœurs', by which the Senator said he intended to attack visually stimulating material. Perhaps he would have gone further than removing mechanical peepshows and risqué advertising had he succeeded in this.[29] Covered with ridicule the Senator retired from the arena. Gourmont's article pointed to the varying meaning attached to the word 'moral' by different races and at different times in history: there is also, he noted, a link between what is considered 'decent' female dress and the prevailing fashions. The first of these arguments is one which Corydon will explore.[30]

Gourmont also had something more to say about 'La dépravation'

74

in his *Promenades littéraires 6ᵉ série*.[31] Extreme depravation was often nothing more than a return to primitive innocence, he maintained. Thus 'historical' stories, including myths, which describe fornication between human beings and animals were once considered normal, although they now scandalise us; de Sade may be disgusting, but the tale of Pasiphae and her bull conceals an ethnographical truth. It is important for us to notice that Gide interpreted myths in an altogether different way and sought their symbolic moral meaning, not their literal one. In the same 1926 collection Gourmont reprinted his preface to Duviquet's book on Elagabalus [32] containing a warning about too great a credulity on the part of a historian of morals: 'To believe that the life of Elagabalus is the epitome of Roman morality in the third century AD is a stupidity which has given rise to several bad novels.' As for de Sade, he had already written in 1898, referring to de Sade's violence:[33] 'subterranean places where the rutting male slowly slits the throat of the girl or his catamite'. Vacher, the criminal, he writes, exhibits this flaw together with another: 'le vagabondage'. 'These beings should be ex-terminated pitilessly and without more ado once they have been suf-ficiently observed.' In the characters of Gide's 'vagabonds' whom we shall have occasion to mention later, it is interesting to observe the relative lack of vice.

In 1901 and subsequently both Gide and Gourmont became involved in a debate concerning freedom on the stage. This is not without relevance to the foregoing discussion, and we shall consider Gide's views later in connection with *Le Roi Candaule*. Gourmont wrote his article on 'La Liberté et la morale à propos de quelques petits faits récents' in December 1901.[34] In this he amplified the call made by Antoine, the Director of the Théâtre Libre and, incidentally, a friend of Gide's: he wanted more liberty, including freedom for the written word, and pointed yet again to the relativity of moral judgements.

> There were long periods from the Middle Ages to the eighteenth century when love and conjugal fidelity would have appeared extremely ridiculous, and a husband's jealousy would have seemed immoral. The morality of love – and this is the greatest part of morality – is particularly unstable. There is not a passing whim or an aberration which has not been accepted and even encouraged from inversion 'pure and simple' to total abstinence.

The notion of original sin and the moral code itself are based on religion; there is, however, a general idea of what is morally acceptable at any given time. There is, as it were, a body of 'negative prejudices'. Referring to Eugène Brieux's play *Les Avariés* (1901) ('Damaged Goods') and doubtless with Ibsen also firmly in mind, Gourmont recalls that there is one code for actions, another for words. We cannot, for example, talk openly of syphilis. Of Brieux he remarks that explicit sexual acts portrayed on the stage will need some form of censorship, for modesty (*la pudeur*) will be outraged and provoke some sort of backlash.[35]

It seems that Gourmont was more libertarian in his attitudes than Gide. Let us say, borrowing an expression from Garnet Rees, that the former was more anarchic. Thus in 1901 he was concerned for the position of women, and was in favour of a draft bill for divorce by mutual consent.[36] Pleading for freedom in 1900,[37] he wrote of a woman accused of engaging in extramarital intercourse: 'The idea of controlling love is among the most peculiar notions which have obsessed and troubled the brains of priests.' He continued: there are examples of religious laws regulating many natural functions, especially eating; men have escaped from these laws, but women have not; France has rejected the dogma of the Church in becoming a secular state, but has kept the Church's moral code; scientists are seen to have contradictory attitudes to continence and sexual freedom. Gourmont holds firmly to the view that moral questions are personal, and are dictated by each individual's feelings (*sensibilité*). The basis of morality must therefore be freedom, he asserts. An act which is freely consented to cannot be held against the person who commits it, nor against the person on whom it is committed.

This position seems both logical and libertarian. But we must not lose sight of the heterosexual basis of Gourmont's thesis. He can appear to be slightly less than egalitarian in his treatment of women, as a passage from his *Lettres à l'Amazone* bears witness.[38] Admitting that he would not understand feminine 'sensibilité' and guilt until he had changed sex like Tiresias, he talked of women's hypocrisy in pretending from primitive times onward 'never to seem to be led by desire, always to clothe themselves with their famous modesty [*pudeur*], and to yield themselves up as victims to the lust of males.' The truth he perceived was that 'Women can control their sexual appetite better than men.' He concludes that we should follow our instincts, and experience no remorse.

Gourmont, like Gide, also has some words to say on Nietzsche: 'Who can agree that the modesty [*pudeur*] of women increases with their beauty?'; and, he writes, Nietzsche more or less maintains that if one thinks highly of a woman intellectually then one cannot love her physically. These remarks are somewhat superficial, and one may easily see how they contrast with Gide's[39]

The role of Woman is important, but the position of the invert is our more immediate concern. Gourmont approached the subject on more than one occasion and clearly did not always have the courage (or imagination) to support his libertarianism. Thus in 1904 we may read his reaction to a reform of the *École Normale* in Paris where many pupils were boarders.[40]

> The École Normale has been transformed. It would have been better to suppress it. Boarding schools are schools of vice for mind and body. Nothing is more unhealthy for the nation than sexual segregation in bringing up our young people. This was the basis of the civilisations of Greece and Rome: the Gynaeceum [a place where women were segregated] created the Theban Band. Heroism was thus obtained by cultivating infamy. Convents have perpetuated these morals. They are groupings of mystical inverts: at certain times they were congregations of real inverts. I do not know what a boarding school for young persons of twenty years of age might signify: I know only too well what happens when they are sixteen.

The important point, however, for Gourmont is that these establishments educate young men in a form of infantilism. As soon as a boy grows hairs he should be living in a 'complete' society, he says; to live only with members of his own sex retards his development, as an example of puerility from Cambridge will bear witness. This system has achieved a regression from 'young man' to 'young girl' – or worse, in the case of adult boarders, 'a Bathyllus character with added blushes'. We may draw the conclusion that Gide would have been hostile to this attempt to deny the educational value of pederasty. Furthermore he would have noticed that, despite Gourmont's liberalism where consenting (mainly heterosexual) adults were concerned, the article reveals a strong bias against countenancing homosexual behaviour among younger persons.

But what of Greek *paiderastia*? Among Gourmont's dialogues between M. Delarue and M. Desmaisons there appeared the following discussion in the *Mercure de France* of January–February 1908.[41] Desmaisons expresses Gourmont's known opinion that inclinations and morals are many and varied. From noting occurrences of heterosexual paedophilia and incest he is led to the view that, whereas at an early 'confused' period feelings doubtless had their origin in carnality, civilisation has led men towards 'sentimental disinterestedness'. Delarue interposes the commonly held unenlightened view that the Greeks confused friendship and love. Among both the Athenians and the Spartans, replies Desmaisons, friendship had a sexual dimension which we can no longer appreciate. This is not a loss but a gain for us, since the majority of modern friendships are founded in material interests. 'I leave homosexualism to one side,' he adds, 'because that is an illness.' He would unravel the mess 'that the Germans have created' and would clearly distinguish 'homosexualism' from 'sensual friendship' (*amitié charnelle*).

Of these two feelings the first is an exclusive choice determined by physical tendencies. The second is a simple confusion of feelings; it is not absolute, it is temporary. The first is a specific feeling, the second is an individual feeling. The homosexual is drawn towards all the members of his own sex; the person who is experiencing a sensual friendship is drawn towards his friend – and only towards his friend. A heterosexual passion might very well orient him at a not too distant date into a path which we consider normal.

Delarue has understood: 'You distinguish the things which result from custom, temptation or imitation from what is due to physiological necessity.' It is reasonable to assume that Gide read this passage, and it is obvious that the views expressed do not coincide with his. What is however interesting is to see Gourmont raising the question of custom and nature which figures prominently in Dialogue II in *Corydon*.

There is no doubt that Gide took notice of an article on 'Innocents' by Gourmont, and that he read it, not on the date of its original appearance on 15 July 1906, but in the collected edition of these *Dialogues* the following year, or shortly thereafter.[42] Desmaisons reports that a moralising novel has just been published, and that the author has followed it up with a printed circular asking the reader to solve 'the problem on page 366'. From the tone of the article we sense that Gourmont's attitude is unsympathetic. 'There exists,' runs the circular,

a permanent conflict between Nature and civilisation which is important for the future of our race. From adolescence onwards Nature endows Man with the ability to reproduce and the creative urge; and Society, by erecting the barriers of morals and material complications, prevents this amorous instinct from being fulfilled before the social time of marriage. Having best regard for health, how can we solve this problem of the impulsive urges of the genius of the species, and the experiences of civilised life?

1. Must man remain chaste until marriage? Is it not to be feared that abstinence will undermine his virile qualities?

2. If you believe that the individual must fulfil his role as a man between the age of eighteen and the time when he can maintain a family, how do you believe he can do so healthily and reasonably without damaging his own future, while avoiding harm to others?

To any anti-Christian heterosexual the answer must appear obvious, and Delarue replies (doubtless in a somewhat cynical tone): 'Innocence, innocence, all is but innocence.'

Having established Gide's awareness of Gourmont's writings, let us turn finally to what from our present point of view is one of the most important of them. In 'L'Amour à l'envers',[43] which first appeared in 1907, we may well be reading the dialogue which prompted Gide to act and cast his contribution to the debate on homosexuality in a similar form. Gourmont was undoubtedly one of those writers who ensured that 'the subject was in the air'; was he also one whom Gide feared would overtake him? If so, Gide need have had no qualms that Gourmont would be expressing the same opinions as Corydon. Once again Desmaisons is Gourmont's spokesman, Delarue his foil. While the latter rejects uranism and is disgusted by it, his interlocutor finds 'l'amour à l'envers' curious – but less curious, he admits, than hetero-sexuality. A doctor or a moralist must have no preferences or dislikes: his primary virtue must be curiosity. Desmaisons proceeds to his ex-planation: 'One is wrong to exclude uranism, for it is a problem worthy of the attention of philosophers, doctors and naturalists.[44] There is no stronger objection to what is commonly called the laws of nature. Even uranists say they are obeying the laws of nature.' Surely Schopenhauer has already provided the answer to this claim, he says.[45]

> He believed he had, but he only established an ingenious comparison between two facts which were equally inexplicable with reference to the laws of nature. He could have drawn up a long list of errors of instinct, and the longer the list the more the laws of nature would have been denied. But uranism is a sufficiently important example to allow us to ignore the rest. One thing is clear, and that is that the sexual instinct is only rarely a sexual or reproductive instinct. It is only perhaps a matter of chance that it ends up in reproduction.[46]
> *Delarue*: Heads or tails?
> *Desmaisons*: Heads or tails, so long as you don't read anything homosexual into the phrase.

He then explains how the sexual instinct is only a need for 'unburdening' the individual. Thus 'tumescence' is involuntary, and 'detumescence' happens by chance. (The terms are Havelock Ellis', and must not be confused with Gide's 'anagénèse' and 'catagénèse'.) If a young male has first experienced the delights of detumescence with a person of his own sex, then here is a uranist, 'for we always return to our first loves'. This is why schools, seminaries, barracks and prisons are breeding grounds of uranism. More seriously, there are born uranists who remain homosexual despite the influence of women. Delarue cites Moltke as an example of such a married homosexual. We must however accept, resumes his interlocutor, that sexual inversion is a natural inclination. It is the logical extension of masturbation. Man is an exceptional creature: 'I do not pretend that inversion is a general law of nature, but I say that it is a law of human nature almost as much so as the law of reproduction.' He reasons that men need a 'release' more frequently than once every nine months, and that they will obtain this by 'one means [*mécanisme*] or another'. This is how occasional uranism could be explained in zoological terms. But a mystery still surrounds those cases where men always reject females, and women males. The theory of 'detumescence', he continues, does not explain aversion to the opposite sex. 'There are all sorts of uranists. There are those for whom both sexes are acceptable; others only fall in love with persons of their own sex; others, being like this last category, also hate and despise the opposite sex.' The simplest and most logical answer is to see them all as degenerates.

But Delarue objects that there are fine artists and men of great intelligence among them. This only demonstrates, replies Desmaisons, that nature is incoherent, and that moral rules are incompatible with the forces that control our lives. Morality, by being general rather than particular, draws a veil of hypocrisy over many of our actions. 'Should a person not declare himself to be a uranist, as others declare that they go for women? Healthy people would then know where they were,' and we could do away with hypocrisy he adds. He points out the lack of intelligence with which people have considered the sexual act.[47] 'Uranism offends my personal sensibilities, but my intelligence can consider it with interest. It is a refusal to conform which astonishes one and gives food for thought. But I want it to be more open. Persons who experience this passion too often admit by their constrained behaviour that they feel all the shame of their lifestyle when they are unmasked.[48] If you haven't the courage to be cynical you should be normal.' If Moltke had openly confessed himself to be a good Lutheran *and* a homosexual he would not have been an object of scorn, he says. Desmaisons' attitude seems, on the whole, to be intellectually honest and not opprobrious.

Gide wrote of Gourmont: 'I suspect he only loves science in order to detest religion the more.'[49] In fact Gide's Protestantism found its antithesis in Gourmont's pagan attitudes which further rejected 'la pudeur féminine' as hypocritical. Gourmont countered abnegation, submission and renunciation, 'the negative virtues of slaves', with an aristocratic code based on the positive virtues of strength, domination and will to power.[50] Gide differs from him in wanting to keep both religious and Nietzschean values in play. Both writers were inclined to derive their philosophical ideas from biology, but they disagreed over the relationship of instinct to intelligence. Both cited the work of Bohn, R. Quinton and de Vries – but Gourmont wrote: 'Our virtues are never anything more than physiological tendencies.'[51] Each writer's attitude to Darwinism is instructive: Gourmont placed Man no higher than any other animal, nor did he see the process of natural selection as inevitably producing humanity as its finest flower. Gide argued simply that mankind is above the animals. It would perhaps in conclusion be fairest to say that Gide was arguing a particular case (that of the healthy uranist), whereas Gourmont wished to seek a more general explanation of human behaviour and morality.

Ward

A large section of Corydon's argument is based on the work of the contemporary American sociologist Lester Ward. While Gourmont was willing to allow the female pride of place among the insects, Ward argued more adventurously – as his preface claims – for a general recognition of the primordial place of Woman in the Universe. Appealing to Ward's gynaecocentrist theory, Gide sought to answer the criticism that homosexuality was misogynistic.

Ward's *Pure Sociology. A Treatise on the Origin and Spontaneous Development of Society* was published in New York in 1903. The French translation by F. Weil which Gide used appeared in Paris in 1906. The section on phylogenetic forces is of particular interest. Reproduction, asserts Ward, is, for society, a form of nutrition in that it permits continuation of the species and of the social structures. He sets out the androcentric theory which claims that male animals and birds are larger and more attractive than the females, and that females have inferior mental, creative and inventive powers. The gynaecocentric theory, which he will advocate, asserts the contrary proposition: namely that male distinctiveness and apparent superiority are only adventitious. Considering in turn the biological imperative, reproduction and fertilisation, he notices the dynamic principle of Nature: all fertilisation is *cross*-fertilisation, and hence he derives the importance of the female. Among animals of the male sex may be seen examples of dowdy and submissive individuals. In the matter of sexual selection: 'While the voice of nature speaking to the male in the form of an intense appetitive interest, says to him: fecundate! it gives to the female a different command, and says: discriminate! . . . here the value of a plurality of males is apparent.'[52] Male efflorescence is seen as an 'over-development', but also as medium of variation and a condition for progress to a higher development. In its earliest stages, society was a gynaecocracy: females are the only ones to stand and fight the invaders of the nest. They defend their young. In the early history of mankind children did not know their fathers, or the fathers their offspring; the mothers were the obvious centres of fertility. Androcracy came into being when men perceived that they contributed to the propagation of the species. The result of this was less promiscuity and the consequent subjugation and ill-treatment of women. The family group came into being. It was a 'slave' system, and an association dictated by economic needs. Marriage in these terms confirmed the inferior position of women. Whereas the history of women has been synonymous with that of anti-feminism, the destiny of women as now perceived, states Ward, may lead us to hope for a freeing of social conventions and a gynandrocratic future.

If we were to classify the phylogenetic forces we would perceive five divisions, he asserts. First stands natural love. This is represented by the male's innate interest in securing fertilisation. It is a dynamic principle. Love is satisfied by possession. Also in this division is to be found phallic worship, and Ward notes the hypocrisy of the odium the world manifests towards this expression of natural love. Second is romantic love. This is a modern convention, derived from natural love and best exemplified in the ideals of chivalry. Its development is due primarily to the greater equality and independence of women. It is further characterised by a slight sense of the illicit, deriving partly from society's disapproval. Third stands conjugal love, in which the aim is to please the partner. This state is monogamous. Fourth is maternal love, which, being instinctive, is to be sharply contrasted with paternal affection. Finally Ward distinguishes consanguineal love, in which he places hope for future society, because he sees it as the antithesis of racial hatred. Overall, man is perceived as egotistical, harsh, brutal and savage, while woman is the aesthete and conserver.

In *Corydon* Gide took special note of passages from Ward's book concerning the position of women. Ward, it must be noted, is not concerned with sexual deviancy. Section three of the second Dialogue sets out what Gide saw as the central ideas of Ward's theory. Thus Ward is represented as the advocate of gynaecocentrism, asserting that, if necessary, Nature could do without the male gender. Variation is found among males, and not among females, because the latter are the centre of gravity of the biological system. Again, Ward is reported to have said that change, or progress as it is called, occurs only among males, and that the female undergoes no transformation. The male is the agent of introduction for new variations in the hereditary constant of the female principle (the ovum); the female is therefore the superior gender. Gide briefly summarises Ward's views on the 'history' of the male element throughout the various degrees of evolution from hermaphroditism among the lower orders to sexual dimorphism. Among the lower animals it is normal to find males more numerous than the females, and this is so that no female runs the risk of non-fertilisation, he says. Nor is the commonly asserted opinion true, he adds, that the so-called 'superior' males spend their newly acquired energy in feeding the female and her infants. In *Corydon* entomological examples from Darwin are also adduced to support these arguments. Ward's distinction between the male decree 'Fecundate!' and the female 'Discriminate!' is also taken up by Corydon.[53] But in the third Dialogue we are reminded of Ward's dictum that for the male *all* females are identical.[54]

Gide made a large number of quotations from Ward which were not used in the final version of *Corydon*. These include remarks on the hypocrisy of many people who suppose that the human race has escaped having sexual relationships which are condemned at particular times and in particular countries.[55] A statement that in primitive ages all females were alike for the male animal and the savage leads to a reiteration of the female's ability to choose: this explains admirably, comments Gide, the primitive aesthetic superiority of the male.[56] The section on the anonymity of fathers in primitive races is reproduced,[57] leading to Ward's conclusion that law and the rights of the mother had pride of place.[58] There was the subsequent development of patriarchal attitudes we have seen. Another extract deals with the influence exercised by man's choice of weak and physically small women:[59] when these desires form the future race women will be reduced to a fully subsidiary status, and this will be but one undesirable result of an androcentrist world. A similar process of selection may be noted among certain birds,[60] and the growth of male secondary sexual characteristics threatens, at least for a time, to reverse the gynarchy which had been so long superior in the animal world. Two more quotations are about the lost cause of gynaecocentrism when the power conferred by choice devolves upon the male.[61] In all these extracts we notice that the centre of Gide's interest is focused upon the struggle for phylogenetic power between the males and females, and that the quotations chosen highlight the desirability (1) of allowing the female to continue her function of improving the species, and (2) of the male, by his variations, being allowed to continue to fulfil his 'secondary' sexual role. Even the quotation in *Corydon* (p. 155) from Napoleon's *Mémorial de Sainte Hélène* (June 1816), observing that one man needs several women, has been taken (with two small omissions) from the French translation of Ward.[62]

Bergson

There are two allusions in *Corydon* to Bergson's *L'Évolution créatrice*, first published in 1907.[63] The thrust of Corydon's argument does not however depend upon a full understanding of Bergson's point of view. The references are probably to be dated to 6 June and 28 July 1908.[64]

Chapter I of *L'Évolution créatrice* deals with the evolution of life, and with the questions of mechanism and purpose. Bergson considers the phenomenon of ageing; transformism; radical mechanism, and biology and 'physico-chemistry' (this is the section containing Corydon's quotation).[65] He then passes on to a search for a criterion, and examines various transformational theories, Darwin and hidden variations, de Vries and abrupt variations, Eimer and orthogenesis, Neo-Lamarckians and acquired heredity. The chapter ends with a presentation of *l'élan vital*.

Bergson clearly gives the physico-chemical theories short shrift, although he approves of Cope's ideas to which he refers. The distinction between *anagenesis* and *catagenesis* is preserved in *Corydon*:

> One of the most notable naturalists of our times (E.D. Cope, *The Primary Factors of Organic Evolution*, Chicago, Open Court Publishing C° 1896, pp. 475–84) has insisted on the opposition of the two orders of phenomena which are met with in living tissues: on the one hand anagenesis, and on the other catagenesis. *The role of the anagenetic forces is to raise the inferior forces* [énergies] *to their own level by means of the assimilation of inorganic substances.*[66] They construct tissues. On the other hand, the function of life itself, if we except assimilation, growth and reproduction, is in the realm of catagenesis, being a downward movement of energy and not an upward one. It is from these catagenetic facts alone that physico-chemistry appears to have borrowed – that is to say in fact from death and not from living forces. And it is certain that the facts of the anagenetic realm do not appear amenable to a physico-chemical analysis, even if they are not properly speaking anagenetic.

We may note that Corydon uses the two key-words anagenetic and catagenetic, and applies them respectively to the theory of feminine and masculine forces which he deploys.

The second reference is to be found in Chapter II of *L'Évolution créatrice*:[67] 'The divergent directions of the evolution of life: torpor, intelligence and instinct'. Bergson's hypothesis of *l'élan vital* is here developed: it is 'an internal thrust which will, through forms which become more and more complex, carry life towards yet higher destinies'. It is neither *merely* an adaptation to circumstances (as Mechanistic theory would have us believe), nor the realisation of an overall plan (as conceived by the Finalists). Evolution is a ceaselessly renewable creation, but is not always a movement forward – there are deviations, retreats and marking time; the philosopher must note that in Nature not everything is coherent. These are not the lines upon which Corydon proceeds, but he borrows a remark from Bergson about the role of sexuality in the plant and animal kingdoms. Bergson is in fact establishing a dynamic of evolution by comparing the nature, properties and definition of animal versus plant life:

> If the plant is distinguished from the animal by fixity and insensibility, movement and consciousness lie dormant within it like memories which

could come to life. Moreover, beside those memories which are normally dormant there are others which are awake and in movement. . . . The following law could be stated: When a tendency analyses itself as it develops, each of the particular tendencies which thus come into being tries to conserve and develop every element of the original tendency which is not incompatible with the function for which it is specialised. This precisely explains the fact of the formation of identical complex mechanisms in independent lines of evolution. Certain deep-set similarities between the vegetable and animal kingdoms have probably no other cause: *sexual generation is perhaps only a luxury for a plant,*[68] but animals had to arrive at this point – and plants must have been carried to it by the same force [*élan*] which bore the animals, namely the original force [*élan*] which existed before the separation of the two kingdoms.

This fits into Corydon's thesis only to the extent that it provides an answer to one of the interlocutor's objections. The point of Corydon's argument here is that, as Lester Ward suggested, the development of the male element is to be held as separate from that of the female. This is not Bergson's concern. (Should one sense a certain irony on Corydon's lips as he speaks of Bergson whom the interlocutor 'admires so greatly'?)[69]

The importance of *L'Évolution créatrice* for an understanding of Corydon's argument lies more in the fact that it provides another hypothesis to explain Darwinian determinism, than that it proposes a cogent explanation of deviant behaviour. Two important points are passed over without comment by Corydon, and both occur within Chapter II. Bergson notes that aborted developments are frequently observed (p. 139). Although individuals themselves are stable, the 'whirlwind' which bears the *race* along is in constant movement. The stability of the race is provided for by the phenomenon of maternal love: 'It shows us each generation caring for the next. It allows us to see that the living being is above all a halt on the road, and that the essence of life is to be found in the movement by which it is transmitted.' The closest Corydon comes to this is in his characterisation of the female as conservative in being and manners (anagenetic).

The other point is the distinction Bergson draws between intelligence and instinct (p. 154). Their roles, he says, are relative – not antithetical. Thus instinct is unconscious, inborn knowledge; intelligence is conscious, capable of acquiring knowledge. The difference is one of degree, not one of nature. These ideas could not be brought easily into line with Corydon's antithesis between what is inherited by nature and what is required by society.

In the *Mercure de France* CXXXV October 1919 pp. 437–65, there appeared an article which illuminates our subject from a slightly different point of view: F. Geneslay, 'Physiologie de l'adolescent'. The thrust of the argument is mainly medical, with tables of weights and measurements. Section IV, however, deals with the sexual instinct and briefly reviews the theories of Gourmont ('the urge to reproduce'), Montaigne ('an evacuation of fluid') and Havelock Ellis ('periodical tumescence'). Section V, 'Deviation and Exaggeration of the Sexual Instinct', is limited to a discussion of 'adventitious' inversion, when satisfaction of a need – not pleasure – determines the behaviour of the individual. Congenital inversion is not discussed. Referring to Edward Carpenter, the writer maintains that the affectionate friendships which occur so frequently in boarding schools for adolescents of both sexes are not to be considered as a vice. Although he says that onanism is an abnormality, citing Balzac's *Physiologie du mariage*,[70] his article carries a reference to socially accepted masturbation among the Hottentots.[71]

Apart from theories and opinions on matters of population, Gide also collected a few statistics. His aim in so doing was to draw conclusions in the fourth Dialogue of *Corydon* from the fall in the birthrate.[72] The relative preponderance of male over female births is a noteworthy feature of the tables at all periods from 1800 to 1960.

A specific reference was later inserted in *Corydon* (p. 81) to an article by Perrier which had appeared in *Le Temps* on 1 August 1912,[73] where the writer had spoken warmly of René Worms' 'remarkable study' on *La Sexualité dans les naissances françaises*. Perrier's newspaper feature is entitled 'Le Monde vivant', and discusses oysters and their annual change of sex.[74] It includes information on the relative frequency of male and female insects (specially marked by Gide, but not included in *Corydon*). Perrier's article doubtless led Gide directly to Worms and to other writings on sexual demography. Worms makes several points of which we must take note. His first section deals with definitions and statistical sources; his second examines the superior number of male births, and relates these to the larger number of female survivors. The discrepancy is reconciled by the greater deathrate of males. In Chapter 5 of this section he advances the theory that the number of males is in direct relationship to poor diet – thus a superabundance of males would not reflect a desirable social situation. (This is the point reported by Perrier and cited by Gide.) The third section presents comparative national statistics, while the fourth considers various influences on the birthrate (regional factors, organic factors – those related to the age of the parents, to hereditary predisposition and so on, psychic factors (which Worms considers erroneous), and social factors – namely those related to economics, morals, race and religion). Worms, for example, provides graphs and four important statistical tables:

(1) The development of male births in France (live births) 1801–1910.

(2) The development of the birthrate and deathrate in France 1801–1910.

(3) The development of male births in France (still births) 1856–1910.

(4) The development of male births in England (live births) 1841–1905. (The latest date for which a 'coefficient of masculinity' is given is the period 1901–5 (103.7).)

It is clear that little of this eventually featured in Corydon's argument. In fact, when he turns his attention to the animal world (pp. 67–8: this passage already occurs in the 1911 edition, being based on Ward), it is rather to conclude that when males are more numerous than females 'variation' will manifest itself. In 1912, however, Gide certainly seems to have contemplated taking additional demographic material into account. The archive contains the following:

Men are more numerous than women from birth to the age of marriage [nubilité]. At that age they tend to be equal as a result of an increase in male mortality. Then the proportion of females soon becomes greater, so that if one takes a population aged twenty and above we find (the latest French census, 1911):

Males	12,120,000
Females	12,944,000
Excess of women over men	824,000

Below the age of fifteen there were:

Males	6,458,000
Females	4,972,000
Excess of males over females	1,486,000

It is to be observed that since the age of marriage is higher for men than for women this disproportion is noticeably increased, thus:

Men between 30 and 55	6,141,260
Women between 20 and 45	7,063,644
Excess of women	922,384

or in every 1,000: 458 males for 542 females.

The average birth rate for the ten years 1901 to 1910 was:

Males	412,000
Females	395,000
Excess of males	17,000[75]

Gide also noted down some figures from the British census of 1911 which showed a similar decline in the excess of males over females 'from puberty onwards'.[76]

CHAPTER SEVEN

Medico-Legal Attitudes

Apart from writers on what might loosely be termed the philosophy of sexuality, or the theory of sexual evolution, Gide's case can also be illuminated by a consideration of the theories specifically concerning homosexuality which were current at the time he was composing *Corydon*. These may conveniently be grouped here under the heading 'medico-legal' analyses in so far as they show that his contemporaries classified homosexuals as a race apart, the investigation of whose behaviour was the responsibility of alienists, doctors and the law.

Corydon contains more than one disclaimer: the interlocutor in the first Dialogue is dissatisfied with the works of Moll, Krafft-Ebing and Raffalovich, and he wants to deal with the subject in a different way. In the preface, dated 1922, a footnote refers the reader to Hirschfeld. Gide's book will not be about the 'third sex', cases of 'inversion', effeminacy or sodomy. Perhaps he should have considered these, Gide concedes, but he maintains that even Hirschfeld's theory does not adequately account for the nature of pederasty. Let us therefore consider in succession the theorists on whom Corydon deliberately turned his back.

Ulrichs

Karl Heinrich Ulrichs,[1] a German lawyer and homosexual, was among the first to suggest in numerous pamphlets published from 1864 to 1879 that homosexuals should be regarded as neither insane nor criminal. His theory of a person endowed with a female soul within a male body was to furnish the starting point for later theories of an 'intermediate sex' – from which Gide in his preface seeks to distance himself.

Krafft-Ebing

Krafft-Ebing's *Psychopathia sexualis*, which first appeared in 1886, was translated and published in French in 1895.[2] In 1895 we can notice an allusion in a letter Valéry wrote to Gide: a particular event is 'very wholesome – morally speaking', and certainly not 'une histoire de Krafft-Ebing'.[3] A new edition, based on the sixteenth and seventeenth German ones, revised and augmented by Albert Moll, was undertaken in 1923 and was published in a French translation by R. Lobstein shortly after 1931. Here the additional material bears particularly on the question of paedophilia, that section being much smaller in 1895. It was also in the first edition that Krafft-Ebing demonstrated the importance of infant sexuality. While maintaining that homosexuality is a perversion of the genital instinct, he considered it as a stigma of degeneracy and/or a state of sexual infantilism manifest in the lack of differentiation of sexual stimuli and response. When seeking to define a 'perverted' act, he wrote that such is any activation of the sexual instinct which does not correspond to the intention of Nature. And that 'intention' is perpetuation of the species by means of reproduction. In analysing the psychology of the homosexual, he observed that such a person has a phobia of the opposite sex, and is for the most part of a timid disposition. He sought to establish a distinction between innate and acquired forms of homosexual behaviour: Moll, in revising the work, added his own comment to the effect that one must carefully distinguish between illness and vice in this regard. Thus the 'perversion' of the sexual instinct must not be confused with the 'perversity' of a given sexual act – for the latter may additionally be provoked by circumstances that in themselves have nothing psychopathological about them. Such circumstances are most frequently provided by prisons, barracks and other institutions where the sexes are rigorously separated. Perversions, furthermore, may be classified into two groups: there are those where the aim of the action is 'perverse' – as is the case with sadism and fetishism; there are those addressed to a 'perverse' object and where the consequent action is therefore also perverse. In this group homosexuality, paedophilia, zoophilia and autoeroticism are placed.

Moll

But Gide criticised Moll's own book, *Les Perversions de l'instinct génital. Étude sur l'inversion sexuelle basée sur des documents officiels*, which first appeared in French in 1893, translated by Pactet and Romme and with a preface by Krafft-Ebing. He wrote to an unknown correspondent in October 1894: 'He doesn't sufficiently distinguish two classes: the effeminates and the others. He continually mixes them up, and nothing could be more different, more "contrary", for one is the opposite of the other: in the context of this psychophysiology what does not attract is repellent – and each of these two classes horrifies the other.'[4] Indeed the French prospectus for Moll's book was prosecuted by the Société de protection contre la licence des rues – but obviously their disapproval was for reasons which were quite different from Gide's, since they believed it to be a 'vile publication' ('livre infâme').

In his opening chapter Moll considers some fundamental differences between men and women: when boys are young they may often fall in love with older women (and he cites the example of Dante). But it is also beyond doubt that love cannot be present for long before the sexual instinct is aroused. We therefore must distinguish between love and friendship: in true friendship jealousy is rarely encountered, he states, and we note without difficulty that *love* between men is often riddled with jealousies. (Gide's view on jealousy was, as we shall see, quite different.) A historical chapter, with examples, takes the reader quickly through the centuries, from the Bible, the Greeks and Romans, the Persians, the Turks and Hafiz, to modern times and the familiar list of important political and artistic homophiles which includes Michelangelo, von Platen and several others.

Chapter three is entitled 'Uranism in Modern Times', and deals with its subject from a social and sexual point of view. In the first part of this chapter Moll stresses the important interchange which occurs across the normally established barriers of class in society; in the second he considers passionate love, and the varieties of taste shown severally in the choice of the age of the desired person. The age range he has in fact observed, albeit somewhat clinically, extends on his figures from sixteen to sixty-four, or even three to sixty-eight. Above all, the observer must note the female mannerisms of this class, he writes. Be they uranists or transsexuals the feminism of their writing, their vanity and other feminine traits characterise the majority. They are very numerous. On masculine prostitution, Moll refers to the work completed and reported on by Tardieu and Coffignon, and dwells on the ever present evil of blackmail and extortion. Chapter five brings us to the pathology of love and discusses sexual 'perversions' as a complication arising from sexual inversion. This distinction will be clearly maintained: thus the author here deals with fetishism, masochism and sadism.

The following chapter, in considering psychic hermaphroditism, repeats the divisions which Krafft-Ebing himself had sought to establish and provides an explanation and aetiology for certain deviant states of sexual behaviour. Thus four divisions are established: the first category, psychosexual hermaphroditism, is not so much a presentation of a

type of bisexual, as a classification of persons who, while being predominantly 'homosexual', also manifest quite overt 'normosexual'
elements. The second is the homosexual, who is here defined as
the person drawn only to others of the same sex. The third state is
effemination, where the patient's psychic element is conditioned by his
homosexuality. The fourth state is androgyny, in which an actual
physical transformation is seen to have taken place. Chapter seven
continues the exposition of the aetiology: homosexuality, or any of its
associated states, is generally inborn, though it must be noted that the
individual's heredity must be very 'onerous'. This is as much as to say
that although the individual is not responsible for his inclinations in
this respect, and that he is consequently neither perverse nor vicious,
he is a victim of neuropathological degeneracy.

But Moll is concerned to locate the seat of this aberrant behaviour,
and this he believes can be done only if the physical location of the
passions themselves can be found with certainty. This is not possible,
and so the psychic aspect must be emphasised. However, he warns, the
observer must be careful to distinguish transvestism from these cases. In
considering curative therapy Moll insists that the doctor must ask
himself whether we may not cause more damage by intervening.
This was a contentious point. Following Krafft-Ebing, Moll adopted
the argument that if these passions are congenital, then prophylactic
measures have no place. Treatment is, however, to be considered
wherever possible: the psyche, not the body, might be changed.
Castration, then, is not seen as a cure; but sexual reorientation and the
avoidance of temptations are to be recommended. To be effective,
treatment must begin at a very early age. Nor is punishment a cure:
punishment should be reserved in this context for rape and 'moral
outrage' (public indecency). Moll's view of pederasty in Greece was not
that it enhanced the position of women, but, on the contrary, that the
more attention men paid to male love the less they honoured their
women. In all situations he saw the uranist, unlike the heterosexual
man, continually beset by an intrusive sexual idea which his make-up
would not allow him to ignore. The more this fruit was forbidden by
the law, he remarked, the more frenetic the uranist became – and the
more difficult he found it to possess it. Moll's final chapter briefly
considers the question of sexual inversion among women, but he has
little of importance to say.

Raffalovich

In Ghéon's letter to Gide of September 1899 to which we shall later
refer,[5] he reported that Laurens had said to him 'but X also likes

women, doesn't he? And he had replied: "Yes – but it's when he's all worked up. He's not a born pederast. He's not a pure, essential one. (Raffalovich's theory.) The born pederast has a horror of perforation, and of women. . . . Wilde – who's not a Sodomite. He finds women ugly."' Raffalovich had published *Uranisme et unisexualité. Étude sur différentes manifestations de l'instinct sexuel* in 1896. 'Uranists may be divided into ultra-virile, virile, effeminate and passive types,' wrote Raffalovich. This sentence from the preface sets the tone: 'In order to restrain the dangers and disorders consequent upon unisexuality it is necessary to restrain the disorders and dangers due to heterosexuality.' Thus minors must be protected, and the greatest danger of 'corruption of morals' avoided. If a cure is attempted, the most probable result will be to turn an 'invert' into a 'pervert', for born 'inverts' are, Raffalovich believed, less vicious, less libertine and more honest and praiseworthy than the majority of 'perverts' who, as voluptuaries, have acquired their 'vice' through deliberate choice.

A large part of the book is taken up with examples and historical accounts of famous homosexuals. The idealised relationship between women and unisexual men is briefly mentioned in connection with Marie de France. In place of an aetiological quest, Raffalovich gives details of the childhood and puberty of virile and ultra-virile uranists, with autobiographical case histories. Inversion through pride, boredom and idealisation is described; as are the ways a unisexual possesses to satisfy his passion – onanism, love and 'platonic' friendship. Chastity, he asserted, is but one way in which the uranist might try to find fulfilment. This positive appeal to the historical role of inversion brings the subject up to date with an attempt to provide an apologia for the uranist. It does not escape, however, from the limits of discussion determined by the clinical and legal theorists.[6]

Ellis

In 1909 there appeared a French translation by A. van Gennep of Havelock Ellis' *Studies in the Psychology of Sex: Sexual Inversion (Études de psychologie sexuelle II: l'inversion sexuelle)*. Gaston Danville, the reviewer in the *Mercure de France*, pointed out that the book was documented from personal observation and contained a historical account of recent work. Presenting Ellis' conclusion in the form 'homosexuality is an economic and demographic phenomenon dependent on the size of population', Danville perhaps attracted Gide's attention by adding that 'we should therefore see in sexual inversion only an accident, a "variation"'.[7] Gide was familiar with Ellis' book and quoted from it in the second Dialogue of *Corydon* (pp. 95 and 99). The material he took was limited on that occasion to citations of examples of homosexual behaviour in the animal world. Thus his references to observations by Bailly-Maître, Muccioli and Sainte-Claire Deville concerning pigeons, rams and dogs are to be found in the opening chapter of Havelock Ellis. Ellis, however, is at pains to show that especially in the case of the latter examples absence of females is sufficient to account for these desires in animals. When we turn to his work we naturally find a wider discussion than is reproduced in *Corydon*.

As Weeks says: 'The aim of *Sexual Inversion* was to present a case *for* homosexuality. . . . The two principles Ellis employed were a form of cultural relativism as applied to moral attitudes, and biological determinism as applied to essential sexual characteristics.'[8] In fact Ellis made the point that although the first modern 'defence' of homosexuality could probably be traced back to Heinrich Hoessli's *Eros* of 1836, the published case histories were few, even in 1880, and those, for example in England, were taken from prisons and lunatic asylums. Sexual inversion, he was to write, is inborn and of organic origin in the same manner as heterosexuality. Moreover, the tendency shows itself at an early age.

The introduction of Ellis' book is largely concerned with definitions of homosexual behaviour in animals, and among the semi-civilised races of the north-western United States, the inhabitants of Albania, China, Japan and Greece. Ellis also has a historical perspective: he discusses the phenomenon of homosexuality in ancient Rome, and among famous people from the Middle Ages to modern times. Thus Walt Whitman and Verlaine are considered before general observations are made on the widespread occurrence of homosexual behaviour in modern Western societies.

'Looking at the phenomena generally, [French version: 'so far as they have been recorded among various lower races'] we seem bound to recognise that there is a widespread natural instinct impelling men towards homosexual relationships, and that this has been sometimes, though very exceptionally, seized upon and developed for advantageous social purposes. On the whole, however, unnatural intercourse (sodomy) [French version: 'the extreme form . . . sodomy'] has been regarded as an anti-social offence, and punishable sometimes by the most serious penalties that could be invented.'[9] There are a few instances, continues Ellis, of sodomy being used to control population growth.[10] More importantly, however, he remarks on the prevalence of these practices in warrior societies.

During war and the separation from women war involves the homosexual instinct tends to develop. [It] has been cultivated and idealised as a military virtue, partly because it counteracts the longing for the softening feminine influences of the home, and partly because it seems to have an inspiring influence in promoting heroism and heightening *esprit de corps*.[11]

After considering examples of male prostitution, Ellis continues:

What may be regarded as true sexual inversion can be traced in Europe from the beginning of the Christian era (though we can scarcely demonstrate the congenital element) especially among two classes – men of exceptional ability and criminals; and also, it may be added, among those neurotic and degenerate individuals who may be said to lie between these two classes, and on or over the borders of both.[12]

Indeed 'prison life develops and fosters the homosexual tendency of criminals; but there can be little doubt that that tendency, or else a tendency to sexual indifference (psychosexual hermaphroditism), is a radical character of a very large number of criminals.'[13] Additionally an awareness of hermaphroditism is to be noticed among artists and intellectuals of the Renaissance, including Muretus, Michelangelo and Leonardo da Vinci. But, in conclusion, a problem concerning social toleration and psychological understanding has to be confronted. Customs are known to vary, and in ancient Greece it was not unknown for reasonable people to expose their unwanted children. 'For this reason,' continues Ellis, 'I am unable to see that homosexuality in ancient Greece – while of great interest as a social and psychological problem – throws light on sexual inversion as we know it in England or the United States [French: 'in modern countries'].'[14]

The main part of Ellis' book is firstly concerned with a review of contemporary opinion as expressed in the studies and case histories reported by Westphal, Hoessli, Casper, Ulrichs, Tarnovsky, Krafft-Ebing, Moll, Schrenck-Notzing, Chevalier, Lydston, Kiernan and Raffalovich. A chapter on sexual inversion in men discusses the relatively undifferentiated state of the sexual impulse in early life, latent inversion and what Ellis considers the rarity of acquired homosexuality. He provides an attempted classification of the varieties of sexual inversion into simple inversion (individuals attracted to their own sex) and psychosexual hermaphroditism (persons attracted to both sexes).[15]

A chapter on sexual inversion in women follows, with case histories and remarks on physical and psychic characteristics. Two further important chapters deal with the nature (ch. V) and the theory (ch. VI) of sexual inversion. These emphasise the importance of the congenital element, taking embryonic hermaphroditism as a key to inversion. Inversion may be seen as a variation or 'Sport', and this type

94

of abnormality is not necessarily to be seen as a disease. 'Jeu' (Sport), as we have seen, was an idea which attracted Gide's attention. Although inversion may be related to degeneration, Ellis states, the animating causes of inversion are seldom operative in the absence of a predisposition toward such behaviour.

In finally posing the question of our present attitude towards homosexuality, Ellis makes a number of interesting remarks which are not without their relevance to an understanding of Gide's point of view. But there are also clear differences of opinion between the two men.

At school there is a need, Ellis states, for coeducation, and for surveillance of moral hygiene. But he is sceptical about the efficacy, or even desirability, of treatment for homosexuals. At its worst such a 'cure' would turn an 'invert' into a 'pervert'; at its best it would produce but another form of masturbation. It is surely preferable to have recourse to healthy gymnastics, he thinks, and if any success is obtained it is rather that the individual finds that he has become bisexual. Hypnotism is in all probability not an effective form of treatment. 'An appeal to the *paiderastia* of the best Greek days [French: 'de la belle époque'], and the dignity, temperance, even chastity, which it involved, will sometimes find a ready response in the emotional, enthusiastic nature of the congenital invert. The "manly love" celebrated by Walt Whitman in *Leaves of Grass*, although it may be of more doubtful value for general use, furnishes a wholesome and robust ideal to the invert who is insensitive to normal ideals.'[16] Here the French translator adds a footnote directing the reader to Edward Carpenter's *Ioläus, an Anthology of Friendship*, although, he says, 'it only deals indirectly with sexual questions'. Gide seems to have taken due notice. He will also have seen Ellis' reference to chastity.

The best method of treatment seems to Ellis to be self-control: 'As both Raffalovich and Féré have lately insisted, it is the ideal of chastity, rather than of normal sexuality, which the congenital invert should hold before his eyes.'[17] But also: 'It can scarcely be said that the attitude of society is favourable to the invert's attainment of a fairly sane and well-balanced attitude.'[18] The function of the law in this matter – and Ellis is speaking expressly of the position in England and Germany – should only be 'to prevent violence, to protect the young, and to preserve public order and decency'.[19] Ellis implies that by 'young' he means boys of the age ranges ten to fourteen *and* fourteen to twenty. 'Whatever laws are laid down beyond this,' he continues, 'must leave matters to the individuals themselves, to the moralist and to social opinion.' The French translator's note refers to the hostile attitude of the jury in the Rémy-Renard case, which we shall consider in our chapter on victims. He adds a remark by Goethe on the existence of pederasty in Nature, the substance of which is taken up by Corydon.

Ellis' book is important for a proper understanding of the history of *Corydon*. While Gide certainly used other sources, the central position occupied by this work provided him with a key with which to explore hitherto unsuspected areas of his subject. It is in this light that we must consider the references it contains to Carpenter's *Ioläus* and *The Intermediate Sex*, to Moll and other theorists, to historical documentation and to the immense amount of material contained in the *Jahrbuch für sexuelle Zwischenstufen*.

Hirschfeld and the Jahrbuch für sexuelle Zwischenstufen

To a conscientious reader of the *Mercure de France* like Gide the first mention made of the *Jahrbuch* in that periodical would have been a source of interest.[20] Volume XLII May 1902, pp. 543–4, under the rubric 'Lettres allemandes', commented that 'the "problem" of sexual inversion seems to interest the Germans greatly', adding that the '*Annales pour les états sexuels intermédiaires*' (the title is given in French) were now in their third year of publication. This, the writer believed, was progress, 'for modesty will no longer be frightened by the slightest allusion to the subject, and we are now beginning to be able to speak more openly about it.' A longer notice by Henri Albert appeared in Volume LVI August 1905, pp. 466–7, when the *Jahrbuch* had completed its sixth year. The reviewer was struck by the unevenness of the articles: 'Medical and legal studies stand next to mediocre literary criticism; there are statistics on the proportion of homosexuals to normal persons, and a psychological study of the great poet and homosexual von Platen.' Possibly the most interesting item in the periodical, he thought, was an article by L.S.A.M. von Römer seeking to establish a continuum between absolute heterosexuality on the one hand and absolute homosexuality on the other, with absolute bisexuality as a state between the two.[21] He drew his readers' attention to the very large bibliographical section devoted to books published in 1903 (pp. 449–646), mentioning in particular several French items, among which occurs *La Nouvelle Sodome* by Edmond Fazy.

In 1907 Henri Albert wrote again and said that a considerable amount of material had appeared in the *Jahrbuch* during the previous two years.[22] Reviewing Volumes VII and VIII, he welcomed the activity of the experts who were attempting to change the German law on homosexual behaviour. This time he was more pleased with the literary articles, singling out in particular an important contribution on

Whitman by Eduard Bertz.[23] He praised the bibliography by 'Numa Praetorius' (that is, Eugen Wilhelm), regretting that it only covered 1904. He was full of admiration for Hirschfeld's article in Volume VIII on the essence of love: 'Vom Wesen der Liebe. Zugleich ein Beitrag zur Lösung der Frage der Bisexualität' (pp. 1–284). Later that year[24] there were two brief mentions of the new *Monatsbericht des Wissenschaftlich-humanitären Komitee*, forerunner of the *Zeitschrift für Sexualwissenschaft*.

In Volume LXXI January 1908, p. 164, Albert mentioned Maximilian Harden, and commented on Hirschfeld's role in the scandal, congratulating him on having shown the 'serious character' of his Wissenschaftlich-humanitären Komitee and of the *Jahrbuch*. In the following month[25] Albert reported that Hirschfeld was again under attack and had just published the first number of his new journal, the *Zeitschrift für Sexualwissenschaft*. Albert added: 'We shall keep our readers informed of developments.' In April[26] the *Zeitschrift* was again mentioned: Hirschfeld was continuing to criticise the authorities in the Harden case. Later the same month[27] Albert praised the *Zeitschrift*'s campaign against paragraph 175 of the German legal code. In his column 'Lettres allemandes' in the *Mercure de France*, LXXIV August 1908, p. 727, Albert drew attention to an interesting article by Max Katte on Schiller's unfinished play on the Knights Templar (*Die Malteser*) in the July number of the *Zeitschrift*. In this dramatic piece, according to Katte, Schiller speaks of 'Knights in love preoccupied with the lives of their beloved friends' – and hence the playwright must finally be supposed to have decided not to continue with a subject which 'presented such difficulties'. Again Albert noted articles which had appeared in the October and November issues of the *Zeitschrift* on the sexual roots of kleptomania (W. Stekel), sexual abstinence (Dr Rohleder), and foot fetishism in China (P. Vaecke).[28]

Volume IX of the original *Jahrbuch* (Leipzig, 1908), and incidentally the last of the first series, was reviewed favourably by Albert in the *Mercure de France*, LXXVII February 1909, p. 733. He said that Hirschfeld had arranged his material with great scientific skill and had avoided the temptation to provide tendentious articles based on 'recent events' (the Eulenburg scandals). Albert commented on the items on Queen Christina and on Sodoma, on Naecke's enquiry into homosexuality in Albania, and on 'Numa Praetorius'' bibliography, regretfully noting the scarcity of French items in the last named section. In 1904 the reviewer had spoken[29] of a separately issued *Bibliographie der Homosexualität* by 'Numa Praetorius', published by Max Spohr in Leipzig. The book in question is actually the second volume of year VII (1904) of the *Jahrbuch*. 'All the "special" books published during 1902 are analysed,' he wrote, 'novels and scientific publications alike. . . . all the particularly "juicy" sections are reproduced or translated [into

German] so that the reader will not miss anything.' Would this have awakened Gide's curiosity?

However, although the *Jahrbuch* was published in Leipzig by Magnus Hirschfeld during the years 1899 to 1908 (vols I–IX of the first series), and again thereafter in a sequence of supplementary volumes until 1923, we are not in a position to state with certainty that Gide was acquainted with this publication. His knowledge of German was reasonable enough for him to have read it, and he did in fact have friends in Germany who might easily have brought it to his attention, in whole or in part. He travelled to Berlin and Weimar in 1903 and on several other occasions. He was in regular contact, for example, with Franz Blei from 1905 onwards, having already commented in the *Mercure de France*, XLVIII October 1903, p. 286, on a report of an article by him. Blei eventually published 'Die Sokratische Freundschaft',[30] and he had been involved in promoting several 'artistic' periodicals of high quality from 1906 onwards.[31] If Gide did read the *Jahrbuch*, he would have found informed articles on matters of historical and contemporary importance, with analyses of pederasty in ancient Greece, and in the literature of the Renaissance and eighteenth centuries and biographies of notable inverts, both historical and modern.[32]

La Revue Blanche

There is no doubt that Gide read the *Revue Blanche* of 1896. He was a member of the circle of literary persons connected with this periodical, and a fragment of *Paludes* had been published in it the previous year. We can well imagine his reactions on seeing the series of pieces which were published there in January–June of that year.[33] A hostile article, 'Bayreuth et l'homosexualité' by H. Gauthier Villars, criticised Wagner and members of the Bayreuth audience.[34] It sought to establish a link between certain aesthetes and the 'conspicuous' unisexuality of Parsifal's knights. This in turn drew an answer from an anonymous reader who pointed to a 'certain anomaly'[35] in Wagner's work. During the same months the *Revue* published a contribution by Alfred Douglas: 'Une introduction à mes poèmes avec quelques considérations sur l'affaire Wilde'. Douglas affirmed that he would have been much better off in Athens, for the English were Philistines, and the French only pointed him out as the lover of Wilde. Ordinary men, he wrote, hate the beauty of passionate friendships, which, of course, he said, can be, and often are, chaste. As for his poems, he asserted that they were not homosexual, although he admitted that some did treat this theme. His righteous indignation was reserved for the Queensberrys of this world, and he attacked André Raffalovich for the hostile attitude he adopted towards Wilde.

In the second half of the same year Jean de Beauvais published in the *Revue* a somewhat ironic review of Raffalovich's *Uranisme et unisexualité*,[36] in addition to an account entitled 'Prostitution, criminalité, uranisme' of a recent French edition of Lombroso's *La femme criminelle et la prostituée*.[37] A short while later Charles Kains Jackson argued in 'L'Amour sélectif'[38] for acceptance of homosexual behaviour of a certain, restrained type. Within a context where he wished to give weight to recent Darwinist theories and to notions of degeneracy in the human race, Kains Jackson wrote: 'At least the lover [*l'amant*] will forward the interest of the race, firstly by choosing his beloved for his merit, and secondly by seeking to elevate this merit to its highest potential.' After all, he argued, 'Fathers only love their sons because they are their sons, not because they possess any natural merit.'

Lacassagne and the 'École de Lyon'

In turning for a moment to other contemporary writers against whose strictly hostile medico-legal views Gide was arguing in *Corydon*, we may briefly notice, as representative of the French school of Lyon, often associated with the work of Lacassagne, the names of Tardieu, Chevalier and Féré.[39]

A seventh, augmented edition of Tardieu's *Étude médico-légale sur les attentats aux mœurs* appeared in 1878. The book had originated from several cases of women who had molested young children. It is divided into two sections: the first considers the rape of women, and rape committed by women on children. The second deals with pederasty and sodomy. Tardieu's experience is limited to those cases which came to the notice of the police and which are therefore often somewhat less than savoury. A feeling of disgust and shame consumes him. Indeed, he remarks, in the necessary context of medico-legal considerations which this crime entails, there is something strange in the way the ancients took no notice of the outward manifestations and effects of this vice. He defines pederasty as the 'vice' practised by those who have sexual intercourse with young boys. Sodomy, he says, is practised on members of both sexes, and there are cases of conjugal sodomy. But, he maintains, both activities lead to male prostitution, blackmail and the underworld of crime connected with this way of life. One may recognise pederasts by their hairstyle and their clothes; they have generally poor health and often show signs of their passive habits. Physical deformation of the anus (infundibuliformity) will often betray members of this class, he remarks.

Julien Chevalier's *De l'inversion de l'instinct sexuel au point de vue médico-légal* was published in 1885. It was reissued with a different title page in an augmented form in 1893, and a short but sympathetic review by Albert Prieur of the 1905 edition (with the new title *Aberrations de l'instinct sexuel au point de vue ethnographique, historique et social*) appeared in the *Mercure de France*, LVI July 1905, in the column 'Sciences'. In his 1885 preface Chevalier provided a historical synopsis of recent theories, and in the body of his book he proposed his own scheme of symptomatology, pathogenesis and diagnostic. Before 1849 the classifications which existed had been founded on an unscientific basis, he claimed. Michéa's *Des déviations maladives de l'appétit vénérien* of that year first established four types, which, in order of frequency, were: (1) 'Greek love', or love for a member of the same sex; (2) bestiality; (3) attraction towards an object; and (4) attraction towards a human corpse. These divisions, too, were rudimentary, having no true scientific basis. However, in 1885, continues Chevalier, Magnan published his *Mémoire* on *Des anomalies des aberrations et des perversions sexuelles* in which he attempted to establish divisions based on physiological criteria. By taking reflex actions he felt he could distinguish between a 'spinal' patient (a vegetative idiot who insists on masturbating); a 'posterior cerebral spinal' (representing the instinctive brutality of the sexual act: a heterosexual example), an 'anterior cerebral spinal' (male/female same-sex libidinal attraction); and, the highest category, 'anterior cerebral' or 'psychic' (platonic lovers, who achieve absolute chastity).

In 1885, Chevalier goes on, Lacassagne, in his lectures, based his theory on the facts themselves, and examined sexual behaviour from the point of view of *quantity* and *quality*. In this way the sexual instinct was to be seen as not essentially different from any other instinctual physical behaviour (for example, sight). Thus the observer must distinguish three possible states: (1) normal; (2) augmented (or diminished); and (3) perverted. But the model remains one of illness and degeneracy. 'These are not distinct morbid entities, but rather diverse symptomatic modalities springing from a unique pathological base, from a unique and deep-seated illness, just as is the case with dipsomania or pyromania.'[40] Chevalier develops these categories and again distinguishes three states. Firstly there is a gradual manifestation: the perversion only depends on the patient's will. It is in some sense factitious, although it becomes a habit – and then it may be considered a vice. Pederasts who become so from a taste for luxury are in this class:

it may be termed 'acquired inversion'. Secondly, the behaviour may be determined by a particular anatomical configuration of the genital organs. This, not being morbid, we may call 'hermaphroditism'. It is termed 'secondary inversion'. The third category is beyond the control of the patient's will and is congenital. This is 'natural inversion', properly so called. Chevalier concentrates on this last category, taking the psychological and medico-legal aspects of the cases particularly into consideration. The argument was, historically, as he quite clearly shows in his discussion of his predecessors' work, one of whether to assign responsibility to the individual for his acts in this area of sexual behaviour. He concludes that inversion is a symptom of a more or less acute state of degeneracy. The pederast who has chosen his way of life through a vicious desire must be distinguished from the sexual invert. The former is more inclined to sodomy than the latter (who is as disgusted by this practice as is the normal man). It must also be noticed, Chevalier states, that inversion is a much rarer state than pederasty. This behaviour is, in the final analysis, a 'striking manifes-tation of an inherited neuro- or psychopathological state': 'the patient is not depraved; he is not guilty – he is a lucid madman'; and again, recalling a happy phrase of Lacassagne's: 'These patients are moral hermaphrodites.'[41]

Féré's *L'Instinct sexuel, évolution et dissolution* (1899) provides a good statement of the most generally accepted view of sexual deviancy in France at the end of the nineteenth century.[42] Féré states: 'The history of sexual perversions proves that they are only developed in individuals who differ individually and in their descendants from the normal type, or whose condition is pathological. Both the absence of control over the instinct and the perversions of it are vices which are no less prejudicial to the individual than to his social environment.'[43] Again: 'Under certain environmental conditions, pederastic habits have been of frequent occurrence, and it cannot be said that perversions of instinct were involved. When, as with the Greeks . . . efforts are made to save Woman's chastity . . . she becomes inaccessible apart from marriage or the gynaeceum.'[44] Sexual inversion, he writes, has only been recognised as a category of behaviour since Westphal's pioneering work of 1870, and the function of a doctor must now be to prevent the consequences of 'sex-dissolution' in society by limiting the number of offspring of degenerates. However, degeneration is the process of elimination necessitated by evolution: it thus makes the precautions advocated by Malthus useless. Féré also provides several paragraphs on deviant sexual behaviour among animals, noting examples from Sainte-Claire Deville on the pernicious dangers of isolating the sexes. This material also occurs in several other writers of the period.

Tarnovsky

V. Tarnovsky's *L'Instinct sexuel et ses manifestations morbides au double point de vue de la jurisprudence et de la psychiatrie* was reviewed by Albert Prieur in the *Mercure de France* in 1904.[45] Tarnovsky's object was twofold: he intended to examine evidence of homosexuality 'as connected with a morbid condition of the organism, whether congenital or acquired', and, in studying the part played by heredity and the phenomena of arrested development and various morbid causes, he aimed to distinguish these characteristics from 'depravity of character, conscious and premeditated vice'. To this end his enquiry establishes three categories of perversion: the first is based on hereditary infirmity, the second on acquired elements, the third includes complex forms of genital perversion. Distancing himself from the 'medical jurist' who would only see depravity, oversatiated lust and inveterate vice in such behaviour, Tarnovsky, as a clinical observer, enters a plea for the necessity of what he terms 'methodical therapeutics'. Thus he wants to cure, not punish. He defines pederasty as a morbid inclination towards persons of the same sex, calling bestiality and sodomy no more than 'variations' of this abnormal genital impulse. His depiction of the individuals who constitute his first category is noteworthy for the emphasis he places on effeminate characteristics. He does, however, admit other groups to this section, such as those whose practice of self-flagellation has led to onanism, those who are attracted only to old men, and finally fetishists of various types. But in many of the cases he describes Tarnovsky fails to distinguish between the (so-called) abnormal actions of homosexual men and irregular heterosexual behaviour, thus blurring his carefully constructed categories. The second category (acquired pederasty) is characterised by the development of 'vicious habits' in boarding schools, ships and prisons. Such behaviour, Tarnovsky repeats with other experts, leads to physical, mental and moral disorders. The book concludes with remarks on male prostitution and blackmail, together with advice to the clinical practitioner on how to recognise homosexuals from an examination of the infundibuliform configuration of the anus.

Saint-Paul

'Dr Laupts' (the pseudonym of G. Saint-Paul) issued his work on homosexuality in two editions: *Tares et poisons. Perversion et perversité sexuelles.* . . . *Préface par Émile Zola* (1896); and, *L'Homosexualité et les types homosexuels. Nouvelle édition de 'Perversion et perversité sexuelles'. Préface par Émile Zola* (1910).[46] The main differences between the two editions occur towards the end, Chapter 5 being rewritten and expanded to form Chapters 5 and 6, with much new material. Saint-Paul rejects Ulrich's identification of an invert as someone who has a female soul inside a male body. His first chapter deals with descriptions, definitions and explanations. In a historical presentation of the views which have been held on the topic, he discusses in turn Schopenhauer, Ulrichs, Mantegazza, Krafft-Ebing, Moll, Ribot, Lacassagne, Chevalier and others. Here is another writer who is careful to distinguish between 'invert' and 'pervert'. Chapter two is a case history, 'Le roman d'un inverti-né', consisting of some documents which were originally sent to Zola. Chapter three is a detailed account of Oscar Wilde's trials and his personality, which also extends the investigation into the realm of art with an analysis of *The Picture of Dorian Gray*. Thus Saint-Paul finds that the description of Basil's feelings towards Dorian Gray, the praise of the latter's beauty, the character of the handsome adolescent Lord Henry whose gestures are so delicate, are all suggestive. 'Dorian Gray,' he writes, 'is a victim of Lord Henry and of the restricted society in which they live.' As for Wilde himself, Saint-Paul defines him as a paedophile: 'he has no effeminate appearance, no feminine vanity [like that possessed by the born invert], and, especially, no taste for strong males. On the contrary, the objects of his love are younger and less masculine – he looks for ephebes.'[47]

The fourth chapter describes the opinions of contemporary philosophers and scholars, including Krafft-Ebing (aetiology), Moll (the distinction between perversion and perversity), Tarde (normal and morbid love) and Raffalovich.

The fifth chapter in the first edition presents Saint-Paul's conclusions. After discussing diagnosis and prognosis, he turns to treatment, considering Schrenck-Notzing's advocacy of hypnotism, and then discussing the merits of counselling, marriage, moral precepts, individual prophylaxis and the pressure which an ideal of chastity may bring to bear on the problem. He then passes on to talk of social influences, detailing the benefits of friendship and sympathy which, when felt for a member of the opposite sex, can provide the first steps for sexual attraction. He identifies the bad effects of 'cerebral hyperactivity', inadequate education (boarding schools, lack of discipline and absence of gymnastic exercises), late marriage and alcohol. 'The health of the mind,' he concludes, 'is indispensable for the physiological functioning of the body; the first element which is necessary for true and complete well-being, for happiness, is calm of mind and confidence in the future.'[48]

In the second edition, Chapter five begins with an analysis of an invert and the questions a clinician must ask. Diagnosis and prognosis are followed by suggestions for treatment: hypnosis (Schrenck-Notzing), and the ideas of A. Nyström and A. Hamon (on hygiene and sexual education). The social causes are also discussed. Among these Saint-Paul notes the more widespread propagation of inversion by 'colonial contamination' (North Africa and elsewhere), the common circulation of books on homosexuality, and late marriage.

Chapter six (second edition) describes how what Saint-Paul (and others) had originally thought of as a psychological phenomenon had now to be considered in a social context. Speaking of developments since the first edition of his book had appeared, he discusses the work of Hirschfeld and the Komitee in Germany campaigning for the reform of article 175. He is sceptical that such a grouping of writers and intellectuals could happen in France, for he believes that except for the occurrence of onanism and unimportant chance encounters Frenchmen are far less inclined to this form of sexual perversion. In some general remarks on the sexual instinct, where he agrees with Havelock Ellis about the importance of economic factors, and on morals, which he sees as a 'function of the species', he demonstrates how far his theories have advanced. He is now no longer happy with his original distinction between 'perversion' and 'perversity'. 'Spontaneous Malthusianism', which ensures the health of the species, is an element which has to be taken into consideration, he states. The book concludes with a brief description of the Eulenburg affair and a bibliography.

Schrenck-Notzing

We have already noticed a number of works by German authors which had been translated into French by the early years of the twentieth century. In addition to these, further mention should perhaps be made at this point of Schrenck-Notzing. Not only was his work important in itself, but his advocacy of the desirability of curing homosexuals was widely influential. Féré had declared himself in favour of chastity on the part of the invert; Chevalier leaned towards the use of bromide in closed institutions and the frequent taking of 'tonic exercise'. Others had recommended castration; Westphal did not believe that physical intervention could cure a mental state. In 1895 Schrenck-Notzing's *Ein Beitrag zur Aetiologie der conträren Sexualempfindung* was intended to show the influence of external conditions. This is the opposite of Krafft-Ebing's 'organic' view where the phenomena in question have a very deep foundation in the physical mechanism. 'Now,' he states, 'by means of suggestion, especially by its application in the hypnotic state, the possibility is demonstrated to us that aberrations of instinctive life from its proper channel may be corrected.'[49] Naturally Schrenck-Notzing claimed a good rate of success for his hypnotic method; equally naturally his opponents accused him of turning his invert patients into perverts. Was it indeed more desirable, they asked, to resort to prostitution in the course of a 'cure'?

In the 1905 review which dealt with the *Jahrbuch für sexuelle Zwischenstufen* in the *Mercure de France*,[50] some details were given of Magnus Hirschfeld's *Berlins drittes Geschlecht*, which was first published in 1905 and appeared in French as *Le Troisième Sexe. Les homosexuels de Berlin* in 1908.[51] The book provides a well-documented picture of the homosexual subculture in Berlin and is, in fact, rather like Coffignon's work on Paris, though less sensational. It objectively describes soldiers, taverns, drag queens – the world of the homosexual and the 'normo-sexual' alike. Gide did not meet Hirschfeld until some time before 1934, most probably in 1928–9.[52] J. Fryer records a visit Gide paid to the Hirschfeld Institute at this earlier date, during which he was shown various exhibits, including a boy with breasts.[53]

Freud

On 16 January 1916 there appeared in the *Mercure de France* a review of two important books by Kostyleff and by Régis and Hesnard.[54] It was in fact through the medium of works such as these that Freud's ideas were able to circulate in France when Gide was composing *Corydon*, for little of Freud had been translated into French before 1920. *Drei Abhandlungen zur Sexualtheorie* had first appeared in Leipzig in 1905.

It is perhaps surprising to read in a letter Gide sent to Madame Mayrisch, a wealthy Luxembourg patroness of the arts, on 2 May 1921 the following remarks:

> Dear Friend, Do you read Freud? So far I haven't read much at all, and I'm very afraid that what he writes may be diffuse and repetitious. But certain extracts from his 'Origin and Development of Psychoanalysis' published in the *Revue de Genève* on 8 February have made me wonder whether he would refuse to write a preface for the German edition of *Corydon* if I were to ask him for one.[55]

In an interesting article on Gide and Freud,[56] D.A. Steel draws our attention to a letter Gide sent to André Lang on 26 December 1921 which also refers to the articles (in the plural) published in the *Revue de Genève*. Here Gide says that his knowledge of German is insufficient for him to read Freud in the original: he is now therefore fortunately able to read *L'Introduction à la psychanalyse*, translated by S. Jankélévitch and published by Payot in late 1921 (actually dated 1922).

The publication in the *Revue de Genève* on 8 February 1921 was the last of a series, presented with an introduction by E. Claparède, which had begun in issue no. 6, December 1920, under the title 'Origine et développement de la psychanalyse'.[57]

The *Revue* claimed to be publishing the first French version of any of Freud's writings, but this is not strictly true, although these articles did constitute the first printing for the French-speaking general public of a substantial work by Freud.

The serialised publication continued in the January 1921 number with material about repression in hysterical illness. It is here we read Freud's assertion that repressed desire continues to exist in the sub-conscious. The issue for February 1921, to which Gide made specific reference, and to which alone he may have had access, deals with dreams. Freud states that the small child always dreams of the fulfil-ment of desires inspired by the previous day's experience: they remain unsatisfied in the real world. An adult's dreams are similarly composed, but they are disfigured. There is a relationship between dreams and an individual's sexual life. In passing on to infantile sexuality Freud's text is interrupted, for 'certain material' will only be published in a special offprint by the *Revue*. A passage on masturbation will have caught Gide's attention: 'Autoeroticism is often not completely conquered, and this is shown by the many varied disturbances to be seen making their appearance throughout life.' The translation ends with a brief description of the Oedipus complex, regression to infantile sexuality, and transference.

Steel concludes in his article on Gide and Freud that Gide should be taken at his word when he says that he had not read any Freud before 1921. This in itself would account for the absence of any Freudian theories from the pages of *Corydon*. And if we believe we can see repression exemplified in the characters of Alissa and Michel, we must therefore seek elsewhere for an explanation of it. The 'repression' which causes the English governess to carve an obscenity on a tree in *Le Treizième Arbre* (1935) is clearly Freudian in origin. In the case of Boris – who masturbates – in *Les Faux-Monnayeurs*, the situation is different again. Steel draws our attention quite correctly to an article by Dr M. Gourévitch in which the credit for influencing Gide is given to a disciple of Freud, Eugénie Sokolnicka.[58] But the influence was limited: in Gide's opinion psychoanalysis cannot cure the child's illness as it is here presented. On the whole we must agree with Steel that Gide's picture of Freudian repression and the technique of analysis is not a coherent one. That this may be due to the fact that the material is presented in a fictional context is something we must certainly take into account.

Let us return to the 'German edition' of *Corydon*. It has a rather curious history. On 26 April 1921, as Gide was writing to Dorothy Bussy, the sister of Lytton and James Strachey, the thought came into his mind that he could in fact pretend that *Corydon* had started life in German and that it had subsequently been 'translated' into French. The German edition (which would then be the true first edition) could have a preface by Freud: 'I must absolutely get into contact with him. Your brother [James] knows him, doesn't he and he wouldn't refuse to introduce me, would he? But there's no hurry. . . . Freud's preface could underline the usefulness and relevance of the book.'[59] Dorothy Bussy replied on 27 April that such a meeting would be easy to arrange as James was then in Vienna translating 'one of his books'. Gide immediately asked for details so that he could have Freud's book printed in the *Nouvelle Revue Française*.[60] The editors of the Bussy correspondence note that the first book of Freud's published by the NRF was *Trois Essais sur la théorie de la sexualité* (1923), translated by Dr Reverchon. 'In fact,' Gide confided to Dorothy Bussy after reading the article in the *Revue de Genève*, 'he doesn't tell me anything I didn't know already; but he puts into proper focus a number of thoughts which were just floating around in my head in, shall we say, a larval state.'

Nothing came of the projected preface – *Corydon* was not to appear first in German – but a year later (4 February 1922) Gide revealed his preoccupation with Freud in his *Journal*: 'Freud and Freudism: for the past ten or fifteen years I've been practising it unawares. . . . The publication of *Corydon* is overdue.' The *Journal* entry for 24 December 1922 shows how the effects of repression (he was thinking of Christianity in particular) reminded him of Freud. In the *Journal* of 19 June 1924, after reading some articles on Freud in the current number of *Disque Vert*, he burst out again: 'Ah! Freud – what a nuisance! we would have managed to find his New World without his help.' On the other hand, Gide felt he should approve of him for having accustomed readers to certain subjects without blushes or protests. 'He is daring,' he remarked, 'or more correctly he has removed a particular false and troublesome sense of shame [*pudeur*].' However, Gide says, had he been a doctor himself, he would have avidly pursued one question in particular. 'What happens when, in order to operate, the sexual function, for social, moral or other reasons, is led to forsake the object of its desire?' In other words he did not find in Freud a satisfactory investigation of the question of the divorce between love and desire which had so preoccupied Corydon. 'When the satisfaction of the flesh finds no agreement,' the *Journal* entry continues, 'and no participation in one's being – and when the self is divided and one part remains behind . . . what secret revenge is then prepared by the part of the self which did not partake in the feast?' Freud is an 'imbecile genius' who has said much that is 'absurd'. Gide takes up the point of repression – if hunger was as often thwarted as the sexual appetite, then this, he maintains, would become the fuel for Freudism, just as water figures in the dreams of thirsty travellers in the desert. This last image seems to have nothing to do, however, with the Freudian interpretation of the symbol of water. Gide's conclusion coincides with opinions he has already expressed: 'Certain forces owe their strength to being bottled in. It is true that sexual desire is capable (if not directly satisfied) of many pretences – I mean can take on many different forms, and hunger can never do that.'

Stekel

In 1932 Gide followed this reading with Hahn's French translation of Wilhelm Stekel's *Neuröse Angstzustände und ihre Behandlung (Les États d'angoisse nerveux et leur traitement)*.[61] 'An excellent book in many places,' he remarked, '– but psychoanalysts have axes to grind: witness Havelock Ellis.' Despite these misgivings, he still wrote to his close friend Roger Martin du Gard on 8 February 1933 that he was 'passionately interested by Stekel's book on anxiety'. In the preface to the English version of this work,[62] Stekel explains how this book was the origin of his differences with Freud. Freud 'asserted publicly', he writes,

> that anxiety states are not curable by psychoanalysis. He differentiated phobias as a constitutional disease from anxiety neuroses [*Angstneurosen*], the latter being the consequence, according to his law, of sexual abuses. He differentiated 'actual neurosis' from psycho-neurosis. The former he asserted to be caused by sexual abuses, the latter by psychic disturbances. I could not agree. . . . I found that *every* state of morbid fear was psychically determinated [*sic*].

And later: 'Besides the influences of sexual life as a cause of neuroses – sufficiently emphasised by Freudians – this book shows the importance of ambition, religious feelings, and the instinct of self-preservation.' Chapter 2 should particularly attract our attention. In it Stekel considers the nature of repression, and finds that Culture itself is repression. We must conform in order to live in society, he states, but repression is not always a desirable acquisition. Repression without awareness of what is being repressed is portrayed as the cause of countless diseases. The other chapters describe various phobias which are provoked, *inter alia*, by trains, birds and the stage.

To be 'passionately interested' in a book does not necessarily mean that one subscribes to the ideas it contains. It does, however, seem that the writings of both Freud and Stekel with their overtones of clinical and behavioural 'illness' fascinated Gide in a way in which the pioneers of psychosexual investigations earlier in the century had failed to do.[63]

Gide continued to show interest in research into the behaviour of the human male, remarking on the publication of Volume One of Kinsey in translation[64] in a letter to Martin du Gard on 30 March 1948. But by now his attitudes had changed, and the climate of opinion was no longer as uncomprehending and puritanical as it had been in the early years of the century. Psychoanalysts might still be inclined to view homosexual behaviour as the result of disease or psychosexual disorder, but at least, Gide felt, the subject had come out into the open.

CHAPTER EIGHT

Natural History and Anthropology

> The best of these thoughts are not those which are found (as Gourmont finds them) in books. . . . The account of an observation, however faithful, objective and detailed it may be, is never as good as the fact itself which I would perhaps have observed differently and for another meaning. For the true naturalist book learning alone cannot suffice; he has no use for interpreters; he understands the hints of the language of Nature and asks direct questions.[1]
>
> *Journal*, 3 July 1927

In the *Journal* for 2 December 1910 we may be surprised to read that Gide thought he could more easily have become 'a naturalist, a doctor, or a pianist than a writer'. Like many cultured men of his generation he was interested in entomology and the study of plants. It is important that we should see this as not only a hobby which had fascinated him from early childhood but something more significant. His research if not particularly rigorous was constantly sustained. With the help of Fabre's studies of insect life and Darwin's *Origin of Species* he investigated the scientific aspect of his subject. This is not to say that he was a Darwinist, nor, indeed, that any other neat label would suit him. It was not his purpose to develop a thesis that would confirm or contradict those of his contemporaries who followed Darwin. Once again, what he wanted to do was to seek a *confirmation* of his ideas, and if in so doing he either fell in line with scientific determinism, or openly asserted the moral independence of mankind, he seems not to have been overconcerned at the resultant contradictions.

Fabre

Souvenirs entomologiques: Études sur l'instinct et les mœurs des insectes by J.H. Fabre, was published in ten volumes from 1879 to 1910. A projected eleventh volume was not completed.[2] Every summer Gide perused these books which he regretfully left behind when he returned from his country property of La Roque in the autumn.[3] In May 1905[4] he had read with interest what Fabre had to say about scorpions. But it is of course the pages of Corydon and the manuscript variants which reveal the true extent of his debt to the entomologist.

He uses Fabre to illustrate a number of points. Firstly there is a question of methodology. Both Gide and Fabre agree on the need for observation, although as the notes on the cerceris show we may not thereby always obtain truth: 'Marchal,' says a footnote (added in manuscript to the 1911 proof of Corydon and subsequently incorporated into the printed versions), 'has controverted what Fabre proposed concerning cercerides (buprestis bifasciata, cerceris quadricincta, etc.)'.[5]

Secondly, there is the question of the relative distribution of males and females and the mechanism which determines this. Fabre, unlike Corydon, has no general answer. The osmiae (osmia cyanoxantha and others) are our first witnesses which are rather charmingly described by Fabre.[6] In the cells which the insect constructs for the larvae, the males are less well accommodated than the females, who are hatched from large commodious cells with a plentiful supply of food. Corydon takes this to support his view that more females are born generally in a time of plenty, fewer in harder times, and he returns to another aspect of this argument later in Dialogue II. The relative numbers can also be affected by the 'difficulty' of the sexual act: and he quotes Fabre's observations on the praying mantis (mantis religiosa).[7] Corydon wishes to draw the conclusion that when desire is precise an 'excess number of males becomes useless'. Fabre, the saddened observer of so much cannibalism among the mantises, limits himself to regretting that he cannot complete his couples 'for there is a tragic consumption of the [males] in my cages'. This last phrase is not quoted in Corydon, and, similarly, Corydon does not take up Fabre's point that in captivity the females chew only a part of their mate: they would have been 'less wasteful' in the wild. Corydon's use of these examples shows his selectivity.

Another of Corydon's points is that there is no intention in pleasure.[8] As a parallel, he cites Fabre's opinion on the noise of the locustidae. That there is no purpose – at least no definite sexual purpose – Fabre would agree, although he allows that this might be a possibility. 'After all,' he wisely says, 'I could not contradict someone who maintained that this was one of its functions.'[9] Fabre also makes the point when dealing with 'La Cigale – le chant':[10] 'These insects sing of their joy in their existence.' By contrast we may read Darwin's assertion that animals emit noise to attract females,[11] and Gide himself talks of 'the love song of the grasshoppers' in Les Nourritures terrestres.[12]

If this noise does not attract male insects, then Corydon argues that a different explanation must be found for the behaviour of the lesser peacock moth.[13] This material, which appears as a footnote in the public edition of *Corydon*, was cast in a different form when it appeared as the appendix in 1911. In both versions, however, the lesson is the same: the smell of the female in season will attract the males – and in the case cited it is the odour to which they are drawn, and not the insect.

Corydon finds only one example of homosexual behaviour among Fabre's insects, which he quotes.[14] There is a critical exclamation in the note: 'O Fabre, patient observer, did you observe that it is truly after being *refused* that these homosexual mountings occurred?' (The male insects had been observed to pile up on top of each other and move their legs vigorously.) 'The cerocome had refused to consummate the final act of wedlock beneath my gaze,' says Fabre, and these words preface the quotation Gide has used. Perhaps Fabre may only be found guilty of coyness.

There are two manuscript notes inserted in the Bibliothèque nationale copy of the 1911 edition, which come from Volume II of Fabre. They are both about sexual 'prodigality' which ensures a balanced proportion of members of a given species. In the first,[15] writing about the *sitaris* (*coleoptera*), Fabre affirms that the number of young larvae is great because the chances that they will perish are equally large. In the second,[16] Fabre cites the example of the *meloe proscarabaeus*,[17] which, according to his observations, does not have the instinct possessed by the *sitaris* for laying its eggs in a safe place. Its fertility is correspondingly greater, he declares, 'for the richness of their ovaries compensates for their lack of instinct'. 'What transcendental harmony,' he exclaims, 'ensures this balance between fertility and instinct!'; and, a few pages further on, in a sentence also cited here by Gide, '"Now instinct fails and fecundity fulfils the need" (p. 317).' These remarks neatly underline the essential points of the relevant part of Corydon's case.

Perrier

The majority of Gide's references to natural history are used in order to establish the point that many so-called 'unnatural' behaviour patterns do exist in the real world. Thus an address by Edmond Perrier, Director of the Museum d'histoire naturelle, given in 1905, is also used by Corydon.[18] Perrier talked about some of the differences between males and females in the higher species, and he made exactly the same point that Corydon expresses. The female demonstrates retention and continuity of features (anagenesis), whereas the male manifests an 'exteriorisation', a prodigality of the sexual element involved in his temperament (catagenesis). These are also points made by Ward, in whose book Gide had first discovered them. A further extract from the same speech is cited in the third Dialogue by the interlocutor.[19] This deals with precisely the aspect of the matter which distinguishes the human race from the rest of the animal world. Among animals the 'favoured' sex is the male, among humans the female. Of course Perrier and the interlocutor take this to indicate the superiority of women who still further beautify themselves with sumptuous ornaments while men remain dull ciphers in dark clothes. It suits Gide's plan well to use this witness as an ironic testimony to Woman's deficiencies. It is with Perrier's interpretation that he quarrels, not with his observations. The address was printed in *Le Temps*, 26 October 1905, and the cutting is included in the Doucet archive:[20] 'It is you, ladies, who have won . . . and have inspired the sensitive brush of Bouguereau,' concludes Perrier. We remember that Corydon had no time for this particular artist.[21]

Gide cut out another article by Perrier[22] on the same subject: 'Les Robes de noces des animaux'. This rather precious title heads a list of examples of mating activities drawn from the life of insects, flowers and marine fauna. All male animals, including crocodiles and birds, make themselves beautiful in order to attract the female, concludes Perrier. Gide did not use the material in *Corydon*.[23]

He did, however, use a third article by Perrier.[24] This appeared in *Le Temps* on 1 August 1912, and it remarks on the disproportion between the number of male and female insects: the *hoplia cerulea* and *rhizotrogus aestivus* show respectively one female for 800 males, and one female for 300 males. These observations confirm other information which Corydon has collected, and more from the same source are deployed a page or so later.[25] The additions are intended to bring further corroboration to Corydon's thesis.[26]

Oysters feature in another manuscript note[27] where Gide quotes from J. Arthur Thomson's *Study of Animal Life*, p. 43. He summarises Thomson's observation that 'Professor Möbius says that out of a million oyster embryos only one individual grows up.' This mortality, Thomson continues, is 'due to untoward currents and surroundings, as well as to hungry mouths.' His point is that physical Nature, as he puts it, is quite careless of life. The example is clearly linked in Gide's mind, however, with observations on the apparently gratuitous over-production of sperm and eggs.

The second Dialogue in *Corydon* also contains several citations from A. Sanson's *Traité de zootechnie*.[28] These observations are added as footnotes to support the argument being advanced in the text. Females, states Sanson, only tolerate coition when they are on heat.[29] Again: the male's sexual appetite is awakened by the odour of the female on heat; the female's instinct awakens at fixed periods, and in addition remains dormant after fecundation and during gestation.[30] And again: secretion from the vaginal glands is responsible for the odour which attracts the male.[31] In the same work by Sanson, Corydon remarks, there is a long section on the mating of domestic horses.[32] Corydon notes the observation that human assistance is necessary 'for the stallion often misses his aim', and draws the further conclusion (not in Sanson) that the 'sexual instinct' does not invariably exist. Sanson actually wrote: 'To avoid tiring the stallion let him not become excited [*se cabrer*] until he is near the female'; and, further: 'In performing the act of coition, much of the fatigue is avoided if the groom himself directs the penis so that it immediately makes contact with the vulva. Moreover, that avoids it taking the wrong route, which would be dangerous.' There is a further use of this material in *Corydon*[33] (loss of vigour occasioned by too frequent mountings).

From another zoological work, by C. Claus (*Éléments de zoologie . . . traduit sur la 4ᵉ éd. allemande par* G. *Moquin-Tandon* (a translation of *Grundzüge der Zoologie*, 1876), Gide noted some observations by W. Kurz on *cladocerans* (water fleas).[34] This is in the same footnote as material cited from Fabre and Perrier. In this case the males generally make their appearance in the autumn although 'they can appear at other times whenever the ambient circumstances become unfavourable'. Corydon has stated in the text that the more food there is available, the greater is the number of females in evidence (this is not, of course, universally true).

Furthermore, the interlocutor (no doubt echoing Gide) admits to some knowledge of the works of Loeb and Bohn. *La Nouvelle Psychologie animale* by Georges Bohn appeared in 1911.[35] In his preface the author states clearly that his constant effort has been to explain psychology by reference to biology. He admits, moreover, that he has little sympathy for finalistic explanations. The book is divided into three main sections: (1) an experimental analysis of the behaviour of lower orders of animals; (2) an analysis of instincts in articulated animals; and (3) an analysis of the psychological behaviour of vertebrates. A section on tropisms from the first part dealing with symmetrical and asymmetrical development under stimulus, and a section from the third part describing cages controlled by mechanical devices (labyrinths and learning-reward systems), have clearly left their mark on the character of Anthime in *Les Caves du Vatican*. The passages referred to by Gide in

Corydon appear in the second part, section iii of Bohn's work, which is an analysis of various instincts.[36] Gide states that he has found similar theories in Émile Waxweiler's *Sur la modification des instincts sociaux* (1907)[37] which he had not read before 1911.

When Ward 'traced the evolution of the male element... at first doubtful, then scarcely differentiated in the hermaphroditism of the coelenterates', then onward to the more sophisticated higher animals, he was noticing what Corydon reminds us 'the delicate Chamisso', the German entomologist of the early nineteenth century, had also in part observed.[38] We note that in the final analysis Corydon's argument does not depend upon a strictly evolutionist view of the existence or function of homosexual characteristics.

Darwin

Darwin is the remaining important writer on natural history whom we have to consider. Gide's interest is apparent in a letter sent to Valéry from Biskra in December 1893.[39] In May 1906 he read to his wife passages from the French translation of the *Journal of Researches into the Geology and Natural History of the Various Countries Visited by H.M.S. Beagle 1832–36.*[40] He had already begun to do this on 3 February 1906 ('Séjour dans les îles océaniennes'), but he continued to read it mostly to himself. On 21 June 1910 he noted finishing reading the *Journal of Researches*. Was this in preparation for *Corydon*? Certainly some references are made in the text to the translation – *Voyage d'un Naturaliste autour du monde fait au bord du navire le Beagle de 1831 à 1836... traduit de l'anglais par M.E. Barbier.* Section 5 of the second Dialogue of *Corydon* contains observations from a footnote in Darwin on the large number of eggs spawned by the white doris (a sort of sea slug).[41] Corydon's point is that a large number of eggs does not ensure a correspondingly large population. Much sexual energy is dispersed. Darwin comes to the same conclusion and is accordingly quoted. So great is this prodigality in Nature that Corydon cites Darwin a third time on the same page in support of the proposition.[42]

It is from the *Voyage* that Corydon quotes Darwin's observations on the beauty of the male inhabitants of Tahiti,[43] giving the impression that Darwin agrees with him in finding that women need ornaments to enhance their charms. Darwin does say that in his opinion women 'appear to be in greater want of some becoming costume even more than the men,' and remarks, as Gide reports, that women wear flowers in their hair. However, in describing the men[44] he specifically mentions their broad shoulders, their well-proportioned physique and their athletic appearance, before going on to talk of their custom of tattooing themselves in such a way that the ornamental designs gracefully follow the line of the body, and generate a very elegant effect. Corydon's suggestion that the men are handsome in their unadorned nakedness is not borne out by Darwin's text.

It is of interest to note that Robert Louis Stevenson is also called as a witness to this point by Gide when Corydon refers to the inhabitants of Polynesia.[45] A note originally printed in the 1920 edition was subsequently deleted: 'Find the passage in *South Seas* or the correspondence.'[46] It is not possible to say exactly which passage Gide had in mind, but it was probably Chapter 5 of *In the South Seas*, 'Depopulation', where Stevenson describes the Marquesas. Here he talks of the previous overpopulation of the islands, of infanticide and cannibalism as social controls on the number of the inhabitants, and of their present depopulated condition. 'Samoans are the most chaste of Polynesians,' he remarks,[47] 'and they are to this day entirely fertile; Marquesans are the most debauched: we have seen how these are perishing; Hawaiians are notoriously lax, and they begin to be dotted among deserts.' In this section we find a criticism (which Corydon also makes) of the Europeanisation brought about by the missionaries: 'Samoa is, for the moment, the main and the most instructive exception to the rule. . . . Their clothing has scarce been tampered with,'[48] and hence there is no moral hypocrisy. These statements, however, apply principally to the dresses of the female natives. There are several remarks about the comeliness of the race as a whole – and many of the other Polynesians are noticeably less handsome, says Stevenson.[49]

To return to Darwin, *The Descent of Man* is mentioned in a note in *Corydon*[50] on the proportionate distribution of the sexes. Darwin is cited again in the third Dialogue at a point shortly after the end of the 1911 version, but the sense of the text clearly indicates that the material had already been prepared in manuscript by then. It is noticeable that Gide covers a great deal of the ground prepared by Darwin, but concentrates on certain areas in particular. Thus in Part I of *The Descent of Man* Darwin deals with variability of body and mind in Man, and with the causes of variability. However, he supposes that the laws of variation are the same in Man as in the lower animals (Chapter 2) and discusses the effects of the increased use and disuse of parts of the body. Corydon does not follow this mechanistic line of reasoning. Darwin, in Part I, also considers the transmission of moral tendencies, however, and the advancement of the intellectual powers through natural selection. Part II, on the principles of natural selection, presents several points which are closer to Corydon's position: thus Darwin deals with the consequences of an excess population of males – which in his view, but not Corydon's, may lead to polygamy.[51] The male alone is generally modified through sexual selection and choice is exercised by the female. The proportion of both sexes is to be seen in relation to natural selection. There follow ten chapters dealing with examples of insects, fishes and reptiles, birds and mammals. There are two points of interest in the last of these sections: firstly, commenting on odour, Darwin writes of its vital role, especially during the mating season – but unlike Corydon he does not limit the importance of this emanation to the female alone (Chapter 18). Secondly, although it is generally true (as Corydon asserts) that males are more ornately endowed than females, Darwin mentions the important exception of the female Rhesus monkey (*macacus rhesus*), the skin of whose face and posterior is more roseate than the male's.

Part III is concerned with the secondary sexual characteristics of man. Here Chapter 19 deals with the differences between men and women; with the influence of beauty in determining the marriages of mankind; with the attention paid by savages of both sexes to ornaments; with the great variation in ideas of what constitutes beauty in a woman, and with the effects of the continued selection of women according to a different standard of beauty in each race. Darwin is more careful in his generalisations than Corydon: 'In most, but not all parts of the world, the men are more ornamented than the women,' he writes; among savages, however, there is the greatest imaginable diversity in ideas of male and female beauty (including colour of skin, the presence or absence of bodily hair, the size and shape of various parts of the body) (Chapter 19).

Corydon[52] quotes Darwin's observation (Chapter 20) that women transmit most of their characteristics, including beauty, to their children of both sexes. But he adds that among animals it is only the males that inherit an 'efflorescence of beauty'. Here is another important distinction which Gide perceives between mankind and other animals. What Corydon does not quote, from the same place, is Darwin's remark on the position of Western Woman: 'Civilised men are largely attracted by the mental charms of women, by their wealth, and especially by their social position; for men rarely marry into a much lower rank.' On another point, however, Corydon and Darwin do come together again: for both, it is a fact that Man, not Woman, has acquired the power of selection.

It is also clear that Corydon does not use the framework of selection established in *The Descent of Man*. Natural selection, as defined by Darwin, applies to external circumstances; sexual selection is governed by the choice of mates and inherited characteristics; the struggle for life, to which Corydon does allude, is best exemplified in the (often unsuccessful) vying for union with the female.

There is no reference in *Corydon* to *The Origin of Species*, but it is clear from a *Journal* entry[53] that Gide read Barbier's translation while he was composing the book. The quotation in the *Journal* is taken from the beginning of Chapter 5: 'Laws of Variation'. 'Variation' (*variabilité*) in the male is a phenomenon for which Corydon wished particularly to account. Darwin states that 'variability is generally related to the conditions of life to which each species has been exposed during several successive generations.' But he also wonders whether these variations, so widespread in domesticated states but less frequent in Nature, are due solely to chance. But chance, he adds, is a word which merely serves to hide our ignorance of the true cause of each variation. We may properly conclude, he continues, that these differences in frequency seem to show a connection between the external conditions to which species are subject, and the variation observed over several generations. What does Gide retain of this? Only that 'beings which stand low in the scale of Nature are more variable than those which are higher'. Since the phrase has been removed from its context Gide's conclusion is also interesting: 'Once the highest level is attained, it is within the individual that this variability is to be found.' This is the plea of the Humanist, and the ground on which Corydon takes his stand. Darwin had written: 'I presume that lowness here means that the several parts of the organisation have been but little specialised for particular functions. . . . Natural selection, it should never be forgotten, can act solely through and for the advantage of each being.'

Corydon shows the interlocutor Darwin's two-volume work on *cirripedia* (of which group barnacles are members), a sub-class of crustacea: *A Monograph on the Sub-class Cirripedia*.[54] *Cirripedia* manifest partial and temporary hermaphroditism, and these characteristics are sometimes acquired by the males.[55] The interesting thing about these animals, says Corydon, is that they are mostly hermaphrodites, but 'according to Darwin' in this particular case there exist dwarf males of an extremely simplified nature, being no more than a sexual implement lacking mouth and digestive tract. Several of these, Corydon says, can be found clustered on a single female and are called 'complemental males' by Darwin. In the main this account is correct, but it is a necessarily inadequate summary of a complicated question. For one thing, one would have liked Corydon to tell us whether the complemental males live on the hermaphrodites as well as on the females, and to have described their precise role in reproduction.

The passage in *Corydon* is a summary of the beginning of Darwin's chapter 'On the Sexual Relation of Cirripedes'.[56] Darwin writes:

Cirripedes are commonly bisexual or hermaphrodite, but in Ibla, Scalpellum, and Alcippe, members of the Lepadidae in the order Thoracica, and in

Cryptophialus in the order Abdominalia, the sexes are separate. . . . The males in the above four genera present a wonderful range of structure; they are attached in the normal way by cement . . . to different parts, in the different species, of the female. These males are minute, often exceedingly minute, and consequently generally more than one is attached to a single female; and I have seen as many as fourteen adhering to one female! In several species the males are short-lived, for they cannot feed, being destitute of mouth and stomach.

However, 'complemental males' in Darwin's terminology is a phrase reserved for certain epizoa – '[they] are the males of the hermaphrodites to which they are attached . . . not exclusively impregnating the ova of a female, but aiding the self-impregnation of an hermaphrodite. Hence I have called these males *Complemental males*, to show that they do not pair with a female, but with a bisexual individual.'[57] 'Cirripedes,' Darwin had written earlier,[58] 'are ordinarily bisexual, in which they differ from all crustaceans: when the sexes are separate, the males are minute, rudimentary in structure, and spermanently epizoic on the females.' The mature males of *Ibla Cumingii* (non-hermaphroditic) exhibit characteristics which are so embryonic that 'they may be said essentially to be mere bags of spermatozoa'.[59] Corydon wishes to use only the evidence which will support his idea that, as evolution continues, the male keeps for himself more and more matter for variation. In this he is inspired by the remarks of Darwin on the non-hermaphroditic types already cited: 'It is the females in the above genera [sc. *Ibla* and so on] which retain the characters of the genus, family and order to which they belong; the males often departing widely from the normal type.'[60] Corydon draws no conclusions from the bisexual state of these crustaceans.

From an unidentified work on zoology he next shows the astonished interlocutor a picture of 'the hideous female of the *chondracanthus gibbosus*, with her dwarf male attached'.[61] Like the *cirripedes*, the *chondracanthus gibbosus* is a crustacean, but unlike them it is a parasitic copepod and is not bisexual. The animal lives in the gills of various sea fish, sexual dimorphism is very marked, and the minute male lives clinging to the female. The conclusions which should be drawn from this example support Corydon's argument even less well.

Perhaps we may sense that Corydon is not a full-blooded Darwinian, even though he is glad of support when quotations can be found. For example, in saying that he values a theory for the fresh stimulus it brings to people's minds rather than for its absolute truth he refers to Darwin, adding that the best theories sow the seeds of their own destruction.[62] As we shall see, he was in fact more hostile to Darwin than might appear. One testimony must give us pause for thought. 'I cannot applaud Fabre's remarks at the expense of Darwinism,' Gide wrote in his *Journal* on 19 June 1910. 'Not that I feel myself to be a convinced transformist (and reading de Vries,[63] far from persuading me, has made me even more wary), but it is quite monstrous to say that Darwinism encourages sloth.' He proceeds to quote Fabre, agreeing only with the final point that it is dangerous for science to acquiesce in the doctrine of evolutionism and not to seek to go further. However, he concedes that he finds Fabre's criticisms often quite sensible. The rest of the passage is not relevant for our argument, since it is about an error in the French translation which misled Fabre, and a further confusion between Charles and Erasmus Darwin.

Other observations are reported by Corydon. In fact a whole menagerie appears, including some from the pages of Havelock Ellis,[64] and an entry on homosexual behaviour among pigeons from G.L.G. Belèze's 'out-of-date' *Dictionnaire universel de la vie pratique à la ville et à la campagne.*[65] This last example demonstrates the diversity of Gide's source books, ranging from the erudite to the obviously popular.

Some observations are from Gide's own notebook. He was clearly very satisfied with the rather long (and some might feel tasteless) account of the sexual activities of the dogs on the boulevard,[66] the whole of which was added in manuscript to the 1911 proof copy. On 5 October 1914 he noted in his *Journal* some problems he was having in mating his own dogs: the bitch was willing, but the male was not. 'How I wish that only people who have raised or supervised animals had the right to speak on sexual matters. They would then perhaps finally consent to understand that many difficulties, deviations and irregularities which they insist on considering "contrary to nature" and abnormal are no less *natural* than anything else.' It was doubtless in this frame of mind that he took a cutting from a periodical which he subsequently decided not to use. Headed '16ᵉ année, nº 12. *Échos et variétés:* "A strange adoptive family"', the piece was about a dog which suckled some piglets. It concluded: 'Moral: among animals, as among humans, maternal love is capable of such devotion that, in spite of the proverb, *the dog may love the cat.*'[67]

CHAPTER NINE

Victims, Martyrs and a Social Conscience

It is open to doubt whether Gilles de Rais and the Marquis de Sade were, in Gide's eyes, truly victims of the sexual attitudes manifest in their respective societies. However, just as we have seen Gide taking an inquisitive and perhaps prurient interest in medical and other books in his late adolescence and early twenties, we may perhaps perceive a similar motive in his note of reading on 21 June 1891 Paul Lacroix (alias P.L. Jacob), *Curiosités de l'histoire de France. Deuxième série: Procès célèbres.*[1] It is a curious fact that the precise bibliographical reference occurs, probably in 1890, on another piece of paper, which is thick and heavily edged in black,[2] not the most appropriate of places, perhaps, for such a jotting. The form of the note suggests that this is information supplied by a friend for further reading. With it there is also a reference to a 'medical dictionary . . . for later' (this is possibly to be equated with the dictionary discussed in Chapter 5).

In his account of 'the original Bluebeard' Lacroix leaves little unrecorded, despite the claim in his preface that he will let the veil of history cover the frightful crimes which were committed by Gilles de Rais. In Brittany, in 1440, accusations and rumours began to circulate concerning the disappearance of many boys and youths between the ages of eight and eighteen. At the subsequent trial Gilles de Rais eventually confirmed the story which two servants, his accomplices, had revealed in testimony. And so Lacroix repeats in detail the terrible catalogue of murders and sexual assaults which had occurred. In his narration he suggestively describes Gilles de Rais' relationship with his pages and his private choristers who remained apparently immune from his homicidal lust, but he highlights the bloody nature of the violent murders which were committed. Only when he reports the details of Gilles de Rais' sexual climaxes does he limit himself to the Latin of the original documents. It is nevertheless clear from the French text that the children were killed after they had been (or while they were being) sexually abused. Gilles de Rais, still a staunch Catholic believer although accused of practising black magic, confessed to an average of 120 murders a year, making a grand total of 'some 800 victims of his perverted lust'. Lacroix records finally how the public trial ended with referral to another court, but that Gilles de Rais was allowed at the instance of the Bishop of Nantes to appear before an ecclesiastical court. He was accused *inter alia* of sodomy, and pleaded guilty to this and to the sin of homicide. His case rested – and this should perhaps remind us of Gide's *Saül* – on the claim that he was besieged, captured and inhabited by demons. Although condemned to be hanged and burned, his body was transferred after execution to the church of Notre Dame, as the model of a repentant sinner.

Unfortunately, we do not know what Gide thought of this story, nor how he reacted to the less lurid account of the Marquis de Sade whom Lacroix rather tritely labels 'the apostle of crime and debauchery'. In not too licentious a vein we are told several amorous anecdotes, and learn of the Marquis' penchant for incest. His life is presented as a quick 'Rake's Progress', including the story of Rose Keller, the prostitute whom he tied up and whipped, and whose lawsuit against de Sade on 3 April 1768 earned him his place in this collection of famous trials. Finally, it is of some significance that only these two stories, out of a total of eight contained in Lacroix's book, were mentioned by Gide in his note.[3]

We are on firmer ground when we turn to a more modern period. 'There have been as many victims as you care to name – but no martyrs. They have all denied it; and they always will' – Corydon's remark may seem unjust, but it is in fact largely true of the men Gide had in mind who were hounded by society and the newspapers. They were shamed into denying their true nature or committing suicide (*Corydon*, p. 22).

The current text of *Corydon* begins with the words: 'In 190– a scandalous trial brought the irritating question of uranism once more before the public.' In the 1920 edition the date given was '189–'. What significance may we attach to this change of date? The only example in the 1890s which was important for Gide was the trial of Oscar Wilde. The other material he cites belongs to the early years of the twentieth century. Gide first met Oscar Wilde on 29 November 1891, and saw him again during the early days of December in Paris.[4] Jean Delay has chronicled the course of the friendship between Wilde, Douglas and Gide.[5] They were to meet again in North Africa in January 1895. Gide's private judgement – 'Wilde . . . that fearful man, the most dangerous product of modern civilisation'[6] – is somewhat at odds with his later public eulogies. In 1891 Gide had read none of Wilde's books, but he could not conceive that they could equal their creator.[7] He did however read *Salome*[8] in February 1893[9] and *Intentions* and *De Profundis* in March 1905.[10]

Wilde is named among the victims listed by Corydon (p. 22). How 'scandalous' did his trial appear to a Frenchman, and how abject his behaviour? Gide followed the reports of the trials in the French newspapers. Like their English counterparts, they found that their impudent and salacious accounts maintained the interest of their readership. On 17 March 1895 Gide wrote to his mother and earnestly asked her to send him 'all the press cuttings' she could find about 'the scandalous case brought against Wilde by the Marquis of Queensberry'.[11]

It was in February 1895 that the Marquis of Queensberry, father of Lord Alfred Douglas, left his visiting card at Wilde's club.[12] The message 'For Oscar Wilde, posing as a somdomite [sic]' led Wilde to institute proceedings against Queensberry for criminal libel. With hindsight we can see how rash a decision this was. The trial of the Marquis happened on 3 to 5 April 1895, in the course of which Wilde's epigrammatic wit, exercised at the expense of the counsel for the defence Edward Carson, enormously entertained the court. Wilde, however, became less certain of himself as the case proceeded. In view of the damaging nature of the evidence, he was advised to withdraw from the prosecution, consenting to the truth of the lesser charge of 'posing'. Defence and prosecution agreed, and a verdict of not guilty was returned in favour of Queensberry.

A warrant was immediately applied for to arrest Wilde because of the evidence which had been disclosed. He was committed for trial on 19 April. In the meantime he was sent to Holloway Prison, and one month later was released on bail after the jury had failed to reach a verdict. This trial took place on 26 April 1895. Wilde and Alfred Taylor had been charged under a single indictment, alleging the commission of acts of gross indecency and conspiracy to procure the commission of such acts by Wilde. Taylor was further charged with having procured for Wilde. It was at this time that society closed its ranks against Wilde: his plays, which were enjoying successful runs in the West End, were taken off, and his books were removed from publishers' lists. Wilde nevertheless bore up with fortitude. Perhaps he believed the jury would not convict him; perhaps he thought that the next trial would result in a definite verdict of not guilty. But the decision to proceed no longer lay with him.

When the new prosecution was instituted, Wilde was encouraged by many of his friends to jump bail and seek refuge in France. He decided to stay. The third trial began on 22 May 1895. On this occasion Taylor and Wilde were tried separately, the conspiracy charge having been dropped. Taylor was found guilty of indecent behaviour. Wilde, who was accused of having committed acts of gross indecency, denied these accusations categorically. There are, however, reports that he appeared physically exhausted and worn down by strain. The result of this final trial is well known: he was found guilty on all counts (except for one which had been withdrawn) and was, together with Taylor, sentenced to two years' imprisonment with hard labour. In *Corydon* Queensberry is seen as Wilde's attacker – as he was indeed in everyday life, though not actually in the law courts, where the state undertook the prosecution in the two later trials.

The Wilde affair provoked many reactions in the French press, but one in particular is perhaps worthy of mention. An article by Paul Adam, an acquaintance of Gide's whom he had met in July 1891,[13] appeared in the *Revue Blanche* for 15 May 1895 entitled 'L'Assaut malicieux' (pp. 458–62). Gide made a note of this among his memoranda for *Corydon*.[14] Adam briefly surveyed the history of Greek love, also referring in a footnote to Schopenhauer's comment on homosexuality, before pointing to a contradiction in people's attitudes to Wilde: should they praise or blame him? The English, he asserts, have not had the benefit of reading Dugas' recent book *L'Amitié antique* (1894), and French moralists condemn Wilde for having seduced Lord Alfred Douglas. Had he seduced a woman they would have praised him for it, yet adultery damages the fabric of society (for syphilitic children are often the result). We condemn those whose habits differ from our own merely because they differ, he writes, adding that the only natural act is simple procreation – anything else is, by definition, anti-natural. *Corydon*'s argument follows the first two of these points.

What has Wilde done which is especially wrong? 'It is odious to be drunk,' writes Adam, 'but it is absurd to congratulate the dandy who has had too much champagne, while reviling someone else who has got drunk on cocktails.' Thus adultery has been accepted for centuries, while unproductive love between males has been condemned. After some arguments of rather dubious validity, Adam comes to the point: Lord Alfred Douglas' passion for Wilde is of the highest sort for it depends neither on instinct nor money.

A poet shows the secret of harmonious thoughts to an unformed adolescent. He captivates him by the cadence of his verse, the beauty of the rhythm. Dazzled by these spiritual marvels the young lord yields himself up to his friend. He listens. He learns. He vibrates before the same shape of splendour. The idea unites them. They are both lovers of the same spiritual flight. . . .

For Adam, there is no greater beauty than that of 'the adolescent seduced by the master's mind and who leaves everything to follow him'. Again this is in accord with *Corydon*'s feelings. Adam concludes: in the choice between adultery and pederasty we should be more indulgent towards the latter because it is less harmful.

The *Mercure de France* published several items on Wilde,[15] and in the issue for January 1914 (from which Gide extracted some material about Ptolemy Auletes)[16] there appeared an article by Louis Wilkinson, translated by H.-D. Davray, entitled 'Sur des lettres inédites d'Oscar Wilde' (pp. 69–78). The letters in question were written between December 1898 and July 1900. This account of Wilde is not unsympathetic, and points out that Wilde 'has become more popular again'. However, Wilkinson continues, 'the question is now frequently asked whether he was not more unfortunate than criminal; whether he was not so much a delinquent as a victim of abnormal mental or emotional conditions which, as people now generally accept, are not incompatible with genius'.[17] The period when these letters were written is, of course, the period of Wilde's decline.

Apart from the recollections contained in *Si le grain ne meurt* there are two places where Gide wrote at length about Wilde, but in both he concentrated more on Wilde's personality and on his tragedy than on his literary works. Was this because, as Wilde is alleged to have told him, Wilde had put his genius in his life and his talent in his books?

The first is an article which was written in December 1901 and published in the June number of *L'Ermitage* the following year.[18] In this 'In Memoriam' Gide does not wish to hide the man *behind* the work (as did his supporters at the trial): he will first show that the man was admirable. Wilde, he says, was like Bacchus, like Elagabalus. In telling his fables he wove spells for Gide. Thus it was for the story of Narcissus whose tale is a model for discipleship: '"If I loved him," replied the river, "it was because, when he leaned over my water, I saw the reflection of my waters in his eyes."'[19] Gide emphasises his interest in Wilde's paradox about Nature and Art: 'The flower of the narcissus is as beautiful as a work of art – and what distinguishes [the world of Art and the world of Nature] cannot be beauty . . . the work of art is always *unique*. Nature, which makes nothing durable, always repeats itself so that nothing which it makes may be lost . . . for God invents Man, and Man invents the work of art. . . . ' Wilde's most ingenious sallies and his most disturbing ironies, however, seemed designed to confront pagan naturalism with Christian idealism and to put the latter at a disadvantage. Gide would have us believe that before 1895 he knew nothing of the scabrous side of Wilde's reputation. He must however have seen that, as rumours about Wilde's friendships spread, public reaction to the stories was similar to the ostracism described in the opening pages of the 1911 version of *Corydon*. It is from early 1895 that Gide reports the witticism: 'Not happiness! Above all, not happiness.

Pleasure! We must always want the most tragic. . . .' And Gide later found a similar thought in Nietzsche. *Dorian Gray*, when recounted by Wilde, was a 'splendid story' but 'Alas! when written down, how great a failed masterpiece it appeared.' There is no comment on the homosexual undertones of the novel and no account of the revisions and suppressions which the publisher obliged Wilde to make to avoid a public scandal. There is a record in Gide's unpublished *Journal* of reading 'Le Portrait de Dorian Gray' in June 1895.[20]

Gide portrays Wilde moving deliberately and inexorably towards his tragedy. 'Scandal,' as he wrote elsewhere, 'must occur' – but 'perhaps,' he added here, 'in some far-off time it will be well to lift this frightful trial out of its abominable filth.' Gide repudiated the assertion made by several German and English newspapers that his recollections about Wilde were contrived. He had not, he said, pointed up the antithesis between the glorious 'King of Life' of the early triumphant days and the pitiful Melmoth of the darker years.

The second article, 'De Profundis', appeared in *L'Ermitage* in August 1905 (pp. 65–73). This is a review of *Intentions* and *De Profundis*, the latter of which had just appeared in French in a truncated form, and in March Gide had already written in his *Journal*, 'I also started reading it at Cuverville in German and in English and will certainly speak of it again.'[21] Each work belonged, as he pointed out in his review, to one part of those 'antithetical' periods. 'Through the excess of pleasure, I admire the secret advance toward a more significant destiny,' he wrote. He was, however, irritated by certain remarks in the translator's preface: 'No, in order to read this work better, regardless of what M. Joseph Renaud [the translator of *Intentions*] says about it, let us not pretend to ignore the drama of the man who, though knowing that it wounds, wished, nevertheless, *to address himself to life*.' But it is the tragedy, and not the homosexuality, which in Gide's view illuminates our understanding. Despite the humility so deeply expressed in the pages of *De Profundis*, Gide remembered from 'elsewhere' a statement of Wilde's which found a deep echo in his own heart: 'To regret one's own experiences is to arrest one's own development. To deny one's own experiences is to put a lie onto the lips of one's own life. It is no less than a denial of the soul.' Likewise, Jacques Copeau, a close friend of Gide's with whom Gide collaborated on several theatrical projects, reports a conversation which allegedly took place in 1905. Gide had said to him:

I am afraid lest I be overwhelmed with remorse when I grow old, and that my intelligence will weaken. I am afraid lest, like Wilde, I write my own *De Profundis*. I have striven so vigorously and so maliciously against myself, I have tried so hard to make myself ordinary as a reaction against my exceptional character, motivated by hatred for the misgivings due to my education and my puritan upbringing. Wilde wrote that if the walls of his prison could speak they would have cried out 'Fool! Fool!'[22]

It is therefore a little paradoxical to read in the *Journal* for May 1905 (p. 157) that in a period of feeling depressed Gide was able to find some comfort in reading *De Profundis* aloud in English and in French.

One may perhaps conclude that for Gide Wilde's example was above all a moral one. The Irishman provided him with elements he was to attribute to both Ménalque and Corydon. Like both characters, Wilde was a self-possessed hedonist shunned and abandoned by society. His influence was liberating, and his role was to clarify in Gide's mind the symbols of Wanderer and Immoralist. Wilde's attitude to life, combined with aphorisms from Nietzsche's works, contributed to the image of 'disponibilité' (openness) and had particular consequences for Gide in the sphere of sexual morality. It remains a curious fact that Gide had so little to say about chastity when speaking of the case of Wilde.

In this early section of *Corydon* the names of F.A. Krupp and General Sir Hector Macdonald appear. Corydon clearly believes that it was because they could not change their nature that they committed suicide (pp. 24–5).

Krupp died on 22 November 1902. This was widely reported in the newspapers, including *Le Temps*, to which Gide's close friend Ghéon referred in a letter shortly afterwards.[23] In a melancholy mood Ghéon wished to celebrate some Arab boys he had known – and then to die. 'How I envy Krupp,' he wrote. But envy was not perhaps the most appropriate reaction. Gide made no comment on this remark. It was in Capri that Krupp had constantly surrounded himself with handsome youths and had given occasion for much scandal. As with Eulenburg, political opponents used this information to discredit him, his associates and those who were close to the Kaiser. Krupp brought an action for libel against the newspaper *Vorwärts* which had published details of his life on Capri, but as he died shortly afterwards the libel action was withdrawn. His funeral was attended by all the best people, including the Emperor.[24] It is no more than a reasonable belief that he died by his own hand. Krupp, to judge from his photograph, was not, according to usual standards, good looking. On the other hand Macdonald and Eulenburg appear intelligent, handsome and noble, even to the most prejudiced observer.[25]

The photograph of General Macdonald, published to commemorate his death, bears this out. A well-groomed British officer, born in 1853, he died on 25 March 1903. Having enlisted in the 92nd Highlanders, the Gordons, he was commissioned after conspicuous gallantry. His career was very successful, but while commander in Ceylon in 1902 it was rumoured that he was involved in homosexual activities with native youths. He returned to London, but on his way back to Ceylon, he shot himself while staying at the Hotel Regina in Paris. This was another scandal which was widely featured in the newspapers.[26]

Eulenburg is the remaining victim named by Corydon, and Harden is rightly singled out as his pursuer (p. 23). The scandal is referred to obliquely later (Dialogue IV) in the context of German militarism (p. 175). But although the contemporary press made much of homosexual corruption in the German army and among the Kaiser's most intimate circle of friends and advisers, this is not the aspect of the affair which seems to preoccupy Gide.

In addition to the articles published (in German) in the *Jahrbuch*, several books on the 'German vice' had appeared in French. As we have already seen, among the most noteworthy of these was Magnus Hirschfeld's *Le Troisième Sexe. Les homosexuals de Berlin* (1908).[27] Another was Oscar Méténier's *Vertus et vices allemands. Les Berlinois chez eux*, Paris: Albin Michel, 1904. There was also John Grand-Carteret, *Derrière 'Lui' (l'homosexualité en Allemagne)*, Paris: E. Bernard, [1908], which reproduces many of the cartoons and caricatures which appeared during the Eulenburg scandal. One book on the Eulenburg trials of which Gide may well have had knowledge was Henri de Weindel and F.P. Fischer, *L'Homosexualité en Allemagne* (1908). Although proceedings in the Eulenburg affair continued until the unfortunate man's death on 17 September 1921, this account gives a good summary of the major skirmishes, and was in fact published at the time of Gide's most intense work on *Corydon*. Weindel and Fischer give a detailed and generally objective account of events up to a date shortly before their book was published. The story begins with the sensational journalism of Maximilian Harden in the paper he had founded in 1892, *Die Zukunft*. The scandalous articles began to appear in October 1906 and from March–April 1907 became much more overt in tone. There was obviously a political dimension to the affair since French and German interests in North Africa would be affected by the outcome. Feelings of nationalism were appealed to – which, as the reader of *Corydon* may notice, did not pass without comment even on the French side.[28] Accusations of homosexual conduct were made in order to discredit persons close to the Kaiser. Thus shortly after the publication of an article on 27 April 1907 the following occurred: Philip Eulenburg, former Ambassador in Vienna, was exiled; Kuno von Moltke, the Military Governor of Berlin, resigned; Count Hohenau, general aide-de-camp of Wilhelm II, was exiled. The scandal also affected Raymond Lecomte, France's Conseiller d'Ambassade in Berlin. The result was a complicated series of court actions. In October 1907 Moltke sued Harden for defamation. Harden retracted what he had written, but did so in such a slippery way as to leave many doubts in the minds of the public. In the course of the trial Moltke and Eulenburg were revealed as very close friends since early youth who continued to be attached to each other in a rather sentimental way. There were stories of orgies, and allegations of Moltke's frigidity towards his wife. Much of this testimony was later discounted, but the case developed into a second trial scheduled for 16 December 1907 and deferred until 19 December. When this occurred, Harden's evidence in particular was discredited, but he pleaded that he wrote his articles in good faith and in the public interest. On 3 January 1908, however, Harden was condemned for defamation and was sentenced to four months' imprisonment.

Soon after the publication of Weindel and Fischer's book Harden brought a libel suit against the newspaper editor Anton Städele for implying that he had been bribed by Eulenburg. Eulenburg was arrested on 7 May 1908, and the trial was opened on 29 June. In September he was released on bail, being now a sick man, and when the proceedings were recommenced in July 1909 they were immediately adjourned *sine die* for the same reason.

Other matters discussed by Weindel and Fischer include the organisation and activity of the police in Germany, the incidence of homosexuality, details of homosexual lifestyles (including prostitution and the criminal underworld), homosexual activity in the army, the aristocracy and the Church. A historical section gives a detailed account of von Platen and Winckelmann. In addition to the Eulenburg affair, other *causes célèbres* mentioned include Hasse, the President of the Tribunal in Breslau, who in 1905 shot and wounded a blackmailer. He gave himself up and was subsequently convicted of homosexual offences. Count Hohenau,[29] too, one of the subjects of the defamatory articles in *Die Zukunft*, was pursued in 1901–2: it appears that he was also probably involved in some homosexual scandals in London. Even the Imperial Chancellor von Bülow was accused by the pamphleteer Brand in 1907, but Brand was found guilty of libel and was condemned to eighteen months' imprisonment.

Both the English and the German victims we have mentioned had something in common which distinguished them from their French counterparts. In England the law exacted harsh penalties from those who were found guilty of having committed sodomy, bestiality or acts of gross indecency. After the passing of the Labouchère amendment (Section 11 of the Criminal Law Amendment Act of 1885) men in Wilde's position were even more vulnerable. Other legislation against homosexual soliciting was incorporated in the Vagrancy Act of 1898.

In Germany paragraph 175 of the Code was similarly oppressive: 'Indecency contrary to nature between two persons of the masculine sex is punishable by a prison sentence and may entail the loss of civil rights.' A note in the *Mercure de France*[30] expressed relief that in Germany in the future 'individual cases would be considered on their own merits', but added the pious warning that 'Justice must protect them from themselves and protect society from them.' This sentiment does not seem to be a case of wartime anti-German feeling, but a reflection of a prejudiced person who thought himself progressive.

The situation in France at this period was quite different. 'Acts contrary to nature' did not in themselves constitute a crime (these only became unlawful under Pétain in 1942), and it was only where minors were concerned, or when an act of public indecency had occurred, that proceedings were instituted. But the situation was not even as simple as this might imply, for the courts had to consider these cases under the headings of 'excitation des mineurs à la débauche' (properly a law against procuring) and 'outrage public à la pudeur'. This, as an authoritative commentator ruefully admitted, had led to a great deal of confusion.[31] A minor, as defined under Article 388 of the French Civil Code, is 'a person of either sex who has not yet completed his/her 21st year'. Minors needed parental consent for marriage, but once married they were legally autonomous. Youths under eighteen and girls under fifteen could not marry unless in exceptional circumstances and with special legal permission. A law of 11 April 1908 ('Concernant la prostitution des mineurs') enacted penalties for minors under the age of eighteen who habitually practised prostitution.[32]

Corydon, who is a decent honest person, has to face public opinion; Wilde and Krupp faced opinion and the law. It is no wonder that the examples (all non-French) mentioned in *Corydon* are victims. They had no other option, for none was subject to the Code Napoléon (mentioned later in the book: *Corydon*, p. 175). They lived outside France.

The English Act and the German paragraph 175 gave many opportunities for blackmail and provoked a number of suicides recorded in the literature of the time, and printed in detail in a special section of the *Jahrbuch*. Corydon in fact has his own story to tell, as we shall see shortly.

Evidence of only two newspaper cuttings concerning the Eulenburg scandals survives among Gide's notes: one is printed in *Corydon*,[33] the other is an account of 'Prince Eulenburg's collapse. Berlin 22 April'.[34] Gide would certainly have known more than this, but what is equally interesting is a small collection of cuttings concerning other events which occurred between 1908 and 1917. Once again, though, it is clear that the extent of this collection is quite arbitrary. It is at most a valuable witness to Gide's concern to establish his 'archive' – a *dossier pédérastie*, as he labelled it.

There is in fact further evidence that he took an active interest in criminal and judicial matters apart from pederasty. In 1912 he made a deliberate effort to become a juror, and was empanelled at the Assizes at Rouen in that year. In the *Nouvelle Revue Française* in November–December 1913[35] he published an account of the cases he had had to consider. There were several instances of 'attentat à la pudeur', all of which were heterosexual. Gide concluded that, among other things, two ideas were of importance – that the crime could be considered an anomaly, and that the criminal may often be regarded as a 'victim' of circumstances or social attitudes. As for the motivation of the criminal, he suggested that it could sometimes be assimilated to his category of 'l'acte gratuit' – a crime without a motive.

In 1930, still preoccupied with the concept of justice, Gide instituted in the *Nouvelle Revue Française* a section entitled 'Ne jugez pas' (an allusion to Matthew 7:1 'Judge not, that ye be not judged'). The first 'dossier' to appear was 'L'Affaire Redureau' (which occurred in 1913), and told the story of a young assassin;[36] the second, 'La Séquestrée de Poitiers', reported the case of a woman imprisoned by her family in 1901. There is also a collection of 'Faits divers', published in 1930 at the end of 'L'Affaire Redureau', which includes a number of suicide cases, including the one (Rouen, 1909) used for an episode in *Les Faux-Monnayeurs*. The articles vary in date from 1895 to 1927, a number belonging to the period 1908–10, although most are from the 1920s. There are no homosexual cases.

The following list[37] gives an impression of the homosexual scandals which were reported in the French newspapers in the period when Gide was gathering material for *Corydon*. It is not of course complete. Cases collected separately by Gide are marked with an asterisk:

(1) An anonymous Englishman [Lord Alfred Douglas], who was enticed by two youths posing as homosexuals, and who was then robbed (*Le Journal*, 26 October 1900).[38]
(2) Two men aged thirty and thirty-four who committed suicide (*Le Journal*, 18 July 1903).
(3) Two men aged twenty-six and forty-two (*Le Journal*, 25 July 1903).
(4) A twenty-five-year-old who was caught in the Bois de Boulogne (*Le Journal*, 2 August 1903).
(5) A case of male prostitution in the Rue Saint Martin (*Le Journal*, 7 August 1903).
(6) A homosexual minor (*Le Journal*, 29 November and 4 December 1903).

131

(7) Incidents in a painter's studio (*Le Journal*, 23 March 1904).

(8) A scandal at the baths in the Rue de Penthièvre (no source given).

(9) The arrest of a homosexual soldier in Nice (*Le Journal*, 1 December 1905).

(10) The arrest of a tradesman in Toulon for procuring youths of sixteen to eighteen years old for a priest (*Petit Parisien*, 9 March 1907).

(11) The arrest of a tradesman at Meaux (*Le Journal*, 15 March 1907).

(12) The celebration of a male marriage (*Le Journal*, 11 June 1907).

(13) The arrest of an army officer in Bourges (*Le Journal*, 16 November 1907).

(14) The arrest of an army officer in Brest (*Le Journal*, 28 November 1907).

(15) A teacher and a male prostitute who were caught in Dijon (*Le Journal*, 27 January 1908).

(16) A police raid on a café, 16 Quai de l'Hôtel de Ville (*Le Journal*, 27 January 1908).

(17) The arrest of a lieutenant in Belfort (*Le Journal*, January 1908).

(18)* A judge from Gnesen (in Germany) who was arrested and sentenced on the same day (*Le Temps*, 20 August 1908).[39]

(19)* The Renard affair (*Le Journal*, 9 February 1909: see below.)[40]

(20)* A man in the provinces who was falsely accused by some children of 'outrage public à la pudeur'. They withdrew their testimony (source untraced, dated by Gide 24 March 1909).[41]

(21) The death of a homosexual in Paris caused by his lover (no source, April 1909).

(22) The arrest of men consorting with youths of fourteen to eighteen years old in Bordeaux (*Le Journal*, 12 April 1909).

(23) A lesbian affair (satirised in *Fantasio*, 1 May 1909).

(24) The arrest of a soldier in Aurillac (*Le Journal*, June 1909).

(25) A raid on a male brothel in Montmartre (*Le Journal*, 22 June and 28 July 1909).

(26)* A lawyer in Macon who was discovered with a telegraph boy (*Le Temps*, 25 September 1910).[42]

(27)* Kiel. Fourteen men were arrested for having had dealings with sailors from the *Preussen* (*Le Matin*, 23 October 1913).[43]

(28)* A young soldier who abducted a fifteen-year-old boy (*Débats*, 3 December 1917).[44]

(29)* Hakki Bey, Turkish Consul in Berlin, disappeared and was wanted for homosexual offences (no source indicated. Dated: '6 August').[45]

There is additionally among the press cuttings an article by Lucien Descaves, 'Invertis et pervertis' (*Le Journal*, 2 March 1910), about the frequency of male prostitution in Paris.

There seems to have been no overriding principle in Gide's collecting, and what survives in the archive suggests a method which was relatively haphazard.

The case of Baron Jacques Adelsward-Fersen need not detain us long. Although this scandal was widely reported in the newspapers (particularly in the *Figaro*, *Le Matin* and *Le Journal*), and Gide cannot have been unaware of it, he has left no comment. Fersen was arrested in July 1903 and charged with misconduct involving boys from well-known schools – the Lycée Carnot, the Lycée Condorcet and the Lycée Janson de Sailly. The place of rendezvous, where other men in their mid-twenties also resorted, was allegedly 18 Avenue de Friedland. Perhaps Gide had this intrigue in mind when he created a similar (but heterosexual) den of vice for the boys in *Les Faux-Monnayeurs*. We should, however, be cautious about assuming this, for the temptation to give too much weight to coincidence is well known.[46] In late November the 9ᵉ Chambre du Tribunal Correctionnel met and, in December, passed judgement: there was a fine, a short prison sentence and five years' 'interdiction des droits de famille' (forfeiture of family rights) for those convicted on the count of 'excitation de mineurs à la débauche'. Fersen left the country and travelled to Capri.[47] We will meet his name again as the founder of the homosexual periodical *Akadémos* (1909), in which he also wrote under the pseudonym of 'Sonyeuse'. Roger Peyrefitte, who gives a somewhat novelettish account of Fersen's life in *L'Exilé de Capri*, tells of a meeting between Fersen and Gide in the Normandy country house of Trouard-Riolle in 1909. This report is unsubstantiated, but Gide is alleged to have told Trouard-Riolle later never to introduce him again to people as disreputable as Fersen and his boyfriend.[48]

The Renard affair of 1908–9 was, however, more important for Gide than the other cases. Anglès reports that Gide followed the proceedings in Le Havre avidly and asked his friend Jean Schlumberger to obtain the lawyers' speeches for him *in extenso*.[49] The facts were as follows. On 7 June 1908 a banker, Monsieur Rémy, was found murdered in his bed. The weapon used was a dessert knife. Of the persons known to have been in the house, Rémy's seventeen-year-old nephew Raingo, some servants and the fifty-year-old butler Renard, suspicion fell on the butler. After Renard's arrest, however, some jewellery was found in the pocket of a young servant named Courtois. Courtois promptly implicated Renard and alleged that the pair of them had committed the murder, having stripped naked in order to avoid bloodstains on their clothes. It emerged that Renard was homosexual. Renard firmly denied being involved in the murder. When the decision of 10 February 1909 sentencing Renard to penal servitude for life and Courtois to twenty years' hard labour had been quashed, the case was taken before the Assize Court at Versailles. Meanwhile Courtois had died in prison. Renard was again found guilty of unpremeditated murder despite the nature of the evidence, which pointed to deliberate conspiracy, if it pointed to anything at all. It was stated at the time: 'A person who starts with homosexuality will logically commit murder in the end.' Renard's appeal to the President was rejected: he was transported to Guiana. There are two cuttings in the archive: one from *Le Journal* dated 9 February 1909, and the other from *Le Matin* 7 August 1909 (quoted at length in a footnote to *Corydon*, p. 178). Gide comments on both. In the first the Avocat Général Rambaud is reported as saying that 'unisexual love' not only corrupts the senses but 'has an enormous influence on morals'. Seeing the drift of this reasoning, Gide appended the following: 'Ped[erasty]. The man who . . . [*sc.* is a pederast] is capable of everything (see the splendid quotation from Malthus).'[50] Rambaud's argument swayed the jury. It is an expression of popular prejudice against which Corydon would presumably have to speak: 'I shall explain why that is unfortunately true to a certain extent – for nothing is so good an invitation to put oneself *outside the law*.'

Traces of this train of thought do in fact survive in *Corydon*: love is a game which is played outside the rules (p. 121); from the point of view of 'natural law' a homosexual is an 'outlaw' (p. 59). And we shall have occasion to note this character trait in Gide's fictional heroes. There are also two letters from Gide dating from 1924 published by Rouveyre:[51] 'It is not the idea of being a uranist which is important, but having first established one's life as if one wasn't one. That is what obliges me to use pretence, cunning – and art'. And again – in rejecting Rouveyre's suggestion that he is drawn towards vice: 'It is precisely my horror of what is forbidden which *obliged* me to revise my code; I could no more be happy with living insincerely than remain outside the law.' The theme of living a life based upon a lie is particularly marked in *Œdipe*.[52]

The remainder of the note on the Renard case highlights the way in which prejudice can outweigh sympathy based on earlier intimacy: 'The high regard felt for Renard by Madame Rémy was such that it was not until some time after the crime had been committed, and only when she had learned of the nature of the relationship between the butler and her nephew, whom she loved as her own son, that she *finally believed* [*sic*] in Renard's guilt.'

The second cutting, from *Le Matin*, illustrates Corydon's contention that 'The current state of our morals tends to make out of homosexual inclinations a school for hypocrisy, malice and revolt against the law.'[53] How should this be? In the words of the journalist,

It has been many years since any accused person has had so many doubts in his favour. . . . But his appeal has been rejected. Public opinion – apart from some obvious [?][54] rare exceptions – has sided with the jury and the magistrates. And why? Because it has been proved that Renard, *even if it is admitted that he did not murder* [Rémy], was an odious and repugnant monster. Because the public had the impression that Renard, *though innocent*, was a worthy member of that collection of persons whom society casts out from its bosom and sends to prison ignobly in Guiana.

This attitude is unsympathetic, illogical and unjust to a degree. It illustrates the contemporary prejudice against homosexuals and likewise society's general hypocrisy,[55] which Gide found so antipathetic.

Gourmont also has something to say about the case and uses it as material for one of his *Dialogues des amateurs* published in the *Mercure de France* 1 March 1909.[56] One should have no illusions about the jury, says Monsieur Desmaisons, for they judge a crime in the same stubborn way that they judge success at bridge; 'But they do so with less competence.' Desmaisons, here the mouthpiece of Gourmont, is bitterly ironic as he tackles the logic of Madame Rémy ('He seduced my nephew, therefore he murdered my husband') and the government Minister. Even Monsieur Delarue is astonished. Desmaisons draws his conclusions: 'All crimes are thereby seen as connected. One sin gives rise to another. And people conclude "This man is not worthy of our interest. If he is innocent of this thing, then he's guilty of the other. Let him pay for his immorality [*qu'il expie ses mauvaises mœurs*]."' Delarue draws his own bitter conclusions, too, for, as he says, this line of reasoning is worthy of the Holy Office.

Cases of a different sort could also have come to Gide's attention. A. Coffignon, *Paris vivant. La Corruption à Paris*, gives anecdotal details on pederasty and male prostitution in the French capital in the 1880s. The book was quite well known, and its tone betrays the author's hostility to his subject matter. The 'active' pederasts are presented as the pimps (*souteneurs*); the 'passive' ones as the adolescent prostitutes (*petits-jésus*). Cases of blackmail, voyeurism and sadism are included. Chapter XXIV, 'Un drame d'amour de pédérastes', records an instance of the death penalty being enforced on 30 May 1885: in the course of police investigations into a theft in 1884 by the 'brothers' Simon evidence of sexual 'misconduct' had also emerged. This incident provides a parallel to the Rémy case.

In the *Revue Blanche*, G. Dubois-Dessaule published on 1 April 1901 (p. 481) an article 'Le Bagne militaire', describing the military penitentiary at Oléron. Here he listed among other things the sexual practices of the convicts.[57] Gide did in fact take note of a short extract of four pages from *Les Réfractaires* (September–mid-October 1913)

135

by Alexander Berkman, author of 'Prison Memoirs of an Anarchist'. Berkman's title was 'Au-delà de l'amour féminin . . .' ('Passing the Love of Women'), and he described how he fell in love with an adolescent, named Floyd, in prison. It is in the form of a confessional dialogue, and the author tells of the gradually increasing sexual attraction he felt towards the youth.[58]

Let us return briefly to the victims who commit suicide. Corydon has intimate knowledge of such a person, and the case history he narrates is not without parallel in the newspaper reports or Havelock Ellis' stories. Corydon was engaged to a young girl whom he loved tenderly but without sensuality.[59] She had a brother, Alexis, who was a few years younger than herself. He was an adolescent, 'full of grace and self-awareness [conscience]', but who on occasion was 'still a child'. He was very fond of Corydon, and Corydon became aware that Alexis wanted his 'caresses' in addition to his friendship. Nothing 'impure' took place, however. When Alexis thus obliged Corydon to recognise his own true nature, Corydon became very severe, calling Alexis' affection effeminate – which it was not. Alexis tried hard to win Corydon's love, but in vain. The boy therefore committed suicide, leaving behind a letter in which he tried to explain his feelings. 'In loving you so deeply,' he wrote, 'I became an object of horror both to you and to myself.' It was for this reason that he 'suppressed his monstrous nature'. Corydon broke off his engagement. Anne-Marie Moulènes and Jean Tipy have drawn attention to the similarities between this story and Henri Ghéon's L'Adolescent, the early parts of which were read to Gide on 14 November 1907 and in February 1908.[60] L'Adolescent was to have described the life of a widower–pederast, and what remains appears to show that Gide was the model on which it was largely to be based. In Ghéon's book the hero meets a twelve-year-old boy who has been injured in the face. He becomes attached to the boy but at first is not aware of this because he visits the house in order to court the boy's sister. He feels no desire towards her because he has learned to dissociate 'reproduction, pleasure and love',[61] but he believes that he loves her sincerely. Their wedding night leaves him with the memory of a 'sentimental ecstasy' without the slightest sensual satisfaction. The boy, called Marcel, comes to live with them, but the wife soon dies in pregnancy, and the man and boy are left to their friendship.

These two narratives could be seen as variations on a theme, for it is not essential to determine the actual event which inspired them, even if it was possible to do so.[62] Indeed what Gide has added by his choice of names is a touching allusion to the idyllic tradition of Vergil's Second Eclogue.

What we should note is Corydon's conclusion. Case histories in the medical or forensic literature lead to condemnation or treatment. In

Gide's story of Corydon and Alexis the drama reveals the truth to the hero and makes him determined to devote himself to his 'speciality'. The cure would consist in teaching these 'victims' that they are not ill. The question whether they should practise their homosexuality has then to be decided.[63]

Part Three

THE LITERARY SOURCES

Il faut arriver à se faire tel que l'on se veut.
Choisissons donc les influences: que tout nous soit une éducation.
le 16 octobre [1888].

ms. Doucet γ 1558

This section of our enquiry deals with literature and is organised on a historical and geographical basis. The bulk of the material relates directly to *Corydon* but relevant books which Gide read at an earlier or a later date have not been omitted. Here, at least as much as in the case of the scientific works we have examined, we are confronted with ideas which influenced Gide's way of thinking, or which seemed to him to corroborate his opinions. We must, however, still remember that his methods were eclectic, and that our record of what he read is incomplete. What strikes us most forcibly is the wide range of his knowledge, and although some of this must necessarily be superficial, it bears witness to an enquiring mind which knew few boundaries. He read most of the foreign works in French translation, and I have endeavoured to identify the editions he used. Several themes occur repeatedly: alongside chastity, there is the important image of sentimental pederasty; alongside pagan temptation appears the figure of the ideal woman. There are many more, and we may notice them change as we observe the content of Gide's reading in the late 1880s and early 1890s, from 1900 to 1914, and from 1920 onwards. In this literary context several contentious debates arise: Gide's arguments with Pierre Louÿs, his polemics on the subject of Verlaine and Whitman, and his differences with Proust. There is, however, no simple pattern which may be imposed on this material: the most that can be said is that this investigation provides us with a context in which to judge Gide's opinions and his own literary works. The 'homosexual novel' as a genre came of age at the end of the nineteenth century, and Gide figures among both the reading public and the creative writers.

CHAPTER TEN

The Ancient World

The following remarks on pederasty in the ancient world are not intended to provide an exhaustive historical account of the subject. Since Gide's approach was not that of a trained historian, we must remember that for this part of his argument he appealed to the testimony of Greek and Latin authors in order to cite corroborative examples from their writings. In this he was not so very different from several of his contemporaries who created their own model of ancient civilisation.

A moment's reflection warns us that great distances in time, geography and social customs separate the Athens of Pericles and Sparta in the fourth century BC from Plutarch of Chaeronea and Lucian of Samosata in Syria in the first and second centuries AD respectively. Strato, the second-century AD writer of paedophile epigrams, has clearly nothing but the grossest connection with the fourth-century BC Athenian philosopher Plato. The situation in Rome under Augustus was different again. These examples of disparity can be multiplied several times over.

Gide relied on translations.[1] His debt to modern commentators is not easy to circumscribe. It is strange that he nowhere mentions L. Dugas' *L'Amitié antique* (1894)[2] nor the important articles in the *Jahrbuch für sexuelle Zwischenstufen*. However, he did use *Le Livre d'amour des anciens* and, more extensively, the second edition of Carpenter's *Ioläus*, as we shall see in due course. He was also aware of a chapter on pederasty in Becker's *Charicles*. In addition his picture of the ancient world was constructed from what he read in Herder, Montesquieu and Michelet, whose historical writings we have already discussed.

Corydon is a polemical tract, and it must be admitted that its portrayal of ancient sexual customs is not particularly balanced. Another way of considering the book is to see it as a dialogue on love. Gide reminded us of this when he drew our attention to Plato. This is also presumably the reason why he added the description 'Four Socratic Dialogues' to the 1920 and subsequent editions. It is not the dialectic which earns it this title, but the association of Socrates with the love of youths. *Corydon*, in fact, has other precursors in Greek literature in the form of debates on the nature and relative desirability of homosexual and heterosexual love. The tradition was a well-established one, and, in addition to Plato's *Symposium*, there survive Lucian's *Amores*, Plutarch's *Amatorius*[3] and a discussion on the topic in the Greek novel *Clitophon and Leucippe* by Achilles Tatius.

Plato

It is particularly difficult to determine the extent of Gide's first-hand knowledge of Plato. Towards the end of October 1891 he recorded in his 'Subjectif' that he had read an essay by Hippolyte Taine on 'Les jeunes gens de Platon'.[4] This is a somewhat sentimental, idealised eulogy of Socrates and his admiring intelligent circle of beautiful youths. But Taine has nothing to say about vice, corruption and homosexuality. In quoting from the speech by the Just Argument in Aristophanes' *Clouds* Taine deliberately recalls the Golden Age and leaves untouched the nature of 'Greek love'. His article is judiciously composed of a large series of extracts from several Platonic dialogues which, taken together, would have provided Gide with some sort of a picture of Plato's beliefs. Taine never explains in what precise way Alcibiades was 'debauched', unless it is that he was perverted by education. The Greeks, he says, achieved the physical perfection of the human race, and this was reflected in their sculpture as well as in the intellectual content of the dialogues he is discussing. 'Human nature was in equilibrium,' he writes; and again: 'The naked body is chaste. . . . what makes nudity shameful is an opposition between the life of the body and the life of the soul' (p. 250). These two ideas are repeated in Gide's *Le Traité du Narcisse* and lie at the heart of his aesthetic appreciation of Greek art.

The *Phaedo* is only mentioned once (in connection with a passage from Milton) in the *Journal* in February 1896.[5] However, one of the most interesting problems centres around Gide's knowledge of the *Gorgias*.[6] Here, it will be remembered, there is a debate between Callicles, the spokesman for self-indulgent pleasure, and Socrates, who argues that control over one's pleasures and passions is the true characteristic of a wise man. The argument moves on to consider whether pleasure is identical with goodness, and whether goodness is identifiable with usefulness. As he attacks politicians and their meretricious rhetoric, Socrates maintains that justice and temperance are the greatest qualities of the soul. These thoughts all have equivalents in Gide's moral system. But the source for Gide's remarks on politics, sophists and the distinction between the useful and the true is A. Fouillée's *La Philosophie de Socrate* (1874).[7]

Indeed, there are in Fouillée's book a surprising number of points of contact with what Gide has to say. For example, the first volume contains a series of chapters on 'La Morale de Socrate' in which we are encouraged to ask whether virtue can be taught (Book III chapter 3). This theme is handled in Gide's *Philoctète*. We are also to consider that wisdom consists in modesty ('la modestie et la pudeur') (*Charmides* 158: Book III chapter 4), for wisdom is to be found not merely in self-knowledge but in knowledge of the Good. Similarly, in Book III chapter 5, Socrates is said to teach that 'temperance is a knowledge of true good things, sufficiently clear to outweigh the attraction exercised by inferior things or pleasures [*voluptés*]'. This is not far removed from the puritanism of Corydon. Book VI chapter 3 is, however, where we must turn for most enlightenment. Love is defined by Socrates, according to Fouillée, as being the bond which unites different souls striving together towards a common goal (p. 203). It is also the first link which is established between the soul of the philosopher and wisdom. Friendship, writes Fouillée, was for Socrates the necessary condition and the instrument of every great and noble influence (p. 204). Thus Beauty and Goodness are synonymous.

However, Fouillée has a method of dealing with the role played by pederasty in ancient Greece which distances him from the idealistic view, in many other ways so similar to his, expressed by Corydon. 'Socrates,' he writes, 'master in love and wisdom, strove to initiate the young men of his time in the noble passions and the cult of true beauty' (p. 206). This meant that their 'impure loves', which were so widespread, had to be converted into a pure and generous affection. On several occasions Fouillée quotes from Xenophon's *Memorabilia*: ' "Socrates often said he was in love with someone; but it is obvious that he was not attached to the beauty of the body but to the openness to virtue manifested by the soul" (*Mem.* IV i)', and, 'on occasion he energetically condemned his contemporaries' wayward behaviour', referring to the example of Critias wanting to rub himself like a pig against Euthydemus (*Mem.* I i). Although Gide had clearly read it, this whole section of the argument has no counterpart in *Corydon*. ' "Wretched man," Socrates would also say to Xenophon, "do you know what would happen to you if you kissed a pretty boy? Do you know that you would cease to be free and become a slave?" ' Thus, Fouillée concludes, Socrates castigates the physical nature of these actions, and criticises them for preventing the soul from attaining its greatest good – namely liberty, the condition for progress towards wisdom. Writing rather regretfully, he admits that Socrates cannot be required to show a delicate sense of modesty foreign to ancient Greece, for he 'makes concessions to these vicious habits' (pp. 207–8). Again quoting Xenophon as witness, Fouillée recalls Socrates' power of self-denial (*Mem.* I iii 14; and the story of Alcibiades in Plato's *Symposium*).

Someone will claim that this vice was so common in Athens that no one was called a criminal on account of it. Doubtless it was common; but it is quite clear when we read Aristophanes' *Knights* and Aeschines' *Speech against Timarchus* that it was a legitimate reason for a man to be excluded from state office. Xenophon, in his *Symposium*, contrasts the customs of the Thebans, who tolerated these loves, with the customs at Athens where such behaviour was dishonourable.[8]

Fouillée's view is tendentious and superficial.[9] It will be interesting to see how in Corydon's discussion of Thebes, dependent not on Fouillée but on Plutarch and on a character study of Epaminondas, an idealised view emerges.

Fouillée also has some words on Socrates' attitude to women and to marriage, and this section is perhaps responsible for suggesting to Gide certain of his remarks concerning the role of the gynaeceum in Greece. Fouillée writes:

> An admiration and love of a husband for his wife which makes of him her *willing* servant. This is doubtless where Socrates' secret preferences lay. It is in the very heart of the family that he dreamed of establishing the sanctuary of love; but the habits of the Athenians made this dream a virtual utopia. ... The purpose of marriage in Athens was to hand down the priestly function from male to male. ... The essential virtues of women were fecundity and chastity. ... Hence love deserted the women's quarters for there was nothing there to tempt it. (p. 210)

In discussing the two sorts of love – the heavenly and the earthly Venus – Fouillée refers again to Xenophon: 'Socrates says in the *Memorabilia* (I vii 13) that "we call the man who prostitutes his beauty for money infamous; but whoever chooses as his friend the person we know to be in love with good and beautiful things, him we call wise."' There is a long quotation from the *Memorabilia* on the superiority of the love of the soul, where there is an important remark on the evanescence of love based uniquely on the physical beauty of the beloved youth. The points contained in a footnote to Gide's 'Au service de l'Allemagne' occur here: 'This union of souls has as its result every virtue, and consequently every joy. It is in this exalted sense that Socrates understands the usefulness [*utilité*] of friends (*Mem.* II vi)' (p. 214). And again, in words which strongly recall the argument of *Le Roi Candaule*: 'It is the privilege of the truly good to give happiness to some men without harming others or depriving them of their proper share (*Mem.* II vi). And friendship is like this, for in it everyone finds his reward [*intérêt*] without seeking for it. It is virtue shared by two, happiness shared by two ...' (p. 215).

Socrates is also shown describing impure love, the opposite of this ideal. Such an emotion is selfish and servile, always prey to desires and unhappy even when surrounded by apparent happiness (p. 216).

Before passing on to a summary of Plato's *Symposium*, Fouillée refers his reader to his companion work, *La Philosophie de Platon*. In this book, too, there is a chapter on love,[10] but Fouillée discusses the topic without mentioning homosexuality. Instead, he summarises ideas on love in nature, and love in the souls of men. Taking as his main ground the speeches of Diotima and Socrates in the *Symposium* he proceeds to a discussion of the principles of love and of its aim to achieve perfect eternal Beauty.[11]

In his book on Socrates, he writes that it is Xenophon's *Symposium* which shows us the moral aspect of love; Plato's shows the metaphysical side. His analysis of Plato's *Symposium* concentrates on the principle of Desire (*Eros*), generation and becoming (pp. 218–31). Here Gide could have read an explanation which has much in common with the pages from Schopenhauer on love, which he already knew.

However, a passing reference in a letter to Paul Valéry in August 1891[12] reveals that Gide already knew Plato's *Symposium* well. He was reading it in October 1894 in a copy given to him by his close friend Eugène Rouart, and praised it highly.[13] Many years later La Petite Dame recorded in early 1921[14] that the Hellenist Marie Delcourt had impressed Gide with her intelligence and modesty. He had also asked La Petite Dame to approach her on his behalf with a request to help him translate the *Symposium*. This project, however, came to nothing.

There seem to be three reasons why Gide was drawn to this dialogue. Firstly, he noticed the homosexual content of the work. Secondly, as he recorded among his manuscript notes: 'My work [*Corydon*] must be serious . . . but not entirely so. It is noteworthy that the only dialogue by Plato which is not serious is the *Symposium* where he does indeed achieve the summit of gravity in Diotima's discourse while nevertheless introducing Alcibiades and Aristophanes as the dialogue proceeds.'[15] Thirdly, Gide considered that, since the question of love was so 'complicated', he should take note of Plato's solution: 'As soon as he wished to speak of love the dialogue form was inadequate, and he used eight interlocutors to present the diversity of their points of view.'[16] We may remember (as Gide most certainly must have done) that this very point was made by Montaigne in his 'Apologie de Raymond de Sebonde' (*Essais*, II 12) 'because of the complexity of viewpoints'. It is of course also true, as Corydon is made to state, that 'as soon as Plutarch and Plato speak of love it is as much the homosexual as the heterosexual variety which concerns them'.[17] Corydon also refers to Aristophanes' speech in the *Symposium*,[18] and uses a citation drawn without acknowledgement from Carpenter's *Ioläus*: 'Plato calls a lover a divine friend.'[19] But such allusions do not take us to the heart of the matter.

There is, in fact, little in *Corydon* which depends directly on the *Symposium* or which can be shown to derive from it, although Corydon's assertion towards the end of Dialogue IV that he knows of nothing better for a youth than a lover[20] is strongly reminiscent of Phaedrus' opinion expressed in the *Symposium* (178 b): 'I know of no greater blessing for a young man than an honourable lover.' However, if we look briefly at Aristophanes' speech, we see that it is used in *Le Traité du Narcisse*. In the *Symposium* Aristophanes tells how when the world was new humans were shaped like globes, with twice the number of legs, arms and other appendages that we now have. But they offended Zeus, and he cut each globe in half. Consequently the separate 'halves' now seek to unite with each other: those who were originally masculine are divided into two males, the feminine into two females, and the androgynes into one of each sex. In this way homosexual and heterosexual love can be explained as the desire for completion, expressed in each imperfect being. In Gide's *Traité* this myth relates to the theory of unfulfilled desire which, as the poet realises, is the moving force of the universe. Without having an explicitly sexual meaning, the story is incorporated into an eclectic framework to explain the nature of being, and an important aspect of symbolist aesthetics. Later in the *Symposium*, with Socrates and Diotima the debate moves on to a more abstract plane, and the philosopher asks why we should wish to possess the beautiful. Love is like desire in that it is an awareness that the things for which we yearn are absent. Good is the name which we give to things which bring us happiness, and this is because we equate what is beautiful with what is good. This in turn mirrors our wish for survival and for the perpetuation of ourselves (or our world) through love. Our desire does not validate the goodness of what we wish for, but a similar impulsion will drive an older man to seek out a younger man with a beautiful soul. The model, however, is an ascetic one. Corydon's ideal of education will likewise tend towards this goal.

We should be aware of two other Platonic dialogues: the *Phaedrus* and the *Laws*. There are allusions to the first of these in *Le Roi Candaule*. This dialogue is important for our argument because the image of self-control is there deployed in the symbol of the two horses. The charioteer has to rein in the black horse of our baser desires, since in its headlong course it will drag the noble white beast, and ourselves, to destruction.[21] But our position on the scale between noble and animal passions depends on our inborn nature: therefore the degree of chastity which is to be exercised is predetermined within the character of each individual. Active indulgence of desire at the lowest level hampers our ascent towards the ideal and the greatest good.

In the *Laws* a somewhat similar but more puritanical view is expressed: 'In another case physical desire will count for very little and the lover will be content to gaze upon his beloved without lusting for him – a mature and genuine desire of soul for soul. That body should sate itself with body he will think outrageous; his reverence and respect for self-control, courage, high principles and good judgement will make him want to lead a life of purity, chaste lover with chaste beloved.'[22]

There is no doubt of the extent to which Plato's puritanism finds a willing echo in the mouth of Corydon. However, Gide is so often self-contradictory that we must not neglect a note from the *Journal*:[23] 'If Socrates and Plato had not loved boys [*les jeunes gens*] what a pity it would have been for Greece and the world. If Socrates and Plato had not loved boys and had not tried to please them, we would each be a little less judicious [*sensé*].' When, much later, Gide returned to Plato in his *Journal* on 11 June 1948 it was because he had recently read an article 'L'Art et la pensée de Platon' in the *Annales du Centre Universitaire Méditerranéen* by a churchman, Father Auguste Valensin. Although he was sufficiently bold to speak of Greek homosexuality, Valensin did not believe that Plato was an advocate of 'vice'. Gide pointed out in commenting on this that Plato's disapproval applied equally well to heterosexuals and homosexuals. For everyone alike the Heavenly Venus[24] was to be preferred. It seems, however, that Gide's own position had changed from what it had been earlier in his life. Now he took Valensin to task for praising an ideal of 'triumphant chastity' which, he said, was no part of the pagan ideal, 'not even (or perhaps only exceptionally) for Plato'. Valensin, he asserted, had failed to come to terms with a question for which Greek society had a ready (and healthy) answer. Gide was now unwilling to believe that contacts between adolescents, and between youths and older men, were chaste. If Plato sublimates 'all that', he asserted, he does so for decency's sake – or because the Greeks took it for granted. For Gide the superabundance of sperm must have a healthy outlet. 'I maintain,' he wrote, 'that the good order of the city is less compromised by contact between young males . . . than when the *libido* directs the desires of these adolescents towards members of the opposite sex.' Here is an older Corydon, less chaste perhaps, but still concerned to promote the moral equilibrium of society.

Lucian

Lucian's *Amores* was specifically drawn to Gide's attention by a German friend who noted down for him in pencil some details about Aeschylus' tragedy *The Myrmidons* from this source. However, the reference to this play in *Corydon* (p. 161) is in fact drawn from Carpenter's *Ioläus*, p. 73. There is no evidence in *Corydon* that Gide considered it useful to base any part of his argument on Lucian's dialogue, although some of the same points are debated. The *Amores* presents Lycinus, an equable person, who tells Theomnestus (a bisexual) of a discussion he once witnessed between Callicratidas, a homosexual Athenian, and Charicles, a womanising Corinthian. Charicles maintains that the argument from nature is persuasive: men ejaculate semen and women are constructed for its reception; among animals homosexual behaviour does not occur, whereas there are many examples of the males' natural inclination towards the female; to conclude, a woman opens up two paths to pleasure, a boy but one. Callicratidas replies that the love of males is the only activity combining both pleasure and virtue. Marriage, though necessary, he says, was only invented to ensure the perpetuity of the race. As for the argument from natural history, lions and bears do not practise homosexual love, because they are not philosophers (that is, lovers of wisdom): this is the essential distinction between brute animals and civilised mankind. There follows a misogynistic diatribe and a praise of the health and bodily virtue of boys. They are fresh and unpolluted. The argument turns from the aesthetic to the sentimental and moral: friends are devoted to each other, witness Orestes and Pylades. And then Callicratidas reaches his conclusion: one should love youths chastely as Alcibiades was loved by Socrates. His advice to young men is to be temperate 'when you approach virtuous boys. Do not for the sake of a brief pleasure squander lasting affection.'[25] The concluding judgement is given by Lycinus: 'Marriage is a boon and a blessing to men when it meets with good fortune, while the love of boys, that pays court to the hallowed dues of friendship, I consider to be the privilege only of philosophy. Therefore all men should marry, but let only the wise be permitted to love boys, for perfect virtue grows least of all among women' (§51).

We recognise several points in common with *Corydon*. But what we also see – and this goes counter to Gide's idealised picture of the role of women in Greece – is that this particular homosexual apologist seems to despise women as a necessary evil. For him they constitute a lower form of moral life.

Gide does not mention Lucian explicitly in any of his published works or correspondences. We only know that it was usual for Lucian to be prepared at the École Alsacienne which he attended in 1877 and 1887.[26] However, the boys would certainly have been shielded from anything judged in the slightest degree immoral. It is all the more intriguing to notice that Gide possessed a presentation copy of Louÿs' translation of Lucian, *Scènes de la vie des courtisanes* (1894), which he disposed of at the sale of part of his library in 1925. The *Dialogues of the Courtesans* contains a series of amusing conversations about the various problems encountered by some *hetaerae* in the course of their amorous adventures. The stories are almost exclusively heterosexual, but there is a passage which describes an example of lesbianism, including cross-dressing. The dialogue in question appears in Louÿs' translation as number 5: 'Les Lesbiennes'. Clonarion speaks to Leaina and asks her if there is any truth in the rumour that she is living with Megilla, who is in love with her, just like a man. 'Quite true,' she replies. 'But I'm ashamed, for it's unnatural.' In response to further questioning she tells how she was picked up at a drinking party arranged by Megilla and Demonassa, and how she was kissed and fondled. Megilla then removes a wig and claims to be Demonassa's husband – but she admits she does not have the requisite 'apparatus', although she has 'a pleasanter method' of her own. Had she changed sex, like the Theban seer Tiresias, she is asked. No: 'I was born a woman like the rest of you, but I have the mind and desires and everything else of a man.' 'You'll find I'm as good as any man,' she adds, 'I have a substitute of my own.' Leaina concludes that she responded to this invitation, but, she warns, 'Don't enquire too closely into the details; they're not very nice.'[27]

Here there are several points to note. Firstly, the story is scabrous, and it seems unlikely that the characters are meant to have a sense of shame. Secondly, although Gide does mention lesbianism in *Corydon*, he only does so in passing. He may well have felt distaste at this sort of anecdote. There is only one reference to pederasty in the *Dialogues of the Courtesans*, and this is passed over by Gide. In Dialogue 10 a youth who is loved by a courtesan is reported to be supervised very closely by his tutor Aristaenetus. 'He's reading with him amorous discourses addressed by the old philosophers to their pupils, and is all wrapped up in the lad,' the girl relates. But the boy cannot wait to make his escape. Finally, in Lucian's *Dialogues of the Gods*, there is an amusing exchange between Zeus and Ganymede – but Gide seems not to have noticed.

Plutarch: Amatorius

Gide could certainly have read Plutarch's *Amatorius* in Amyot's translation or, just as easily, in the collection *Le Livre d'amour des anciens* (pp. 195–240). Amyot, in a preface added to the Dialogue, thought this the most dangerous part of Plutarch's writings for young men to read, since many things are said against marriage and support is given to that 'execrable nastiness [*vilenie*]', the love of youths.

Autobulus tells how his father Plutarch had once witnessed a debate on love. His narrative is punctuated by a romantic upheaval in the nearby town where a rich young widow is trying to seduce and marry a handsome youth. The presentation of the dialogue is therefore dramatic, and can be divided, roughly speaking, into three parts. The debate is first between the adherents and opponents of pederasty; secondly the widow abducts the youth; thirdly, when only the serious participants are left, the talk turns to the praise of Eros, the god of love, and to a discussion of his power and the benefits he confers. A section attacking conjugal love has been lost, and this part ends with a description of the role of married women. The dialogue concludes with the celebration of the young widow's marriage to the youth.

Protogenes is the spokesman for homosexual love. Genuine love, he maintains, has no connection with the women's apartments; it attaches itself not to the body but to a young and talented soul. The object of desire is pleasure and enjoyment, whereas the object of love is friendship and virtue.

> There is only one genuine love, the love of boys. It is not 'flashing with desire' as Anacreon says of the love of maidens, or 'drenched with unguents, shining bright'. Its aspect is simple and unspoiled. You will see it in the schools of philosophy, or perhaps in the gymnasia and palaestrae, searching for young men whom it cheers on with a clear and noble cry to the pursuit of virtue when they are found worthy of its attention.[28]

Finally, 'It is not gentlemanly or urbane to make love to slave boys: such a love is mere copulation, like the love of women' (751 b). We notice the same emphasis on virtue as before, again coupled with contempt for women.

Daphnaeus responds, taking up the argument in favour of marriage and the love of women. It is interesting to see him refer to the example of Solon, the Athenian lawgiver, whose life appears to foreshadow the ideal set out by Corydon. This should not surprise us, for it was typical of a generally held Greek view of society: 'After the pelting storm of his love for boys [he] had brought his life into the peaceful sea of marriage and philosophy' (751 e). Other apothegms correspond less well with Gide's position: 'Boy love denies pleasure; that is because it is ashamed and afraid. It needs a fair pretext for approaching the young and beautiful, so it pretends friendship and virtue' (752 a). Among other interjections at this point Plutarch comments ironically: 'So marriage is to be a loveless union, devoid of God-given friendship' (752 c).

The dialogue then proceeds to a general discussion of the power of love, citing the superior examples of friends in battle. Although this is again an especially Greek *topos*, one may notice this argument deployed by Corydon. 'It is not only the most warlike peoples, Boeotians,

Spartans and Cretans, who are the most susceptible to love, but also the great heroes of old' (761 d). Witness Achilles, Epaminondas,[29] and also Hercules, who loved Iolaus and Admetus (it was love for Admetus which spurred him on to rescue Alcestis from Death). Women, we are told, have no part in Ares (war), despite the often asserted link between love and battle. A distinction is drawn here between Aphrodite (sensual love, of women) and Eros (an ethereal power of Love) (761 e). Among the benefits of Eros is his ability to make a man 'clever, single-hearted, generous and high-minded' (762 b). In a concluding passage which reminds us of certain Platonic ideas, Plutarch says: 'Love draws us to the beauty of that Other World, that divine and blessed entity which is the real object of love. Yet most men, since they pursue in boys and women merely the mirrored image of Beauty, can attain by their groping nothing more solid than a pleasure mixed with pain' (765 f). Yet here also is a call to abnegation: 'But the noble and self-controlled lover has a different bent. His regard is refracted to the other world, to Beauty divine and intelligible' (766 a), ending with a remark which might seem to the modern reader a statement of the poise achieved, theoretically, by the bisexual: 'The lover of human beauty will be fairly and equally disposed towards both sexes. . . . Beauty is the "flower of virtue"; yet it would be absurd to deny that the female produces that flower' (767 a,b).

There is no obvious reason why Gide should have ignored this dialogue completely. The character of Daphnaeus seems on several occasions to fill the role allotted by Gide to Corydon's interlocutor. Perhaps the major reason for its having been put to one side is to be sought in the nature of Gide's puritanism.

Achilles Tatius

After *Corydon* had been composed, Dorothy Bussy wrote to Gide on 22 December 1924 and told him that she had just discovered the Greek novel *The Loves of Clitophon and Leucippe* by Achilles Tatius.[30] She was very enthusiastic and asked whether he had heard of the work before. He replied a few days later that he did indeed know the name, but that he had not read the novel itself. The story is a picaresque and sentimental account of two heterosexual lovers who are for most of the time separated from each other. At one point (Book II 35–8) the hero discusses with two homosexuals, Menelaus and Clinias, the relative merits of hetero- and homosexual forms of love. Clinias is distraught because he has just inadvertently killed his beloved Charicles. ' "You know not, Clitophon," said Menelaus, "the sum of all pleasure: the unsatisfied is the most desirable of all.'[31] There is no need to emphasise how well this corresponds with Gide's often expressed idea. 'I hold that there are two kinds of beauty conversant among men, the one heavenly, the other vulgar. . . . No woman ever went up to heaven,' (36) says Menelaus, but, he continues, Ganymede most certainly did. Clitophon's reply praises the beauty of women: 'Woman's beauty seems the more heavenly of the two because it does not rapidly fade' (37). The discussion then continues on the subject of the relative pleasure of kissing women and boys:

> The beauty of a boy is not fostered by the odour of perfumes . . . the fresh natural odour of a boy has a sweeter smell than all the anointings and perfumery of a woman. And you can, before the consummation of your love, wrestle in close embrace with him and openly enfold him in your arms. And his embraces have no shame. There is no soft tenderness of flesh in the close pressure of love, but your bodies press hard together and wrestle in very bliss. His kisses have not the cunning artifices which a woman's kisses have; nor do they trick you with an idle deceit, but he loves as he knows best, and there is no art; his kisses are the kisses of nature. And this is the likeness of a boy's kiss – even as nectar set firm upon your lips. And in kisses you can never have satiety, but, the deeper draughts you drink, the more you thirst for love.[32]

Corydon, quite simply, seems unwilling to admit openly to this degree of sensuality in his love making.

Corydon invokes the ancients for three reasons. First by citing Plutarch he argues a moral case. Secondly he presents what might be termed a romantic picture by referring to ideals of sentimental friendship and the naive Arcadia of Theocritus, Vergil and other poets. A third category of examples could be labelled 'licentious', and consists of anecdotal details from a variety of sources.

Plutarch: Lives

Corydon remarks that Plutarch spoke as readily of homosexual love as he did of heterosexual attraction (p. 161). This, as we have seen, is certainly true of the *Amatorius*. The observation is also true, albeit in a slightly different sense, in respect of Plutarch's *Lives*, where, however, there is no debate on the relative merits of the two forms of love. Plutarch's aim in writing is seemingly to present the lives of great men as models of virtue for his readers. In any case, the impression which Corydon tries to give us is perhaps misleading, for Plutarch does not concentrate on his heroes' sexuality, nor does he appear to have a coherent view about the desirability (or otherwise) of their individual sexual behaviour. What he does highlight are certain aspects of the social customs of the Greek city states of Thebes and Sparta.

It is on these states that Corydon also focuses. Gide took as an exemplar the character of the Theban commander Epaminondas. From this point he turned to the Sacred Band of Thebes, to Sparta and, therefore, to the valour and virtue of martial states (p. 166). The extracts from Plutarch printed in the text of *Corydon*, together with the citations remaining in the unpublished files, are taken mostly from the *Lives* of Pelopidas, Lycurgus, Demetrius and, especially, Agesilaus.

On pages 166–70 Corydon quotes at length from the *Life of Pelopidas* xix, xvii and xviii, which deals at this point with the Spartans and the Sacred Band of the Thebans.[33] These are warrior societies, states Plutarch, and the Thebans have shown that brave, honourable men are not born solely in Sparta. The Sacred Band is formed of men in love with each other, so that each will shun the disgrace of appearing unworthy of his lover. Corydon repeats Plutarch's observation attributed to Pammenes[34] to the effect that while one member of the pair would fight for love of his friend the other would fight fearing lest not to do so would bring dishonour. Plutarch does not report the relative ages of the lovers in each couple, and we do not know whether they are of equal age. Are they like knight and squire who entertain a chivalrous love for each other, the squire being the significantly younger member of the pair? Both Edward Carpenter and John Addington Symonds discussed this question. If Plutarch's remarks suggest anything to the modern reader it is most probably that both young men were in the flower of their manhood. Perhaps this impression is reinforced by memories of the statues of the Athenian tyrant-slayers Harmodius and Aristogiton.[35] The question of relative ages, however, is not one to which Corydon addresses himself here, preferring to concentrate instead on establishing the moral virtue of these comradely associations.

At this point in *Corydon* there is a long quotation from Plutarch's *Life of Agesilaus* (xi, 7). The extract concerns moral rectitude. This time Corydon reports a relationship between an older person – Agesilaus, one of the Spartan kings – and the young Megabates, who would probably have been in his early adolescence. Agesilaus is strongly tempted to yield to his love, but he holds back his kisses even though as a result he is consumed with an intense fire when the boy goes away. Here the absence of martial concerns makes the point of Gide's example clear. In this, as in the previous case, our attention has in fact been directed to the element of self-sacrifice in the relationship. Agesilaus has an additional reason for acting as he does, for he wishes to remain faithful to his ambition never to be conquered. However, the anecdote about Agesilaus tells us that he was unwilling to yield to sexual impulse, which at the time he felt debased him. The Theban story tells us no such thing about what happened at night among the army tents. Corydon's repeated quotation, once in Pierron's translation and once in Amyot's,[36] from the *Life of Lycurgus*, the Spartan lawgiver, does not clarify this point, but moves on to highlight another important function of male relationships. The education that an older person may profitably bestow on a younger lover is above all an education in virtue. Perhaps Rousseau, who so admired Plutarch's heroes, would have been better served in this way than he was by Mme de Warens, Corydon slyly suggests (p. 182).

After these lengthy quotations from Plutarch, Corydon offers 'many more' which would 'fill an entire volume' were he to recite them in full to his interlocutor. Several in fact survive among the manuscript notes. It is obvious, however, that Gide was principally interested in collecting information concerning Epaminondas. We have already noticed that he copied out an extract from Montesquieu in 1904 which mentioned this Theban general.[37] In *Corydon* itself (p. 159) he summarises material from Walckenaer's article on Epaminondas from the *Biographie universelle*, Volume XII: 'Cicero relates that Epaminondas was the greatest man produced by Greece and he was the perfect model of a great captain, patriot and wise man. Plutarch's *Life* is lost, but we can obtain information from the *Lives* of Agesilaus and Pelopidas.' In a footnote, not retained in *Corydon*, Walckenaer judges that 'unfortunately' it seems from Plutarch's treatise on love that Epaminondas was 'addicted to that infamous inclination to which the Greeks, and especially the Boeotians, attached no shame'. Further on in the article we read: 'Epaminondas had observed the advantage derived by the Lacedaemonians over the other Greeks for which their sobriety and temperance accounted. He sought by his own example to inspire in his fellow citizens the same notion of austerity.' The manuscript notes contain the substance of this article and are quite extensive.[38] Further research on Epaminondas led Gide to record a note in Brunschvicg's edition of Pascal: 'Note the admirable praise of Epaminondas by Montaigne.'[39]

Several extracts from the *Life of Agesilaus* were made by Gide to accompany those we have already seen from the *Life of Pelopidas*. Hence we read[40] that Agesilaus, knowing that his fellow king Agesipolis was as fond of boys as he was himself, often brought the conversation round to this while they were at table. Plutarch says that Agesilaus helped Agesipolis get what he wanted, but Gide only copied out: 'In these Spartan love affairs there is nothing shameful, but on the contrary there is only modesty, honesty and zeal for virtue.' Gide was looking for examples of temperance and chastity, and found them here,[41] together with descriptions of Agesilaus' simplicity and moderation. From the same source,[42] he copied down the details of the love affairs of Archidamus, son of Agesilaus, and Cleonymus: 'Agesilaus knew his son's inclination and did not attempt to dissuade him, for Cleonymus from his childhood showed every sign that he would become a good [honnête] man.' This very Archidamus, Gide noted, would later be described as 'valiant above all men, brave, courageous and quick in support of his men against the enemy'.[43] 'Immediately after this passage,' the manuscript continues,[44]

> we have the following, which clearly shows the Spartan conception of uranism as a school of virtue: 'Isados, son of Phoebidas, was singularly admired, not only by his fellow citizens, but even by his enemies. He was a very handsome youth, tall, and at the age when boys pass from puberty to maturity retained all the gracefulness of youth. Completely naked, without defensive weapons or garments, with his body well rubbed with oil, holding a javelin in one hand and a sword in the other he ran from his house. . . .'

The sequel, which Gide had read and intended to copy, recounts how this brave warrior was rewarded for fighting well, but, such being the City's respect for obedience to the laws, was fined for hazarding himself without protective armour. The whole of the extract was in fact included in the 1920 proofs, but was then deleted.[45]

There are two independent citations of a particular text from the Life of Lysander in the archive,[46] where Gide recorded that Lysander had formerly been the lover of Agesilaus. Lysander, however, he noted, is credited by Plutarch with daughters – and therefore his uranism did not preclude marriage. We may see the same notion emerge at the end of Dialogue IV in Corydon. It would be interesting, Gide adds, to establish the relative ages of Agesilaus and Lysander. He clearly realised that one was significantly older than the other as the quotation[47] from the Life of Agesilaus shows: 'When Agesilaus was among the groups of children brought up together, he was beloved by Lysander who was especially attracted by the beauty of his natural qualities.' But Agesilaus was lame. For the ancient writer this would have signified that his lover was not attracted by the superficial beauty of his body; for Gide the lameness could be taken as a symbol of an individual anomaly and could doubtless fit neatly into his theory of 'le héros malade'.

Moving to an associated question, another extract from the Life of Lysander[48] calls our attention to the Spartan cult of male beauty. The Spartans wore their hair long: 'Lycurgus stated that long hair increases the possessor's beauty.' Gide omitted the following part of the sentence: 'and makes ugliness even more terrifying.' 'Lysander,' Gide noted, 'is shown with long hair; and this is not at all an indication of effeminacy

for Plutarch continues "His manly courage, proof against all temptations
[voluptés], knew no pleasure other than that which procures public
esteem and which is the recompense for fine actions. This is a luxury
[volupté] which the youths of Sparta may indulge without shame."'
Gide copied the first few words of this final sentence, but feeling
perhaps that he had noted sufficient, and that his argument would not
be well served by a hint that shame might attach elsewhere, he deleted
what he had written.

The link between virtue, courage and beauty was one for which he
had also cited the Life of Pelopidas xix 1–2 in the proof copy of the
1920 edition of Corydon, but deleting the text before publication.[49] He
quoted Plutarch's remarks that pederasty in Thebes was due not to Laius'
passion for Chrysippus 'as the poets would have us believe', but to the
lawgivers who wished to calm the naturally violent behaviour of
the Thebans; furthermore, he says (quoting Plutarch), this is why
Harmonia, daughter of Ares and Aphrodite, was their divine pro-
tectress, for the spirit of a warlike people, softened by grace and
persuasion, creates the best of governments. Passages designed to illustrate the range of homosexual behaviour, from the bestial and cynical
conduct of the tyrant Alexander of Pherai,[50] 'who forced the youngest
brothers of Thebe to serve his vile lust', to the most noble and graceful actions of lovers and youths,[51] were also deleted from the 1920
proofs.[52]

The Life of Demetrius ('Poliorcetes') afforded Gide two anecdotes
concerning virtue in relation to homosexuality. But, as we can easily
see, both could be interpreted in a hostile sense.[53] The first tells how
Demetrius gave himself up entirely to his vices and pleasures. He was,
however, temperate in war. One day his father Antigonus, learning
that he was ill, paid him a visit. As Antigonus went in, a handsome
youth came out. Antigonus felt his son's pulse, and Demetrius replied
that the fever had now left him. '"Yes I know," replied Antigonus, "I
met it on the way out." Thus it was that the father gently condoned his
son's vices from a concern for the help which he hoped he would
give.'

The second relates how Democles, a young boy who was not yet
adolescent, was pursued by Demetrius. Plutarch does not propose to
reveal all Demetrius' turpitudes, but says he must tell us this story to
illustrate the boy's wisdom and virtue. Democles was forced to stop
frequenting the gymnasium. He had to bathe in an out-of-the-way
steam room. Eventually Demetrius, having spied upon the boy, followed
him into the steam bath, whereupon Democles had no other recourse
than to jump into the boiling vat of water.

Neither of these anecdotes is particularly attractive, and neither
shows the tyrant in a good light. The question is whether Gide chose

them merely as anecdotes – which seems unlikely – or whether he perceived in them an acceptable form of virtue. If the latter is the case, then only one character in each tale can reasonably be called honourable – Demetrius (in war) and Democles (in love). It is just possible to imagine that they might have been destined for the use of the hostile interlocutor in *Corydon*.

One remaining example of a noble death is quoted by Gide from the *Life of Agis and Cleomenes*:[54] faced by insurmountable odds, Panteus, a Spartan warrior and former lover of Cleomenes, committed suicide instead of surrendering when all the other members of his band of soldiers were dead.

It is of some interest to note a passage on Aspasia, the mistress of the Athenian statesman Pericles, which was deleted from the 1920 proofs at the point where Corydon had been speaking of modern adultery and the purity of women among the ancient Greeks.[55] The material for this part of the text derives ultimately from Plutarch's *Life of Pericles*,[56] but Gide transcribed his remarks directly from the article on Aspasia in the *Biographie universelle*. There is no evidence that he ever read the *Life of Pericles* itself. The point in question is the moral standing of Aspasia. In answer to the interlocutor's remark that she was a courtesan, and therefore a disreputable character, Corydon was to have explained (as the article had explained, and Plutarch beforehand) that Aspasia was born in Miletus in Asia Minor and, as a foreign woman, could not marry an Athenian citizen. Since her children were in consequence classed as illegitimate, the author of the article surmises that this was why she was thought of as a courtesan. Corydon concludes that she ran an intellectual *salon*, and not an establishment where love was sold. The rest of the article (not quoted by Gide) places emphasis on the 'glory of Aspasia's life [which] consisted of the sincere and lasting feelings she inspired in Pericles [this is mentioned by Plutarch]. . . . Plutarch relates that Pericles felt the most perfect conjugal tenderness towards her: could such feelings be inspired by a depraved woman?' (The question is not Plutarch's.) There are several other details in the article which are of less concern to us. However, it is worth remarking that Plutarch included further information about her numerous lovers, that she was thought to have influenced the most powerful among them to sympathise with the Persian cause (an activity which was widely considered to be disreputable), that she did run a house of prostitution, and that she was accused by playwrights of being a prostitute herself and of procuring free-born women for Pericles. Later she was prosecuted for impiety and escaped condemnation thanks to the eloquence of Pericles. It is evident that Corydon's words form a partial and idealised portrait of Aspasia extracted from what was a tendentious account of the ancient testimony.

Plutarch: Other Works

Before leaving Plutarch, we have to notice two extracts in the archive taken from the *Moralia*. The first (probably in Gide's handwriting) is a citation, in Latin, from the Oxford edition by Wyttenbach of 1797 and relates the death of Adonis. Some say, reports Plutarch, that Bacchus was the lover of Adonis, and he quotes two lines from Phanocles' erotic poem on homosexual loves: 'Bacchus, wandering over the mountains, caught sight of divine Adonis and, while traversing beautiful Cyprus, snatched him away.'[57] The second extract concerns the story of the sin committed by Laius when he fell in love with Chrysippus and carried him off:[58] 'Pelops, son of Tantalus and Euryanassa, having married Hippodamia, begat Atreus and Thyestes; and from the Nymph Danais he begat Chrysippus whom he loved above all his legitimate children. But Theban Laius fell in love with Chrysippus and ravished him, and when caught by Thyestes and Atreus he obtained Pelops' pardon because he had acted under the power of love.' The translation Gide used this time was Amyot's. What probably caught his attention was the final phrase – or was it the unexpected anecdote about Laius, the father of Oedipus? In fact not all ancient versions of the story record that Laius was pardoned – and few modern readers realise that the tragic fate of Oedipus had its origins in a case of homosexual rape. There is a problem connected with the date at which this extract was copied, but we can probably assume that it was during the composition of *Corydon*. Gide wrote his *Œdipe* between 1927 and 1931. In 1933 Roger Martin du Gard appended a postscript to a letter to Gide, presumably in response to a request for information.[59] His note reads:

M.H.F. Meier, *Histoire de l'amour grec*:

p. 25. The epic poet Pisander (635 BC) wrote a *Heraclea* in which he presented Laius as the inventor and first example of this sort of love. Chrysippus, contaminated by Laius, killed himself with his own sword. And because the Thebans did not punish Laius' criminal passion, Hera sent the Sphinx to chastise them for their blameworthy forgiveness.

p. 29. Aeschylus wrote a *Laius* whose subject was Laius' impure love for Chrysippus, son of Pelops.

p. 30. Finally Euripides in his tragedy *Chrysippus* described, or mentioned, the rape of Pelops' son by Laius and the attachment which united them beyond the grave; and he represented this as the first example of pederasty in Greece. Plato shared this opinion.[60]

In interpreting the moral opprobrium evident here, it seems valid to enquire whether Laius' 'sin' consisted simply of making homosexual advances to a boy, or whether his actions in ignoring (or failing to obtain) the father's permission went beyond the bounds of good behaviour expected of a guest. However that may be, we will notice a further allusion to this incident below.

An ink note appended to ms. Doucet γ 885.5 (Laius' story) reads: 'Tantalus made himself odious to Jupiter by the rape of Ganymede. To check.' We do not know the immediate source of Gide's information, nor whether he was able subsequently to verify it. The story is recondite, and certainly does not constitute one of the reasons commonly alleged for Tantalus' punishment in the Underworld. It is to be found in Tzetzes' commentary on Lycophron's *Alexandra* (line 355) which mentions Tantalus' love for Ganymede and how he engaged with Ilus in a contest for possession of the charming youth. Neither this story, nor any of the ones extracted from the *Moralia*, has the moral force of the material which Gide drew from Plutarch's *Lives*.

Romantic Love

Let us now turn to Corydon's portrayal of the 'sentimental' and 'romantic' aspects of Greek love. In the second edition of Carpenter's *Ioläus* (1906), Gide found some particularly interesting material. He did not, however, go further and include in his arguments any general socialist attitudes which would directly have reflected the political views of the English writer and his ideal of a humanitarian comradely love of man for man. In fact the 1920 proofs of *Corydon* contain a deleted footnote which clearly demonstrates Gide's indebtedness to Carpenter in one particular respect: 'It would be appropriate to reproduce here the very important passage [*sic*] cited in Carpenter's *Ioläus* (2nd edition) pp. 67–74.'[61] The material in question comes from the beginning of the section in *Ioläus* entitled 'Poetry of Friendship among Greeks and Romans', and is mainly about the friendship of Achilles and Patroclus as described in *Iliad* XXIII (together with some comments by J.A. Symonds, and some remarks from Plato's *Symposium* and Athenaeus XIII on the same heroes). It was taken up and cited in part in the text of *Corydon* (pp. 160–1).

Carpenter states in his preface: 'The degree to which Friendship, in the early history of the world, has been recognised as an institution, and the dignity ascribed to it, are things hardly realised today. . . . I have been much struck by . . . the way in which they point to a solid and enduring body of human sentiment on the subject.' In *Corydon* Dialogue IV (p. 160) Gide repeats a quotation from Symonds, cited in Carpenter, telling how the whole subject of the Iliad is the passion of

Achilles for Patroclus:[62] 'the love of Achilles, passing the love of women, for Patroclus, which induced him to forego his anger and to fight at last.' Gide also took Symonds' statement on Plato from Carpenter and the material was incorporated into the text of *Corydon*:[63]

> Plato, discussing the *Myrmidons* of Aeschylus, remarks in the *Symposium* that the tragic poet was wrong to make Achilles the lover of Patroclus, seeing that Patroclus was the elder of the two, and that Achilles was the youngest and most beautiful of all the Greeks. The fact however is that Homer raises no question in our minds about the relation of lover and beloved. Achilles and Patroclus are comrades. Their friendship is equal.[64] It was only the reflective activity of the Greek mind, working upon the Homeric legend by the light of subsequent custom, which introduced these distinctions.

Corydon's point is that there can be no doubt about the nature of their affection (but some critics have of course demurred). Shortly afterwards, a note in *Corydon* refers us to a list of lovers, whose happiness derives from the fact that their love is reciprocal: Theseus and Pirithous, Orestes and Pylades, Achilles and Patroclus. The material is taken from *Ioläus*, and Gide's quotation of Bion is adapted from Leconte de Lisle's translation of 1869. Carpenter had also attracted Gide's attention when speaking about the similarities between Greek friendship and mediaeval chivalry. Here, printed in the 1920 text of *Corydon*,[65] we read a note: 'Look up Plutarch III 77 and aspecially J.A. Symonds Volume I page 97.' The second reference was obtained from *Ioläus* (pp. 15–16) where there is a long quotation from Symonds' *Studies of the Greek Poets* Volume I p. 97. Symonds talks about fraternity of arms among the ancient Greeks, and names Hercules and Hylas, Theseus and Pirithous: 'The chivalry of Hellas found its motive force in friendship rather than in the love of women.' It does not, however, seem that Gide knew Symonds' *A Problem in Greek Ethics*, where much of this material is more amply developed.[66] Carpenter (p. 23) quotes the story recorded in Plutarch's *Life of Pelopidas* xviii about the vows of loyalty and devotion which lovers swore on the tomb of Iolaus. However, Gide appears to have taken what Corydon says of this (p. 169) directly from Plutarch. Again, the report that Plato calls a lover a divine friend is found in both Carpenter and Plutarch. These romantic feelings were not limited to the pagans. As we have seen,[67] Corydon also cites from *Ioläus* the example of St Augustine's sentimental feelings, and, from the same source, refers to several anecdotes concerning this type of friendship in Eastern countries.

Asceticism: Lucretius

Four quotations which Gide took from Lucretius' *De rerum natura* when he was composing *Les Cahiers d'André Walter* illustrate the anguish which may arise from enforced asceticism, more particularly in the case – which was Gide's – of suppressed homosexual desires. But it is still something of a paradox for a young Protestant to seek enlightenment in the words of an Epicurean poet, one of whose aims was 'to free the reader from the bonds of religion' (IV 7). Another reference which Gide made to Epicurus at this time helps us to understand: ' "[Epicurus'] pleasure [*volupté*] was not sordid; he lived so soberly that the Church Fathers sometimes quote his example to shame the Christians." La Mothe le Vayer (*Vertu des paiens: II Épicure*).'[68] It is reasonable to assume, however, that a helpful friend suggested that he should read what the Latin poet had to say on love. Book IV 1030–6 describes nocturnal emissions, and continues thereafter (1037–1287) to deal with the subject of sexual behaviour more generally, presenting in turn the physical origin and character of heterosexual love, a criticism of the way in which it undermines the true pleasure of the mind, a description of its insatiable nature (for lovers can never fuse their bodies into one entity), a comment on its evil consequences and delusions, and an account of the physiological details of conception, sterility and the effects of habit. Lucretius is at times scathing about women, but he does not deny the naturalness of sexual pleasure, and thinks that physical desire should certainly be satisfied. He does, however, warn against its delusions. There is one reference in this section of the poem to homosexual attraction, but it is rather casual: 'he who receives a wound from Venus' arrows, be it a boy with girl-like limbs who strikes his heart, or a woman [and so on]' (1052–3).

The first two of Gide's quotations appear in the description of the narrator's need for caresses, when even the sight of statues exacerbates his thirst.[69] The series of Latin verses makes the sense more clear:

> quoniam nihil inde abradere possunt,
> Nec penetrare et abire in corpus corpore toto.

IV 1110–11

('[Even when finally the lovers embrace, and they eagerly kiss, all is in vain] for they can tear nothing away, nor enter and dissolve entirely into the other body with their own.') A few lines further down the same page of Gide we read: 'Nec satiare queunt spectando corpora coram' (IV 1102: '[Like a thirsty man who dreams, so, in love, Venus mocks the lovers with vain images] nor can they satisfy their bodies by gazing openly on the beloved'). This second citation is clearly intended to reinforce the image of thirst which appears in the text.

The third quotation[70] takes up another Lucretian theme, but cleverly reverses the sense. Lucretius' text reads:

> quoniam medio de fonte leporum
> Surgit amari aliquid quod in ipsis floribus angat.
>
> IV 1133–4

('Since from the heart of this fountain of pleasures arises a bitterness which causes them pain among the very flowers.') In *André Walter*, only the words 'surgit dulce aliquid' appear, and the French text echoes the new variation: 'Keen-edged enjoyment [*l'âpre jouissance*] in the midst of suffering'. Here, it should be noticed, the phrase still scans, but the fuller version transcribed in the manuscripts does not: 'And we have passed. "Surgit dulce aliquid de medio fonte dolorum" ['Something sweet arises from the heart of this fountain of sorrows'].' All that is needed is to write 'medio de fonte' and the fault is repaired: Gide appears to have been helped by someone who knew Latin better than he did.

The fourth quotation occurs in the unpublished *Journal* on 11 July 1887.[71] It is a fuller version of our second quotation:

> Nec satiare queunt spectando corpora coram
> Nec manibus quidquam teneris abradere membris
> Possunt – errantes incerti corpore toto.
>
> IV 1102–4

('Nor can they satisfy their bodies by gazing openly on the beloved, nor can they tear anything away from the delicate limbs as their aimless hands move over the whole body.') This is the same idea as the one in IV 1110–11, expressed in slightly different words.

But perhaps the full significance of this last quotation can be judged from an unpublished *Journal* entry dated 20 July 1888 where the three lines occur again, but now accompanied by part of a line from Vergil: 'Huc ades, O formose puer' (*Eclogue* II 45: 'Come hither, O handsome boy') and with the comment: 'But my sickness [*mal*] is so dark that I cannot speak of it.'[72] The homosexual connotation of these words is obvious, and so, too, is the link Gide forged with Lucretius' text. A little over four weeks later (21 August 1888)[73] he wrote beseechingly: 'A friend, a friend; my heart needs to spread the affection which weighs it down.'

Some Mythological Characters

In *Divers* there is a footnote referring to the epic poet Nonnus. Gide is criticising the symbolic interpretation of myths, epitomised by the early nineteenth-century German scholar F. Creuzer, whose *Symbolik und Mythologie der alten Völker* was very influential. The material Gide uses is taken from a bilingual Greek–French edition of Nonnus' *Dionysiaca*, edited by Le Comte de Marcellus, who also provided an extensive commentary on the poem. In the particular note which Gide cites, the editor accuses Creuzer of identifying Ampelus with Phaethon.[74] We can be fairly sure that Gide was not the sort of person to read Nonnus from start to finish. The poem is a long and intricate account of the fortunes of Bacchus, written in an obscure and, to some minds, tedious style in the fifth century AD. What drew Gide's attention to the translation, and to this section in particular, was less likely to be mythographical interest than the character Ampelus. Nonnus, in detailing the triumphal progress of Bacchus, dwells in particular on the love he had for Ampelus. There are numerous passages of homosexual interest, but among the more evident is one in Book X where Marcellus in his notes refers unsympathetically to this 'abominable passion', and another in Book IX (v. 300 ff.), from which Gide has drawn his quotation. The entry under the name Ampelus in the *Biographie universelle*, which we know Gide often consulted,[75] would be sufficient by itself to explain his interest: 'A young satyr . . . ravishing descriptions of their games and amusements in Nonnus. . . . Soon the delicate adolescent dies. Bacchus waters the lifeless corpse of his young friend with his tears. . . . "Ampelus", a feminine noun with a masculine ending . . . seems expressly made to be the name of a young man who serves the God his master as a woman.'

In the mythological compendium of the *Biographie universelle* there are entries for 'Ganymède', 'Chrysippe' and 'Orphée'. The first recalls how Zeus fell in love with the boy and caused him to be transported to Olympus. The writer adds that of all the less edifying stories of the gods the Romans remembered this one in particular: 'In general the cup-bearers [*échansons*] in great houses were handsome long-haired adolescents whose services as the master's favourites rounded off their grand official function.' The story of Chrysippus is briefly told and, although his beauty is mentioned, there is no reason given to explain why Laius abducted him. The third youth, Orpheus, in whose story Gide was interested from an early date,[76] is famous for his love for Eurydice. The article concludes with an account of his death at the hands of a band of frenzied women, adding 'for we will not mention [although we do!] Ovid's infamous account in which Orpheus is sur-rounded by many a Ganymede and Alcibiades.'[77]

Typical of these mythological allusions is another manuscript note referring to the myth of 'Cypressus' (that is, Cyparissus).[78] Gide remarks that it is treated in Ovid, *Metamorphoses* X 121 (actually X 106–42. The subsequent story is that of Ganymede), and then observes that it is likewise to be found in Vergil's *Georgics* I 20. He also states that the material occurs in Marlowe's *Hero and Leander* and Spenser's *Faerie Queene*.[79] According to Ovid, Cyparissus, a youth of Cea, was beloved by Apollo (or by Sylvanus, according to Vergil). When the boy had inadvertently killed his own favourite stag he was seized with im-moderate grief and metamorphosed into a cypress. There are some other stories to which Gide alludes. There are references in the manuscripts to the well-known love of the Emperor Hadrian for Antinous[80] and to Bathyllus (the beloved of the poet Anacreon).[81] These are familiar tales, and it is not reasonable to trace them to particular texts. Nisus and Euryalus are also mentioned,[82] and it will be remembered that their story is told by Vergil in *Aeneid* IX 176 ff.: Nisus avenged his beloved's death and then, throwing himself upon Euryalus' dead body, expired. Even quite unexpected sources yielded information about the loves of beautiful youths. Thus a cutting from the theatre journal *Comoedia* features in the archive.[83] It is an article by Polti, from his regular column 'Le Museum des personnages'. In it a contrast is being drawn between the sickness of modern society and the idealised beauty of antiquity:

> IX ADOLESCENTS, misfortune increased your beauty. Balder, pale northern sun, Attis mourned for by powerful Cybele, Qaïaïp his Californian brother, Adonis with eyes the colour of violets, and you, charming ephebes so far removed from our hideous modern homosexuals: Hylas at the spring, Ampelus victim of the bull and for ever longed for by Bacchus; Abderus the favourite of Hercules, devoured by man-eating horses entrusted to him by the conqueror of Diomedes; Hyacinthus, and a thousand others right up to Antinous with his melancholy brow – did he not drown himself to save the Emperor Hadrian, his lover, in accordance with the oracle?

Arcadian and Bucolic Poetry

When Gide turned to Theocritus and Vergil his interest in their bucolic poems was undoubtedly sentimental. He found in them a true ex-pression of natural simplicity. Corydon observes that the rustic charac-ters of Theocritus were more natural and naive than people corrupted by modern society (p. 144). He also remarks that the Vergilian Menalcas takes his pleasures with Amyntas naturally and easily (p. 144). For him this poetry is inspired by homosexuality (p. 144) and only became false to itself when the poet ceased to be in love with the shepherds he describes. This is a partisan rather than a scholarly view of Greek bucolic poetry, for there is as much evidence there of heterosexual as of homosexual attraction. However, the important point to note resides in Corydon's name, itself a direct echo of Vergil's second Eclogue.

Gide had read a little Theocritus when he was young, as we learn from an unpublished *Journal* entry of November 1894.[84] Already by this date, however, he regretted that he had forgotten most of what he knew. References in his works to Theocritus are merely associated with the charms of shepherd boys.[85] He may well have read the other bucolic poetry printed in Leconte de Lisle's collection from which he took the translation of Bion we have noticed.[86]

The case with Vergil is quite different, for Gide had an intimate and long-standing acquaintance with his poetry. However, the first part of his life is marked by frequent readings of the *Eclogues*, while in his later years he turned almost exclusively towards the *Aeneid*.

In 1891 he wrote enthusiastically in his 'Subjectif' (p. 106: 30 May– 13 June): 'I have finished the *Eclogues*, having read them in Latin, one each morning. The first is, I think, the best, together with the fourth. I do not like the 'Silenus' (the sixth), and the eighth is tedious. I know numbers II and X by heart.' On the whole he admitted to being a little bored with them because of 'the monotony of their themes and their rather soft [*flasque*] quality'. Another comment appears in the unpublished *Journal* of 10 June 1891.[87]

> Vergil is delicious [*exquis*]: I was quite sure he was – and I'm glad, for I love making discoveries. These *Eclogues*! and what sensuality [*volupté*]! They are replete with moments of titillation, and are still quite innocent [*ingénus*] – how terribly depraved the Latin race is! or rather we are – but in the last analysis each appears depraved to the other. Several of the Eclogues are badly composed – the second, and the 'Silenus'.

The first Eclogue is a dialogue between Tityrus and Meliboeus on the delights of home, however poor it is, and the hardships of exile. (In his own writings, Gide was later to reverse the meaning of these two themes.) The fourth, about which he later became far less enthusiastic,[88] is the celebrated 'Pollio' Eclogue in praise of the heavenly child, which some commentators have interpreted as a reference to various contemporaries of the poet, and others as a prophecy concerning Christ. Eclogue X, 'Gallus', expresses the poet's warm affection for Gallus who, in describing his own frustrated love, says: 'O how soft a sleep would my bones enjoy, could I but feel that a pipe of yours one day would tell of my passion! Nay, indeed, would that I had been one of you myself – the shepherd of a flock of yours, or the dresser of those full ripe grapes! Then at least, whether it had been Phyllis, or Amyntas, or any other love; and what if Amyntas be brown? violets are dark, too. . . .'[89] The second Eclogue is the description of Corydon pining for his beloved Alexis, a youth who does not respond to his passion. Menalcas is dark, Alexis is fair – and the poet invites Alexis to live with him and share the delights of Arcadian bliss. Amyntas is jealous of Damoetas' affection for Corydon: but, Corydon, asks the poet, 'What madness has possessed you? You will find another Alexis, even though the present one may scorn you.' In the sixth Eclogue Tityrus tells the stories of Silenus, the Creation and several mythological tales; in the eighth, the power of love is described. Of the remaining Eclogues, III and VII are song contests where the shepherds vie with each other and sing the delights of an idealised rural existence: Menalcas and his darling Amyntas (III), Daphnis, Corydon, Meliboeus, Alexis and Lycidas (VII) make their several appearances. The fifth Eclogue is in praise of the shepherd Daphnis; the ninth is the tale of Fortune's wheel, told by Lycidas and Moeris, mentioning Tityrus and Menalcas again.

Vergil is the ancient writer to whom Gide most frequently turned. There are a number of epigraphs which he chose from the *Eclogues*, neatly summarising the subject of the works to which they are prefixed (for example 'Quid tum si fuscus Amyntas', *Ecl.* X 38, epitomises the sensual delight he found in dark-skinned Arab boys and stands at the head of Book VII of *Les Nourritures terrestres*). Vergilian characters were also endowed with an individual symbolic meaning by Gide: Tityrus, Meliboeus and Menalcas all appear in his early writings – *Mopsus* and *Amyntas* are titles which he gave to two of his travel pieces.[90] The choice of 'Corydon' speaks for itself. Vergil's Arcadian shepherds appear in Book VI of *Les Nourritures terrestres*, and in this work the narrator is clearly intended to stand in relation to the youth Nathanaël as the older man does to his shepherd boy in the *Eclogues*. Again, in Book VII (p. 234) we read: 'These are my flocks, I hear the flute of the shepherd whom I love. Will he come? Or shall I go to him?' Indeed Gide recalled in a letter to Jeanne Rondeaux, his future sister-in-law, in February 1894: '[Here] the shepherd boys play on their flutes as they do in Vergil.' This was not, after all, as innocent a literary allusion as might at first have appeared to her.

Gide also used the symbol of Ménalque with a clear reference to himself in a letter to Jammes on 22 April 1897: 'Ménalque has unfolded Italy before him. He has been re-reading Vergil on the slopes of those same valleys which listened to the poet's voice. Ah! would that I was one of you, Arcadians! and, if it please the gods, shepherding your flocks or picking your ripe grapes.'[91] This is not simply a literary affectation, and the leitmotif may be recognised in private letters and diary entries alike. 'Ah! why am I not one of you – and may the gods grant my wish! – you children who wander on my road [qui vagabondez sur ma route].'[92] And again: 'Ah! how many hours I lost like this on the slopes of the Apennines . . . following the sheep . . . in the company of shepherds, myself a shepherd, listening to the song of their rustic flutes murmur to my heart: Utinam ex vobis unus [Would that I was one of you].'[93] 'Vergil speaks splendidly of Menalcas,' he also remarked in the epigraph of the letter to Jammes – but did Gide wish his correspondent to understand the hidden truth of his words? Menalcas' example is explicitly referred to in *Corydon* (*Ecl.* III 66).[94]

Licentious Writings

The licentious aspect of Gide's reading is revealed when we follow him in his perusal of *Le Livre d'amour des anciens* (1912). The book is, as the title makes clear, a general collection of texts translated from Greek and Latin authors dealing with love in many of its aspects, both heterosexual and homosexual. The material ranges widely from Aristophanes to Athenaeus, and from Horace and Martial to the writers of the *Augustan History*. The main part of the work is in fact based on Forberg's *De figuris Veneris* with some additions and omissions. There is a translation of Plutarch's *Amatorius*, the *Boyish Muse* of Strato, and selected amatory epigrams from the *Greek Anthology* and Martial. We know from the archive that the section to which Gide paid most attention was 'De paedicando' (pp. 65–96).

It is scarcely to be doubted that he read more of this collection than he happened to refer to in his notes. Strato's epigrams (included in the *Greek Anthology*), for example, do not feature in *Corydon*, nor are they among the manuscript material. They vary from the romantic to the overtly obscene, although there are only a few in the latter category. They contain many references to the age at which a boy ceases to be attractive when his beard begins to grow. We read in Epigram 4: 'A boy of fourteen is the flower of love, at fifteen he is more lovely still, sixteen is the age of the gods, and at seventeen he is fit for Zeus himself.' Other poems deal with unrequited love, the advantage of a boy's anatomy over a girl's, the praise of beautiful boys, and the poet's erotic address to fair and dark youths alike (Epigram 165). Epigram 192 openly declares: 'I like boys, dusty and dirty from their athletic exercises, limbs gleaming with oil. Refinement only belongs to women.' Despite his silence, we may well imagine that Gide enjoyed reading these poems.[95]

Two notes which are printed in *Corydon* (p. 172) derive from *Le Livre d'amour des anciens*. The first quotes Herodotus' statement that the Greeks taught the Persians the love of boys.[96] The author of *Le Livre d'amour des anciens* professes not to know whether this 'evil' (*mal*) came from Asia to Greece or vice versa, for ancient authors do not agree on the point. Corydon is more definite, for he sides with those who believe that Eastern luxury undermined the manly strength of Greece. However, other writers who are cited in *Le Livre d'amour* express differing opinions: Athenaeus, for example, reports in the *Deipnosophistae* (XIII 79): 'According to Timaeus the love of boys arose first in Crete and passed from there into Greece.' There follows (from Athenaeus) the story of Laius and Chrysippus. The tale of Orpheus who 'introduced this fetid pleasure into Thrace' is related, and, from Vergil's *Georgics* IV 516–22, how he was torn to pieces by the Thracian women who considered themselves despised by him. Athenaeus' report that the Celts mocked the men who did not love men is also quoted: 'The Celts prefer boys, so that often some of them sleep between two mignons.'[97]

The second note in *Corydon* relates to two separate items from Athenaeus.[98] The first of these refers to Sophocles' love of boys and Euripides' love of women.[99] The second is about Sophocles' erotic success with a boy who shortly afterwards stole his cloak. The way in which this material is integrated into Corydon's argument, however, is interesting and instructive. Questionable gossip is used to make a moral point about the high position of women in art and society being due to pederasty. Furthermore, Corydon attempts to argue from this dubious premise that modern society would benefit from adopting similar behaviour. It seems reasonable to assume that Gide's knowledge of Book XIII of the *Deipnosophistae*, which deals with both homosexual and heterosexual love, is limited to what he read in 'De paedicando' and in the relevant pages of *Ioläus* where Book XIII is cited.[100]

In the unpublished part of his *Journal* for October 1887 Gide noted that he would read to his cousin Madeleine the section in Aristophanes' *Frogs* which showed the opinion the ancient Greeks had of tragedy. The page number he gives (p. 417) shows that he was reading C. Poyard's translation, which first appeared in 1860; the passage to which he refers contains the beginning of the debate between Euripides and Aeschylus (lines 826–44). This is, of course, innocent enough, but Poyard's translation is elsewhere remarkably free of euphemisms and deleted passages. Thus in the same play Gide must have read the exchange between Heracles and Dionysus when the latter is asked if, on a particular occasion, he desired a woman, a boy, a man – or the notoriously effeminate Clisthenes (lines 56–8); the description of Hades where men are put who have cheated boys of the money earned by their 'complaisant behaviour' (lines 145–8); and the notes explaining Clisthenes' readiness to be 'boarded' like a ship (line 48); not to mention a simple Latin explanation of the exclamation 'Divine ecstasy [*divine jouissance*]': 'Semen emittere mihi videor [I think I'm coming]' (line 753).

On 10 June 1891 Gide wrote in his *Journal* a list of authors he intended to read. It included 'the strong [*nerveux*] and especially the masculine [*mâles*] – Aristophanes, Shakespeare, Rabelais'. Did 'mâle' include the debate scene in Aristophanes' *Clouds* (lines 973–4)? There the Just and the Unjust Arguments discuss the correct behaviour for youths, and how boys should smooth out the impression left in the gymnasium sand after they have been sitting down, the better to curb temptation among prospective lovers. We could add the description in the *Birds* (lines 139–42) of the Ideal City where boys' testicles can be caressed (Poyard explains in Latin), and the reference at the opening of the *Peace* (lines 11–12) to the Dung Beetle's favourite food supplied by boy prostitutes (with explanatory Latin note). However, the allusion in *Corydon* to the playwright is a mere mention of his name (p. 158). A reference to him in 'La Licence, la dépravation et les déclarations de M. le Sénateur Bérenger' clearly shows that Gide thought then that 'art' can coexist with 'pornography'.[101] But this gets us little further. We can surmise that Gide perhaps read the *Thesmophoriazusae* in Poyard's translation, where the precise sense of the obscene puns and allusions is given in Latin in the footnotes. This play tells of the adventures of Euripides and his ancient relative among a crowd of women who are celebrating the Festival of the Thesmophoria. It contains amusing portrayals of Agathon (an effeminate tragic poet) and Clisthenes, and some of the plot depends on men in female disguise.

It is, however, possible to imagine that these homosexual jokes would have proved too shocking for Gide. If this is so, then his silence on another subject might well be explained in a similar way. It is scarcely likely that he was ignorant of Petronius' tale of the amorous adventures of Encolpius, Ascyltus and the young boy Giton,[102] but there is no mention of this author in his published works or correspondences.

It is curious to note that Gide's one reference to Apuleius' *The Metamorphoses* (*The Golden Ass*) also occurs at about this same early date in *Les Cahiers d'André Walter*.[103] Unlike many other books, Apuleius' is one which the narrator is unwilling to share with his beloved. In response to her mocking smile, he closes it: but it is not possible to know precisely what Gide had in mind. Apart from the rather innocent fable of Cupid and Psyche (to which he was clearly not referring), the story does contain several episodes which are overtly pornographic. There are descriptions of heterosexual adventures, rendered with varying degrees of fidelity in the translations to which Gide had access. Spice is also added to some of these by the fact that the hero is no longer a man, but has been transformed into an ass. Furthermore, there is a noteworthy description of the effeminate priests (the *galli*) of the Syrian Goddess,[104] their lascivious attitudes and their lewd behaviour with a handsome peasant they take back home with them.

Nor does Gide make any comment on the Roman satirists Martial and Juvenal. Perhaps the images in the former's poetry were often too gross for him; and perhaps they too often concerned forms of sodomitical intercourse between adults, which he found distasteful. Juvenal's accounts of the pathics' excesses in Satires 2, 6 and 9 would also, one feels, not have appealed particularly to him except in so far as they might have underlined how pure was his noble ideal of educational friendship. Again the historians Suetonius and Tacitus are passed over almost in silence. Gide paid no particular attention to the former's account of the alleged amorous excesses of the Emperor Tiberius.[105] Although he claimed to read Tacitus with some enjoyment we can catch only two glimpses of him in the *Journal*. The first is dated 14 July 1893 and refers to *Annals* XIII: 'that admirable book in which Nero gradually loses his softness and his original fears'. We may recall that some of the chapters in question provided the main source for Racine's tragedy *Britannicus*, and it was probably in connection with this play that Gide's attention was drawn to them. The crimes and outrages of Nero are recounted in this and subsequent books of the *Annals*. The second reference occurs in the spring of 1906[106] and relates to *Annals* XI 1–3 in which Tacitus describes the Empress Messalina and the disorders at the court of Claudius. Again, Sallust was one of the authors he said he intended to read in 1904.[107] Did he in fact do so? In the 'Feuillets' for 1918,[108] Sallust's *Catilina* V 4 is referred to, but this is of no immediate importance. There is, however, a reference to homosexual behaviour later in this work (XIV 5) – and Gide would have seen it had he persevered.

From articles and books by modern writers, Gide was obviously prepared to hunt out material for possible use. An interesting example of this is provided by a cutting preserved in the archive[109] among the material taken from an article on 'L'Île sainte d'Isis' by P.H. Boussac.[110] The temples at Philae were about to be submerged, and the author considered it appropriate to describe the sculptures, inscriptions and later history of the site for the educated amateur. His account is anecdotal, rather than scrupulously archaeological. Gide abstracted pages 103–6, and drew a line opposite the text on pages 105–6 where there is a section on the debauchery of Ptolemy Auletes: 'Thus the mocking Alexandrians gave him the surname of Auletes [flute player].' Boussac compares him with Nero, asserting that he dressed as a woman, led a dissolute life, obliged the citizens to follow his example, and joined in the Bacchic frenzies. Gide also marked the two inscriptions reported by Boussac: 'Strouthion the *cinaedus* [catamite] was here, with his friend Nicolaus' and 'Trypho the *cinaedus* of Dionysus the Young [Dionysos le nouveau] came to Isis at Philae.' There are some etymological explanations: 'cinaedus' is said to derive from the dance in which the buttocks are vigorously wiggled; 'Strouthion' is alleged to recall the lascivious reputation of the bird of this name, the sparrow.[111]

Two references of a licentious nature occur in *L'Immoraliste*. The first is to the orgiastic worship of the Phrygian goddess Cybele and her priests, the *galli*; the second is to the subject of Michel's historical studies, Procopius' *Gothica* I 2, which tells of Athalaric. This youth, the historian records, met an early death through intemperance. A lover of women and drunkenness, he gave himself up to a life of debauchery and corruption. No homosexual encounters are credited to him – but he is the very model of a type of moral suicide (and hence a fitting topic for Michel to study).

Elagabalus (see Plate 1) the youthful Roman Emperor who was renowned for his homosexual excesses and who died young, is referred to by Gide only in passing, but it is worth remarking on the conversation in which his name arose. In the *Journal* for 4 February 1902, Gide reported that the actor Édouard De Max, a friend of his, mentioned three roles he would like to play – Racine's Oreste and Néron, and Corneille's Polyeucte – and three historical costumes he would like to wear: those of Julian (the Apostate Emperor), Elagabalus and Henri III (of France – noteworthy in this context presumably because of his homosexuality). Gide did not record his own reply.[112] Although we do not know whether Gide read the relevant chapters from Herodian or the *Augustan History*, it is easy to assume that the Emperor's story was familiar to him through allusions in Montaigne and many other writers.

Gide also alludes to historical facts or to opinions which could be represented as such. He seems to have selected them, however, in a rather random fashion, and even though they doubtless do not represent the full range of his knowledge on the subject they do bear witness to his eclecticism.

The first set of such facts is Corydon's mention of homosexuality among the Celts. According to Diodorus Siculus, he says, the Celts were not very attached to their women and much preferred 'to roll on the ground on animal skins, each together with his lover'. The translation was specially provided for him (possibly by his friend Arnold Naville) on a sheet of paper together with an extract from Aristotle's

Politics.[113] But what Corydon does not quote is the sequel in Diodorus which was also part of his friend's translation: 'But strangest of all, and in spite of all natural modesty [indifférents à leur dignité], they readily offer [ils livrent facilement à d'autres] the flower of their youth. Far from finding any dishonour in this conduct, they consider themselves dishonoured if their offers are refused.' Corydon also mentions the Aristotle extract[114] which says that in Sparta Lycurgus omitted to frame laws for women, and this can lead to great abuses 'especially when men are inclined to let themselves be dominated by them. Energetic and warlike races are prone to this [an argument contradicted by Corydon in Dialogue IV as we have seen]. However, I exclude the Celts and some other nations who openly honour masculine love.' It would indeed be interesting to know whether Gide actually referred to a copy of St Hilaire's edition of the *Politics*, for the index contains an entry on 'amour viril'. Here a note in section II 7 (part of Gide's reference) is mentioned. It runs:

> This vice, so widespread in Greece, was protected by the laws. In Aristotle's day it was commonly believed that the Cretans were the first to practise it (Heraclides Ponticus, p. 508). Plato asserts that it was they who invented the story of Ganymede, to find a divine excuse for their disgusting behaviour (*Laws*, Book I p. 203). The scholiast on Aeschylus (*Septem* 81) maintains that Laius, father of Oedipus, was the first Greek to soil himself with this baseness, and that his death and the misfortunes of his race were punishment for his crime. Hippocrates, in the *Oath*, severely forbids his followers to have commerce with men,

and so on. St Hilaire ends by remarking: 'To have done with this revolting subject', Plato in the *Republic* (Book V p. 251) offers his warriors the love of their young companions as supreme recompense for their courage. 'It does not however seem that, according to Socrates, these caresses should go beyond the expression of a simple and pure friendship, albeit somewhat keen [*vive*].'

The second group of historical remarks concerns the 'Ionians' and the 'Dorians'. This distinction was used by Gide to describe his relationship with Louÿs, as we shall see. An extract on the Ionians, taken from the French translation of Ernst Curtius' *Griechische Geschichte*, can be found in the *Corydon* archive.[115] It reads: 'The most famous of the chroniclers . . . is Ion of Chios, a true Ionian who possessed a complex, rich and subtle nature. . . . But the most charming picture which Ion gives us is his meeting with Sophocles at Chios. . . . Here, at a feast, he describes the poet arguing with a pedantic schoolmaster and defending some lines of Phrynichus while craftily stealing a kiss from a beautiful boy cupbearer. By this means Sophocles wished to give the lie to Pericles, who was in the habit of saying about him: "He's a good poet but a poor general." '[116] Shortly before this extract, Curtius, who has been speaking of Greek historiography, characterises the Ionian race who, when they wrote history, 'threw themselves enthusiastically into the living present and freely translated the impressions their most eminent contemporaries made upon them'. This brief description is the counterpart of a simplified picture of Dorian manliness. Curtius was also twice quoted in the 1920 proofs of *Corydon* and then deleted. The first example provided additional material to characterise the Dorians.[117] The second example, intended as a footnote, was about the decadence of the Greeks, particularly at Athens.[118] The quotation from Curtius connects this with the decline of the gymnasia in the education of the young. This observation, let us remember, was also made by Montesquieu and others (and noted by Gide),[119] but *Corydon* was to have used it to illustrate his theory of the debilitating effect of the soft Ionian east.

Becker's *Charicles* has to be considered in this context, too, for another manuscript fragment (which has the appearance of an aide-mémoire) refers to 'Becker's *Charicles* "Zweiter Excursus zur fünften Scene", where one can find a collection of information on the love of boys (*Knabenliebe*).'[120] Becker's theory that homosexuality was a specific institution of the Dorian race, intimately connected with their warlike customs (which he describes), would have been familiar to Gide but is now widely discredited. The book was again referred to in the deleted footnote from Curtius in the 1920 proofs which we have just discussed.[121] The ostensible reason for mentioning Becker was the educational role of the gymnasia (a subject to which Excursus I of Scene 5 had been entirely devoted).

In fact, Gide had long been acquainted with other expressions of similar views. In the early 1890s, for example, he was an avid reader of Taine, and this philosopher, whose pen was generally chaste and whose picture of antiquity was idealised, drew a particular conclusion from the Greeks' love of beauty. The culture of the body became widespread in that civilisation, Taine noted, and this resulted in 'presenting bodily beauty as the chief aim of human existence, thus extending admiration of the form achieved until it became a vice'. 'Greek vice,' unknown in Homeric times, he wrote in his *Philosophie de l'art en Grèce*, began with the creation of the gymnasia. Taine referred for corroboration to *Charicles*. The development of athletic games, contests and gymnastic exercises all had an important part to play, wrote Taine, in the Spartan concept of masculine beauty, and in the work of sculptors from the rest of Greece. Moreover, the so-called Dorian mode in music had a moral advantage, being 'serious, virile, elevated, very simple and even very harsh, but excellent for inspiring patience and energy'. Athletes, the ideal which such a splendid culture produces, he said, harden themselves in mind and body: 'They abstain from pleasure and excitement, they condemn themselves to continence.'

A last example of Gide's zeal in documenting himself comes from Strabo's geographical work and was probably provided by Jacques Heurgon, the classicist and dedicatee of *Thésée*, with whom he was staying in North Africa during the Second World War. The translation he used was by A. Tardieu in four volumes, and he merely noted in the margin of his manuscript of *Thésée* into which he incorporated the material: 'How Minos regulated pederasty in Crete. See Strabo Book X Chap. 4 §21 [= Tardieu, Vol. II pp. 373–5].' Strabo's account takes two aspects of Cretan pederasty into consideration: the actual ritual of the custom, and the reasons for which it was performed. In *Thésée* this material is reduced to its essentials and provides a suitably Cretan motive for the intrigue. Thus Gide, following Strabo, records: 'One of the island's customs is for the lover to seize the youth he desires and take him off to live with him for two months, after which the boy declares publicly [whether he likes his lover][122] and whether he has been treated decently.' Gide also follows Strabo in relating that the intending seducer warns the boy's father (in *Thésée*, King Minos) several days before the abduction takes place. (This, states Strabo, is so that a token show of force may be made.)

It is interesting to find in Gide the same motivation as in Strabo for the parties' attitudes: 'Every adolescent who reaches manhood without being chosen by an older man [ms. variant: lover] is ashamed, and considers this neglect a reason for dishonour; for it is commonly held that if he is handsome then his rejection must have been occasioned by some vice of mind or feelings.'[123]

It will be as well to conclude our discussion of classical material with a glance at Euripides' *Bacchae*, for Gide's comments on this play are as illuminating as many of the remarks we have already noticed. His attention was not attracted to the sexual implications of Pentheus dressing as a woman, nor yet precisely to the Eastern softness of the youthful Dionysus. The play does not, of course, deal overtly with homosexuality, though there is a suggestion of a homosexual element in Pentheus' feelings towards Dionysus.[124] We need simply take note of Gide's general moral attitudes. He was surprised that the Hellenist Marie Delcourt accorded so little space to the play in her book *La Vie d'Euripide*, which he read on 2 January 1931 (*Journal*) and again some seven years later. On 21 August 1940, after a conversation with her and several other friends during which she allegedly said that she found the *Bacchae* as 'boring' as Shakespeare's *The Tempest*, he noted in the *Journal* that he re-read the former play in consequence. His reaction was different from hers, reinforcing his first acquaintance with the *Bacchae* when his emotion had been overwhelming. 'I first encountered it,' he wrote, 'when I was still struggling against the bonds of puritan morality. Pentheus' resistance was my own, as I reacted against what a secret Dionysus was proposing. On the path ahead I was afraid I would only find disorder and disharmony. . . .' The maenads, Gide asserted, become furious only when they are threatened with constraint. He believed that Euripides' *Hippolytus* also shows how a god exacts retribution for a similar puritanical denial. This seems to have caught his imagination more forcibly than Hippolytus' diatribe against women's craftiness and his praise of chastity.[125] The thought was not new to him. In his *Évolution du théâtre* (1904) he had written of the god taking vengeance on the man who has denied his instincts. The same idea occurs in the *Traité sur la mythologie grecque* (*circa* 1919).[126] So strong is this image that we encounter it again in the *Journal* on 17 September 1935: 'If one only lives long enough the things one has suppressed in one's youth rise up and exact vengeance – as did Aphrodite and Dionysus in the Greek tragedies.' The classical model which Gide adopted seems to have been so complex that it had necessarily to embrace a Dionysiac acknowledgement of desire and a Socratic worship of restraint.

CHAPTER ELEVEN

The Orient

Gide was no Orientalist. For him Algeria was a country where he, no less than his fictional hero Michel, was able to find a means of liberating himself from a restrictive morality. In October 1893 he sailed to North Africa. He deliberately left his Bible behind, but then wrote to his mother to forward it to him. His Arab servant and companion Athman introduced him to the life of the cafés, to the licentious puppet shows of Karagöz, and to the often sentimental stories and popular songs about love in its manifold forms. As Gide wrote in March 1899 to his friend Ghéon[1] describing one of these songs:

At first Athman did not want to translate because it was an 'Egyptian' song:

I crave pardon
And the brown-skinned lad offered me his cheek. . . .
I crave pardon.
He has unsheathed the roses in his garden,
And I have fasted for seven months
For having once kissed him on the mouth.
Pardon, pardon, pardon.

Although the café was insalubrious, as Athman said in Abu Nowas' words:

The wine is always good
When the boy who pours it is handsome.

But here again we have to remember that Gide was above all a person whose culture was *literary*, and so we must turn towards the books which formed his picture of Oriental boy-love. He mentioned that in addition to Galland's old-fashioned bowdlerised version he only knew the early nineteenth-century German translation of the *1001 Nights* by Weil.[2] But this did not remain the case. Among the manuscript notes for *Corydon* there is one in German in Gide's handwriting which reads: 'Ped. See "The Man's Dispute with the learned woman concerning the relative excellence of male and female". *1001 Nights* by

Greve. Vol. VI pp. 181 et seq.'³ The book referred to is in fact based on Burton's English translation, and that the note must date from after 1908 is clear from Greve's date of publication. The story in question is told on Nights 419–23 and takes the form of a debate which is not very different in its essentials from the discussions we have noted in Plutarch and Lucian. Scheherazade tells how two men go to consult a wise woman who sits behind a curtain while her beautiful brother waits upon them. One of the men is captivated by the youth, and therefore a debate ensues about the relative attraction exercised by boys and girls. The man's speech is a panegyric of males 'for each is worth two women, as the Koran says', and a man is the model of human action to which appeal is always made. Men are cleaner than females. He quotes verses from Al-Hariri's Makámát in praise of beardless youths, and from Abu Tammám (the author of the anthology known as Al-Hamásah).

The woman quotes poetry which castigates the love of boys, and recalls the condemnation of sodomy in the Koran (xxvi, 165 ff.: the Lord speaks to the Sodomites, the people of Lot). She denounces the literal filthiness of sodomites and contrasts their bodies with the wholesome cleanliness of girls. In fact she could not agree less with her adversary: girls are more beautiful than youths (she utters a fulsome panegyric) – and youths when handsome, she says, are in fact often compared with girls.

Mardrus' new French translation of the 1001 Nights was published by the Revue Blanche in sixteen volumes between 1899 and 1904. The first volume was dedicated to Paul Valéry, the fourth to Gide. The publishers noted: 'For the first time in Europe a complete and faithful translation of Alf Lailah wa Lailah is presented to the public (the English translations by Payne and Burton were also complete, but were privately published in small limited editions and are nowadays extremely difficult to find.'⁴ Gide was shown the manuscript of the translation before it was submitted to the Revue Blanche; he reviewed the book as it began to appear.⁵ It was so much greater, richer, stranger and more sensual, he said, than Galland's version, which he had admired since childhood. In fact, rather than draw attention in his review to any story in particular, he emphasised the notion of 'sensuality promoted to the degree of a cardinal virtue' which, in his opinion, gave this work its unique value. 'A splendid, persistent, indecent sensuality,' he wrote, 'permeated with laughter'.⁶ It was not so much the accounts of the disreputable exploits of the homosexual Abu Nowas which he valued as 'a demonstration of a sensuality which consists simply of considering as an end, and not as a means, the present object and the present moment. That is what I also admire in Persian poetry; that is what I admire especially.'⁷ The whole of Persian literature, he added with perhaps pardonable exaggeration, appeared to him like the golden palace in the well-known story. Of the numerous doors which open on to views of riches there is a fortieth, forbidden door which closes off a darkened room whose perfumed atmosphere is intoxicating and makes one faint. 'It is a room where you nevertheless enter and where you find a strange, beautiful black horse which unfolds its wings as soon as you mount. It carries you to the heights of unknown heavens, and then suddenly descends, unseats you, and blinds you in one eye with the tip of its wing.' The commentators on Omar Khayyam and Hafiz call this the 'mystical sense of the Persian poets'. But Gide, continuing the metaphor, admits that he does not enjoy these flights. He appreciates still less the partial loss of vision. And so he is quite happy to explore the other delights revealed in the gardens and the orchards.

In his review of Volume IV, Gide singled out for comment the story of the 'Shepherd and the Young Girl'.[8] The girl tries her utmost to seduce the shepherd, but her charms are to no avail, even despite the fact that she is sufficiently beautiful to be mistaken for a beardless youth. The shepherd withdraws into a life of asceticism and the girl disappears. Abu Nowas appears in Volume VI, in the story 'An Adventure of the Poet Abu Nowas'.[9] 'At last,' says Gide in his review:[10] but the truth is that here the 'adventure' is libertine and heterosexual, although Abu Nowas is in a 'cabaret mal famé' with a boy when first the Calif sends his eunuch to find him.

But Gide did not give up his pursuit of Burton's translation. When he was in Cambridge in 1918 he commissioned his friend André Ruyters to obtain from a London bookseller a copy, complete with its 'Terminal Essay' in Volume X which deals with homosexual practices in the East.[11] In his review of Mardrus' translation in 1899 he had explicitly denied knowledge of Burton's book, saying that he regretted he did not understand English. Now, presumably, he could read it, but he did not use it for writing *Corydon*. In particular he made no mention of Burton's theory of a 'Sotadic Zone' where pederasty was endemic, avoiding these ideas perhaps because he found them ideologically unacceptable. Burton's views would in any case have already been familiar to him from the preface to Van Gennep's translation of Havelock Ellis' *Sexual Inversion*.

Gide remembered that in Florence in 1895 he had made the acquaintance of a young orientalist, Fédor Rosenberg:[12] 'We began to talk. An American lady had left FitzGerald's translation of Omar Khayyam on the table. This provided an opportunity to speak of Persian poetry. At that date I was very keen on Hafiz and Firdousi, but I only knew their work through German and French translations.' He also records reading Hafiz (and Goethe) in Italy in early 1898.[13] In 1899, he advised his readers 'to avoid Nicolas' French translation of Omar Khayyam, it is literal: FitzGerald's is beautiful. There is also an

THE ORIENT

excellent recent French one by C. Groulleau. As for Hafiz, if you cannot obtain Rosenzweig's read Hammer's German translation. Sa'di and Firdousi may be read in French in their entirety but I prefer Omar Khayyam and Hafiz.'[14] Given Gide's poor command of English, we may well be sceptical about his ability to judge the quality of FitzGerald's version at this date. There are three poems from Hafiz and Sa'di in English translation in Carpenter's *Ioläus*.

Hafiz

Hafiz, a Sufi, lived in Shiraz, capital of the province of Fars, in the fourteenth century, 'a time when pederasty flourished in the most open – I almost said most official – manner'.[15] His Odes (or 'Erotic poems' or 'Ghazels') were first translated into French by A.L.M. Nicolas in 1898. Gide was familiar with this version. Only Ghazels 1 to 13 are printed in this collection, and despite frequent invocations to the cup-boy to pour out the wine, the translation is strictly heterosexual in tone. Hammer's German version to which Gide refers is fuller. It is, however, characteristic of the Ghazels, Arthur Guy noted in his fuller French translation of Ghazels 1–175 in 1927, that descriptions of the beloved are devoid of all indications that the person is a woman – in fact, indications that the beloved is a boy are very numerous. The problem (*sic*), Guy writes, is not solved by saying that the substitution of the masculine sex is a convention due to the impropriety of talking openly of women: can the listener imagine a young girl, he asks, 'going to the inn, drunk, with cup in hand' (Ghazel 37)? As for wine, Hafiz 'demonstrates an inordinate delight in the graceful ephebes who serve him.' But 'let us notice that these portrayals of passion for the winecup or for the Beloved [*l'aimé*] are without any deliberate sensuality'. 'This is a pure love; *to be near* the Beloved. The lover must sacrifice everything to the object of his affection – worldly goods, glory, riches, honour – and, finally, personal vanity.' There is another way of looking at this love: if one takes the poet's expression as symbolic or mystical, then, in accordance with the traditions of Sufism, we may with certainty identify the Beloved with God.

The common definition of a Ghazel is a poem whose most frequent subject is the beauty of the beloved object, the description of the lover's feelings, and love itself. In this sense Nicolas' selection is hardly representative. As Gide wrote to Ghéon on 19 March 1899: 'Alas! the fruits are there, and the night, and the nightingale, and the roses, and the glass is full of the same wine, alas! but the cup-bearer – where is he? (Have I already read you that in Hafiz?)'[16]

179

Omar Khayyam and Firdousi

J.B. Nicolas' translation of Omar Khayyam appeared in a bilingual edition in 1867. It consists of 464 quatrains, and, as Gide said, has no great literary pretensions. He noted in his manuscripts[17] an extract from this version: 'pp. 104–5. Quatrain 205 "En compagnie d'un ami aimable – (ici une note) = ('Dieu')". . . .' ('Together with a bosom friend – (a note) = ("God")'). Nicolas' text reads: 'Together with a bosom friend what I like is a cup of wine. When I fall prey to sorrow, what I require is that my eyes fill with tears. O, since this abject world cannot last for us, what is best is to live our lives dead drunk!' There is nothing, it should be added, in Nicolas' introduction about pederasty, or about affection for the youths who pour the poet's wine. Omar Khayyam is far from being a licentious poet and, in FitzGerald's poetic version too, he is remarkably chaste. We may all make what we please of the recurring invocations to pleasure and the cup-bearer.

Firdousi has less to offer for our enquiry. The *Shah-Namah*,[18] or *Book of Kings*, is an epic poem of the early history of Persia, and has none of the wistful, lyrical tenderness of the poets we have so far been concerned with. For this we have to turn to Sa'di.

Sa'di

The *Journal* of 4 April 1906 contains a remark about Marie de Regnier reading Sa'di aloud to Gide, but the precise verses are not specified. Several partial or bowdlerised translations of Sa'di's *Gulistan* or *Rose Garden* had appeared before N. Semelet published his full French version in 1834. It is perhaps surprising that Gide said he was so relatively unattracted by Sa'di's work, for Chapter 5 contains a fulsome account of pederastic affection under the title 'Of Love and Youth'. But he knew it well enough: 'As Sa'di says: "What have I to do with repentance?" . . .'[19] Semelet's preface to Chapter 5 discusses lesbianism in the harem, the sexual use of boys, pederasty among the Tartars, and the institution of polygamy. In all countries, but especially in the East, he notes, homosexual behaviour results from the separation of the sexes. However, he offers an observation by way of compensation: a young man will no more be corrupted by reading Chapter 5 than he would be made a criminal by reading the *Mémoires* of Vidocq, the ex-convict police chief.

Story 5 is not untypical:[20]

A schoolboy was so perfectly beautiful and sweet-voiced that the teacher, in accordance with human nature, conceived such an affection for him that he often recited the following verses:

> I am not so little occupied with thee, O heavenly face,
> That remembrance of myself occurs to my mind.
> From thy sight I am unable to withdraw my eyes,
> Although when I am opposite I may see that an arrow comes.

Once the boy said to him: 'As thou strivest to direct my studies, direct also my behaviour.' . . . He replied:
'O lad, make that request to someone else because the eyes with which I look upon thee behold nothing but virtues. . . .'

Story 11 points a different moral:

> When a beardless youth is beautiful and sweet
> His speech is bitter, his temper hasty.
> When his beard grows and he attains puberty
> He associates with men and seeks affection. . . .

Other stories illustrate the fires of love, the sadness of separation from the beloved and the passion of desire. If Sa'di gives his hearer a moral lesson it is contained in story 21, an 'envoi' to the chapter on love:

> Tie thy heart to the heart-charmer thou possessest,
> And shut thy eye to all the rest of the world. . . .

However, unless these words are to be taken, like some of our other examples, as instances of religious metaphor, they have to be understood in a fully erotic sense. Perhaps Gide perceived this, and perhaps he also noted the absence of a call for abstinence.

Earlier in date than either Sa'di or Hafiz is Damaghānī Minuchihrī, a Persian poet of the eleventh century AD (fifth century of the Hejira). Gide does not mention him, but he might have known the translation of his *Divan*, which appeared in a partial selection in 1876 and in a complete edition in French in 1886. The poet composed in distichs which are collected together into poems of differing lengths. Most of his work is panegyrical, but there are a number of drinking songs and a few poems which are overtly erotic. Bearing in mind how vulnerable a reader is when he relies on the gender of pronouns in translation, it is nevertheless to be observed that in the complete collection there are several homosexual poems. There are, of course, heterosexual ones too, and we encounter the commonplaces of Oriental poetry – nightingales, gardens, tulips, roses, forlorn journeys across the desert, and boys to pour the wine. The translator tells us in his preface that there was as yet no trace of Sufi mysticism in these verses – for that lay two centuries into the future. We have only to beware of the fulsome praise of beauty which a panegyric requires. Thus poems XLI, XLII and XLIII in praise of the young Sultan Mas'oud have a distinctly suggestive tone when they celebrate the young man's beauty. The boy who pours the wine is likened to the moon, and called young Turk of the race of houris (XI couplet 14), or, in another poem (LXIII couplets 13–18), has honeyed lips and honeyed words, and seduces whoever beholds his angry looks, his eyes, his face and hair. Poem LXIX is distinctly erotic as the poet addresses the friend with whom he is sitting on the fresh grass: 'Let us sit among the violets, and I will ruffle the downy hair of thy cheek until both hands rumple the heart and the feet of the violet' (couplet 2); 'And when we have finished the wine and the dessert we will provide something to make up for them, for we are resourceful. I will savour the juice of your mouth and believe it is wine; we will exchange two or three kisses and will take them for sweetmeats' (couplets 4 and 5). Poems L and LXXXV are apparently addressed to an unresponsive youth, and XCI is a reproach to a handsome young man, a former friend, who has snubbed the poet. Poem XXXVII is a lament for the absence of the poet's friend. Although it is somewhat of a common-place, the joy of a forbidden delight is expressed in another poem in terms that have a somewhat Gidean ring: 'I love this slave boy and the cup of wine – that is no reason for reproof or blame. I know that both these things are forbidden – but pleasure lies precisely in what one should not have' (LXXV, couplets 10 and 11).

Several years after the end of Gide's close friendship with Pierre Louÿs there appeared in 1902, under the imprint of the Mercure de France, a small collection of 'Arabic' love poetry entitled *Anthologie de l'amour arabe*,[21] with an introduction by Louÿs, whose tone is firmly heterosexual: we will read, says Louÿs, poems addressed to girls who are 'virgin, chaste, discreet and passionate'. Aged between ten and twelve, he writes, they are beauties without veils, and younger than one would expect in Western poetry. He is forthright about certain conventions: 'From a particular [unspecified] date the beloved was disguised under the name of a man – and, let us be quite clear, this was through modesty [*pudeur*], not at all through perversity.' Louÿs' notion of modesty can thus be seen to differ radically from Gide's. But so also can his idea of heterosexual poetry, for there are two poems which are (to my mind) homosexual. If Gide knew of this collection – and it is reasonable to assume that he did – his attention must surely have been caught by the poems by Moudrik el Chaibany and Beha el Din el Amili.

The first of these poets was a teacher in Baghdad who fell in love, so the biographical note tells us, with his young pupil Amr. The boy was in consequence taken away, and only allowed back to console the poet on his deathbed.

'Will this young fawn,' laments the poet, 'ever grow dim in my memory? Is it more difficult to forget the boy or gain his friendship?' There follows a hymn of desire, 'for his cheeks are smooth and his eyes are dark'. 'This youth is the master of my soul, and my heart is consumed by the fire of his cheeks. My strength ebbs from me as I look upon his girdle. I grow impatient with waiting as I think of his young beard, and my body trembles.'

The second poet was born in Kazan in 1525 AD and died in 1572. This idyll describes a beautiful boy who comes to the poet's tent. They kiss. On the second night they drink together: the poet lays his hand on the boy's cloak, requesting a second kiss. But this is refused. 'All night long,' the poet writes, 'he slept, his head cradled in my arm. And my delight was to contemplate the innocent happiness of his sleep.'[22] In this poem chastity and sensuality are both beautifully expressed.

We may also note in passing Edmond Fazy and Abdul-Halim Memdouh, *Anthologie de l'amour turc* (1905), also published by the Mercure de France. Fazy was the author of a sodomitical novel whose intrigue is set in Constantinople, *La Nouvelle Sodome*; the book was reviewed by Rachilde in the same issue of the *Mercure de France* which contained his 'Vers d'amour'. Some of these poems are about graceful adolescents.[23] It is again difficult to ascertain whether Gide knew these works, although it is probable that he was aware of their existence.

In February and March 1916 Gide started to undertake a translation of some poems by Kabīr,[24] the Indian mystic who was born in or near Benares in about 1440. In all probability he had in front of him a copy of the English collection *One Hundred Poems of Kabīr, translated by Rabindranath Tagore, assisted by E. Underhill* (London: Macmillan, 1915).[25] In this poetry it is possible to discern a very strong sensual call. Kabīr was alive at the time when the impassioned verse of the great Persian mystics, among whom we should place Sa'di and Hafiz, exercised a widespread influence in India. Although married, he idealised divine love in his rapturous songs. Showing contempt for those ascetics who wished to renounce a world permeated by beauty, love and joy, he wrote of God as the supreme object of love, 'the soul's comrade, teacher and bridegroom'. The preface of this edition draws particular attention to eleven poems which clearly show 'his lovely and delicate sense of intimate communion with the Divine Friend, Lover, Teacher of the soul'. In this English translation of Kabīr, however, one notices that although the poet is most warm in his praise of the Lord, there is little imagery which is overtly carnal. Thus there are no cup-boys and no languorous descriptions of the body of the beloved.

Of the one hundred poems in the collection the following sentiments might well have touched a chord in Gide's sensibility: 'Kabīr says: "When you unite love with the Lover, then you have love's perfection"' (poem 93); 'Dear friend, I am eager to meet my beloved! My youth has flowered and the pain of separation from Him troubles my breast' (poem 51); 'When I am parted from my Beloved, my heart is full of misery: I have no comfort in the day, I have no sleep in the night. To whom shall I tell my sorrow?' (poem 52). The preface tells us that we should identify the Friend and the Beloved with God. We are close to the world of Gide's *El Hadj*.

After *Corydon* had been published, there appeared a translation of Djami which also deserves a brief mention. In 1925 the first volume of the series 'Les Joyaux de l'Orient' contained the first French version, by Henri Massé, of the *Beharistan*. The 'Fifth Garden' describes the nightingales in the garden of love and tenderness, and how the butterflies' wings are burned by desire and affection. 'This love,' says Djami, 'a necessary quality of man, calls for purity and chastity. Love which consists of natural concupiscence and sensual desires belongs to brutes and wild beasts.' There follow examples of heterosexual loves and male pederasty. Boys are deserted when their beards begin to grow (a beard is 'the cheese grater which rasps the heart'). The true lover should love the soul.

Gide's own account of his travels in North Africa may be read in *Amyntas* (together with *Feuilles de route*, which had appeared previously). He does not report having had a surprise similar to the one experienced by Gérard de Nerval (recalled in *Corydon*, p. 146). The relevant chapter of Nerval's *Voyage en Orient*[26] is called *Les Khowals* (male dancers). These performers permitted by Moslem custom must be distinguished from 'almées' (plural: *oualem*), who were female singers, and from 'ghawasies' (female dancers). Nerval, excited by the exotic sensual dance which he witnessed, did not properly distinguish them and, as Corydon reports, only found out his mistake just in time. The event is recorded in *Corydon*, but the original text is fuller:

> There were two who were very beautiful, with a proud visage, and Arab eyes heightened by *kohl*; their cheeks were full, delicate and lightly painted. But as for the third, it must be said that a less tender sex was revealed by a week-old beard. So that examining the matter properly, and when at the end of the dance I could make out more clearly the features of the other two, I was not slow to come to the conclusion that we were dealing with 'almées' who were male. O life of the East, this was yet another of your surprises, and I was on the point of imprudently burning for one of these doubtful creatures.

Gide does not retain the final phrase 'êtres douteux'. It is curious that this text is cited to support Corydon's contention that an adolescent's beauty has no need of paint. The evidence of both Montesquieu and Nerval points equally towards another conclusion: in a different civilisation from the West it is the custom to enhance a boy's beauty with ornaments.

The East held many promises for Gide. In an acute juxtaposition of asceticism with sensual pleasure, the images of the veil, nightingale, rose and cup-bearer are witness to the doors which, as it is written in the Koran, open on to Paradise.

The Bible

Gide knew the Bible extremely well and frequently quoted from it. It is therefore surprising that none of the Biblical passages explicitly referring to homosexuality or onanism is mentioned in his writings. Corydon is silent on these matters.[27] However, the narration in 1 and 2 Samuel forms the basis of Saül, as we shall see later in Chapter 20. There is also a reference to 1 Corinthians 6 in Les Cahiers d'André Walter (p. 160): in the text this occurs at the end of the 'Cahier noir' during the final stages of the hero Allain's madness and shortly before his death. It reads: 'Know ye not that we shall judge angels' (1 Corinthians 6:3). In the manuscript contemporary with the composition of the book,[28] this quotation recurs, together with several others, notably 1 Corinthians 6:12: 'But I will not be brought under the power of any.' The words do not seem to be particularly relevant to our enquiry, but there follows the remark: 'Meditate on the end of 1 Corinthians 6.' Claude Martin (ad loc.) draws our attention to 1 Corinthians 6:12–20, 'a sermon against fornication', which tallies well with the puritanical tone of much of the book. Gide (or his hero) experiences temptation at the very moment when he denies the flesh. But it makes even better sense to treat the manuscript comment as a purely personal one, for the author's eyes alone – a 'Journal' entry in fact – for if we look at verses 9 and following we discover a specific injunction against homosexuality of which Gide was clearly well aware: 'Know ye not that the unrighteous shall not inherit the kingdom of God? Be not deceived: neither fornicators, nor idolaters, nor adulterers, nor effeminate, nor abusers of themselves with mankind. . . . And such were some of you. . . .' Unfortunately, the manuscripts do not reveal the fruit of his meditation, but we may surmise that he recognised the nature of the sin towards which he felt himself inexorably attracted.

There is, finally, a passing reference to the Sodom story in a letter from Gide to Vielé-Griffin in the summer of 1897.[29] In thanking him for his recently published collection of poems, La Clarté de vie (Paris: Mercure de France, 1897), Gide used a rather startling simile: 'An extraordinary and brilliant light [clarté] disconcerts people almost immediately: your readers are like the ancient inhabitants of Sodom, who, being suddenly dazzled by celestial light, can no longer find the doors of their houses where they might commit their former sins [leurs vieux péchés].' This is no more than a figure of speech, and does not refer literally to the content of Vielé-Griffin's poems. What it does tell us, however, is that Gide was sufficiently aware of the Biblical text to turn it into a neat compliment in praise of the compelling novelty of these poems which, in several respects, he considered were similar to his own Nourritures terrestres.

CHAPTER TWELVE

Sixteenth and Seventeenth Centuries

'I read in Taine (*Littérature anglaise*) the details of the feasts and customs of the Renaissance. Perhaps that was what true beauty is – entirely physical. Some while ago this display of riches would have left me cold. I am reading it at the right moment, when it can intoxicate me the most. My thoughts become voluptuously impious and pagan.' Gide wrote these words in June 1891.[1]

Montaigne

When we turn our attention to Montaigne we are dealing with a writer whom Gide held in very high regard. We are also in the presence of a man with whose moral outlook Gide claimed at moments he could identify. If Montaigne had a profound sense of his own humanity, seeking to understand himself and act in accordance with his nature, then this is the model which Gide wished to emulate.[2] There are references in Gide's earlier writings to Montaigne, for there does not seem to have been a period of his life when he was without a copy of the *Essais* ready to hand. On 9 June 1891 one entry among several in the 'Subjectif',[3] quoting from Flaubert, bears witness to this: '*Correspondance* III p. 296: "I re-read the chapter in old father Montaigne 'Quelques vers de Virgile'. What he says about chastity is exactly what I think, too. What is admirable is the effort – and not abstinence in itself."' Furthermore we read in *Corydon* of that conflict between nature and custom which so exercised the ancient writers and which in turn prompted Montaigne to note: 'The laws of conscience which we maintain are born of nature, derive from custom.'[4] What then is Nature? For to act according to one's nature is to ensure happiness, as Gide noted in 1929:[5] 'The words which embody the whole of his moral teaching "Happily because naturally" (*Essais*, III 36).' Nor, he again noticed in the same place, can we err in matters of health if we follow Nature.[6] To follow our instincts is not, however, to live in a correct manner, for, as Gide says:

> Yet I am aware how easy it is in [Montaigne's] case to juggle with words, and bring oneself to find in his teaching little more than the advice to yield to one's own nature and blindly follow its instincts to the point of allowing full play even to the vilest, which always seem to be the most sincere – that is to say the most natural – and which by virtue of their density and their weight, are found sturdily surviving in the ultimate deeps. . . . But this, I think, is seriously to mistake Montaigne who, although he then gives full due, perhaps more than their due, to those instincts we share with the beasts, knows how to rise above them. . . . [7]

What then in Gide's view is Montaigne's definition of vice? 'To my mind this increasingly steady reliance upon the counsels of nature alone' – which Gide sees as particularly characteristic of the 'latter part of the Essays'[8] – 'is more nearly related to the pagan wisdom of Goethe. Montaigne disclaims more and more all contentiously upright virtue: ". . . it is a vice," he declares, "to tie himselfe to any strictnesse" (III 365) . . . "Whatsoever cometh contrary to nature's course, may be combersome, but what comes according to her should ever please" (III 368)[9]. . . . And finally his concluding words: "Nature is a gentle guide: yet not more gentle than prudent and just. I quest after her track; we have confounded her with artificial traces . . ." (III 383)'.[10]

Bearing in mind Gide's great familiarity with the *Essais* it is reasonable to look at several of them in particular. We will see how they do not accord on all points with the position which Gide defends. We should first take the 'Apologie de Raymond de Sebonde' (II 12), to which reference is made in *Corydon* (p. 92), and we must particularly remember what Gide said about his difficulty in persevering with reading the 'Apologie' in 1906 and 1911.[11] In a discursive manner Montaigne comes round to speaking of the behaviour of animals, and with examples drawn from natural history finds that friendship is stronger among animals than it is among men. 'In truth animals live much more according to rule than we do ourselves, and contain themselves more moderately within the limitations dictated by Nature, but then not so exactly as to escape some comparison with our waywardness.' There follows the curious and somewhat grotesque example of the elephant who fell in love with a girl, and the extract cited by Corydon (p. 92) referring to 'certain animals who yield to the love of males' ('de leur sexe' – that is, they are also male. Corydon finds that the observation is expressed 'assez bizarrement'). Nothing more is made of this by Montaigne, who continues with examples of animals' fidelity and warlike behaviour. His argument, however, is that many things are contained in Nature, not just the ones in which we believe: 'There are countries where men are born without heads, with their eyes and mouth positioned in their chest; others where they are all androgynes [and so on].' There are, in short, many curiosities in the world, but Gide's Corydon is not interested in oddities and aberrations.

The subject of the 'Apologie' changes, but we still have material which Gide may well have noticed – for example, the following story to illustrate the uncertainty and partial nature of human knowledge:

> Solon had not sufficiently seen how debauched they were, for Diogenes, masturbating in public, declared openly among the bystanders that he wished to satisfy his belly by rubbing it. To those who asked him why he did not choose a more comfortable place to eat than in the road he said: 'It is because I am hungry in the road' [Diogenes Laertius, VI 69]. . . . These philosophers placed the highest value on virtue and refused all other disciplines than morality.

At this point we may briefly glance at *Essais*, I 23, 'De la coutume et de ne changer aisément une loy receüe', to which we have already alluded and from which Gide quoted in *Corydon* (p. 47): 'The laws of conscience which we say are born from Nature derive from Custom.' Here we read of countries where there are public male brothels and marriages between men; of other strange customs whereby, for example, while eating, men wipe their fingers on their thighs or on their testicles. These are situations where public opinion dictates our behaviour, for, as Montaigne remarks: 'Plato attempts to drive out the unnatural [*dénaturées*] and preposterous [*prépostères*] loves practised in his time by a method he considers sovereign and unassailable – namely that public opinion should condemn them, and that everyone, including the poets, should give them short shrift. And this method would ensure that the most beautiful girls do not provoke their fathers' love, nor the handsomest youths the love of their sisters.' He adds, a little later: 'Truly modesty is a fine virtue and one whose use is widely acknowledged, but if one were to consider it and bring out its value with reference to Nature, this would be as difficult to do as it is easy to base oneself on common practice in commending the value of the laws and rules of conduct.' We have seen that Gide did not care to highlight Plato's condemnation of homosexuality expressed in the *Laws*.

In 'Sur des vers de Virgile' (*Essais*, III 5), Montaigne speaks, among other things, of love, chastity and the uses of pleasure. He quotes many ancient examples (these are not cited in *Corydon*): 'There was a nation where in order to dull the lust of those who came to pray, boys and girls were kept for pleasure at the churches ['églises', that is, temples], and it was a matter of ceremony to make use of them before the service'

(Herodotus, I 199; Strabo, XVI p. 1081; and elsewhere). The philo-sopher Phaedo, we are reminded, prostituted the flower of his youth in order to earn his livelihood when his native city Elis had been captured (Diogenes Laertius, II 105). Again, Montaigne says of Measure: although Socrates is stimulated by touching shoulders with his beloved as they both read from the same book (Xenophon, *Symposium* IV 27), philosophy does not strive against 'natural desire' ('les voluptez naturelles') provided that measure and moderation are called upon too. Why are we complaisant towards youth, but not towards age? 'Among the most ugly things I count artificial beauty. . . . the ugliness of an evident and admitted old age is less old and less ugly in my opinion than another, painted and smoothed over.' This also was the opinion of Arcesilaus, whose authority is cited (Diogenes Laertius, IV 34). Again, though: '⟨Love only seems to me to be properly and naturally in season at an age close to childhood. And similarly with beauty: for Homer extends it to when the chin begins to darken and Plato himself noted it as rare;⟩ and it is a matter of note that the sophist Dion [*sic*] called the delicate hairs of adolescence "aristogitons" and "harmodians" [after the two Athenian lovers, held in public esteem as liberators of the state from tyranny].'[12] Montaigne has often seen weakness of intellect excused by beauty of body. Finally, he remarks: 'Plato makes provision in his laws [*Republic* V 468 c] for the man who has performed a noble warlike deed to receive a kiss or other amorous favour from whomsoever he wishes during the campaign without fear of refusal. What he finds so just as a reward for military virtue may surely enter into account for some other value?' This may seem to suggest – and Gide's references may enhance this impression – that Montaigne has few misgivings when dealing with the question of Greek pederasty.

In turning now to 'De l'amitié' (I 28), we will see that Montaigne did have reservations and that his attitude was equally certain whether the case was classical or modern. Here we must clearly distinguish between the profound – and some would say sentimental – friendship which Montaigne experienced towards his dearest companion Étienne de la Boétie on the one hand, and, on the other, the type of sexual friend-ship which was more honoured by the ancient Greeks than by modern society and by Montaigne himself. Perhaps, writes Montaigne, the difference could be more neatly marked by citing Cicero and Seneca, placing their writings in contrast with that 'friendship against Nature which was common among the Greeks'. As for this latter manifesta-tion, even Aristotle says that 'the wise legislator takes more care of friendship than of justice' (Aristotle, *Eth. Nic.* VIII 1). But in reporting this, Montaigne is sceptical: 'If such a free and voluntary union could come about where not only the souls but also the bodies took full delight and participated fully, it is probable that friendship would be more total and more complete; but this sex [sc. the masculine] has shown by no example that it can achieve this, and that other Greek licence [sc. pederasty] is justly abhorred by our morals. And pederasty, moreover, according to their custom, because it requires so necessary a difference between the lovers' ages and positions, did not sufficiently answer to the ideal of perfect union and agreement which we now require.' Love for boys is based only on their external beauty, Montaigne asserts, and if this friendship has any value it is only when the beloved youth is taught by example to aspire to the nobility of soul which is possessed by his adult lover.

In his rather long account of the idea of ancient boy-love we must notice two things. Firstly, that Montaigne, while idealising these relationships, is only willing to see value in them when sexuality has disappeared and the educational process has been fulfilled, resulting in the knowledge of the Good. In this he is expressing the Ideal we can read in Plato. Secondly, the friendship of which Montaigne speaks is of *equals*, conceived of as without overt sexual expression, and finding fulfilment in perfect ideal union: 'This perfect friendship of which I speak is indivisible, and each gives himself so completely to his friend that he has nothing to share with anyone else.' Boy-love, despite the claims which may justly be made for its educational value, is essentially unequal.

What did Gide think of Montaigne's affection for La Boétie? 'Nothing could be more suitable or more natural than the friendship of these two men. Montaigne reveals La Boétie as eminently worthy, not only of the affection he immediately felt for him, but also of a general esteem, respect and love. And he himself, intelligent, supple, attractive, was bound to be irresistible. . . . Lovely as this friendship may have been, one must ask whether for Montaigne it was not something of a constraint. . . .'[13]

There is evidence to show, however, that Gide was more particularly acquainted with Sainte-Beuve's appreciation of Montaigne's cult of friendship, and this has doubtless coloured his views.[14] He referred to the passage in his 'Notes de lecture' in January 1902,[15] and in his commentary on Montaigne.[16] He added a reference when this text appeared in Volume XV of his *Œuvres complètes* (pp. 16, 64). The phrase which had caught his attention was from Pliny's letters: 'I have lost the witness of my life. . . . I fear that henceforth I shall live more negligently.' This reference, of course, is here connected with the recent death of Madeleine Gide, whereas Sainte-Beuve was writing of the bonds of friendship which are most strongly forged in youth. But the article throws an interesting light on Gide's understanding of male affection. It need hardly be added that neither writer's view is a Greek one. Sainte-Beuve writes that La Boétie and Montaigne were united by

191

a bond of love and virtue. La Boétie, he says, Montaigne's elder by two years, enjoined his friend to exercise restraint: he was to follow 'the gravity of morals which is the foundation of wisdom'. Their friendship was an 'amitié-passion' which bound the two men together: 'it was born with the unexpected quickness of love'. However, Sainte-Beuve also records La Boétie's advice to Montaigne when counselling him to avoid immoral conduct (libertinage): 'For you, Montaigne, what has bound you to me for ever and despite all that may happen is the strength of nature, the most pleasing aspect of love – virtue itself.' Sainte-Beuve then quotes from La Bruyère: 'Beauty pierces us in a flash; but friendship takes time to form.' Once formed it lasts over a long period. He also quotes La Fontaine, who seems to him to have thought of friendship as being as keen as love 'and sometimes mixed with it in charming confusion. In his Deux pigeons are these husband and wife? two brothers? we do not know for sure. They could be two friends. At the end it appears that the poet was thinking of two lovers.'[17] Sainte-Beuve next discusses La Fontaine's Les Deux Amis du Monomotapa, Seneca, Montesquieu, Saint-Évremond and d'Aubigny while making the point that Montaigne's friendship was especially warm (chaleureuse). Saint-Évremond, according to Sainte-Beuve, 'returns to the common agreement of the Schools which rejects women when perfect friendship is discussed'. Sainte-Beuve enlarges on friendship between man and woman, and ends by submitting that this type of heterosexual liaison would have been too soft and delicate for Montaigne.

There are other parts of the Essais in which we may look to find material which recalls Gide's concerns with sexual morality and sexual oddities, the role of women, and the conduct of Epaminondas and of the Spartans.

Thus in 'De la force de l'imagination' (I 21) there is the story of Marie Germain, who underwent a change of sex and grew a beard, having at Vitry le François 'made some effort at jumping, and thus her virile member appeared'. The same story is reported in Montaigne's Journal de voyage and in Estienne's Apologie pour Hérodote.[18] Montaigne discourses on the coquettishness of women (we remember what is said in Corydon)[19] and recounts how the ancient Gauls thought it offensive to have commerce with women under the age of twenty.[20] Gide had noticed that Montaigne, although a lover of women, was abusive of them, and remarked that his friendship with La Boétie was more keen.[21]

Sophocles, reports Montaigne, was criticised for having praised a young boy.[22] And in the same chapter we read a study of the character of Epaminondas. Doubtless this passage and others were in Gide's mind when he penned the note in the fourth Dialogue: '[There was no shame:] See the passages from Pascal, Montaigne – and the accounts of the death of Epaminondas' (p. 160). In fact there are many references in Montaigne to Epaminondas – but none to his love of boys. He is praised for his valour and for his refusal to take riches and power (II 1 and 19; II 8 and 11). He is placed by Montaigne above Caesar and Alexander (II 36: 'Des plus excellens hommes'). In 'Sur des vers de Virgile' (III 5) the Spartan King Agesilaus' opinion on love is reported, but this is not retained in *Corydon*.

Marie Germain and contemporary events in Italy give us reason to turn for a moment to Montaigne's *Journal de voyage*, in which he described his journey to Rome undertaken in 1580. Among the unpublished documents for *Corydon*[23] are two extracts from Lautrey's edition of Montaigne's *Journal de voyage*, published in 1906. The first (p. 185) tells how Montaigne was amused at the various offers that were made for his pleasure and enjoyment as he journeyed towards Florence. 'There was nothing that they did not promise' – and the editor adds a footnote, retained by Gide, to the effect that in the early editions a note specifies 'anche ragazze e ragazzi' – both girls and boys. The second describes something which Montaigne learned at Rome (p. 248):

> In the Church of S. Giovanni Porta Latina certain Portuguese gentlemen, several years previously, had entered into a strange fellowship. They married each other, male with male, with religious solemnity, and, with the same ceremonies with which we conduct our marriages, they célebrated Easter communion together, would read the nuptial Gospel, and then slept in the same bed and lived together. . . . There were eight or nine Portuguese who were members of this fine sect.

And the editor appends a note, also copied by Gide: 'Eleven, including Spanish and Portuguese, were burned. 1578. A. d'Ancona'.[24]

Although he does not refer to them, Gide must also have noticed the story of the transsexual Marie Germain, retold here with a footnote referring to Ristelhuber's edition of Estienne's *Apologie pour Hérodote*, and an anecdote concerning the scholar Muret which leaves the reader in no doubt as to the latter's reputation. Muret is also mentioned in *Essais* I 26 ('De l'institution des enfans') as one of the best contemporary orators known to Montaigne. It is not surprising to find Montaigne in conversation with him and other scholars in Rome on the merits of Amyot's and Estienne's translations of Plutarch.[25] A footnote by Lautrey attracts our attention. Did it also attract Gide's?[26]

> Marc Antoine de Muret, born at Muret near Limoges in 1526, died in Rome in 1585, taught at the Collège de Guyenne in Bordeaux in 1547. Montaigne who was then studying logic at the Faculty of Arts in that town, counted him among his 'précepteurs [domestiques]' (*Essais*, 1582 and 1588, I 25), and while at school he acted in a Latin tragedy written by the young teacher.

193

Muret next taught the Humanities at the Collège Cardinal Lemoine in Paris. Moreri reports: 'While at Toulouse he indulged in criminal misconduct with one of his schoolboys, François Menge Frémiot by name, a native of Dijon, and was condemned in 1554 *in absentia* to be burned, together with his disciple, in the Place St Georges at Toulouse. Having been warned by a councillor of the measures which were being taken against him he fled to Italy where he found people who justly prized his merits, especially in Venice.' This last sentence is not maliciously intended.

It must surely not have escaped Gide's notice that in 1547 Muret was twenty-one-years old and Montaigne fourteen.

In the *Mercure de France* in 1896 there appeared an article by Rémy de Gourmont on the life of Étienne Dolet which Gide may well have read.[27] It is allegedly based on a seventeenth-century manuscript written by a certain 'Marcus' and is quite brief. It mentions Dolet's atheism and the 'other' crime of which he was accused, saying that here 'Marcus' is more discreet: 'If Dolet frequented youths of doubtful moral conduct and boys who were too familiar "he was motivated by a pure love of humanity and literature",' wanting to spread his philosophical and political doctrines among them. 'Marcus' tells us that ' "in order to gain their allegiance he gave apple-sugar to the youngest, while to the adolescent ephebes he offered fine books recounting the pleasures of the Olympic games, and all sorts of stories which would encourage the beauty of the soul and the taste for bodily grace." He expounded these works himself, "not being loth to strip off his clothes in order to perform the games and their due rites".'

If Gide had referred to Ristelhuber's edition of Estienne's *Apologie* he would have found several references to the prevalence of 'sodomy' in sixteenth-century France and Italy. This behaviour, it is alleged, was formerly less frequent in France; travellers learned about it when they went to Italy or Turkey. It is true, remarks Estienne, that Athenaeus reports that the ancient inhabitants of Gaul were 'addicted to this vice', but we must also remember the epigram which tells that Siena boasts of four things: its towers, its bells, its bardashes and its prostitutes.[28] Chapter 13 is specifically entitled 'On the Sin of Sodomy and the Sin against Nature in Our Age'. Sodomy is the sin which true Christians cannot even think about without a sense of horror, Estienne asserts. There is the story of Pietro Luigi Farnese, Duke of Parma and Piacenza (1545–7), who abducted the Bishop of Fano and abused him. The Bishop soon died of the disease he had thus contracted, and the Duke was so weakened by his abomination that he was unable to defend himself when finally killed with a dagger. The 'sin against nature' is different: here are stories of shepherds and their sheep, and of the

Italians with their goats during the siege of Lyon. There is an example of the transsexual behaviour of a girl who lived at Fontaines near Blois: she dressed as a man, married and was burned when the truth was discovered.

In the course of his reading Gide discovered several passages which had a more or less direct bearing on this period. Sometimes the text refers to love; sometimes to homosexuality. Thus in *Corydon* (p. 184) we have a small quotation from the sixteenth-century poetess Louise Labé: '"La lubricité et ardeur des reins n'a rien de commun, ou que bien peu, avec Amour." Débat de folie et d'amour, Discours III.' ('Lust and the fire in our loins have nothing – or only very little – to do with love.')[29] The Dialogue from which the citation is taken is simply headed: 'Cupid comes and greets Jupiter,' and the god of love warns him that the strange shapes which Jupiter assumes when courting earthly women will not guarantee true affection. To see Gide's quotation in context is to understand that the ideal of love is disinterestedness. This form of disinterestedness comes close to the notion of ideal courtly love, but is this what Gide wished to emphasize? I think not, for his citation leans more on the idea of chastity. In Labé Cupid says:

> Riches will obtain for you the love of miserly women – they will not bring love. For this desire to gain what is in a person's heart chases away true and complete Love, which does not look for its own selfish profit but seeks the advantage of the beloved. . . . Man is the only courtly and gracious being, for he can make himself subject to another's feelings, and increase his beauty and fine graces by a thousand new conceits, and can make the beholder cry, laugh, sing and grow passionate. Lust and the fire in our loins have nothing – or only very little – to do with Love. . . . Love delights in equality . . . for there is as much pleasure in being kissed as in kissing and in being in love.

Jupiter must therefore make himself less godlike and become the equal of his beloved earthly women. The notion of equality in love is, however, one which Corydon does not always keep in view.

But it is clear that except in a rather haphazard way Gide was either ill equipped or not strongly inclined to pursue the history of his subject exhaustively. He would be satisfied with references met with in the normal course of his admittedly extensive reading. Thus we come to Calderón. A note in the *Corydon* archive[30] reads: '"You must therefore be a sodomite. I can see no other reason which would oblige you to so absolute a silence." Calderón (Cabellos de Absolon) Day 1. Frequent allusions already in Gongora, Quevedo etc. In Madrid in 1636 an association was discovered, and the names of 80 prominent citizens were recorded. Two of them were publicly burned in December. See: Memorial histórico español t. XIII pp. 508 and 541.'[31] The text and

195

note, together with the reference, are given in Rouanet's French translation of Calderón's *Drames religieux*, 1898. Amon has a deep secret which he feels he cannot reveal. Jonadab replies with the witticism that he must be a sodomite; Amon retorts that Jonadab must be mad. The editor notes that although this sort of allusion is frequent in Gongora and Quevedo it is his opinion that this joke is derived from a contemporary scandal (in 1636) which he briefly outlines. We remark here that as far as Gide's argument is concerned this evidence has notably more connection with what he called 'sodomy' than with pederasty and the love of boys.

Pascal

The *Journal* records in 1905 (I p. 178) Gide's first methodical reading of Pascal's *Pensées*. He was using Brunschwicg's edition of 1904, and noted at this date (2 September 1905, p. 176) that he was principally attracted by the 'Prières pour demander à Dieu le bon usage des maladies'. Let us not forget that he had earlier integrated a related idea into his own general reflections on the 'uses' of illness: 'Illness is a source of disquiet [*inquiétude*]. Nothing can be expected from those who are "satisfied".'[32] This is in fact seen as a validation of the hero and of the individual, for 'Illness proposes a new source of disquiet to man which must be legitimised [qu'il s'agit de légitimer].' This way of thinking of the distinction and difference which an individual may epitomise is of a piece with Gide's rather botanical view of what he termed the Spartan question: 'Why did Sparta produce no great men? [We note the absence from Gide's mind of Agesilaus here.] The perfection of the race prevented the individual from being exalted. . . . the finest flowers are often given by plants which appear the most puny.' In the period when he was preparing *Corydon*, Gide frequently turned to Montaigne, but he turned even more readily to Pascal on some occasions.[33] In Pascal's *Lettres à Mlle de Roannez* which he was reading in 1908,[34] the following commentary on the needs of the flesh and of the concept of sin is to be found: 'The Jansenist has a horror of sin, but not of the flesh, and imagines the latter as by no means necessarily sinful, but [creating] a victim.' During a religious crisis in 1916 Gide reopened his Pascal[35] and felt that he could (perhaps arbitrarily) identify with his present experience that state described by the religious philosopher: ' "Our passions distract us from ourselves [nous poussent au dehors] even when exterior objects do not stir up those passions. . . . Thus philosophers say in vain 'Withdraw into yourselves, there you will find your Good'; they are not believed, and *those who do believe them are the emptiest and most foolish."* The Devil also says this to me.' The last few words are Gide's, and his comment is revealing. We should not, however, expect a man's attitudes towards sin and the demands of the flesh to remain consistent over a long period. An easy answer is not to be found by someone who prized chastity yet recognised temptation.[36]

The name of Pascal may then at first sight seem surprising in an investigation such as ours, but we must return to the argument concerning the relative importance of Nature and Custom: 'I am afraid lest this nature may not be itself but a first custom, as the first custom is a second nature' (Sect. II Pensée 93). And again: 'The nature of man is natural, *omne animal*. There is nothing that cannot be made natural. There is no natural quality that cannot be destroyed' (Sect. II Pensée 94). And again: 'Doubtless nature is not so uniform. It is custom which brings that about, by constraining nature; and sometimes nature overcomes custom and maintains a man within his instincts, in spite of all customs be they good or bad' (Sect. II Pensée 97).[37] It is clear how these can be made to fit into the debate which we noticed above had already engaged Montaigne's mind. Pensée 89 in this edition, which Gide did not quote, introduces a sequence of ideas about the relationship of Nature to Custom. 'Custom is our very nature: whoever grows accustomed to faith, believes, and can no longer not fear Hell, and does not believe otherwise. . . .' Brunschwicg comments: 'The role of custom is clearly indicated in these fragments: a belief is, in its origins, *possible*, and in this is similar to other beliefs; habit, by increasing the strength of this belief, makes it dominant, then exclusive. In consequence, it appears *necessary*, and becomes inherent in our nature.' To Pensée 94 Brunschwicg adds the note that *omne animal*, which occurs twice in the Vulgate (Genesis 7:14, and Ecclesiasticus 13:19), should be taken to mean 'every animal' and not – as he asserts Pascal takes it – 'entirely animal'. Corydon takes Pascal's sense. The third citation, from Pensée 97, is not, in Pascal, about the sexual nature of man. It reads: 'The most important thing in life is the choice of a career – and this is ruled by chance. Custom creates masons, soldiers and thatchers. . . . From having heard these skills praised and others condemned while they were yet children, men choose. . . . So great is the force of habit [*coutume*] that from what nature has made mere men, all sorts of conditions of men are made; for in some districts everyone is a mason, in others all are soldiers, etc. Doubtless nature is not so uniform.' Corydon's quotation (p. 53) begins here.

On p. 160 of *Corydon* Pascal's praise of Epaminondas is referred to. In the archive we have a surviving note in which Gide reminded himself that he should refer to 'the admirable praise by Montaigne quoted by Brunschvicg'. Pascal's Pensée (Sect. VI Pensée 353) is as follows: 'I do not admire the excess of a virtue as something of value if I do not see simultaneously an excess of the opposite virtue, as was the case with Epaminondas who had both extreme courage and extreme kindness. One does not demonstrate greatness by standing at one extreme, but rather by touching two at once and by filling in the interval between them.' Brunschvicg notes: 'This judgement is borrowed from Montaigne "Des plus excellents hommes" (II 36) (and also III 1). . . . "It is a miracle to be able to unite to such warlike actions some image of justice; but it was due to the rigour of Epaminondas that he could unite to them softness and the ease of kind, innocent and pure conduct."'

Here we move away from the more sexually explicit comments on behaviour towards those which confirm other points of Gide's moral outlook, namely chastity and self-control, the implications of temptation and extreme behaviour. Another Pensée (Sect. II Pensée 103) also suggests itself for consideration: '⟨The example of Alexander's chastity has made fewer continent men than has his drunkenness intemperate ones.⟩[38] It is not shameful to be less virtuous than him, and it seems excusable not to be more vicious than him. One believes oneself not to be sharing the vices of ordinary men when one sees oneself sharing the vices of these great men; and yet one takes no notice that in that respect they belong to ordinary men. . . . if they are greater than ourselves it is because they bear their heads higher; but their feet are as low as our own.' Here Brunschvicg adds: 'Pascal contrasts the delicacy with which Alexander treated the wife and daughters of Darius with the fury caused by his drunkenness which led him to kill Clitus and which doubtless brought about his own death. See Montaigne II 1 and 19.'

In Section XIV Pensée 922, it is true, there are allusive definitions of certain crimes among which figure 'les sodomistes', but there is no note in Brunschvicg's edition, and no explanation. In three cases (usury, simony and vengeance) Pascal gives two definitions – one of the act as a crime, but another which excuses the perpetrator.

There is a reference in the *Corydon* archive[39] to Mme de Lafayette's well-known description of Monsieur, brother of Louis XIV: 'The miracle of kindling this prince's heart was not in the power of any lady at Court.' Gide has taken this from a French history of Henrietta Maria, wife of Charles I of England. In *Corydon* itself (p. 173), the period of the French Renaissance and the reign of Louis XIII are singled out by Corydon as the times when artistic achievement and pederasty went hand in hand. Havelock Ellis, it should be added, was of the same opinion.

Bussy-Rabutin had a more salacious interest in court gossip, and Gide noted in his *Journal* in 1890 that he intended to read his '*Histoire des*

Gaules. Chap. II La France devenue italienne'.[40] To make love 'à l'italienne' was a euphemism for sodomy (and is so used of intercourse with a woman in one of the episodes in the book).[41] The pamphlet in question was published as a sequel to the *Histoire amoureuse des Gaules*, which had earned its author a period of imprisonment in the Bastille in 1665. It covers the period roughly speaking from 1670 to 1686, and describes various disorders, intrigues and acts of debauchery at court, including the behaviour of members of a certain secret society who took vows to abjure the love of women. What they did instead is darkly hinted at by the pamphleteer. The King was seriously displeased on learning about their conduct, and they were in consequence whipped or sent into exile.

Towards the end of Dialogue IV in *Corydon* Gide refers quite incidentally to La Bruyère, who in his *Caractères* (III: 'Des femmes') mentions boys he has known who, between the ages of thirteen and twenty-two, have shown a desire to be beautiful girls. Corydon's only comment is that twenty-two is rather a late age to have chosen.[42] Could Gide have selected other passages from here? He most certainly would have known of one in Chapter VI ('Des biens de la fortune') but this would only have served his purpose had he been writing a diatribe against mature and effeminate homosexuals. Eumolpe and Giton, two affected courtiers, are promenaded to satirise some of the excesses at court: the names of course recall the behaviour of the characters in Petronius' *Satyrica*.

La Rochefoucauld's maxim, 'There are people who would never have been in love if they had not heard it talked about first,' quoted in *Corydon* (p. 50) to support the proposition that society encourages us to conform, is repeated in the *Journal*, 10 February 1929, to make a similar point about conventions which are too readily accepted.

It is, in conclusion, difficult to see that Gide made a deliberate effort to represent the attitudes of these earlier writers towards the question of homosexual behaviour and to place their comments in an historical framework. What general remarks we may make with certainty are relatively few. In his reading of Montaigne in this regard Gide recognised the essayist's awareness of the complexity of human views and actions, coupled with an attempt to understand the needs of the individual in the context of the debate between Nature and Custom. The former was absolute, the latter relative. To this must be added an understanding of a philosophical stance which although Stoic in essence derived ultimately from a certain interpretation of Plato and the Academy (to which Gide himself did not subscribe). There are, in addition, the examples of the behaviour of notable men in Greek society which caught Gide's attention. He also noticed the anecdotes. We must not however overlook Montaigne's hostility to pederasty and his enthusiastic praise of reciprocated and selfless friendship between equals. Gide saw many things in Pascal's writings, but principally a certain puritanism which derived its value from the individual's effort to achieve greatness through exploration of his limits. This does not express a sexual, nor yet a social morality in this context – but rather an individual code whose resonances we shall explore later, and which buttressed Gide's thoughts in several ways at different times in his life.

CHAPTER THIRTEEN

The Enlightenment and After in France

Rousseau's education was clearly marred by his mistress Mme de Warens, Corydon asserts (p. 182), and the Spartan model would have been more beneficial for him. Perhaps the point where Rousseau was most at fault is the one mentioned by Corydon in Dialogue III. We are there reminded of Rousseau's proposition that Art was responsible for the corruption of Greek morals (*Corydon*, p. 133). This is of course an echo of Plato's diatribe against musicians and artists in the *Republic*, although 'corruption' takes on a different meaning for Plato since he is more concerned with the battle waged by truth against the imaginative inventions of playwrights. Rousseau is also referred to in *Corydon* in a section discussing the arousal of desire, and Mlle Quinault is similarly called upon (*Corydon*, p. 128) when she says: 'We have yet to decide whether all those objects which excite so many good and bad feelings within us because we cannot see them, would not have left us cold and unresponsive had we always been able to gaze upon them.'[1]

Mme d'Épinay

It is worth remaining a moment longer with Mlle Quinault, for the opinions Gide has just quoted are to be found in the *Mémoires* of Mme d'Épinay.[2] In the *Journal* he noted on 2 December 1905 that he was continuing to read and take extracts from this book, and, comparing it with what he read in Rousseau, he found the *Confessions* a more rewarding work. From this latter source he transcribed a brief anecdote about Rousseau's kindly feelings towards a man who was both a friend and a rival in love for his mistress. We will see the significance of such an attitude when we consider *Le Roi Candaule*.

The relevant section in the *Mémoires* (pp. 213–27) is the record of a conversation between five persons who included the *philosophes* the Marquis de Saint-Lambert and Duclos. Mlle Quinault, a former actress, though famous for her dramatic abilities was also considered rather fast. While the others discourse seriously about the modesty of the natural man she interjects some frivolous and facetious remarks. Mme d'Épinay is apprehensive lest she should spoil the debate. To the proposition made by Mlle Quinault that to be naked is to be natural and only ugly persons develop a sense of modesty (*pudeur*), Saint-Lambert replies that when one is alone, whether one is ugly or handsome, there is no *pudeur*. It is a matter of social convention, he asserts. Mlle Quinault agrees when Duclos supports this with the observation that *la pudeur* is put on with the rest of one's clothes every morning. The Prince believes that vice and virtue are relative to different societies, but that a universal moral sense exists. Duclos points out that savages, who at first naked, only clothed themselves because they were cold, and in reply to the Prince's idea that surely Nature was responsible for suggesting the veil of modesty, both he and Saint-Lambert exclaim that if that was Nature's first intention she would not have waited as long as she did.

Mme d'Épinay, a lady more decorous than the philosophers, remarks that modesty (*pudeur*) cannot be separated from shame: Saint-Lambert derives this feeling from a sense of imperfection. Faults confessed, says the Prince, thereby become virtues. But, adds Duclos, if you had not been given ideas of shame (*pudeur*) by your education you would not have had them. The natural man, he argues, is unaware of them. The Prince replies that it is ironic that only mankind blushes at natural things; Saint-Lambert believes it is good to follow the dictates of Nature – this will acquaint us with tender friendship. It is here that Mlle Quinault ironically makes the interjection quoted in *Corydon*: it is clear that Gide, when he used it, did so in order to suit *Corydon*'s argument and not to represent Mlle Quinault's position.

In the *Mémoires*, there follows a dithyramb by Saint-Lambert on natural marriage which, curiously enough, exhibits points of contact with material Gide also knew from his reading of Malthus and Pierre Louÿs. The Prince is puzzled by the fact that such a *natural* action as intercourse has become hidden from the general view. Duclos explains that since desire is intimately connected with possession, Man is like a dog with a bone who jealously guards what he has discovered. Jealousy is the seed of modesty, he says. We must notice that this idea is fundamental to a correct understanding of *Le Roi Candaule*. The Prince is not totally convinced, for there are surely other natural functions which are kept private – and these do not arise from jealousy. Mme d'Épinay is afraid that the conversation will get out of hand. There is a bashful modesty (*pudeur timorée*), she suggests, characterised by innocence and delicacy. But she need not have been afraid that *her* modesty will be offended, for the dinner party breaks up and the conversation comes to an abrupt end. Her conclusion is a reflection on the central concern of the guests and on Rousseau's *Discours sur l'inégalité* (1755): 'Unless one is insane one cannot hope to bring Man back to the state of Nature.' The question which the whole of this discussion neatly raises for an understanding of *Corydon* is the relative merit of the arguments for and against Nature and Custom. But it will also be noticed that Gide is far from advocating Duclos' libertarian attitude in its totality.[3]

'The important thing is not to get cured, but rather to live with one's ills' ('L'important n'est pas de guérir, mais bien de vivre avec ses maux')[4] is an aphorism attributed by Corydon to the Abbé Galiani, who was writing to Mme d'Épinay, but the phrase does not occur in the standard edition of the Abbé's *Correspondance*.[5] In fact the Abbé, who considered his life in Naples to be a form of exile from the witty society of Paris, made remarks in his frequent letters to Mme d'Épinay which seem to indicate a different outlook on life.[6] What may be no more than a curious coincidence must be noted here, although an explanation of it might be sought in the confusion of quotations on small scraps of paper with which Gide worked. We know that the phrase in question appears in the 1911 edition of *Corydon*; we also know that Gide began work seriously on *Les Caves du Vatican* in that year. The epigraph to Book V of the latter work bears closely on our subject. It is a quotation, in English, from Conrad's *Lord Jim* which, but for the fact that we know its pedigree, might seem to be the English sentence from which Galiani's French was made: 'strictly speaking, the question is not how to get cured, but how to live.'[7] Whatever the truth of the matter, both these quotations, which are so very similar as to awaken our suspicions, have clearly been chosen to underline the state of responsible self-awareness which should be the hallmark of a hero. Finally, it is perhaps of some interest to note that Gide made no mention of the Abbé's *Dialogue sur les femmes* which would surely have attracted his attention had he perused it. In this *Dialogue*, Galiani's Marquis disagrees with the Chevalier's proposition that woman is naturally weak and prone to illness, whereas man is strong. He replies that all this is an aspect of corruption in society, and not a state of nature. Corydon could have used this argument to good advantage.

Diderot

The debate between Nature and Custom also provides the main subject of Diderot's *Supplément au voyage de Bougainville*. Among the notes printed in Gide's *Journal* and placed after the year 1911[8] is an extract from this dialogue in which character 'A' asks his friend 'B' what he understands by the word 'mœurs' (morals, or customs). 'B' replies: 'I understand a general obedience to, and behaviour dependent on, laws which may be good or bad. If the laws are good, people will behave well, etc.' This particular point is one which Gide also encountered in Montesquieu,[9] but its consequences in Diderot's argument take us further, and illuminate a paradox concerning our assumptions as to what is acceptable behaviour in society.

'B' continues: 'How do you expect people to observe the law when they are told rules which contradict each other?' He specifies three such sets of rules: the natural, the civil and the religious codes. These, he maintains, have never been in agreement, and people are therefore forced to disobey one or the other of them. The conclusion we should perhaps draw from this, suggests Diderot, is that the civil law, which we would do well to obey in order to avoid anarchy, should be modelled on the 'natural law'. But what is the Law of Nature, the reader might ask? The topic, as the dialogue has revealed, is well illustrated by the example of the inhabitants of Tahiti. A Rousseauistic praise of the virtues of living a natural life forms a substantial part of 'Les Adieux du vieillard' (section II of the *Supplément*) in which an Elder predicts the troubles consequent upon the arrival of Europeans and their civilisation in the Pacific. This is followed (section III) by a discussion between a priest (l'Aumônier) and an inhabitant of Tahiti ('L'Entretien de l'Aumônier et d'Orou'). The island is presented as a paradise where no false sense of shame sullies the naturalness of the sexual act, and where the birth of children is always a cause for rejoicing no matter what their parentage. Tahitian morality (*honnêteté*) is good because it is natural; Christianity is 'contrary to nature' when it enjoins chastity, marital fidelity and celibacy. In Tahiti, Orou tells us, libertinism as understood by Christians does not exist, but the islanders have their own definition of immoral behaviour (section V). Since sexual immaturity, sterility, old age or congenital defect (*vice de naissance*) will either yield no children or children who are less than perfect, persons within these classes who engage in the sexual act are considered to do so 'un-naturally'. Thus the Tahitians know of no absolute prohibition against fornication, incest and adultery, the moral good in the island being the pursuit of 'the general good and individual utility'. 'Vice de naissance' is not further defined, but it seems to me unlikely to mean homosexuality, since Diderot is only discussing heterosexual unions which culminate in children. Orou demonstrates by his arguments the hypocrisy of Christian virtue, and emphasises the value of acting in accordance with the rules of Nature. Are not the inhabitants of Tahiti remarkable, he asks, for their bravery and their beauty?[10] This is a sentiment with which Corydon agrees.

The concluding section of the *Supplément* discusses marriage, sexual behaviour and *pudeur* (modesty; sense of shame). According to character 'B', 'Vices and virtues – all are equally present in Nature.'[11] 'B' is forced to agree with 'A' on a series of propositions: that marriage, courtship (*galanterie*), flirtation (*coquetterie*), constancy, fidelity and jealousy are all 'natural'. As for 'pudeur', 'B' will only agree that 'the joys of love are followed by a weakness which makes one vulnerable to one's enemy', for, he maintains, any other aspect of it is the direct result of a definition imposed by society. He adds, referring to part of the Aumônier's report which he has not read out aloud, that men in Tahiti are not ashamed of 'involuntary' signs of sexual attraction. It is, he continues, only when women become the property of men, and 'furtive enjoyment is seen as theft', that the words 'pudeur', 'retenue' (restraint) and 'bienséance' (decency) come to be used. Here he perceives the origin of imaginary vices and virtues which erect barriers between the sexes and inhibit the natural expression of affection. 'B' also has some remarks to make on 'volupté' (sexual pleasure) which he believes is more marked in women, for, as he says, men are more direct and more sure of themselves. We return to two points expressed by 'B' towards the end of the dialogue, which have clearly helped to shape the opinions formulated by Corydon although they have not been expressly stated in Gide's book. The first is an assertion that what has contributed to the unhappiness of the human race is the fact that society has engendered an artificial man who has been grafted on to our ancestor the natural man. The second is the statement that whoever on his own initiative contravenes a law which he considers bad thereby authorises other citizens to break any other law, even if it is a good one. Diderot does not refer to irregular (that is, homosexual) behaviour in the *Supplément*, and concentrates on the general question of naturalness and freedom in the sexual sphere.

The edition of Diderot's *Œuvres choisies* from which Gide quoted the foregoing extract also contains the *Entretien entre d'Alembert et Diderot* and *Le Rêve d'Alembert*. It does not include *La Suite de l'Entretien*, but it would be very surprising indeed if Gide had not read the last-named work in another edition. In fact none of these three works is specifically mentioned in the *Journal* or in *Corydon*, and this is perhaps curious because Diderot addresses himself in these dialogues to some moral questions which are directly relevant to Gide's discussion of nature and society. In *Le Rêve* Mlle de l'Espinasse's 'mad idea' that 'Man is perhaps only a monstrous version of Woman – or *vice versa*'[12] is supported by Dr Bordeu's evidence of physical similarities between the genital organs of the two sexes. Later in the same discussion Bordeu explains how the emission of seminal fluid is a pure case of physical action and reaction. His explanation appeals to mechanical laws and does not depend on the need for the propagation of the species (p. 360).

In the *Suite* Bordeu and Mlle de l'Espinasse pursue their discussion into more delicate areas. Bordeu develops his argument in favour of masturbation, for the 'results of rigorous continence are dire, especially in the case of young persons.'[13] Nature, he avers, should be given a helping hand, although he admits he would not doff his hat in the street to someone who he knew practised these habits. Even so, he can envisage that these actions can be solitary or shared with 'a similar being, male or female, for one's sex – or even the use of one's sex – is of no importance in this case' (p. 379). He replies to Mlle de l'Espinasse, who reflects that she is trying to square 'these combinations which seem contrary to nature', with the statement of his view of Nature. 'Everything which exists can be neither contrary to nature nor outside nature – and I don't even exclude chastity and deliberate continence which would be in the forefront of crimes against nature (if one could sin against nature), and among the greatest crimes against the social laws of a country in which actions are weighed in other scales than those of fanaticism and prejudice' (p. 380). They then discuss interspecific sexuality. 'From where,' Bordeu is asked, 'do these abominable appetites arise?' He answers with the final words of the *Suite*: 'Everywhere from a poverty of organisation among youth, and from corruption in the minds of older persons; from the attraction of beauty in Athens, from the lack of women in Rome, from the fear of the pox in Paris. Adieu' (p. 385). He has not mentioned homosexuality explicitly, but we are free to imagine that he had this topic in mind. The interesting aspect of Bordeu's libertarian attitude is that it is founded on a healthy observance of Nature's laws. He, too, has the reputation of being a person of the purest moral standing (p. 379).

After the publication of *Corydon* Gide continued to find memorable phrases in Diderot's writings which brought the issue of pederasty to the fore, even when the philosopher clearly had had no intention of speaking out publicly on the question. Hence the *Journal* entry for 4 October 1931, discussing the obtuseness of people unacquainted with homosexuality, refers obliquely to a sentence in a letter to Sophie Volland which had been printed in the *Nouvelle Revue Française* 1 March 1929 (pp. 353–63). Gide's eye had been caught by a curious example used to illustrate the courage needed to avoid hypocrisy. Diderot had written: 'But one must be very courageous to be open about everything. It is perhaps easier to accuse oneself of intending to commit some great crime than of harbouring some small, obscure, vile and low feeling [un petit sentiment obscur, vil et bas]. It would perhaps cost one less to note down: "I have wished to obtain the throne at the expense of the life of its occupant" than to write: "One day I was at the baths with a large number of young men, and I noticed one of them who was strikingly beautiful and I could not in the least resist going up to him"'

(p. 355). It is scarcely to be doubted that Gide would have rejected Diderot's hostile description of these feelings, while still agreeing with the need for honesty illustrated by the anecdote.

Bayle and Voltaire

The friend who suggested to Gide that he should read Bussy-Rabutin also indicated the article on Thomas Sanchez from Bayle's *Dictionnaire historique et critique* and pointed him towards Voltaire's *Dictionnaire philosophique*. All three names occur together in a manuscript reading list which can be dated shortly before 1891.[14] Bayle's article must have been something of a disappointment. Sanchez was the author of *Disputationes de sancti matrimonii sacramento*, which was first printed in 'Genoa' (but really in Madrid) in 1602. There were several re-editions. The book caused a great scandal, for although the Spanish Jesuit in question was renowned for his sobriety, chastity and application to study, it was this latter quality which had enabled him to list in detail for the benefit of confessors all the shocking and aberrant behaviour of which married couples were capable. The fairly long article in the *Dictionnaire* alerts the curious reader to the existence of Sanchez' 'scandalous' book, and Bayle was criticised for publicising it. He did not, however, cite examples, and so Gide, who very probably never read the work itself, was not much the wiser. Nevertheless, we should bear in mind Corydon's remarks about the occurrence of irregular behaviour within marriage.[15]

Voltaire's *Dictionnaire philosophique*, first published in 1764, is more fruitful, but the tone of the articles in question is undoubtedly hostile to pederasty. In the first ('Amitié'), friendship is defined as contact between two souls when both persons are virtuous and responsive, and Voltaire takes care to exclude debauchees, courtiers and self-interested parties from the category of friends. He notes that 'the Greeks and the Arabs were more enthusiastic in their friendships' than the French of his own day. This leads him to observe that 'friendship was a point of religion and of law' among the Greeks. In illustration he cites the Sacred Band of Thebans, which, he says disparagingly, some people have wrongly taken for a band of sodomites. Nothing could have been further from the truth, he adds. Nevertheless, 'pederasty was unfortunately tolerated in Greece – but the law must not be held responsible when it is shamefully abused'. Much the same theme is spun out at greater length in the article on pederasty itself ('Amour nommé

207

socratique'), and Voltaire here offers an explanation for the existence in nature of so unnatural a vice. In youth, he suggests, the sexual instinct is often misled, for although heterosexual desire awakens at an early age, the fact that adolescent boys often look effeminate means that when they are brought up with persons of their own sex their inclination is to seek out something which looks like the natural (that is, heterosexual) object of their love. There is, he thinks, more excuse in warm climates for such confusion and such behaviour, and he is filled with disgust at the thought of passions of this sort 'in a Dutch sailor, or in a Muscovite canteen-keeper'. Next he returns to the Greeks and the Theban Band of youthful warriors instituted by Laius (sic), not wishing to see in them anything other than the finest example of the achievements of discipline, 'for each swore to die for his friend'. He is very sceptical of the existence of laws promoting homosexual practices in ancient Persia, though he acknowledges the widespread occurrence of boy-love in Rome despite the provisions of the Lex Scantinia.[16] It was, he says, the third-century AD Roman Emperor Philip who revived this law and chased the boy prostitutes from the city. Voltaire's attitude is neatly summed up in his exclamation: 'No. It is not in human nature to enact a law which contradicts and violates nature – a law which would extinguish the human race if it was observed to the letter.' His emotional hostility is so great that it seems he has forgotten to distinguish between a law which enjoins a particular action and one which merely allows it.

Editors of the *Dictionnaire philosophique* generally print additional matter from the 1769 edition concerning the burning of Deschaufours when the Abbé Desfontaines, who had been accused of sodomising boy chimney sweepers, had been let off. This contemporary manifestation of victimisation provoked Voltaire into protesting against a travesty of justice rather than upholding the value of a sodomitical way of life. The third of the relevant articles on love ('Amour') is about heterosexual passion. It does, however, use examples from the animal kingdom, citing horses (which enjoy sexual contact) and fishes (who, unfortunately for them, have no contact). Man is described as happier and superior to them both in so far as his amorous experience engages his whole body. He can also make love whenever he so desires. The only drawback which Voltaire perceives is the presence of venereal disease, which, as he acidly remarks, arose not from debauchery but from the innocent haunts of the natural savage. Is it not odd, he comments, that Nature should be so anti-natural: 'but all is doubtless for the best.' Although several of the ideas expressed in these articles find their counterparts, either with agreement or denial, in *Corydon*, we unfortunately cannot know precisely how Gide reacted when he first encountered them.

Among the points raised by Corydon there are several which in their original context were not directly related to homosexuality. They must, however, be taken into consideration because of the part they play in his argument. They concern the role of mistresses, the stimulation of desire and the ideal of chastity. For example, Gide noticed a wide variety of quotations which he thought might sustain Corydon's argument in a more general manner. One, taken from Beaumarchais' *Le Mariage de Figaro*, and not in fact carried forward into *Corydon*, has a bearing on the relationship between man and wife:[17] 'Truly, Suzanna, I have often thought that if we pursue elsewhere that pleasure which our legitimate wives afford us, it is because they do not sufficiently study the art of sustaining our interest, of renewing their love and reanimating, in a manner of speaking, the attraction of our possessing them by the charms of variety.' In the context of the play this is an excuse for the Count's inconstancy and immorality. We shall never know how Corydon would have deployed it, for its libertine message appears to denigrate the role of the wife, and this, one assumes, would not have met with his approval. Perhaps it could have found a place among the remarks about heterosexual immorality. It is, incidentally, noticeable that Gide makes no comment on the advances which the Count mistakenly makes to the page Chérubin.

Laclos' *Les Liaisons dangereuses*, we are told by Gide in 'Les Dix Romans français que . . .',[18] exhibits an example of how 'debauchery begins at the point where love and pleasure are no longer connected', but the book can also be seen to offer the reader a mechanism similar to that employed by Henry Fielding in *Tom Jones*: Danceny experiences a pure love for the young and beautiful Cécile Volange (*Corydon*, p. 183), and in this case the older woman – Mme Merteuil – takes advantage of his idealism to become his mistress. Similarly, says Corydon (p. 182), Hugo in *Les Misérables* persuades the reader that Marius would more readily have had a casual affair with another girl than he would have mentally lifted the hem of the dress of his idealised sweetheart Cosette. These examples both pave the way for Corydon's assertion that the uranist can similarly respect the woman (or man) he most profoundly worships.

Stendhal

In *De l'amour*[19] Stendhal has nothing to say about homosexual love; in *Vie d'Henry Brulard* there is, it is true, an extremely affectionate depiction of his feelings for a young manservant when he himself was but a boy. However, he must be considered here because of his short novel *Armance* and the preface which Gide wrote for it in 1921.[20] There are many references to Stendhal in Gide's *Journal*, but the most significant praise bestowed on the author of *Armance* was that he served him as a whetstone for his mind, not as a model to be slavishly imitated.[21] In a conversation, recorded in the *Journal* on 5 January 1902, the talk turned to Stendhal's attitude to love and women. Gide thought that Stendhal felt much more *interest* in women than love for them, and that he paraded his wit rather than his body. There is no mention here of a possible sensitivity on Stendhal's part to masculine beauty or male sentimentality. Examples of both these feelings can in fact be found in the pages of *La Chartreuse de Parme*.

Gide knew *Armance* well and re-read it with great enthusiasm as he prepared to write his preface for it. There is an early reference to the hero of the novel in his manuscript 'Voyage en Bretagne' of 1889[22] when, conscious of the social barriers which separated him from the common people and the pleasures he desired, he wrote: 'And when I am surrounded by fishermen's sons and I watch them swimming, I involuntarily think of Octave.' Stendhal's work describes the love which comes into being between Octave, a rich but impotent young nobleman, and Armance, a poor refugee of noble family. Each has reasons, real or imaginary, for giving the other the impression that his (or her) deep love is not truly reciprocated. Their love is resolved, and the marriage takes place, at the price of Octave's immediate departure for the Greek War of Independence – and death. Octave's impotence is a secret he cannot reveal; and Armance does not want to be mistaken for a mere fortune-hunter. It is on Octave's belief that is it impossible to declare his love that Gide focuses. In doing so he incidentally uses three examples he deployed in *Corydon*. They are Fielding's *Tom Jones*, Hugo's *Les Misérables*, and Louise Labé (with the same quotations). They all describe a dichotomy between 'pure love' and 'carnal desire' which appealed to Gide. He considers whether an impotent person (*impuissant*) can fall in love, and then passes on to comment on Stendhal's own experience with women, returning to the topic of the divorce between love and pleasure. 'If a grain of passion enters one's heart, then a grain of possible *fiasco* also enters,' Gide quotes from *De l'amour*. Stendhal, he remarks, describes his hero in such a way that his impotence is not betrayed by his physical appearance: contrary to general opinion, such people are not necessarily effeminate, nor do they possess falsetto voices. Gide cites a case with which he is personally acquainted and which he tried to solve with the help of a pretty young actress. Thus pleasure (*volupté*) can remain divorced from love, he concludes. It is of course axiomatic that sufferers from impotence will never in fact have such a choice. Gide then advances his opinion that an impotent love can sometimes free itself, and even achieve a greater ecstasy, in so far as it does not seek carnal satisfaction. He does not believe that Stendhal is interested in the case of an *abnormal* person – the case of Octave is a *particular* case.[23] The remainder of the preface consists of some solutions to Octave's problem suggested by Gide: 'I imagine Octave marrying Armance; I imagine her puzzled at first, then sad and resigned (– I only speak here of the resignation of love; but for many women having to renounce motherhood is doubtless much more cruel and long lasting).' He concludes by returning to the topic he has often considered: the tragedy of the alcove is among the most dreadful mankind can know. A way of avoiding this is offered to whoever is able to experience a love divorced from carnal desire.

Cristallisation is the name Stendhal gave to an operation in the lover's mind which endows the beloved with qualities which are not necessarily present. This in turn gives rise to *fiasco*, and creates barriers for the lovers. We will see that this has a part to play in the love of Édouard and Olivier in *Les Faux-Monnayeurs*, but long before that date Gide had written in his *Journal* in 1887–8: 'Enthusiasms lie hidden within us . . . but the object of admiration is not important – admiration matters most (Stendhal, 'cristallisation').'[24]

Balzac

Balzac's name does not appear significantly in the main text of *Corydon*, but Gide does mention him in the course of his open letter to Porché (1928) printed as an appendix to the current edition. It would of course be absurd to assume that silence means that Gide was not acquainted with certain novels included in the *Comédie humaine*, but his reading list, the 'Subjectif', brings some welcome detail. The titles in question are these:

La Fille aux yeux d'or (read 8 February 1892);
Illusions perdues (read 19 February 1892);
Splendeurs et misères des courtisanes (read 27 February 1892);
La Dernière Incarnation de Vautrin (read 2 March 1892);
Séraphita (read 10 October 1892);
Louis Lambert (recorded under two dates: July 1890 ('re-read'), and March 1893);
Le Père Goriot (4 November 1889; 13 February 1892; July 1893).

We do not of course know whether these notes indicate complete readings of the texts (it appears doubtful that they do in some cases). Gide also records reading *Le Cousin Pons* (18–25 January and September 1892). This novel portrays a close sentimental friendship between two men no longer in their prime. I doubt whether it could – with propriety – be called a 'homosexual novel'. For the sake of discussion these works may be roughly separated into two groups, namely those novels where the character Vautrin appears, and those books which, like Gautier's *Mademoiselle de Maupin*, describe an ideal creature of indeterminate (but angelic) sexual status.

Alluding to *Le Père Goriot*, and comparing Oscar Wilde to Vautrin, Gide wrote to his mother on 28 January 1895: 'He seems to have depraved him [Lord Alfred Douglas] to the marrow, like a Vautrin who is, I think, more terrible than the character of that name in *Le Père Goriot* – because he does everything in the name of aestheticism.' Gide's paradox is almost worthy of Wilde himself. The context of his remark leaves it unresolved as to whether he has homosexuality – or corruption in a more general sense – in mind. He never discussed homosexuality openly with his mother in his letter, although he did refer to Wilde's 'compromising' presence and to Douglas being 'devoured by an unwholesome thirst for infamy' in a letter he wrote to her on 30 January 1895.

'In speaking of Balzac,' Gide wrote later to Porché, 'you seem not to know his extraordinary *Vautrin* – the play whose run was curtailed by the censor (?) in 1840' (*Corydon*, p. 192). Gide was aware of the story behind the composition of *Vautrin*, and the play's subsequent problems with the political censor.[25] However, his *Journal* entry for 26 April 1918 speaks of his amazement on reading it: 'Had I read it already?' If he had, he adds, he cannot have been paying attention for 'this is where we can catch Balzac unawares – much more so than in *Le Père Goriot* and *Illusions perdues*. This is where he makes a more significant confession.' Gide underlined all the passages which could be quoted in this context, and 'especially the dialogue with Raoul de Frescas.' Here, then, he says, is Vautrin without the mask (*Corydon*, p. 192). Indeed the character of Vautrin has provoked various comments. In the play he is a social outcast, but one with a conscience and a need to protect the weak. It is he himself who has a weakness, however, for attractive youths – and this is why he extends his 'protection' to Raoul de Frescas, who has been dispossessed of his fortune. He educates the young man and instils in him a love of truth and virtue.[26] One might be inclined to see this as an ideal education were the play not so impossibly melodramatic. Despite Gide's implied judgement that the relationship was pederastic, *Vautrin* was probably censored because the chief actor dared to caricature Louis-Philippe.

Philippe Berthier[27] bases his interpretation of passages in *Splendeurs et misères des courtisanes* on contemporary awareness of the widespread occurrence of homosexual practices in prisons and in the hulks, where convicts were chained together, producing a pattern of devoted 'clients' and 'servants'. As he says, we must read between the lines and pay attention to hints that a man's appearance or behaviour may be effeminate. Thus the relationship between Lucien and Vautrin seems to him not only far from being aberrant but 'to obey a law of nature', since the youth is this man–woman ('cet homme–femme'), and Vautrin, who is characterised by his abundant body hair, is a veritable 'homme–homme'. Nor can Vautrin be seen as a 'common pederast': and Berthier's analysis of the relationship with Lucien brings out the extent to which Balzac is also dependent on the Romantic tradition of the satanic hero. It is indeed this last element which, it seems to me, separates the demonic manipulative power of Vautrin from the sentimentalism of Le Cousin Pons. Generally speaking, Berthier argues, sexuality must be seen as an aspect of the power relationships described in Balzac's novels. Homosexuality is not the whole of Vautrin's character, he adds; but without it he is not fully comprehensible. From a need to counter the structure and forces of society Vautrin is necessarily 'pedagogue and pederast', according to Berthier, for homosexuality transcends all social boundaries.

Vautrin also devotes himself to Eugène de Rastignac (in Le Père Goriot), and in the course of the narrative confronts his young protégé with advice on how to succeed in society. Moreover, the reader is very aware that the conversation, by the particular way in which Vautrin deploys his arguments, represents something like a metaphysical seduction of the young man. Eugène is innocent, and we are witnessing the perversion of his naive provincial virtue. Vautrin's physical strength is a symbol of his power to subvert society, not an indication of the homosexual charm his body may exert on adolescents. As Hunt has written: 'The only hint of turpitude [sic] in Vautrin's relations with men is made in regard to Théodore Calvi, one of his galley-associates whom he saves from execution in La Dernière Incarnation. Vautrin has a mania for devoting himself to handsome young men. . . . He is a woman hater . . . "Pour moi la femme n'est belle que quand elle ressemble à un homme" ["I only find a woman handsome when she's like a man"]' (p. 365).[28] But it is not clear whether the 'resemblance' is to be thought of as physical, moral – or both. Lucien de Rubempré is the young hero of Illusions perdues who is rescued from a watery suicide at the end of the novel by the timely arrival of Vautrin ex machina. He is then transported to Paris as the older man's secretary, and another work of 'education' begins. The purity of this relationship has also been suspected. Lucien is described as 'almost like a woman' ('une femme manquée')[29] but this is perhaps merely a particular stereotype of a youth of the Romantic period. Vautrin's affection for him is not jealous, but supremely paternal. On occasion, as Hunt remarks (p. 365), it could also be called maternal. His grief knows no bounds when he learns of Lucien's suicide. Are we then right in concluding with Hunt: 'All this is significant enough, but it is gratuitous to suppose that it was only Balzac's discretion that prevented him from suggesting physical depravity [sic] between the two' (p. 365)? If Balzac had described 'physical depravity' this would undoubtedly have undermined the sympathy, understanding and admiration he wished to arouse in the reader. In a word it would surely have been impossible for him to have been explicit in this regard, even if he had wished to be so, and we are left perhaps with the sole resource of paying attention to M. de Charlus and Gide as they read between the lines. To the pure all things might be pure, but there is sufficient emotional power in the depiction of Vautrin's relationships for them to be considered homosexual by a reader committed to that interpretation. We might surely add that Gide would have been particularly sensitive to the portrayal of an older man taking care to 'protect' and 'educate' a younger one. He passed no comment on Lucien's effeminacy.

Before considering our second grouping of works from the *Comédie humaine* a word ought to be said about a heroine who is in fact far from angelic. This is Paquita in *La Fille aux yeux d'or*. She is a lesbian, object of the passion of de Marsay and his half-sister. De Marsay pursues her, and determines to kill her when he finds out that he has in fact been used as a 'front'. His half-sister beats him to it, and slashes the girl to death. It is of course difficult for the reader not to see in all this a heightening of the excitement of passion by the use of melodrama, but the important point for our purpose is to notice that Paquita's love for de Marsay has been occasioned by his effeminate appearance. Members of both sexes may sometimes thus be observed to resemble each other, as we will see in discussing Gautier, and the circle of elegant young men to whom de Marsay belongs provides the very epitome of a somewhat immoral dandyism.

With *Louis Lambert* and *Séraphita* we are dealing with a more occult expression of the power of souls to transcend their earthly envelope. Briefly, *Louis Lambert* is conceived as the story of a schoolboy contemporary of Balzac, and it charts the hero's metaphysical development through early manhood towards love, marriage, madness and an early death. He reaches a plane of 'angelic existence', so to speak, where, in an echo of Swedenborg's doctrine of revelation, he achieves his state of lucidity through contemplation of the soul. Hunt (p. 51) reminds us that 'in an afterthought added to the text in 1842 Balzac suggests that the true reason for [Lambert's] collapse had been the realisation that the physical pleasures of marriage would be an obstacle' to such a state of internal perfection.

While expanding the final version of *Louis Lambert*, Balzac was working on *Séraphita*. This is another novel to some extent inspired by Swedenborg's writings, and in it Balzac develops further the figure of an angel on earth. The central character (one hesitates between the name of hero and heroine) is androgynous. This mythical person, who appears to Wilfrid as a beautiful woman and to Minna as a strong, wise man, is the incarnation of someone who has passed beyond mere earthly love. However absurd the book may appear – and it is far from being one of Balzac's most persuasively realistic productions – it expresses through the person of Seraphita–Seraphitus certain Illuminist ideals which were current at the time of its composition. What a modern reader may make of this 'transsexualism' is of course another matter. Gide has not vouchsafed us his opinion, but we would do well to place the book beside *Mademoiselle de Maupin*, of which it is a less sensational and more didactic companion.[30]

Flaubert

We may enter upon a digression here with Flaubert because of the way in which he perceived the relationship of literature to documentary testimony and to observed reality. Whereas Balzac was clearly willing to believe himself capable of exploring metaphysical phenomena, Flaubert anchored his imaginary world in historical fact, even when he was portraying the nightmarish temptations which assailed the fourth-century ascetic St Antony. He revealed a sexual world which was hitherto unknown to the nineteenth-century reader, and it is interesting to see how Gide reacted to it.

La Tentation de Saint Antoine, which is mentioned on several occasions in *Les Cahiers d'André Walter*,[31] appealed to Gide because it evoked in his mind the profoundly disturbing conflict between asceticism and sensual temptation. On 28 February 1889 he noted that he had 'shivered' as he read the text aloud, and he found the dialogue between the Chimaera and the Sphinx in section VII especially powerful.[32] He had no comment to make on section V which features Cybele, the *gallus* (or high priest) of her cult, and Attis who castrated himself in furtherance of his mystical worship of the goddess.

On 10 February 1890 Gide recorded having read an article by H. Fouquier on Flaubert's *Salammbô*,[33] and he was later, in 1908, to note that he had read another one on the same novel by Pezard in the *Mercure de France*.[34] Pézard's article he found 'foolish', because it insisted on considering this historical novel as if it was historical *fact*.

'What a splendid book,' Gide exclaimed, adding that it had gone up in his estimation on a second reading. 'It is perhaps somewhat childish – but it is a poet's childishness and this disarms criticism.' Flaubert, so Gide asserted, sought an authorisation in his documents, and his intention was not slavishly to repeat facts. But among these 'facts' – and Gide does not comment on this – are certain details describing male love. With some exaggeration, Flaubert wrote to Jules de Goncourt at the beginning of October 1861 that the section of his novel on which he was working was 'A shower of shit and a procession of pederasts'. The book is savage, but it is also beautiful. Among the details relevant to our enquiry we may note the attribution of certain effeminate manners to some contingents (especially the Lydians) in the Barbarian army, and, most striking of all, the episode when pairs of lovers are ordered by the triumphant Carthaginians to slaughter each other. Presumably Flaubert modelled his account on material drawn from Plutarch and other ancient sources.[35] But nowhere does Flaubert describe the sentimental educational aspect of pederasty which would have found an echo in Gide's mind. There is a passing reference in *Corydon* (p. 95) to the observations on the sexual behaviour of partridges in Flaubert's *Bouvard et Pécuchet*, but nothing is said of these heroes' attempts to educate Victor and deal with his 'bad habits'.

Gautier

With Théophile Gautier we return to the point at which we left Balzac, and consider the metaphysical notions implicit in the image of the androgyne. But we are now dealing with a creation which is more sensual and more titillating than *Séraphita* or the mere loves of the angels. Gide records having first read Gautier's *Mademoiselle de Maupin*[36] towards the end of December 1889. He remarked that he disliked the style. He also found Gautier's preface absurdly intransigent. However, 'The double love of Rosalind is charming and the night shared between Frédéric and Rosette is a poetry of which dreams are made. [(Rosette-Théodore-d'Albert)].'[37] *Mademoiselle de Maupin* is again referred to in *Corydon* (p. 141) where an extract is quoted from Chapter IX of the book.[38] Mademoiselle de Maupin, like many members of the 'third sex', is a hero–heroine, promising all things to both men and women.

The novel has a heroine *en travesti*, and critics have called attention to links between the book and Shakespeare's *As You Like It*. It will be remembered that in the play, which Gautier's characters enact in the course of the story (Chapter XI), Orlando is in love with Rosalind, and that when they seek refuge in the Forest of Arden, Rosalind disguises herself as a youth. Phoebe, a shepherdess, falls in love with this supposed young man, but there is also the important scene (Act 3, scene 2) in which Rosalind, in disguise, persuades Orlando to treat her as if she was the person with whom he is in love. She thus invites him to love her as a man. This will, she asserts, cure him of his love for Rosalind, remarking as she does so that both boys and women are fickle in their loves. It is also important to note that when Rosalind first disguises herself as Ganymede, she considers her 'manliness' as in outward appearance only: '[In my heart] lie there what woman's fear there will . . . swashing and a martial outside. . . .' On 10 February 1890 Gide noted, after reading *As You Like It*: 'It is the *genre*, rather than the play itself, which I find most attractive. . . . The idea of the sonnets and madrigals pinned to the trees is delicious – and so is the notion of the pretended love of Phoebe for Rosalind.'[39]

Gautier, it need hardly be said, was writing within a different tradition. What he is able to exploit is the Romantic notion of an androgynous soul,[40] and he explores the realm of perversion in a way reminiscent of Baudelaire. One recent editor was clearly upset by this: 'If one is a normal (or nearly normal) reader, and if one thinks that it is natural to love according to the rules of nature, one will hardly notice the slightly "free" pages entailed by the depiction of a beloved woman *en travesti*.'[41] The section referred to extends over Chapters VIII and IX, culminating with a confession in Chapter X. But the passage which Gide prints is in fact about love in antiquity. It has a place in *Mademoiselle de Maupin* as part of the hero's self-explanation; in *Corydon* its purpose is rather to lend weight to the long history of pederasty. 'The strange loves of which the ancient poets write in their elegies, and which so greatly surprise us, being beyond our imaginings, are therefore likely and possible . . .'; and the habit of modern translators who substitute female for male pronouns 'only shows how little we have understood the genius of antiquity'. It would be interesting to look in closer detail at this text.

Gautier, through the mouthpiece of his narrator, declares the hermaphrodite to have been 'one of the most ardently cherished but empty dreams [*chimères*] of idolatrous antiquity', and proceeds to a fairly lascivious description of the well-known statue of Hermaphroditus. But the morality of antiquity will always have to be confronted with the 'virtues' of Christianity, he writes. Thus: 'Virginity . . . was unknown in the ancient world – a flower without a fruit. . . . That vigorous and healthy world would have trampled it underfoot. The three words "virginity", "mysticism" and "melancholy" were unknown to the ancients, and are three new diseases brought by Christ'; a woman's role in antiquity was that of a slave to our pleasures: Christianity has not improved her status in the eyes of the literary hero. And this hetero-sexual eroticism continues throughout the text in the form of delirious descriptions of the charms of women. 'Unlike erotic poetry written since the time of Christ, my poems are not concerned with one soul asking another soul to love because it is beloved,' and classical poetry, he asserts, is a hymn to the immediate satisfaction of heterosexual desire.

Perhaps Gautier was a not altogether happy choice to sustain Corydon's argument. The immediate context of the quoted passage gives the lie to the notion that Gautier's hero is altogether reconciled to being in love with a man: 'That is how it is. I love a man, Silvio. For a long time I tried to close my eyes to the facts. I gave a different name to what I felt, and I clothed my feelings with the epithet of pure, disinterested friendship. . . . I blush when I think or write of it. But it is only too true: I love this man not merely out of friendship, but with love. . . . What I feel for this young man is truly unbelievable.' And again: 'Pity me now for being in love, and especially for loving the person I love. What misfortune, what mad, culpable and odious passion has taken possession of me. It is a shame whose blush will never depart from my brow. It is the most deplorable of all aberrations. . . . I doubt whether I am a man or a woman. I horrify myself.' This is extravagant. There follows a sensual description of the beloved's person, and the narrator confesses that he cannot touch him without being seized with trembling from head to toe. He seeks an explanation, however, and concludes: 'Théodore must be a woman in disguise; it's all quite impossible otherwise. This excess of beauty – which would be remark-able in a woman – is not a masculine beauty, even if he was Antinous the beloved of Hadrian, or Alexis the friend of Vergil. He's a woman, and I'm mad to torment myself about it. Such beauty belongs only to the angels and to women.' At the end of the chapter the hero muses after a tirade on sensuality that 'what is most strange is that I scarcely now think of his sex, and I love him with a feeling of perfect safety'. If, after all, Théodore is a woman in disguise he cannot account for her behaviour; if he really does turn out to be a man, 'I'll go mad – but probably still love him.'

Is such a feeling presented as natural, or as *merely* immoral? Part of the answer lies in Gautier's notion of the Beautiful (*le beau*). 'There is now, alas! only one thing beating in my breast and that is the horrible desire which carries me towards Théodore. My moral notions are reduced to this: what is physically beautiful is good, and what is ugly is evil.' Hence a lady poisoner is morally acceptable provided she is beautiful. In this sense, visual satisfaction is what is really craved, and the purity and polish of form and line are what are most immediately accepted. 'It is *this* which explains the singular aberrations of classical love. Since Christ, no one has made a single male statue where the beauty of the adolescent was idealised and conveyed more carefully than was the case with the ancient sculptors. Woman has become the symbol of moral and physical beauty.' She may still of course be a mere pleasure machine (*machine à plaisir*).

Our hero is an unregenerate heterosexual, and spends most of his energy praising women. If the nature of love is rage and extravagant sensuality, then the nature of morality is beauty. We must distinguish between the hero's relationship with Théodore, and his friendship for Silvio, the recipient of these confidences. It is pointed out quite clearly that although Silvio inspired the deepest affection he did not stimulate the hero's sexual desire. Hence we are to conclude that here at least androgynous beauty appeals to the sensual appetite.

In conclusion, we may for the moment ignore the extravagant tone, and note Gautier's emphasis on immorality and vice. We are more firmly in the satanic world of Baudelaire's *Le Vampire*, *Lesbos* and *À celle qui est trop gaie*, than we are with Gide and his 'honest puritanism'. When Venus is to be praised, Gautier, placing himself far from the chaste adoration which Gide bestowed, declared: 'We can see her: she hides nothing, for modesty is only for women who are ugly – modesty is a modern invention, the daughter of Christian scorn of form and material.'

Peladan

Gautier's hermaphrodite is in many ways a precursor of the androgynes of Joséphin Peladan. The name of this mystic Rosicrucian is not one which we readily associate with Gide. We do know, however, that he read at least two of the novels in the series *La Décadence latine* early in 1891. We also know what he thought of them: 'There are certainly proper times for reading particular books – and this wasn't the right time for reading that one [*À coeur perdu*]. I read it as badly as possible. I can still remember passages of great lyrical beauty, but they were sublimated and they sparkled too much [*sublimées, trop miroitantes*]' – it is not at all clear what Gide means.[42] *Le Traité du Narcisse* and *Les Cahiers d'André Walter* also offer us evidence of a certain sort of mysticism which may derive in part from a reading of Peladan. Four sections of Peladan's novel-cycle must be considered: *Éthopée IV*, *À coeur perdu* (Paris: G. Edinger, 1888); *VII*, *Coeur en peine* (Paris: E. Dentu, 1890); *VIII*, *L'Androgyne* (Paris: E. Dentu, 1891); and *IX*, *La Gynandre* (Paris: E. Dentu, 1891).

The hero of *À coeur perdu* is Nebo, a spirit-cum-magician-cum-succubus who in a mystical–sensual adventure falls in love with a princess, Paule, the epitome of Womankind. 'A woman who cannot pray will be incapable of love' (p. 64); 'love which must remain a dream – or, for an intellectual, a state of sentimental androgyny – remains in spite of what is daily learned the only means of softening that fierce, stupid animal called the man of instincts' (p. 65). These, and thoughts like them, pass through the mind of the Princess and give a good impression of the book's quality. She sees her relationship with Nebo as like that of brother and sister. Perhaps this was as far as Gide read, for his note in the 'Subjectif' refers to pages 40 and 51. Perhaps, though, he was marking points of especial interest. On page 40 Nebo refuses to possess Paule in a common manner (*vulgairement*) – for 'to be merely lover and mistress is less than we are worth'. They both desire nobility in love, and Nebo in particular wishes to deny the flesh even though he is strongly tempted by it. On page 51 Nebo fears he will be put into the woman's position and be violated: he will be 'absorbed', if he does not escape. He wants a companion for life, not just a few nights with a beautiful princess. Since Paule wishes to be a sister to him, he is conscious of the tempting sin of incest. It is possible to perceive a link between this literary expression of sinfulness and Gide's relationship with his cousin, particularly if we bear in mind Gide's own literary deployment of it in *Les Cahiers d'André Walter*.

Book 1, Chapter xxi (Extaticon viii) brings us nearer our point of interest. Paule asks Nebo: 'Do you not think that modern art and literature are quite unjust when they present the physical side of men? And women who write about love, are they not very hypocritical – or poor artists? Do you not think, as I do, that since the time of Athens we have lost the appreciation of masculine beauty?' But Nebo replies ironically: surely she does not believe that nakedness was responsible for beauty in the plastic arts? Such is Nebo's rejection of sensuality that we see in these words the contrary position to the one later adopted by Corydon. But when Nebo is erotically tempted (Chapter xiii (Extaticon ix)), Paule is dressed in a 'boyish jacket', and later (Chapter xviii (Extaticon xiv)) as an androgyne, 'adorably perverse . . . with her undulating walk echoing the movements of a belly dancer and the quickness of a page's step'. To Nebo, Paule seem lacking in modesty (*impudique*), in so far as she tries to seduce him with her fleshly charms. Thus the figure of the androgyne suggests a distancing of love not so much away from the heterosexual mode as towards an ethereal plane which is disengaged from sexuality. To love an androgyne is to love the spirit. Indeed Nebo, himself called 'le Platonicien', is often described as possessing the soft beauty and grace of a boyish adolescent (Book 2, Osculon xiii). In the Epilogue Nebo confesses his sin to his spirit-mentor Mérodack who replies: 'My dearest brother, only the spirit can love well and forever.' 'Your heart,' Nebo responds, 'is sweeter than the heart of woman, o Mérodack my Saviour.'

Coeur en peine continues in much the same vein, with passages on 'the fourfold word androgyne' and other Rosicrucian mystifications. Some sentences recall expressions in Gide's early works: 'Then the poor soul cries out in panic "Whosoever has not the strength to pursue his dream loses all rights to happiness"' (p. 43). There is also a dialogue on love in which Tammuz, another androgynous spirit, is addressed by 'Elle': androgynes are beautiful adolescents with evanescent souls, and after she has met one, everything else seems colourless and of lesser value. Tammuz replies: 'Woe to him who includes Woman in his thoughts. . . . The life of the body and the heart may be lived by two people, but the life of the Spirit is lived in solitude' (p. 258). Here is a strong echo of that desire for spirituality (*angélisme*) by which André Walter is beset; here also we perceive a doctrine of renunciation which is a fundamental part of Gide's attitude to sexuality.

We do not know for certain whether Gide read the other two books by Peladan. *L'Androgyne*[43] is described by the author as 'The monograph on puberty and the beginning of the oelohite Samas' voyage towards the light; the description of love and delight [*amour et volupté*]. A recreation of Greek ephebic impressions viewed through catholic mysticism. . . . ' The definition seems promising. Peladan's novel deals with love affairs at school, but then, after Part One, the hero passes on to relationships with women. Although the boy Samas is 'an adolescent sworn to remain a virgin', he is told by his Jesuit schoolmaster: '"What a man does with a woman is natural and excusable . . . whereas the kiss of Tanis [another boy] is worse than adultery, worse than incest – it is the kiss of Sodom. . . ." "In that case," exclaimed Samas, "if Agûr and I kiss that is the worst debauchery of all!" The ephebe remained pensive' (p. 173). In this novel, too, the Rosicrucian ideal of the androgyne features prominently. There is, for example, a 'Hymne à l'androgyne' whose eight long stanzas set out in parallel the charms of both sexes, emphasising in each case those elements each shares with the other. The poem moves from a description of adolescents towards its conclusion that angels are the perfect expression of the androgyne: 'O sex original and definitive, the absolute of love, the absolute of form, sex which denies sexuality, sex of eternity! Praise be to thee, o Androgyne!' One may easily be forgiven for seeing in the earlier stanzas an expression of homosexual eroticism. But the 'third mode' which is being celebrated is purity, transcending sexuality:

Ephebe . . . union of coming strength and fading grace. O uncertain moment of body and of soul. . . .

Man who captivates . . . Siegfried yet unaware, Cherubino starting to awake . . . the first down is on your lips, and your heart feels its first tremblings; pretty stammerer, disclosing at your neck your flesh as white as any woman's arm! . . .

Adonis or Tammuz . . . Alcibiades; ideal chrysalis whence spring the angels, and from where men fall to lower manliness. . . .

Intangible Eros, uranian Eros, for the gross men of moral times you are a nameless sin; they call you Sodom, celestial contemner of all sensual pleasure. . . .

La Gynandre, which has a certain amount to say about lesbianism, reworks much of the same material but in a different form. In a section on the nature of the androgyne (Book 5, Chapter ii, pp. 253–5) the hero Tammuz defines it thus:

Why should a man whose purpose is to think develop his muscular structure and wear heavy boots and rough clothes? I am effeminate and I dominate the most uncooperative women. I make myself feminine to be closer to women and re-establish sexual correspondence. The androgyne has been maligned. Ideally it is a boy who is a virgin – but in practice it is the man of feelings, the thinker, the artist . . . who strives for autocomplementarity.

We must notice several points in conclusion. Firstly the androgyne is an image which occurs in Gide's very early published works; secondly, it has strictly speaking little to do with Corydon's defence of pederasty; and thirdly Peladan's novels (and this is true of many of our other examples) nevertheless convey a profound atmosphere of heterosexuality which could find but little echo in Gide's own sensuality.[44]

Lautréamont

At first sight Lautréamont's *Les Chants de Maldoror* may seem a work too cynical and too sadistic to have appealed to Gide. This is the book of which André Breton, applying Swinburne's judgement on the Marquis de Sade, said: 'a cold shudder of infinity is felt to move through these accursed pages.'[45] The evil which takes shape here seems far removed from Gide's morality. Or is it? The aesthetic attraction of *Maldoror* might seem more in tune with the irrational nightmare world of the Surrealists than with certain aspects of Gide's consciously controlled realism. Perhaps the meeting place of these opposing viewpoints is not impossible to discern. As Breton noted, evil is best displayed when based on prohibited desires which derive their expression from forbidden sexual impulses.

Although we only know for certain that Gide admired the sixth *Chant*, a manuscript note in the *Corydon* archive refers to the fifth, and we can assume that he was probably familiar with the remainder.[46] A preliminary question which has to be asked, however, is at what date did he first become acquainted with *Les Chants de Maldoror*. The book was announced in the *Mercure de France* in January 1891 (II p. 55), and this was followed in February (pp. 97–102) by a review by Rémy de Gourmont in which he spoke of the 'frightening' quality of the work, the novelty of its imagery and the madness which it revealed. He made no mention of its sexual irregularities. There is no record of Gide's reaction to all this, but it is not without significance that he acquired a copy of the 1874 edition in that same January.[47] Did he read it immediately, or did it remain unopened for some time? As we shall see shortly, he says that he discovered the sixth *Chant* as late as 1905. Our suspicions that he looked at it earlier might well be aroused by some general points of apparent contact between *Les Nourritures terrestres* and *Maldoror*: the subject matter of both includes a demonic element, sensual attraction towards boys, and the image of the Wayfarer. In both, the style is incantatory and lyrical. O'Brien and Steel[48] have recognised some more precise similarities which, in their opinion, establish that Gide knew at least the first *Chant* in the mid-1890s,[49] but to me there seems nothing sufficiently distinctive here to prove a connection. There are, moreover, significant points of dissimilarity: it is far from clear that the threatening atmosphere of vampirism and the innocent, though anxious, happiness of the parents in *Maldoror* are genuine counterparts of Ménalque's seduction of the boy to a life of vagabondage and the diatribe against the stifling atmosphere of the family.

Gide did not look at the book properly until he was preparing *Corydon* in 1905. On 23 November of that year, he wrote in his *Journal*:

> I have just read, first to myself, then aloud, the extraordinary sixth *Chant de Maldoror* (Chapters I, II and III). By what accident did I not know it before? . . . This raises me to the very peak of excitement. In one moment he leaps from the detestable to the excellent. The letters which pass between Maldoror and Mervyn, the description of the family dining-room, the picture of the Commodore, the small brothers 'their caps adorned with a feather torn from the wing of the Carolina fern-owl, their knee-length velvet trousers and their red silk stockings' who 'hand in hand, go off into the drawing-room, taking care to tip-toe on the ebony parquet'. . . . What *mastery* in the 'deliberateness' of these lines!

The next day he read the sixth *Chant* enthusiastically to his friend, the actor–manager Jacques Copeau. On 28 November, he recorded that his recent reading of Rimbaud's *Les Poètes de sept ans* and Lautréamont had made him ashamed of all his own previous works. He was disgusted with everything 'that was only a result of the cultivated mind. It seems to me that I was born for something else.' Perhaps there was still time to mend this state of affairs, he reflected. It was doubtless in this mood that he turned to the composition of *Les Caves du Vatican*. We may surmise that what was 'detestable' in Lautréamont was violence (not much in evidence in the sixth *Chant*), while what was 'excellent' was the presentation of the visions of childhood. Among other things, the sixth *Chant* contains a portrayal of an adolescent awakening to the call of affection.

Maldoror makes that call almost irresistible. The sixth *Chant* takes the form of a 'novel' whose subject is the evil genius Maldoror and his prey, called Mervyn. Maldoror, in the grip of the Minotaur of his perverse instincts, glimpses a passer-by whose youth and beauty excite him strangely. Mervyn is sixteen years and four months old, a 'son of fair Albion' ('fils de la blonde Angleterre'). Maldoror draws near, then retreats, but follows the youth home and spies on him. This is how he witnesses the patriarchal scene and the well-behaved younger brothers from whom he plans to lure Mervyn. But the seduction will not take place immediately, for he has 'ulterior plans' for this shy adolescent. Section III contains the letter Maldoror sends to Mervyn, signed with a mysterious group of three stars:

> Young man, I have an interest in you; I wish to make you happy. I will take you away as my companion and we will journey far off to the isles of Oceania. Mervyn, you know that I care for you [que je t'aime], and I do not need to prove it to you. You will give me your friendship. . . . I will keep you safe from the dangers which your lack of experience will incur. I will be as a brother to you, nor will you want for good counsel.

A rendezvous on the Pont du Carroussel is fixed.

Mervyn replies in his letter: 'If it is appropriate to accept the friendship of an older person, so, too, is making him understand that our characters are not similar.' He is doubtful about his correspondent's real age, for how can he reconcile 'the coldness of your syllogisms with the passion which emanates from them'? He will not leave his parents, but he will come to the bridge. Overwhelmed by this 'attachment' which he cannot explain, he avows that he is certain of one thing above all else – 'that I shall meet you there and touch your hand, provided that this innocent gesture of an adolescent, who even yesterday was still worshipping at the altar of modesty, should not offend you by its respectful familiarity. For should one not acknowledge familiarity in the case of a strong and ardent intimacy [intimité], even when the loss of one's soul [la perdition] is serious and certain?' 'When I think of you,' he continues, 'my breast throbs with the noise of an empire as it falls in ruins. . . . When in your hands, I yield up my headstrong feelings, those fresh tablets of marble innocent of contact with a mortal being.' This is indeed the 'guilty letter', which shows him so beautifully falling into temptation. Here, also, is the end of the section to which Gide paid particular attention. The story continues in its satanic way to tell how God has sent one of His archangels to save the adolescent from certain death, how Mervyn is shoved into a sack by Maldoror, how he is rescued by the butcher's friend who wants to look inside before they use their sledge-hammers to beat the sack and its contents to pulp, and how, finally, Mervyn is attached to the column in the Place Vendôme and whirled around. He flies loose and crashes into the dome of the Panthéon.

It is not difficult to see in the seduction of a youth by an older man a theme which is common to both writers. Did other pederastic elements in the earlier *Chants* also come to have an importance for Gide after 1905? The answer is, unfortunately, that we have no further record of what he thought about them.

Chant 1 describes a sadistic attack on an adolescent – 'Blindfold him while you tear the throbbing flesh' – and then the reader can pretend to rescue the boy, tasting his tears and his blood as a reward.

Chant 2 tells how Maldoror talks to an eight-year-old boy on a bench and tries to persuade him to murder and rob in order to obtain fame in life. So far the scene is a satanic reminiscence of Vautrin's corruption of Rastignac in *Le Père Goriot*. The boy, however, has a seizure. A hermaphrodite is described: 'This sweet adolescent face simultaneously expresses the most virile energy and the grace of a celestial virgin.' But the solitary creature despairs at not being like the other members of the human race. Maldoror, too, is in search of a twin soul, but this he can find only in the nature of a ferocious shark. The young boy whose grace and beauty made flowers spring forth is rejected, and the beautiful sixteen-year-old who survives a shipwreck is murdered on the beach.

Chant 5 contains a yet more vigorous and satanic description of pederasty (and this was the section referred to in the brief note in the *Corydon* archive): 'O incomprehensible pederasts, I will not be the one who insults your great degradation; it will not be me who will pour scorn on your infundibuliform anuses. For shameful and almost incurable illnesses besiege you and bring their inevitable chastisement with them.' It is possible for the reader to imagine that parts of Maldoror's prayer are addressed to young persons of either sex. Finally, he cries out that he will break the 'sphincter of the universe'. This and what follows can scarcely have found a willing reader in Gide, despite the preferred age of the beloved and the age of the seducer: 'Meanwhile let him who burns with fire to share my bed come to me. But I make one condition for my hospitality – he must not be more than fifteen. Let him for his part not believe that I am thirty [Gide became thirty-six in 1905]; what does that matter? Feelings do not diminish with age. I do not like women, nor yet hermaphrodites. I need beings like myself.' There follow several appeals to the reader which remind us perhaps of Gide's call to Nathanaël: 'If only I could gaze on the face of him who reads me through these seraphic pages. If he has not yet reached puberty, let him come near. Hold me close to you. . . .' There is a new distance between Maldoror and Gide when the former confesses that he has always felt an evil inclination (*caprice infâme*) for pale schoolboys and 'aetiolated factory children'. However, the word 'pederast' is clearly used by Lautréamont to indicate the *younger* partner: 'Human justice has not yet caught me *in flagrante delicto*, despite the incontestable dexterity of its police. Not so long ago I even assassinated a pederast who did not lend himself sufficiently to my passion. . . . Why, o adolescent reader, do you shudder in fear? Do you think I will do the same to you? You are unjust . . . but you are right. Beware of me, especially if you are beautiful. . . . God opens the heavenly gates and welcomes in the catamite [*pédéraste*].'

One final word must be said: despite the fact that in the early 1890s Gide was undeniably attracted to books in which a violent expression of sexuality could be found, by 1905 his attitudes in this respect appear to have become far more moderate. In short, we have every reason to believe that Maldoror's satanism was too greatly nourished on blood and sperm to have appealed to Gide as a witness to the purity of pederasty. This may well be the reason why, despite the sentimentality of the seductive letters exchanged by Mervyn and Maldoror, there is no mention of this 'exciting' reading in *Corydon*.[50] It is satanism of a quite different character, albeit still sexual, which the reader encounters in *Les Caves du Vatican*, and, different yet again, in *Les Faux-Monnayeurs*.

Rimbaud and Verlaine

In his 'Subjectif' for 18–25 January 1892, Gide records that he read the 1884 edition of Verlaine's *Les Poètes maudits*. He had previously read the section on Rimbaud from the same book on 16 November 1889.[51] He bought a copy of Verlaine's *Bonheur* and Rimbaud's *Illuminations* in April 1891.[52] The Rimbaud travelled in his suitcase in 1895 together with Goethe's *Poésies* and Nerval's *Voyage en Orient*.[53]

Gide wrote to Ducoté early in 1900[54] that he was preparing something on Rimbaud. It was not until 1941 that the periodical *Poésie*

published in its number 41(vi) for October–November a short article
by him on the poet. In this piece Gide recalls his enthusiasm, dating
from the early 1890s. He remained, however, a 'secret worshipper',
although Rimbaud's later popularity gave the lie to his original belief
that here was an esoteric poet writing for the happy few. But Rimbaud
also appeared to Gide as a 'demon poet' and a poet accursed ('poète
maudit'). He 'gloried in the heady taste of Rimbaud's cup of poison'. He
was reassured when Claudel patronised the poet and brought his poems
before the public with his preface to the edition prepared by Paterne
Berrichon in 1916. Claudel's initiative, Gide wrote, was not so much
due to the dictum 'Unto the pure all things are pure' (Titus 1:15) as to
the equally Biblical notion 'And the violent take it by force' (Matthew
11:12). To his mind the Catholic who drew Rimbaud to his breast was
like the Spartan boy who stoically kept a fox concealed beneath his
cloak although the animal bit him cruelly.[55] Rimbaud's violence was
not to be tamed, he said, but, for Gide, true poetic quality resided in
being many things to many men. Although Rimbaud's youthful poetry
demonstrated 'his thirst for open spaces, escape, risk and adventure, his
blasphemies and his sensual delight (*gourmandise*) in forbidden things,
we must not forget his later bankrupt life.' This short article addressed
to the Catholic publisher Seghers concludes by applying the lesson of
Rimbaud's excessive individualism to the France of 1941: it would, in
Gide's eyes, be as imprudent to suppress this force as it would be to
indulge it freely.

If we return to 1905 we learn from the *Journal* of 23 November
that Gide's reading of *Les Chants de Maldoror* coincided with that of
Rimbaud's *Les Poètes de sept ans*. In his preface to the subsequent
edition, Claudel speaks of Rimbaud the primitive mystic ('un mystique
à l'état sauvage') and talks of the spiritual conquest which his life
represented. He discerns three periods – the first is the violent outburst
of blind genius. The second is the period of the 'seer' (*le voyant*)
containing the alchemical attempt to explain the poet's vision. *Les
Poètes de sept ans* belongs here, he remarks, and reveals Rimbaud's need
to escape which may only end in death and that desire to 'see' which
called him as a child to press his closed fist into his eyes. Claudel notes
that metaphors are less frequently used and hallucinations replace
them. The third period comprises *La Saison en Enfer*, 'a dark, bitter
book, yet one shot through with a mysterious softness'. Claudel praises
the music and the prosody of this section, and clearly sees the inspiration as an act of God.

But Gide was not satisfied with this. When he met Claudel on 19
November 1912, shortly after publication, he remarked that he thought
Claudel had not done justice to the 'ferocious' side of Rimbaud's
character.[56] Claudel replied that he had wanted to concentrate on *La

Saison en enfer, for which *Les Illuminations* could be seen as a sort of preparation. As for Rimbaud's 'anomaly', Claudel considered that the fact that he had lived with a woman in Dakar who had borne him a child 'was sufficient to discredit those rumours of bad habits which are still occasionally connected with his name. For if he had had them (and it is apparently very difficult to cure oneself) it is obvious that he would have continued to manifest them in a country where they are so accepted and facilitated that without exception all officers live quite openly with their "boy".' This anecdote, with its generalisations and insensitivity, tells us more about Claudel than about Rimbaud.

Five numbered manuscript sheets dated 'June 1907'[57] contain a 'Note on Verlaine', commenting on Lepelletier's book on the poet.[58] Anglès records that Drouin had shown the work to Gide, and suggests that this had provoked him to write on the subject.[59] It must be added, however, that a polemic against Lepelletier began in the pages of the *Mercure de France* in March 1910 with the first of a series of articles by Paterne Berrichon, 'Rimbaud et Verlaine', who however agreed with him in denying that the poets' conduct was homosexual.[60] This drew a reply from Lepelletier in April (pp. 570–1). A later contribution by Paul Escoube, 'Paul Verlaine et l'amour',[61] supported Lepelletier, and, without going deeply into the question of homosexuality, averred that 'whether Verlaine was abnormal or not does not detract from the beauty of *Sagesse*'. The debate even continued after the war with Marcel Coulon, 'Le Problème de Rimbaud – sa solution',[62] who asked whether the kisses were not symbolic, or the homosexuality other than carnal. It is obvious from a remark written at the end of his text that Gide had thought of publishing it as it stood in an appendix to *Corydon*, probably in 1920. The general purport of this material is somewhat similar to Gide's remarks on Bazalgette's *Whitman*, and this may well explain its eventual exclusion. He was, however, obviously more satisfied with what he had written on Verlaine and Rimbaud, for he judged the Bazalgette 'very mediocre' and 'needing to be completely redone'.[63] The substance of what he says is as follows.

Lepelletier's book is more interesting than he had expected – but the passages about Rimbaud and Létinois are particularly irritating. With an ironic flourish reminiscent of parts of *Corydon* ('I am not a good judge of these matters') he admits that he should perhaps 'bend' his conclusions in order to fit in better with general opinion. But this gives him a stiff neck, 'the point being whether to consider Verlaine as dishonoured if his love for Rimbaud, Lucien Létinois or others was more than merely platonic'. Doubtless a writer who defends Verlaine must choose facts which will enable him to praise him – and if he wrote too warmly on the other matter this would mar the picture. (This is of course also ironic.)

Gide continues: Must we speak of 'the legend of Verlaine' as we have spoken of 'the legend of Baudelaire' (for quite different reasons)? If Wilde's trial had not made such an impact, Wilde's devoted friends would now be speaking about his 'legend'.

And phrases like Lepelletier's 'exceptional impurities which only existed in his imagination' can easily be called upon to salvage a writer's reputation. Then in order to be on the right side you add: 'Pharisees, fools and malicious people can write with hostility about the attraction which Verlaine felt throughout his life for his special friends.' I am such a fool [writes Gide ironically] but without malice, and when I read at the beginning of Lepelletier's biography 'Did it remain theoretical or did he succumb to the desire to practise it?' I say I don't know. [Lepelletier talks of] 'the perfect innocence of his masculine affections' and naively adds that he never made a formal confession.

More particularly when we consider the relations between Verlaine and Rimbaud, we note that in addition to remarks by the people concerned this 'excellent' Lepelletier only quotes from letters which Verlaine sent him. And Verlaine must have known or sensed that Lepelletier was impervious on this matter, and quite lacking in awareness. If he had had something to confess he might have chosen Lepelletier to tell it to – but Lepelletier categorically states that there was nothing to say because nothing was said. I find that irritating. May I simply point out that Verlaine's conduct often gave rise subsequently to similar imputations – whereas according to Lepelletier the first experience should have warned him off completely [eût dû singulièrement l'échauder]. Rimbaud was ten years younger than Verlaine and was only sixteen when Verlaine called him to Paris. Although he wasn't exactly very beautiful, he was furiously provocative, despotic and authoritarian. And without going as far as Gourmont in his disgusting portrait of Rimbaud,[64] I cannot help but think that Lepelletier considered it an amusing duty to remove Verlaine from women and domestic life,[65] and that any means of controlling this grown-up child appeared good to him. Lepelletier quotes rather too victoriously the lines:

> On ripostait par le courage
> La joie et les pommes de terre[66]

and is rather cavalier in dealing with the lines of Laeti et errabundi which refer to this friendship:

> Car les passions satisfaites
> Insolemment, outre mesure,
> Mettaient dans nos têtes des fêtes
> Et dans nos sens, qui tout rassure,
>
> Tout, la jeunesse, l'amitié,
> Et nos coeurs, ah! que dégagés

Des femmes prises en pitié
Et du dernier des préjugés,

Laissant la crainte de l'orgie
Et le scrupule au bon ermite,
Puisque quand la borne est franchie
Ponsard ne veut plus de limite.[67]

[Gide does not mention the preceding poem 'Ces passions qu'eux seuls nomment encore amours'.] That doesn't *prove* anything, I know, even when Verlaine calls Rimbaud his 'grand péché radieux' ['splendid, radiant sin']. But it certainly doesn't prove the *opposite*.

For I think it correct to say that Rimbaud with an 'originality' of feeling more obdurate than Verlaine was his presiding 'evil genius' – rather as Douglas was Wilde's. And that for Verlaine as for Wilde, after a great intellectual exaltation resulting from an ecstasy due more or less to love, there was an attempt at self-recovery – and then moments when he let himself go.

As for sentences like the following, whose aim is to forge a legend: 'I remember that poor Verlaine's life was filled from beginning to end with one single, immense love for a woman!' Even if that wasn't grossly exaggerated, we all know what that proves. [One recalls here Gide's feelings for his own wife.]

In this otherwise well-documented book (but documented in one direction only) he doesn't breathe a word of Verlaine's rushing off as soon as he left prison in February 1875 to find Rimbaud, who was then a teacher in Stuttgart.

As for the medical examination which Verlaine proposed [to prove that he and Rimbaud were 'virgins' – an attempt to deal with the accusations made during the divorce proceedings brought by Verlaine's wife] I find it repugnant and grotesque. And what does it prove? Nothing. And surely Verlaine was crafty enought to know that. Even Lepelletier agrees after first taking it to be a proof of innocence (p. 28), or at least of Verlaine's good faith (p. 350). Alas, perhaps we should see in all this a cynical abuse of the 'legend' in many minds which makes a sodomite (*enc[ulé]*) of any pederast. (It is monstrous! and after that, people are astonished that Krupp and Macdonald committed suicide!)

I find truly admirable the assurance with which Lepelletier, wishing to protect Verlaine and Rimbaud, cites Achilles and Patroclus (without bothering about the 'evidence for the prosecution' preserved in Aeschylus' play), Nisus and Euryalus (why not Alexis and Corydon), and even the 'heroic Theban legend'.[68]

Gide continues at this point with the substance of his remarks on Epaminondas and the Theban Legend, drawn from Plutarch and the *Biographie universelle*, which he incorporated into *Corydon*, Dialogue IV

230

(pp. 159 and elsewhere). He then goes on: 'The lack of awareness with which Lepelletier writes is quite admirable when he says: "Since unlike the emperor Hadrian he was unable to raise a mausoleum of stone(!) to this Antinous from the Ardennes (Lucien Létinois) Verlaine constructed a lyrical monument in *Amour* which seems indestructible." ' This country boy has now achieved his fame and is ' "an immortal companion of Bathyllus [the beloved of Anacreon, or possibly the actor–boyfriend of Maecenas] and Corydon". But doubtless Lepelletier, who is neither "pharisee" nor "foolish" nor "hostile" [*méchant*], leaves only me with the notion that Antinous, Bathyllus and Corydon were not pure Sunday School figures.'

'Furthermore,' Gide concludes, 'and especially as regards Lucien Létinois, I don't myself think that anything happened. But I maintain that if homosexuality had not been a part of Verlaine's temperament this love would not have declared itself.'

To this attack Gide added a small personal footnote, addressed to someone unknown (possibly Ghéon?). It perhaps explains the warmth with which he attacked the pious hagiography of both Lepelletier and Bazalgette, although their respective subjects were not as open about themselves as Gide was to become. 'Will I astonish you greatly if I say that such books further increase my resolve to make a posthumous masquerade impossible in my case by using my writings *from now onwards?*'

One cannot say that Gide greatly misrepresented Lepelletier, but in arguing his case so concisely he might be thought to have shown less than a full picture of the critic's position.

Lepelletier recalls in his book that he was a close friend of Verlaine and his wife; he disapproved of Rimbaud, who behaved very badly on the one occasion when he, Lepelletier, invited him to dinner. If Verlaine had a moral failing it was fondness for drink, he considered, and Rimbaud hastened his friend's decline into 'pathological dipsomania'. It was Rimbaud who separated Verlaine from his wife by his generally disagreeable behaviour and the vicious power he exerted over him. Rimbaud 'was responsible for the suspicions of unnatural passion which were alleged during the divorce proceedings'. And these rumours, Lepelletier adds, 'which stain the memory of Verlaine, will be shown to be false'. Verlaine was pitiable and weak ('pauvre, faible'); Rimbaud was a depraved but amiable urchin ('ce gamin vicieux et génial') – the author of all his moral and physical misfortunes'. Lepelletier is unwilling to give him credit for inspiring any of Verlaine's poetry.

It is true that Lepelletier quotes the letter of 23 September 1872 in which Verlaine offers, with Rimbaud, to undergo a medical examination, and this could well have been a 'farce'. But what requires more serious consideration is a short passage quoted from another letter from Verlaine (p. 294, of about the same date): 'All this stuff about unnaturalness which they have the infamy to charge against me is just intimidation (or blackmail).' In a proposed pamphlet he would 'give a very sober but clear sort of psychological analysis, with no rhetorical flourishes or paradoxes, of the highly honourable and sympathetic motives of my very real, very deep and very persevering love for Rimbaud – and I won't add "very pure", tut!' The tone of this is itself obviously 'rhetorical', and encourages us not to treat the statement at face value. In June 1873 Verlaine wrote to protest against a homosexual interpretation of certain poems. Lepelletier adduces this to strengthen his argument (p. 328), but, as Gide realised, one cannot use isolated facts to arrive at a general conclusion. Only particular poems are in question: 'May I never more move if in writing those lines I was thinking of anything "imphame" [a hybrid Greek and Latin pun: "unspeakable"], or, if you prefer, "infemme" ["womanless"]. The small pieces, *Le Piano*, etc. *Oh! triste! triste était mon âme* and *J'ai peur d'un baiser*, *Beams* and some others are quite good testimony – if required – of my perfect love for "le sesque" ["le sexe": "woman"].' And here again Verlaine's bantering tone makes it difficult to reach a firm interpretation of his attitude.

As Gide states, Lepelletier does 'affirm' more frequently than the facts allow. For instance, Lepelletier discusses the affair in Belgium when Verlaine shot and wounded Rimbaud, and he argues that there is nothing in the legal documents to suggest that the question of homosexuality was raised by the authorities, except for a brief question to Rimbaud, who did not deign to answer; that the police would certainly have explored any suggestion of sexual misconduct (*mœurs infâmes*); and that therefore to interpret the shooting as arising from 'unnatural jealousy' is wrong. If there was an argument, Lepelletier states, it must have been a domestic one about money, and he refers to lines from *Laeti et errabundi*:

> La misère aussi faisait rage . . .
> On ripostait par le courage,
> La joie et les pommes de terre.

('And poverty was rampant . . .') 'Une intimité poétique et pot-au-feu' ('A poetic and kitchen-sink friendship'), he remarks (p. 338). This is, of course, the passage we have seen singled out by Gide.

Is this all? Lepelletier states: 'In order fully to describe the character of the relationship between these two friends, let us affirm that the intimacy between Verlaine and Rimbaud was entirely intellectual and based on common interests. Historical examples are frequent which show comrades living in profound intimacy with all sexuality excluded.

If necessary, a hundred famous examples could prove that friendly and intellectual bonds have existed between men, without any shameful accusation being justified or even made with sincerity or probability' (p. 337). But Lepelletier is nevertheless forced to concede that there are 'enigmatic or equivocal passages' in Verlaine's work. The warmth of his affection has misled people, he says; however, the following lines are 'quite prosaic and in no way passionate':

> Le bonheur de vivre à deux hommes,
> Mieux que non pas d'époux modèles,
> Chacun au tas versant des sommes
> De sentiments forts et fidèles.[69]

Indeed! We may well wish to agree with Gide.

Lucien Létinois, a country lad, was born in 1860. He was a pupil of Verlaine's, and in 1881, after having set up a farm, the two went off to London. Lepelletier explains this affair by pointing to the attractions which the boy's religious attitudes held for Verlaine, and by reminding us that since his own son[70] had become estranged, Lucien doubtless awakened in him paternal feelings. Lepelletier speaks of Verlaine's 'greed for affection', but because of the special relationship he finds it necessary to explain further. Here, while admitting that these feelings are homosexual, he wishes to emphasise their purity (something Gide has chosen not to notice):

Science and history have defined the purely cerebral character of these homosexual feelings – the platonic character, to use the common expression. The most famous philosophers in antiquity showed an affection towards some of their disciples which seemed to go beyond ordinary friendship. Plato has discussed this matter very explicitly. . . . Socrates considered that he should propagate his teaching, unite the souls of others to his own, and dominate men's minds. A psychical communion was established between master and disciple. The same can be said of other religious people. . . . Socrates was accused of debauching the youths who gathered around him, eager to hear his learned words and savour the honey of his wisdom.

Lepelletier makes the common mistake of failing to distinguish between moral corruption as defined in the nineteenth century (homosexual, or other so-called deviant behaviour), and the accusations against Socrates which concerned atheism, and an alleged encouragement to his pupils to act unlawfully.[71]

'Other teachers, too,' Lepelletier continues, 'have been accused of seducing their pupils.' This, in fact, happened to the Saint-Simoniens in 1840.[72] The argument is unpersuasive, but typical of its time. We know that Verlaine's affections were blameless, Lepelletier concludes, because he showed them in public and never behind closed doors. So open were they that the whole village soon gossiped about Lucien and Verlaine. After the boy's untimely death 'the same note' was sounded in the poems celebrating the sincerity and absolute purity of their friendship. However, these poems themselves gave rise to rumours. Basing himself on quotations from *Amour* and *Bonheur* Lepelletier underlines what he sees as the spiritual nature of this friendship:

> Il n'est dans la légende actuelle et l'ancienne,
> Rien de plus noble et de plus beau que deux amis.[73]

As for the women in Verlaine's life, Lepelletier clearly has an idealised picture of the poet's wife, while he cannot ignore the rapacious female 'attendants' of the years 1892–6. In his decline 'Verlaine wasn't very fussy about his women,' he writes. 'After all, he hadn't known many' (p. 535). It is interesting to contrast Lepelletier's pious wish to save the poet from calumny with Gide's more realistic relish for truth. It must, however, be obvious to the reader that Gide, too, had a Romantic view of certain special friendships.

Gide records that Valéry told him when they were in their early twenties that statues would be erected to Verlaine and to Rimbaud, despite the fact that at that date the latter's poetry was considered 'monstrous and inhuman'.[74] One of the earliest entries in Gide's *Journal* records a visit paid to Verlaine in January 1890, and a later entry in the 'Feuillets' (*circa* 1918)[75] recalls Verlaine's correction of the judge's word 'sodomiste' when he was in court. A still later reference on 4 July 1933, dealing disparagingly with François Porché's recent book on Verlaine, links the 'perfect spontaneity' of the verse with the 'lack of self-control with which he is nowadays reproached'. Gide thought of Rimbaud in a similar fashion as one 'in whose heart God has planted that nomadic instinct, that unquiet love, impatient with what is agreed, always seeking adventure . . .'[76] Let us remember also that Bernard, in *Les Faux-Monnayeurs*, is shown to like Rimbaud for having preferred life.[77] Life? Art? Perhaps we should not at present observe the dichotomy too closely, for it is a fictional character who is speaking.

Gide likewise judged that Verlaine was an incomparable poet because he obtained his success, not by self-constraint, application and effort, but simply by lack of discipline (*laisser aller*).[78] His early poems are, for this reason, to be considered as much finer than his later ones. Speaking of Rimbaud's influence on Verlaine, Gide did not feel that it was particularly great. Their meeting was of course important, he thought, for Verlaine's life was completely thrown into turmoil as a consequence, and because 'following a strange drama which remains mysterious despite the light which people have shed on it since, Verlaine was sent to prison. . . . Because, as a consequence of this drama, Verlaine flung himself upon religion and produced what is in my opinion unquestionably his finest collection [probably *Sagesse*]. And because the memory of this passionate and reckless period later inspired one of the most pathetic poems that he wrote.' In this *Conférence* Gide turns to Lepelletier's book, and quotes his account of the publication of *Sagesse*. In the next collection, *Amour*, published eight years later, Gide remarks that the 'fine series of poems' devoted to Lucien Létinois may be found. 'Moreover, I would not wish to ask you to look with too severe an eye at these poems from his decadent period.' One of the actors present at the *Conférence* was particularly requested to read aloud 'J'ai la fureur d'aimer', which, commented Gide, would 'not only move you with the pathos which holds back the breath', but would also interest the audience because they 'would feel how the excess of his most exquisite uncontrolled qualities' could 'lead Verlaine to the very worst'. After saying this, Gide admitted that in *Parallèlement* he could only find a few 'curious' items. What these were we cannot be sure, but he might have been thinking of 'Ces passions qu'eux seuls nomment encore amours', '*Laeti et errabundi*' and 'Sur une statue de Ganymède'. He considered there was 'virtually nothing of note' in *Bonheur* and did not mention poem XV in that section.

Finally, there are two other collections of poems to be considered, *Femmes* and *Hombres*.[79] The first of these was published in Brussels in 1890 with the date '1891', and is characterised by the emphasis the poet places on the carnal aspect of his love for women. It is this edition which features among the books Gide read on 7 July 1891.[80] *Hombres*, a series of erotic homosexual poems, was published anonymously 'Sous le manteau et se vend nulle part', most probably by Messein in 1903. 'Sur une statue de Ganymède' is also included here. There is, however, no record that Gide saw a copy of this book, although he could clearly have been aware of its existence.

Polti, Sardou and Rostand

We have already seen that Gide took a cutting from an article by Georges Polti, the theatre critic, on the beauty of adolescents in classical antiquity.[81] There is good reason to think that his name was well known to him, for, in an amusing reference to the critic in a letter to Gide on 11 November 1894, Pierre Louÿs pretended that the manuscript of *Paludes* would be burned: 'It's a dramatic situation which M. Polti has not foreseen – the hero's work destroyed by his friend.'[82] Louÿs was referring to a series of articles which began to be published in the *Mercure de France*, X March 1894.[83] This (almost) exhaustive catalogue of dramatic possibilities included, in Volume XII (September 1894, pp. 51–4), as part of 'Situation XXVI', 'Crimes of Love (the Lover and the Beloved)'. Love, Polti averred, was an essentially comic subject – but this particular 'Situation' was its only tragic manifestation.

He distinguished eight types of erotic crime. The first was onanism – the solitary vice which provokes no action, and provides either 'elegiac shadows' (Narcissus and *Charlot s'amuse...*) or grotesque forms (Aristophanes), unless it be used to study the collapse of the will (as, for example, authors might do with drunkenness and gaming). The ensuing types cover rape, prostitution, adultery and incest. The sixth type is labelled 'Unisexuality in both its meanings: pederasty and tribadism'. Pederasty (defined as 'A man loves another man who yields to him') is illustrated by the examples of Vautrin (admittedly from a novel), and Aeschylus' *Laius* and Euripides' *Chrysippus*. These two plays survive only in an extremely fragmentary form, but Polti reconstructs the story of the *Chrysippus* with some plausibility, a few obvious errors and a great deal of melodrama: Atreus and Thyestes kill their brother Chrysippus for having yielded to Laius' love, and Laius learns the truth from his beloved's dying lips. Polti imagines how great the monologue of the first man on earth to feel and satisfy these passions would be. Sapphism, on the other hand, he writes, does not have the horrible, grandiose nature of pederasty; 'it is a weak, cowardly bad habit of dissipated or sickly girls, and does not offer the tragic poet the brutal unnatural frenzy rooted in powerful barbaric youth which we see in the criminal passions of heroic times.' The seventh type, bestiality, is 'not theatrical', but Polti cites the example of Euripides' lost play *The Cretans* in which Pasiphae's love for the bull was described. This is held to be 'the Ultima Thule of sexual madness'. He has little to say about his eighth and final type, the abuse of minors, remarking that it derives its elements from the previous seven categories and, if the reader wishes to pursue this subject, which is 'so modern, so English', he will see the pathos it can achieve in skilful hands by reading the *Pall Mall Gazette*. The scandals to which he refers concerned the prostitution of adolescent girls in London. The French public was in fact able to read a translation of articles from the *Pall Mall Gazette*, published in 1885.[84] When Polti's work was published in volume form it received a very hostile review from Louÿs in the *Mercure de France*.[85]

In the context of dramatic representations of sexual permissiveness it is of interest to note Gide's reactions to seeing Sardou's *Divorçons!* on 30 October 1889: 'The play is extremely strong and marvellously made. It even frightened me a little by its extreme boldness.'[86] The intrigue of the play, first performed in December 1880, can be summarised quite simply. At the date when a new divorce law is about to be voted on by the National Assembly, M. and Mme Des Prunelles are trapped in an unhappy marriage. The wife, her lover and her husband settle down to talk of the divorce, and adultery is suggested as a means to speed up the proceedings. The rest of the conversation is also quite 'free'. Later, the husband and wife have a dinner to celebrate their forthcoming divorce and the lover arrives unexpectedly. He is annoyed that the husband is 'seducing' the wife. There is also a discussion between husband and wife about the number of hours they have spent making love since the beginning of their marriage. The wife emerges somewhat tousled from behind a screen where her husband has been fondling her, and this is taken by the policeman for indecent behaviour with a third party. The play has a happy ending as the married pair are reunited. What Gide probably found most shocking was the cynical discussion of divorce and the means of achieving it. However, in January 1893 he did not feel any constraint, it appears, at reading Ibsen's *Ghosts*, which raises the issue of venereal disease, aloud to his mother,[87] noting in the *Journal*: [88] 'But one must be careful not to be too amused by the scandal.'

On 20 June 1910 there is a reference in the *Journal* to Rostand's *Chantecler*. This may not of itself seem particularly important, for Gide remarks on the portrayal of a poet as victim of the mob. The name of the work also recurs in Gide's attack on Gourmont but with praise for the quality of Gourmont's judgement of Rostand.[89] There exists, however, in manuscript[90] a section of dialogue which did not eventually find a place in *Corydon*. The piece is headed 'Uranism – subject': 'Truly, I do not see much in modern times apart from *Chantecler*,' says Corydon. The interlocutor shows his astonishment, and Corydon continues with some irony: 'Do you not then know this play? Is it possible that the fuss that has been made has not reached your ears? The subject is rather unwholesome but the author set the play outside a human context in a supernatural world so that the story seems perfectly natural.' The following lines are deleted: 'I shall tell you the story from the point of view of a naturalist, for you know that I don't understand much about the idealised pictures of poets.' Corydon continues:

M. Rostand starts from the fact that particularly among birds certain females assume the shining livery of the males, thereby renouncing love and all the prerogatives of their own sex. This is how one may exceptionally see a female pheasant whose plumage is normally fairly dull appear in the splendid guise of the male. In this masculine clothing Chantecler immediately falls in love with her. I don't remember the rest very well: the female probably allows herself to be moved [by Chantecler's desire – *deleted*]. The drama must derive from the fact that the female can only love Chantecler if she forgoes [*heavily corrected text*] that masculine display which made her so desirable [in Chantecler's eyes – *deleted*]. The author did well to set all that among the birds.

The play was first performed at the Théâtre de la Porte-St-Martin on 7 February 1910, and published in the February and March numbers of *L'Illustration*. It is a poetic extravaganza on the theme of the pride of a cockerel. When his beloved, the hen pheasant, effectively prevents him from waking the sun by his cry – and Nature continues in her normal course – he is for a moment subdued but lives to crow again. There is a debate between the magnificently dressed peacock and Chantecler. The hen pheasant is undoubtedly an exotic creature too, who describes her splendid 'outfit'. But need we take this bird lore so very seriously? I doubt that Rostand was appealing to natural science in the same manner as was Corydon.

Louÿs

It is when we come to consider Gide's erstwhile friend Pierre Louÿs that we return to the argument concerning chastity. Louÿs and Gide were at school together at the École Alsacienne and their friendship developed during the years 1888–92. Whether because of a fundamental in-compatibility of spirit or a schoolboy love of practical joking which Gide found difficult to accept, their friendship became markedly cooler until a definitive break in their private relations occurred in 1895. In May of the following year Gide still agreed to contribute 'La Ronde de la Grenade' to *Le Centaure*, a new literary periodical edited by Louÿs. The poem is a hymn to sensuality, later incorporated in the *Nourritures terrestres*. This in fact is the last significant contact between the two writers, for their disagreement was made public and Gide withdrew from further collaboration because he judged the tone of *Le Centaure* too licentious.[91] The event serves to underline the paradox of Gide's viewing his liberation from a puritanical standpoint. Perhaps after all as the two friends attained adulthood it was their attitudes towards religion and sexuality which separated them most radically. Louÿs' books are marked by a strong element of sensuality which is both heterosexual and pagan. His contemporaries considered him out-spokenly pornographic, particularly in such works as *Aphrodite. Mœurs antiques* (1896), *La Femme et le Pantin* (1898), *Scènes de la vie des courtisanes* (a translation of Lucian of Samosata) (1894), *Les Chansons de Bilitis* (1894 and 1895), and *Les Aventures du Roi Pausole* (1901).

Louÿs is mentioned twice in *Corydon* (pp. 128 and 163); on the first occasion Gide has *Le Roi Pausole* in mind, and on the second *Aphrodite*.

We ought nevertheless also to consider two articles of a slightly later date, for they are central to Louÿs' definition of sexual liberty. In Gide's eyes they place Louÿs in company with Gourmont on the side of the demons.

The first of these articles is the 'Plaidoyer pour la liberté morale'[92] which appeared in the *Mercure de France*, XXIV October 1897 (pp. 7–15). Here Louÿs considers that it is disgraceful that in modern times nudity and love should be thought scandalous. (We note ironically in this context Gide's own Biblical counter-battlecry: 'Il faut que le scandale arrive!' – 'It must needs be that offences come', Matthew 18:7). What women are allowed to reveal is decided irrationally, he writes, and it varies throughout history. (Gide appeals to the same type of relativistic argument in *Corydon*.) We have arrived at such a state, Louÿs asserts, that, if what everyone wants is in fact produced on the stage at the Opéra, everyone will be scandalised at the sight of this splendidly naked woman ('admirablement nue'). He is against the hypocrisy generally manifested in society, and in appealing to beauty would have us be enriched by the 'fecund emotions' to which it gives rise: 'If the human form inspires shame, remove all statues from the museums!' As for love, although it is the universal mystery, it may not be shown on stage. Only murder and crime have that privilege. In a sentence reminiscent of what was recorded by Mme d'Épinay, Louÿs confesses that he considers that the marriage night is a religious ceremony. This is a new religion, for Louÿs believes that our new prudery coincides with the triumph of one particular element in Christian thought. Christ, he avers, was not against nudity. We have listened too much to St Paul and the Lutherans, he says, who were all responsible for an 'invasion of ugliness'.[93]

The second article, 'Liberté pour l'amour et pour le mariage', was printed in *Le Journal* in November and December 1900.[94] Louÿs argues that the birthrate should be increased in France, since a recent demographic survey shows that an alarming decline is taking place. (As we have seen above, Gide also paid attention to these figures, but drew quite different conclusions from them.) The current propaganda, Louÿs argues, is in favour of chastity and virginity. This should be done away with, and women should be made proud of childbrith; in the case of illegitimate births, the mothers are currently stigmatised and unsupported by the social services. (Both these ideas are close to Gourmont's views.) Marriage, he considers, is not the obvious solution, for 'far from encouraging conception, it is frequently a mutual school of voluntary sterility'. He inveighs against many petty fiscal and legal obstacles to marriage and concludes with a strong argument for lowering the age of majority in sexual and marital matters.

The 'Plaidoyer' has an interesting footnote in which Louÿs complains that he has been misrepresented by a 'Professor of Law in the South of France, M. Charles G., a Protestant' (probably a reference to Gide's uncle, the economist, who in 1910 was to take over the presidency of the Fédération des Sociétés contre l'Immoralité Publique from Senator René Bérenger).[95] The professor had seen a plea for universal nudity in Louÿs preface to *Aphrodite*. What the preface actually says refers specifically to the Greeks. One nevertheless has a strong feeling that Louÿs would welcome a rebirth of their civilisation, at least in so far as it allowed freedom to the heterosexuals. He will not write, he says in the same preface, that he has painted sensuality (*la volupté*) as it is, in order to exalt virtue. However, this is a novel about courtesans in ancient Greece: 'The Greeks considered love and all its consequences the most sublime and virtuous of feelings. They never associated with Love those ideas of shamelessness and lack of modesty which the Jewish tradition has introduced among us through Christian doctrine.' Herodotus (I, 10), he says, wrote quite naturally: 'Some barbarian peoples consider it shameful to appear naked [in public],' and, moreover, there is a tendency, when defending Greek morality, to quote the teaching of some philosophers who condemned sexual pleasures. This, he remarks, is muddled thinking, for these 'exceptional moralists' were criticising excess in indulging sensual appetite wherever it occurred. Louÿs, who was sufficiently well informed to realise how far short of historical truth this judgement of his fell, may easily be seen to be arguing a biased case in favour of his novel's courtesans. He nevertheless makes a significant point by noting the importance of 'sensuality' for the Greeks, although here again he is obviously unwilling to extend the franchise beyond the world of the heterosexual. He writes:

> Cities where the legislator intended to introduce a narrow, unproductive and artificial virtue were condemned to total death from the very start. This is what happended in Sparta which in the midst of the greatest surge which has ever uplifted the human soul produced not one poet, not one painter . . . and scarcely the common fame [*renom populaire* – not *gloire* (glory)] of a sort of Bobillot [a clown] who managed to get himself killed with 300 men in a mountain valley, and not even win [Leonidas at Thermopylae].

The tone of these remarks about homosexuality, the only ones Louÿs makes here, is hostile and dismissive. (The same historical facts are mentioned in *Corydon*, pp. 163–4, with a reference to Louÿs.) With a flourish Louÿs introduces the reader to his novel: 'Let us for a moment relive that moment in the past when human nakedness, that most perfect form which we can know . . . would be revealed in the figure of the sacred courtesan,' and let us in consequence leave behind the black, ugly modern world of religious prejudice.

The ideal of the nude concubine is also to be found in Louÿs' *Psyché*, where Aracoeli is depicted at ease only when naked, although she occasionally wears a precious stone in her ear.[96] Corydon (p. 128) doubts whether in the city of Tryphême, dreamed up by Louÿs, the frequent and frank exhibition of their charms by the fair sex would not bring about a result contrary to the effect Louÿs predicted. Might not familiarity breed contempt? or at best coolness? The reference is to the city in *Le Roi Pausole*, which the King visits in Book IV Chapters 5 and 6. Pausole, wishing his subjects to be as free as he is himself, has passed a law to enable them to enjoy their liberty. In Tryphême the public orators describe the sexual freedom of their customs. Not all the citizens are naked, but some young girls ride nude upon their horses, and a guard of honour is formed of 1,800 'jeunes filles nues'. Other naked girls are walking around the streets. In the Epilogue, the narrator cautions us against taking 'the Fantasy for the Dream, and Tryphême for Utopia'. The book, however, is undoubtedly a piece of 'soft' pornography. Tryphême, admits Corydon, could be said to have existed 'fifty years ago' – as in Tahiti, before the missionaries arrived. He quotes Darwin's description to support his assertion, giving us the impression that in *this* Paradise the men outshone the women. As for the criticism of the missionaries, the idea is perhaps a commonplace, or more probably was suggested by passages in Stevenson's *In the South Seas* which we have noticed above. But here, surely, is a contradiction – and one not un-connected with Gide's puritanical attitude towards the role of women. It is also obvious that his homosexuality plays its part in his recognition of Tahiti as Utopia.

We do not know whether *Aphrodite* furnished material for conversa-tions between Louÿs and Gide, for the manuscript was finished in early 1896, being serialised by Alfred Vallette in the *Mercure de France* from November 1895. 'There is nothing more sacred on earth,' wrote Louÿs in the preface to *Aphrodite*, 'than physical love, and nothing more beautiful than the human body.' Did not Gide also believe in love? He explained the difference which separated him from Louÿs by appealing to Greek models. 'Pierre Louÿs was too Ionian and I was too Dorian for us to get on well together,' he wrote in his *Journal* in January 1907.[97] The courtesans of *Aphrodite* are 'Ionian'; the homosexuals of Sparta and the Sacred Band of Thebes are 'Dorian'. The mark of the Ionian is sensuality; the Dorian is recognisable by his austerity and discipline. We will see in connection with *Le Roi Candaule* (1899) an extension of Gide's argument with Louÿs in the form of a plea for restraint and modesty in a work of art. And did not Gide write in fact to Louÿs in 1890 responding to an anonymous note from 'Emmanuelle': 'As soon as the Person shows herself She becomes just anyone'?[98]

Barrès

In Dialogue III (p. 137) Corydon maintains that Barrès in his *Le Jardin de Bérénice* (1891) drew the picture of a girl so close to nature, and so obedient to her instincts, that her lesbian attachment was quite normal: 'It is only through *education* that he brings her up to the level of heterosexual love.' To the quite reasonable objection that Barrès had nothing of the sort in mind, Corydon responds that Bérénice represented for her author 'the mysterious force which moves the world'. And Gide's text assigns to her an 'anagenetic' role which suits Corydon's argument well: 'The serenity of her function which is to bring to birth everything which comes to her'. It is Barrès whom Gide took to task for promulgating the doctrine of National Roots (*enracinement*)[99] and certain nationalistic attitudes to race and literature. In the midst of a number of observations recorded in the *Journal* in June 1910 we find his name mentioned. Gide is noting some botanical and entomological examples which are connected with material referred to in *Corydon*. He says that he cannot agree with Barrès, for he has observed that a law of Nature makes every animal drive away its offspring as soon as they can fend for themselves. Where Barrès sees the family group as essential, Gide sees a 'natural' reason for escape and liberty. This idea is frequently expressed in Gide's writings and is at the very base of his understanding of the adolescent.

Contemporary Imaginative Works with Homosexual Themes

During the period when Gide was writing *Les Cahiers d'André Walter*, *Les Nourritures terrestres*, *L'Immoraliste* and *Corydon* a number of novels and other creative works with homosexual themes were published in France. We often have proof of his knowledge of them, but where this is lacking it is generally reasonable to assume that he was aware of their existence. A detailed examination of them will therefore provide a context in which we can consider Gide's own literary output. After the First World War, and the completion of *Corydon*, he continued to take note of writings of this sort which interested him.

Huysmans

In his unpublished *Journal*, Gide noted on 27 February 1889 that he had finished reading Huysmans' *À rebours*.[100] The novel had first appeared in 1884. Des Esseintes, the hero, is the aesthete who believes that 'artificiality is the distinctive mark of man's genius'. In the course of the centuries, males in his family have become more and more effeminate; his superior sensibility ensures that by the time he reaches his majority he has tasted the delights of so many women that his appetite has become jaded. His favourite author is Petronius, in whose *Satyrica* he relishes the portrayal of 'a decaying civilisation' and the 'adventures of a band of Sodomites'. He sees parallels between it and his favourite modern novels. However, his library encompasses many authors of the late Roman Empire, and his idol in the pictorial world is Gustave Moreau's *Salome*. One episode in the novel describes how des Esseintes meets a sixteen-year-old orphan, Auguste Langlois, in the street, and takes a liking to him. The purpose of this affection is to try to turn him into an assassin by buying the delights of a sumptuous brothel for him. The excesses committed by des Esseintes increase his neurotic state. In the list of his past loves, Miss Urania, an American circus acrobat, makes an interesting appearance. As he observed her perform he perceived 'an artificial change of sex in her' – her 'female simperings' diminished, and gave way to the 'agile and powerful charms of a male'. And so he becomes effeminate in order to complement her masculinity. Unfortunately, she turns out in bed to be an ordinary woman, with none of the 'athletic brutalities' he both desired and feared.

Among his other memories is a youth who asked for directions. He was an ill-dressed schoolboy, with large eyes and sensual lips. He lowered his gaze, and, coming closer, his arm had touch des Esseintes'. 'From this chance encounter,' the narrator remarks, 'was born a mistrustful friendship which lasted for some months. Des Esseintes no longer thought of it without a shudder. Never had he endured a more attractive and a more commanding serfdom. Never had he known such dangers; never had he felt himself more painfully satisfied. This reciprocal attachment dominated all others' (pp. 145–6). Finally, overwhelmed by the world's mediocrity, and victim of more hallucinations, des Esseintes prays for a form of redemption. It may readily be seen that explicit homosexuality plays a minor role in this story, for our few examples are far outnumbered by the lists of excessive sensual experiences of other kinds which cause the decadent nerves of des Esseintes to vibrate as he continues his effete search through the worlds of literature, music, perfumes, food and the Church. In these pages effeminacy is linked to degeneracy, implying a generalised physical and moral debility.

Bonnetain

Charlot s'amuse . . . , a 'scientific' novel whose hero suffers from an irresistible urge to masturbate, was published in 1883 by Paul Bonnetain, a disciple of Zola.[101] The book caused an outrage and was prosecuted by the police a year later for public indecency. However, the novelist won his case, and a full edition reappeared in 1885 with all the alleged obscenities included and specially indicated. Charlot has a terrible hereditary background – a drunken, suicidal father and a nympho-maniac mother – so his neurosis, his lack of willpower and his vitiated genital urge can easily be shown to lead to uncontrollable masturbation, and then to epilepsy, anaemia and the general collapse of his moral health. As a pretty child he is seduced and abused by several priests (the anti-clerical tone of the book is clearly marked), and when he moves on to secondary school he forms an attachment with Lucien, a more 'masculine' youth one year his elder. This union is also corrupt-ing, for despite some idyllic interludes Charlot is taught to dissimulate and throw inquisitive doctors off the scent. But Lucien grows out of his infatuation, turns to women, rejects Charlot and joins the army. Having now learned to masturbate efficiently, Charlot frequently con-soles himself in this manner and becomes progressively more sickly and effeminate. One of the consequences of his behaviour is his indifference to women, for when he is eighteen he is attracted not by some fisher-girls whom he sees but by their young brothers: 'He was filled with a sort of unhealthy misogyny . . . a distaste for women which is, as it were, the punishment for self-abuse' (p. 170). Relief from temptation comes when he in turn joins the army and is too busy to think of anything but chores. But when his duties are lightened and he is alone in his sentry box his devil tempts him all over again. A visit to a prostitute does not cure him; an affair with Fanny, a nymphomaniac, is only successful as long as they both continue to indulge their appetite for 'ecstatic orgies of lust'. When Fanny abandons Charlot, leaving their baby with him, he is inconsolable and plunges back into his vice. Finally, having found a book entitled *Family Advice for Fathers*, he reads that 'solitary vice, when it does not lead to frightful diseases, inevitably results in madness or suicide'. He therefore decides to pre-empt his destiny, and, taking the child with him (for he fears that the boy will have inherited the family curse), he drowns them both in the canal.

The notoriety of this novel was so great that it is very likely that Gide knew of it, although he may not actually have read it. The dangers of solitary vice which it illustrates exactly correspond with the descriptions of onanism contained in the medical books which Gide consulted.

Descaves

The name of Lucien Descaves occurs in a press-cutting in the *Corydon* archive.[102] An article by him on 'Invertis et pervertis' had been printed in *Le Journal* for 2 March 1910, and Gide cut this out. Descaves is concerned about the frequency of male prostitution in Paris. Male prostitutes, he asserts, are undesirable because their trade encourages idleness, and, in this respect, they are unlike female prostitutes. He writes of heterosexual sado-masochism on the boulevards but retains his most violent denunciations for the urinals, the 'Vespasiennes' – 'those disgraceful trading posts with their public notices and messages'. This was the author who had published *Sous-Offs* in 1890. Gide does not in fact mention the book, but it caused a great scandal when it appeared. An 'indelicate and unpatriotic' novel about military life, it includes one character Laprévotte, a sodomite, who is caught in Le Havre with a group of seven boys (p. 44). It was proceeded against for indecency ('outrage aux mœurs'), and the defendants were acquitted in March 1890. The prosecution mainly took exception to the portrayal of the French army as a crowd of cowards, thieves and verminous rascals. The affair was much talked about in the press from November 1889 to March 1890.[103]

Rachilde

Les Hors Nature, by Rachilde (who became the wife of Vallette, the proprietor of *Le Mercure de France*, with which Gide was closely connected), was published in 1897, and ran to several editions in the same year. It was reviewed by Ghéon in *L'Ermitage* VIII May 1897, immediately after his account of *Les Nourritures terrestres*: 'From a situation which might appear repugnant or ridiculous, she has been able to extract a tragic case – and she has given us a psychological study of homosexuality[104] in its complete form, both sensual and mental.'

It is the story of two brothers. Paul Éric de Fertzen, the younger, is an exquisite. Described in Part Two of the novel as manifesting a 'terrible hermaphroditism', he is madly fond of women and has several affairs in high society. His elder brother, Reutler, is 'masculine' and 'severe'. They are of Franco-Prussian descent, and this isolates them and requires that Reutler watch over his younger brother. Their close friendship is very affectionate, but soon grows unhealthy and oppressively jealous. Eventually Reutler, who is often tempted by the violent idea of suicide, recognises the 'tiger of his passion' and the 'forbidden love' which he nurtures in his breast. By force of will he keeps this to himself, but in a long ecstatic monologue he gives expression to his ardent yearning for Paul: 'You are my body and I am your soul.' Although he fondles Paul's feet with loving adoration, he will only admit that his love has 'nothing unhealthy [*maladif*]' about it since 'there is no *desire*'. The story comes to a melodramatic climax when after a series of rows and reconciliations Paul is given a thrashing by Reutler. This he enjoys, and becoming daily more effeminate he admires the manliness of his groom, demonstrates the pathological and violent side of his character, and seduces a peasant girl against her will. She is in fact a pyromaniac whom the two brothers had rescued (the burning church has also provided a dramatic backcloth for Reutler's passion). She now sets fire to the castle and, in a final scene as the brothers are trapped in a tower, Reutler, after taking poison, strangles Paul in a last, long, loving embrace. The book is a curious mixture of gothic sensationalism, and the suave effeteness of Huysmans' À *rebours* and Wilde's *Picture of Dorian Gray*. The characters are shown as undoubtedly corrupt and destined to the flames by which they are eventually consumed. It is hard to believe that Gide would have enjoyed reading it.

Eekhoud

Escal-Vigor by G. Eekhoud[105] first appeared under the title *Le Comte de la Digue* in the *Mercure de France* in 1898 (vols XXVII and XXVIII September–November). It was published in book form the following year and, like *Les Hors Nature*, also ran to several editions. Here again the style is somewhat gothic, but the book is generally speaking less melodramatic than Rachilde's. When, in fact, she reviewed it for the *Mercure de France*, XXIX February 1899 (pp. 466–8), she called it 'this sad and scarlet novel', adding, in the course of a passionate defence of Eekhoud, that he showed how 'by the despair of love, love is purified'. The novel tells the story of a pederast, and one could easily imagine that Gide could have found it congenial. However, it is not without its stereotypes. Henry de Kehlmark, the noble hero, had been a beautiful adolescent, but being highly strung and over-sensitive he had become withdrawn and artistic. He had suffered from migraines in the past, but through healthy exercise he becomes cured. His muscles develop. Blandine falls in love with him and Henry in turn adores her – but 'the season of the flesh did not last long'. In fact Guidon, a young lad from a rough family, is introduced to him. He is a dreamer, and when Henry makes chaste advances to him, promising to teach him to read, he is fired with ecstasy. A happy intimacy is established but Guidon's 'fanatical affection' gives rise to gossip. Blandine becomes a little jealous. Henry and Guidon sit for hours holding hands and talking. One day Henry tells him the story of two young men, one of whom is powerless and in a frenzy when his friend contemplates marriage. Henry describes their idyllic love, and then tells how these friends die at last, together, embracing forcibly in the fire. This is Henry's declaration of love; Guidon answers that he submits entirely, and seeks his friend's lips.

Henry consequently tells Blandine that he is in love with Guidon. She is horrified but continues to be devoted to him. The story is complicated by several subsidiary heterosexual intrigues, some of which involve Blandine. But because her love is true she becomes the worthy recipient of Henry's confession: 'I was an object of horror for myself,' he tells her. 'I believed that I was cursed, possessed by the devil and destined for the fires of Sodom.' His homosexual reading has been wide: Shakespeare's Sonnets, Michelangelo's poems for Tommaso Cavalieri, Montaigne, Tennyson, Wagner, Whitman, Carpenter, Plato, Plutarch on the Sacred Band, the life of Hadrian – and several more. 'I communed with all the noble virile passions of antiquity and the Renaissance, which masters praise so at school without mentioning the superb inspiring eroticism of absolute art.' The speech turns into a rather melodramatic confession as Henry speaks of his temptations and likens himself to the monster Gilles de Rais. (His relationship with Guidon has given us no reason to believe that he was so pathologically affected.) Having asked for comfort from religion he was anathematised and confined 'like Tannhäuser to the Venusberg – or rather the "Uranienberg"'.

Blandine says that he must have suffered extremely. With great compassion she offers him the comfort of living with both Guidon and herself in chaste devotion. This he accepts for 'with these two he felt himself strong enough to create the religion of absolute love, both homo- and heterogenic'. But such pious hopes are not to be fulfilled, for a revenge plot has been coming to the boil in the background. During a fête Guidon is attacked by a band of furious maenads and Henry rides in to the rescue. Both of them, however, are assailed by the mob with stones and arrows and are severely wounded. When they regain consciousness they are both near death: 'They looked at each other, smiled, recalled the slaughter, grasped each other in a close embrace and, their lips now pressed against each other's never to separate, they awaited the moment when each would draw his final breath.' The angelic Blandine is there to close their eyes.

What is surely remarkable about this novel is the idealised portrayal of the devotion of Henry for his younger beloved. Blandine symbolises a noble chaste ideal of womankind (her few lapses from chastity do not detract from this). The diatribe against sodomy can be seen as either a gesture towards the rules of conventional morality (which it undoubtedly is) or, within the context of the story, an attempt to focus the reader's attention once more on an ideal, ethereal love where the soul (but not the flesh) is allowed to express itself. What essential difference, we might ask ourselves, is there between the romantic agony of Henry and Guidon, and the plight of many a nineteenth-century

247

pair of star-crossed operatic heterosexual lovers? In both cases a noble death dictated by fate authenticates the moral value of their love.

Eekhoud's book was prosecuted unsuccessfully in Belgium. In this period the author was contributing a regular series of articles 'La Chronique de Bruxelles' to the *Mercure da France*, and in one of these he took the opportunity to write at some length about pederasty.[106] As part of his case he gave details about the prosecution and the support he had received from prominent men. The *Mercure de France*[107] had in fact sponsored a petition, and among the numerous signatories were Gide, Léon Blum and Bazalgette – strange bedfellows indeed! Eekhoud then proceeded to remarks about Hirschfeld's initiative in launching the *Jahrbuch*, giving examples of famous homosexuals and significant passages describing uranian love in other books (notably Goethe). In his own defence he maintained his right to artistic integrity and spoke strongly of the relevance for a modern audience of the portrayal of pederasty. Was this not, he remarked, as much a sign of our times as Werther's suicide was a sign of his? And did not some unenlightened members of the public judge it just as severely, calling it 'immoral'? His was, he said, another step along the trail blazed by Zola.[108]

Rouart

La Villa sans maître, written by Eugène Rouart, an intimate friend of Gide's, was published in 1898. It is heavily influenced by *Les Nourritures terrestres*, and even contrives to mention Gide in the text under the pseudonym 'Valentin Knox'. The book's adolescent hero has two friends who represent different aspects of his personality: Gabriel, the solace of his soul who replaces his mother's love, and Ménalque (a Gidean avatar), who is a symbol of adventure and debauchery. Marie-Anne, the hero's girlfriend, dies in due course in an arctic landscape somewhat reminiscent of the setting of part of Gide's *Le Voyage d'Urien*. Most of the sexual imagery in the novel is not homosexual, the exceptions being the descriptions of half-naked boys in the bakery and lusty farm lads. Feeling that his life has been a failure, the hero eventually seeks refuge in the desert after killing Gabriel with the knife given by Ménalque. This symbolic act leaves him in a bitter solitude where his only comfort is his adopted son. He hopes for repose in God and death. The book provides an example of Gide's influence on another writer rather than the reverse, but there are nevertheless some intriguing similarities between *La Villa sans maître* and *L'Immoraliste*. The latter was not published until 1902, but Gide's friendship with Rouart spans the period of its gestation.

Schlumberger

Another novel, *Heureux qui comme Ulysse* . . . was written by a close friend of Gide's, Jean Schlumberger, and published in the *Cahiers de la Quinzaine* in 1906.[109] When Schlumberger made the 'mistake' of reading it to his family it was not warmly received. Ghéon cried when he was read the final chapters, and was responsible for a short review in *L'Ermitage*, XVII September 1906; Gide, in October of that year, found it 'fearfully interesting' – but he was possibly motivated by a sense of inferiority in saying so. The book was generally judged too laconic, even by its author; and the sequel, *L'Inquiète Paternité*, found no more enthusiastic a welcome when it was read to Gide at Cuverville in 1909.[110]

The story concerns Cyrille, a sailor, who returns home after a long absence to find his wife and young son waiting for him. But he has a deeper and more loyal sentimental attachment to his long dead youthful friend Germain. As the tale unfolds, the reader gradually penetrates the mystery surrounding the birth of the son, Rémy. The secrets of old relationships are revealed, and we learn that it was Cyrille who encouraged Germain to make love to his wife. Rémy is thus a reincarnation of a lost love, and this explains the hesitant sensual affection Cyrille undoubtedly feels towards him. This sensitive work concludes with the departure of the mother and the boy. Gide's *Le Roi Candaule* had appeared in 1899, and this had developed a similar idea of a man who shares his wife with his closest friend, but Schlumberger makes something different out of the story.

Binet-Valmer

Lucien is by G. Binet-Valmer, an author listed among the 'collaborators' in the first issue of the *Nouvelle Revue Française* in 1908. It was published by Ollendorff in 1910, and reviewed by Rachilde in the *Mercure de France*, LXXXVI August 1910 pp. 497–8, where she noted 'with pleasure that today's *hors nature* are strikingly like those of yesteryear'. The story is narrated in the tradition of the scientific, naturalist school of which Zola had been the foremost exponent. It begins as a police novel. Certainly one is reminded of a similar narrative device in *Les Faux-Monnayeurs*, but this is probably quite coincidental. Lucien is an effeminate youth. He is spineless and has a shifty look. His physical nature is degenerate, for he has inherited his mother's tainted blood. Lucien's father, a famous doctor, decides to help his son, whom he suspects of being a degenerate: 'Confess. I promise you that I will listen not as a father with the right to punish, but as a doctor whose sole wish is to save a man who is ill.' To this Lucien replies that he has done wrong to become involved in scandal, but that he is not ill. He does however collapse hysterically in tears and soon tries to commit suicide. His father sees Lucien as a 'monster', and Lucien asks him to help him become a man of genius. The world of Lombroso is not far from our minds here, with references to the degree of sanity which distinguishes the ordinary member of society from persons who deviate from the norm.

Lucien's lover is called Reggie, and it is for him that he feels this 'frightening love [*épouvantable amour*]'. But, he cries, 'I want, I do want to be pure!' An attempted cure is then embarked upon, in which Marie becomes Lucien's fiancée. Eventually, however, he breaks out into a cold sweat when he touches her breasts. Although the novelist does not say so, this is clearly a treatment recommended in contemporary textbooks of clinical psychology. Within its own terms the novel offers a realistic presentation of the attitudes of men like Lucien's father. The final section consists of two letters, one from Lucien to his father explaining why he has committed suicide, and one to Marie urging her to forget him after his death. But there is a noteworthy reversal at the end of the story. Batchano, Lucien's counsellor and his father's colleague, reflects sadly on the poor abandoned cadaver of Lecamus which is undergoing an autopsy: Batchano nourished a strong affection for Lucien and is profoundly moved by the tragedy which such love entails. Clearly society should not claim the lives of these youthful victims. But Lucien and Reginald are not dead. They are now enjoying themselves in Italy, and will be off to Naples as the novel closes.

The interesting thing here is that among so many stereotyped representations of personality and behaviour the story ends on an openly optimistic note. The reader is intended to feel that the hero has escaped his fate. A review of the book appeared in Le Matin on 24 June 1910 and is among the Corydon press cuttings.[111] The reviewer, Henry Bernstein, summarises the story and concludes: 'The book is about a struggle between two abnormal people – the father has a maniacal desire for fame and the son is a slave to his pitiable impulse. . . . Like all good novels it has no "winner".' Similarly an extract from the review by Ernest Charles which appeared in the Vie Littéraire, 25 July 1910 p. 399, was copied out on to a small piece of paper by Gide: 'M.B.V. has analysed in great detail the illness or the vice of Lucien, the taint [*les tares*] which inevitably arises from this illness or this vice, and – for example – the mad vanity or the inescapable lying [*le mensonge irrésistible*].'[112] Although Gide has left us no comment of his own on this book, it is clear that Charles' criticism must have done more than awaken an echo in his mind, for Corydon takes his stand on the avoidance of lying.

Akadémos

In 1909 there appeared in Paris a monthly literary periodical, Akadémos. The venture lasted only one year. The same issue of the Mercure de France which contained an announcement of the appearance of Gide's newly founded Nouvelle Revue Française also carried a favourable notice of Akadémos, singling out for mention Laurent Tailhade's article on 'Les Carnets de Stéphane Baillehache (souvenirs sur Verlaine)'[113] There were to be six other mentions in the Mercure of the periodical in the course of the year.[114] Perhaps the second of these, in May (p. 160), should attract our attention, for here the reviewer, Charles Henri Hirsch, noted on the same page a 'regrettable' article by Gide, 'Mœurs littéraires: Autour du tombeau de Catulle Mendès', which had just appeared in the NRF.[115] On no occasion, however, did he draw attention to the homosexual nature of the contributions in Akadémos. The periodical's manifesto was a call to adopt a new classicism. 'We come from those luminous skies... where Plato walked and Vergil used to sing.' And again: 'Let us liberate the classical land of France from Slavonic decadence, German heaviness, Saxon slang and Judaeo-Christian prejudice, which deform the naturalness of paganism. . . .' The paganism favoured by this 'Revue mensuelle d'art libre et de critique' was both of style and of content. Thus the first few issues contained one or two overtly pederastic poems together with a contribution by Deligeorges ('La Lande ithyphallique'), which describes an Inferno populated by 'soft and yielding beings with bodies painted carmine' ('les êtres doux et mols, au corps teint de carmin'). The sixth, eighth and ninth issues contained an article by Peladan: 'Théorie amoureuse de l'androgyne'. This, however, was not particularly new, for it repeated what he had said about the image of Adam and Eve, complementary but each insufficient, to illustrate the solipsism of love. Peladan went on to describe the sex of the soul (a true androgyne is an ethereal substance) and concluded with a section on the realisation of the Eros of imagination in Art.

In the July issue (pp. 1–24) there appeared an article by Guy Delrouze,[116] 'Le Préjugé contre les mœurs: son origine, sa valeur, ses dangers', bearing as an epigraph a quotation from Gourmont with which Gide would doubtless have disagreed: 'Of all sexual aberrations, chastity is not the least odd.' This contains a plea for greater tolerance of homosexuals together with an historical account of the topic. In the main Delrouze follows Gourmont's arguments. Modesty, he writes, began when man invented property. His call for less victimisation is based on rejection of the prejudice which exalts chastity and condemns the flesh, for these are in his view survivals of the old family prohibitions of the early legislators. He agrees that a *crime passionnel* when committed with violence is not to be tolerated, but asserts that protection of children seems to him as much of a fiction as the corruption of children. Given that it is desirable, he writes, that too early an initiation into love should not hinder the development of an adolescent, it is by no means established that such would be the case at least among healthy individuals: 'Pleasure is only dangerous if indulged in to excess.'

Gide would only have agreed with him when he is talking about the resilience of healthy adolescents and the dangers of excessive pleasures. Like Gide, and Gourmont, Delrouze is astonished at the judge in the Renard case equating homosexuality with violent crime.[117] The remainder of the article contains a brief view of contemporary opinions and a sketch of attitudes in Greece and Rome, followed by some remarks on Europe and the East. Among modern theories the writer retains the following: both men and women are fundamentally bisexual creatures; the body may go in one direction, the nervous system in a contrary one; such a phenomenon exists in nature; there is a spectrum of the degrees to which any individual is predominantly homosexual or heterosexual. Several other observations are made: we may ask whether a nation's decadence arises from debased morals, or is the reverse the case? No society has been able to outlive luxury, wealth and happiness. Among other examples Delrouze briefly alludes to Burton's 'Terminal Essay' in the *Arabian Nights*, Dante and Brunetto Latini, Henri III of France, Elizabethan England and Christopher Marlowe, Stendhal (on Napoleon), Wagner and Ludwig of Bavaria, and Whitman (whom he calls a 'hypersexual' – one who can love men passionately without crossing the boundary of conscious desire). His remarks on contemporary events are somewhat superficial: he is quite naturally aware of recent developments in Germany; in speaking of English schools he draws a conclusion about the inborn homosexuality of the British. The French, he observes, are far more heterosexually inclined than their English or German counterparts. In Italy homosexual practices constitute 'a national industry', and he has several equally inadequate remarks on India, China and Japan. Again there is not much here to remind us of Gide's arguments except perhaps a point which is made in *Corydon* in the course of discussing the situation in France. Despite what he has said, Delrouze still insists that homosexual activity among Frenchmen must be recognised – and so must that state of 'veritable hermaphroditism' which lasts but a brief time during puberty. This latter idea also occurs in *Corydon*.

Other material of interest in this periodical is four erotic Arabic poems (translated by Ary-René d'Yvermont, 15 August 1909 pp. 193–7: 'No other people has celebrated with so much warmth the fever of boy love'), and a poem to the Boy Eros (τῷ παιδὶ ἔ ρωτι) by Sonyeuse (*ibid.* p. 268). In the September issue there is a play by Robert Scheffer, *Hadrien sur le Nil*, in the course of which the Emperor's beloved Antinous exclaims, 'I am the slave of my beauty and I long for death as a release.' After a love scene on a boat, Antinous plunges naked to his death in the Nile. October saw a piece on the charms of boys at school (Achille Essebac [A. Bécasse], 'Palestres d'aujourd' hui', pp. 515–18), and in December there appeared three poems by Jacques Adelsward-Fersen. One was on pagan Rome, one on pederastic love and one was misogynistic. Throughout the various issues there are a small number of pieces of minor interest, including a serialised novel by 'Sydney Place', *Les Fréquentations de Maurice (mœurs de Londres)*, which contains several suggestive incidents and descriptions. It seems probable that Gide read the issues of this periodical, for he noticed that number 3 contained no mention of his own new venture, the *Nouvelle Revue Française*, among its listing of 'Periodicals Received.'[118] However, he left no record of what he thought of the articles, and we may surmise that, since the general tone of the periodical was somewhat libertarian and erotic, the contributors would have been more in tune with Gourmont's ideas than with Gide's. There is no evidence that it influenced the composition of *Corydon* except perhaps in the witness it bore to the 'subject being in the air', and hence in spurring Gide on to complete his project.[119]

Proust

We turn now to some works which Gide was acquainted with but which mainly because of chronological factors, we can be confident exercised no influence on the composition of *Corydon*. Thus, we know that by a curious coincidence Proust probably started to work on an article on homosexuality in 1908, largely inspired, it seems, by the contemporary Eulenburg scandal. The text eventually formed the basis of *Sodome I* in *À la recherche du temps perdu*. This essay, as Painter notes,[120] can be identified 'not with the novel itself, but with the preliminary sketch for the first and second chapters of *Sodome et Gomorrhe* which forms Chapter Twelve, 'La Race maudite', of *Contre Sainte-Beuve*'.[121] Proust spoke of this to Robert Dreyfus in May of that year, and suggested that he was thinking of having it printed in the *Mercure de France* when he had completed it. It is doubtful, however, whether Gide knew of Proust's views on homosexuality before 25 February 1916,[122] although it is certainly of some significance that Ghéon reviewed *Du côté de chez Swann* in the *NRF* on 1 January 1914 (pp. 139–43).[123] It was in 1912 that Proust himself had learned that Gide and Ghéon were practising homosexuals;[124] in 1892 Gide and

Proust had frequented the same *salons* and might possibly have met by chance.[125]

Apart from a brief mention, there is nothing in Gide's *Journal* about the 1916 encounter. It is later, on 14 May 1921, that we can read a more detailed account of another meeting with Proust. This was the year in which *Sodome I* was published. Gide tells us that as soon as he arrived, Proust started to talk of uranism, and that he then interrupted himself to ask Gide some detailed questions about the Gospels. Gide was bringing him a copy of the 1920 edition of *Corydon* (concerning which Proust promised he would remain silent). It was on this occasion that Proust allegedly advised him that he could tell all provided he never said 'I'. 'That doesn't suit me,' wrote Gide, but he reports that in this conversation Proust did not hide his homosexuality, 'glorying in it, rather'. Proust maintained that Baudelaire[126] was homosexual, and that the way the poet wrote about Lesbos was for him sufficient proof. Gide protested that even if Baudelaire was that way inclined the poet was almost certainly unaware of it, and the idea that he was a practising homosexual was inconceivable to him. But Proust was convinced: how could one doubt it! Gide was finally tempted to believe that this was so, and also that homosexuals were more numerous than he had at first thought.

We must remember that we only have Gide's word for the foregoing, but we have no specific reason to question his veracity on this occasion. Moreover it is doubtless this conversation, and perhaps others like it, which lie behind the note dated November 1922 which Gide added to the preface of the 1924 edition of *Corydon*:

> Certain books, and Proust's in particular, have accustomed the public to be less timorous, and to dare to consider unemotionally those things which they pretended not to know about, or at first preferred to ignore. Many people willingly believe that they cause not to exist whatever they do not mention. But I fear that these books have also significantly helped to mislead people. The theory of a man–woman, of 'sexuelle Zwischenstufen' (intermediate stages of sexuality) which Dr Hirschfeld launched in Germany some time before the Great War – and with which Marcel Proust seems to agree – may well not be false. But it only explains and is relevant to certain cases of homosexuality which I am precisely not concerned with in my book – inversion, effeminacy and sodomy. . . . They stand revealed as much more frequent than I at first believed. And let us suppose that Hirschfeld's theory satisfies these readers. This theory of a 'third sex' will never explain what we customarily call Greek love – 'pederasty' which contains no element of effeminacy on either side.

Gide is decidedly concerned to distance Corydon from the Baron de Charlus. Despite this, Gide was very enthusiastic about the portrayal of

Charlus which had appeared in the extracts published in the *NRF* on 1 June 1914,[127] and he returned to the subject in his next letter of 14 June, replying to Proust's letter of [10/11 June]:

M. de Charlus is a splendid portrait by means of which you have contributed to the popular confusion between a homosexual [*homosexuel*] and an invert [*inverti*]. For the shades of meaning and distinctions which you include in your letter will not apply to them. Charlus, who is a single individual, will be taken for a type and will give rise to generalisations. What I am saying is in fact in praise of your picture. (Did you know the strange Baron d'Oazans (I forget how his name is spelled) who died some five or six years ago? and of whom Charlus sometimes reminds me?)[128]

It is in the first part of *Sodome et Gomorrhe* that Charlus and Jupien meet and are watched by the narrator.[129] The reader is given a deliciously humorous description of their encounter together with some more general remarks on 'the race accursed' ('la race maudite'). The narrator perceives a feminine element in M. de Charlus, and he finds Jupien's simpering posture antipathetic. Despite this, the scene has for him a natural beauty of its own (p. 605). Charlus would like a sleeping-car attendant, a bus driver – or anyone else like that – the sort he calls masculine (p. 611). Jupien is the type of invert who, fortunately for Charlus, is attracted to older men (p. 607). This, for the narrator, illustrates a general principle: Charlus belongs to the race of those beings who are less contradictory than they appear at first sight, for 'their ideal is masculine precisely because they have a feminine temperament'. The 'race' is also one on which a curse weighs heavily. Because they seek a sexual complement to their nature, two inverts can never make a satisfactory 'match', for a feminine temperament will seek a masculine man who, by definition, will only be interested in women. There are other curses: despite the idealism and asceticism which undoubtedly exist on occasion (p. 616),[130] they are the victims of society which regards their defects with disgust. They are forced to live in hypocrisy. Their illness is only seldom curable. In justifying their tastes they forget when they appeal to the Greek world that 'there was no [deviant] homosexuality' where homosexuality was the norm.[131] Only opprobrium defines what is criminal (pp. 616–17). Even nowadays homosexuality can be found allied with great moral value.

Despite this, however, the major part of the narrator's picture is negative. Homosexuals, obliged to keep their secret safe from society, have created a freemasonry of their own. This is not to say that they are all of one type (pp. 619–20). There are convivial sodomites, those who are overtly feminine and grotesque, and those who despise women and classify themselves among the intellectual and artistic elite by appealing to the example of great men who were homosexuals. There are solitary types who, thinking they are the only homosexuals in existence, often experience a chaste love by a redirection of their impulses (pp. 619, 624). The narrator describes their quest, and with the exquisite simile of the orchid and the jellyfish underlines the often sterile beauty of their life (pp. 626–7). There are those who take their pleasure with members of both sexes (p. 622), and those who make their partner jealous, and who are jealous themselves. Finally, in a return to the episode which has provoked these reflections, the narrator describes how there is in the case of most of these men and adolescents evidence of the spirit of a woman enclosed within the body of a man (p. 621). It is as if the invert, he writes, is more nearly related to that early stage in the development of life on earth where the hermaphrodite was manifest among the plants and animals (p. 629). This underlines inverts' strangeness in modern society, and also, he asserts by appealing to examples from botany and biology, their naturalness.

If they have little else in common Gide and Proust have an engaging and sympathetic interest in natural history. But, it must be added, they are in this respect both inheritors of nineteenth-century tradition. Proust in dwelling on the effeminate or unwholesome aspects of inversion distances himself from Gide, even though he uses the image of primitive monomorphism to explain his categories.

Gide's apologetic letter to Proust of January 1914[132] gives as his excuse for having first rejected À la recherche the fact that he had believed Proust was a snob – 'du côté de chez Verdurin' – and therefore out of sympathy with the NRF. He had also opened the manuscript at a couple of places where an unfortunate impression had been made by 'a cup of camomile' (sic) and the syntax of a sentence which implied an anatomical impossibility. In other words his reaction was not conditioned by what Proust said about sexuality. What he does not state is that Ghéon was instrumental in drawing to the attention of the NRF panel of readers the merit of Proust's novel. Ghéon's enthusiasm encouraged them to reconsider their verdict.[133] But what this in turn obscures is the fact that Ghéon's original review of Du côté de chez Swann was hostile and largely dismissive. On 2 January 1914 Proust wrote to Ghéon to complain of the way in which he had been treated, and in answering the charge that his book was full of irrelevant material cited the case of Charlus and the manner in which he had been introduced:

Some people may think that I have reproduced a quite ordinary situation in showing Swann naively entrusting his mistress to M. de Charlus who, these same readers believe, is betraying Swann. It isn't like that at all.

M. de Charlus is an old homosexual who will fill the whole of the third volume, and Swann, with whom he fell in love at school, knows that in entrusting Odette to him he is incurring no risks. . . . When people have read volume three, if they turn back to volume one and to that single passage where M. de Charlus makes a brief appearance, they will see that he fixes me with a stare and will understand why.[134]

From Proust's next letter to Ghéon ([6 January 1914] – Ghéon's replies are lost), it is easy to see that Ghéon had quickly revised his opinion – no doubt influenced by the promise of more on Charlus. Except for a very few letters, we do not possess Gide's part in the correspondence. However, on 11 June 1914 Proust wrote to thank Gide for being 'indulgent' towards M. de Charlus, adding that he had tried to portray a homosexual attracted by virility because 'without being aware of it, he is a Woman'. He continued:

In no way do I assert that this is the only type of homosexual. But he is a particularly interesting one which to the best of my belief has never been described. Moreover, like all homosexuals he is different from other men – in some respects worse and in others infinitely better. . . . I am convinced that M. de Charlus owes to his homosexuality his understanding of so many things which are a closed book for his brother the Duc de Guermantes, as well as his sensitivity and his discrimination. I have shown that from the start. Unfortunately, my striving for objectivity in that regard as elsewhere will render this book particularly hateful. Indeed, in volume three where M. de Charlus (who only makes a brief appearance here) occupies an important place, the enemies of homosexuality will be revolted by the scenes I shall depict. And the rest of them won't be happy either at their virile ideal being presented as being a consequence of a feminine temperament.

Gide had obviously read the particular passage in the earlier volume where Charlus first appears. When the extracts were to be published in periodical form in the NRF Proust warned Gide that he would see 'nothing of Monsieur de Charlus, although he does appear in volume two and has quite a long conversation with the narrator in Paris after the scene which you have read (at Balbec).' The description of this 'original' character does in fact differ a little from the picture Proust had conjured up when he had first approached Gallimard in 1912: 'He's the virile pederast, in love with virility, loathing effeminate young men, in fact loathing all young men, just as a man who has suffered through women becomes a misogynist.'[135]

On the occasions when Gide visited Proust in 1921 their conversation had mostly been about uranism.[136] Gide learned that everything graceful, tender and charming among Proust's homosexual memories had been transposed to provide a fuller picture of heterosexual love in the novel. Consequently only the grotesque and the abject remained for Sodom. Gide would rather have had Eros depicted in all the youth and beauty of the God. Proust allegedly replied that youth was the element most easily transposed – and beauty seldom attracted him, having little relationship with desire. Proust maintained that he had not wished to stigmatise uranism. 'I eventually understood,' wrote Gide, 'that what the rest of us consider ignoble and the object of laughter or disgust does not appear to him to be so repulsive.' In addition to the moral questions raised by effeminacy and debauchery, we therefore have to remember that a difference of aesthetics also separated the views of Proust and Gide. The question of Proust's 'divided nature' is one which Gide did not pose, though he was clearly out of sympathy with what he saw as the writer's 'duplicity'. But if in his eyes Proust was 'dishonest ', it was not merely because he thought the autobiographical aspects of À la recherche misleading and often contrary to what he knew of Proust's sexual experiences. Dishonesty lay in painting an ugly picture of homosexuality, and in aligning it once again with hostile medical and religious stereotypes.

Yourcenar

Marguerite Yourcenar's Alexis, ou le traité du vain combat first appeared in Paris 'Au Sans Pareil' in 1929, and another novel of hers with a homosexual theme, Coup de grâce, was published in 1939. It was Gide's friend, Roger Martin du Gard, who wrote to him on 30 June 1930 enquiring whether he had read the first of these books. We do not know Gide's reply, and his only other reference to Yourcenar occurs in the Journal for 9 September 1940 when he mentioned an article by her on Cavafy and his poems.[137]

Alexis is a confessional novel, written with gravity and decorum when the author was twenty-four. In bidding farewell to his wife Monique, the hero explains the feelings which have dominated his life since his adolescence. In his youth, he relates, he was pure. He was brought up by women, but lived a solitary life. He idealised his sisters and his sisters' female friends, and extended this esteem to other women. He was unhappy at school, but when he eventually returned to his home he had a homosexual experience which revealed the dazzling power of love. This episode is not described in detail, but the sense of sin which it revealed was to remain with Alexis. In his early twenties, he had many furtive relationships. He divorced sexuality from love. He depicts the disarray of the adolescent, dwelling on his temptations and his faltering acquiescence. He reminds Monique how he was drawn to her by her seriousness, and reveals how an awareness of his vice made him hesitant to progress from their engagement to marriage. For him marriage, when it came, meant that he renounced his happiness. There was no true intimacy, and he felt himself destroyed. Despite the birth of their child he felt that they were strangers to one another.

The book finishes partly on a note of despair, for Alexis cannot love Monique. He has, however, found once again the beauty and mystery of his body – and so he craves understanding and forgiveness for his actions. *Alexis* does in fact seem strongly influenced by a Gidean view of the world: 'virtue has its temptations', 'virtue consists in striving to achieve', 'wisdom, like life, is made of continuous progress and new beginnings'. With these and similar aphorisms, and with a sense of sin and guilt which has to be overcome, the hero strives for self-knowledge in a manner which recalls Michel in *L'Immoraliste*.

Martin du Gard

Roger Martin du Gard's play *Un Taciturne* was first performed on 28 October 1931 at the Théâtre Louis Jouvet (Comédie des Champs Élysées) in Paris. A second, slightly altered version appeared in 1948. It was on 2 March 1931 that Martin du Gard wrote to Gide that he was planning a play on an 'involuntary and unconscious sexual attraction' but he refused to say more. Gide encouraged him with a telegram. A number of further letters were exchanged from then until the play was produced, and Gide proffered several suggestions. He wanted to help his friend rewrite a passage where Wanda expresses her sexual disgust, and said that he was willing to come to Paris especially to do so.[138] The drama centres around Thierry, a homosexual who is unaware of his true nature, and Wanda, a lesbian, who is a little more perceptive about herself. Thierry commits suicide when he realises that he is homosexual. Martin du Gard foresaw Gide's discomfort at the melodramatic dénouement when he wrote on 17 March 1931: 'This will seem to you (and to the fanatics at La Souco, too [Dorothy Bussy])[139] a concession to traditional morality. But in my opinion it is simply the logical act of a given character in a particular situation. If it is psychologically true nothing else matters.'

Gide's contribution to the play consisted largely in what he saw as improvements in the dialogue to achieve a more stylish effect on stage. His reaction to the depiction of Thierry is not particularly easy to ascertain. Martin du Gard records that Gide found the whole concept of the play 'very bold'[140] when they were trying to get it put on in Paris. Gide wrote in his *Journal* on 4 October 1931: 'Roger is complaining that he can't find a young actor who is sufficiently seductive. . . . If there is no sensuality, the pistol shot at the end has no meaning. Roger is beginning to understand that he was not perhaps correct in maintaining that no man, however slightly inclined towards Sodom, can remain insensitive to the charms of a Ganymede. He must nevertheless convince himself that some people remain completely blind in that respect. . . .' Gide goes on to make the point that the young actor must be sufficiently attractive to make the action comprehensible. 'As Hippolyte with Phèdre,' he adds. The play gave rise to further reflections on 12 November 1931: All the Thierrys whom Gide knew had 'found their own solution'; it was not a question of choosing whether 'to be cured or to shoot oneself' – which was the advice offered by a cousin of Martin du Gard in a critical article. 'Thierry must have been terribly busy not to have noticed his tastes until so late,' is Gide's final rather unsympathetic comment.[141]

Cocteau

We cannot conclude this chapter without a brief word about Jean Cocteau, whom Gide had known since 1912, or possibly earlier as the inclusion of Cocteau's name in a list of subscribers for the statue to Verlaine in 1910 might imply.[142] The problem here, however, is that we risk entering a world of biographical anecdotes. Most of the comments which Gide made on Cocteau's work refer to more general questions of aesthetics. It is no secret that Gide was out of sympathy with many of the enterprises in which Cocteau was engaged, and that he regarded his modernism as singularly lacking in depth. *Le Livre blanc*, an account of some of Cocteau's homoerotic adventures, was probably written towards the end of 1927, and was first published in an anonymous limited private edition in 1928 (Paris: Les Quatre Chemins), and reprinted in 1930 (Paris: Éditions du Signe). On 11 October 1929 Gide recorded in his *Journal* that he had read the book while waiting for the copy promised by Cocteau. 'What empty agitation in the dramas he narrates! What a contrived style! how he plays to the gallery! what artifice! But certain obscenities are told in a charming manner.' Whether he had in mind the episodes with adolescents, or the boys ejaculating in the bath house observed from behind a mirror we do not know. 'What are shocking – and particularly so – are the pseudo-religious sophisms.' It is interesting to observe that whereas Gide had felt that Proust's portrayal of childhood in À *la recherche du temps perdu* was more successful than his own in *Si le grain ne meurt*[143] (despite their disagreements over the nature of homosexuality), he had a very low opinion of Cocteau's reminiscences in *Le Livre blanc*. Gide was not to be pleased, as the character of Passavant in *Les Faux-Monnayeurs* bears witness.

CHAPTER FOURTEEN

British and American Literature

How well did Gide know English? On 10 April 1910 he confessed in a letter to Edmund Gosse that he was ashamed that his knowledge of the language was so poor. He had begun to rectify this state of affairs by taking classes, but it is clear from entries in the *Journal* for 1912 (I p. 364; and elsewhere) that his progress was not very fast. It was only in 1918, during his visit to Cambridge, that he was able to improve matters. However, his knowledge of English literature and his contacts with English men of letters dated from well before the First World War. Gide met Oscar Wilde in Paris in 1891 and again in North Africa in the company of Lord Alfred Douglas in 1895. In 1896 Henry-D. Davray,[1] whom Gide knew through his contacts with the *Mercure de France*, started a column in that periodical called 'Lettres anglaises' in which he chronicled the latest literary events in England. 1908 witnessed Gide's brief trip to England in the company of a group of friends which included Henri Ghéon. In December 1911 Gide dined with Gosse and met Henry James, and in the same year he made the acquaintance of Arnold Bennett through the agency of Valery Larbaud. Larbaud was also with him when he met Joseph Conrad and Arthur Symons. This particular visit was quite different from the one recorded in *Ainsi soit-il* when the young Gide had gone there under the strict supervision of pastor Élie Allégret. Another journey to England occurred in 1918 when Gide took Marc Allégret with him to Cambridge and made important contacts with Dorothy Bussy (the sister of Lytton Strachey), and other people associated with the Bloomsbury group.

Gide's reading in English was wide, but it must be remembered that, before he was truly proficient in the language, he was limited to reading what was available in French, either in book form or in the literary periodicals. Information was also undoubtedly mediated through friends, and, more significantly, through secondary works like Taine's *Histoire de la littérature anglaise*, which his mother gave him in May 1891.[2]

Shakespeare

If we turn first to Shakespeare, we have seen, in our discussion of Gautier's *Mademoiselle de Maupin*, the charm which Gide discovered in the love scenes in *As You Like It* in 1890. On being urged by his close associate Jacques Copeau to translate the play, Gide wrote in the *Journal* on 18 June 1914 that he was quite taken with the idea, but when he read it later he recorded on 28 May 1921 that he had not liked it very much. It may be that on this occasion the effort of tackling it in English took the edge off his enjoyment. As for *Twelfth Night*, which contains a similar travesty role (Viola disguised as Cesario, giving rise to a love entanglement based on mistaken gender), Gide passed no detailed comment except for a reference in the *Journal* on 23 February 1930 which clearly shows he was familiar with the play. It had been staged by Copeau at the Théâtre du Vieux-Colombier on 22 May 1914.[3]

In 1891 he copied out, in French, into his notebook:

The finest passage in *The Tempest*:

> Ariel: Do you love me, master? No?
> Prospero: Dearly, my delicate Ariel.

– but he is not of the same nature.[4]

It is, I think, obvious that the lines caught his attention because of the way in which they lend themselves to a homosexual interpretation. After all, we need only imagine the spirit Ariel as a playful boy in order to enter Gide's frame of mind. His comment on the relationship: 'but he is not of the same nature', is not obscure if we recollect similar observations of Gide's in the early 1890s. As he said in the example of Castor and Pollux,[5] he believed that natures which are too similar to each other cannot fulfil their love. Perhaps being able to see man and boy as beings from two different spheres helped him provide an explanation of what he felt.

It might be thought, and pardonably so perhaps by many Englishmen, that Gide would turn to Shakespeare's Sonnets as the most flawless expression of the love of a man for his younger friend. Curiously enough, he does not seem to have found them particularly attractive.[6] He wrote in his *Journal* on 25 September 1914 that he had read a few Sonnets, and later, on 18 July 1923, he noted that he had read 'the whole collection again for the third time'. He found several of them frustratingly difficult (*exaspérants*), although he had re-read several of them at least a dozen times. On a previous occasion, on 23 September 1914, he had shared the pleasure of reading some of them with Jacques

Raverat, the friend who had spoken to him warmly of Rupert Brooke and with whom he had further discussed the possibility of translating *As You Like It*.[7]

It is common knowledge that any list of famous homosexuals will give pride of place to Shakespeare. We are therefore not surprised to find a judgement of this kind in *Corydon* (p. 173). Ruskin, whom we shall turn to in a moment, taught Gide that Shakespeare's heroines are images of pure women; it was Gide who tried to forge the link between this image of purity and the playwright's homosexuality.

Marlowe

He seems to have found it more rewarding to read Marlowe. He noted in the *Journal* on 5 July 1937: 'Finished Shakespeare's *Venus and Adonis*', and considered that certain passages suffered from the effects of rhetoric. He judged Marlowe's *Hero and Leander* superior to it 'if I remember it correctly. I'll have to re-read it'. In both poems, however, he recognised 'a burning gust of sensuality'. But, he added, '*Venus and Adonis* has the reputation of being "artificial and cold", for it is especially the beauty of Adonis which Shakespeare is captivated by and which he celebrates.'

Marlowe's name also appears prominently among lists of famous homosexuals, and Corydon is possibly thinking of Piers Gaveston and the King in *Edward II* when he refers to him (pp. 161–2). Havelock Ellis mentioned Marlowe in the preface to *Sexual Inversion*, and had edited a selection of his works in the Mermaid Series. Here, in the unexpurgated edition of 1887, he printed a transcript of the documents alleging Marlowe's heterodox sexual and religious views. It is rather unlikely that Gide had access to this book while he was writing *Corydon*, although he does quote from John Addington Symonds' preface to it in his *Retour de l'U.R.S.S.* (1936).[8] It is more likely that he knew of G. Eekhoud's 1896 French translation of *Edward II*. If he did, the case is an interesting one. The play was performed at Lugné-Poë's Théâtre de l'Oeuvre.[9]

There is, as we know, the amorous dialogue between Jupiter and Ganymede at the opening of Marlowe's *Dido Queen of Carthage*. Eekhoud quotes from this in his preface to *Edward II*. He then passes on to a brief analysis of the play he has translated (and adapted), and in so doing brings out the following particular details. The King invites Gaveston to share the kingdom with his dearest friend; Gaveston's plans for their mutual pleasures are quoted at length:

Sometime a lovely boy in Dian's shape
With hair that gilds the water as it glides. . . .

The King, made desperate, nevertheless gloriously bears witness to his 'subversive loves' until the very end. 'The character of Edward II is treated by the author with an admirable elevation and charity. . . . The abnormal passion of Edward II is so sincere and so inescapable, so all-consuming, that we forgive him and even take his side and Gaveston's against the Queen and the barons, the more so since being guilty he expiates his weaknesses by a long humiliating agony and fearful torture. This love consumes and poisons him so greatly that we are reminded of Nessus' shirt and Hercules.' 'After Gaveston's death Edward II is faithful to his instinct and brings his forbidden affection to bear on young Spencer – or rather he only provides himself with a successor for the assassinated Gaveston so as to defy the pack of his enemies. Ordered by the barons to repudiate this new favourite . . . he embraces him proudly.' 'This is a noble and tragic theatre,' concludes Eekhoud.

Among the manuscript fragments there is an intriguing scrap, referring simultaneously to Spenser, Ovid and Marlowe.[10] The text (in French) reads:

Corydon.
    See the myth of Cypressus. Ovid. Met. X 121 alluded to in Marlowe: Hero and Leander.
    (Doubtless the whole passage should be translated)
as well as in Spenser F.Q. VI 17 . . .[11]

The passage in Marlowe[12] is brief;

> There might you see the gods in sundrie shapes,
> Committing headdie ryots, incest, rapes . . .
> Love kindling fire, to burne such townes as *Troy*,
> *Sylvanus* weeping for the lovely boy
> That now is turned into a Cypres tree,
> Under whose shade the Wood-gods love to bee.

This is indeed only an allusion to a tale of mythological pederasty. We might more easily have expected Gide's attention to be caught by the far more sensual description of Neptune's amorous playing with Leander later in the poem (II 155–226):

> He clapt his plumpe cheekes, with his tresses playd,
> And smiling wantonly, his love bewrayd.
> He watcht his armes, and as they opend wide,
> At every stroke, betwixt them would he slide,
> And steale a kisse . . .
> And dive into the water, and there prie

264

Upon his brest, his thighs and everie lim,
And up againe, and close beside him swim,
And talk of love: *Leander* made replie,
You are deceav'd, I am no woman I.
Thereat smilde *Neptune*. . . .

It is no wonder that we read in the *Journal* the entry for 13 November 1912: 'I am discovering *Hero and Leander* and as I get further into this ardent and magnificent poetry I become quite dazed and intoxicated by it.' He reiterated his enthusiasm when he wrote to Edmund Gosse on reading Marlowe's poem 'and several cantos of the *Faerie Queene*' on 28 November of the same year. The *Journal* entries for 10, 18 and 23 November also tell us that he was spending time with these two works. He records reaching the end of 'Le deuxième chant' of Spenser (presumably Book II, or possibly canto 2 of Book I), but little more need be said here of the *Faerie Queene*. The stanza alluded to in the manuscript we have noticed above is Book I vi 17, and tells how Sylvanus, on seeing Una, is reminded of the 'lovely boy' Cyparisse, though he finds that she is more comely than the youth. Cyparisse, so the legend goes, died of grief after Sylvanus had killed his favourite hind. It is easy to see that in Spenser this is merely a classical allusion to illustrate the text. There are in fact several other apparent allusions to 'homely' manifestations of pederasty among Spenser's peasants, but Gide does not refer to these.[13]

Fielding and Smollett

A passage by Addison from the *Spectator* is quoted in English in *Corydon* to show the naivety of certain remarks about Nature's adornment of male birds and women's cultivation of their own inherited charms: 'The peacock in all his pride does not display half the colours that appear in the garment of a British Lady, when she is dressed either for a ball or a birthday. . . .' 'Or should we,' adds Gide, 'see this as ironic?'[14]

Defoe is also appealed to, but this time the illustration is even further from our main concern: Corydon finds himself (pp. 166–7) in a position where he thinks he might be unwisely giving the interlocutor the impression of being the only man in the world who has seen the truth. But he has a duty to speak out, he says, citing, in English: 'He that opposes his own judgement against the current of the times ought to be backed with unanswerable truth, and he that has truth on his side is a fool as well as a coward, if he is afraid to own it, because of the multitude of other men's opinions. Tis hard for a man to say, all the world is mistaken, but himself. . . .' This extract is not taken directly from Defoe, as is clear from the printed text, but from Taine's *Histoire de la littérature anglaise* (vol. IV p. 87), where Taine is discussing Defoe's 'presbyterian' attitudes.

These two examples demonstrate quite neatly how Gide often wished to give his ideas a certain weight and authority by illustrating them with evidence that others had held similar opinions. Strictly speaking, such quotations often do not advance his argument, nor do they bring fresh evidence to bear. But these remarks are not entirely true of the eighteenth-century English novelists whom Gide came to admire so greatly. Although their influence on his works is perhaps best seen when he was composing *Les Faux-Monnayeurs*, Fielding, Smollett and Sterne all made an impression on him. On 15 February 1918 he wrote to Ruyters that he was reading Fielding's *Amelia* aloud to his wife; on 9 May he wrote in his *Journal* that his interest was beginning to flag. This was doubtless when he added the note to the section of Dialogue IV in *Corydon* (p. 183) which mentions the 'frequent occurrence' of selfless love combined with passionate affection in *Amelia*. A glance at the book will illustrate what attracted Gide's attention, namely the portrayal of an obviously innocent relationship between an older man and his young servant.[15]

The young man is Amelia's foster-brother, and it is this fact which endears him to the narrator Booth. He enlists and serves as Booth's batman. His affection is particularly in evidence during a storm at sea, and is described in the following terms:

> I am going to relate to you an instance of heroic affection in a poor man towards his master, to which love itself, even among persons of superior education, can produce but few similar instances. My poor man being unable to get me with him into the boat, leaped suddenly into the sea, and swam back to the ship; and when I gently rebuked him for his rashness, he answered, he chose rather to die with me, than to live to carry the account of my death to my Amelia; at the same time bursting into a flood of tears, he cried, 'Good heavens! What will that poor lady feel when she hears of this!' This tender concern for my dear love, endeared the poor fellow more to me than the gallant instance which he had just before given of his affection towards myself.

It is true that Booth talks of an emotional tie between himself and his servant, and he does state that he 'was very easily prevailed upon to list one of the handsomest young fellows in England'. All this may indeed provoke a sympathetic reaction in the mind – or heart – of a homosexual reader. But *Corydon* appears to have forgotten that these men are characters in a novel; that the evident sentimentality of the epoch dictates the attitudes portrayed; that the actions are firmly linked to the heterosexual element in the plot; and that many reflections are made on the relative sophistication of persons in different stations of society. The two characters are man and master. Such affection, and it is an idealised literary convention, may be witnessed in any number of adventure stories from *Robinson Crusoe* to *Coral Island*, and might even have been perceived by Gide in *Kidnapped!*, which he read in Albert Savine's translation in 1905.[16]

Gide records reading Fielding's *Tom Jones* (how much of it one cannot tell) on 3 July 1911.[17] He emphasises how in his opinion Fielding only likes *natural* virtue – a certain goodness of character that makes Tom shoulder the whole blame for the misconduct he has shared in with his friend. 'If Tom regrets anything,' he adds, 'it is when he thinks it might have upset Sophia.' He reminds us that Fielding wrote that he did not intend to present *perfect* characters in his narrative. In *Corydon* *Tom Jones* is referred to (p. 182), not because the hero is a pederast (far from it!) but because in Corydon's view the book demonstrates a clear connection between Tom's large number of casual sexual affairs and the real love he entertains for Sophia. Such a notion, need one add, borders on the grotesque.

In Smollett's *The Adventures of Roderick Random* a nobleman makes amorous advances to the hero in Chapter 51. The conversation develops with much the same arguments as are used by Corydon – although it is only fair to add that neither Corydon nor his creator ever mentions the book. Gide did however ask Ruyters on 7 July 1918 to check that the copy of Smollett's works which he had ordered had been despatched.[18]

'At this day,' says Lord Strutwell,

> it prevails not only over all the east, but in most parts of Europe; in our own country it gains ground apace, and in all probability will become in a short time a more fashionable vice than simple fornication. Indeed, there is something to be said in vindication of it; for, notwithstanding the severity of the law against offenders in this way, it must be confessed that the practice of this passion is unattended with that curse and burden upon society, which proceeds from a race of miserable and deserted bastards. . . . And it likewise prevents the debauchery of many a young maiden, and the prostitution of honest men's wives; not to mention the consideration of health, which is much less liable to be impaired in the gratification of this appetite, than in the exercise of common venery, which, by ruining the constitutions of our young men, has produced a puny progeny, that degenerates from generation to generation.

But we must remember that Strutwell is a rogue and Roderick a dupe.[19]
The Adventures of Peregrine Pickle contains some amusing episodes

which Gide may well have noticed. In Chapter 49, an Italian marquis and a German baron are caught by the landlady fondling each other and are soundly berated by her. Pallet, the 'virtuous painter', witnesses the Italian's advances, and 'conscious of his own attractions,' is 'alarmed for his person'. He is scandalised, and Pickle entertains 'a just detestation for all such abominable practices'. However, in the following scene Pallet is inviegled by Pickle into dressing as a woman for a masquerade. There he is pursued by a (male) masquerader, who, having been thumped on the ear for having made an improper advance, demands to know whether the 'lady' is 'either a male or hermaphrodite'. Virtue is protected by a hasty exit, which unfortunately lands the two heroes in the Bastille.[20]

Byron

Byron's *Lara* portrays a mediaeval chieftain and his page. Gide read the poem and noted in his *Journal* on 18 February 1888: 'The first canto is disturbing [*d'un intérêt troublant*] – the charm and the danger of these books is that one identifies oneself too closely with the hero and absorbs his passions.'[21] This leaves it open to us to guess at the precise nature of his feelings, and it suggests that he found more in *Lara* than he did in *The Corsair*, which he read at the same date. Did he only see in *Lara* 'A thing of dark imaginings'? In Canto I the reader learns how Lara, a melancholy but proud man, has returned from self-imposed exile, accompanied by

> a single page
> Of foreign aspect, and of tender age,

I 4 47–8

who is mysteriously – and entirely – devoted to him. The solitariness and beauty of Kaled the page are described:

> Of higher birth he seemed, and better days,
> Nor mark of vulgar toil that hand betrays,
> So femininely white it might bespeak
> Another sex, when matched with that fair cheek,
> But for his garb, and something in his gaze
> More wild and high than woman's eye betrays.

I 27 574–9

Before the fatal battle in Canto II, Lara looks at Kaled and lays his hand on his. When he is mortally wounded, he is tenderly succoured by Kaled. The page faints when his master dies, and is then found to be a woman. She dies of grief, but does not reveal her past, leaving the reader still unsure whether Lara loved her as a woman or as a boy, although there are hints in the poem which make the former supposition more probable. In fact the story puts a veneer of respectability on the relationship since the heterosexual element is disguised and there is no overt expression of sexuality. Cotnam[22] is inclined to conclude that Gide was drawn to the dark romantic image of the hero and that he assimilated the relationship to what he perceived of his own feelings towards his cousin Madeleine. That is possible: but we may equally well suppose that the disturbing portrayal of an older man's feelings for an attractive boy is what he remarked upon in Canto I. There is, let it be added, little in common except for superficial details between Kaled's disguise and the dual hermaphroditic nature of the characters in Gautier and Peladan we have discussed in the previous chapter.

Dolben

There is some evidence that Gide took an interest in the work of English uranian poets. On 27 March 1912 his friend Valery Larbaud wrote to him with a recommendation to read the recent edition by Robert Bridges of the poems of Digby Mackworth Dolben (1848–67), a pupil at Eton who was drowned at the age of nineteen. Larbaud's remarks reveal that those in the know in London were debating the extent of Dolben's homosexuality: 'an English mystical poet – not Socratic: Uranian, rather. . . . [There is] an accusation of sodomy made by some idiots who had not read his poems which until recently were only in manuscript.'[23] This division between 'sodomy' and a more etherialised 'uranism' is closely related to Corydon's distinction between the two. Dolben's poems are characterised by homoerotic feeling and an emotional and sentimental religiosity where it is often difficult to separate an address to the Deity from one to the beloved boy.

Ruskin

What we have to say of Ruskin is quite different from the foregoing. Although Gide was exasperated by *Praeterita* when he came to read it

eventually in 1925,[24] it was in *Sesame and Lilies*, in Proust's translation of 1906, that he found an idea similar to his own on the value
of Woman. This is not to say, of course, that Ruskin intended this or
any of his remarks to be understood in a way which could add respectability to homosexual behaviour. Such a thought was never present to
his mind. The standard text of *Corydon* reads: 'We also owe to pederasty these pure images of women. I do not think it too bold to say that
this applies to Shakespeare too,' and a note in the 1920 edition adds:
'Note the long and important passage on this in Ruskin (*Sesame and
Lilies* II §56–58).' Here, in Ruskin's 'Of Queens' Gardens', Woman
is indeed put on a pedestal: reading, we are told, enables us to understand such matters as the worth of womankind – and so 'we must turn
to Shakespeare'. In Section 56 Ruskin maintains that Shakespeare
has no heroes, only heroines (except perhaps Henry V), and 'there
is hardly a play that has not a perfect woman in it, steadfast in grave
hope, and errorless purpose'. Catastrophes (Section 57) in Shakespeare
are caused by man's folly; woman's virtue and courage are wrecked by
man's stupidity. There is only one weak woman in the plays – Ophelia
(Section 58). It is true that there are three unpleasant principal women
(Lady Macbeth, Regan and Goneril), Ruskin concedes, but we immediately realise that they are 'awful' exceptions to the ordinary rules
of life. 'He represents women as infallibly faithful and wise counsellors,
– incorruptibly just and pure examples – strong always to sanctify,
even when they cannot save.' (What, one wonders, did Ruskin think
of Tamora, Cressida and the Queen in *Cymbeline*!)

The importance of Corydon's appeal to Ruskin's authority lies in
this: here is evidence from an allegedly unbiased source which will
help the reader complete the syllogism: All homosexuals respect women,
Shakespeare was a homosexual, therefore . . . It is a curious form of
misogyny, one might comment, which treats women as outside the
pale of humanity because they are so superior to it.

Walt Whitman

Two notable English-speaking contemporaries of Gide must also be
considered: Walt Whitman and Oscar Wilde. We have already spoken
of the latter in the earlier Chapter 9.

In the literary periodical *L'Ermitage* III 15 June 1892 pp. 337–49,
there appeared a translation by H. Bérenger of Havelock Ellis' article
on Walt Whitman. Ellis commended Whitman for having introduced
the Greek spirit into art. His naturalness and health, he wrote, ensured a more vigorous element than what was revealed by the nerveless
nudes of Bouguereau[25] and Leighton. Ellis perceived that in the inti-

mate physical affection of friends and lovers, Whitman had discovered the roots of universal love. Concentrating on *Leaves of Grass*, he averred that the love of comrades was the central point from which the whole of Whitman's moral world derived. Could Gide have read this? His actual connection with the editorial staff of *L'Ermitage* most probably began with the March number of 1893.

The first mention of Whitman's name in the correspondence exchanged between Gide and Ghéon occurs in a letter from Gide dated 19 March 1899. In a clearly Whitmanesque way they both took up with enthusiasm the poet's term 'comrade' (*camarade*). It was several years later that Gide was to be so offended by the 'flat-footed' translation of the poems by Léon Bazalgette[26] which appeared in 1909. In this translation 'Calamus' occupies pp. 156–298, and the version is less than honest. Indeed it fully earns Gide's criticisms. The preface is also very circumspect. A new version of 'Calamus' by Bazalgette did appear in 1919 and this was more open:

> Whitman bears us away from this noisy world to where the symbolic reed grows, and confides his heavy secret to us which he only dares tell us surrounded by the wilderness, solitude and silence. This is the need to cherish men like himself who are virile and loving, natural and free, – to be for example one of that pair of youths with lusty blood who adventure throughout the world, hand in hand; or one of those manly but soft companions who pass along with an arm around each other's shoulders as if to bear as one the precious burden of fraternal love.
>
> This great desire for a fuller and more intimate love of man for man encounters a thoughtful sadness, and painful strivings [*ardeurs*], the sharp pang of a passion which is not satisfied in its measure because it is measureless.

This is quite explicit, and Bazalgette had progressed since 1909. It must, however, be added that Gide had also promoted a translation of Whitman in the meantime (NRF, 1918), and whether we should see a curious form of literary leapfrogging, with each author vying with the other, is not altogether certain. We do nevertheless know that, although Gide never alluded to Bazalgette's second, improved version, he thought that the 1909 edition was a definite disservice to the poet. Gide's collaborative effort of 1918 was an attempt to put the matter straight.

We can follow the history of Gide's Whitman translation from March 1914. In this month, during a fortnight's stay in Florence, Gide saw Louis Fabulet, a mutual friend of his and Ghéon's since 1899.[27] He helped Fabulet with his portion of the work,[28] and in June he was revising his own translations and helping another close friend, Jacques Copeau.[29]

One collaborator they were not able to engage was Claudel, who, having learned that Gide was a pederast, had announced that he could not co-operate on the book.[30] There then seems to have been a period when work was understandably suspended in view of the war and Gide's involvement with the refugees at the Foyer Franco-Belge in Paris. He took it up again in late 1917,[31] also, at this date, attempting unsuccessfully to secure the co-operation of Paul Valéry.[32] The following year he pronounced his satisfaction with the general preface by Valery Larbaud.[33]

In the event Gide was responsible for the following poems, since 'Calamus' had been given to Louis Fabulet:

Song of Myself (§24)	'Walt Whitman, a Kosmos . . .'
Children of Adam	'From Pent-up Aching Rivers'
	'O Hymen! O Hymenee!'
	'I am He that Aches with Love'
	'Native Moments'
	'Once I Pass'd through a Populous City'
Drum Taps	'Beat! Beat! Drums!'
	'A March in the Ranks Hard-Prest'
Autumn Rivulets	'You Felons on Trial in Courts'

It is obvious that homosexual themes have not dictated this choice, although the first and fifth poems contain significant references to the subject. The hand of a homosexual poet is, however, betrayed by some of the imagery in *From Pent-up Aching Rivers* ('The swimmer swimming naked in the bath . . .'; the poet possessed by a 'master'; and so on). The use of the phrases 'the bedfellow's song' (line 8), referring to the poet, and 'relief from the bedfellow's embrace in the night' (line 47), presumably indicating the woman with whom the poet sleeps, is as awkward for the English reader as it is for the French translator. Gide has in general avoided the traps set by the need to specify the gender of nouns in French, but he speaks of 'compagnon de lit' in both places, making the second example unmistakably masculine. Similarly, he translates 'O tender waiter' (line 53) (that is, the poet is addressing the woman who waits for him) as 'O tendre attentif', thus creating an unwelcome homoerotic resonance. One line, 'Two hawks in the air, two fishes swimming in the sea not more lawless than we' (viz. the poet and his mistress) is quoted in *Les Caves du Vatican*,[34] and is there suggestively applied to the relationship between Protos and Lafcadio. There seems to be little doubt that Gide thought of this poem as particularly homosexual, despite Whitman's careful phrase 'singing the phallus, Singing the song of procreation' (lines 4–5).

It would also be fair to point out that many pieces from the *Song of Myself* which contain a vibrant expression of the love of man for man have not found their way into this particular anthology. It is futile to speculate on the further reasons which lay behind the choice of poems which were included.

Whitman had died in 1892, but there is a group of articles which Gide cut out and kept among his notes. They date from April 1913 to February 1914 and deal mainly with allegations that there was an orgy at Whitman's funeral. There are also comments on his alleged homosexual behaviour, and some evaluation of his poetry. The extracts are mostly taken from the *Mercure de France*, in which a number of other items on Whitman had appeared in earlier years, and are as follows:

(1) *Mercure de France*, 1 iv 1913 pp. 658–9 (an allegation that the funeral was an orgy. Unsigned). Ms. Doucet γ 885.33.

(2) *Ibid.*, 16 iv 1913 pp. 890–2 (an answer to Apollinaire's description of the funeral as an orgy, saying that it was no such thing. By Stuart Merrill). γ 885.34.

(3) *Ibid.*, 1 vi 1913 p. 671 (a letter from Benjamin de Cassérès praising Merrill's defence of Whitman). γ 885.32.

(4) *Ibid.*, 1 vii 1913 pp. 204–10 (an article on Whitman by Édouard Bertz, answering Merrill: 'It was Whitman himself who thought up the story of his six children (there were no women in his life), believing that he could thereby deny any accusation of homosexuality. He did not manage to. . . . Whitman loved a *large number* of young men.' Bertz quotes part of 'Hours continuing long, sore and heavy-hearted' (1860): 'Sullen and suffering hours . . . harbor his anguish and his passion', against which Gide has added his own translation of the following two lines in the margin:

> Sullen and suffering hours! (I am ashamed – but
>   it is useless – I am what I am;)
> Hours of my torment –   I wonder if other men ever have
>   the like, out of the like feelings?

Bertz continues: 'No trick of interpretation can hide the truly homosexual nature of this passionate despair'). γ 885.30.

(5) *Ibid.*, 1 x 1913 pp. 654–5 (a letter from Édouard Bertz about Whitman, attacking Bazalgette: Bertz supports the idea of Whitman's homosexuality and refers to an article in the 'Archives d'anthropologie criminelle' by A. Lacassagne (15 June 1913) where mention is also made of W.C. Rivers' 'Walt Whitman's Anomaly'). γ 885.29(1).

(6) *L'Effort libre*, Nov. 1913 pp. 113–18 ('Les petits fils de l'honorable James Harlan' by Léon Bazalgette (Harlan was the civil servant who had Whitman dismissed in Boston), referring to Rivers' 'W. Whitman's Anomaly'. Bazalgette is anti-Rivers and

anti-homosexual, and contributes a rhetorical diatribe against 'modern Europeans' who want to claim that Whitman was homosexual). ɣ 885.29(2).

(7) *Mercure de France*, 16 xi 1913 pp. 329–36 (an answer to Bertz by Stuart Merrill, stating that Whitman was not homosexual). ɣ 885.29(3).

(8) *Ibid.*, 16 xii 1913 pp. 864–5 (a note by Guillaume Apollinaire: 'it seems to me that S. Merrill . . . confuses unisexuality with the basest debauchery . . .'). ɣ 885.29(4).

(9) *Ibid.*, 1 i 1914 pp. 222–3 (another letter from Eduard Bertz: Merrill is naive if he thinks he has disproved Whitman's homosexuality, and referring, *inter alia*, to Bertz's essay 'W.W. ein Charakterbild' in *Jahrbuch für sexuelle Zwickerstufen* [sic], 1905 pp. 265–6). ɣ 885.29(5).

(10) *Ibid.*, 1 ii 1914 pp. 669–671 (an article by Albert Schinz, saying that the poems must be considered separately from the life of Whitman, and that there was no orgy at the funeral). ɣ 885.31.

The polemic in the *Mercure de France* raged from 1 April 1913 until 1 February 1914, and Gide, in the character of Corydon, entered the debate. An interesting footnote is provided by the *Journal*. The entry for 29 July 1930 reads: 'Traubel, in his *Whitman in Camden*,[35] quotes a fine letter from John Addington Symonds. Whitman (who perhaps did not dare to speak frankly to Traubel) seems disturbed [*gêné*] by the quite precise interpretations to which his *Calamus* could give rise. And I can perfectly well understand that he should prefer to leave every reader free to discover in it what he likes.' The last remark strikes one as a typically ambivalent Gidean comment.[36]

Two versions of Corydon's attack on Bazalgette's translation survive. There is the one printed in Dialogue I of *Corydon*, and an earlier draft of the same material in manuscript.[37] Remembering that Gide judged his first attempt inferior to the note he had composed on Verlaine,[38] we can see that the differences are instructive although the thrust of the polemic remains the same. The material on Whitman as it stands now in *Corydon* (pp. 17–19) is relatively short and consists of some exchanges between Corydon and the interlocutor. The pretext for their conversation is Bazalgette's recently published volume of translations and his biography of Whitman. The interlocutor, as can be expected, takes Bazalgette's part. Corydon answers him, and begins by making the intelligent statement that Whitman's poems are admirable whatever the private behaviour of the poet might have been. Bazalgette has proved nothing, he maintains, for what he says amounts to a syllogism: homosexuality is contrary to nature; Whitman was a healthy *natural* man; therefore he was not a pederast. He continues: 'Even though

Bazalgette translates "love" by *affection* and *amitié*, and "sweet" by *pur*, when the words are addressed to a comrade,[39] it is obvious that all the passionate sensual tender pieces are what you would call "contrary to nature".'

Corydon's syllogism is as follows: Whitman is a typical *normal* man; Whitman is a pederast; therefore pederasty is normal. The interlocutor prefers Bazalgette's question-begging to Corydon's; Corydon replies that it is truth he is concerned with, and that he is writing a rejoinder to Bazalgette. What follows, in a footnote, is the substance of Gide's draft, which was not printed in the editions of 1911 or 1920: it is the case that Bazalgette has to choose a particular gender when translating – for example he uses the feminine 'amie' when the poet speaks of 'the friend whose embracing awakes me', but, having introduced this bias into his text, he has no right to draw conclusions from it. Bazalgette, Corydon continues, candidly confesses that the story of Whitman's intrigue with women is 'purely' imaginary, but he still has a desire to introduce females everywhere into his translation: the sea heaving 'like a breast' (*comme un sein*) is 'absurd' and 'profoundly anti-Whitmanesque'. And Bazalgette invents other examples: Whitman seeks kisses 'from the [female] peelers of apples', and so on. There is no excuse and no authority for these interpretations, Corydon concludes. There are other literary deformations; they traduce the writer, but 'a discussion would lead us away from the topic in hand'.

In *Corydon*, Gide reduced to a minimum the material which he had prepared in all probability before 1911 and with which he declared himself dissatisfied.[40] Manuscript γ 885.11–16 presents the more detailed argument. We may summarise as follows.

Gide sets out on the offensive. Bazalgette's argument is the syllogism we have seen will be used in *Corydon*: Whitman is healthy; pederasty is a neurosis; Whitman is therefore not a pederast. But Whitman, writes Gide, was a pederast[41] – and all his work proclaims this. 'Therefore one of the premises must be wrong and I shall attack the second: Whitman is healthy; Whitman is a pederast; therefore a healthy man can be a pederast. Nor shall I argue from the particular to the general. Bazalgette does, and if I chose him as an example I would generalise (the Greeks took this line).' Secondly, Bazalgette says Whitman was a 'simple inverti'. Gide dislikes this because (1) 'inverti' shows Whitman in a bad light; it implies a falsification of and deviation from the natural order; and it begs the question. Other words are possible, but all seem derogatory to right-minded people; but, however insulting they are, they do not imply a theory which would allow Bazalgette to 'prove' his point. (2) The second reason for dislike is the adjective 'simple'. 'This either means nothing; or it assigns Whitman to a predetermined class, as one might say "a common scoundrel" [*vulgaire goujat*]. But, anyway, Bazalgette is correct in one thing: Whitman is not a pederast.[42] Furthermore, Bazalgette quotes the only two [sic] lines in the whole of his works where Whitman celebrates heterosexuality: he glosses over all the other examples which show his sexual orientation.'

The important point in this discussion, says Gide, is to define where homosexuality may be said to begin; and here it would be indelicate to be precise, but everyone has his own idea which will in turn determine the answer. 'Even if it is proved that Whitman committed none of those acts which are commonly called indecent [infamants] with his everyday comrades, I would still consider him to be homosexual.' It is quite sufficient that he should be attracted to and inspired by young men.

> Even if I freely agree with Bazalgette that his contacts with men were mostly chaste, it only proves that he was naturally chaste and wrote poetry instead of indulging in debauchery. And I agree that we can conclude (taking Whitman's normality as an example) that a normal healthy man is hardly inclined to debauchery [peu débauché]. There is, however, undeniable sensuality in the love Whitman expresses for the Comrade: this is not the brutal satisfaction of lust. It explains how the only melancholic poems of Leaves of Grass are homosexual.

Gide continues: Bazalgette sees in 'A Woman Waits for Me' (from Children of Adam) 'a proof of Whitman's non-homosexuality: I see an argument against Bazalgette's position there. The poem is not about love – for Whitman only professed this towards young men.' The figure of the woman is indeterminate and the poem is about procreation. 'Whitman, a natural man [naturiste], necessarily speaks of procreation, for this is part of his healthiness. Furthermore, it is absurd to conclude that since he had six children he had six love affairs. The most it need mean is that six times in his life he went with a woman, and apart from the procreative act had nothing to do with her.'

'If I do allow myself to argue from the particular to the general,' concludes Gide, 'I believe that healthiness is closer to chastity than to debauchery. One may refer to the admirable poem already quoted where Whitman speaks of his powerful reserves of sperm [Whitman's text actually reads: 'I dare not withdraw till I deposit what has so long accumulated within me']. But this observation is independent of any tendency, be it homo- or heterosexual.'

It may be seen from the foregoing that both versions of Gide's commentary on Whitman are polemical. Neither seeks to argue the literary merit of the poet's homosexual verse. The earlier, fuller attack is best seen as a contribution to a war of pamphlets. Whatever the faults of Bazalgette's translation, and they are many, Gide's attention is focused on the poet's naturalness and health.

Bazalgette's portrayal of Whitman in his biography of 1908 shows some interesting similarities with Gide's view on this last point. But this is scarcely surprising, for in addition to his image as a socialist and democrat, Whitman's contemporary admirers saw in him the epitome of vitality. Where there was a divergence of opinion was clearly over the poet's sexual life, and while everyone concluded that it was exuberant, the direction it took remained in dispute. Relying on Whitman's own statements and those of the 'official' biographer, Bazalgette undertook, as Gide saw, to square a difficult circle in the following terms. 'Walt was not a young gallant [*demoiseau*],' he wrote in Part 2 Chapter 3 of his book.

> When an adolescent and young man, his indifference to women was noticeable. . . . There is no girlfriend's silhouette and not the slightest love affair to be discerned in his twentieth year, a time which was both exuberant and thoughtful, petulant and serious. This was how that strange boy was made: the torments of love seemed foreign to his heart. A woman was essentially no different from a male for him: his friendship knew no degrees appropriate to the sex of those who surrounded him. Open and tender-hearted, bold and trusting towards everyone, his bearing, his expression, the beatings of his heart, the tone of his voice remained the same when confronted by the roughest fisherman as when he met the freshest young girl. And there is every probability that his youth was chaste until at the age of twenty-two he returned to New York. Shortsighted critics were later to base their allegations on this apparent coolness and were to try and pass Walt Whitman off as a mere invert ['simple inverti' – the phrase picked out by Gide]. For those who have a real knowledge of the man and his work there is no need to show the ridiculousness of this opinion, and we will have an opportunity of mentioning this more usefully at other times in his life. But it is nevertheless certain that Woman and love, in the usual sense of the words, did not play the decisive and capital role in the poet's life which they do in the life of the average man.

A little later he does indeed refer again to this point: 'What has misled some people and induced them to say, for example, that Walt seemed to "detest women" is probably his absolute ignorance of all the small attentions, gallant words and playful exchanges which a civilised man in any country will use to convey his amorous inclinations.'

If Gide was previously unaware of Symonds' letter and Whitman's reply, he could have learned about it from here. Bazalgette believes there were six children, the fruit of several women – for 'Walt was a wanderer'; he supposes this happened in Louisiana, and that Walt was so splendidly handsome that some Creole (or possibly French) woman just could not resist. He quotes as evidence:

Once I pass'd through a populous city imprinting my brain
    for future use with its shows, architecture, customs,
    traditions,
Yet now of all that city I remember only a woman I casually
    met there who detain'd me for love of me,
Day by day and night by night we were together – all else
    has long been forgotten by me,
I remember I say only that woman who passionately clung to
    me,
Again we wander, we love, we separate again,
Again she holds me by the hand, I must not go,
I see her close beside me with silent lips sad and
    tremulous.

Children of Adam[43]

In Chapter 3 of Part 4, Bazalgette turns to the question of comrade-ship. 'Un Coeur de camarade' deals with material from the Civil War, the hospitals, Whitman's letters home describing the soldier boys, their joy in him and their need to be embraced. This affection is presented by Bazalgette as platonic, though expressed in the warmest terms. Whitman's feelings, we are told, arise from his sense of the tragic destiny of Man. Comradeship is the key to his gospel: 'In every individual he perceived the seeds of a tender, serious emotion which was awakened by contact with another individual, and this natural attraction which was both physical and moral drawing man to man was, according to him, the very basis of social cohesiveness [*solidarité*].' This, concludes Bazalgette, is the meaning of that 'flight of the pure feeling of virile friendship'.

Let us note as a final point a strange agreement between the two critics: both Gide and Bazalgette, for their own quite different reasons, wish to claim that Whitman's virile love was chaste. But let us also remember that in *Si le grain ne meurt* (p. 596) Gide likened himself to Whitman, 'satisfied often by the most fleeting [*furtif*] contact'.

CHAPTER FIFTEEN

German, Scandinavian and Dutch Literature

Goethe

Gide said that when he began his study of English in 1909 he abandoned German.[1] But this is not entirely true. Nor does it follow that he suddenly became deaf to the charms of one of his favourite authors, Goethe, of whom he wrote on 4 November 1927 that he was the greatest influence he had undergone, adding, however, that as a general rule he recognised in other people thoughts which were already his own. It was certainly what he called Goethe's 'paganism' which he found most attractive and sensual. But he admitted that, despite impressions to the contrary, in the well-known distinction between self-control and ecstatic abandonment to sensuality, it was Nietzsche whom he perceived in the company of Dionysus, while Goethe was on the side of Apollo and serene restraint.[2] Was this an opinion he would have expressed earlier? There is room for more than a little doubt. At the outset he remarked on Goethe's having sensed the importance of suffering and illness. This is in the 'meditation' in the *Journal* for 1896 about the wholesomeness of the Spartans, which we have already discussed above in Chapter 10.[3] Just as Gide took up again the idea of the need for a flaw or an anomaly to validate the man of genius, so he returned to one particular observation of Goethe's: 'The best part of man is his unease' ('le tremblement', 'das Schaudern').[4] This has its part to play in Gide's apology for homosexuality.

In the third Dialogue of *Corydon* (pp. 138–9), Chancellor Müller's report of Goethe's opinion on pederasty is quoted in German and French:[5]

Goethe explained how this aberration really derived from the fact that according to the pure aesthetic rule the male body was far more beautiful and more perfect and more complete ['vollendeter', 'accompli'] than that of a woman. Once such a feeling has been awakened it easily deviates towards the bestial. Pederasty is as old as the human race and we can therefore say that it is natural, that it depends on Nature although it goes against Nature. What Culture has won and gained from Nature must never be relinquished. It must never be yielded up at any price.

The paradox to which Goethe points is that pederasty may well provoke our feelings of disgust, but it is undeniably natural. What Corydon's argument requires is that the natural (that is, pederastic) state should be considered the norm, and therefore good. The 'unnatural' civilised state will then be represented by the educational effort required to ensure a degree of heterosexuality. The idea has its counterpart in the examples from Barrès and Rousseau also cited by Corydon. It is of some interest to see that Goethe continued with a sentence which Corydon did not repeat: 'So, in addition, the idea of the sacredness of marriage is a similar cultural achievement of Christianity, and it is one of inestimable value notwithstanding the fact that marriage is, properly speaking, unnatural.' Presumably Gide did not want to complicate the issue at this point by introducing the question of marriage and Christianity.

The debate between culture and nature is, however, one we shall leave to one side for a moment, for when we turn to Goethe's writings we perceive that on occasion sensual awareness finds a different mode of expression.

Gide knew the story of *Der Erlkönig* well: the elf king pursues the boy, and, despite the father's loving care, manages to ravish the child. The poem ends with the boy's death, and, although it has often been considered as homosexual in tone, the Erlkönig's triumph may at least also be seen on an allegorical level (Death), or as a macabre element of folklore (the evil supernatural forces of Nature). True perhaps to his perception about 'das Schaudern' Gide imagined that the child was less terrorised than charmed.[6] But this new interpretation is probably only another curious, though minor, example we can add to many others where Gide tries to give a rather startling twist to a well-worn story. It is significant that he does not develop his ideas on *why* the boy is attracted to the Erlkönig. Perhaps he is to be thought of as attracted by the unknown? or flirting with evil? or welcoming a force against which he will have to pit his strength?

With *Wilhelm Meister*, the *Römische Elegien* and the *Epigrammen* we come to more substantial matter. There is an early reference to *Wilhelm Meister* in the 'Subjectif' in 1892.[7] In the following year, a note appears in the *Journal* (p. 41). But there is no further comment. There are in fact two episodes in the novel which call for our attention, and both occur in the *Wanderjahre* in Volume 2 of the translation Gide most probably used, although at this date his command of German appears to have been quite reasonable.[8]

The first is in a letter from Wilhelm to Natalie in Book II, Chapter xi. Wilhelm is recalling a day in summer in his early youth when he was down by the riverside with Adolf, the son of a local fisherman. The heat is so intense that Adolf undresses and goes for a swim. Wilhelm follows his example. 'When he climbed out of the water,' the description continues, 'he stood erect in the sunshine to dry himself, and my eyes were dazzled by the sight of that human body of which previously I had had no conception. He appeared to be looking at me with similar intensity. We dressed quickly, but it seemed to us that we were still naked; our souls were drawn together, and, with ardent kisses, we swore eternal friendship.' They run back home together, 'already inseparable', but when a little later Wilhelm wishes to tell Adolf how he has just fallen in love with the bailiff's daughter tragedy intervenes and Adolf meets a sudden death by accidental drowning. Amid the sensual descriptions, the foregoing episode bears all the hallmarks of an idealised Romantic distinction between 'friendship' and 'love'. But the reader may clearly derive from it what pleasurable stimulation he wishes.

The second episode occurs at the very end of the novel.[9] Felix, unhappily in love with Hersilie, is galloping along the river bank when it caves in. He is rescued and brought back to life when Wilhelm bleeds him. 'The young man fixed his piercing gaze on Wilhelm and cried out: "If I must live, let it be with you." So saying he threw his arms around his saviour's neck and wept bitterly. They held each other in this embrace like Castor and Pollux meeting on the threshold of Orcus.'[10] When Felix lies down, Wilhelm gently smiles at him and covers him with his cloak. He looks at him with joy, compassion and sweetness, for his body is beautiful, a 'sublime image of God'. Felix's clothes are spread out in the sun so that when he awakes he can once more appear decent.

It will be noticed that in both these examples there is a heterosexual motif which is an integral part of the story. Notwithstanding this, the beauty of the youthful male body and the emotions it gives rise to are equally important.

Gide knew the *West-Östliche Divan* and read it with great pleasure. The lyrical sensuality he found within its pages was a fitting complement to the Oriental poems we have examined. Section IX *Saki Nameh, Schenkenbuch* (the Book of Saki, the cup-bearer) perhaps offers the closest resemblance to the works of the Sufi poets. Here we read a number of poems about delicious wine and the ecstasy it provides. The poet is poised in his devotions between Saki (the boy), and the girl Suleika. Saki will keep watch outside his master's tent until he receives a kiss as his reward (poems xiv and xx); the poet celebrates the glorious sensation of the present time, and sings of his enthusiasm for the handsome cup-bearer. The boy is beautiful, and the poet will watch him sleeping, with love and care (poem xxi). Although their sensuality is enhanced by their gentle lyricism, these poems, clearly inspired by Persian poetry, remind one of the abnegation expressed by the Sufi poets in their search for God.

Suleika has a book of her own (VIII), while there is a book explicitly dedicated to Hafiz (II). In this latter, the poet mostly addresses his master Hafiz. There is little direct imitation of Hafiz' love poetry, but Goethe delicately unfolds a pattern of sensuousness and scepticism. One of Hafiz' lessons strikes our memory: the cup-bearer will be educated by the poet until his beard begins to grow. Nor must we ignore the *Uschk Nameh* (III: *The Book of Love*) which beautifully enumerates the joys of the senses. Here there are deft allusions to the pederastic loves of the Sufi poets. But the love is transcendental, and is presented as the lyrical figuration of a desire to perceive and worship the eternal Godhead.

One clear implication of what the *Römische Elegien* and *Venetianische Epigrammen*[11] meant for Gide is revealed in an aside made in the *Journal* in May 1905 (p. 160). He was re-reading both these works: 'Four years ago, on such a night as this, I would have prowled till dawn.' The particular sensuality of the poems answered his mood. Poems 39 and 88 of the Venetian series may have more especially stimulated his emotions.

Without wishing to analyse here the extent of Gide's debt to Goethe, for that would take us far beyond the scope of the present investigation, we should note, as Ross has suggested,[12] that Goethe's ideal of *Knabenliebe*, although different from Gide's sexual and instinctive interest in youth, proposed a social and pedagogic role by which the French author often justified his own actions. In addition to this, it is significant that we find Gide's interest in Vergil and bucolic poetry stimulated by Goethe, and that his enthusiasm for Hafiz and Persian literature was also inspired by him.[13] Saki appears as a cup-bearer in Gide's *Saül*, and receives the kisses of his fond master in the *Divan*.

In *Werther*, one indication of the strength of passionate friendship is the vision of the bailiff's eldest son clinging to the hero's lips when Werther has committed suicide. In Part 2 of *Faust*, Mephistopheles (Act 5, scene 4) makes some lewd suggestions to a pretty boy-angel, but this is clearly in keeping with his satanic immorality. Gide mentions neither of these episodes specifically, although the knew both works well from quite an early period, for on 10 March 1890 he recorded reading 'a large part of *Werther* in German', adding 'I must re-read it before I comment on it.'[14] The most important way in which the *Nourritures* owes a debt to Goethe, however, is in the portrayal of the charm of adolescent sensuality. For Gide, Goethe represented an ideal of naturalness. In his writings Gide found a type of pagan hedonism tempered with an ideal of chastity. But it was a chastity that allowed free rein to the sentiments.

Gide noted that Goethe shared with Winckelmann the view that Art and morality coincided at certain privileged historical moments, of which the best-known examples were Periclean Athens in the fifth century BC and the Renaissance. It is no accident, Corydon's argument goes, that pederasty flourished quite naturally then, too. Lambert relates a conversation early in 1948 in which Gide showed him the very fine pages Goethe had written on Winckelmann, on his cult of passionate friendship (*amitié amoureuse*), and on the connection between this passion and Winckelmann's worship of the classical ideal of beauty.[15]

In *Ioläus* (pp. 149–50),[16] Carpenter quotes an extract from Goethe on Winckelmann:

> The relation to women, which among us has become so tender and full of meaning, hardly aspired [among the ancients] beyond the limits of vulgar necessity. . . . More to them than all other feelings was the friendship between persons of the male sex. . . . In these cases of union between two youths, the passionate fulfilment of loving duties, the joys of inseparableness, the devotion of one for the other, the unavoided companionship in death, fill us with astonishment; indeed one feels oneself ashamed when poets, historians, philosophers and orators overwhelm us with legends, anecdotes, sentiments and ideas containing such meaning and feeling. Winckelmann felt himself born for a friendship of this kind – not only as capable of it, but in the highest degree in need of it; he became conscious of his true self only under the form of friendship.

When writing to Edmund Gosse, on 21 December 1916, Gide referred to Pater's comment on Winckelmann's end: 'It seemed as if the gods[17] had given him a death which, for its swiftness and its opportunity, he might well have desired.' The quotation is from Pater's *Studies in the History of the Renaissance*[18] where a case is made out for Winckelmann's essential paganism, despite the fact that he converted to Roman Catholicism and that he received the sacraments not long after being mortally wounded by Arcangeli, the ruffian whom he had befriended. Pater had found it impossible (p. 161) to gloss over the special nature of Winckelmann's attraction towards ancient Greece: 'That his affinity with Hellenism was not merely intellectual, that the subtler threads of temperament were interwoven in it, is proved by his romantic, fervid friendships with young men. He has known, he says, many young men more beautiful than Guido's archangel. These friendships, bringing him in contact with the pride of human form and staining his thoughts with its bloom, perfected his reconciliation with the spirit of Greek culture.' For him, maintains Pater, the Greek ideal of male beauty expressed itself pre-eminently in sculpture (p. 182), although it must always be remembered that 'the beauty of the Greek statues was [for him] a sexless beauty' (p. 194). Although a sense of shame had been introduced in the Middle Ages into Christian art, says Pater, paganism returned in the Renaissance: it remained true that the Hellenic ideal was one 'in which man is at unity with himself, with his physical nature, with the outward world' (p. 196). This idea of Pater's was one to which Gide gave full assent. Thus Pater perceived an intimate link between Winckelmann's friendships and his sensitivity to the living form of antique sculpture. This constitutes a further comment on Hegel's judgement, in his *Lectures on the Philosophy of Art*, cited by Pater (p. 146): 'Winckelmann by contemplation of the ideal works of the ancients received a sort of inspiration through which he opened a new sense for the study of art.'[19]

The German poet von Platen[20] has long enjoyed a reputation for the sensitivity with which he portrayed his homosexual love. It was not, however, until 11 August 1934 (*Journal*) that Gide noted having read his *Tagebücher*, adding that although he found their style attractive he felt little in common with those who 'moaned' (*les plaintifs*). Two of von Platen's sonnets are included, in an English translation, in Carpenter's *Ioläus*, and Gide could therefore easily have read them: 'Since pain is life and life is only pain', and 'Oh! When I die, would I might fade away' (on the death of Pindar in the arms of his young friend Theoxenus). 'Platen, however, was unfortunate in his affairs of the heart,' remarks Carpenter, 'and there is a refrain of suffering in his poems.'[21]

Gide discovered Schiller's *Don Carlos* during his second stay in Munich in May 1892.[22] However, on 29 September 1942 he confided in the *Journal* that he found the play unimpressive when compared with Goethe. He had nothing to say of the deep bond of friendship between Carlos and Posa. We have already discussed Schiller's *Die Malteser* briefly above.[23]

In a postscript to a letter which he wrote from Algiers to his mother on 28 January 1895, Gide refers to a 'deplorable' article on Hermann Sudermann by Arvède Barine (the pseudonym of Mme Charles Vincent). He adds: 'What an aversion I'm beginning to feel for the whole of this young German Realist school.' Gide nowhere else mentions the work of the dramatist Sudermann, but there is an obvious possibility that he knew of *Sodoms Ende*, which had been first published in Germany in 1891. There is no French translation, and the play was not performed in France. Its subject is the rise of a talented but morbidly weak-willed heterosexual artist, Willy Jankow, who has painted *The Fall of Sodom*, complete with Lot's wife gazing on the town, which becomes in the course of the drama an allegory of the delirious sensuality of the wicked characters inhabiting modern Berlin. Sudermann shows in a fairly conventional Realist manner the conflict between the quiet virtues of home life and the corruscating temptations of Art. The link we must make with Gide's preoccupations on this occasion has nothing to do with eroticism, but refers to his aesthetic and social attitudes. His allegiance to non-utilitarian Symbolist tenets alienated him from the realistic treatment of the social subject matter of Sudermann, Ibsen and others like them. If he had maintained an interest in them earlier, as may be reasonably supposed, his patience with socially committed writing was running out, as we can clearly see from two other letters written to his mother during this period (20/21 November 1894, and 11 December 1894).

It is unfortunately not possible to say how much he knew of the poetry of Stefan George. An entry in his *Journal* for 7 April 1908 records their first meeting, but Gide had clearly been wanting their mutual friend Albert Mockel to introduce them for some time. He was impressed, as many others had been, by the severity of the poet's dress and manner. 'I admire his work,' Gide wrote, 'whenever I manage to understand it.' The remark is probably not meant to be uncomplimentary, for George's symbolist poetry is often allusive, being greatly influenced by Mallarmé whom he had known in Paris. Did Gide read *Algabal*, a collection of poems by George published in 1892, the hero of which reflects the spirit of the homosexual Roman Emperor Elagabalus? The three parts into which it is divided (*Im Untergrund, Tage*, and *Andeken*) reveal echoes of the violent sensual exoticism of Huysmans in the deliberate interplay of tenderness and cruelty. Love of women is largely absent from George's poetry, and one of the characteristic figures in his early poems is the beautiful youth, symbol of 'das schöne Leben', later most clearly developed in part four of *Der Siebente Ring* as the handsome Maximin, who manifests the ideal of the Perfect in his perfect body. Maximin is also at the heart of one of George's last poems (published in *Das neue Reich*, 1928: 'Du schlenk und rein wie eine Flamme' ('You, pure and slender as a flame')), a moving evocation of the boy and all that he had meant to the poet. These delicately sensual poems, one feels, Gide must have known.

As for other writers, we do not know his opinion of Thomas Mann's *Der Tod in Venedig* (first published in 1912).[24] The plays of Wedekind (as, for example, *Frühlings Erwachen, Erdgeist, Die Büchste der Pandora* or *Tod und Teufel*) set us a similar problem, although these may well have been works with which Gide was familiar. He had after all read (or seen) Wedekind's *Minne Haha* in Germany in 1903.[25] It was in the *Mercure de France*, LXX November 1907 (pp. 168–70), that Henri Albert gave a review of a recent German performance of *Frühlings Erwachen*. Originally dating from 1891 it was, he reported, now no longer neglected in Germany, although he thought that a French audience would find some of the dialogue ridiculous. The work is a powerful attack on moral hypocrisy. We have no actual evidence that Gide was acquainted with the large number of German books with homosexual themes published between 1890 and 1924, details of which may be found in the bibliographies in the *Jahrbuch für sexuelle Zwischenstufen*. We must conclude that, except for Goethe, the German literary influence in this context on Gide was less important than the effect of the scandals which occurred in Germany in the early years of this century.[26]

Scandinavia

Only a chance citation in *Corydon* has revealed the significance of the Danish writer Jacobsen's *Niels Lyhne*.[27] Upholding the principle of passionate and self-denying love between boys Corydon quotes: 'Does there exist a more delicate or more noble feeling than that passionate yet timid friendship felt by one young boy for another? The boy who is in love dares not express his affection by a touch, a look or a word. This is a clear seeing tenderness which is hurt by the slightest fault in the beloved. It is composed of admiration and self-forgetfulness, of pride, humility and serene joy.' This gives a misleading impression of Jacobsen's novel on two counts. Firstly the story is not about a homosexual and his relationships. It is about boyhood. Secondly the author's comment which has been quoted should be set more precisely in context. Two young boys, Niels and Frithjof, hero-worship the older Erik. 'Physical exercises requiring strength, a steady hand and a skilful eye, these were the things which Erik liked.' And again: 'Jealousy spurred Niels forward, for he had become attached [*s'était epris*] to Erik who let himself be loved coldly and with a shade of disdain. Does there exist a more delicate. . . .' The picture is therefore more complicated than Gide suggests. Nor does the sentimental relationship occupy the centre of the reader's attention. In this respect *Niels Lyhne* differs from other novels we have considered. Perhaps in so doing it points us more clearly to one of Gide's major interests, namely an idealisation of boyish or adolescent love which owes nothing to clinical theory.

Holland

It was on 23 October 1934 that Gide first met his Dutch friend Jef Last whose novel *Zuydersee* (1934) was to be published in French by Gallimard with a preface by Gide in 1938. The story is about the building of the great dyke, and includes a touching description of two young fishermen, Teun and Auke, who, in a very natural way, become aware of their homosexuality. Last's *Het Huis zonder Vensters* (1935), which owes much to his stay with Gide in Morocco in the spring of 1935, also features a homosexual character. Commenting on the 'naturalness', of *Zuydersee*, Gide said that he considered German homosexual literature too sentimental, while French readers, he thought, could not conceive of homosexuality without a notion of crime.[28] In his actual preface to *Zuydersee* Gide is anecdotal, for which he was rather defensive in his letters to Last. He says nothing about the book's homosexual elements, but likens Last (rather unexpectedly, perhaps) to the Norwegian writer Knut Hamsun, of whom he had written in the *Journal* on 9 April 1908: '*Pan*... bouquet and flavour, but nothing more. No meat. . . .'

CHAPTER SIXTEEN

Italian Literature

Dante

Dante was another of those great writers whom Gide acknowledged among his most important influences, having read him carefully and patiently in his youth.[1] Indeed, he said that he had read him with almost as much love and attention as he had read his New Testament. It might therefore seem strange that *La Divina Commedia* is given so little space in *Corydon*.[2] This neglect of Dante is corrected in Gide's open letter to François Porché in the Appendix.[3] Gide refers to two French translations, the one by Lamennais (1856) and the other by de L'Espinasse-Mongenet (1912). Dante, according to Gide, leaves it to the reader of Canto XVI of the *Inferno* to imagine for himself the crime some particular individuals have committed. He says that we must infer their fault from what we know of the life they led. Jacopo Rusticucci, for example, was married to a sharp-tongued wife, and so left her and indulged in unnatural debauchery (*d'infâmes débauches*). The previous Canto, he remarks, seems also to have been concerned with this same class of sinners, and this is perhaps why Dante remains so 'chastely imprecise': 'They were all besmirched with the same sin when they were in the world[4] [Dante says] mentioning the group which also includes his master Brunetto Latini.' Mme de L'Espinasse-Mongenet has more to say on this matter than Lamennais, and so Gide appeals to her opinion that Cantos XV and XVI speak of those who sin against nature. Gide reports that additionally she believes that they form two groups, namely the sodomitical men of letters of Canto XV and the warrior–statesmen of Canto XVI. Thus, says Gide, Guido Guerra, Tegghiaio Aldobrandi and Jacopo Rusticucci are, for her, all valiant upright men. He could have added that she, too, repeats the story of Rusticucci's shrewish wife and the 'downward path of the baleful passion of Sodom'. In fact she does make a few more remarks of which it would be well to take note. On Canto XV, line 83, she writes:

> The tenderness and respect which here appear in the words Dante addresses to his master have seemed to some to be bitterly ironic. . . . There is, however, no reason for surprise if one remembers the strict orthodoxy of Dante's attitude. One mortal sin, if it is not absolved before death occurs, is enough to damn a soul however fine and well endowed it might otherwise be. Dante does not want to be unjust towards Ser Brunetto. He wants to recognise that he is great and good. But the weakness of Brunetto for this vice which is punished in this circle of Hell forces Dante to condemn him.

Gide returns to this question a little later in a footnote, but does not give it the prominence it deserves. It is essential to see that for Dante true repentance is more important than the sin itself. If we refuse to recognise that the condemned souls in Cantos XV and XVI are sodomites, Gide concludes – 'and if we are unwilling to see Dante praise them' – we must nevertheless accept that he places Sodom not in Hell but in Purgatory (Canto XXVI). And in this case, he adds, there is no doubt of Dante's leniency: 'O souls, sure one day to be at peace.'[5] These are again the souls of famous contemporary poets, he notes. Furthermore, this concern might be Dante's own, or could be introduced by 'cortesia' towards his revered guide and master Vergil.

There are here again a number of interesting points. The two groups of *Purgatorio* XXVI lines 33–104 are condemned to cry out as they meet each other 'Sodom and Gomorrah' or 'Pasiphae enters the cowhide so that the bull may rush to its vice'. In each case this reflects the sin for which they are being punished. Thus the group who cry 'Sodom' committed the act which Caesar committed when he was allegedly Nicomedes' minion.[6] The other group say 'Nostro peccato fu ermafrodito'. Gide judges this 'mysterious and unsuitable in the context', questioning Lamennais' note which says: 'This word indicates the bestial union of men with animals.' But this is, as Gide himself felt, a difficult interpretation. For one thing, it is not clear whether by 'naming' themselves 'Pasiphae' they label themselves as the active or passive partners in such affairs. If passive, then one sees little difference between their position and Caesar's, if both groups are homosexuals. If active, then this might be sufficient to distinguish the groups. But since Dante's image is allusive we cannot know for certain. It may however be said that no distinction can be perceived here (or in the *Inferno*) between pederasty and sodomy practised by adults.

A number of these matters are elaborated in another letter printed in the Appendix to *Corydon*. Dated 18 January 1929, a reply by Léon Kochnitzky to Gide's open letter, it deals with Gide's representation of Dante's treatment of the sodomites. Kochnitzky concludes (1) that there can be no doubt that the damned souls in Cantos XV and XVI are inverts; (2) that Dante was not particularly indulgent towards homosexuals, but that his moral criteria did not depend on a particular method of practising physical love; (3) that far from being 'chastely imprecise' Dante gives an almost 'clinical' description of this love. In deploying his case, Kochnitzky refers closely to the text and quotes the opinions of Boccaccio and Benvenuto d'Imola. Gide is very willing to agree with his 'erudite correspondent' that Dante was not particularly indulgent towards homosexuals, and that if he speaks of them at length in the *Divina Commedia* it is because 'there was a great number of them at that date and many famous people were among their ranks'. This opinion, of course, is in agreement with Corydon's view of Renaissance Italy.

Leonardo da Vinci

'Quand l'amant est près de son aimé, il se repose': 'When the lover is with his beloved he is at peace,' says Corydon, as he cites this dictum of Leonardo de Vinci (p. 144). The phrase appears to come from Peladan's translation of extracts from Leonardo which was published by the *Mercure de France* in 1907. It is, however, strange that Gide, who was normally quite careful when he copied texts, changed the phrase 'uni a l'aimé' (united with the [male] beloved) to 'près de son aimé' (near the beloved). The other words are identical. In this collection, Chapter III 'Morale', section 84 (pp. 66–7), the whole aphorism appears and reads as follows:

> The lover [*l'amant*] is moved by the thing he loves; as the senses with what is to be perceived [*le sens avec le sensible*] they bond together and form one whole.
>
> The work of art is the first thing to be born from this union. If the thing which he loves is base, the lover debases himself. When the thing to which he joins himself is suitable [*convient*] to the person who so unites himself, the result is one of delight, pleasure and peace.
>
> When the lover is united with the beloved, he is at peace. (T.6.r [cod. Mediolanensis]).

This is clearly an attempt to describe the birth of a work of art and to account for its transcendent beauty in terms which recall certain Platonic doctrines. Gide's emphasis in *Corydon*, however, is quite different, for he wants to characterise the quality and nature of homosexual love.[7]

In his youth, Leonardo was accused of pederasty in Florence, but the accusation was later withdrawn. Havelock Ellis, who reports this story, goes on to say that it seems that his hermaphroditic conception of beauty probably derived from his own physical characteristics.[8]

Michelangelo

Michelangelo, said Havelock Ellis,[9] was definitely an invert and recent biographical studies had shown conclusively that he was 'of a nervous disposition, and a little morbid; indifferent to women and very sensitive to male beauty; his friendships were very enthusiastic and tender. However, nothing authorises us to believe that he had physical relationships with men.'[10] Havelock Ellis saw in these facts something which we notice corresponds to one aspect of Gide's attitude: 'Homosexuality which did not develop into sodomy was tolerated,' and this, in the art of Michelangelo, he wrote, gave rise to the marvellous depiction of male beauty, while female beauty was simultaneously given a grave dignity, clear of any sexual attraction. It was Ellis' opinion that there was only one case during Michelangelo's long life 'of evidence even of friendship with a woman'.[11]

Gide copied out two short extracts from Hermann Grimm's Leben Michelangelos[12] on Riccio, Michelangelo and a group of youths. But it is upon the question of Michelangelo's attachment to women that two other items in the Corydon archive focus.[13] The first of these is an extract from Le Temps where A. Mézières in an article 'Michel-Ange et Vittoria Colonna' attempts to answer the question: why did Michelangelo compose his love poems? He is writing in reply to a recent book by Pierre de Bouchaud, Michel-Ange, Paris: Grasset, 1912. Gide marked certain passages in the margin (here indicated by *): 'He loved physical beauty as someone with an admirable knowledge of the body*.' 'He chose the name of Tommaso Cavalieri as a blind to hide Vittoria Colonna*.' 'The letter to Cavalieri is full of humility, and we are astonished when we see that there are three drafts of this letter among his papers: the second letter appears even more strange because of the amorous expressions which it contains*.' 'It was not rare [sic] in amorous poetry in romance languages to replace the name of the beloved woman by the name of a man in order to put people off the scent – it is not impossible that Michelangelo copied this tradition*.' 'No trace of sensuality appears, even in the description of Vittoria Colonna's physical charms.' 'He describes her handsome features, and her fair hair*.' 'Michelangelo worships her from afar, chastely' – and, like Dante he allows himself plays on words which 'are like a concession which genius pays to fashion*.'

One may well imagine how Gide was tempted to ironise at the expense of M. Mézières. In the event he contented himself with a brief note on a separate sheet of paper, intended perhaps to find its way into print eventually: 'and these morals became so widespread that M. Mézières can write [deletion] just as nowadays a p[ederast] would hide his passion beneath a feminine name'.[14]

Mézières' idea is indeed ludicrous, but the second manuscript fragment shows Gide being at least as ingenious (and equally unpersuasive). Fragment γ 885.24 is part of the conversation between Corydon and his interlocutor which was not used in the printed version: ' "– Than Tommaso Cavalieri, you mean?" "– I don't really know, for there were several of them [sc. Michelangelo's lovers]." ' Corydon continues, saying that he does not believe that Vittoria Colonna held the important place in his life and works that some critics believe, for 'it is not sufficiently often recognised that when he met her for the first time he was almost sixty and she was past fifty. Their relationship (I cannot say "their love") remained platonic. I am also willing to believe that those other connections he made in later life were platonic too, but I do know that before Vittoria appeared there is no mention of any woman in his life.' Corydon adds that it was 'under the exalting influence of his passionate friendships that he achieved his finest works'. Furthermore, 'the man who finds his happiness and comfort – his resolution almost – in the frescoes in the Sistine Chapel has every right to remain a platonic lover. These frescoes are the worthy children of the noble Uranian Venus.'[15] Corydon concludes: 'And I do not think that is the only example where homosexuality can be seen leading to chastity and not to debauchery.'

The Sonnets of Michelangelo enjoy a similar reputation to those of Shakespeare. There is, too, a brief eulogy of Michelangelo in Carpenter's *Ioläus* (p. 129) which Gide read when he was revising *Corydon*. 'For him the body was the symbol, the expression, the dwelling place of some divine beauty,' Carpenter had written. The Sonnets, Carpenter states, were for the most part written to male friends – although this fact was disguised by the pious frauds of the poet's nephew, who edited them in the first instance. Carpenter prints three, in an English translation by J.A. Symonds, with which Gide was most probably acquainted. But Corydon does not allude to the poetry. As we remember, there is instead a photographic reproduction of the Creation of Adam symbolically placed above his desk.

Cellini

A work of more peripheral interest may be mentioned at this point, namely Cellini's *Autobiography*, which Gide bought in November 1890:

the translation in question is probably by Leclanché.[16] As is well known, Cellini's life was boisterous, and he recounts many hetero-sexual adventures. Three episodes, however, catch our eye: the first is an occasion during his stay in France when Caterina accused him of treating her 'in the Italian fashion [that is, sodomitically]' – a charge which he denied vigorously.[17] The second story is how Pier-Francesco Riccio, the jealous majordomo of the Duke of Florence, plotted with Gambetta, the mother of Cellini's young apprentice Cencio, to accuse Cellini of having indulged in unnatural intercourse with the boy. This was also firmly denied.[18] The third example occurs in a dispute be-tween Cellini and his rival Baccio Bandinelli, who shouted at the sculptor in the presence of the Duke, 'Shut up! filthy Sodomite.' De-spite his anger, Cellini tells how he was sufficiently master of himself to answer: 'Would to God that I had been initiated into so noble an art, for Zeus and Ganymede exercised it in the heavens, and the great-est emperors and princes practise it on earth. Unfortunately, I am but a poor humble man who cannot aspire to so admirable a thing.' The court was greatly amused, and Cellini's biting irony concealed the outrage which he felt at such an insult.[19] It is clearly quite another matter to turn from the *Autobiography* to his statues of youths (notably 'Perseus', 'Narcissus' and 'Apollo and Hyacinthus') and to attempt to perceive in them what Gide called the homosexual inspiration of the Renaissance.

Part Four

IMAGINATIVE WRITINGS

Nous ne valons que par ce qui nous distingue des autres; l'idiosyncrasie est notre maladie de valeur; – ou en d'autres termes: ce qui importe en nous, c'est ce que nous seuls possédons, ce qu'on ne peut trouver en aucun autre, ce que n'a pas votre *homme normal*, donc ce que vous appelez maladie.

Valentin Knox, in *Paludes* (Pléiade, p. 120)

We should not make the error of assuming that a writer is merely the sum of the influences he has undergone. Nor should we believe that he is incapable of the imaginative feat of creating his own world of fictional characters and events. We must, however, recognise that Gide's homophile outlook often contributed an important element to what he wrote. Sometimes it is to be found overtly expressed; at other times it forms a subtle and suggestive atmosphere. It may be limited to ideals of hedonism, of abnegation, of sin, of noble chastity or of true self-fulfilment. Nevertheless, it is difficult to escape the conclusion that a need for self-confession sometimes dictated the inclusion of scenes with strong pederastic undertones.

Just as Gide changed his viewpoint in the course of writing *Corydon*, so we may notice that he changed his portrayal of sexuality during his lifetime. The rate of change was not constant, but it is always perceptible, the greatest watershed being provided by the First World War. It is therefore important to pay attention to two things: first, the chronology of the composition and publication of each work; second, homosexual themes in the context of Gide's particular moral and aesthetic views at the time of writing. In addition, we will notice that a number of significant ideas and symbols occur more than once, and provide an intertextual richness which ensures that no one work can be viewed in isolation. What we have to remember is that autobiographical details take on a new significance once they are incorporated into an imaginative work with its own structural coherence. It is also clear that myths allowed Gide a freer expression of his thought, and by using them he was able to present certain moral issues in an abstract form. When, on the other hand, he created his fiction from the life he knew, he highlighted a moral dilemma which had a more immediate personal resonance. Thus the artificial figures of Prométhée, Nathanaël and Ménalque are essentially divorced from life, whereas Michel is only too obviously enmeshed in its toils.

The writings we shall consider fall quite naturally into two categories: prose and theatre. In the former, the works which require special notice are obviously *L'Immoraliste* and *Les Faux-Monnayeurs*, but other *récits* and *soties* also have a claim on our attention. Among the plays, *Philoctète, Saül* and *Le Roi Candaule* raise interesting problems of interpretation. What is striking is the variety of forms which the figures of the desirable adolescent and the aspiring lover assume in plays and prose fiction alike. We shall trace these images from the puritanical expression of *Les Cahiers d'André Walter*, through the comparatively calm self-acceptance of Édouard in *Les Faux-Monnayeurs* and beyond, to the serene amorality of *Thésée*.

CHAPTER SEVENTEEN

Early Prose Works: Asceticism

'Je vous délivrerai de toutes vos souillures'
Ezechiel XXXVI, 29

(Late August 1887, ms. Doucet γ 1558)

Les Cahiers d'André Walter

Les Cahiers d'André Walter, published anonymously in 1891, is a fictional work which is greatly indebted to the biography of its author. Indeed so intimate is the link between the fiction and its creator that every temptation exists to use the text as a document for the understanding of Gide's psychology. This temptation must be resisted, or at most relegated to a subsidiary position, for the conscious effort of the writer was undoubtedly to compose a work about the conflicts within a soul devoted to an ideal of chastity. The narrative has its own coherence, and the debate on asceticism which it presents can be given additional support by arguments and examples from Gide's life. It seems to me that Jean Delay, despite an interesting chapter on Gide's homosexuality as revealed in the pages of *Les Cahiers d'André Walter*, is too inclined to see the work as confessional literature.[1]

In *Les Cahiers d'André Walter* the narrator addresses his beloved, Emmanuèle, and describes the torment of his soul. There are two 'cahiers' – the 'Cahier blanc', which is characterised by angelic fancy, and the 'Cahier noir', which describes the narrator's fall into madness and despair. Emmanuèle is married to T*** at the end of the first 'cahier'; she dies in the course of the second. The antithetical presentation of the material is strongly marked, the most important 'dialogue' being between the body and the soul. The narrator's quest for chastity is constantly threatened with compromise – or with temptation. We can distinguish three levels of narration: there is the voice which tells the story, Allain (the hero of the book which the narrator is writing), and Gide (whose presence is assured by the use made of early notebooks and *Journal* entries reflecting his relationship with his cousin Madeleine Rondeaux, whom he was soon to marry). Of these three, the first two have the greater right to our attention as fictional creations, and although Allain remains embryonic his existence is required as a mirror-image of the narrator. Narrator and hero both career impetuously towards madness and self-destruction. It is therefore difficult to say what is uniquely personal to Gide, for the factual elements have been closely interwoven with the imaginary ones.

André Walter, the narrator, wishes to repress the desires of the flesh. This is the import of two descriptions of his horror when accosted by prostitutes or loose women (pp. 54, 115). Similarly, there is a terrifying nightmare he experiences when his struggle has already depraved him and led him to the brink of madness: 'She appeared; she was very beautiful, dressed in an embroidered robe which fell like a stole in folds to her feet . . . a prancing monkey came up to her; it lifted the edge of her coat, causing the fringe to swing. And I was afraid to look. . . . Beneath her dress there was nothing; it was black – as black as a hole; and I sobbed with despair. Then, with both hands, she caught the bottom of her dress and threw it across her face. Like a sack, she was turned inside out' (p. 157). Gide made several purchases of engravings by Félicien Rops in 1891,[2] and the source for this dream may well be found in another, of which there is no mention in his notes, *Impudence*.[3] The coincidence of a monkey and a woman in an obscene position in this picture would seem to point strongly to this possibility. Rops shows a woman facing the viewer, slightly turning to her left, wearing black stockings to just above her knees. Her dress is rolled up in front above the navel; her upper arms are covered, but her breasts are bare. She places both her wrists on her hips, and her elbows are jutting out. The pubic hair is shown. In front of her sits a monkey, with its knees drawn up and a long tail emerging from between its feet. There is a huge grin on its face. It can easily be seen that Gide has altered the emotional and moral impact of the image.

With this dream we can consider another one which is narrated a few pages earlier (p. 145). Here the tone is excited, but the expedition it gives rise to is equally fruitless:

A dream full of visions. . . . And in the river I saw again the children I had seen from ***. Their lithe bodies were swimming and diving, their sunburned limbs enveloped in this freshness. And I was angry that I could not be one of them, one of those vagabonds upon the highways, who all day long and in the heat go stealing. At night they sleep in ditches, careless of the frost or rain. And when they have a fever they dive quite naked into the freshness of a stream. . . . Neither do they think.

The dream is of children, but is not explicitly linked to love. Nor does it have an expressed connection with homosexual desire, despite the Vergilian echo: 'Would that I was one of you.'[4] Of its several possible meanings, the symbolic call to sensual awareness seems best to suit the immediate context. And yet there is a sequel, for, fired with his excited enthusiasm, André Walter sets out at five in the morning to find the substance of this vision:

The caress of the air frightened me; I walked on as if in a delirium; my sharpened senses caused me almost fear, so extraordinary were their vibrations. . . . I began to run. . . . I was like a drunken man; in my ears all the frenzy [fureurs] of the scherzo in C minor[5] sang with the resonance of the full orchestra. . . . In pain I savoured my loneliness; I peopled it with beloved beings; – at first quite vague, the supple forms of children playing on the beach danced before my eyes. Their beauty still pursues me. I would have liked to bathe as well, near them, and with my hands feel the soft sweetness [la douceur] of their brown skins. But I was alone; I shuddered deeply, and I wept for the fleeing dream I could not grasp.

However, the vocabulary reveals an ecstasy which still has no particular explanation in the text other than a call to freedom of a more general kind. Thus the narrator's words require a further elaboration which is withheld: 'la caresse de l'air', 'le délire', 'mes sens aigus', 'vibrations extraordinaires', 'je jouissais douloureusement' – all bear witness to a hyperaesthesia which is perhaps more of a literary conceit than anything else, but which gains in significance once we know the details of the author's biography. In fact this passage originally appears in Gide's manuscript version of his journey in Brittany in 1889,[6] and is clearly a description of actual events. It was not included in the published version of his travelogue, 'Notes sur un voyage en Bretagne', which appeared in La Wallonie in 1891 under the title 'Reflets d'ailleurs'.[7] In real life the beauty of the children on the beach, a group of local boys aged twelve to sixteen, was offset by the disgust Gide experienced when he returned later in anticipation of seeing them swimming nude and found that only one of them remained, encrusted with mud as he hunted for crabs at low tide. That this has no analogue in André Walter demonstrates the author's wish to focus attention on his hero's febrile excitement. We may add that other homoerotic descriptions in 'Le Voyage en Bretagne' were left unpublished.[8]

The choice of these images is of course not fortuitous, for we shall see the vagabond recur in later writings. Delay asks what is the nature of André Walter's fantasy, and cites both the passages from the Cahiers.

In the second case he concludes that since the only beloved beings mentioned so far are Emmanuèle, André's mother and Lucile, the boys must bear privileged witness to the tastes of André Walter 'being in [his] dreams the fantasy which will be the one present in Gide's homosexual life until his death'. Having undeniably recognised the source of the image, however, Delay fails to emphasise the message the symbol bears, namely Man's inability to satisfy Desire. The theme appears in *Les Cahiers d'André Walter*, in *Le Traité du Narcisse* and in many of Gide's early writings.

Allied with this idea, and also expressed in terms of vagabond contacts, is an image describing the future path rejected in despair by the solitary wanderer André Walter, as he passes through our vale of tears (p. 154): 'Life beyond would be new affections... and I would still have smiles for all the companions I should meet with by chance along the roads, and I would love them, and, as everything fades away, would new affections console me for those gone by? Ah! Why?' It is, he remarks, a condition of life that the bonds of affection be broken despite our effort to remain faithful until death. Thus the innocent children will learn of sadness when André leaves them: 'And would I go, taking with me my remorse at having made them love me despite myself, and leaving behind unconsolable grief?'

Scandal is mentioned twice, once in each 'cahier'. The first is in a 'Journal' entry for September 1887 (pp. 52–3): 'Your advice is admirable, O Ar ***. And your teaching! "Free the soul by giving the body what it asks," you say, – and you would think more highly of me if I did so.... But, my friend, the body must ask for what is possible; if I gave it what it asked for, you would be the first to cry scandal; – and could I satisfy its requests?' These words are to be compared with an entry in Gide's unpublished *Journal* which contains notes for *André Walter*.[9] Three pages describe confiding in a male friend, and the friend's embarrassment: 'Henceforth it will be between myself and God. I will not speak of it to anyone.' We can only speculate as to whether the scandal concerned masturbation or pederasty. The rest of the passage in *André Walter* explains that the temptations of the body are sexual in a general way and take their place within the battle fought between body and soul for the triumph of chastity. The second example is in a similar vein (p. 123): 'Language is only made for average emotions; the extremes avoid all effort to reveal them. Always excessive in everything, how then could I speak?... It is not that I lack daring, but I would thereby perhaps make sad some weaker hearts whom I hold dear, and I would be for some an object of scandal.'[10] Here also the exact nature of the 'excess' is not specified.

The dissociation between pleasure and love in this text upon which Delay has remarked[11] is very noticeable, so much so that everything which is said about it can be understood to relate to the esoteric debate on chastity. Furthermore, we are able to read between the lines (for Gide is not explicit on the point) and conclude that André Walter's besetting temptation was onanism. Some explanation of this sort is required for the few dark hints that the hero makes about his desires. The phrase 'continence dépravée' also occurs (p. 158), but whether the 'depravation' be purely mental or otherwise we are left to guess at. Delay sees it as a consequence of the debate about chastity,[12] although, of course, it is more probably to be seen as the very definition of the terms discussed.

In 1893 Gide recorded in his *Journal*, 'I lived until the age of twenty-three completely virgin and depraved; so greatly maddened [*affolé*] that everywhere I sought some flesh where I might place my lips.'[13] These words again reflect the temptation, the self-repression and fear of the flesh to which we have referred above in our discussion of Greek statuary and Lucretius' poem.[14] In his madness the narrator concludes that chastity is vanity (p. 158), for it is pride in disguise. No sooner is the Devil forced to retreat on one front than he returns in another form. The worst temptation of all (Origen's self-castration) is fortunately prevented by our pride, he says. But now the Devil is again tempting the narrator to blaspheme.

Les Cahiers d'André Walter was written before Gide's travels in North Africa, but not before he had become aware of his sexual temptations. It is a young man's book where, despite many arresting passages, a lack of precision, intended to enhance the otherworldliness of a soul in strife, prevents us from calling the hero a pederast. There is no doubt that here the author dared not give this love a name. The last words lead us forward to the arctic images of *Le Voyage d'Urien*, and, indeed, to the adventures of Boris in the snow in *Les Faux-Monnayeurs*: 'The snow is pure.'

Le Traité du Narcisse

There is, in the early unpublished section of Gide's *Journal*, a note for 14 May 1887 describing the 'melancholy of Narcissus' – 'the only example among the ancients – his love for an empty image is betrayed, his love for a reflection which makes his lips greedy is broken by his arms tormented by desire – his pose, bending like a water flower, his look, his hair weeping on his brow with the yielding disorder of a willow tree'.[15] But it was in his *Journal* on 8 May 1890 that he first committed to paper his intention of writing *Le Traité du Narcisse*. In the following year, he wrote to his close friend Paul Valéry on 23 June that he was continuing to work at this book which, thanks to their conversations, he now viewed in a slightly different light. We can also trace the influence on the *Traité* of several of Gide's contemporaries. Mallarmé, whom he greatly admired,[16] Moréas, René Ghil and Stuart Merrill were among many whose poetry speaks of the Pure Notion proceeding from poet's words.[17] But although Valéry at this date did not have the stature of Mallarmé, it is undoubtedly the case that his influence on Gide was crucial. They were first introduced to each other by their mutual friend Pierre Louÿs in December 1890,[18] and they had each begun to compose a *Narcisse* quite independently. Valéry's sonnet 'Narcisse Parle', dated 28 September 1890, was sent to Louÿ's on 19 November 1890 for publication in the latter's literary magazine, *La Conque*, where it appeared the following March. On one occasion during these Christmas holidays Gide and Valéry talked, seated on the supposed tomb of Narcissa, the daughter of the poet Young. The tomb bore an epitaph, 'Placandis Narcissae manibus', which Valéry used as his epigraph; Gide dedicated his *Narcisse* to 'My friend Paul Ambroise Valéry with whom I dreamed this dream', adding an apposite epigraph from Vergil's second Eclogue (v. 25) which he liked so well: 'Nuper me in littore vidi' ('Lately I saw myself on the shore'). In Gide's letters to Valéry of February 1891 we can follow his critical comments on his friend's poem,[19] but there are many differences between the two works. Valéry's fundamental concern was speculation on the nature of Mind and Existence; Gide's *Narcisse* evokes a more personal mythology.

It is not in the *Traité* that we should look for Gide's reaction to Valéry's poem, but rather in *Le Narcisse secret* which Gide submitted to his friend on 21 March 1892. Although this piece was destined for *La Conque* XIII, it never appeared there. It bore another epigraph from Vergil (*Eclogues* II 48) which indicated how close a relationship it had to his friend's poem: 'Narcissum et florem iungit' ('[She] binds together the narcissus and the flower [of the fragrant dill]'). The chief point which Gide intended to make occurs at the end of the *Traité*: 'First some myths sufficed. Then people insisted on explaining them; the pride of a priest who reveals the mysteries in order to be worshipped himself . . . . ' Valéry's Narcisse speaks; Gide's is silent. This is their fundamental difference. And Gide's poetic fragment hints at the destructive consequence of revelation and profanation: the water is coloured by the blood flowing from the 'ripe vulva of the careless nymph . . .'.

It has been suggested that Wilde may have had some influence on Gide's choice of this myth and its treatment. We have seen how in

In Memoriam Oscar Wilde Gide does indeed recount a story about Narcissus which Wilde told him on one of their early meetings. The point of that story, however, is not the point of Gide's *Traité*: Wilde demonstrates how a disciple deceives himself and only really sees his own reflection in his master. Furthermore, the greater part of the *Traité* had been written by the time Gide met Wilde for the first time in Paris, in November 1891.[20]

It is the image of silence which holds the key to the moral attitudes expressed not only in the *Narcisse* but in other works like the *Philoctète*. It is an image which is part of a closely related group of words: the others are purity, chastity, wholeness and Paradise. The group expresses the Ideal of which the imperfect counterpart is the transient world that we know so well. This correlation is what Gide offers to account for the eternal need for renewal which we observe. In this he follows Schopenhauer, and he was not particularly original in doing so. Thus if absolute beauty exists, it only does so as an abstract Ideal. What we know on earth is Desire – the eternal Unfulfillable. The three characters who feature in the *Traité*, Narcisse, Adam and the Poet, show us how through contemplation and solitude the Truth may be made manifest; this is the only way to counteract the fragmentation of our illusory world. Thus Gide's argument is both aesthetic and moralistic. If Desire exists we have surely to find rules with which to deal with it, and it is, at least in theory, open to us to negate its imperative in order to regain Paradise.

At the start of the *Traité* Gide took great care to write that Narcisse was handsome, *and therefore chaste*. Narcisse is naked – but not for that reason tempting or attractive. He is naked because nakedness represents a state of Paradisal completeness. Adam, it will be remembered, was naked before he tasted the fruit of the tree of knowledge. If nakedness represents perfection, the need for clothing symbolises the fall from grace. In the first case, although naked, we experience no desire; in the second, we do experience desire, but this is a necessary punishment for sin. Thus the emphasis placed on Paradise shows the Ideal towards which we strive – an Ideal which dispenses with sexuality. The Ideal, as we have seen in our discussion of Plato, Schopenhauer and Clement of Alexandria, depends on abnegation, denial and self-control. For Gide, Plato's (and Peladan's) original hermaphrodite is not the symbol of sexual excess but the image of the Absolute. It is Narcisse who, when he is self-regarding, is self-complete.

We may judge much in this *Traité* artificial and derivative. We may think it jejune. But with its awareness of sin, coupled with a hero who is, in his perfection, both beautiful and naked, it reveals important aspects of Gide's moral pose.

Le Voyage d'Urien

In the title of this work, begun in 1892 and fully published in 1893, critics have seen more than one possible pun: 'The Naughtical Journey', or 'Travels of a Uranist'. It is indeed difficult to decide whether Gide intended the second of these – and hard to believe that he could have overlooked so obvious a play on words.

What may be said with certainty is that he offered the work to his readers as a Symbolist novel. 'Symbolist' is to be taken in the sense of a representation of a 'paysage d'âme' – an evocation of a soulscape. One might add, with Brée, that it is a journey towards the education of the Self. In describing this vision Gide is undoubtedly successful. But it is also true that beneath the surface level of the narrative the reader may discern several suggestive elements. These relate to moral and sensual awareness, and a great deal of Gide's disquiet was due to the obsessive emotional state which he experienced while he was composing the book at La Roque. He explained this in *Si le grain ne meurt* (p. 593), but he gave the work its own coherence. As he pointed out in a preface published in 1894:[21] 'The central emotion in this book is not a specific one: it is an emotion arising out of the dream of life which is experienced from the astonishment of birth, to death, where no answer has been found; and my sailors who have no definite characters become in turn either the whole of humanity – or merely myself.'

The important point is in what follows:

> They do not know what the future holds in store and do not steer their ship, but a desire for Will [*un désir de volonté*] deceives them and makes them believe that the chance route taken by their ship has been properly decided upon. Faced with sensuality [*toutes les voluptés*] they control themselves – not because they hope for future rewards which would not satisfy them, but because they aim at glorious deeds which test their strength so that they may keep it whole. They are perhaps foolish – I do not say they are wise. They would suffer most greatly from having no battles to wage, no conquests to make. Even then they would not say that their abstinence was futile, because their inner strength remains: they *could* conquer. Perhaps this is tempting God – but that feeds their pride. . . .

It is in the light of this doctrine of Renunciation and the power of the individual Will that we must judge the sensual temptations experienced by the crew of heroes, several of whom bear Arthurian names. Our keys to understanding must be the words *désir*, *voluptés* and *privation*; our symbols are those remarked upon by Valéry – ice and purity, heat and ardour. Brée (p. 54) additionally draws our attention to 'will' (*volonté*), and stagnant introspection (self-knowledge), adding that there is also a whole system of unconsciously expressed homosexual symbols. She sensibly advises great prudence in giving them a psychological interpretation. Labuda, following Delay, did not heed her warning.[22]

Gide's ship, however, is not a ship of fools in the allegorical sense of Sebastian Brandt's *Stultifera navis*. He drew for inspiration on less recondite sources such as contemporary engravings of polar explorations; the *Odyssey*, a tale of fantastic adventure he had long cherished; Poe's *The Adventures of Arthur Gordon Pym*; and the *Arabian Nights*, which, as we shall see, contributed more than a hint of Eastern mystery and luxury. Haiatalnefus' fetid court may have been suggested by the story of the Lemnian women in the tale of Jason and the Argonauts.[23] These are only a few of the possibilities. Since without a doubt there is on occasion a strange troubled sexual element present in the tale, there is a temptation to look towards *Les Chants de Maldoror* (and, in particular, at the evocative description at the end of *Chant* 5). In Lautréamont, too, we find Gide's familiar call to be a 'vagabond' and travel towards 'distant lands and unknown oceans', rejecting the family and the past, 'amid polar seas and torrid climes'. These, for Lautréamont at least, are the haunts of the hermaphrodite.[24]

And so, Gide tells us, our souls have embarked upon a new voyage. Since it is dawn, the whole of life is set temptingly before us, and much of this exotic adventure lies in the Orient. A Syrian boat brings a cargo of slaves, but despite their beauty these half-naked girls are sad (p. 16). The Sirens are more to be feared (pp. 20–3), for they have conjured by their song a miraculous city, resplendent with minarets, by which the sailors have been tempted. The mirage suddenly disappears, and the Sirens are revealed. But each of the crew has a different picture of them, and each has fled for a different reason. Morgain alone gives an explanation which reveals a fear of heterosexual contact: 'They were like women; they were very beautiful – and that is why I fled.' But when he describes their song he likens its charm to a shady valley and cool water for a feverish man. Then Morgain is silent: he is sad that the Sirens have gone.

If this scene is to be interpreted sexually (and this is by no means essential) then, it seems to me, the meaning is clear: Morgain has not the courage to yield to these temptations. If the image is a metaphor, and this would well suit Gide's Symbolist aesthetic, then the precise example will stand for a more general statement, namely that Morgain is the soul (or personality) in quest of self-fulfilment which dares not satisfy itself.

We visit the palace of Haiatalnefus (the Queen named in the *Arabian Nights*) in the company of the crew. It is a place of delight whose beauties we will not see again (p. 32). Is this the equivalent of Homer's island of the enchantress Circe in *Odyssey* X? The sailors are first met by some women whose lascivious advances they reject. The people on the island have a hermaphroditic charm: there are boys with women's faces, and women who look like boys. These women are so deprived of men that they hunger for them. The sailors are lost, for with the exception of twelve resistant souls, they succumb to the temptation of luxury and lust. The twelve remain silent, and daily grow more austere (p. 34). Now a desire for noble action is born; but on several occasions they do not yield to temptation – they will not swim, for fear. Their monotonous life continues, but still the faithful band do not yield to temptation. They nearly do so: warm baths and the seduction of women's clothes almost induce that languor which is the prelude to illness. But the fear of too much suffering warns them against such pleasures. Taken literally, this clearly shows an association of sexual pleasure with the 'price' to be paid – venereal disease; taken metaphorically, the image is another in the chain illustrating Desire (or Will) debilitated by indulgence. A plague occurs; bodies are more beautiful, but febrile lust increases. Kisses are devourings – and when hand touches hand, it bleeds. There is a fetid atmosphere of illness, symbolising moral decay. This splendid passage describes the frightening scene witnessed by the twelve 'good' men. The twelve ascetics watch their companions die, and then, uncertain what to do, they are eventually forced to leave because of the stench of decomposition.

What is the meaning of this horror? Some critics have interpreted it as an authorial confession; they say that Gide is expressing his disgust at heterosexual intercourse. Delay suggests that the plague is a symbol of venereal disease which contaminates the sailors as soon as they follow the women,[25] and he talks arbitrarily of 'the wound and defilement involved in the [heterosexual] sexual act'. That may be so, and Gide's motive may have been disgust, or fear. But what must equally be said is that this is a portrayal of the consequences of *any* luxurious indulgence of the flesh.[26] The twelve who escape are able to do so because they are pure. And this, as we have seen, is a recurring theme.

Ellis is the Ideal Woman in the *Voyage*. She is the ultimate companion Urien seeks; she is his 'sister'. For her, he is her 'brother'. This pure union of souls, free from sexual temptation, is again symbolic (p. 60). The depiction of her is sometimes ironic and occasionally amusingly off-beat (p. 42), but it is Ellis who is closely connected with the mystical appearance of the twelve ghostly women with their sheep. These symbols of purity are evanescent, but they inspire Ydier, Nathanaël and Urien with awed respect and care. It is with Ellis that the remaining heroes travel with joyful will (*volontés joyeuses*) towards the radiance of the divine city (p. 52). The irony will be that their goal will always lie beyond their grasp. It is not necessary to identify

Ellis with Madeleine (as Delay would have us do) in order to understand the meaning of these symbols.

If a brief examination of the figures of women in the *Voyage* leads us to this conclusion, may the same be said of the male characters? What relationships are established between them?

Children are mentioned on three occasions. First, in a deserted and disgusting landscape symbolic of the baseness and madness of the world, a boy sits fingering his 'loathsome penis' (p. 24). Next, children pursue the men who swim in the warm water of the pools (p. 29): this, as we have seen, is a symbol of luxury and decadence. Last, a mysteriously quiet and attractive boy, 'with eyes the colour of the northern sea', whose voice is sweet and soft, is in direct contrast with the foregoing images. The perfection of his solitude is calm, thoughtful and symbolically Ideal (p. 31). It seems to me that when we come to the description of children in this book we cannot wholeheartedly agree with Delay.[27] Although he correctly discerns the function of the 'free child who excited Gide's desire' (and one recalls the longing description of the bathing boys in *Les Cahiers d'André Walter*), he is wrong to see intimidation expressed in the person of the grave mysterious child. There is, of course, as he points out, a literary prototype here, for the character owes something to Novalis (*Die Lehrlinge zu Sais* (part 1), where the image has no homosexual connotations); but he is not correct in this context to cite Adler's definition of paedophilia: 'a tendency and practice provoked by the subject's fear of his sexual partner'.[28] Moreover, Adler's dictum is itself far from obtaining common consent.

Nathanaël, the youth to whom the *Nourritures terrestres* is addressed, makes an appearance here. He realises that the men are 'living their dream' (p. 18), and he is among the twelve just men who are saved from Temptation. The whirling dervishes are obscene in their frenzied dance, for they are losing their self-control. The cabin boys and sailors, asleep on deck, writhe with unfilled desire, reaching out their arms towards each dreamer.

Delay has an interesting observation on Éric the swan-slayer: 'The Eskimos symbolise the Puritans and Gide finds their doctrine intolerable, for it leads to a mutilation of the being through refusing the demands of the body.[29] Opposed to that idea is the healthy vitality of Éric, who satisfies his instincts spontaneously and cynically.' But if he is right in saying this, then an impossible paradox arises for Éric kills the symbol of purity. When Delay says that Éric represents the aggression of the male,[30] he is correct only in so far as he does not imply that such a person enjoys a moral superiority.[31] Brée (p. 55) sees Éric as another 'Adam-Androgyne' who necessarily disturbs the peace of paradise; he is a 'Lafcadio before his time' – introducing life, as he dispenses death. (We irresistibly recall the Biblical image of the seed that must die to be reborn.)

Clearly, if one can say that the *Voyage* is 'about' rejection of Woman and the need for companionship, then much of the description which shows disgust for women is readily explicable. But this is not an easy explanation to adopt for the whole book. Even though there is complaisance on the part of the author when he describes the men, the sailors and the nude divers (p. 28), this does not commend licentiousness within the narrated story. In fact, these travellers are divided not between heterosexuals and homosexuals, but between base persons who yield to temptation, and the ascetics whose 'sterile virtue' is roundly condemned by the philanderers (p. 26).

La Tentative amoureuse and *Paludes*

Two other early works require brief mention: *La Tentative amoureuse* (written and published in 1893), and *Paludes* (written in 1894 and published in 1895). Neither has anything particularly direct to say about homosexuality, but both explore a sexual ethic. In the case of *Paludes* this is admittedly marginal.

When *La Tentative amoureuse* was republished in 1899, Gide gave it a subtitle: the 'Traité du vain désir'. This we will have to bear in mind when we look at the subtitle to *Philoctète*. The story relates the sentimental attachment of two lovers, Luc and Rachel, and tells how they experience the 'fervour of love'. In fact they do little of the sort, for their love is essentially a love of two souls, and the character of the hero leads him at first to reject the consummation of the flesh. But here Gide plays with his reader and with his creation. Having first recognised the fragility of Rachel and therefore refused her proffered advances, Luc possesses her, for, in the words of the narrator (Gide): 'To make one's inventions always like oneself is a laughable obsession' (p. 74). An accompanying sentence ('Luc was frightened at the thought of carnal possession as he would have been at something damaged [*une chose meurtrie*]') will remind us simultaneously of Michel's attitude to Marceline in *L'Immoraliste* and of Alissa's cry in *La Porte étroite*: 'We will no longer ask God to raise us to a state of happiness.' But the sentence occurs *before* Luc changes his mind. It therefore belongs to the puritanical asexual stratum of the story. The *récit* is another parable of the virtues (and the dangers) of an ascetic life.

Paludes is also ironic, but in a different manner since it is a satire on an enclosed, stagnant way of life. The stagnation is largely aesthetic. But escape from an aesthetic, Gide implies, carries moral implications. Of those elements which concern us at present, we may first note the defintion of normality (*l'homme normal*) (pp. 120–1). Valentin Knox, one of the characters, expounds the paradox that normal people are not worth bothering with. They have nothing to distinguish them from anyone else, and an individual only has value in respect of his idiosyncrasy. (This is also part of the teaching of *Le Prométhée mal enchaîné* (1899), where the inability to recognise this fact lies at the heart of Damocles' misfortune.) Health and normality are thus not enviable, for they represent only a state of equilibrium. It is the quality of being different which constitutes the worth of a human being. And here we perceive not only an echo of Nietzsche's praise of individualism but also the importance of Corydon's pride in being an outlaw. It follows from this that all true heroes have an illness, an anomaly, which enables them to excel. But this doctrine of the 'héros malade', enunciated in Gide's *Journal* in the mid-1890s,[32] did not significantly outlast the First World War.

A second point makes us return once more to the doctrine of renunciation. We may still, of course, perceive a biographical element in the story without thereby diminishing the moral force of the argument. The narrator characterises Angèle as someone 'who fears pleasure [*la volupté*] as something too strong which might have destroyed her'. He has also composed a poem for them both: 'We are not among those, my dear, of whom the sons of men are born.' The reasons are a desire for ascesis and a fear of sensuality. It will by now have become obvious that while Gide does not condone fear (for it is a denial of individual Will), he insists on the integrity of purity.

Le Traité des Dioscures

At some time before 1906 Gide was working on a treatise which he called variously 'Castor et Pollux', 'Le Traité des Dioscures' and 'Considérations sur la mythologie grecque'.[33] He made several statements about his intentions. To André Rouveyre he wrote on 11 April 1928 that the subject was to have been one which reflected the interest he had shared with Pierre Louÿs in the myth of Leda, the mother of the Dioscuri, to whom Zeus had made love in the form of a swan. To Paul Fort, on 8 December 1906, he said that he had intended to expound a heroic ideology based on an interpretation of certain Greek myths, notably those of Theseus and Hercules.[34] But as the years went by he clearly changed his mind about what he wanted to say and finally abandoned the project.

The legends of the Greek heroes Castor and Pollux (the Dioscuri) are complex and varied. Some writers record that while Pollux was a child of Leda by Zeus, and therefore immortal, Castor was the son of Leda and her mortal husband Tyndareus. When Castor fell in battle, his grief-stricken brother agreed to share his fate and to live alternately one day under the earth and the other in the heavens.[35] Their relationship can in this manner be seen as symbiotic and reciprocal, and this is the point on to which Gide originally fastened. In 'Cahier 1' (unpublished) of the *Journal*, which is clearly datable to his first visit to North Africa in 1894, there is an interesting note on Castor and Pollux which takes up the concept of the impossibility of love ever being fulfilled. This is another instance of the idea which frequently makes its appearance in Gide's writings of the early 1890s. Here the heroes' alternating natures ensure that they never meet, and it is not without significance that both are male: 'Castor and Pollux do not flee from each other – on the contrary, they seek each other out, in parallel. They find it impossible to meet because of the equal nature of their love.'[36] This is strikingly similar to the statement in *Les Cahiers d'André Walter*: 'The souls cannot know each other, and the most similar of them yet remain parallel.'[37]

CHAPTER EIGHTEEN

Early Prose Works: Ecstasy

The following group of works have one distinct and important feature. They are inspired less by Western traditions than by writings of Middle Eastern and Persian origin. Gide's experiences in North Africa are clearly also significant and must therefore be taken into account.

Les Nourritures terrestres

> Jesus saw Nathanael coming to him, and saith of him, Behold an Israelite indeed, in whom is no guile!
>
> John 1:47

Les Nourritures terrestres was published in 1897, although several pieces ('Le Récit de Ménalque' and 'La Ronde de la grenade') had appeared the previous year. Gide began work on it during the winter of 1893–4, and he here came closer than ever before to creating a lyrical description of sensual delights. The themes he deploys are those of 'vagabondage' and 'ferveur'. The traveller is constantly delighted by new experience, and it is the very freshness of the unknown which constitutes his joy. In a fervent denial of rooted fixity (*enracinement*), Gide sings of the tremulous excitement (*inquiétude*) of discovery. His major discovery was that God could be praised both through the soul – which he had learned already – and through the senses. This was new, but still did not make him an irreligious pagan. Although this book was to teach individual salvation, the most precious part of that teaching was contained in the word 'dénuement' – a form of asceticism which could none the less accommodate each new experience. In such a way would the body quench its thirst with more pleasure for having deliberately crossed the desert to reach its goal. Gide may well be in favour of sensual delight: he will not countenance debauchery. The editor of the Pléiade edition reminds us how contemptuous he was of his fellow contributors when he saw his *Ronde* printed in the *Centaure* (p. 1485). Is this contradicted when the author says to Nathanaël that he no longer believes in sin (p. 171)? We shall have to leave this question open.

Although much of the atmosphere of *Les Nourritures terrestres* is Eastern, we must also mark the influence of Vergil's *Eclogues*, which lend an idyllic charm to certain descriptions. If Corydon and Alexis are not here, then their places are well filled by dark-skinned Amyntas and the other shepherds. I do not, however, agree with O'Brien's remark[1] that 'in form *Les Nourritures terrestres* reflects the pastoral Vergil even more than in subject', for the book is not, like the *Eclogues*, a series of poetic statements with differing moods unified only by their Arcadian setting.

Hafiz and Sa'di are called upon and cited in the text. The loves they sang were, as we have seen, the boys who poured their wine. But these are not mere literary reminiscences, for together they create part of the very atmosphere Gide has enjoyed and wants to celebrate. To these names must be added Goethe's. Nor must we forget the Bible, for both in his praise of God and in his thematic use of the Old Testament Gide uses it to provide a coherent strand to link the episodes. Thus both Nathanaël and the Shulamite figure prominently here.

Who is Nathanaël? He is most importantly the youth for whom this book is written – and the disciple whose continued presence Gide finally does not want. The 'Envoi' makes this clear. Gide is his teacher, but a teacher whose sensual ecstasy is calculated to awaken his pupil's:

Nathanaël, I can begin no line of verse without your sweet name recurring to my mind.

Nathanaël, I want you to be born again – to life.

But there is a sorrow in his words:

Nathanaël, do you sufficiently understand the pathos in my words? I want to be yet more close to you.

And as Elisha did for the Shulamite's son 'and put his mouth upon his mouth, and his eyes upon his eyes, and his hands upon his hands: and he stretched himself upon the child'[2] my loving heart shining on your still shaded soul, I wish to spread myself on you, my mouth pressed to yours, my brow against yours, your cold hands clasped in my burning hands, and my beating heart . . . (and it is written 'and the flesh of the child waxed warm') so that you awake to pleasure [*la volupté*] – *then you must leave me* – for a life which is exciting and unruly [*palpitante et déréglée*].

Nathanaël, here is all the warmth of my soul – carry it away.

Nathanaël, I want to teach you ecstasy (*la ferveur*). (p. 171)

This apparently ungoverned ecstasy has its justification not in the delight of the author but in the ultimate value of the lesson. The aim is Nathanaël's self-awareness and liberation. Nor is Nathanaël a privileged person: *everything* has its own individual importance (p. 171).

Nathanaël is taught to delight in the present, and to use his lips while they are still fresh and sweet. The future will otherwise bring regrets. This is a common theme of the Persian poets. Furthermore, the author expresses his regrets that he is unable to conduct Nathanaël back in time to savour his own youthful joy (p. 245); the time is past when he knew Lossif and his flocks: 'Nathanaël, what would constitute a room for us? A shelter in a landscape' (p. 223). Thus the author impresses upon us the transient and temporary nature of this affective relationship.

'Utinam ex vobis unus' is a Vergilian cry we have heard Gide use personally on several occasions.[3] Here it expresses the narrator's view of the delights he wishes to find in the shepherd-boys' paradise. The experiences described belong to the author's two 'worlds' – the burning heat and the cool shade of North Africa; the moist countryside of Normandy. Are the two identical? It is in Normandy that he wishes to recapture that past moment when he played with the farmer's children 'whose sweating flesh smelled so good' (p. 212). Other pictures also belong to this bucolic farmland scene: two handsome barefooted lads (p. 156); returning home in the hay wagon with the rough young farm labourers at La Roque (p. 210); a smile and a caress for the little boy at the forge (p. 205). Other images belong to Algeria: shepherd-boys in the gardens of Biskra (p. 180); and shepherds drinking from their cupped hands (p. 218). The 'Ronde de la grenade' celebrates, among other portraits, the naked children and the delicious sensual pomegranates (p. 195). If Athman, the shepherd-boy, is impatient, then the narrator is soon to be there as witness of the spring: they will resume their friendship (p. 232. In real life Athman was Gide's Arab servant-boy). This recalls the rather mysterious address at the beginning of Book 5 (p. 204) to 'Tu': 'You said we would make love in the spring . . . but in the summer you were waiting for a woman who did not come.' This is in Normandy, and perhaps for that very reason the promise of the spring did not come true.

Other examples are more explicit, and reveal not only a depth of tenderness but an intimate desire. Thus Gide writes that he hears the flute of the shepherd whom he loves: 'Will he come? Or will I have to go to him?' (p. 234). And this is followed by a direct call to the boy (p. 235). Indeed, caresses are exchanged with a child in a shady garden, which is a symbol of delight (p. 176). The narrator lies at night with the groom in the stables (p. 208). Although on some occasions courtesans have come to him, he has often waited in his turn for the presence of young lads (p. 221).

But there is another side to this canticle of sensuality. On the occasion when a Kabyle boy shepherd proffers a cup of palm wine, the gift of drunkenness is not much to the author's taste (p. 172). Here is a hint of the asceticism which is also to be found in Hafiz. At another time, two boys take the author to the pools at Gafsa, 'places of dangerous charm' where temptation lies in wait (p. 233).

We must remember that although many of these examples are taken directly from Gide's travel notes, their function within *Les Nourritures* remains literary and self-conscious. Thus if Nathanaël is addressed by the author as 'my little shepherd' (p. 215) and is thereby idealised, so also are the other boys and youths. After all, 'The wandering life is the life of shepherds' (p. 222), and *Les Nourritures* is nothing if not a celebration of *adventure*.

Like the sailors in *Le Voyage d'Urien*, the youths symbolise the call of the unknown and make it more beautiful with their graceful strength (p. 199). Among the narrator's ultimate companions with whom he celebrates the joys of desire and thirst, there is Hylas, known from legend as the youth beloved by Hercules. For Gide, however, another message is now more fit for Hylas' lips. It is he who sings the 'Ronde de la grenade'.[4] This song is in praise of joy, but also underlines the observation that no soul may attain happiness. Sensual delight has a bitter taste. When every one of Hylas' senses has its own desires, then he is besieged and overcome by them. In this he is exactly like Saül. And when he yields to drunkenness he sacrifices his soul and is lost.

Ménalque seems at first glance to be the amoralist *par excellence*, but on closer inspection his attitudes do not appear to diverge too widely from those which we may reasonably suppose to be the author's. The section in which he recounts his life, the so-called 'Récit de Ménalque', was, we know, composed separately from the *Nourritures* at the express request of Edmond Ducoté, who wanted something of Gide's for the literary periodical *L'Ermitage*. Gide wrote to Valéry on 24 January 1896: 'I don't care for it very much – I wrote it in a hurry.' This statement may, however, be designed to elicit praise from his correspondent, for there is no hint here of what Gide wrote in his *Journal* on 24 March 1935 with the hindsight of one who has changed his moral position: 'I disapprove . . . the irony is not sufficiently well marked . . . it goes against the most precious element in the work – the praise of self-denial [*dénuement*].' In fact the 'Récit' (and the character of Ménalque) functions as a story within a story, a technique which Gide used elsewhere and called 'mise en abyme'. The device enables a single topic to be presented from more than one view point. In this case the topic is manifold, but can be resolved into the notions of desire, love, God and selfhood. Furthermore, Gide admitted that he feared that too great a similarity betwen Ménalque and himself might mislead his readers.

We have seen that Nathanaël is a youth chosen by Gide, and that the author is his mentor. In the same way, Ménalque watches for a youth. He sees him at school.[5] He speaks to him, and four days later the boy follows him. Here we are reminded of *Maldoror* and *À rebours*. Ménalque's lesson is simple. 'I opened his eyes to the splendour of the plain; he understood that it lay waiting for him. I therefore taught his soul to rove more widely, to be more joyful, then I taught him to detach himself from me and know his solitude' (p. 186). Solitude, one has to add, is a source of Ménalque's own pride. Ménalque's love and fervour are indiscriminate. Every object and every moment are the reasons for his joy. Thus it is not 'perverse' of him to fall in love, albeit fleetingly, with the least handsome of the four cabin boys on board his boat (p. 190).[6] Ménalque's existence is divided into several periods. He first studied until he was eighteen, then his life began and he embarked on his adventures. At twenty-five he settled down to a time of civilised learning. At fifty he sold everything he had, not wishing his world to be limited by possessions: this was a prelude to further travel. What can be said of Ménalque and his possessions can also be said of his affections and his friendships. As Nietzsche scorned charity, so Ménalque will only tolerate those youths sufficiently able to appreciate his lesson and leave him. He has known the love of women, and his attitude towards the opposite sex is sensual and opportunistic.

The narrator, on the other hand, responds with more delight than did Ménalque to female charms, and, although this may well be a literary artifice, the presence of the women is essential for the balance of the book's moral view. After all, one 'should not limit one's choice'. Ménalque, as we have seen, is presented as a bisexual, although he may often reject sexual adventures (as on the occasion when he leaves his companions to their pleasures, p. 188). However, after his love for the ill-favoured cabin boy, he relates an affair with a Venetian courtesan whose beauty eclipsed all other loves. But he escapes after three nights (p. 190). There are other references in the main text to heterosexual intercourse. One relates to Meriem, an *Oulad*, the native girl whom Gide himself knew during his early visit to Algeria (p. 223). Another refers to the courtesans who wait for the narrator (p. 221); a third cites the custom of Arab women who wash you after you have made love (p. 237). At Biskra, couples fornicate on low divans (p. 232); in the Italian gardens where the friends of both sexes are gathered, pleasure is tasted in the dark (pp. 202–3). Térence, one of these companions, is in love with a Kabyle girl-child (p. 200).

Nearly all these pictures are Oriental. There are but few references to women in the Normandy countryside – and when they appear it is, for example, at a moment which allows the narrator a kindly smile for them and their children (p. 205). These are descriptions which are more chaste, as are those of Arab women at the spring (pp. 218, 234, 246), of village women at Biskra (p. 231, excluding the courtesans), and of others, unseen, protected within their houses (p. 236). Immodesty is to be found in the women dancing in the cafés, it is true, but there is nothing here to compare with Nerval's descriptions of the effeminate dancing boys recalled in *Corydon*. It has been said that the Biblical *Song of Solomon* finds many echoes in *Les Nourritures terrestres*. Strictly speaking this is not so, for the Shulamite is only mentioned twice, first in the 'Ballade des plus célèbres amants' (p. 197), and secondly, in the apple-store (p. 213). But it is nevertheless true that she stands as a symbol of passionate sensual love. The famous lovers of the 'Ballade' are heterosexual (is this deliberately made the 'fault' of Mélibée[7] who sings the song?), and they are also Oriental except for Theseus and Orpheus, who in the last two stanzas underline the moral of these (and other) loves: there is a time for loving – and a time for leaving those loves behind.[8] Thus the lesson once again returns to the teachings of Ménalque.

This points us finally to a significant conclusion about the relative importance of boys and women for Ménalque (and for the narrator). Both may be objects of sensual and sexual delight, but the youths stimulate a sentimental and moral need for education. In this last-mentioned element may be said to exist the soul of the pederastic relationship. One lesson which Nathanaël has to learn is that every act of fecundation is accompanied by pleasure (*la volupté*) (p. 213). But there are many pleasures besides: the narrator declares, indeed, that he has known every passion and every vice (p. 158). Which vices remain sterile is not stated. But the narrator's purest pleasure will come from chastisement of the flesh (p. 154). This leads to 'love', but love is to be understood as something essentially divine. The opening section of Book 1 develops this idea, and it is stated in Book 2 in the 'Ronde des belles preuves de l'existence de Dieu' (pp. 169–70): 'God is proved by the love one feels for Him. . . . I have preferred many things to men, and men are not the objects I have most loved while on earth. . . .' Gide concludes with a somewhat typical ironic concession: 'I have perhaps overdone my praise.' But this does not detract from the main idea expressed in *Les Nourritures terrestres*. If 'bonté' (goodwill) and 'tendresse' (tenderness) are human qualities, then love is the experience we feel in and for God. What we need is love, not 'sympathie' (p. 156). This latter word, 'the communion of loving souls', was an important leitmotif in *Les Cahiers d'André Walter*, linking the hero to his beloved cousin in an ascetic joy which they were scarcely able to sustain. *Les Nourritures* bears witness to a stronger statement of a particular sort of religious fervour. The narrator's deep affection for the sleeping child, leaning against his shoulder (p. 206), is love precisely because it transcends sexuality. Although it is based in 'tendresse', it bears witness to a greater love. It is the love of the Persian poet watching his beloved slumbering.

It is hard to avoid the conclusion that important though the sensual elements in this book are, they constitute symbols of a greater truth. In *Les Nourritures terrestres* there is no *one* particular person who is the object of passion. Gide's praise is of openness and accessibility to *everything*.[9] 'I have passionately loved everything that has no home' ('tout ce qui vagabonde', p. 206) is the formula which expresses this fervent self-denial. 'Ah, Nathanaël! The finest thing I have known on earth is my hunger!' (p. 167). Does then the *object* of his love matter so very much, so long as it allows him in the course of casual encounters to find his way towards the greater love, the love of God?

There is undoubtedly a confessional element in this work, and it was with this in mind that Gide wrote in his preface that he had drawn a picture of himself 'without disguise, and without modesty [*sans pudeur*]' (p. 153). This does not mean that the moral of the book is 'immodest' – merely that the author believed he had revealed truths about himself more clearly than before.[10]

Les Nouvelles Nourritures

This work was begun in 1916 and published in 1935. Several fragments (which I shall indicate where appropriate) had already been offered in 1919 to Philippe Soupault for inclusion in his periodical *Littérature*. In many ways the book is Gide's considered response to what might have seemed the egotistical hedonism in the earlier work. Although its emphasis is again on God and abnegation, and its illustration largely provided by chance meetings on the journey through life, its tone is more sombre. Nathanaël has become the author's 'Comrade' (though now less 'plaintif') (pp. 299 and elsewhere), and this reflects Gide's newfound Communist humanism.

It is interesting to note that Gide still addresses his work to an adolescent: 'I write so that an adolescent such as I was when I was sixteen – but freer and more aware than me – can find an answer to his urgent question [*interrogation palpitante*]' (p. 256. 1919 fragment). A little earlier, the text includes the exclamation: 'O child, you whom I love! I want to carry you away with me in my flight' (p. 255). Together with this, we must consider the call to the comrade – the comrade who is

Gide's companion and who must leave home, as Nathanaël had been urged to do, for the protection afforded him by his mother will weaken him (p. 298). These images can also be found in other works. For example, *Le Retour de l'enfant prodigue*, which was written in 1907 during the composition of *La Porte étroite*, describes the Prodigal Son talking to his younger brother, an adolescent. 'One loving word would have sufficed,' he tells the youth, and the object of this love is escape – not comfort and security (pp. 486–9).[11]

Book 1 includes a series of 'Rencontres' which illustrate *inter alia* those relationships or contacts which have enlarged the narrator's experience. The first belongs to the 1919 group of fragments and describes the joy of being with a younger 'comrade'. This is in fact an undisguised account of Gide's own joy of being with Marc, a love affair on which he had recently embarked and which gave him for the first time a knowledge of sensuality linked with intimate friendship on the deepest level. He describes their play, and likens it to a dance. This love is both spontaneous and joyful. There is equality in their participation: 'We excelled in matching our movements to each other's [*les mouvements d'ensemble*]', he writes. But he also adds, a trifle cryptically: 'The dance of the perfect pal [*copain*] is danced as a solo' (pp. 257–8).

The other 'Rencontres' are not like this. They are sorrowful: a poor negro; an old decrepit man; a poor fifteen-year-old in Florence, in some way involved with a young girl who commits suicide. These are images of despair and destitution (pp. 262–8). Again, when the author visits a sick friend, the picture provides a pretext for humanitarian concern and a protest against facile optimism (pp. 282–3). This invalid (or perhaps it is another) is consumed by the regret of never having known the Vergilian joy of 'embracing the beloved for whom he burned with desire' (p. 281), only to be warned by the narrator that his desire would not thus have been satisfied: 'For memory hurts more than imagination' (p. 281). The explanation which is offered for this proposition is that possession is of less worth than pursuit (p. 281). It is no wonder that the invalid is shown refusing the narrator's proffered words of consolation.

What then is the nature of love described in these fragments? At the time when he was writing, Gide felt himself to be old and possibly near death (he became fifty-one in 1920). He also regretted the things he had done less than the things he had not done: 'For it is at the age when both body and soul are most ready for love, are the most worthy of love and of being loved, when embraces are the most powerful, when curiosity is at its most acute and instructive, when pleasure [*volupté*] is most prized – it is at that age that the soul and the body find most strength to resist the call of love' (p. 286). It is interesting to compare this with the closing pages of *Corydon*, and to speculate on how a man who considered himself to be no longer young pleaded the case against restraint. 'I now repent of having darkened my youth, of having preferred the imaginary to the real, of having turned aside from life' (p. 287). If he asserts that there are many forms of happiness we still have to bear in mind that this does not mean that nothing is forbidden. Among his 'enemies' he lists 'those who pervert, enfeeble or slow one down' (p. 288). We shall see more of this side of relationships in *Les Faux-Monnayeurs*, for the history of men is to be distinguished from natural history. 'Man is counterfeit,' writes Gide (p. 297), while in the natural world 'it is the voice of God we must learn to listen to'.

What teaching is there here for the adolescent? Gide is clear: we must look towards the future; we may only make progress by putting our past behind us. And in a strikingly amoral sexual image he makes his point: 'History relates how Lot's wife was changed into a pillar of salt for having stopped and looked back. Turned towards the future, Lot then sleeps with his daughters. So be it [*Ainsi soit-il*].'[12]

One may in conclusion perceive certain apparent contradictions in this text. At the beginning of the first Book there is a reminiscence of the *Nourritures terrestres* in the description of amorous desire, recalling *Corydon*: 'All nature strives towards pleasure [*volupté*].' The more loving such desire becomes, the more imprecise are the boundaries which define it (pp. 253, 281). Similarly, the role of abnegation is still maintained: 'All affirmation culminates in abnegation' (p. 261). Beside this, the perception of suffering (*la misère*) makes one ashamed of one's happiness (p. 269). If the experience of falling in love with Marc has led to ecstasy, then one must perceive the sorrow of others. Perhaps the answer is indeed still love, but love of a wider sort anchored in humanitarianism (p. 284). It is a movement away from individual egotism towards others – 'autrui'. The difference is that now Gide is more concerned about 'autrui' than he previously appeared to be.[13] His advice to his 'disciple' remains nevertheless religious in the wider sense: 'Comrade, do not accept life such as men offer it to you. Never cease persuading yourself that life could be more beautiful. . . . From the day when you begin to understand that Man – not God – is responsible for all life's misfortunes, you will no longer participate in them' (p. 300). Once more, then, Gide sees his role as educator of the youth of whom he is fond. The youth is now his comrade.[14]

El Hadj[15]

El Hadj was composed during July–August 1896 at the same time as large sections of *Les Nourritures terrestres*. It was published in *Le*

319

Centaure in 1896, and subsequently in book form in 1899. With its subtitle 'Treatise of the False Prophet' it is a work which owes much to Gide's picture of the Koran and the Bible. It is another book whose subject is the desert and the nature of love. El Hadj stands in relation to his mysterious Prince as the poet Hafiz to his master.

This is the book characterised by Yvonne Davet in her notes to the Pléiade edition as having 'an equivocal amorous style for the relationship of the Prince and El Hadj'.[16] She further points to the correct identification of the Prince with God, for the narrative is a religious parable. Anglès (I p. 32) says, with slight exaggeration, that of the books written during this period *El Hadj* is the one in which Gide's paedophilia is the least concealed. The fact that it is a parable, however, does not preclude an examination of the equivocal amorous elements in the tale. But before we do so we shall take into account a manuscript note from the *Journal* which seems to date from 1888: 'I must compose something poetic which is Oriental and passionate [*brûlante*] on the words – "In my bed, for many nights, I sought him whom my heart desires. I sought him and did not find him." Then, rising by degrees to a mystical level and freeing oneself from the bonds of the flesh, take up the words "I seek the Lord [and so on].'[17] The point to notice here, surely, is that despite the probably homosexual origin of these remarks Gide clearly intended to develop his idea in order to give voice to the ultimate religious experience of the soul in quest of truth. This may also be perceived as a cry of anguish when the soul is faced with the solitude of existence and the unattainability of perfect love. The key passage ('In my bed . . .') was recast, with a change in the gender of the person sought, in a fragment destined for the original version of *Proserpine*.[18] It was used in that place to express Demeter's despairing search for her beloved daughter. There is another parallel in the early *Journal*, including a poem in an Oriental mode, when the hero weeps at night for the absent woman who is the mystical object of his love.[19]

When the pilgrims set out, El Hadj sings songs of love, for there are no women in the party (p. 346); later, women are allowed, but their presence and activities are strictly regulated (p. 353). They are no more than convenient chattels. The chief relationships which are depicted are between El Hadj and the Prince, and between El Hadj and the flock of pilgrims. The duty of El Hadj is to serenade the Prince. It is true that at an early point the Prince asks for a song of love about a garden where a woman waits for him, but he adds: 'Do not tell me of her' (p. 352). Each song is an expression of the poet's love: 'Prince! my soul sighs; my soul languishes for you' (p. 351); 'Prince, by loving, I believe thee' (p. 352). And he spends half the night in song (p. 353). El Hadj's heart is filled with love for the Prince (p. 353); his language is the language of the soul thirsty for love: 'El Hadj,' replies the Prince, 'how small is your love' (p. 354), and the poet's tenderness increases as his ardour mounts. Although the Prince is beautiful (as El Hadj at length perceives), his beauty is not of this world (p. 356). After his death, El Hadj disposes of the Prince's corpse and gives voice to a sentiment with which we are familiar: 'At length despairingly delivered of the love of my soul, alone in the night I could shout my joy, and pushing away the past which was dead, I could let my hope sing out' (p. 362). El Hadj's soul is free, and the significance of this lies precisely in the relationship of love. The Prince has triumphed because he died only for El Hadj, and El Hadj was the only one who adored him (p. 362). There is a parallel to be drawn here with Christ's sacrifice as an expression of His love.

The tone of El Hadj's songs seems openly homosexual, but we must remember the allegorical nature of the eroticism of Gide's model Hafiz.

> My sweet friend sleeps beneath his tent.
> I stay awake so that he may sleep.
> When I am alone it is because I am waiting for my friend.
> I only go to him at eventide.
> Now is the fiery time of midday . . .
> It is the time . . .
> When the virtue of the pure grows thirsty[20]

> So great is thirst desire of love
> And love is thirst for touching . . .

> Because of my friend
> I await the sweet night without fear.
> When the evening comes, my friend awakes;
> I go to him; we console each other for a long space of time.
> He teaches my eyes to see the garden of the skies. . . .

pp. 354–5

If we turn to El Hadj's love for the people, we find that it only comes into being with the death of the Prince. Furthermore, this new love is made of pity (p. 359). After the Prince's death, the poet leads his people onward, into the desert – but his role is now the role of the false prophet of the title. The people finally reject him and return home. Faced with this result, El Hadj has become severe in his solitude like other Gidean heroes of this date. If he hates the Prince it is because 'I grow weary, with hunger and tiredness, because I loved you so greatly. And the memory of your nights makes me feel my solitude more desolate' (p. 359).[21]

The end of the narrative also has a counterpart in other books by Gide, and it is not without a suggestion of the educative role which an older man can play. We recall the boy at the end of *L'Immoraliste*, the young brother in *Le Retour de l'enfant prodigue* and Caloub in the final chapter of *Les Faux-Monnayeurs*. 'Here, here, within the palace in the town, I know that a young brother of the Prince is growing up. . . . Does he await my voice to guide him? And will I begin again with him and with a new people a new story?' (p. 363). It is hard to see this as strictly religious symbolism. It is rather as if Gide was now calling to another Nathanaël.

CHAPTER NINETEEN

Philoctète

The appearance of *Philoctète* was first announced in the *Tentative amoureuse* (1893), where it was subtitled 'The treatise of the unwholesome wound' (*Le Traité de l'immonde blessure*), and it is clear that its composition was well under way by the end of 1894, as we learn from a letter Gide wrote to Drouin in September of that year.[1] He finished writing Act 2 in August and Acts 4 and 5 in October 1898.[2] It was first published in the December number of the *Revue Blanche* in 1898 and appeared in its *édition originale* in the following year, with the subtitle changed to *Le Traité des trois morales*.

It is important to establish the play's date of composition, since this shows several suggested interpretations to be unlikely or impossible: Martin Chauffier's idea that the play is a parable of the Dreyfus case[3] is implausible, since, although Dreyfus was arrested in 1894 and condemned to transportation in January 1895, general public feeling reached its climax only when the retrial occurred in 1898–9. Furthermore, even in 1898 Gide seemed relatively indifferent to the fate of Dreyfus: 'Is Dreyfus innocent? guilty? That's not very important. France matters to me much more – roughly speaking.'[4] The likeness between Philoctète's island and Devil's Island is surely quite fortuitous. The most that can be said is that *one* character (Ulysse) represents current nationalistic attitudes, while some of the issues raised by the Dreyfus affair are debated in Gide's play. Equally improbable is the suggestion by Y. Louria that the drama of Philoctète, a victim of society, was intended to mirror that of Oscar Wilde. This idea need not be seriously entertained, since the trial and downfall of Wilde took place in 1895. Delay[5] thinks that an equation may be made between Gide's mother, Ulysse and the concept of Duty on the one hand, and Gide, Philoctète and the ideal of devotion to the Self on the other: it seems to me that since the play has its own artistically coherent message it is unwise and unnecessary to interpret it so strictly in what Delay calls 'psychobiographical' terms. Similarly, Gide's own somewhat disingenuous remark mentioned by Heyd in his edition of the *Théâtre complet*, that the play is merely on the theme of 'le robinsonisme' (wanderlust), seems too superficial to be accepted as a totally adequate interpretation. Watson-Williams[6] has seen *Philoctète* as 'excessively' serious, maintaining that the play is chiefly about the dangers of intellectual aridity, while other critics have thought it much less so. The play must, I think, be grouped with the other symbolist treatises that Gide was engaged upon at this time: *El Hadj*, *Proserpine* and *Le Voyage d'Urien*. It has much in common with the earlier purely aesthetic writing of *Le Traité du Narcisse*, and, in addition, shows a preoccupation with moral values. It is also clear that Gide, as a self-conscious symbolist writer, would probably have avoided contaminating his art with so immediate a concern as politics or social crusading.

The key to a correct analysis of the play lies in an examination of Gide's source-material and models, of which the most important are Goethe and Sophocles, and in his development of certain symbols. The direct influence of Nietzsche's ideal of the Individual must probably be discounted, since although Gide was to some extent familiar with these theories by 1895,[7] he had not yet read any of Nietzsche's works.

At this period, Gide was profoundly influenced by Goethe[8] and read, among other works, Eckermann's *Gespräche mit Goethe*, which contains a long discussion on the possibilities of the Philoctetes legend, together with an account of the versions of it that were written in antiquity.[9] Goethe also remarks on the great resemblance between Philoctetes and the Oedipus of the *Oedipus Coloneus*, a comparison which Gide, with his interest in the two heroes and the idea of 'le héros malade', would obviously have found very attractive: 'We see these heroes deprived of help. They are old and infirm. Oedipus has his daughter to support him, Philoctetes has his bow': Goethe draws attention to the potential symbolic value of the bow, Philoctetes' wound and the solitude in which the story is set. Moreover, he does not neglect the question of the subordination of an individual to the state, which, as we shall see, was one of Gide's main concerns. The idea may thus have presented itself to Gide of giving the basic legend a new, symbolist interpretation.

It is only in broadest outline that Gide follows the plot of Sophocles' play. Ulysse, the wily soldier–politician, and Néoptolème, a youth, come to the island where, on account of his pestilential wound, Philoctète has been abandoned by the Greeks. They intend to obtain his bow from him so that the Greeks can win the Trojan War. The subtitle *Trois Morales* which Gide chose for his play relates to the question posed by Néoptolème: 'What is virtue?' Each protagonist has a different conception of *vertu* to propound. Ulysse and Philoctète both teach theirs to Néoptolème, who finally frees himself from his previous errors, only to accept a third form of virtue. Gide defined the three attitudes in a letter to Drouin of 26 March 1898: 'The fact is that of the three duties the catechism enjoins – towards others, towards God, towards oneself – the first seems to me reducible to the second, and the second to the third.'[10] Although the desert where Philoctète develops his moral system reminds one of the cold, glacial setting often found in the writings of the Symbolists, it is also a symbol of freedom peculiar to Gide.

Ulysse's ideal of virtue is to accept a fate dictated by military and political necessity. Philoctète, on the other hand, has evolved since he ceased to be among other men, and he can now do without them. He has been able to develop a *vertu* which has its end in itself and in him: it is not narrowly egoistic, for its aim and justification is rather the purification of the Self. Néoptolème, who is at first undecided in his allegiance, finally resolves his dilemma and chooses Philoctète in preference to Ulysse and the state. He does so in a spirit of love and devotion to the person he now considers to be his friend, so that he sees virtue as a duty which he owes to another individual. It is also important to realise, as McLaren points out (p. 22), that Néoptolème personifies 'the inquiring, searching mind that Gide so admires in the adolescent'. A distinction is to be drawn between duty and virtue: Néoptolème asks Ulysse to define the former, but seeks and accepts Philoctète's teaching on *vertu*. The first is composed of worldly necessity, the second transcends this into a sphere of moral – and almost mystical – values. The final victory is obviously obtained by fulfilment of the self, since neither Néoptolème nor Ulysse attains the apotheosis which is Philoctète's after he has asserted his will to control his acts. Although indeed he has not succeeded in achieving a perfect victory, the fact that he *has chosen* is of prime importance, even in the eyes of Ulysse. On the one hand he cannot attain perfect self-fulfilment because his ideal of virtue is superhuman, on the other he establishes his theoretical superiority over the other two protagonists. Néoptolème has failed because his love for Philoctète prevented him from accomplishing his *own* acts: he, too, was subservient.

Gide's insistence on the hero's superiority is neatly shown in the last act of his play if we compare it with the Greek model. In Sophocles, Philoctetes ironically asks whether the birds will come and feed him when he is deprived of his bow, his only method of obtaining food; whereas in Gide, after the bow has been symbolically removed, the birds actually do come and feed him. The bitter jest in Sophocles has been used by Gide to point his own moral: sacrifice of this sort leads to happiness and regeneration. Elsewhere, we see that silence is equated with fulfilment and the cessation of vain desire: 'Orpheus only sang when he was distressed. When he possessed the *reality* of his love he was silent',[11] and this is closely analogous to the situation of Philoctète. Gide was to use the symbols of secrecy and silence again in *Le Roi Candaule*. The idea of the power of self-control is expanded: Philoctète has learned more about himself since he has ceased to speak to men, and thinks more deeply as a result of his silence (p. 160). He peopled the solitude with his own words: he filled the silence with *himself*. But when he is asked to recite more poetry, he cannot speak: the presence of others, who distract him from his self-absorption, prevents him (p. 162). Similarly, in the scene between him and Néoptolème, he is unable to speak and convey his conception of what is above the gods. He knows, but cannot express the idea in words: it is knowledge, therefore, which comes from introspection and may be demonstrated only in deeds (pp. 169–70). The difficulty found in trying to express it lies in the fact that the individual must *make manifest* his self-found truth.

This intensely personal moral system, developed necessarily in solitude and silence, cannot be communicated: all that can be shown is the way by which self-discovery has to be attained. If anything is needed to point out the relative value of Philoctète's moral attitude and that of Ulysse, it is this remark by Néoptolème who has 'understood': 'Do not speak too much, Ulysse. . . . Philoctète used to be silent' (p. 172). It is only a virtue to be quiet when silence has been established as a symbol of Truth and the way of attaining it. When Philoctète does cry out something definite, 'There is no virtue, Néoptolème' (p. 176), it is only a momentary break in the thread, for Philoctète (like Christ on the cross) has his human weaknesses. But the message is not received by Néoptolème, for it is nullified in silence. Philoctète's silence prevents Ulysse from knowing the truth about the sacrifice of the bow: his virtue achieved in silence remains intact. It is this silence which both protects and nurtures his progression towards self-knowledge and subsequent self-assertion: to those who talk and dissipate their energies, this progression is refused. As McLaren has seen (p. 20), *Philoctète* demonstrates the triumph of individual liberty.

Another problem concerned with the interpretation of the play still remains: is Philoctète *un héros malade*, as his pestilential wound might lead one to expect? Certainly Sophocles emphasised his misfortune and aroused a feeling of pity for him, but his name is absent from the list of such heroes which Gide wrote down in his *Journal* in the 1890s. The point he was then making was that the pain of illness enabled those heroes he mentioned to exemplify desire, rather than the satisfaction of complete possession or achievement. In *Philoctète*, this Gidean dilemma is stated in a different way. Philoctète's present attitude has been evolved out of his pain, since in the numerous retellings of it in his solitude, his song (and therefore his self-sufficient virtue) has become purer and more beautiful. His 'loathsome wound' (*immonde blessure*) had the primary merit of driving him into solitude. It is important, however, that neither Ulysse nor Néoptolème has undergone similar suffering.

There are those who have seen a strong homosexual element in the play, and who have tried to identify Philoctète's wound with Gide's 'anomaly'.[12] To equate wounds, loathsome or not, with sexual acts (as Ireland does)[13] is in any case arbitrary. Moreover, this notion was only proposed after the image had become a Surrealist commonplace which in turn depended upon an interpretation of Freud. There is undoubtedly a very equivocal atmosphere, especially in some of the scenes between Néoptolème and Philoctète, as Valéry was quick to notice when he wrote on 6 July 1899 to Gide: '*Philoctète* revealed a very interesting Néoptolème. . . . I expected to see the young man more or less raped [*violé*] subsequently. But nothing came of it.' But ideals of self-fulfilment are being sought, and the characters are not symbols of abandonment to the senses: the dialogue on virtue does not extend into the realm of sexual morality. Brée believes (pp. 125–6), wrongly in my view, that this play is linked with *Saül* and *Le Roi Candaule* by the fact that all three feature a youth who is handsome and unknown, raising the threat of (homosexual) temptation for the hero. Her subsequent analysis of *Philoctète* is, however, quite acute. If we turn again to Sophocles, we may be able to clarify Gide's intentions: in the Greek play, the ideal of friendship and honour which fires Neoptolemus is something more adult than the reactions of the character in *Philoctète*. Gide has reduced the warrior's age to that of a child, so that Néoptolème's quest for enlightenment may appear more acceptable. If he was a little self-indulgent in depicting the scenes between Philoctète and Néoptolème, he may well have been influenced by his conception of Greek homosexual love, where he saw the lover in the role of moral guide and teacher. We must conclude that here again we undoubtedly have an example of Gide's homosexuality influencing his portrayal of the characters.

CHAPTER TWENTY

Saül

Saül, dans le désert, à la recherche des ânesses – tu ne les retrouveras pas, tes ânesses – mais bien la royauté que tu ne cherchais pas.

Les Nourritures terrestres, VII (Pléiade, p. 240)

Aussi loin que mes pieds m'ont porté, j'ai marché, comme Saül à la poursuite de ses ânesses, à la poursuite de mon désir; mais, où l'attendait un royaume, c'est la misère que j'ai trouvée.

Le Retour de l'enfant prodigue (*Théâtre*, III p. 43)

Gide had already conceived the idea of writing *Saül* as early as 1894.[1] It was eventually composed between the summer of 1897 and the spring of 1898, and published by the Mercure de France in 1903. Despite several attempts to have it performed (notably with De Max in the title role) it did not reach the stage until 1922 when Jacques Copeau put it on at the Vieux Colombier. The story is derived from the Biblical narrative of Saul, Jonathan and David.[2] There are some deviations from the Biblical account, notably in the manner of Saul's death and in the defection of David to the forces of the Philistines on Gilboa, but more important changes have been introduced in the moral and psychological attitudes of the characters. There are some elements, too, which Gide's play has in common with its source: these are the political problems caused by a change in the succession to the throne; David, the handsome young harpist, who fights and kills Goliath; Saul's antagonism towards the magicians and his violent fits of madness; the affection of David and Jonathan; Saul in the presence of Samuel and the Witch of Endor.

Gide's chief invention is to develop the notion that Saül has a 'secret'. At the start of the play this is the secret we read of in the Bible: Saül wishes to enquire into the future of the kingship (p. 26). As the drama proceeds, Gide associates this question closely with another secret – namely the sexual desire which Saül gradually realises is at the basis of his attraction towards David. Here the two secrets unite, for David is the answer to both questions, and Saül is thereby shown to be destroyed by what he finds most desirable. This is an attempt to link Saül's political downfall directly with his psychological weakness and moral defeat. Brée considers (p. 141) that there are three distinct dramas in Saül which are not perfectly integrated: first, the demons possess Saül; second, Saül vainly seeks to know the future; third, Saül thirsts for self-abandonment and sensual gratification. McLaren's view is simpler (p. 15), but he puts the case too starkly when he says that the play is a study in the pathology of moral degeneration.

There are at the outset some interesting comparisons to be made between this play and Le Roi Candaule, for both are about excess causing a man to fail to achieve happiness. Thus Candaule wishes to enjoy the friendship of Gygès (Saül is attracted to David); Candaule and Gygès are the same age (Saül is older than David who is seventeen, and Saül is sexually attracted towards the youth). The equal-age relationship in this play is a reciprocal one between David and Jonathan. The former is strong, the latter rather soft. Candaule is king, Gygès is poor (Saül is king, David is poor). Gygès kills his wife to assert his power of possession (Saül kills his wife because he always hated her). We will see that the themes which are repeated are used in new combinations to explore the implications of different relationships. Apparent similarities must not be used as evidence of strict parallelism between the two works.

How is corruption made manifest in Saül? The King welcomes what destroys him (p. 93), and this is present in the form of the devils. They are the figuration of his desires, as they explain (pp. 14–15): the sixth demon symbolises anger or madness, and Saül will find him in drunkenness; the fifth demon stands for lechery (luxure), which he will find in bed; the fourth demon is fear and doubt; the third is domination, which will not support him in his weakness; the second is vanity – the royal robes will not protect Saül against the cold, for he will be naked but for them, and when the weather is hot this demon will be called indecency; the first demon, echoing Mark 5:9 and Luke 8:30, is called Legion. These roles correspond in some degree to the deadly sins, but as the play proceeds they become more clearly identified with Saül's sexual temptations. In Act 2 they besiege the King, and on his friendly invitation come and sit very near to him (pp. 62–3). The second demon takes Saül's smile as an invitation to snuggle closer, and the fifth acts as his cup-bearer. Saül feels somewhat stifled, but allows the game to continue until the rowdy boy-like creatures all push and fight at once so that the wine is spilled. Here we are reminded of Hylas' song from Book 4 of Les Nourritures terrestres:

Each of my senses had its desires. When I wished to return home I found my servants and serving maids seated at my table. There was no room for me to sit down. The place of honour was occupied by Thirst; other thirsts were vying for the best seat. The whole table was in uproar, but they united against me. When I tried to reach the table they all rose against me and were already drunk. They chased me from my house; they dragged me outside, and I went and gathered bunches of grapes for them. (p. 200)

The singer is a victim of imperious desires which he finds too tempting to resist. Saül cannot resist the ones which call to him: at the end of Act 2 they tempt him with sensual delights (p. 64, the coolness of morning, the dew, the baths, the sherbets). The most significant temptation is that of the seventh demon, who would like to hear David sing.

In Act 4, scene 2, Saül is in the desert (pp. 112–14). The King is looking for his donkeys – a symbolic quest for the innocence of his former youth – but he does not find them. Instead he finds a demon who is dark-skinned and progressively more handsome as he is stripped naked by Saül. Is he too dark? That, the demon responds, depends on your tastes.[3] They disappear together behind the dunes, and Saül caresses him.[4] The King yields again to temptation (Act 5, scene 3, p. 141) when he enfolds a small demon in his robes and gives him wine to drink. Jonathan comes in and sees them: he is sad, and Saül is ashamed at being observed. At the end of scene 5 Saül declares that his demons (desires) have completely dominated and destroyed him (p. 149).

As Christ met his temptations in the desert, so does Saül. In Gide's world the extremes of thirst and aridity symbolise desires. It is the individual's responsibility to turn them to good use, and in this Saül does not succeed.

Saül cannot pray, for his senses are too alert (p. 16), and at the start of the play he cannot achieve a state of drunkenness although he would very much like to do so (p. 19). He was handsome in his youth before his decline began – that is to say, before he gave himself to vice and the cares of kingship (pp. 21, 90). The Queen observes two important elements in his character: he never knows what he wants (p. 37), and he has reached out beyond the range of his will (*volonté*) (p. 56). This last point is of the utmost importance, for even the pederastic suggestions contained in the play are subordinate to a demonstration of the need for an individual to know his limits and remain within them. Saül is presented as a character who sees an antithesis between his love for his wife and his attraction towards the demons and David. He has, indeed, never *loved* the Queen (p. 26); and in Act 2, scene 9, pausing to wonder what his own secret is, whether it is connected with David, and if the demons wish to learn it, Saül understands why he was not fond of her: 'In my youth I practised chastity too easily. I practised many virtues' (p. 60). This statement makes it clear that renunciation of the path of virtue is the work of the Devil.

Saül is jealous of the affection between David and Jonathan,[5] but his own relationship with David is not built on mutual attraction. It is not correct to say, as does McLaren (p. 17), that Saül is prevented from 'externalising' this 'problem' by his 'position and prestige'. David is first introduced as a harp player to Saül by the Queen, High Priest and the Barber in order to obtain the King's 'secret', since they cannot get rid of the cup-bearer Saki and they have to invent a new appointment. David's privacy is invaded when the King uses the affectionate name 'Daoud' (pp. 50–1) without authorisation. David remains cool and dutiful, singing the King songs of praise, not songs of love.[6] There is obviously something unwholesome and troubled in Saül's infatuation with the youth. But David does not appear to understand the sexual element present in it (p. 110). For him, Saül's 'madness' is an inexplicable contagion affecting the army.[7] The political relationship is worked out in these terms: as a postulant for David's love, Saül divests himself of the outward marks of kingly authority (the crown, p. 74; his beard, p. 82). The removal of his beard is not simply an exercise in making himself more attractive although it incidentally has this effect. Nor, of itself (*pace* Hytier), does it establish Saül's homosexual identity. McLaren notes (p. 18) that Saül is too mentally ill (*sic*) to analyse logically the tragic repercussions of this act. In *L'Immoraliste* a similar event marks Michel's transition from Old Adam to New Man.[8] These are attempts at self-revelation, but they are not necessarily successful. 'Let my passion serve my interest for once,' Saül pathetically declares before he goes to the Witch of Endor (p. 86). He is corrupted by his desire for friendship, whereas Jonathan is not.

Jean Vilar recorded in 1951 Gide's indications of how the play should be interpreted: 'Saül is chaste; but he is sensual. I mean that at first he does not recognise his proclivity. David reveals it to him. He only yields with horror and fright. All the sentences which express his *desire* for David must be spoken harshly, gravely and almost painfully.'[9] Much earlier than this, Gide had already written to Valéry on 22 October 1898 explaining the role of David (but sidestepping the question of homosexuality): 'He symbolises the personal drama which stems from any vice – welcoming and loving what is harmful to oneself.'

The relationship between David and Jonathan which causes Saül so much jealous anger is quite different. The two youths are of the same age. The intimate name 'Daoud' is quickly on Jonathan's lips. Brée (p. 139) calls this (rather unsympathetically) 'sensual marivaudage'.

But here we have to notice the character which Gide has chosen to give to each youth. David is handsome, strong, courageous and virile. Seemingly not only the King but also the Queen is captivated by his beauty. His manliness of bearing prevents sentimental feelings from being mistaken for either vice or effeminacy. Yet if he is victorious, it is because he relies not on his strength alone but also on the help of God. This point is made several times. He possesses, in fact, a truly noble quality: piety. He loves Saül as his King; he loves Jonathan more than himself (p. 72). In these two different loves he shows himself loyal and obedient in the first case, self-sacrificing in the second.

Jonathan is not the prince we read of in the Bible. As the Queen, his mother, says, he is legitimate, but weak and sickly (p. 26). He is handsome, and his weakness is not without some grace (p. 27). He is tender, and sensitive (p. 33). In several ways he reminds us of the Olivier to come in *Les Faux-Monnayeurs*, while David can be compared to Bernard. Jonathan is less strong than David, and when his mother introduces David to him, saying 'You will love him as your brother' (p. 41), he smiles. He is enthusiastic and sentimental about his friendship (p. 48). He is lacking in a sense of royal power: and in his feebleness of body he would willingly abdicate the kingship and give it to his friend. His gift of his royal clothes to David is in fact drawn from the Biblical narrative.[10] This also is a sacrifice, and one that springs from love. But it is different from David's abnegation, deriving its reason from weakness. It would be wrong to call Jonathan 'effeminate', for this word is too opprobrious. It is sufficient to say that he has the softness of character calculated to make a foil within the play to David's firmness of purpose.

The love 'passing the love of women' of II Samuel 1:26 may be said to take the form here of sentimental homosexualism. Most Biblical commentators would see it in the Old Testament as a love more innocent and devoted than the love one entertains for women: this is not at all the way Gide presents it. In this relationship we witness moments of deep friendship, but perhaps none more poignant than the leave-taking of the two youths (Act 4, scene 1). In fact, David needs the support of Jonathan in order to depart. All pleasure will also disappear, sighs Jonathan, and, far from David, his own strength will ebb away. But David is forced to leave because of Saül's behaviour. Moreover, he will desert to the enemy and arrange for his beloved (and for Saül) to be safe when the Philistines attack and rout the Hebrews (pp. 108, 131). However profound David's love for Jonathan may be, the funeral dirge he pronounces on learning of his death on Gilboa is very brief in Gide's version. This is not to show the character's indifference, but to demonstrate the power of manly virtue to confine itself within due bounds.

Given Gide's tastes, the cup-bearer is presented in a somewhat un-expected way. We might have thought his duty was to minister to Saül's diseased appetites, or perhaps to offer temptation in his turn. However, Saki, whose name is redolent of Persian poetry and Goethe's *Divan*, has really no such role to play. He is simple, naive and very young. He is a boy. His job is to stay on the terrace with the King and pour his wine. This gives rise to some malicious speculation among the courtiers, but the audience has a more correct appreciation of Saül's temptations (pp. 12, 123). Saki transfers his childish affections to Jonathan, and Jonathan questions him excitedly about what he knows of David's triumph over Goliath. Subsequently, Saki keeps Jonathan company more often (pp. 58, 107).

There is little difficulty in identifying the theme of homosexuality in this play. The problem lies in understanding its function within the dramatic structure, and in assessing the moral value we are invited to attach to it.[11]

There is an ecstatic declaration of desire expressed by Saül for David at the close of Act 3: 'Full of delight! Delight. Why am I not with him, near the streams, watching his flocks. . . . In the heat of the air I would burn! I would then feel my heart less on fire – which the song makes alive – which leaps – from my lips – towards you – Daoud – delight' (pp. 105–6). The first part of this quotation is a direct echo of the Vergilian 'utinam ex vobis unus', redolent of the Arcadian joys of the shepherds with whom delight is to be found.[12] In another context, too, the very different love of Jonathan finds similar expression in this phrase as he wishes to be like David, naked beneath a simple sheep-skin (p. 76). It is in this scene, witnessed by Saül, that Jonathan experiences his tremulous anticipation at the sight of David: 'I do not know if it is from joy or cold, from feverish anguish or from love, that now I am trembling in my linen tunic.' David's reply is similarly erotic: 'You are more handsome in your white tunic than wearing your royal finery. I did not know how elegant you are, nor how your weak-ness adds graceful charm to your body.' When Jonathan weeps at this, David offers him consolation 'within [his] arms'. He is less restrained in his words when later he tells Jonathan where they will meet in the hidden cave: 'Jonathan! my brother! my soul has sobbed with love. . . . Adieu! Do not forget . . . (He moves away, turning to look back.) More than my soul, – ah! Jonathan! more than my soul.' These are the accents of passionate friendship (p. 111).

A.L. Lerner's study of *Saül* is a conscientious attempt to relate the play to its Biblical sources and to take into account a variety of critics' views. Certain of her assertions, however, we simply cannot accept. It is, for example, not true that 'David . . . enters into a sexual liaison with Jonathan' (p. 88). Nor is it helpful to talk of 'Gide's carefully constructed triangular homosexual relationship' (p. 88), for this places the emphasis where it should not be. Lerner sums up: 'Yet, at the play's conclusion, we can only have learned how one should not act. . . . We know that one should not be "asservi par ses désirs" ["slave to one's desires"]. . . . *Saül* seems to counsel balance. This balance seems to be the difference between Saül and David' (p. 84). If this means that one form of homosexuality is shown to be acceptable and another is not, we will not demur but insistence on seeing the play in these terms of balance also leads Lerner to assert (p. 47): 'The differences between the two cases [of homosexual behaviour] may relate to freedom – Saül is trying to impose himself on David; David and Jonathan are moved by mutual love and desire [*sic*]. This question of the degree to which a person may be free is one with which Gide struggled constantly. In his relations with David Saül himself is not free.' This judgement, although partly true, is improperly argued, for in an important sense David and Jonathan are not free either, and Saül is the character who is dominated by his desires.

Brée raises an interesting question about the definition of homosexuality in this play. If it is true, she says, that Saül journeys towards a discovery – be it moral or political – of his repressed homosexuality which is symbolised by his total defeat by his demons, what are we to make of the positive nature of the relationship between David and Jonathan, for is that not also homosexual? She concludes (p. 144) that their manifest affection detracts from the symbolic force of Saül's pederasty. The answer, I believe, is clearly that not all homosexual attraction is similar merely in virtue of being homosexual. This is a point that Corydon himself recognises.[13] In any case, it is, I consider, too simplistic to say that the play *Saül* condemns homosexuality *per se*.

It has been suggested by several critics that in Saül's downfall we should see an analogue of Oscar Wilde's. This is possible, of course, but if we need an exterior explanation of the play we may just as readily appeal to Gide's own desires. Gide was eventually to give the point wider application when, in 1942, he wrote of Racine's *Phèdre*: 'Phèdre does not renounce what brings about her fall [that is, her incestuous love for her stepson Hippolyte], and she seeks how she may use her sense of shame in order to satisfy her love.'[14] Saül's conflict is an inward one, but his desires and will to act have an outward manifestation. As he teaches Jonathan in Act 5: 'There is a time to act – and a time to repent one's acts.'[15] But he admits that he did not act: hence we see the larger significance of his desires: 'I know, I know. I've especially desired. But of that, too, my son, the time comes for me to repent' (p. 138). Repentance will not be possible, for later as he prays he finds he makes no further progress. Surrounded by demons, he asks: 'Will I find a remedy for my desire, except the satisfying of it?' This is the conclusion to the scenes where Saul has called on his will in vain to act (p. 145). There is nothing solid in this man, everything yields to the desires with which he is assailed. He has no inner firmness, no support (p. 139), and this is symbolised by the sensual memory of '[David's] admirable supple limbs'. What Saül best likes in David is his *strength* (p. 139).

Where then does Saül's happiness lie? The prophecy of the Witch of Endor reaches beyond mere mortal *bonheur* (pp. 87–8). Saül will in effect learn this when she provides a revelation of his 'secret' by conjuring up the ghost of Samuel. But *déchéance* (corruption, defeat) is the other side of the medal, for as Saül sententiously but truly utters: 'With what will a man console himself for his destruction except that thing which caused his fall?'

Saül's weakness lies both in his powerlessness to resist and in his eagerness to welcome temptations. Samuel warns Saül: 'He who wounds you is welcomed by you' (p. 93). The Witch of Endor warns: 'O King, deplorably open and welcoming, close your door' (p. 99), and in her (non-Biblical) death agony she repeats: 'Close your door! Shut your eyes! Stop your ears – and no longer let the perfume of love reach your heart' (p. 100). In his madness, which is provoked by David, Saül remembers this advice, but he is incapable of pursuing it. Thus his love, the symbol of his general weakness of will, imposes itself on him in his dream (p. 105). Even the boy Saki will tell the King not to open the flap of the tent and let the demons in (p. 140).

These are then the dangers of openness (*accueil*). Gide wrote much later to Victor Poucel, a Catholic critic, on 27 November 1927: 'The danger presented by the doctrine [expressed in *Les Nourritures terrestres*] appeared so clearly to me that I immediately composed *Saül* as an antidote[16]. . . . Its subject is the ruin of the soul, the fall from grace [*déchéance*] and the powerlessness [*évanouissement*] which lack of re-sistance to temptations entails.'[17] The same point was made to the Protestant minister Ferrari on 15 March 1928:[18] 'The disintegration of the personality to which too passive an openness [*accueil*] leads is the subject of *Saül*.' Six years earlier Gide had written to François Mauriac with perhaps pardonable exaggeration: 'I have certainly never written anything more *moral* than this play – I mean, more full of warning.'[19] This is the very anguish, distress and disarray which Gide saw as the counterpart of the joy of *Les Nourritures terrestres*, men-tioned in a letter to his brother-in-law Marcel Drouin as early as 1896.[20] In 1895 he had already written to the same correspondent: 'I shall write a poem where I shall compare my desires to Lear's daughters, for I feel I am like that dispossessed King in that I have listened to passions which flatter me.' In the event it was an entomological ob-servation which allowed him to glimpse the central idea around which he was to construct his *Saül*: one day, he records, he found a chrysalis which had been completely invaded and eaten away by parasitic insects which filled the interior. It was in a similar manner that Saül was consumed.[21]

McLaren's conclusion (p. 19) has a different emphasis: 'The moral lesson of this play, therefore, lies in the warning that suppression of the personality results from a destruction of that inner dialogue which . . . Gide considers the prerequisite of artistic creation and the essence of life itself.' This is not persuasive. A more correct interpretation is surely that nobility resides in the restraint shown by David in his love for Jonathan, and that Saül's surrender to the temptations of vice is to be deplored.

L'Échanson

Another aspect of Gide's 'immoralism' appears in the *Journal* entry for 4 February 1902. What is said is intriguing, for it refers to a theatrical project which was never completed. 'One day I really will write *L'Échanson*. I do not know why procurers have always been shown as monsters and vile creatures. What one feels a vocation for appears good [*beau*]. I envisage a splendid play about Joseph, and especially the scene in the prison: Joseph between the butler [*échanson*] and the baker.' The story which is alluded to occurs in Genesis 40. Joseph interprets the dreams of the two servants of Pharaoh, predicting rewards for the butler and the punishment of death for the baker. How could this have been used to illustrate the role of the procurer?

The answer is to be found in a public lecture, 'De l'importance du public', which Gide delivered in Weimar on 5 August 1903.[22] Speaking of the purveyors of worthless works of art he turned again to Joseph. The two servants who ministered to Pharaoh's needs are likened to men who seek to nourish the public with their art. He concludes: 'The first of these was the "échanson", he who pours that men may drink. Pharaoh, remembering him, had him brought back to his court. He is also called Ganymede and intoxicates the gods. The second was the baker who brought food, and he was hanged. He is also called Prometheus and was chained to the Caucasus.' The relevance of these images lies in the following sentences: 'Oh! false modern bringers of nourishment, you need have no fear! If nobody thinks of hanging you, it is because you bring no food. But neither do you intoxicate us, and that is why you are detestable.' It is not his purpose, Gide states in a footnote, to talk here about *true* nourishers who are the only ones worthy of the hatred of men and gods. They must do without public approbation and bide their time. As Stendhal and Nietzsche had said before, they will be understood by future generations.[23]

It therefore appears probable that in *L'Échanson* the two servants of Pharaoh would not have been portrayed as ministers to tempt the appetites of men. They would not have been like Saül's demons. Nor would they have played the relatively subordinate role of Saki. In the English Bible the first servant is called 'the chief butler', which in accordance with early English usage could mean 'chief cup-bearer'; in French he is the 'grand échanson', and this surely enables Gide's mind to lend him more youthful characteristics, especially when he compares him to Ganymede. Would this uncompleted project have portrayed an ideal of ecstasy to which the closest we come in Gide's other works is Ménalque – but substituting, in this case, the figure of a boy as the eulogist of pleasure?

CHAPTER TWENTY-ONE

Le Roi Candaule

Le Roi Candaule is based on a classical legend. It was written during a brief span of a few months in 1899 and was printed in *L'Ermitage* in September to December of the same year.[1] Henri Ghéon, Gide's companion in debauch, helped him in its composition by drawing material to his attention.[2]

The story of Gide's play is simple: by means of a magic ring Gygès, a poor fisherman and boyhood friend of King Candaule, is enabled to see the naked beauty of the Queen Nyssia. In revenge for such an outrage she orders Gygès to kill the King. He does so. As we shall see, Gide constructs around these bare elements a play in which he explores the nature of friendship, happiness, the ideal of a hero, the concept of an individual's limits and the dangers of openness (*accueil*). Despite its homosexual undertones, *Le Roi Candaule* is about neither pederasty nor the education of youth.

In his preface Gide refers disingenuously to a 'simple reading of Herodotus' and to Plato, who tell two different versions of the tale.[3] The central feature of Herodotus' story is the importance the Lydians attach to modesty; Plato writes of a magic ring which confers invisibility. Gide should also have mentioned a third source, a luxury edition of a short story by Théophile Gautier, which Ghéon had told him about.[4] Gautier's Gygès is described at twenty-five as 'the handsomest young man in Asia' (Gyges apparently meaning 'beautiful' in Lydian according to Gautier), and his Candaule, built like Hercules (from whom he was descended), is presented as 'a young man full of strength'.

'Fate', for a Gidean hero, is an internal psychological force, not an external supernatural one.[5] With this in mind, and in the light of Gide's Protestant and Nietzschean beliefs, we can understand the quest for happiness (*le bonheur*) and the conditions for its successful achievement. The most substantial of these views is contained in one of Gide's notes to his preface: Candaule is too generous, '"Generous to a fault [*jusqu'au vice*]", writes Nietzsche; and again: "It is curious to note that excessive generosity does not exist without a loss of modesty." Modesty is a reserve.' Similarly, Gide intended to write a novel on this theme: 'X. has a generous nature – he is even chivalrous and somewhat utopian. He emulates Christian feelings (he is a Jew); generosity without morality. He offers his wife to Y, an unhappy friend of his who has been eating his heart out for the last five years. Y and the wife do not consummate their adultery. . . . The husband starts to struggle with the ghost of scandal; he cannot maintain his noble attitude; the rottenness of society reduces him to the level of a common cuckold.'[6] It is of particular interest to see that the motivating factor in the story was to have been 'generosity without morality'. Candaule hardly acts altruistically, as was the case with X, but his generosity leads equally to failure. This is its 'vice', for it destroys the agent. It is a vice, too, because it treats friendship on a par with mere material objects. Straightforwardness and power are the elements of an ethic of Nietzschean proportions which Gide said were to be displayed in the 'real characters' of the 'new drama'.[7] Furthermore, Gide appealed to the Greek model unfettered by Christian conventions 'which placed the sovereign good in the nobility of the soul, the strength of the body and everything that makes men bold'.[8] Nor must the element of jealous possessiveness to which this vice gives rise be ignored. Here is the clue to the difference between the heterosexual and so-called homosexual relationships in the play. As we shall see in discussing *Les Faux-Monnayeurs*, Gide distinguished between the jealousy felt by men in a strong heterosexual love, and a different emotion in 'other loves'. There is much of this 'different emotion', he said, in *Le Roi Candaule*. His comment refers to the notion of the Queen's purity being damaged when she is 'exhibited' in public.[9] One may adduce parallels with other Gidean heroes who, like Saül, succumb to the dangers of openness. 'Accueil' in *Saül* and 'générosité' in *Le Roi Candaule* are two aspects of the same fault and show how the doctrine of *Les Nourritures terrestres* could only be a snare for the weak.

The play is structured around two contending groups of courtiers (the sycophants and the noble-minded), two contending protagonists (Candaule and Gygès) and two women, each dependent on one of the protagonists.

The women are scarcely important: Trydo, Gygès' wife, is simply one of his chattels. The Queen's function is to bring about the dénouement. 'Nyssia,' wrote Ghéon in his review of the play, 'is a woman who is educated for modesty [*formée à la pudeur*]. She is simple, too, but more perceptive [*plus fine*]. She believes in Candaule – when she no longer believes in him, she believes in Gygès. She has to believe.' This explains why her change of allegiance is so sudden – and, it must be admitted, a trifle unprepared – at the end of the play. Her motive for having the King killed is not outraged decency as it had been in previous versions of the story, but more simply the need for someone to love her exclusively. With Gygès she is sure of this, and we should bear in mind her own reaction to her situation: 'There are some happinesses one kills rather than shares' (p. 184). It may further be noted in this connection that Nyssia and Trydo in the ancient sources are variant names for the Queen. Ghéon had done some supplementary research for Gide and was able to report this, together with Anatole France's comment that the name 'Trydo' was 'rougher and perhaps more meaningful'.[10] An interesting point arises here, for one is tempted – mistakenly – to see this 'duplicated' woman as an embodiment of two aspects of Gygès' experience. Indeed, a common view of the Candaules story in the early nineteenth century was that it symbolised the mythical duality of the sun and moon: 'L'éternel Androgyne se dédouble.' Such an interpretation may be found in the pages of the *Biographie universelle* (*Partie mythologique*) which Gide knew well, under the entry for 'Gygès'.[11] Candaules was held to represent the moon and Gyges the sun, his conqueror. But we look in vain for androgynes in this play. We know, moreover, from what Gide wrote in 'Un esprit non prévenu'[12] that he reacted strongly against this method of interpretation, and we have no reason to think that Trydo plays a significant symbolic role.

The groups of courtiers have the important function of representing attitudes against which Candaule and Gygès may be measured. On the one hand are the worldly flatterers, more interested in the fleshly delights of the flute girls and the feast than in an honest moral duty to their King. Nicomède speaks for them when he says: 'To accept with joyous heart one's benefit is the greatest secret of happiness', and Sébas, Archelaüs, Syphax and Pharnace agree. Their attitudes are seriously challenged by the second, smaller group of Phèdre, Simmias and Philèbe.

Of the persons in the first group, Nicomède is the name of the King of Bithynia who was the lover of the young Caesar (his grandfather, Nicomedes II, is the titular hero of Corneille's tragedy). Archelaüs was possibly suggested by the General who fought for Mithridates against Sulla. Gide was interested in Sulla as we shall see, but Archelaus, King of Macedonia and patron of Euripides, is also a candidate since his court is reported to have been very luxurious and the King himself a homosexual.[13] A third person, Archelaus, the preceptor of Socrates, is perhaps most likely, for the report that he was Socrates' lover is mentioned in Montaigne's *Apologie de Raymond de Sebonde*,[14] with which Gide was very familiar. Syphax was the Numidian prince who fought against the Roman General Scipio, and appears in Corneille's

Sophonisbe. Sébas seems to have been taken from the Greek word *sebas* meaning 'reverence' or 'sacredness', although there is probably contamination with the name of Cebes, the close friend of Simmias in Plato's dialogues. It is also possible that Ghéon had done some research on this name, too, and had discovered that *sebas* is applied to the thighs of the dead Patroclus by Achilles in a quotation from Aeschylus' *Myrmidons* cited by Athenaeus and Plutarch.[15] Pharnace is probably from Racine's *Mithridate*, but it is perhaps not without significance that he was reportedly a connoisseur of boys, having many castrated in furtherance of his pleasure.[16]

The names in the second group are all Platonic: Phaedrus and Philebus are titles of dialogues (as well as names of participants – Phaedrus (Phèdre) we remember from the *Symposium*). In the *Philebus* we read (11a): 'Philebus holds that good, for all animate beings, consists in joy, pleasure, amusement and in all like things.' Simmias is a speaker in the *Phaedo*, a Theban philosopher, disciple of Socrates and friend of Cebes. In Gide's play Phèdre, Simmias and Philèbe engage in a dialogue on friendship and happiness which, as we shall see, reinforces the symbols in the drama. Simmias' ideal is a friendship which one would never gamble away; Philèbe thinks that 'to believe oneself happy is better than to attempt to be so' (p. 175); Phèdre is Simmias' friend and so shares his opinions (p. 178). All three extol the keeping of one's treasure. In this way they are dramatically opposed to the group of Syphax, who misunderstands the nature of the King's danger when he twice toasts his happiness (p. 179), and of Sébas and Archelaüs, who are only too selfishly glad of the King's largesse since it enables them to indulge their appetites. In this context drunkenness is shown to be less praiseworthy than sobriety, and so it follows that Candaule's own hedonistic dismissal of 'la pudeur' is wrong: 'Drunkenness . . . renders to each man the very thing which from excessive modesty he kept secret' (p. 185). Phèdre and Simmias sit next to each other at the banquet[17] and are emphatically sober (p. 185). If their attitude is contrasted with that of the dissipated courtiers who surround them, their importance becomes evident: they are 'honnêtes' in the sense that they keep to the ideal approved by Gide. They are a pair of 'Platonic' lovers who obviously respect each other and live for each other. It is Phèdre who speaks with reverence of the 'value [*prix*] of friendship' (p. 176), and Simmias who reproaches the King for talking of gambling away friendship. They are largely silent during the feast, but their few interruptions thereby gain in importance. They are obviously self-sufficient, secure in the knowledge that neither will betray the other. They finally decide to leave Candaule's court together. They therefore provide a structural contrast not only to the group of profligates but also to the King.

It is Candaule who enviously refers to Simmias' friendship (p. 178), wishing to enquire about his ideals and participate in them. Thus he begins to expound to Phèdre and Simmias his ideal of happiness based on experiment. Zest for life and action are needed, he maintains, not the philosophical calm of Phèdre's existence. In a scene only printed in *L'Ermitage*[18] the debate continues:

SIMMIAS: The generosity you spoke of just now is only vice.

CANDAULE: Just so, Simmias! It must be that, for one to take so much pleasure in it.

SIMMIAS: But whereas desire holds sway over love [amour], it is good opinion, Candaule, which presides over friendship [amitié].

CANDAULE: Who teaches you to speak so well, Simmias?

SIMMIAS: Phèdre, my friend.

CANDAULE: Does Phèdre have a good opinion of you?

SIMMIAS: I dare not say so, but I hope he does.

CANDAULE: Well said. Phèdre, do you have a good opinion of me?

PHÈDRE: If I did not already possess Simmias' love, as truly as I live I would wish to be your friend, Candaule.

CANDAULE: Phèdre, thank you. I crave pardon, Simmias. I envy you.

With the equivocal use here of the words 'amour' and 'amitié' it is quite clear that there is a homoerotic element in this friendship. This is not, however, the major point: 'amitié' clearly depends on Gide's understanding of the Greek ideal, but it is also shown to draw its strength and cohesive power from mutual respect. This is in direct contrast to Candaule's attempt to buy Gygès' affection.[19]

It is important to clarify Candaule's position with regard to the happiness motif. *Le bonheur* has always been a precarious matter for him: he has always been of a giving nature, but since he has such great wealth, the thing which would make him happiest is denied him (p. 176). It is certainly the case that he has a beautiful wife, but that is not sufficient: he desires true friendship (p. 178). The symbol of Candaule's *bonheur* is, however, in this respect the Queen herself, since she is the most prized of his possessions which he wishes to reveal to the courtiers. It is significant that not until Gygès' appearance does the King decide to win friendship by actually giving away his Queen: this act, he hopes, will constitute his happiness. The King contradicts the courtiers who assert that the mere possession of beautiful things must render him happy (pp. 193–4). He cannot be happy alone, and needs to share. It is almost as if other people's happiness not only reinforces his own, but may even replace it (p. 195). Allied in his mind with this is the thought that only the poor are preoccupied with happiness. His form of happiness is that of the rich man who gambles away his possessions – and here we are reminded of Ménalque. But obviously this equation of happiness and risk is valid only so long as one's dearest possession is not true friendship. Candaule admits the correctness of Simmias' remark. Thus the reverse side of Candaule's conception of happiness reveals itself: he wants to buy Simmias' friendship in the same way as he will try to buy Gygès'. The King's last thought when he leaves the Queen and Gygès together is to wish that everyone around him will be happy. This reflected happiness will, he believes, be his own. At the last minute, however, he seems to see for the first time the error of his action, for he discovers what has been the secret of Gygès' happiness: sole possession.[20]

Without agreeing completely with Edmond Jaloux,[21] we may nevertheless see a large element of truth in his assertion that 'Candaule is, in fact, fond of Gygès [aime Gygès] and not of Nyssia . . . he does not give Gygès his most precious possession [this is a doubtful statement] but one which he slightly despises and by means of which he wants to attach Gygès to himself.' McLaren (p. 33), referring to this suggestion, comments that it seems 'more likely, however, that Candaule's actions have an intellectual rather than a physical or emotional bias', but he misses the point when he continues: 'his careless [sic] sacrifice of Nyssia is but a manifestation of an illusory, unrealistic approach to life.'

It is at this moment in the play that the King and Gygès display their opposing positions most forcefully. The friendship between the protagonists is not reciprocal, for Gygès is convinced that a poor man calls forth pity, not friendship. Therefore all Candaule's efforts to share anything with Gygès are bound to fail. Candaule does not understand the fisherman's mistrust. It is true that they used to play together on the beach when young, but now wealth and power have separated them. It is because the King admires Gygès' strength in killing Trydo that he wishes to cultivate him: perhaps he hopes that some of this power will become his own. But it is clear when they are alone that the King's need is emotional (p. 205) despite the fact that he is still materialistic (p. 209) and cannot readily grasp the trusting nature of friendship. Candaule asks Gygès whether he would accept a friend who seduced his wife, only to receive the reply: 'O King! how could a friend think of deceiving me?' (p. 212).

Gygès values the same equality in friendship as do Phèdre and Simmias. The King's question after he was offered his Queen: 'Do you still doubt my friendship?' meets with the answer: 'Yes, so long as it is always you who give' (p. 214). When it can be proved that Gygès has also given something to the King, namely the magic ring, there is a swift reversal in his attitude: 'Am I now really your friend, dear Candaule?' (p. 216). The unnatural brusqueness of this change points to manipulation of a symbolic character, and not to psychological realism. The gift does not make Gygès into Candaule's *alter ego*,[22] but it allows him to be balanced more equally against the symbol of the King. Exchange and parity, therefore, are shown to constitute the essential conditions of friendship, although the King does not realise this. In consequence (and to underline the symbolism), it is because the relationship has been entered into upon these terms that Gygès suffers at having possessed the Queen. He suffers even more when Nyssia orders him to kill Candaule who has changed from mere benefactor into friend. In consternation (*épouvanté*; *désolé*) he rushes to him, crying 'Candaule, mon ami . . .'.

On this level the play appears to be about friendship and happiness, but a further analysis of Gygès shows that this feature is subordinate to the moral position of a man of strength. Gygès is in fact the hero of the play, and is presented in such a way as to show up the weakness inherent in Candaule. As Ghéon acutely wrote in his review, Gygès is 'simple, healthy and strong . . . he has the honesty of a man who *possesses* something'; and again: 'Candaule is at the summit of sensual, intellectual and moral culture.' Furthermore Gyges is happy fishing since the fish belong to no one before they are caught: his happiness does not consist, therefore, in appropriating others' goods. This has its relevance when the Queen is offered to him. McLaren (p. 35), however, goes a little too far when he writes of Candaule's 'evangelical attitude' to Gygès and his desire 'to control and influence another's personality'. Gygès is careful to define the quality of his poverty: 'I am not unhappy [*malheureux*] – but poor [*misérable*] (p. 198). When he learns that he is not in sole possession of his wife Trydo, he solves the threat to his happiness by simply killing her. Outrageous as this may seem, he is in fact reasserting his possession of her by disposing of her in the way he thinks fit. Again, it is the *dual* possession imposed on Nyssia which causes him anguish: by this means Candaule has forfeited all rights to her. When Gygès enters into sole possession of the Queen, however, at the close of the action, he dominates her with his strength and forces her to put on her veil. If Candaule reminds us of Saül, then Gygès should remind us of Gide's pre-1918 ideal of a Nietzschean Superman who symbolises the doctrine of 'passer outre'[23] (persevere and break the bonds), based on self-knowledge and consequent inner strength. He complements Candaule symbolically and structurally point for point.

Apart from the ideas represented by these several spokesmen in the play, two important objects also hold the symbolic and dramatic structure together. These are a magic ring and a woman's veil. At first glance the ring seems to offer several possible interpretations. The most obvious, namely that its magic is necessary to facilitate the dénouement, is also the most obviously trivial. The second, that it is a sexual symbol – particularly a homosexual one – seems more attractive: on examination, however, one is led to conclude that the 'Platonism' of the play is non-hedonistic although at times admittedly sentimental. The ring cannot meaningfully be said to cement an erotic union between the King and Gygès. Nyssia (in more than the obvious sense) does not get a look-in. The third view is the orthodox emblematic interpretation: a ring is a circle symbolising completeness, truth, eternity. Gide was doubtless aware of this tradition, but the idea of completeness resides in the symbolic character of Gygès – and nowhere else in the play. The meaning of a symbolic object which changed hands – and was notably the gift of an unworthy person, Candaule – would hardly be clear. The fourth interpretation is the most likely: the ring, despite all the Jungian symbology it might conceal, is not important *per se*. It is its engraved message to which we must pay attention: *eutychian kryptô*, in Greek in the text, 'I conceal happiness.' As the object which it 'conceals' (that is, renders invisible) is now Candaule, now Gygès, it follows that the 'happiness' to which it refers must be the nature of the concept which the King is seeking. It is true that in another sense it 'conceals' Nyssia (that is, holds in store the night of love with her), but this contrived explanation diminishes the power of the symbol. It cannot be identified with one character in particular, although the moral import of the message approximates to what we have seen in Gygès.

When considered in conjunction with the veil, the ring clearly teaches the necessity for modesty (*la pudeur*), for we remember Sébas' question about the Queen: 'Why was she hiding?' and Archelaüs' reply: 'For modesty's sake' (p. 173). The veil has two possible symbolic meanings, each of which depends on the important notion of hiding the truth. First, it may be seen as an indication of hypocrisy – in much the same way as blindness is used in La Symphonie pastorale to point the differences between the morally blind and the morally clearsighted. It does not, however, seem to me that the major characters in Le Roi Candaule are hypocritical in this sense: at most Candaule may be said to be perversely unaware of the truth. The second interpretation is more promising: the veil is to serve as a protection and a guarantee. The fact that Nyssia appears at the banquet without her veil leads directly to Candaule's downfall: Gygès, on the other hand, affirms his power by telling her to put it back on at the end of the play. This is both a symbolic negation of 'générosité' and a proof of the moral correctness of 'pudeur'. There is also a danger to 'bonheur' itself as the Queen remarks: 'I fear that Candaule's happiness will fade if it is left uncovered' (p. 194). The veil symbolises the need for the beautiful and the sacred to be kept intimate, so that we are reminded of the aesthetic and ethical motif of Le Traité du Narcisse and remarks in Corydon.[24] The point which Gide was discussing with Louÿs thus becomes clear: Gide's message was not altogether puritanical, but a beauty unveiled will only be defiled by the mob and cause one's own downfall into the bargain.

The author's desire for a veil to hide beauty is not peculiar to this work.[25] Its inclusion in *Le Roi Candaule* is obviously due less to a concern for local colour than to Gide's wish to use it as a symbol of puritan restraint. Its structural purpose is therefore similar to that fulfilled by the magic ring.

We have noticed what Phèdre and Simmias have had to say about friendship. The relationship between Gygès and Candaule is not like theirs. The erotic, as distinct from sentimental, tastes of Gygès and Candaule are explicitly heterosexual (pp. 211, 214). It is true that the 'poem' recited by Syphax and Nicomède in praise of the cup-bearer (*l'échanson*) (pp. 227–80) echoes lines by the homosexual Abu Nowas from the *Arabian Nights*. We recall Ghéon's collaboration here, for Gide enthusiastically cited these verses in a letter to his friend in March 1899.[26] This is, however, a minor detail and does not affect the point at issue. The play has a dual structure: an aesthetic and a moral message are both concealed within the plot. It is true that the moral issues are well to the fore, but it would be a mistake to see *Le Roi Candaule* as a debate on the relative merits of heterosexual and homosexual love. For one thing, the veil has a part to play in the former love but not in the latter, and the two experiences are not confronted as they are, for example, in Plutarch's *Amatorius* or Lucian's *Amores*. Nor is the play about the war of the sexes, as Delorme suggests.[27] Gide made this clear in a *Journal* entry for 2 December 1905, commenting on a passage in Rousseau's *Confessions* he had recently read: '"Indeed, however violently I burned for her, I found it as sweet to be the confidant as to be the object of her love, and never for one moment did I consider her lover as my rival, but always as my friend. People will say that that is not true love: yes – but it was therefore more". . . . One can make a curious comparison with Myshkin and Rogozhin and Nastasia Philipovna in Dostoievsky's *Idiot*. The expression of this feeling (which is also the feeling in my *Candaule*) . . . is of the greatest importance.'[28]

In exploring the relationship of the individual Man of Power (Gygès) to his society, Gide was focusing on a facet of the debate between the merits of nature (Gygès) and culture (Candaule).[29] This, as we know, is a dichotomy he keenly felt and was to deploy in a different manner in *L'Immoraliste* and in *Corydon*.

Sylla

This project was announced in *L'Ermitage* in August 1901 as 'Scylla, pièce en 3 actes', and the title immediately raises a problem: *Sylla* or

Scylla? It is irrelevant to suggest[30] that the play's subject could be Scylla, daughter of Nisus, because of the interest Gide manifested elsewhere in Cretan legends. The key is surely given by an entry in the *Journal* on 8 August 1905: 'It is strange how high the value of *Humanity* has risen since the Greeks, or even since Shakespeare. Nothing is more harmful to drama than this over-valuation. That is more or less the exact subject of my *Sylla*.' What Gide seems to be calling for is a dramatic character who does not pander to the happiness of the multitude but who, driven by a kind of apparent Devil, allows the strong tension between good and evil to create the action. Together with Nietzsche, Gide wishes to turn away from the Parsifals of the world. Both *Saül* and *Le Roi Candaule* illustrate this proposition.

We have therefore to consider the character of the Roman dictator Sulla to whom Gide referred more than once.[31] In the *Journal* entry of 16 January 1916 he was obliged to see the reverse side of the power he had perhaps too enthusiastically praised before the war: 'Faced with this continuous procession of misery which deeply moved me, I became ashamed of all superiority, and repeated the words of Montesquieu's Marius to myself: "the price of raising onself above mankind is too great".' The quotation is from the *Dialogue de Sylla et d'Eucrate*, in the course of which, after abdicating power, the dictator Sulla tells his questioner Eucrates how he has now resigned himself to mediocrity through no fault of his own. He was only competent at performing great actions, he says – at conquering, destroying and founding states. When he reached the summit of his power, he continues, he was dissatisfied, for he needed some goal to lead him on. The blood that he had spilled had permitted his greatest actions, since it was not through kindness that he had governed. He did not, however, kill for the love of the state as did the earlier Romans of the Republic, he says: he was born to be free on earth and therefore he acted to secure freedom for the individual. Condemnation of this attitude is implicit in the cross-questioning which Eucrates carries out. The final – and most serious – reproach which can be made to a man of Sulla's morals must be this: that he was cruel for love of his own freedom, and that he set up Crime and Dictatorship as an example for people to follow. The mob, says Eucrates, will take no notice of Sulla's moderation, and it is therefore useless; the secret of obtaining liberty at the head of the state by spilling blood has been revealed, and those with opportunities for doing the same will look to it with relish.

Laboulaye's edition of Montesquieu was, as we saw above, used by Gide while he compiled his notes for *Corydon*. Laboulaye's preface records Villemain's praise of the *Dialogue* which focuses on the essential power underpinning domination: 'Republican passions combine in Sulla with his great desire to dominate – and from this strange amalgam is formed that bloodthirsty and arrogant scorn of the human race which is the soul of the *Dialogue*. . . . Montesquieu supported with perhaps too much application the stupid and fatal illusion of men which makes them admire the boldness that crushes them.' Laboulaye added his own belief that Montesquieu was wrong to have 'poeticised' a brutal soldier and given him 'refined ideas and feelings that make him into a character worthy of the stage'.

Michelet in his *Histoire romaine* throws extra light on the exploits and vices of Sulla. The characterisation of the Gracchi, too, which Gide quoted from Michelet, may not be without its particular relevance here: 'The Stoics who reared the two children, as they had reared Cleomenes the reformer of Sparta, taught them the politics of levelling which serves tyranny so well, [and the classical fables of the equal distribution of possessions under Romulus and Lycurgus].'[32]

Recalling Dostoievsky's glorification of crime (as Gide understood it), and remembering Gide's own interest in the anomalies of an individual like Lafcadio, one can see that Gide may have considered Sulla as a morally perplexing character, the more so, perhaps, because of one particular attribute: homosexuality.

Michelet can see no good in Sulla, and passes the following verdict on him: 'This hero, this God who was carried to his tomb with so much pomp, had long since been nothing more than corruption. Consumed by loathsome vices [*maux infâmes*], devoured by indestructible vermin, this son of Venus and Fortune – as he wanted to be called – had up to the day of his death continued to indulge the filthy passions of his youth. The minions, the low comedians, the fallen women with whom he spent his days and nights and their share of the booty. . . .'[33]

We may be sure that Gide's distaste would not have been so great, nor his censure so severe. Could it be that this passage suggested an analogue to the downfall of Saül, and to that King's inability to resist the demons of homosexual desire?

Alexandre aux Indes

There is another project which we may associate with *Saül*, *Le Roi Candaule* and *Sylla*. Many historians writing of Alexander the Great speak of his homosexuality, but Plutarch does not devote much space to this aspect of his character. When speaking of Alexander's closest friend and comrade Hephaestion, he narrates the King's great grief at his sudden death.[34] He mentions an incident when Alexander was obliged to kiss and tenderly embrace his favourite (*erômenos*) Bagoas in front of the whole army.[35] Otherwise he chronicles Alexander's many wars and, when sketching his portrait, emphasises his sobriety and self-control.[36] Indeed, Alexander was reported to have been very angry when it was suggested that he might like to buy some boys. He would say that sleep and sexual intercourse, reports Plutarch, made him conscious of being mortal.[37]

In 1896, as we have seen, Gide referred to Pascal's dictum that Alexander's chastity had found fewer imitators than his drunkenness.[38] An entry in the *Journal* for 1921[39] repeats the point, putting it in the context of those who seek to gain authority for their conduct by appealing to an 'influence' or an 'example'. The idea of 'authorisation' is one Gide illustrated by means of the sons of Œdipe in his play of the same name, but in 1912 he would more probably have been inclined to use Alexander's life as a symbol of the Individualist's autonomy. In the *Journal* in January of that year,[40] he noted the preoccupations which were leading him to compose *Alexandre aux Indes*: can a person recognise that he has come to the limits of his experiences, and, if so, can he renounce future temptations? Can he synthesise the experiences he has already undergone? It is difficult, he wrote, for an individual to be both master and servant of his own will since desire (which enriches) has always to be held in check. If one stops being uniquely oneself and cares too much for others, then one's domain becomes too large and there is nothing solid at the core of the individual.

The symbolism which Gide wished to attach to Alexander's march to India is thus made clear. His journey of conquest prefigures each man's attempt to ascertain the limits of his own being. Gide considered that what is important is the way in which such an exploration is carried out: 'It is as a conqueror, not as a traveller, that Alexander advances into new territories; he is seeking the limits of the world.'[41] In other words, the adventure is as necessary as the strength and the will to accomplish it. Nor are these concerns separable from the wider moral issues arising from sexual temptation. Saül and Candaule demonstrate this, for they lack the strong inner core of being. Uncontrolled desire leads to destruction, whereas an inner security permits one to adventure, like Thésée, into the labyrinth of desire.[42] 'The constant vagrancy of desire [*constante vagabondage du désir*] [is] one of the principal causes of the deterioration of the personality.'[43] Presumably, Alexander's sobriety could have been used by Gide to provide a positive lesson in resistance.

CHAPTER TWENTY-TWO

L'Immoraliste

IMMORALISTS. Moralists must now put up with being rated as immoralists, because they dissect morals. He, however, who would dissect must kill, but only in order that we may know more, judge better, not in order that all the world may dissect. Unfortunately, men still think that every moralist in his every action must be a pattern for others to imitate. They confound him with the preacher of morality. The older moralists did not dissect enough and preached too often, whence that confusion and the unpleasant consequences for our latter-day moralists are derived.

Nietzsche, *Human, All Too Human*[1]

Although *L'Immoraliste* was finished on 25 October 1901 and published in May 1902, the period of its gestation covered approximately the previous fifteen years. It is clear that many of the incidental details and a number of character traits owe much to the author himself and to the life he led in Algeria. But this is not the perspective from which we will view the book. We shall not ask questions of a biographical nature. It will be more interesting to see to what extent the moral attitudes expressed in this work of narrative fiction coincide with those of Gide's other books written during the same period. Did he not say that if he had been able to he would have composed all these works *simultaneously*, and that they are therefore all explorations of a closely related set of themes? Furthermore, by choosing a deliberately provocative title, there seems little doubt that he intended his book to take its place alongside other decadent works of fiction of the 1890s, even though it differs from them radically in the debt which it owes to the author's Protestant ethic. Throughout our analysis we must bear in mind one important idea: we know before we begin that Gide was a pederast, but we will not know until our conclusion in what way or to what extent his creation Michel is similarly inclined.

Gide often used epigraphs to direct his reader's attention to the underlying point of his narrative. He did this here and placed at the head of his book a dedication which serves this purpose. The dedicatee is Henri Ghéon, his 'franc camarade' (a Whitmanesque allusion), and this name appears together with a quotation from Psalm 139:14: 'I will praise thee; for I am fearfully and wonderfully made' ('Je te loue, ô mon Dieu! de ce que tu m'as fait créature si admirable'). Thus the book is placed under two signs: the sign of openness, and the sign of the beauty of mankind which is not without religious overtones.

But the reference to Ghéon is more than an acknowledgement of indebtedness to a friend. Two important episodes in the book owe much to adventures in which both men shared in North Africa and Normandy. This is, of course, a matter of documentary source-material and will open our eyes to the original nature of experiences which eventually found their artistic expression in the text. Thus the editors of the Gide–Ghéon correspondence draw our attention to what occurred when Ghéon, Gide and his wife visited Algiers, Constantine and Biskra in late 1900:[2] 'Gide's joys [*exaltations*] were doubtless much more cerebral or more sentimental than Ghéon's.' Moreover, not a little of this material is recalled in the travel notes published in *Amyntas* (pp. 162–3). As for Normandy, it is clear that the two friends shared in the 'secret history of the farm' at La Roque, Gide's property, where Ghéon had been invited in October 1898.[3] This does not mean that Gide, or for that matter Ghéon, is to be identified with Michel. Nor does it mean that the moral implications of Michel's story are directly transposed from real life. Thus Guérard (p. 109) is correct in seeing the strength of the *récit* in 'its controlled *transposition* of personal experience' (my italics). He also (p. 115) draws an interesting parallel with Mann's *Tod in Venedig.* That both Gide and Ghéon had homosexual adventures is not the only thing that matters.

L'Immoraliste is not a book which preaches a lesson. Gide makes this clear in his preface, which was purposely written in July for the first public edition (November 1902), and in a letter to Ghéon dated 6 July [1902] commenting on an article on *L'Immoraliste* by Rachilde.[4] He wrote: 'I wanted my book to be neither an accusation nor an apology, and I have taken care not to sit in judgement.'[5] He adds that the word 'drame' is more suited to Michel's situation than the word 'problème'. And it is a drama which takes place within his hero's soul. This is not to deny its more general application, and, he remarks, 'whether Michel succeeds or fails, the "problem" will continue to exist'. Success or failure, then, is a more interesting point than the reasons for the 'drame', and we remark on Gide's reticence in not directing us to the source of Michel's temptations, be they homosexual or other. The author did not intend the story to be taken as a case history ('l'exposé d'un cas bizarre'). It is not a contribution to the clinical study of 'aberrant' behaviour.

This, for what it is worth, is the author's opinion, but the 'Préface' is itself part of the structure of the book, and is intended to throw a particular (but not unique) light upon the subject. After the author's preface, comes a letter from one of Michel's friends commending Michel to a highly placed official. Can Michel serve the state? He is intelligent and has inner strength. He is devoted. 'In a short while,' this witness remarks, 'he will only be devoted to himself' (p. 369). On this view, Michel has not yet become a complete egotist and still possesses great merit.

The third and most important level of narration is provided by Michel himself, who tells the story of his life from his marriage to the death of his wife Marceline. He adds a few words to describe his present existence. Thus what we know about Michel derives from his own lucid self-awareness. What we know of his wife and their relationship also comes from this source. What we know of love and the nature of desire is similarly derived. In the course of the narrative, Michel reports his meetings with Ménalque, and in these cases alone do we feel that a system of beliefs foreign to Michel's enters into account. Michel allows Ménalque to speak in his own behalf.

It has often been suggested, quite correctly in my view, that Ménalque is a symbolic character[6] in a fictional world which may generally be described as realistic. He is a person who has a positive philosophy of life. He appears three times in the récit.[7]

On the first of these occasions, the description we are given of his meeting with Michel is strikingly reminiscent of the opening section of the subsequently published Corydon (1911 version). Indeed Michel seems to be the counterpart of the interlocutor in that book, and Ménalque is for all the world like Corydon whose 'scandalous' behaviour has placed him outside decent society. But 'decent' means nothing more than hypocritical. In L'Immoraliste the nature of the scandal is not specified. We note two points: Michel had previously been alienated by Ménalque's insolence and self-sufficient pride – now this is a reason for Michel to warm to him. Secondly, Michel makes a public gesture of comradeship because he feels drawn to Ménalque 'by a secret influence'. Although Michel appreciates his charming but infrequent smile, we learn no more about a possible secret which they share.

The discussion turns to the young Arab Moktir and the scissors he had stolen from Michel. We are not told how Ménalque became acquainted with the boy. The conclusions Ménalque draws from the incident are clearly intended to explain the character of Michel. They are that Michel likes children more than he likes his wife, and that he has no sense of property. Michel was unaware of either of these traits of his personality. The fact that Moktir knew he was being observed as he stole the scissors is of no importance for our understanding of this point. Ménalque enlarges on the theme of property: possession encourages quiet repose, and, for a person who is in love with life, excitement is essential. Ménalque has no use for the good or bad opinion men may have of him. And, as for Michel, Ménalque believes that for someone who has no sense of property he has too many possessions. In other words, we are being shown that there is a disparity between Michel's character and the life he leads. Michel does not understand this, and at the end of the first interview Ménalque leaves him with an ironic smile.

By the time Ménalque makes his second appearance Michel has learned that his own sufferings are due to the fact that he wishes to preserve his possessions. But he has learned his lesson badly, because he still wants to preserve the objects *intact*, and unsullied by life.

Ménalque is elegant and 'almost handsome'. His expression conveys courage and decision rather than goodness of heart (*bonté*). The fact that Marceline does not like him indicates the distance which separates their views on life. The newspapers now recognise him as a famous explorer and praise his qualities. Leaving to one side the irony levelled at fickle public opinion, Ménalque's virtues are nevertheless apparent. He is devoted, bold and capable of self-denial (*abnégation*). This is again a description which reminds us of Corydon. He explains his philosophy: his only wish is to be natural, and pleasure is for him evidence of the authenticity of his acts. He does not obey other people's rules. Nor does he imitate their behaviour, for an imitator is afraid of being himself. Rather he chooses the rare element which distinguishes him from others. But he has a word against 'constraint': people who live according to that rule are only happy when untrue ('ne se plaisent que contrefaits'). Obviously he does not believe in the virtues of 'abnégation' *per se*. Michel's reply incurs Ménalque's scorn, for it is a stupid reiteration of a commonplace. What Michel also reveals to the reader is that this phrase has in fact been borrowed from Marceline. Thus once again Ménalque and Marceline are shown to represent opposing attitudes. Despite his egotism, however, Ménalque is profoundly devoted to his friends.

The third encounter occurs at the very moment when Marceline has her miscarriage. Michel has thus significantly abandoned her for the temptations of an opposite philosophy. But what do we learn of Ménalque this time? In his opinion, a man must choose and know what he wants. It is wrong to hunger after another's happiness, for each individual has his own and must be true to it. There are many forms of happiness in the world: this is a reiteration of the teaching of *Les Nourritures*. In developing his thought, Ménalque draws a conclusion about Art. If it is not directly connected with life, it is but a dead letter. Thus the Greeks, he says, who lived life 'naturally', were great artists and philosophers. (Corydon will make the same observation and relate it to the pederasty their civilisation encouraged.) However, Michel's earlier lecture (p. 424) made a different point: culture born from life kills life itself. Another thing Ménalque says takes up an idea which had gone through Michel's head shortly before this interview: of the three moments of existence past, present and future, Michel feels an urgent need to project himself forward into the future. Ménalque rejects the past, but lives in the future realised in the present. For him, feelings of joy are soon corrupted and pass away, best forgotten. Those memories which provoke repentance are the joys he has experienced. Ménalque's happiness is made of disquiet (*inquiétude*). Michel, with his 'bonheur calme', is first forced to acknowledge that Ménalque's philosophy, though disturbing, reveals an important truth for him. 'My thought was laid bare,' he says – but then he reacts, becomes irritated, and returns to that very safety Ménalque has scorned. He finds it destroyed by the miscarriage.

The author appears to be suggesting that we should see Michel as a sort of Ménalque *manqué*, or at best as a Ménalque who has not the strength of character to assume the role of individualist. Michel, however, characterises Ménalque's joy as 'cynical'. This is not necessarily a judgement which should command our assent, but it reveals something about Michel's own attitudes.

On the evidence provided by the text it is difficult to say what was the nature of the scandal which surrounded Ménalque. The details of the exploits recounted in *Les Nourritures* have been removed. Why? Here it is only possible to speculate. Gide may have wanted to simplify his portrait in order to convey the moral message more clearly. Or he may have had personal reasons for being less overt in his portrayal of a pederast. Again, he might have felt that to portray Ménalque as a homosexual would lead the reader to conclude that Michel, in emulating him, was following the same path. And this would quite justifiably raise a very pertinent question: would Gide have been satisfied to show his hero as an immoralist and a failure if he was an avowed pederast?

We have seen Michel briefly in his relationship with Ménalque. Let us also remember that his character cannot be understood without reference to his wife and to the love he has for her. Indeed the symbiotic nature of their lives is also a typical element in the Gidean narrative structure. Just as in the *Prométhée mal enchaîné* (p. 317) the relationship between the hero and the conscience which devours him (symbolised by his Eagle) is described in the words of John 3:30, 'He must increase, but I must decrease', so in *L'Immoraliste* there are noteworthy sets of opposites which balance each other. Equilibrium is not achieved by this means, for Gide's aim is rather to keep in play the requirements of mutually exclusive but interdependent systems of values. The story is set in two environments which are at opposite extremes – the heat of Algeria and the cool dampness of Normandy. In each place the quality of the hero's desire is different. Michel's father was an atheist, his mother a devout Huguenot (p. 373): he forgets his mother's example and moves towards paganism. Michel evolves from being able to recognise the Old Adam to attempting to refashion himself as the New Man. But by far the most important alternating structure is provided by the image of illness and health. As Michel moves from a tubercular state to good health, so Marceline goes in the opposite direction. This is an example of the weak being sacrificed to the strong. But even so there is a paradox in the morality represented by our healthy hero. It is by no means obvious that *mens sana* is to be found *in corpore sano*, for as Michel becomes stronger he also indulges in excesses of immorality which lead him to the very brink of failure. So here is another polarity: a sound body and an unhealthy mind. This is one facet of what Gide meant by Michel's 'drama'. If it is true that the hero's leading characteristic is a quest for self-knowledge, we will most surely see the gradual revelation of the answers when we examine his marriage. We will also see answers in what he seeks outside that marriage.

Michel did not marry his wife for love (p. 372), but to please his father. At this date, however, he loved no other woman (p. 373). On their honeymoon he describes his attitude as cold courtesy ('galanterie froide') rather than love (p. 375). When he is ill, he recognises the powerfulness of Marceline's love for him (p. 380). When he regains his health, he regains his desire for Marceline, albeit somewhat slowly (p. 396). But Michel has changed, and he realises that the New Man which he has become is not the person Marceline had married. He therefore becomes more and more false in his dealings with her (p. 403).[8] However, paradoxically, dissimulation increases his love for her (p. 403). An important event occurs: Michel has a fight with a coachman whose drunken driving has endangered Marceline's life. As a direct result Michel makes love to his wife for the first time, but he ascribes his delight to the newness of the experience, to its unexpected quality and to the fact that they had waited until now.[9]

This moment in Sorrento is crucial for our understanding of how a sexual element can assume symbolic significance, for Michel adds: 'So much does one night suffice for the greatest love to express itself,' and: 'I believe that in love there is a single highest point, and that later, ah! the soul seeks in vain to go beyond it. . . . Nothing prevents happiness as much as remembering past happiness.'[10] On this point Ménalque and Michel agree, though Michel later seems to have forgotten it. When Marceline becomes pregnant, Michel cares for her tenderly and with love (p. 410), but in turn her tenderness and love cause him some anguish (p. 410).

The first turning point in his marital love occurs when the child is stillborn and his hope in the future is destroyed (p. 438). A moment before, he had been talking to Ménalque and 'clinging on to [his] doubtful happiness' (p. 437). He was anxious but 'pretended' that his anxiety sustained his love. This comment is obviously made with hindsight as he recounts the story. Michel's attitudes may, however, seem to have the contradictoriness of real life, for when Marceline is ill on this occasion, he watches over her, his 'heart beating in time with hers . . . hoping by the power of my love to instil some of my life into her body. And though I no longer thought much about happiness, my only joy, though sad, was to see Marceline's occasional smile' (p. 438).

When the scene moves to Normandy and Michel goes out on his poaching expeditions, it is nevertheless Marceline's faithful lamp which guides him home (p. 449). He is now caught between two forces: he needs the secure affection of Marceline, but feels an imperious desire to leave the house (p. 450).

A second turning point is marked by his awareness that 'everything is going to pieces' around him (p. 453). Marceline is ill; he kisses her. He promises that he will love her as he did that time in Sorrento (p. 453). Here the past is clearly intruding on the present and preventing useful, honest action. At the beginning of Part III (p. 454), Michel makes an important statement: he has tried to grasp his love and hold it in his hands (he should know that love is winged and cannot be possessed like a mere object). Now he also realises that he has no use for calm happiness. The love which Marceline offered him was as useless for him as repose for a man who is not tired. But he is not a monster of egotism: although he does not love her in an absolute sense, he cares deeply for her and feels her suffering most keenly. He is ready to be hypocritical in his love for her if only that will bring her some comfort. And so they travel south towards the places where Michel was ill and was cured. This is another example of the past intruding on the present. He spends lavishly in order to procure her health, but he has an ambiguous attitude towards this expense (p. 456). He loves her passionately (p. 460), and describes his feelings in detail. However, he is conscious of a battle between his will and his love: 'When sometimes I left her for an hour to walk by myself in the countryside, I would hurry back, drawn by a loving care . . . ; and sometimes I would call upon my will [volonté], protesting against this power that held me, and would say to myself "Is that all you're worth, false great man!" and I would force myself to extend my absence. But I would come back with my arms laden with flowers' (p. 460).

When they reach Sorrento Michel's dream has fled. They do not find their remembered joy. In this section of the story, Michel's adventures increase, but we are not told what he does in the course of his prowlings in Naples, Palermo and elsewhere. We are not told because the importance of these adventures lies in the fact that during them he is separate from Marceline. But he does not want to be separated from her completely: he cradles her lovingly, but still goes out and leaves her alone (p. 467). As Michel's actions become more and more manic, Marceline passes judgement on him: 'You like inhumanity' (p. 468). Has she understood the real quality of his professed affection for her? has she seen through the appearances and discerned the truth at the core of Michel's personality? Or is this the cry of despair, similar to Christ's, as she realises that her love will never be reciprocated in kind? It is all these. A final scene reveals the horror of the situation. 'With a last semblance of virtue I remained by her side until the evening.' Then Michel goes out, returns because he is apprehensive, but then goes out again. This time he will remain out all night in the company of the Arab youth Moktir, and make love to Moktir's mistress. On his return Marceline, very close to death, has rejected her rosary and with it her faith and her love. This is the comment of austere virtue on the life Michel now leads. We have been listening to a story of love denied, but this love has had a sexual and sentimental expression. Although I agree with Ireland (p. 197) that when Marceline sees the threat to their happiness, Michel 'plunges into a subterranean world of spontaneity and disorder until he no longer has any taste except for the most violent forms of life', I cannot follow him when he says: 'Only what is hidden can satisfy Michel, since only what is hidden is authentic.'

Michel did not have a child of his own, but it is towards children that he is drawn. This is the other side of his life, and it is symbolically represented by the adventures which it offers. As the story progresses, so the nature of these relationships changes. Michel's formulation of his conduct, though true, is too simple to be applied universally throughout the *récit*: 'Since my illness I have been living without rules [*sans loi*] like an animal or child' (p. 397).

Arab boys occur in two episodes in the story: firstly when Michel is ill, and secondly when he returns to Biskra after his recovery. On the first occasion their charm and beauty symbolise the healthy vigour Michel so ardently desires. It is Marceline who begins by bringing him a young 'friend', Bachir (p. 381). The boy is at first frightened, then a friendship develops and he goes on walks with Michel (p. 381). On one occasion Michel sees that he is naked beneath his gandourah, but nothing more is made of this. There is a public garden frequented by children; Michel and Marceline watch their innocent games and talk with them (pp. 387–8). Michel grows tired of Bachir and gets to know a fourteen-year-old named Ashour 'who would have been handsome if he had not been blind in one eye'.[11] Here one may note a preference which already demonstrates an incompatibility between Michel and his wife: Marceline prefers children who are sickly (*chétifs*) and studious, while Michel prefers active boys (pp. 389, 393–4). It is worth remarking that this motif is particular to *L'Immoraliste* and serves to underline the symbolic structure of the *récit*, for if we consider Ménalque in *Les Nourritures* we remember that attraction lay for him in everything, and he fell in love with the ugliest cabin boy. As Michel's health improves, he no longer needs the help of Marceline in his relationships: indeed he is becoming self-sufficient (he carries a useless shawl in order to engage in conversation with children, p. 390). When he is with his wife he cuts his walk short, for she 'doesn't understand magic' (p. 392). The allusion is to a secret garden within whose shaded confines a shepherd boy plays on his pipe (pp. 391–2).[12] Michel then returns there alone and meets Lassif, a handsome twelve-year-old. The next day he meets Lassif's brother Lachmi, who is a little older, but not so handsome. He notices Lachmi's 'sunburned nakedness' as the boy climbs down a palm tree (p. 393). There are other boys, and Michel encourages them to talk and play.[13]

What the reader notices about the whole of the passage in the text is the innocence of the events described, and the writer's keen awareness of the physical presence of the boys. But this is not a story about a character's development from sexual innocence to sexual depravity. The debate is a more generalised one about breaking society's taboos. The tone of sentimental pederasty derives more directly from the author's tastes than from the inclinations of Michel. Moktir now appears, and he is different. He is the only one of Marceline's protégés whom Michel does not dislike, and this is 'perhaps because he has now grown handsome' (pp. 394–5). It is Moktir who performs the important symbolic act of stealing. He thereby betrays Marceline's ideals and defines himself as an 'outlaw', rather like Bernard at the start of *Les Faux-Monnayeurs*. As a consequence, he moves over to Michel and becomes his 'favourite' (without this implying any special sexual attraction). There occurs in a deleted section of the manuscript (reproduced in the Pléiade notes, p. 1525) Michel's comment on witnessing Moktir's theft: 'I admired how one of the first manifestations of that instinctive and unformed soul I was calling into being . . . was an incorrigible pleasure in seeing Moktir steal. . . . Should I accuse myself now of not having accused the thief? If I determine in advance the point where I experience pleasure . . . that will again impose constraints. . . . Let us not judge. Let instinct alone be my guide.' Leaving aside the Biblical echo of Matthew 7:1 ('Judge not that ye be not judged'), this passage makes clearer the importance Michel attaches to instinct beyond the rule of law. As a result of the theft, Michel lies to Marceline and this in turn marks another boundary of virtue and mutual understanding within their marriage.

The second visit to Biskra occurs late in the story when Michel is unable to recreate the conditions of his past happiness. Michel's awareness of the boys underlines this theme. The youths are now unrecognisable (p. 465), they are ugly and grown-up ('affreusement grands') (p. 466), and have lost their original innocence. They are marked by toil, vice and idleness.[14] Michel lists them one by one. But again Moktir proves to be an exception. He has just left prison, and, unlike the others, is still the image of strength and beauty. This can only mean that he has the immoral charm of the vagabond. We have already seen how he is instrumental in separating Michel from his dying wife: he and Michel are happy to be in the desert, away from her (p. 467).

There remains one Arab boy we have not mentioned. This is Ali, who figures briefly in the prefatory letter to the *récit* and at the end of Michel's story. The narrative is equivocal. Ali is the boy who brings Michel food in return for 'a little money and some caresses' (p. 471). He has a prostitute sister, an 'Ouled', who slept with Michel for a while but who left when Ali became jealous. That a child might express such possessiveness could seem quite normal to the reader. Ali's sister, however, jokes that Michel prefers the boy to her and that that is why he keeps him there. The text concludes: 'Perhaps there is a grain of truth in her idea. . . .' This does not concede much. It is of course suggestive, but the author has deliberately denied us a precise insight. There are, after all, many reasons for being fond of children. The reader is tempted to remark that Gide is playing at cat and mouse. A more honourable interpretation might be that, given the intimate nature of the book, the author is risking making a confession through the mouth of his fictional creation, but is doing so in a way which will not commit him irrevocably.

Michel's relationships with the youths on his Normandy farm are diametrically opposed to those in North Africa. Being a member of the gentry, he wishes to break the mould he is in. He prefers the farm labourers.[15] There is Pierre, a vagabond, who is tall, handsome and follows his instincts (p. 442). The youth attracts Michel for these reasons, but he is dismissed by the bailiff. Bute, another disreputable youth, ministers to Michel's curiosity: his stories exercise the same fascination on Michel as the tales of the Goths had done (p. 446). He becomes Michel's accomplice, but is finally sent away through Michel's fault (p. 451). Another boy, Alcide the poacher, becomes Michel's associate (pp. 447–9). Alcide's life is a mystery, and Michel's unhealthy curiosity is greatly stimulated. To obtain a deeper intimacy Michel compromises himself more and more, but he is still unable to enter into his confidence. Alcide suddenly goes away, and Michel is left 'unbearably alone'. This is an expression of desire, rather than love, but it is not a desire which is overtly sexual. It is a wish to capture another person's 'bonheur' – the very sin against which Ménalque has warned. Michel wants to become a vagabond like all three youths, but constantly has Marceline at home who is anxious at his absences (p. 448). What reinforces the reader's sense of Michel's desolation is that Pierre, Bute and Alcide are shown in increasing order of amorality.

In Italy, on the second journey, there are similar examples of vagabonds and drunken sailors in Syracuse (p. 463), but there the lesson is quite clear, for Michel pessimistically comments: 'In Syracuse the brutality of passion still assumed in my eyes the *hypocritical* aspect of healthiness and strength' (my italics). Such contacts are not profitable, for when he slept in the open next to some Arabs his only reward was fleas (p. 465). These scenes are evidently denials of the beauty of sensuality, to be explained by their position towards the end of the narrative charting his moral decline. But there is a momentary (though unfulfilled) compensation in the form of the handsome Theocritean coachboy in Taormina (p. 462). (One might almost conclude that, since this is not totally consistent with the other indicators in the text, it is an attractive incident from real life which the author felt impelled to insert.)

Charles is a youth who is nearer to Michel's world than these vagabonds and foreigners. Here is a form of companionship to which Michel is initially drawn. That he rejects Charles later shows his distaste for middle-class values and the virtue of prudence. At first, however, Michel's joy is aroused as their hands meet underwater when they hunt for eels. Charles trains a horse, and Michel is tempted by the pleasure he feels in his company to go riding with him. On neither occasion is Marceline present (pp. 413, 417). Here the first moments of delight are undeniably sensual. That they are also innocent is probably one of the reasons why they develop no further.

Michel has very few real friends. They number but three, and date from his schooldays (p. 369). It is true that as a gesture of friendship he places his hand on Ménalque's shoulder (p. 435), but this should not blind us to the truth. The paradoxical reason why Michel has so few friends is that he has always devoted himself not to individuals but to friendship (p. 374).

The fact that Michel is an historian gives an added dimension to comments in the text on the relationship of an individual with the past, present and future. To an important degree Michel's interest in youths is also linked with these perceptions. When he was young he wrote a successful book on Phrygian cults (p. 373), and, although the implications of such a work are not made clear, the significance lies in the pagan sensuality of the orgiastic worship of the fertility goddess

Cybele and the god Attis whose devotees castrated themselves. Later in his studies Michel concentrates on the Goths and on Athalaric in particular (p. 407).[16] The picture he forms of this fifteen-year-old youth is a symbol of what he himself desires. He acknowledges this later (p. 457). Thus he projects on to history a wish which should more properly be fulfilled in the present:

> I imagined him revolting against his mother Amalasontha, reacting against his Roman education, rejecting culture like a horse which finds its harness too constricting, and preferring the society of the uncontrolled Goths to that of Cassiodorus, who was too well behaved and old, tasting in the company of some rough companions [*favoris*] of his own age a violent, voluptuous and unbridled life which would lead to his death at eighteen, spoiled and drunk with debauchery.

Here, he reminds us, he found in this 'tragic thrust towards a state which was more savage and more whole something that Marceline smilingly called my "crisis" [*crise*]'. He tried his best to learn a lesson from the frightful death of Athalaric (p. 407). But if this wish had been fulfilled, would the end have been so very different from the final moments of the story he relates?

Later, in Normandy, as his life requires that more order be put in the management of the farm, Michel still seeks refuge in the past and in his books. He becomes more attracted by the uncontrolled morals ('l'éthique fruste') of the Goths, and seeks too boldly to praise their lack of culture (p. 418). He applies this lesson to his present responsibilities. Was it wisdom, or was it rather folly, he muses (p. 418). His lecture, as we have seen, draws the conclusion from Athalaric and the Goths that they serve as examples to show that Culture, born originally from life, will end by destroying it (p. 424).

In Part III, Michel, in love with life, happy merely to eat and sleep, is only interested in historical research as 'a means of psychological investigation' (p. 457). Now young Athalaric, he tells us, would rise in vain from the tomb. The past cannot provide an answer for the urgent modern question 'What may a man *yet* do?' Thus the concern expressed on the eve of his meeting with Ménalque ('How dangerously our happiness relies on hope! and on an uncertain future', p. 434) has turned, in the course of his disenchantment with his marriage, to a new awareness of the present moment. In parallel with this, lies another discovery which has to be actualised: the Old Adam must be recognised (p. 398), and the New Man achieved (p. 403). If boys have a role to play in this revelation, it is again not a specifically sexual one. We must return to the symbols of health and illness: Michel begins to hate erudition[17] as he recovers, for it is a reminder of his past life and an intimation of death (p. 398). Ménalque's phrase is perhaps the most apposite: 'How pale are words when compared with actions' (p. 429).

Can any action, regardless of what it is, be considered good? Gide explores this question in several ways. One of Michel's early characteristics was austerity (p. 373); he finds on his later journey to Italy that privation increases his exhilaration (*ivresse*) (p. 458). The difference between the two epochs in his life is marked by this: in Italy his appetites are unrestrained, whereas earlier they had been kept under control. As we have seen, the boys and youths bear witness to this, but also show the sordid wages of 'sin'. Ménalque instructs both the reader and Michel: 'I hold that sobriety offers a more powerful intoxication: I keep my lucidity' (p. 426). This is after he has said that he would have provided some Shiraz wine at dinner. The significance of these words must be that what is recommended is the sensual asceticism celebrated by the poet of Shiraz, Hafiz. They do drink together on the third occasion. Michel, when later reflecting on joy, concludes that there are 'strong joys for the strong, weak joys for the weak' (p. 461). In one sense this is correct, for strong joys suppress the weak person; but in another sense it is delusive, for strength does not justify self-indulgence to the point of 'ivresse'.

The 'immoralities' which are specifically mentioned in the text are incest (Michel is attracted by this, p. 446), and wanderlust ('la débauche vagabonde') (p. 462). The reader will probably also wish to include Michel's adultery with Moktir's mistress. Michel becomes a prowler (*rôdeur*) as he prefers the instinctual to the civilised (p. 442). Thus his search for happiness is as doomed to failure as is Alissa's in *La Porte étroite*. He has sought *excess*, not restraint, in his self-abandonment. His pederastic tendencies, if they exist, are repressed. His unbridled thirst for novelty destroys him: 'It is no longer as it was before, a smiling harmony. . . . I no longer know which dark God I serve. O new God! give me yet more new races to know, and unexpected types of beauty!' (p. 467). This is almost the cry of an insatiate Don Juan. Brée (p. 159) also points out that Michel's 'homosexuality . . . is only one of many suppressed tendencies . . . one of Michel's hidden demons'. Furthermore, she identifies each of the youths as a representation of Michel's desires (p. 166): 'His drama is not the drama of homosexuality, but of lack of self-knowledge [*inconscience*] and the ensuing bad faith.'

Guérard (pp. 102–16) expresses a different and more committed view, in which, by insisting on the importance of the theme of 'latent homosexuality', he is led to over-emphasise the sexual elements to the detriment of the wider moral questions. Despite his many pertinent remarks, we may yet disagree when he writes: 'The novel's overall "meaning" is reducible to the barest Freudian terms, but Michel as a character is not' (p. 108). We must, however, assent to his acute

362

observation that *L'Immoraliste* dramatises as clearly as Dostoievsky's *Gambler* the compulsion to risk – and lose' (p. 107. It is a pity that he adds: 'Payment must eventually be made to the internalised parental authority'). Where he is less correct is in stating (p. 116) that nearly everything is related to Michel's sexual problem.

J.C. Davies seeks to diminish but not completely discard a Freudian interpretation of the story. In drawing our attention to earlier drafts of *L'Immoraliste* he records Michel's 'frenzied renewals of his own virility' after Marceline's miscarriage. He believes that Michel's homosexuality is hinted at during the book, to become openly declared at the end. This view is also one to which J. Meyer subscribes, who quite rightly notes[18] that the 'traditional connection of homosexuality and high culture' (which he observes in *Corydon*) is in direct contradiction with 'Michel's (admittedly spurious) repudiation of culture as the destroyer of life – and of homosexuality'. However, like so many critics, he places too much emphasis on Michel's supposed homosexuality. Moreover, he does not see that an attraction towards Ménalque is not at all the same thing as a desire to be with a boy. Nor does he understand that these temptations are no different in essence from the other satanic delights which destroy the hero who welcomes them too easily.[19]

Gide himself reports an amusing anecdote in his *Journal* on 26 November 1915. Paul Bourget, whom he had just met, lost no time in asking him whether his Immoralist was, or was not, a pederast. Gide was taken aback, he says, and in answer to the question 'I mean: a practising pederast?' could find nothing better to say than 'He is more probably [*sans doute plutôt*] a pederast who doesn't realise he is one. . . . I think there's rather a lot like that around.' It is clearly unsafe to place too much trust in this view of Michel's character, for the conversation is reported very much in the tone of someone telling a joke against himself.

At the date of publication, Gide, writing to Ghéon on 20 June 1902, quoted with evident approval some very perceptive comments on *L'Immoraliste* he had been sent by Mme Mardrus: 'I believe that even in *Le Roi Candaule*[20] you have never delved so deeply into the drama of complication and thirst. And this veiled adventure of a soul is further complicated by adventures of the flesh which make one shiver. . . .' The role of pederasty in the book can be seen as either anecdotal or symbolic: it is anecdotal if we attend to the biographical and documentary aspect of the *récit*. It is symbolic if we see it as forming part of the structure of the ideas expressed. One thing may be said with certainty: in so far as Michel perceives these tendencies, however dimly, he is conscious within himself of his status as a would-be 'outlaw'.

Finally, another privileged and intelligent critic is Ghéon himself, to

whom Gide wrote warmly in commendation of his recent article in
L'Ermitage.[21] Ghéon drew his readers' attention to the war between
instinct and culture in the *récit*. The sexual aspect of the story is of
secondary importance, he maintained. When Michel seeks his Instinct,
he added, we see that he will only be able to find Vice. 'I think the
most profound axis of the book and the point around which everything else develops,' Gide quoted approvingly, 'is what you say. "Once
learned, instinct is no longer instinct, but a negative force, quite simply
the negation of its opposite, culture."' Here, Gide has not chosen to
develop the antithesis between Nature and Custom in the sense in
which Corydon pursued the question. The whole discussion is to be
seen in the context of Nietzsche's definition of Immoralists with which
we opened this chapter.

CHAPTER TWENTY-THREE

Les Caves du Vatican

The original idea for writing this *sotie* seems to date from 1893, and Gide returned to it on several subsequent occasions, notably on 3 September 1905 (*Journal*) before he seriously began composition in 1911. The book first appeared in 1914.[1]

What is a *sotie*? According to Gide, it is a flippant treatment of a serious idea – an excuse for using parody and the unexpectedly bizarre. We therefore have to judge which elements are comic and which are not, and, in the context of our present discussion, determine the meaning of any sexual elements within the story. The 'problem' of homosexuality does not, however, feature among the serious concerns of *Les Caves*. Nor does it form part of the 'drama' of the hero's life, as was the case in *L'Immoraliste*. The questions Gide raises deal with the truth of an artist's life and the relationship of this to his fiction; free thought and rigid belief; chastity and marriage; and the liberty of the individual. In this last category we should place the *acte gratuit*, for it appears more as an affirmation of free will in general than as an excuse in any particular circumstance to break society's moral codes. Indeed, it has been rightly said that such actions are gratuitous not in the sense that they have no explanation, but that they have no motive of profit for the individual who commits them.

Nevertheless, in Lafcadio, a youthful vagabond, the reader has to face a character who is both beautiful and amoral. As Valery Larbaud remarked, certain pages – notably the rescue scene – do remind us of *Maldoror*. At the beginning of the story Lafcadio is nineteen: a photograph of him aged fifteen shows him sitting naked and happy on an upturned canoe at the feet of Faby (one of his 'uncles') and a mysterious, beautiful woman. Julius, whom we will come to in a moment, is intrigued. Lafcadio's curious ethic is summarised in his private notebook: it is reasonable to conclude that he punishes himself for lacking self-control at certain apparently innocuous moments. There follows a brief physical description when he appears in the room: 'The adolescent in the photo had scarcely grown more mature. . . . He looked little more than sixteen' (p. 718). Both Julius and, later, Fleurissoire are attracted by his youthful grace (pp. 732, 824). He is tender as well as indifferent, and sometimes cruel (p. 730). He is, as Protos recognises, seductive (*séduisant*) (p. 859). The Pléiade editors reproduce a description which was not included in the final version:

> *Lafcadio*: On his arms, his thighs and from the nape of his neck down to that place (the axis)[2] where Greek sculptors positioned the satyr's tuft of hairs, he still had that fair silky down which his mother laughingly called his 'milk hair', by analogy with a child's 'milk teeth.' She liked to see him naked, and, far from being scandalised, she was amused at his lack of modesty. In fact one could say that he only discovered what was socially acceptable later when he learned about hypocrisy. I believe he first found out about this from Baraglioul [Julius]. . . . Baraglioul was sometimes very sad at not being alone in contemplating the secrets of this magnificent body. . . .

Another manuscript sketch of Baraglioul shows him hypocritically 'hiding his wedding ring beneath an enormous cornelian' (p. 1573).

The nature of Lafcadio's relations with his 'uncles' is suggestive but obscure. His mother had 'given him five', all of different nationalities, and three of them diplomats. What were they, apart from being his mother's lovers? Proust had no doubt that these 'uncles' were 'aunties' (*tantes*: the French equivalent of 'queens').[3] That they were severally attracted to this handsome blond young man 'of a feline nature' (p. 824) goes without saying. Uncle Faby gives him presents – as would, of course, be quite natural in perfectly innocent circumstances (p. 716). Uncle Wladimir takes a boyish delight in a midnight escapade with him (p. 825). In his life story, as he recounts it to the inquisitive Julius, there are more details (pp. 738–43). Uncle Prince Wladimir Bielkowski 'paid particular attention' to Lafcadio 'as did all those who wished to please my mother'. 'It seemed that he was paying court to me – but what he did, I think, was not done deliberately, for he always followed his bent. And he had several of those! He looked after me more than my mother knew, and I was continually flattered by the attentions he bestowed on me. This strange man changed our way of life overnight. . . . He brought a sort of wildness to the exercise of his pleasures.' This is suggestive. Another uncle, Ardengo Baldi, joins the group: he is a juggler, conjuror and a very entertaining companion. The boy is amused by his antics, but soon this 'education' is interrupted by the departure of Bielkowski and Baldi. Uncle Fabian Taylor, Lord Gravensdale, now appears. Faby, Lafcadio later recalls (p. 824), was at first embarrassed at being attracted (*épris*) to him, but when he had confided in Lafcadio's mother he felt a lot better. The boy and he later laughed about this in their tent, but at the time Faby's restraint (*retenu*) had considerably annoyed him! It is Uncle Faby who was responsible for Lafcadio's 'natural' existence in the nude by the seaside, captured in the photograph. Julius comments primly that when posing for the photograph Lafcadio could have been more decently dressed, to which Lafcadio laughingly replies that Faby had locked up all his clothes, including his underwear, 'on the pretext of getting me sun-burned'. Although not explicit, this suggests a stronger element of sexual interest than in the previous cases. His mother was amused: she was 'not scandalised' (was there then a risk of scandal in this behaviour?), and she told her guests that they need not remain if they did not so wish. They stayed. Faby next takes the fifteen-year-old Lafcadio to Algeria ('a splendid trip'; 'it was, I believe, the best time in my life'). Here again there is only innuendo. Nothing is made explicit, and it is only by referring these details to patterns we have found in Gide's other books and in his own life that we can truly attach a 'scandalous' meaning to them. That we are meant to do so probably forms part of the author's intention to play at tantalising and mystifying the reader.

On his return from Algeria, Lafcadio is 'confined' to a boarding school where he meets Protos. This relationship is not presented in a particularly suggestive way, but it is intimately linked with the other forms of immorality explored in the *sotie*.[4] From here he runs away to Baden, where he rejoins his mother and his uncle Le Marquis de Gesvres (pp. 742–3). De Gesvres is a dandy who teaches Lafcadio the importance of clothes and the rules for satisfying his whims, desires and appetites. He soon disappears without there having been any indication of affection or sexual attraction. His function, like Ménalque's, is to expound a set of rules about the conduct to be adopted by a superior man of taste.

Julius' father, Count Juste-Agénor de Baraglioul, Lafcadio's bene-factor (and progenitor), occupies a special position in the world of 'uncles'. After the tender and affecting interview Lafcadio has with him, his paternal benevolence even induces the young man to reflect that 'he would have been one of the best uncles' to have had (p. 730). The author uses this moment for a little comic irony. Quite different, however, are the worldly Protos' commentaries upon these 'affairs', and he obviously regards all such relationships between uncles and Lafcadio as 'merchandise' of some description. After all, in Protos' world nothing is obtained for nothing: ever since Lafcadio acquired some money and dropped Mlle Venitequa (Lafcadio's erstwhile girlfriend – a person of dubious morals) 'your connections with Count Julius have become – my word – rather intimate. Would you care to explain why? Lafcadio, my friend, in the past I've known you to have had several uncles [*Je vous avais connu de nombreux oncles*] . . . . What would you like people to think? Unless of course you owe your present good fortune directly to Monsieur Julius, which would, if I may say so, seeing how seductive you are, Lafcadio, seem quite scandalous.' The alleged scandal is of course meant to be in the mind of the unliberated bourgeois reader. True or false, it provides the reason for Protos' suggesting blackmail, 'for blackmail is a holy institution, necessary for the maintenance of morality'. Earlier (p. 856) he has said how Lafcadio's beauty can be used to attract women and blackmail men. Let us not, however, jump to the conclusion that Gide believes everything his characters say. Lafcadio recalls how Protos was one of the older boys in his class, whereas he himself was one of the youngest. Protos was scornful of what their masters taught, but he was quick to take advantage of a situation. He soon earned the admiration of the younger boy, and thereby exerted an influence over him (p. 737).

There is, however, one episode where we are not left in doubt as to the nature of the temptations which the characters undergo. It is important to remember that the information is provided by the amoral Lafcadio, who is perhaps imputing motives to the quarry he observes. He adds a revealing commentary on his own reactions. The passage occurs during Lafcadio's train journey (p. 824). He reminisces about his meeting with the Curé of Covigliaio,[5] who was 'débonnaire', but 'not in the mood greatly to deprave the boy he was talking to'. In Lafcadio's estimation the Curé was obviously being careful. Lafcadio is also attracted to the boy, and connects this in his mind with his relationship with Uncle Faby. He would willingly have made the boy his friend (camarade): 'What nice eyes he had.' The boy is less than five years younger than him: fourteen to sixteen is the attractive age, at which Lafcadio himself was a 'stripling, full of desires [convoitise]'. Their eyes had anxiously sought out each other's. Lafcadio turned away, but certainly not out of disgust. The fact is that he makes conversation with the ugly Curé and, despite wanting to be unpleasant, can only succeed in charming him. This is an ironical depiction of a scene of flirtation. Another comic element is introduced with the immediate appearance of Fleurissoire, who, far from being a pederast, is charmed by the childlike innocence of the reassuringly friendly Lafcadio. This balances the innuendoes of the previous scene. But Fleurissoire is an idiot, and, in leaving a compartment where he felt threatened by a middle-aged Italian, has a worse fate in store at the hands of Lafcadio, who, in his famous acte gratuit, will push him from the train. It is fatuous for him to suppose that Lafcadio's frank expression and good clothes indicate the innocence of a schoolboy on holiday.

Lafcadio clearly possesses the indeterminacy of sexuality which Gide believed characterised adolescent youths. No sooner has he lost his mother and the protection of Uncle de Gesvres than he finds Carola

Venitequa, Protos' ex-mistress. He lives with her, but throws her out for having let Julius intrude into his room (pp. 731, 736, 744). Later, he will reflect on how he owed to her 'his most mediocre pleasures' (p. 824). Her underclothes are indiscreetly displayed on a chair in his room: this leaves no doubt as to their relationship (p. 713). She will reappear in the Roman brothel to which Fleurissoire is unsuspectingly lured (pp. 781, 784–5). There is a not altogether unflattering portrait of her here, where the author suggests she was not a totally abandoned and corrupted being. The physical description of her on her first appearance was slightly unappetising: 'a young woman, quite well built – or rather slightly on the fat side but shapely and of healthy aspect. Her features were common, but not vulgar and quite engaging; she had a soft, animal, sheep-like gaze' (p. 714).

Lafcadio has other relationships with women. During the fire, he is attracted by a young girl who is simply but elegantly dressed, and who promises a reward to the man who will rescue the children from the house. In a moment of adventurous enthusiasm Lafcadio does so: his chivalry extends to kissing her purse and asking if he can keep it in memory of her (p. 725). The following day he is still thinking of her 'a little' (p. 732), and follows her in the street. She is Geneviève de Baraglioul, eldest daughter of Julius. She finds Lafcadio handsome; he nobly and romantically kisses her hand (p. 734). In all this the reader may suspect there is something too histrionic to be quite natural. The novelist does not, however, ask us to question the fact that they are mutually attracted. Geneviève does not reappear until near the end of the story. Lafcadio is once again struck by her beauty, but he does not speak to her directly. Later, she comes to see him unexpectedly during his sleep (pp. 870–3), and the scene is rather comic in its mock-romantic overtones. The *sotie* terminates with the author's comment that we take poetic leave of the lovers at dawn: Lafcadio is lying on top of Geneviève. When he gets up he does not contemplate her charms (which are enumerated), but he goes to the symbolically open window, framing a new day. Lafcadio, the author tells us finally, thinks a little less highly of Geneviève since she has begun to love him more. (He is, after all, her step-uncle, though Gide does not capitalise on this.)

Of the heterosexual and homosexual relationships described in *Les Caves* we may, I think, say this: that the descriptions of the former seem anaemic (and sometimes mock-heroic), the portrayals of the latter suggestive and provocatively sensual. Lafcadio's relationship with Geneviève places him in a position where he despises or rejects love; his adventures with his uncles and his thoughts in the train bring delight. In a word, the experience of heterosexual love seems more cerebral and more inclined to cause the participants to reflect in a general way on moral issues. This is not to say that the homosexual world is without a sense of indecency. Bardolotti, for example, a splendidly comic creation, is an ageing satyr who poses as a cardinal. He is the person addressed by Protos as 'Ma Vieille' ('Darling'), but his face reveals no token of real age or sex. He is equally at home with the girl whose breasts bounce jauntily beneath her blouse, and with the boy Dorino, his partner in sexy horseplay (pp. 800–1). Protos, disguised in the train as Judge Defouqueblize, is supported by an accomplice dressed as a well-groomed widow who inadvertently reveals an alarming and well-formed calf muscle in scarlet stockings.

Marriage is not a state to which Lafcadio aspires: it is too redolent of bourgeois convention. The marriages of Anthime and Julius are not proposed as models we should emulate, nor is anything positively complimentary said about them. In the first case, Véronique is stubborn, unattractive and hard working. She smiles, however, and her husband is pleased with her *for all the bad qualities she does not possess*. But their home is not a happy one after she deliberately feeds his experimental rats (p. 687). In the second case, we witness the ironic depiction of Julius and his wife Marguerite as they go to bed, and talk of his difficulties with his latest novel.

The family presents a problem, for it is the context within which an individualist like Lafcadio (a bastard) may have to come to terms with himself and other people. One element in the plot, let us not forget, is the integration of Lafcadio into his true (but hitherto unknown) family – the family of Julius' father. The scene (p. 728) when the old Count meets Lafcadio is touching, and the warmth of the family bond affects Lafcadio for a moment – before he decides to reject all his past (p. 730). 'My child,' the Count has also said, 'a family is a great, closed thing: you will never be more than illegitimate' (p. 728). Bastardy, in Gide's symbolic language, means freedom.

If in this work marriage is not presented in a particularly engaging light, neither is friendship. Indeed, the ludicrous aspects of the affection between Fleurissoire and Blafaphas are emphasised, and neither character can be said to have escaped the author's irony. What would each have been without the other? They were so close that at school they were nicknamed the 'Blafafoires'. The author says of them, with a comic mixture of metaphors: 'To each their friendship seemed to be like Noah's ark, an oasis in the pitiless desert of life' (p. 760). But they are dull and mediocre students. Their friendship does not inspire them or stimulate their imaginations. It provides not an 'opening' (*ouverture*), but a common ground where they can continue to stagnate. We should contrast the stimulation Lafcadio experiences from his close contacts with Protos at school, where his excitement perhaps resides less in the abstract quality of friendship than in the immoral nature of the people involved. We might be strengthened in this view when we infer

Blafaphas' reaction on learning that his best friend is engaged to their mutual girlfriend.

> However great was Fleurissoire's naivety, could he really suppose that his friend would share his happiness to this furthest point? Quite out of countenance, he took Blafaphas in his arms (the street was empty [!]) and swore that however great his love might be, his friendship would be even greater, and that he didn't intend it should be in any way diminished by his marriage, and finally that rather than feel that Blafaphas was suffering the pangs of jealousy, he was ready to promise on his word of honour that he would never make use of his conjugal rights.

This scene is obviously ludicrous, and reminds the reader of the mock-heroic insanity of Flaubert's *Bouvard et Pécuchet*. It also takes up a theme which we have seen expounded in *Le Roi Candaule*. But in *Les Caves du Vatican* no sympathy is evoked for these characters and their feelings.

One final word remains to be said about another boy who features in the story: Beppo. Anthime Armand-Dubois notices him in the street in Rome, buys a cricket from him and tells him he will soon need 'a few rats' for his experiments. The boy is an orphan, aged about twelve or thirteen. The relationship which develops is interesting: Beppo adores the scientist and watches the vivisections with admiration. Anthime's crabbed heart beats a little faster when, in his lonely laboratory, he hears the approaching sound of small bare feet. What he wants, however, is not the boy but the bag of wriggling specimens. There is in fact no real bridge of affection between the two characters, and later, when Anthime wants to put an end to his wife's pious 'nonsense', Beppo will not help him (p. 699). What then are we to make of some of the details of the description of Beppo which, taken together, suggest particularly attractive characteristics? Arriving at the laboratory, 'he would take four steps forward and shout out in his fresh young voice a "permesso" which filled the room with light. The voice sounded like an angel: he was an executioner's assistant' (pp. 682–3).[6] Later, he helps Véronique to place her pious candles in the niche on the wall: 'he is at present a slim fifteen-year-old adolescent' (p. 697). This is surely an authorial intrusion, not an observation by Anthime's wife! What we should also notice is a similarity between Beppo and Lafcadio. They are both in a sense murderers, and they both have a limpid, fresh expression in their eyes.

We must conclude that one of the themes Gide sets out to illustrate is the education of youth. It is Julius who explains this when talking of the hero of his novel: 'Let us take him when he is an adolescent: I want the elegance of his nature to be recognised by this means, that above all he acts in the spirit of a gambler, and that he usually prefers pleasure to self-interest' (p. 837). This was part of the education received by Lafcadio from Baldi and certain other uncles. But the end of such an education leads towards constraint and self-control. This is the lesson inculcated also by Protos, and developed in Julius' conversation with Lafcadio. An example of Gide's technique of 'mise en abyme' emphasises this: an element within the plot (Julius' novel) echoes the concerns of the characters at large. Furthermore, links may be established with other works: 'Nous vivons contrefaits' ('Our lives are counterfeit') is the message of Defouqueblize–Protos which has already featured in *L'Immoraliste*. This does not seem to destroy the author's exclamation towards the close: 'O vérité palpable du désir' ('O truth of desire, manifest to the senses') (p. 873), reminiscent of *Les Nourritures terrestres*. There is, however, no good reason to conclude with Brée (p. 231) that Lafcadio is in any way similar to Michel.

It is noticeable that in this *sotie* sexuality is divorced from ideological questions of good and evil. This differs from what we observed in earlier works, and applies equally well to heterosexuality and homosexuality. The moral questions centre instead on other propositions: the place of unmotivated crime in the novel (p. 837), the 'gratuitous act', the bastard state and the nature of individual freedom (p. 854, and elsewhere). If Protos, Lafcadio and the *subtils* are lawless – a phrase reminiscent of Corydon's description of pederasts – then this has more to do with the inconsequentiality of an adolescent's acts than with his sexual proclivities.[7] Something else, too, is reminiscent of *Corydon*: the description of Lafcadio's *acte gratuit* in terms of *jeu, risque, dépense* and *luxe* – the very determinants of masculine variation. In the final analysis, Lafcadio is a youth, not an adult like Michel. His story is therefore open-ended, and was indeed 'open' as it unfolded during the telling. What he has experienced is not a tragedy. He is one of the beautiful vagabonds, those 'feline' creatures, towards whom Gide felt attracted. As the author wrily puts into the mouth of Julius, adapting the latin comic writer Terence's phrase:[8] the novelist entertained 'the flattering illusion that nothing human should remain unknown to him' (p. 712). Julius, an avatar of Gide, will live again in the character of Édouard in *Les Faux-Monnayeurs* where he will form different relationships from those he entertains in this *sotie*.

CHAPTER TWENTY-FOUR

Les Faux-Monnayeurs

The plot of *Les Faux-Monnayeurs* is, as is well known, centred around two actual events: one concerns the circulation of counterfeit money,[1] and the other a schoolboy suicide in Clermont Ferrand on 5 June 1909. Although the idea of writing the novel had been in his mind for some time, Gide seriously began composition in 1919 and published parts of the book in 1925. It appeared finally in 1926. The title itself dates from 1914, but it is clear from the *Journal des Faux-Monnayeurs* that the original conception of the characters and moral purport of the novel underwent a radical revision after the First World War. There is no doubt that this was due to changes in Gide's life: the Great War marked a period of growing humanitarian awareness on his part, of confrontation with the suffering of mankind, of religious doubts, and, above all, the birth of a very deep affection for the young Marc Allégret, echoes of which can be perceived in *Les Nouvelles Nourritures*. Although the novel contains many other details drawn from life, I do not believe that *Les Faux-Monnayeurs* is essentially a *roman à clef*. Consequently, in the following discussion I wish to put to one side all biographical details in order to concentrate more precisely on what I consider the essential points of the novel in the terms in which they are presented. Although Gide chooses to use his work partly as a confessional,[2] he may also say that, as creator, he is not one character but several, and that his thoughts are to be found expressed in many ways throughout his book.[3] Thus Édouard is not coterminous with Gide,[4] nor Passavant with Cocteau, nor Olivier with Marc. An additional level of narrative complexity is created by the existence of the Author, who makes comments from a standpoint entirely outside the fiction, but who is not to be identified with Gide himself. Moreover, the characters have their own lives within the novel, and the situations which are described enjoin a consideration of a range of moral questions.

There are connections between *Les Caves* and the early conception of *Les Faux-Monnayeurs*. Julius, the novelist, was to reappear as Édouard; Lafcadio was to be the young hero. Indeed Lafcadio, ultimately to be transformed into Bernard, shares with Bernard a fondness for looking into other people's suitcases. The pages of Gide's notebook, *Le Journal des Faux-Monnayeurs*, preserve some interesting details of these early ideas. In 1919 we read: Lafcadio is a youth who has 'new needs' and must continually move onward (p. 17). In this he shares the aspirations common to the truly young: whosoever remains true to his *jeunesse* does not renounce ambition and desire (p. 13). Édouard is to be his mentor and manipulate him (p. 18). If it is true that Lafcadio is rootless, then it will fall to the lot of another vagabond to establish a link between him and Édouard (p. 28). On 3 May 1920 Gide noted (p. 42) a further idea: Édouard senses that Lafcadio has an advantage over him – 'He feels that the most elegant way of disarming him is to win him for himself. Lafcadio suggests this to him, delicately and unobtrusively. However, this intimacy, which was at first imposed, grows into a warm friendship [*sentiment véritable*]. Furthermore, Lafcadio is very attractive (he is not yet too aware of this).' Several pages from 'Lafcadio's Diary' are reproduced in the *Journal des Faux-Monnayeurs* and belong to these early states of the novel. In them an aspect of the relationship between Édouard and the boy is revealed. Édouard advises him to be a patient observer, and to resist what he is attracted to. 'Whatever differs from us is of most importance. . . . What I want from you is cynicism, not insensitivity. . . . Beware, emotion easily brings lack of skill in its wake . . . but if you seek to escape from it, all is lost. . . .' Édouard defines sensitivity (*sensibilité*) as 'most often a joyful vibrant energy of life most keenly felt when one is most actively engaged' (p. 135). Édouard wants to know if Lafcadio has a mistress. The boy replies that he is more concerned with freedom than with tying himself down. Later (pp. 137–8), Lafcadio confides in his diary: 'An affair is what I fear most. . . .' He is full of contradictions: 'I was going to write that I have a taste for pleasure [*volupté*], but I must admit that I find love [*amour*] boring. . . . What I find most boring in love is romance – pleasure [*plaisir*] so long postponed, tender gestures. . . . For I am always in love – with everything and everybody. I would not like being tied down to one person.' All this is reminiscent of the *Nourritures terrestres*. Gide's original intention was to make Lafcadio the narrator who would gradually discover what was going on – and participate in the events as a curious observer, an idle spectator and a source of corruption. What he finally decided to do was to compose a more complex novel where events, characters and moral issues were perceived from more than one viewpoint. He had already foreseen this problem in 1919 when he wrote in his notes that however thick he wished the texture of the novel to be, he could not think of including everything within its pages (p. 10). His solution would be to adhere rigidly to the principle that ideas should only be expressed as a function of personalities (*tempéraments*) and characters. The novelist's view is that 'opinions do not exist outside individuals'.[5] This will allow for a certain proliferation of points of view, but will also have a bearing on the range and interpretation of the moral attitudes which are expressed. Gide's aim can therefore best be summarised in his own words: 'It is not so much in putting forward a solution to certain problems that I can perform a real service for the reader – but rather in forcing him to reflect on these problems to which I do not myself admit that there can be any solution other than an individual and personal one.'[6]

Along with other elements which characterised *Les Caves*, the egotism of the hero and the wayward eccentricity of the narrative are absent from the final version of *Les Faux-Monnayeurs*. In their place are a new technique and a presentation of new experiences. Most importantly, a new humanitarianism shapes the story as a result of Gide's use of a revitalised Édouard as the central unifying feature of his fiction. There are, however, certain constants which link the book with Gide's previous writings: the nature of happiness (*le bonheur*) and the conditions for its existence; the function of true and false values in society (*les subtils*; *les contrefaits*); the education of youth; the role of family life; the symbolic value of bastardy; and the individual's need for freedom. These are familiar Gidean themes, but in *Les Faux-Monnayeurs* the Author and the characters express attitudes towards them which differ in important respects from those which we have noticed before. To all this is now added friendship.[7]

As the title of the novel suggests, Gide's major concern is with 'reality' and 'appearance'. Are things only as true as they seem to be? or is it possible to distinguish between 'real' and 'false' appearances? Édouard states this a little differently: 'The conflict between the real world and the representation of it which we make. The way in which the world of appearances imposes itself on us, and the way in which we try to impose on the external world our own personal interpretation. This is the drama of our lives' (p. 1096). But, one may add, this is peculiarly a novelist's perception and a novelist's problem. It is primarily of aesthetic importance. May we go further and see this dichotomy in evidence in the novelist's moral world? I believe we can, for as it is true that the values in this fictional world are symbolised by the use of true and counterfeit coinage, so the Devil plays an important role in the delineation of character and events. On inspection characters are less complex than they at first seemed: their relationships are an intricate web skilfully woven by the novelist, but they can often be defined according to whether they belong to the world of the damned or the (relatively speaking) saved. The use of a variety of narrative viewpoints does not suceed in entirely camouflaging this fact: what it achieves is a richer presentation without recourse to an omniscient narrator. This in turn is intended to fulfil Gide's aesthetic aim of echoing the untidiness and partial comprehensibility of 'real' life. However, the Demon and his counterparts circulate freely through these pages, and this ensures a quite noticeable bipolar construction in the text. To be sure, this type of opposition is not new in Gide's writings, for we can see such balancings from the eagle and hero in *Le Prométhée*, through the illness and health of Michel and Marceline, to the *subtils* and *crustacées* in *Les Caves*. What is new is that a major opposition is described between two figures who are respectively a force for good and a force for evil: Édouard and Passavant. They are both novelists; they are both homosexual; they both pursue Olivier. We will consider them in detail in a moment. Among the evil forces we should include Vincent and most of the hypocritical residents of the Pension Vedel. Among the angels are the pure Bronja, and Bernard with his quest for self-knowledge. There are characters who balance each other in another way: Bernard and Olivier each have a relationship with Édouard – but on different terms. The difference is largely dictated by their personalities. Sarah and Armand are set antithetically against the purity of their sister Rachel. Many of the other characters are associated with one or other of these two 'worlds'. An antithesis may also be perceived between the existence of the free individual (Édouard) and the stifling family groups (Molinier). There are bad and good heterosexuals (although it must be admitted that the latter are quite rare). One thing it is difficult to say with certainty is whether there is a debate between the homosexual and heterosexual lifestyle. If the outcome is to be measured by the happiness achieved, then Édouard's eventual relationship with Olivier is more successful than many an ordinary marriage.

The novel opens with a portrayal of Bernard. He is an adolescent who, on learning that he is illegitimate, answers the call to enjoy his newfound freedom and leaves his family. He becomes more mature as the story unfolds, and a rather immature wish to be free is gradually replaced by a serious concern for honest self-sufficiency which life (and his angel) teach him. Depicted as naive and handsome (p. 1034) on his first visit to 'save' Laura and help her, he is at this point in the story a melodramatic adolescent who suddenly realises that what he is engaged in is not a game. Later, in Switzerland, he is still described as an 'adolescent plein de grâce', and Laura is like his 'elder sister' (p. 1077). It is in his mouth that a truth which Gide held dear is placed: he is mature enough to have learned that there is 'nothing that is good for everybody' (p. 1089). This perception allows him the best use of his abilities and the best occupation for his virtues. It is indecision which he has learned to call a cardinal sin. Laura perceives that repentence is not in Bernard's nature (p. 1093). He learns in due course how to understand the strength of his character, but even now he admires the qualities of probity and steadfastness of purpose. The Author having allowed (or pretended to allow) Bernard to display his personality, passes provisional judgement on him at the end of Part 2:

Bernard is too young to conduct an intrigue. He boasts that he will protect Boris: the most he can do is keep an eye on him. . . . I wrote . . . 'I ought to have mistrusted Bernard's extravagant act at the beginning of the story . . . it is as if he has exhausted his reserves of anarchy. . . . His habit of revolt and opposition makes him revolt against revolt itself. . . . There was perhaps no more to be expected of him. Perhaps he gave up self-control too soon.' But these remarks no longer seem to me to be correct. I think he must still be given credit. There is generosity in him. I feel he has manliness and strength. He is capable of feeling indignation. He listens to himself too much – but then, he speaks well. I mistrust feelings which are too quickly expressed. He is a very good pupil, but new feelings do not flow easily in channels that have been learned. . . . He has read and remembered too much, and he has learned much more from books than from life. (pp. 1109–10)

Bernard, we may add, experiences heterosexual desires.

When Bernard escapes from home, he seeks out his closest friend Olivier. At this early point in the story Gide describes the nature of several schoolboy relationships, but we will deal with these later. Olivier appears very much the opposite of Bernard: how serious he looks among these schoolboys, although he is younger than the majority of them (p. 935). 'His face and his expression which are still somewhat childlike reveal a quick mind. He blushes easily. He is kind-hearted [tendre]. Despite being friendly towards everybody, a secret aloofness or modesty keeps his comrades at a distance. He is hurt by this.' Olivier, remarks the Author at the end of Part 2, is gentle and sensitive but open to flattery (p. 1110): 'Everything goes to his head.' He is perhaps a little vain. 'Sensuality, resentment [dépit] and vanity – what an advantage that gives anyone over him.' He is, however, 'still young – and there is still hope for him'. It is vanity which is evident in Olivier's invitation to Édouard to attend the Argonautes' dinner (p. 1152), but the moment has passed for him to be proud of Passavant's friendship when Bernard disapproves. And it is characteristic of Olivier to take more pleasure in praising his friends than in being praised himself (p. 1170). The real change in his life will come with the recognition of Édouard's love – but then, curiously perhaps, he will fade from the novel.

The relationship between Bernard and Olivier seems perhaps at first sight to have definite homosexual overtones. After discovering the letter, Bernard feels the need to go and see 'son cher Olivier' (p. 934). 'Olivier, my friend,' he muses, 'the time has come to put your willingness to help [*complaisance*] to the test, and for you to show me what you're worth. The fine thing about our friendship is that up till now neither of us has used the other.' Let us note here the tone and the role of friendship between young people of the same age. Bernard has appealed to the nobility of their disinterested relationship and now speaks of value (*valeur*) and service. But Olivier shows a weaker attitude. He blushes as he sees Bernard approaching: 'Bernard was his closest friend, and so Olivier took great care not to seek him out' (p. 935). In a few words Gide sketches the essential characteristics of the two boys, suggesting as he does so that Olivier's timidity complements Bernard's adventurousness. Without Bernard, Olivier would suffer even more from his sense of isolation.

Bernard spends a night with his friend, and the following morning is ready to follow his own destiny (pp. 975–6). Immediately he wakes up, he gets dressed, and, without waiting to say goodbye, he leaves the house. He seems indifferent to feelings of affection, but he does subsequently reproach himself with this: 'Olivier might have been upset – and wasn't he the person Bernard preferred in all the world?' (p. 994). Their bed was narrow – but Bernard did not take advantage of this. On the contrary, he showed himself attentive to Olivier's well-being, and disengaged himself with great care. Gide may probably be convicted of self-indulgence here in singling out the suggestive facts that Bernard was only wearing a 'short shirt', and that Olivier's arm was resting 'indiscreetly and heavily' across him. The possibility that his friend was not really asleep scarcely crossed Bernard's thoughts. However, Gide does let us suspect that Olivier's attitude is somewhat different from this. On the previous evening Bernard had refused his help ('That would be cheating,' p. 959), but the attentive reader is quick to notice Olivier's emotion as he waits for his friend to arrive, when he clasps him in his arms (p. 951), and when he admires his boldness (p. 952). 'He broke into sobs; he held Bernard in a strong embrace. "Promise that you never . . ." Bernard hugged him and then pushed him away, laughing' (p. 952: the allusion is to Bernard and loose women, and is clearly inspired by a similar incident recorded in *Si le grain ne meurt*, pp. 485–6). Olivier invites him into his bed and then tells him how disgusting he found his own visit to a prostitute: Bernard is congratulatory, solicitous, and gently chiding – for he does not share his friend's distaste.

When Bernard reads a passage in Édouard's diary (p. 1023), he becomes disturbed because he can now understand more clearly the true nature of friendship. 'His own friendship for Olivier,' Bernard reflects, 'was undoubtedly very deep . . . his feelings clung to this in a way that was almost excessive. But Olivier and he did not understand friendship in quite the same manner.' As he continues to read, it seems to Bernard that Olivier is capable of hiding a part of the truth from him. Up to that time he had not suspected anything. On another occasion, the resentment (*dépit*) he feels (it is not jealousy) when he sees Olivier take Uncle Édouard's arm (p. 1023) has its structural counterpart in the jealousy which Olivier feels on reading a letter from Bernard. And this letter itself (p. 1069), which recounts Bernard's life as Édouard's private secretary, finds a further counterpart in Olivier's letter describing his adventures with Passavant (Part 2, vi). When Bernard writes his letter and speaks of his enthusiasm during the trip to Switzerland (p. 1069), the Author comments on the characters of the two adolescents:

> Bernard was too spontaneous, too natural and too pure – he did not know Olivier well enough to realise what a flood of hideous feelings his letter would arouse. It was like a high tide of resentment, despair and anger. He felt he was simultaneously displaced in the hearts of both Bernard and Édouard. . . . He was especially tortured by one phrase . . . 'In the same bedroom' he went on repeating to himself – and the abominable serpent of jealousy unwound itself and writhed within his heart. 'They sleep in the same room' . . . . His mind was filled with impure visions which he did not even try to dispel.

It is significant that Olivier is fully conscious of the physical elements implied by such a friendship. His reaction shows the presence of the Demon at work. It is as a direct consequence of receiving this letter that Olivier visits Passavant (p. 1070).

As a result of his experiences with Count Passavant, Olivier's need to see his friend once more on the day of the *baccalauréat* is not confined to the expression of pure friendship: 'Who will say that he is not keener to show himself to Bernard than to see him again?' (p. 1141). Bernard, however, greets him with an exclamation, 'Oh, how nice he looks,' and, with natural joy, is pleased that Olivier has come. Olivier has learned to be sophisticated (unnatural) – and therefore immediately suspects irony and duplicity. He has become false, as the ensuing conversation demonstrates. Bernard is honest. The next time we shall see them is at the banquet (pp. 1167 ff.). After this, Bernard will give his place as Édouard's secretary to Olivier, who has been redeemed. This is what the Author said at the end of Part 2 that he himself would have preferred to happen.

Let us turn for a moment to the relationship between Bernard and Édouard. In order to understand it, we must enquire into motives. For Bernard, it is firstly a desire for adventure which spurs him to take the suitcase and become involved in Édouard's and Laura's lives. Secondly,

Olivier's words put into his mind the thought of a possible meeting with Édouard (p. 957). We must remember, though, that Édouard is not an object of desire for him, but an object of interest. When Édouard confronts Bernard, the bond is forged between the novelist and the apprentice-thief by the latter's daring and Édouard's sense of amusement when faced with the unexpected. This is of course reminiscent of Lafcadio. It is for this reason that Bernard will become Édouard's secretary, and Olivier will in consequence go over to Passavant (p. 1040). If these are the links between Édouard and Bernard, it is perhaps also true to say that in Gide's view the most important thing they have in common is a concern with the understanding and representation of reality. Bernard and Édouard are both novelists (Part 2, iv). Bernard is in love with Laura, and then with Sarah, whom he soon rejects; he prefers Rachel's lesson of self-sacrifice (Part 3, xiii). He seeks a healthy virtue, nourished by honesty (pp. 1093–4). What then can Uncle Édouard teach him through his loving friendship? The answer is little: at the end of the Swiss episode, Édouard admits that they have both made a false start (p. 1106). Bernard is of the same opinion. We therefore see that here we have two individuals of different ages but of a somewhat similar disposition. Bernard is too independent for Édouard to be able to help him in the fullest sense. In other words, Édouard is not in love with him, for he does not see in Bernard a sensitive being who stands in need of his affection.

This last remark, of course, could not be applied to Olivier, whose character is very soft. Olivier is capable of offering himself to Passavant as well as to his friend Bernard, and he is most particularly drawn towards his uncle, whom he will meet secretly at the station (p. 957). He is in fact unable to tell Bernard exactly why Édouard is 'all right' (*très bien*): it is simply a feeling which he has. Moreover, he senses that Édouard 'is interested in lots of things which don't interest my parents'; previously Olivier had felt uncomfortable at his uncle's way of looking at him (p. 957) – but he does not understand why this should be so. Édouard had given him some advice, honestly and straight-forwardly (p. 958). The particular example concerns Olivier's bad poetry, but Édouard's manner is significant. The enthusiasm they had both felt at the prospect of a meeting soon evaporates. They are each thrown off balance by the great emotion they feel, and consequently fall victim to a *fiasco* of the type described by Stendhal. This in fact bears witness to the depth of their love. The older man recognises what is happening, but the youth is bewildered and clumsy. Each misunderstands the other's feelings (another Stendhal element).

As we have seen, it is through Bernard's eyes that we first learn the truth about Édouard's feelings for Olivier (p. 1004). Édouard had written in his notebook: 'As soon as I saw Olivier on that first day, as soon as he sat down at the table, as soon as I first looked – or rather as soon as *he* first did so, I felt his glance take possession of me, and I realised I was no longer master of my own life.' It is this glance which makes Olivier blush, despite his not understanding what it means (p. 957). Before discussing the development of this relationship, however, let us take stock of the character of the two men, Édouard and Passavant, who represent the two moral extremes to which Olivier is attracted. Both are homosexuals, but neither is particularly criticised on that score.

Édouard, during his recent trip to England, has been 'dreadfully deprived of pleasure' (p. 985), and so he determines that the first thing he will do on reaching Paris is to visit 'a place of ill-fame'. There is an echo of this in the *Journal des Faux-Monnayeurs* (p. 56: a note by Gide, dated August 1921); and we may thereby attach a personal moral resonance to it – 'The most dubious indulgences of the flesh have left my soul more peaceful than the slightest incorrectness of my mind; and it is when I leave a society reception that I find my conscience most ill at ease – not when I come out of the b . . . [brothel, or, more probably, 'bain turc'].' Ten years previously, Édouard had had a love affair with Laura (p. 986: a diary entry written in uncomfortably similar terms to Gide's eulogy of his own wife), and had worshipped her. She was sixteen at the time, he was twenty-eight. 'But,' he comments, 'whosoever truly loves renounces sincerity.' We shall return to this proposition later. In Switzerland, Laura gives Bernard a brief description of Édouard's character: 'He is never the same for long. He does not fix himself to anything, but nothing is more attractive than his flight. . . . His being endlessly forms and re-forms itself. You think you've got hold of him – he's Proteus, he's changed. He takes on the shape of the person he's in love with. And in order to understand him you have to love him' (p. 1094). This is another facet of his character, not perhaps perceived by Olivier. The Author judges Édouard more harshly and, he maintains, more 'realistically' (Part 2, pp. 1108–10). Thus Édouard is probably 'imprudent' to entrust Boris to the Azaïses: he does so because he cannot resist experimenting. Although he is curious, he is not ill-natured. He is just careless. If he is destroying the purity of a boy (Boris), he must be listening to the Devil, for he would be sharp enough to reject these plans if anyone else were to suggest them. His behaviour towards Laura is irritating for the Author – and at times revolting. His motives are at fault, and the Author perceives that Édouard is not honest with himself. That is surely important if Édouard is to look after the happiness of his beloved. Another aspect of his difficulty in being honest is revealed later when he realises he is making public the fact that Olivier has decided to live at his house – 'something he would have preferred to keep quiet' (p. 1191). 'I must carefully respect everything in Édouard which prevents him from writing his book. He understands many things, but through everything and everybody he is forever pursuing himself.'[8] What Édouard will find is that love, once achieved, ennobles his soul, but does not prevent life from continuing.

Count Passavant is a corrupt (and corrupting) character. Édouard's first reported reaction to him is illuminating: 'Everything that Passavant does makes [Édouard] feel ill. . . . He pretends to be enlightening public opinion – that means he skilfully bends it.' Édouard has met him occasionally and found him charming, but he considers Passavant a charlatan (*faiseur*) (p. 983). Passavant's recent book, *La Barre fixe*, is judged by Édouard with the same severity that Gide used in his own *Journal* on 18 May 1923 about Cocteau's *Le Grand Écart* (to which, with its play on gymnastic terms, the title punningly alludes). Brée (p. 362) is right to say that, as far as Gide's novel is concerned, it does not matter if we identify Passavant with Cocteau – or not. Later, Édouard has reason to be more harsh when judging the bad influence the Count exerts over Olivier (p. 1108). There is, of course, another scene when Édouard goes to Passavant's house in order to retrieve Olivier's belongings – Édouard is triumphant, and is therefore able to forget his erstwhile hatred of his rival (p. 1191). But (according to the Author) he does not know the Count's personality. Passavant cannot stand being the loser; he is angry, but hides his discomfiture under a show of nonchalance (p. 1192); he can always control his emotions, and he can always persuade himself that the 'adventure' he has had with Olivier has outlived its interest. The Author is suggesting that Passavant *uses* people; he also adds a somewhat personal note of attack to his description: 'Passavant could not resist the pleasure of pouring some drops of his poisonous treachery over Édouard's happiness' (p. 1193). But did Lady Griffith, one of the members of Passavant's circle, see this side of him, too?

When Passavant is first introduced, the Author sneers: 'Robert de Passavant, who now calls himself Vincent's friend, is the friend of many people' (p. 960). He likes the company of younger men: he is thirty years old (p. 967). Lady Griffith and Passavant callously manipulate Vincent. She has a view about Passavant's abilities as a novelist: he is vain, hypocritical, ambitious, versatile, egotistical – and will never write well because he does not know how to listen. She makes innuendoes about Passavant's motives for frequenting young men (pp. 968, and elsewhere), and, particularly, about an arrangement to meet Olivier (p. 982). In this way a morally very unattractive character-portrait emerges. Another facet of Passavant's superficiality is revealed in his disingenuous remarks to Olivier about his own book (p. 1044). Honesty in things connected with novel-writing is one of the touchstones of Les Faux-Monnayeurs. In Passavant's speech there is little truth and less good faith.

Passavant's double standards are equally in evidence when it comes to brothers, and how one should treat them. He has one of his own, Gontran, a somewhat seraphic fifteen-year-old (p. 965), who develops a form of asceticism protected by hard study (pp. 1136–7). Passavant ignores him. However, this does not prevent the Count from being sententious when he advises Vincent to take greater interest in Olivier, his brother. Of course we know the reason: Passavant wants an introduction. This is advice dictated by self-interest (p. 1055). These are the very attitudes which suggest to Édouard the title of his novel, Les Faux-Monnayeurs – 'he was thinking of certain colleagues, and of Passavant in particular' (p. 1085). Let us allow the Author to have the final word on the Count's character:

> Passavant . . . let's not speak of him. Nothing causes more damage, nothing is more highly praised than men of his sort – except perhaps women like Lady Griffith. . . . Such people are cut from cloth which has no substance. . . . America exports them in quantity, but is not the only country to produce them. Wealth, intelligence, beauty – they seem to possess everything, except a soul. . . . They feel the weight of no past; no sanctions affect them. They are without laws, masters, or scruples. They are free and spontaneous, and they are the despair of a novelist for he can only obtain reactions from them which are devoid of value. (p. 1110)

If the reader looks on this as a totally negative catalogue he risks being confused, for Gide's own preferences went often enough towards the lawless, be it in the realm of morals or the aesthetics of the novel (p. 1080).

For every personality as yet unformed, a wholesome education is of the greatest importance. An adolescent is in such a position, and, if he hesitates, it is because, like Hercules, he has come to the crossroads which will lead to either vice or virtue.[9] This is the case with Olivier. Which mentor will he choose? The society in which he finds himself offers values which are worthless. Families, as we shall see, are hidebound or hypocritical institutions.

The relationship between Édouard and Olivier has, as we have remarked, its peripeteia.[10] It starts with their equal inability to express their love (pp. 991, 994). The reader is allowed to perceive both sides, and also to peruse Édouard's more particular confession in his diary (pp. 1004–5). 'How greatly I appreciate that in Olivier there is so much curiosity, so much dissatisfaction with the past' (p. 1007). 'In him everything attracts me, and still remains a mystery' (p. 1009). If Olivier had been an orphan, Édouard would have liked to make him his secretary, but he thinks that Olivier does not care for him (p. 1031).

Édouard therefore pretends to be indifferent, and does not force his attentions on the youth. Instead, he only watches him when Olivier is not looking (p. 1031). On other occasions in this section of the novel, and notably when Olivier has started to frequent Passavant, Édouard finds communication with him difficult and discouraging (p. 1057). Édouard, it will be remembered, is invited by Olivier to the Banquet of the Argonautes:[11] he uses the distant, polite form of address (*vous*) to Olivier, who is dismayed at this departure from past familiarity. Soon, however, Olivier becomes very drunk and, after a brawl, he is led away to safety by Uncle Édouard. Both now use 'tu', thus declaring their affection for each other (pp. 1170, 1175). The realisation of their love overwhelms Olivier. His happiness is so great that he can conceive no higher bliss. This is why he attempts to commit suicide, albeit on the rather literary model of Dostoievsky's Dmitri Karamazov. Édouard is understanding, comforting and sane. Lovingly, he looks after the young invalid. All this is perhaps a trifle sentimental, but none the less devoid of melodramatic description and exaggeration. Édouard finally watches over his friend as he sleeps (p. 1181). When Olivier recovers, the boy has a confession to make: he is ashamed of his recent behaviour. But this shame is not connected with his love: he feels he has disgraced himself by becoming drunk (and consequently devoid of self-control), and by acting so badly during the recent months. In a word, he asks forgiveness for having 'prepared the ground so inadequately for meeting Édouard' (p. 1190). In reply, Édouard cradles him forgivingly in his arms. They remain together until the morning, and Olivier is too happy to sleep. Édouard's sense of being in love is profound: 'It is by him and through him that I feel and live.'[12]

Earlier, the Author maintained that Olivier was upset by the fact that Bernard had become Édouard's secretary instead of him. 'It is Olivier whom Édouard loves.'[13] 'With what care would he not have brought him to maturity? With what loving respect would he not have guided his steps, supported him and raised him to his own level? Passavant will damage him, I'm sure. Nothing is more pernicious for him than being unscrupulously smothered in this way.'

The case of Olivier and Passavant is far less noble. We remember that Olivier, piqued at learning that Édouard seems to prefer Bernard, seeks out the company of the Count (p. 1070). He had, of course, been there already, timidly falling in with the arrangements made by his brother Vincent (pp. 1040 ff.). That was the moment when Passavant, with a great deal of social charm and flattery, proposed the editorship of his periodical to Olivier. The boy's timidity and social awkwardness are frequently mentioned here – but Passavant does not manage to overwhelm him completely. In talking of Olivier's mother, for example, and of possible ways of manipulating her, he oversteps the mark.

'Olivier did not answer. He loved his mother tenderly, and was displeased by the bantering tone Robert had adopted when he spoke of her' (p. 1042). Passavant again reveals his flashy superficiality when he proposes some catchphrases for his new literary movement. Slowly, and despite his natural good judgement, Olivier is won over by the Count's social ease, his cigarettes and his glasses of port. The dedication Passavant writes in the copy of his book he gives to Olivier states clearly the quality, but not the precise nature, of his friendship for the boy: 'For Olivier Molinier, his presumptive friend' ('ami présomptif': a play on words – Passavant is presumptuously assuming that he will next succeed to Olivier's friendship). This is written as an addition above a quotation taken from the book itself. Except for the name, the thought crosses one's mind that this is perhaps a standard form for several young dedicatees: 'Please, Orlando, come a little forward. I am still not sure that I dare to understand you perfectly.' There is an appositeness in this: the sexual ambiguities of Ganymede (Rosalind) and Orlando in As You Like It, where Olivier is Orlando's wicked elder brother, cannot have been far from the Gide's mind.

It is to Vincent that Passavant confides that he finds Olivier quite charming (p. 1055), and this remark is a prelude to another request for a manipulation of Olivier's mother to ensure that the Count can take Olivier away with him. He will succeed this time. He is, however, sensitive to the possibly ironic, mocking smile of Vincent. It is from Olivier's letter to Bernard that we learn what has happened since Olivier has joined Passavant, and how his character has developed (pp. 1102–5). Olivier now seems arrogant and pompous. He writes superficially of things (like his examination) which are important to him. He is sententious. He approves of titillating and scabrous material, and he has in fact compromised his honour by agreeing to write such an article, on a subject dictated to him by Passavant, despite the pain it will cause his mother. 'But that's life [tant pis]. As Passavant says: "The younger you are, the less affected you are by scandal."' The sum of this false brilliance is the measure of his education by Passavant. Olivier also admires the Count's elegance,[14] his rudeness and vulgarity. 'He knows how to use ideas, pictures, people and things splendidly. I mean he makes capital out of everything. He says that the great art in life is not so much to enjoy things as to learn how to profit by them' (p. 1105). In endorsing this view, Olivier is seen to be approving a disgraceful opportunism.

These attitudes reappear when Olivier meets Bernard during the examinations (p. 1142), and they are subjected to Bernard's criticisms. Olivier has learned his false definition of truth from the Count. He seems able only to reproduce secondhand ideas which are all the more tarnished and worthless for having come from Passavant. Bernard recognises that they express the opposite of what he knows his friend really believes. They are not authentic. The morality of Passavant, and therefore of Olivier, is dubious. Things will improve, as we have seen, and Olivier will be brought back to the truth. This process begins as the warmth of Bernard's genuine friendship melts the cold frost of Olivier's distress (p. 1148).

Passavant is quick to disclaim the idea that there was any real affection between Olivier and himself. When things become awkward he denies and rejects Olivier, on the pretext of avoiding 'unfounded' scandal. He does not even have the courage of his vices. There are hints that his relationship with 'Olive' (his nickname for the boy) is affected and effeminate (p. 1103). The corruption of Olivier is summarised in a paragraph of notes, printed in the *Journal des Faux-Monnayeurs* (p. 76). As before, a character's attitude to literary values reveals the worth of his general moral position: 'Olivier was very concerned not to speak of things he knew hardly anything about; but as this principle was not shared by any of the people who frequented Robert and who did not restrain themselves from making instant judgements on books they hadn't read, Olivier preferred to believe that he was much more ignorant than they were, whereas he was only more conscientious.' Marchand (pp. 122–8) writes cogently about these two ideals of education: Passavant is self-regarding – a pederast who perverts his pupil materially, morally and intellectually; Édouard believes in encouraging the better part of self and in ensuring the emancipation of his pupil.

The question of integrity is central to this discussion. Although Édouard is often inconsistent and unpredictable (at least in the opinion of Laura and other witnesses), he is not lacking in integrity. Conscientiousness is another facet of this virtue. Bernard develops into a person who will possess mature integrity; Passavant has none at all. Whereas Édouard's friendships are firm, Passavant is unreliable in his ('Affairs of the heart' bore him, he says cynically, p. 969). Furthermore, the other friendships Passavant cultivates are an indication of his character. These are not necessarily homosexual, although his reasons for wishing to meet 'le petit Léon' are presumably of this order (p. 1199). The Count corrupts Vincent as he exploits his weaknesses and tempts him into a life of gambling and reckless love with Lady Griffith. Strouvilhou, the anarchist, is also one of his associates: this satanic figure circulates the false coins, and is another corrupter of youth (pp. 1146–7). In an extended conversation with Passavant (pp. 1195–1200), Strouvilhou describes his amoral and destructive philosophy: the Count has clearly misjudged the seriousness of his attitudes, and so he prudently decides to take some precautions against any violence which might be offered to his person or his possessions. '*Ex uno disce omnes*,'[15] says Passavant himself (p. 1200). Strouvilhou epitomises hatred and a racial theory which Gide now (1925) found unacceptable. That the race could be improved by 'selection' might seem to connect with orthodox biological theory – but, as Bernard states a few pages later, it is the happiness of others which will thereby suffer (p. 1213). Alfred Jarry, the eccentric writer widely rumoured to be homosexual, makes a grotesque appearance at Passavant's literary banquet (p. 1173). Cob-Lafleur is another 'original' ('like an old wrinkled baby, made up with cosmetics', p. 1227). Despite his own unwholesomeness, he is disgusted by Passavant and repudiates him.

Armand, however, is the important link between the worlds of Passavant, Édouard and the puritan boarding house of the Azaïs family. He is another renegade, and another satanic character.[16] He is attracted to Passavant because 'I like what makes me sick' (p. 1228). In other words, he is as much in love with evil and self-destruction as his sister Rachel is in love with purity. In this he represents, perhaps, the counterpart of Édouard's attraction to amoral vagabonds if we call to mind the original concept of Lafcadio.[17]

Olivier, whose judgements are generally benevolent, thinks that Armand is 'the most intelligent and interesting member of the family' (p. 1010). Armand's behaviour is in fact outrageous. He is ironic about his parents' puritanism and the wish of other people to romanticise love. Édouard thought (and still wishes to think) that Armand has a sensitive soul: he is surprised to find him so vulgar. (He attributes this to the drink.) It is not possible, however, to share Édouard's innocent optimism: in a later conversation between Olivier and Armand, Armand's character is fully revealed (pp. 1158–63). He is not a liar: his type of immorality is the opposite of hypocrisy. He is deeply ironic, negative and salacious. His life and his room are sordid. His conversation, ideas and literary projects are determinedly vulgar. His poem is called 'Le Vase nocturne' (The Chamberpot), whose philosophy he describes to Olivier. Olivier is upset.[18] Armand's quest is to discover the limits of experience and to determine the point at which something innocent will become something dangerous. This is the nature of his anguish, and he seeks to diminish it by acts of iconoclasm against the sexual purity which is enjoined upon him by precept and example. His self-hatred is again in evidence in another conversation with Olivier when Armand has taken over the literary editorship of Passavant's magazine. This stupid iconoclasm extends to placing moustaches on the *Mona Lisa*. He now admits, however, to being a creature internally divided against himself. He is immoral, but says that he respects his sister Rachel 'because she is virtuous'. 'She is, I think, the only person I love in the whole world' (p. 1231). Is he sincere? 'The sincerest thing about me is my horror and hatred of everything which is called Virtue' (p. 1232). This evil is the result of his puritan education. His revolt is intimately connected with the doctrine of purity and sexual repression.

Bernard also wants to meet Armand and his younger sister Sarah. Bernard's judgement is that Armand is a 'counterfeit' (p. 1140). He does not measure up to Bernard's ideal of probity. Sarah, however, is introduced to Bernard by Armand, and her intrigue with Bernard is encouraged by him (pp. 1165, 1176). The sense of sin, as exemplified in this sexual relationship, is very marked. Sarah is more amenable than Rachel, and she is shown not only welcoming joy when it appears (p. 1216), but also receiving it from Bernard only through the media- tion of her brother. It thus almost appears as if this sexual joy is experienced by proxy: from an incidental remark that Sarah's room is contiguous with Armand's (p. 1159), we pass to the disturbing double value of Armand's 'pleasure . . . temporary indulgence. . . . It was so that he could subsequently condemn them more severely' (p. 1165), the more so because of his complaisant act of locking them in together (p. 1177).[19] Additionally, Sarah has flirted with Olivier (pp. 1019, 1165), and Armand suggests that there is a touch of lesbianism in her behaviour towards the English girl who shares her room (p. 1014).[20]

Would we be justified in seeing other heterosexual desires and rela- tionships in the novel as antithetical to Virtue? After all, Bernard rejects Sarah's easygoing attitudes when he finds the path of true self- knowledge (p. 1212). As a consequence of the struggle with the Angel: 'Rachel's voice was so sad that Bernard immediately understood what she wanted to say to him. He did not answer, but stood with bowed head – and then out of pity for Rachel he suddenly began to hate Sarah and contemplate with horror the pleasure he had enjoyed with her.' The relationship between Lady Griffith and Vincent is a corrupt one. On the other hand, Laura has idealised her emotions for Édouard, and Bernard has formed an idealised attachment for Laura (pp. 1077–8, 1090–1, 1150–1). Laura, as we know, has had an affair with Vincent from the consequences of which she is rescued as the novel proceeds, but her husband Félix cannot be called an inspiring companion (this, for what it is worth, is Édouard's opinion) – a fact which may explain if not excuse her behaviour.[21]

These relationships, too, are in their various ways unsatisfactory. People in 'settled' marital situations are shown at no less disadvantage. The Vedel household is corrupt with hypocrisy; La Pérouse is victimised and misunderstood by his wife; the Profitendieus have with effort secured a bourgeois compromise; the Moliniers do not understand each other. In fact the father and mother in this last-mentioned family each have an important part to play in commenting on the behaviour of the young people in the novel.

Molinier *père* appears as a complacent, sententious and rather vulgar bourgeois in his conversation with Édouard (pp. 1117–19). It is ironic that he is pleased that his children have formed friendships with 'the best people': Vincent with his 'prince' (but not the corrupting affair with Lady Griffith of which Molinier knows nothing), Olivier with Passavant, and Georges with Adamanti (a boy who also features in the schoolboy criminal activities). On the other hand, he condemns Olivier's friendship with Bernard, whom he wrongly suspects of being implicated in the sexual scandals at the 'tea shop' (his euphemism for the brothel). His reason for believing this rests on his knowledge that Bernard is illegitimate, 'for one can expect nothing good from a child born in these sorry circumstances'. 'The fruit of disorder and insub-ordination will always carry the seeds of anarchy.' All this is, of course, false; and the reader can see that it is so. (These are arguments of the sort used by the prosecution in the Rémy case, but one must wonder how Gide squared his hostile portrayal of Molinier's logic with the sympathetic representation of Lafcadio and other bastards.) The real problem in the marriage itself is that Molinier has been unfaithful and now thinks that his guilty secret has been uncovered by Pauline, his wife. 'When we are young,' he sighs, 'we want our wives to be chaste without knowing what their virtue will cost us' (p. 1115).

But Pauline has in fact known about his misconduct for some time. She is intelligent and understanding. She even covers up for him. The present crisis has come about only because Georges has stolen his father's love letters: this she quickly realises. She also exercises a more watchful control than her husband's over their offspring. The signifi-cance of some events nevertheless escapes her. Édouard notes that he did not suspect how much resignation she hid under an appearance of being happy (p. 1153). Although her husband placed the responsibility for allowing Olivier to go off with Passavant on her, she says that had the decision been hers alone she would not have let him go (p. 1154). One of her principles is to make a virtue out of necessity. Another is to devote herself to the well-being of her children. It is in this last capacity that she pronounces judgement on Édouard's affectionate rela-tionship with Olivier (pp. 1186, 1189):

> I cannot pretend to you that I disapprove when I don't. I have learned from life. I have understood how delicately balanced is a boy's purity, even when it seemed most firmly secured. Morever, I do not think that the most chaste adolescents later make the best husbands. . . . But I am afraid for them lest they encounter debauchery and form demeaning connections. Olivier is easily led. You will make it your fondest duty to restrain him. I believe that you can do him good. . . . Olivier will make you a better man. What may one not obtain from oneself by love? (p. 1187).

Here Pauline is the spokeswoman for *Corydon*, taking up part of the teaching of Dialogue IV: 'I doubt whether a young man can arrive at marriage more damaged than certain heterosexuals today.'[22] It is important to set against these words Édouard's doubts, for we are reminded that in this novel (in so far as it is a reflection of life) very little is absolutely and necessarily true: 'Pauline accepted my friendship with Olivier much less easily than she professed to do – less easily than she accepted all the rest. I'm willing to believe that she doesn't quite condemn my feelings, and even that from a certain point of view she's quite satisfied with them, as she told me. But perhaps without admitting it to herself, she feels some jealousy. . . .' But Pauline is, after all, 'an exceptional woman'.

Among examples of adolescent and childish sexuality, the novel touches on masturbation. Here again there is a use of the images of vice and virtue. Boris is a timid boy who has a secret. His companion and counterpart in the novel is Bronja, an angel of purity, with whom he talks and plays in Saas-Fee. Bronja is in fact the daughter of the psychiatrist Sophroniska: her mother hopes that her friendship with Boris will help to cure him and relieve him of his sense of guilt. Édouard records a typical conversation between the two children in the course of which Boris reveals the odd contradictoriness of his personality (pp. 1070–2). Furthermore, Bronja falls into a fit after telling her mother that on their walk Boris had wanted to undress and roll naked in the snow (p. 1087). 'I think Sophroniska's educational methods excellent in theory,' Édouard drily notes, 'but perhaps she is mistaken about the children's stamina.' When Bronja dies, Boris is left more isolated in the world (p. 1235). Sophroniska's method is to break down Boris's defences and violate his privacy. Thus she learns that when he was nine he made friends at school with a boy 'one or two years his senior who initiated him into clandestine practices' which they called 'magic' (p. 1097). The manner in which this is connected with the main theme of the novel is clear: 'They honestly believed they had discovered a secret which consoled them for real absence by an illusory present.'[23] Additionally, their overexcited imaginations were enhanced by sexual pleasure (*volupté*). These are not Sophroniska's terms, but Édouard's. Nevertheless, the picture of the deleterious effects of masturbation is not far removed from the orthodox views expressed by medical opinion of the early twentieth century which we have already noted. In fact Gide has not properly resolved a chronological difficulty here, for although the novel seems to be set in the 1890s there are several features – most notably the hints at Freudian psycho-analytical techniques – which belong more properly to the inter-war period. This should not, however, affect our conclusions.[24]

Boris 'cures' himself of his baleful habit, only to succumb again in a moment of stress when he is cruelly tormented by the boys in the Pension Vedel. They leave his talismanical message ('Gas, Telephone,

100,000 Roubles') anonymously on his desk; he resists the call of his dark past until the evening when 'with nothing to help him fight against it, as soon as he reached his room, he yielded' (p. 1237). This also is expressed in terms of Heaven and Hell: 'but he took pleasure in falling from grace and in this very act of perdition he found his ecstasy [volupté]' (p. 1237). It is here that Sophroniska's methods are recognisably those of a modern psychiatrist, and we know that she is modelled on Eugénie Sokolnicka.[25] Her main aim is to encourage the patient to come to terms with his past. Boris must be brought to a stage where he can admit everything – and then, she claims, the cure may be effected (p. 1074). There is no more immodesty in this undertaking, she adds, than in the simplest medical examination. Édouard concludes that if Sophroniska is lacking anything it is aesthetic (and perhaps imaginative) sensitivity. She would never make a good novelist (p. 1076). It is even possible to doubt whether for her the words 'evil' and 'purity' have a precise moral sense, for she admits that what confuses her most about Boris is her belief that he is 'extremely pure'. 'Because,' she continues, 'in that case I don't know where to look for the root of his illness. Nine times out of ten you find at the base of such a disturbed personality a great shameful secret' (p. 1075). Has Sophroniska not heard of the 'divided self'? and is she totally satisfied when she discovers the 'shameful' secret of Boris' private vice? Édouard does not believe that Sophroniska's method is successful. Of course, he himself is also wrong when he thinks the boy will be cured by going to the Pension Vedel, but his objections to the psychoanalytical method still bear some weight. He recognises that the symptoms of Boris' disorder have disappeared, but he thinks that 'his illness has simply sought refuge in a deeper part of the self, as if to escape the inquisitive glance of the doctor; and that now it is his soul itself which is affected' (p. 1100). Sophroniska nevertheless accepts that Boris' newly acquired mysticism (certainly 'less effortful and less destructive of his organism') is as effective a way of deflecting his energies from real life as was his onanism. In Édouard's words, 'without believing in the dogma of the Church she still believes in the efficacy of faith'.

Bernard is one of the people towards whom Boris looks for protection[26] (p. 1235). The boy is now aged thirteen, and his tender soul needs someone to whom he can offer his nobility and purity (p. 1236). The other boys, however, are not like Bernard. When Boris first arrives at the Pension Vedel he feels out of place, and, compared with them, 'seems like a little girl' (p. 1136). This weakness is exploited by them. At first they are hostile and spurn him because of his softness and girlish appearance (p. 1236). Then they realise that they can use him for their homicide plot, and with hypocritical guile surround him with expressions of false friendship. In his lonely innocence he believes them

(p. 1239). The important thing to note here is that the 'talisman' is simply used as a means of manipulating the boy. No connection is made in the schoolboys' minds between vice (for they do not know what the 'magic' is) and its punishment. There is, in fact, no sexual dimension to this motif outside the private struggle of Boris with his demon.

In the course of the novel, a number of persons express their opinions on friendship, love and marriage. The boundaries of these subjects are not well defined, and one must expect the words to describe a varied range of affections. Nor is it to be supposed that a coherent view will emerge from a variety of opinions expressed by individual characters. Thus Brée (p. 288) may talk of the 'picaresque nature' of love in the novel, but one must beware of taking this as the final word on the matter. Gide noted in the *Journal des Faux-Monnayeurs* (p. 77) that as the novel progressed Bernard's character was to become more precise *as a function of his love affairs*: 'Each love, each adoration brings with it devotion and loyalty. Perhaps he regrets this at first, but he quickly understands that it is only by limiting himself that his field of action will become precise.'[27] The essence of Bernard's early concept of his friendship for Olivier is duty and worth. Its noble quality is its altruism (p. 934). The finest quality of Édouard's affection for Olivier is its devotion and its protective tenderness. In this case one also has to add its ecstasy. But, as we have observed, Édouard has had other relationships – notably with Laura – which have given him the opportunity to express his friendship. It is to this that Laura alludes when she calls his sympathetic help the finest thing she has known. She would, herself, have used another word – love (p. 985) – but she is forced to recognise that in his affairs (at least as far as she knows) Édouard is always a free agent (p. 1094). When Bernard has fallen in love with her, it is she who does not reciprocate, calling her affection 'friendship'. The effects on Bernard are important, for through this experience his character is developing and changing. 'I love Laura more and more,' he tells Olivier. 'I think it is the nature of love never to remain the same; it must always grow larger, under threat of becoming smaller if it doesn't. And that's what distinguishes it from friendship' (pp. 1150–1). Olivier says ('sadly') that friendship can also grow weak. He then questions Bernard about desire. Does he have any desire for Laura? No: the 'strange thing' is that since he has known her he has experienced no desire. He is totally and uniquely in love with her beauty, but he feels only veneration for her: 'All thoughts of the flesh would be impious.' She is the ideal he wishes to serve. His conception of love for her is therefore simultaneously chivalric and puritanical. Love is not desire. If we compare it with the description Édouard offers of his feelings towards Laura, we perceive some similarities; the differences lie in Bernard's positive attitudes, his wish to serve and his naive enthusiasm. Each worships his beloved with chaste adoration. The effect on Bernard of being in love with Laura has been to make him less egotistical, and he has even suspended that inner dialogue with himself in which he used often to indulge (p. 1150). As an adolescent, he feels these aspirations confusedly and without being able to understand their meaning. The affair with Sarah has had quite the contrary effect on him, and this is why he renounced her. It is also fairly clear to the reader that Sarah's belief in sexual equality is not to be taken as a reasonable ideal, for her analysis of her sister's piety is unsympathetic and her attitudes are immodest (p. 1165).

Édouard's reaction to Laura is different. How could he make her understand that since there is no central core to his existence he is not made for marriage (p. 987)? We notice that the reason he gives is in no way connected with his affection for Olivier. (Indeed, his love for the boy might even appear to give the lie to Laura's analysis of his inability to love, but the Author speaks of Édouard's 'amorous respect' for Olivier (p. 1110).) The key is surely this: in both cases a degree of purity is attained in so far as the love transcends merely sensual appetites. This is true of homosexual and heterosexual attachments alike. The relationships are, however, seen differently by each partner. Édouard comments on the devotion of women: 'The man she loves is most frequently only a peg on which she can hang her love' (p. 1006). He is speaking of the 'sincere ease' with which Laura is able to substitute one beloved for another. As Gide has pointed out by selecting a quotation from Chamfort at the head of Part 1, viii: 'One must choose to love women, or to know them. There is no middle course.' This could not be said of the guileless and more innocent love of a boy.

If love 'crystallises' in the sense which Stendhal described,[28] then Édouard observes this and also admits he is more interested in the phenomenon of decrystallisation within a marriage first grounded on love. For Stendhal, crystallisation is the work of the imagination. The consequence is that disillusion will soon occur when the lovers' original ardour fails (pp. 988–9).[29] Such are the comments reserved by Édouard for his affair with Laura. This is what is demonstrated by the numerous marriages within the novel: the Azaïs–Vedel household has 'progressed' until it is now an empty hypocritical shell, the Molinier and Profitendieu families are caught in a web of disillusion. More especially, we are made privy to the sad deterioration of M. and Mme La Pérouse's domestic life: an intolerable irritation is occasioned by the slightest roughness of contour, and if two persons living together both have such roughnesses, then with 'reciprocal friction, married life becomes pure hell' (p. 1059). The novel also depicts other elements in these relationships: thus La Pérouse regrets the austerity of his youth (p. 1027), and Vincent, when setting out on his immoral path, does at least have misgivings about corrupting Laura (pp. 959–60). Unlike Olivier, none of these hetero-sexuals would have contemplated suicide at the height of bliss – although it was Bernard who first raised the idea, giving it a different application, and, perhaps, a rhetorical shade of unreality (pp. 1152, 1180).

In the *Journal des Faux-Monnayeurs* (p. 22) there is a definition of 'amitié' which refers to the earlier, rather amoral, plan for the novel: 'I note the definition Méral gave me of friendship: "A friend," he said, "is someone with whom you would be glad to do something wrong."' This could of course apply to the group of young boys among whom Georges features – but the final version of the novel embodied a purer ideal of friendship.

It might seem that both love and friendship are equally able to provoke jealousy, but the fact that we do not observe this to be the case in this novel requires some explanation. We have already remarked on the presentation of a case of jealousy in *Le Roi Candaule*. Olivier, as we have seen, is jealous of Bernard's relationship with Édouard, and in consequence he listens to the promptings of the Demon. Pierre-Quint recalls a conversation on the subject of jealousy: 'Gide: Jealousy is a feeling which is only experienced violently in a strong heterosexual love: it is the hatred of the male for the male. In other love [sc. homosexual, pederastic] jealousy is of a quite different nature, and I think it is much more rare.' Gide goes on to talk of a relationship which may well have determined some of the elements described in Édouard's affection for Olivier: 'My hatred for C[octeau], my greatest suffering, my need to react violently, my life completely turned upside-down – I was Pygmalion finding his statue damaged and his creation destroyed. My work, my careful education, my way of thinking were completely debauched by someone. . . . It wasn't jealousy, it was some-thing else.'[30]

In the novel, Édouard comments: 'One understands that Othello is jealous: he is obsessed by the picture of the pleasure his wife has had with another man. But a Douviers [the weak husband of Laura] must needs imagine that he *should* become jealous in order to be so' (p. 1201). This again presupposes the truly 'manly' character of jealousy.

As Gide wrote in the *Journal des Faux-Monnayeurs*: 'Everywhere life presents us with the beginnings of dramas, but it is rare for them to develop and show themselves in the way a novelist links them up' (p. 104). This is one of the reasons which explain the labyrinthine nature of the relationships in the novel. An extra dimension has been added to the structural complexity by Gide's frequent development of con-trasting and complementary groups of characters and events. This is why the question of pederasty in *Les Faux-Monnayeurs* cannot be con-sidered in isolation. It is, however, obvious that two forms of ideal relationship are shown to exist. The first is the chaste adoration of a worthy member of the opposite sex (this, in the context, is naturally seen from the man's point of view). The second is a tender friendship for a younger boy who needs to be raised to the level of virtue by loving care. Such an *amitié particulière* provides a sentimental and educational role for the older man. Is Édouard really innocent and chaste? Gide is discreet, for he only tells us that Édouard and Olivier 'stayed together until the next morning' (p. 1190). Nobody doubts that he is good. His honesty and openness are in total contrast with Passavant's (and other people's) double-dealing and falseness. In the novel, Édouard is not married. He has no 'drame', unlike Michel in *L'Immoraliste*. He is the writer who tries to see the actions of the characters clearly and note the moral consequences that flow from them. Because he is a homosexual he provides a touchstone when love is discussed. By studying his attitudes the reader may arrive at a satisfactory moral conclusion. But Édouard is human, all too human perhaps, and can be tempted. He is puritanical, but not unduly so. He is not the paragon of virtue whose curiosity is only stimulated by one boy. He loves Olivier. There was Bernard. There is Georges (whom he sees stealing a book). And to take us forward into the future there is young Caloub . . .

CHAPTER TWENTY-FIVE

Thésée: A Homosexual Codicil

Thésée, which takes the form of a first-person historical novel, represents a return to a world of satirical mythology. Most of the book was written shortly before and during Gide's residence in wartime North Africa, and the first draft was completed on 21 May 1944. It was finally published in the USA and France in 1946.[1]

The legend of Theseus, the Athenian hero, fascinated Gide over many years. There are four main episodes in *Thésée*,[2] each with its particular importance. We begin with Thésée's childhood, then pass to the Cretan expedition which set out to kill the Minotaur. Next we witness the founding of the city of Athens, and finally we listen to Thésée's confrontation with Œdipe. The second of these episodes is subdivided into smaller sections: Thésée and Dédale, Thésée and Ariane, Thésée and Phèdre. The whole story is told by Thésée in his old age. Hippolyte, his dead son, is the dedicatee, but this is an obvious literary subterfuge which permits Gide to speak to a younger generation. Thus it is simultaneously a confessional and an educational work, and may even be seen as an allegorical account of the evolution of Gide's own moral position throughout his life.

This last interpretation is more obviously acceptable if we glance for a moment at the ideal the hero Thésée represents. Thésée deliberately creates his acts: he abandons Ariane and causes his father's death quite intentionally. Without this interpretation, Gide maintained, Thésée's story is turned into a children's fairytale: the hero's essential characteristics are self-awareness (*conscience*) and purpose (*résolution*). What tempts Thésée is a challenge (*le défi*).[3]

These elements are used in particular to describe Thésée's early life. He is lawless. He is a vagabond with a restless soul (*âme insoumise*).[4] 'Scarcely has he arrived at Minos' court than he suborns Ariane. Nothing shows that he loves her. But he lets her love him for as long as he can use this love.'[5] He is egotistically heterosexual, and there is no hint that he has other inclinations.[6] Is Thésée then an anti-feminist?

Whatever Gide's changing interpretation of the symbol of Theseus, Ariadne always stands in the same relationship to the hero. He abandons her to Bacchus so that he can continue his journey:[7] 'Creusa,[8] Eurydice, Ariadne – a woman is always hanging back, always afraid, always anxious about letting go and seeing the bond snap which ties her to her past. She it is who restrains Theseus and makes Orpheus turn round.'[9] The sophisticated symbol which Gide has constructed is his own. How much it owes to his attitude to women in general, and to Madeleine Gide in particular, is difficult to assess. Gide's Ariane is to Thésée as love is to the hero: she fetters the power which otherwise would (and should) leap forward. The epigraph from Nietzsche which Gide used in *Divers* 'Who knows who Ariadne is, apart from me', refers to an incident in the philosopher's life retold in Halévy's *La Vie de Nietzsche* (pp. 362, 380), a work which was, as it so happens, used in *Corydon*, too.[10]

In Gide's book several members of Minos' family have experience of sexual irregularities: Minos' mother, Europa, was carried off by a bull, and Pasiphaë, his wife, made love to another one. Léda, whom Pasiphaë calls her 'cousin' (there is no ancient authority for this relationship), had intercourse with a swan. Phèdre's incestuous passion adds another example. The cases of Léda and Pasiphaë are, however, of long-standing interest for Gide, as we can see from the joke at the end of *Le Prométhée mal enchaîné*: Pasiphaë there, in giving birth to a calf, points the moral that intentions are not a guarantee of precise results. The tone in both *Prométhée* and *Thésée* is flippant. In the latter, Gide alleges, through the mouthpiece of Pasiphaë, that this experience is a good training for Minos as future Judge of the Dead. On a more serious level, these examples could symbolise Freudian imperatives, or the relative character of moral judgements, or the unruliness of human nature when contrasted with the orderliness of custom and law. They raise the question of an individual's responsibility for his (or her) acts. The particular example is Phèdre, who fell in love with her stepson: her family and her environment are blamed, but she cannot escape the responsibility of having falsely accused Hippolyte. Thus, we are to understand, there are some people who are wholly responsible for their acts, and there are others who cannot escape their inner destiny. In neither case is there any justification for avoiding the truth.[11]

One other allegorical figure needs to be discussed. The Minotaur, the result of Pasiphaë's bestiality, is a symbol of lust. He is a monster with whom Thésée has to grapple before he can live a satisfactory life. He is beautiful and few men resist his charms. He is the personification of Thésée's particular desires, tempting Thésée until the hero sees that the animal is a brute. Symbolically, the labyrinth the monster inhabits is in everyone, taking on different shapes and pandering to the desires of the individual. This thought had already been in part expressed by Étéocle and Polynice in *Œdipe*. Thus Icare's labyrinth is metaphysical, and Dédale's is architectonic. The Minotaur is a Gidean avatar of the Sphinx: a hero must conquer his monster. It is, however, a little difficult to see what precise hidden desires in Thésée the Minotaur is intended to represent. If they are homosexual appetites, then they are not the hero's, for he says, 'Although I'm Greek, I'm not at all attracted to members of my own sex, no matter how young and pretty they are' (p. 1441). Moreover, Thésée has already told us that women are both his 'strongest and his weakest suit' (p. 1417). He contrasts himself with his 'cousin' Hercules, and does not envy him his boyfriend Hylas in the least (p. 1441). He has already been rather derogatory about Hercules' subservient relationship to Omphale, the Queen of Lydia, who was responsible for making Hercules effeminate (pp. 1418–19). If specifically homosexual, these desires must be the author's own, for if they mean anything in Thésée's case they can only be more general, standing for curiosity and appetites which lead him away from his central heroic purpose.

This is not to say that Thésée is presented as devoid of aesthetic sensibility where young men are concerned. The Minotaur is 'young' and 'handsome' (p. 1439); Icare is 'beautiful' (p. 1434). A special case has to be made out with regard to Thésée's companion Pirithoüs, who does not enter Plutarch's narrative until after the point where Gide's story breaks off. In other words, Gide deliberately changes the chronology of his source and integrates Pirithoüs among the companions sailing to Crete. Their relationship therefore begins now in their early youth, but there is nothing overtly homosexual between them. They are the same age, and they are both devoted to the pursuit of women.[12] Had Gide read Xenophon's *Symposium*[13] he would have discovered that it was commonly believed in ancient Athens that the two men were lovers (like Achilles and Patroclus). Socrates' view, as expounded by Xenophon, was that this opinion came about not because they slept together, but because they were firm friends.[14]

In Gide's story, Pirithoüs comes up with a pederastic scheme for leaving Crete, and this earns Thésée's exclamation about his own heterosexual *bona fides* (pp. 1440–1). As we have seen,[15] the details in *Thésée* concerning Cretan pederastic customs are taken directly from Strabo. The problem is that Thésée is in love with Phèdre but has also given Ariane reason to believe that her advances are not unwelcome. He can only escape with Phèdre if he smuggles her on board ship disguised as Minos' son Glaucus. No one will mind this in the least, Pirithoüs says, and Minos will feel highly honoured if his 'son' is being abducted. This is entertaining burlesque, and Gide is no doubt intending to startle the modern reader with such a casual description of 'shocking' habits. Something in Plutarch may nevertheless have put the idea into his mind, for there[16] a story is told of how two of the 'maidens' who originally sailed to Crete in the tribute from Athens were in fact youths, chosen for their girl-like appearance and dressed to deceive the guards.

Is it not strange that Gide was strongly drawn towards so hetero-sexual a hero? He did not idealise him on account of his beauty, nor was it because of his sexuality. Thésée represented the hero *par excellence*, the man of power who gains strength through self-knowledge and conflict with himself. Secondly, the story of his life is an allegory of Gide's teachings. His tale is in these terms the author's last will and testament. The adolescent may indulge in a careless life of the senses. This was young Thésée before he received his training. When he obtains his weapons, he has achieved inward strength through educa-tion. His virtues are 'common sense, willpower, courage and ambition'. The next stage is to preach the supremacy of man. Thésée is, at the beginning, the adolescent who shakes off the constricting past in order to forge a new life for himself. He lives firstly by his senses and, as in the *Nourritures terrestres*, his desire becomes dominated by the taste for transcendence (*dépassement*) and greatness (*grandeur*). The necessary condition for heroism is the abandonment of secure comfort, and Thésée sets out like the *Enfant prodigue*. His heroic ardour and thirst for action lead him on, but when he has learned to 'Go Beyond' (*passer outre*) his aim is no longer to satisfy successive desires. Thus it is that at the close of his life he turns his energy towards humanitarian actions and founds his City. The problem of religious belief is now seen more simply: there are different ways of attaining peace and nobility. Œdipe, in this book, is a mystic; Thésée is a materialist. One must learn only how to avoid the ambiguities and traps of mysticism which, for a person who is not suited to them and who needs to *act* (as did Gide), are pernicious. Gide's last word on the subject of pederasty assigns an ironically trivial role to this form of love. The author's final concern, then, is not with sin, temptation and moral depravity, but with indi-vidual authenticity.

Epilogue

Woe unto the world because of offences! for it must needs be that offences come; but woe to that man by whom the offence cometh!

Matthew 18:7

In the Bible, the Greek word *skandala* (snares, or stumbling-blocks) is rendered in English as 'offences', but in French as 'le scandale'. Granted that Gide assented to the proposition that 'Il faut que le scandale arrive,' he could not have been other than profoundly conscious of the burden which is placed upon the man who is the cause of such offences. In referring to this passage he doubtless also had in mind the preceding verse: 'But whoso shall offend one of these little ones which believe in me, it were better for him that a millstone were hanged about his neck, and that he were drowned in the depth of the sea.' The earliest Gidean example of this thought is placed in the mouth of the fictional hero of *Les Cahiers d'André Walter*: 'People would say "He is mad"; they would laugh, and shrug, and turn their backs on me. I am not lacking in courage, but I would perhaps sadden some weak persons who are dear to me, and I would be an object of scandal for several. And yet these things are in my very soul.'[1] Later, a similar formula appears in the 1922 preface to *Corydon* – 'saddening a soul, dearest to me among all others'. The publication of *Corydon* was a 'scandalous' (though carefully contrived) act. Whatever the roles of prejudiced interlocutor and honest pederast within those dialogues may suggest, Gide was fully conscious of two imperatives. The first was a need to bear witness. The second was a rejection of the role of victim. These required courage.

In his polemical and imaginative writings there are, as we have seen, inconsistencies in his attitudes towards the expression of homosexual desires. There is also a degree of firmness in his advocacy of purity. He took pride in being a creature of contradictions. Non-resolution was, he maintained, the key to his character. A latter-day Proteus, the sea god

401

who changed his shape in order to elude a questioner's grasp, he believed that so long as his teachings carried within themselves a healing antidote, their conclusion would be reached not in the author's words but in the reader's mind. He claimed that there were two simultaneous but opposite tendencies present within himself, and that these manifested themselves in many ways. A structure of systems of opposition is fundamental to the presentation of his thought. We may thus observe that, for him, the importance of the dialogue form lay in the fact that propositions are often set within more than one frame of reference. Even equations of a relatively simple kind, such as the identification of health with moral firmness, and illness with moral weakness (as in certain pages of *L'Immoraliste*), enable the author to present opposing points of view and to avoid definite conclusions.

But what becomes of truth? and where does Gide stand on the question of pederasty? The most profound dichotomies which run through his pages are the struggles of pagan and Christian values, and the conflict between Nature and Culture. Pagan desires are encapsulated in his awareness of sensuality, freedom and naturalness; the Christian ethic is founded on a consciousness of Evil, and a need for ascetic self-control. The world of the Greeks, Gide considered, was centred upon the experience of being uniquely human; he came to believe that the teaching of St Paul was too oppressive. If there was ever to be a resolution between these two opposing moral viewpoints, it would have to be found, Gide seems to say, in the characters of Ménalque, Édouard and others like them, who base their wisdom on self-knowledge carefully and judiciously acquired. 'Know thyself', the device over Apollo's temple at Delphi, is a necessary preliminary to the next exhortation: 'Be thyself'. But the Biblical injunction to remember that the seed must first perish before it may bring forth fruit (John 12:24) recalls the need for sacrifice.

For our particular subject of enquiry we have noticed the importance of defining Gide not simply as a homosexual, but more precisely as a lover of teenage boys. Bearing this in mind will help to clarify the various roles which they play in his books and explain the nature of the moral dilemmas expounded in his writings. What he says, however, must be read against the background of contemporary medico-legal theories and the novels with homosexual themes which were published at the time. With few exceptions, the scientific community saw homosexuality as an illness, although writers differed on whether the condition was acquired (perversion) or inborn (inversion). The sociologists were little better informed, though Corydon managed to turn Ward's gynaecocentric theories to good advantage. Gide called upon the world of natural history specifically because it was the terrain where, since Darwin, such matters had to be debated.

Gide's question is first: Is this conduct natural? Then he asks whether it is desirable. He thus reopens the centuries-old discussion between the imperatives of Nature and Custom, and explains the particular needs and the special responsibilities of the pederast. But his answers are complex: although we have seen that he described Corydon as a healthy individual, we must also bear in mind his earlier definition of the ideal hero and man of power in which he insisted on the importance of the illness, defect, suffering or *difference* which sets a man apart and makes him unusual or unique.

Corydon's argument must also be contrasted with those used by Rémy de Gourmont and his followers. Gide rejected Gourmont's permissiveness, and argued firmly for a morality which was higher than the mere freedom to act according to one's animal nature. One might have expected him to take as his model the Greek attitude towards homosexuality. To a certain extent, of course, he did – and in this respect he resembles a number of homosexual apologists who in addition, like him, called on antecedents from the Renaissance and elsewhere. Where he differs from many of them is in incorporating this material into an argument which also borrows ideas from scientists and sociologists. He is above all interested in the multiplicity of human attitudes. To observe these he paid the price of abandoning any sort of coherent investigation. Except in *Corydon*, however, it is noticeable that Gide used remarkably little of the documentary evidence which he had collected. In his fiction a refashioning of elements from his own personal experience predominates.

Despite Gide's constant awareness of Satan, we have perceived a change of focus over the years in the imaginative works. In his early writings, the literary stereotype of the sexually indeterminate soul, combined in *Les Cahiers d'André Walter* and *Le Voyage d'Urien* with a tortured rejection of sensuality, gives way to portrayals of individual men like Saül and Michel who are beset by temptations. A further aspect is represented by the cavalier irony and mock-heroic amorality of *Les Caves du Vatican*, while after the First World War and the growth of Gide's love for Marc Allégret a fourth demonstrates a radical move towards a more humanitarian depiction of pederasty. There is an attempt in *Geneviève* to deal with lesbianism and the emancipation of women. A final word, in *Thésée*, suggests by its off-handedness that pederasty is simply in the natural order of things.

For Gide, however, the ideal of Woman is constant. Although she may symbolise a negative constraint, she is, generally speaking, a creature of purity – or, on occasion, of noble maternity. In an important sense the attraction she asserts is asexual and unconnected with desire. She is the model of 'pudeur' (modesty) and reserve. His other ideal is the love bestowed on boys. It is this that we see through the eyes of Corydon and Édouard, although the latter (perhaps because he is portrayed as a novelist) is more in touch with the moral untidiness of life. For both of them the main justification of pederasty is educational; the main excuse sentimental.

It is when we come to temptations that we enter a more exciting and more disturbing world. 'My function,' wrote Gide, speaking of *Les Faux-Monnayeurs*, 'is to disturb' ('Inquiéter, tel est mon rôle'). To be a pederast is to be outside the normal moral law. Hence Gide is profoundly conscious that much of what he feels is 'lawless'. This thought he also erected into an aesthetic principle. Such an idea will explain his rejection of the family unit as a suitable school for adolescents. It will explain his attraction towards outsiders, and his longing to escape in order to be one of their number. It will help us understand the force of his deployment of the symbolic *acte gratuit*, and the fascinated interest he showed in nonconformists at the Assize courts and elsewhere. Subsumed under the label 'Vagabond' this temptation is a vital force in his attitude towards life. Another temptation is sensuality. The degree to which an individual is thereby enriched is in direct proportion to his ability to control his desires. Desire itself, indeed, is given a philosophical expression in *Le Traité du Narcisse*, a poetical and religious one in *Les Nourritures terrestres* and a scientific one in *Corydon*. It is perhaps possible to maintain that all these contradictory forces reach an uneasy resolution in *Les Faux-Monnayeurs* with the relatively successful outcome of the love of Édouard and Olivier, but even here we must be mindful of the transient nature of pederastic relationships.

Awareness of evil is the specific contribution that a Protestant conscience brings to bear on the temptations of the flesh. A forbidden fruit is luscious, but full of corruption.

APPENDICES

APPENDICES

Pederasty and Art

Gide held one belief in common with many men of letters of the late nineteenth century, namely a firm conviction that Art and Morality were not separable. He often argued that beauty of body was to be equated with beauty of mind, and, in October 1903, while composing material for 'Le Renoncement au voyage' to be published in *Amyntas*, he reflected on the relationship between life and Art. Art was born, he considered, from the horror of death; Arabs did not have this fear, and so their art was inferior to that of the Greeks, who, in their 'denial of death', protested against it to the very edge of the tomb.[1] Art – and particularly Greek art – is, for Gide, the celebration of life, and thus of its pleasures. Its appeal is not only to the cerebral part of the beholder, but also to his flesh. Ghéon recounted to Gide with delight how, in a conversation in 1899 with the artist Pierre Laurens, an intimate friend of both men, he had been able to offer a definition of pederasty: 'All in all, true pederasty is a prolongation of artistic emotion. "To see and to touch," as Wilde said – and that entails no moral deformation.'[2] However, in *Si le grain ne meurt* (p. 386), Gide describes his childhood visits to the Musée du Luxembourg, where much to the horror of his nursemaid Marie he fell into ecstasies contemplating the nudes in the pictures – and more especially the statues. At this age, he takes pains to point out, these images were quite divorced in his mind from sexual pleasure. He particularly mentions Idrac's *Mercury*[3] (see Plate 2), but even here his 'profound amazement' remained idealised. The examples he cites from later in his life are mostly works from ancient Greece and the Italian Renaissance. At these periods, he believed, Art and Morality most closely coincided in an ideal of harmony.[4]

Among the books which Gide consulted on Greek art was M. Collignon's *Histoire de la sculpture grecque*. He recorded having first finished reading it in Italy in early 1898.[5] This authoritative and well-illustrated commentary on Greek sculpture in two large quarto volumes is further referred to in the *Journal* on 17 and 22 November 1905, at the time of writing *Corydon*. Gide recorded: 'From nine until midnight – lost in a religious contemplation of some photographs of Polyclitus.' The illustrations which so inspired him were probably the *Doryphorus* (a young warrior) (see Plate 3), and a *Hermes*. It is clear from an incidental reference in *Corydon* to 'the "molliter juvenis" [*sic*] of whom Pliny speaks' that Gide took his note from Collignon (the extra comment: 'more desirable and desired than desiring', *Corydon* p. 185, is Gide's own). Pliny was contrasting the statues of a youth cast in a languid pose with a boy cast in a manly one. Collignon commented: 'According to Pliny the *Diadumenus* is a young man in whom is still united the grace of early youth [*molliter iuvenis*] and the vigour of manhood; the Latin writer seems thus to be contrasting him with the *Doryphorus* who is a few years older. If we are tempted to find this distinction rather subtle, we only have to remind ourselves of that Platonic dialogue where the friend of Socrates appreciates in the manner of a true connoisseur the beauty of Alcibiades: "I must admit that the other day, as I was taking delight in looking at him, he seemed to me to be still very handsome, even though he is now a man." What changes a few more years can bring about in the form of youths, and what importance these slight differences assumed for the Greeks who were in the habit of measuring by eye the age and complexion of their athletes.'[6]

Gide recorded a citation from Pierre Paris' *La Sculpture antique* to take up not an aesthetic point but a moral one.[7] It fits in well with the idealised form of friendship Corydon describes: 'Harmodius and Aristogiton. The strength of each seems doubled by that of his friend, and separated from Aristogiton Harmodius would have appeared lessened, just as Aristogiton would have done if separated from Harmodius.' Paris is in fact discussing the sculptor's aesthetic achievement in creating a group of two individuals who nevertheless constitute a coherent and necessary whole. Three pages earlier, at the beginning of this section, Paris had touched on a distinction which Gide put to use: 'It could be foreseen that the Ionian genius, in Attica, would not let itself be outflanked by the Dorian genius – or rather that it would have taken the lead' (p.176). Harmodius was the younger of the two (there is a reproduction in the text). In *Corydon* itself (p. 158) Phidias, the Athenian sculptor of the mid-fifth century BC, and Lysippus, the celebrated fourth-century BC sculptor from Sicyon, are both praised briefly.

A few quotations will demonstrate Gide's sensual attraction to works of art, particularly when the subjects of the statues he praises coincide with his sexual preferences. For example, as early as *Les Cahiers d'André Walter*, we read: 'Whether it be loving, adoring or passionate I am obsessed with touch [*caresse*]: I want an enfolding, absorbing embrace –

Plate 1 *Portrait bust of Elagabalus.*
Capitoline Museum, Rome.

Plate 2 *Mercury Inventing his Wand.*
Idrac. Louvre, Paris.

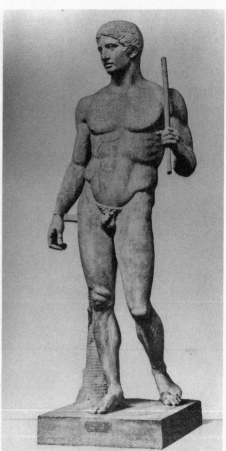

Plate 3 *Doryphorus*. Polyclitus. From an illustration in Collignon, *Histoire de la sculpture grecque*.

Plate 4 *The Spinario*. Capitoline Museum, Rome.

Plate 5 *The Barberini Faun.* Glyptothek, Munich.

Plate 6 *David*. Donatello. Bargello, Florence.

Plate 7   *David*. Pollaiuolo. State Museum, Berlin.

Plate 8   *Pastoral Concert* (detail). Giorgione. Louvre, Paris.

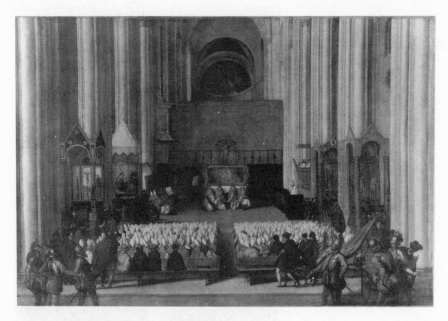

Plate 9   *The Council of Trent.* 'Titian'. Louvre, Paris.

Plate 9a   *The Council of Trent.*
Bystanders (detail).

Plate 9b   *The Council of Trent.*
Bystanders (detail).

Plate 10   *Love Disarmed.*
Bouguereau. Private collection.

Plate 11   *Breton Boy.* Gauguin.
Wallraf-Richartz Museum, Cologne.

or else self-forgetfulness, rendering ecstasy extreme. This is why I suffer so greatly when I behold a statue's beauty – because my deepest self does not melt into it but reacts against it. . . . This marble is so diaphanous that some flesh still seems to be there. Desire to possess it torments me, and I suffer intensely in my body and my soul at the feeling of the impossible; the *Spinario* [see Plate 4], the *Apollo Sauroctonus*, the damaged torso of the *Diana Reclining* – looking upon them does not quench my thirst: it awakens it.'[8] This is from the first part of the book, the 'Cahier blanc', and has its counterpart in the second, the 'Cahier noir', where caresses are rejected in favour of asceticism and chastity (p. 122).

Such a reaction to the statues was in fact the author's own, as can clearly be seen from a reference in the *Journal* (Rome, January 1896) to the *Spinario* and the *Diana Reclining*. Gide says that he prefers neither the *Niobid* in the Beaux-Arts nor the *Barberini Faun* in Munich, adorable as they both are, to the *Spinario*. Gide had earlier referred to the 'extraordinary beauty' of the *Faun* (see Plate 5) in a letter to his mother on 30 March 1892 (wrongly attributing it to Praxiteles). He also adored the 'extraordinary' *Mercury Fishing* in Naples (this statue is possibly the well-known *Seated Mercury*, but the identification is not certain): 'No softness in spite of so much grace; and the astonishing light slenderness of this small undeveloped [*impubère*] body does not cause one to regret that the forms are neither more childlike nor more full.'[9] In the *Journal* the remarks which he made on 26 and 30 December 1895 about Donatello's *David* (see Plate 6) and the description he gave are of the same order but more detailed: 'these delicious shapes, that line in the stomach immediately below the ribs where the breath holds it in . . . and that extraordinary fullness of the hips immediately above the sacrum . . .'. If this point needs to be reinforced, it is interesting to see Gide quite naturally talking of an attractive youth in terms of Greek statuary: 'Émile X . . . when naked he is admirably at ease; it is when he is dressed that he appears awkward. . . . His skin is entirely fair and covered in down; on the dimples in the sacrum – in exactly the place where the ancient sculptors position the faun's tufts of hair – this light down becomes more dark; and truly, yesterday afternoon, in his Praxitelean pose, with one shoulder leaning against the wall in the swimming baths, and standing quite naturally like the *Apollo Sauroctonus*, with his slightly snub-nosed mocking face, he looked just like a latter-day faun. He is fifteen.'[10] This was doubtless the nature of the attraction which Gide felt towards certain works by Michelangelo and Pollaiuolo. In Berlin in 1907 he saw the former's *St John the Baptist*,[11] and it was also in this museum that he noticed Pollaiuolo's *David* (see Plate 7). As early as 5 March 1889 he had remarked[12] that Leonardo da Vinci's picture of St John the Baptist in the Louvre 'had something of the hermaphrodite' (though, of course, this point is commonly made). He added: 'It is disturbing, and disappointing [*troublant et décevant*]', but how it fell short of his expectations he did not say. Something similar may be perceived behind a reference of his to Ingres' use of adolescents in a picture to charm the viewer (*Journal*, 22 April 1905), and a remark on seeing Verrocchio's *David* (*Journal*, 30 December 1895). A judgement on Holbein's portrait of Edward VI reveals the same sensibility: 'the openness [*disponibilité*] of the face, the uncertain expression of a child – a countenance which is still exquisite, but which will soon cease to be so' (*Journal*, February 1902, unpublished). There was a change when in 1938 he appealed again to the example of Michelangelo's sculptures (*Moses*, *The Slaves*, *The Medici Tomb*) and mentioned Greek statuary (the *Discobolus*, the *Diadumenus*, the *Apollo Sauroctonus*, the *Barberini Faun*). At this later date he wished to demonstrate that there was a 'reason' behind the conception of these works, and that one could in consequence perceive an 'artistic truth'.[13] Such an idea finds an echo in what he had to say elsewhere about the rational spirit of classical Greece.

Gide found a great deal of satisfaction when his courtship of a youth included pedagogical visits to admire the Greek statues in the Louvre. 'Pederastic love,' write the editors of his correspondence with Ghéon, 'must be *via* the contemplation of works of art', and they draw our attention to Corydon's hypothetical book 'which would be a history of the connection between uranism and the plastic arts (*Corydon*, p. 133)'. In fact, the section on the arts in *Corydon* is quite brief.

Corydon, as a typically 'sensitive' homosexual, professes 'a certain taste for works of art', and has a reproduction of the *Creation of Adam* from the Sistine Chapel above his desk. The interlocutor mentions later in the course of his argument that the 'reason' why Michelangelo painted nude youths on that ceiling was that the sight of them was anodyne, whereas women would have stimulated the viewers' desires. For Corydon, the promotion of Woman is the indicator of an art that has become less natural.[14] Thus he considers that the most naive and honest art derives from those times (Renaissance Florence and Venice, and Periclean Athens) when uranism and consequent respect for women held pride of place. The interlocutor's (quite reasonable) hope that Giorgione's *Pastoral Concert*[15] (see Plate 8), which shows two naked women and two young musicians who are fully dressed, will not be taken as an example of decadent art is met by Corydon's comment that here is the antithesis to ancient Greek art: the youths are clothed, and, probably, this culture did not generate much good sculpture.[16] When the interlocutor counters by asking whether this art demonstrates that pederasty was at a low ebb, Corydon answers that Titian's *Council of Trent*[17] (see Plate 9) (which Gide had seen in the Louvre) shows that it was not, for the courtiers who are depicted 'in the shadows in the foreground' are 'in positions which leave no room for doubt' (*Corydon*, p. 135). Moreover, asserts Corydon, the soldiers' 'indifference' clearly shows that such behaviour was accepted and caused no adverse reaction. But the facts do not support this interpretation: in the foreground, on the right, there is a group of soldiers, one of whom, having been provoked by a young man, is being restrained from drawing his sword by another soldier. Well out of the shadows, in the centre foreground, there are, however, two young men in their twenties, seen from behind, one with his left arm tightly around his companion's waist; the latter is pointing forward into the assembly with his left hand. In the left foreground, also seen from the rear, there is another young man whose companion, dressed in a long cloak, is standing close behind him and apparently leaning with his right arm on his shoulder. These two pairs of men are the ones to which Corydon refers, but the explanation of their behaviour is not necessarily sexual. Indeed, their gestures need be no more than indications of affectionate friendship, and they are, in any case, typical Mannerist poses. Together with some persons who are shown in a bored or non-committal attitude, the depiction of these secular figures serves as a frame for the serried ranks of bishops intent on the sacred proceedings of the Council. But Corydon interprets the men's behaviour as 'pederasty turning rather into sodomy', saying that the picture and 'contemporary Venetian chronicles' bear witness to his assertion.[18] The contrast which he wishes to make is between the good, spontaneous sexuality of youth, and the tired, vicious debauchery of more cynical mature men. It is surprising that Corydon's judgements are so superficial: Gide has made no real attempt to argue the case. Furthermore, the views expressed by both the interlocutor and Corydon are specious, and some of the latter's – it must be admitted – although self-revealing are grotesque.

In February to April 1891 Gide purchased a group of erotic heterosexual engravings by Félicien Rops which provide a surprising contrast to what has been said so far. The most noteworthy is *La Pudeur de Sodome*, where a statue of a middle-aged man, in Egyptian style, facing the viewer, is covered from the stomach downwards with a curtain drawn across by a woman seen from the rear. She is nude except for her fan, lace stockings, belt, armlets and necklace, and wears a small black mask on her buttocks. The mask is a device Rops used in other drawings to symbolise hypocrisy, and here its position clearly suggests the meaning of the title 'The Modesty of Sodom'.[19] Perhaps the reason for Gide's interest in Rops' work is to be found in their modish popularity. We might also speculate that they represent a young man's prurient fascination with 'forbidden' subjects, especially when a friend and adviser like Pierre Louÿs was close at hand. At any rate, they exemplify a type of art which Gide was soon to castigate as immoral when the distance between himself and Louÿs became greater.

Gide recognised the role played by sensuality in Art. This is the central point of his attack on Bérenger in 1906: 'Do not remove Pleasure from literature and the arts; I wish *talent* to ensure for Pleasure the most inviolate of sanctuaries – yes! the sanctuary of Pleasure!'[20]

Corydon: Introduction to Dialogue I (1911) *

Il fallut tout le désœuvrement d'un été désert à Paris, pour me décider à monter chez Corydon.

On rencontre Corydon dans la rue, au café, dans de rares salons; on ne va pas chez lui. Corydon a mauvaise réputation. Corydon est un garçon de grande valeur; je le connais depuis bientôt dix ans; j'avais pour lui, je l'avoue, certaine affection, tempérée par beaucoup d'estime; ses études en médecine furent des plus brillantes, et ses premiers travaux forcèrent l'admiration des gens de métier; Corydon est doux, spirituel, obligeant, généreux, bien né; parfois il me prend des regrets d'avoir dû rompre avec lui, mais qu'y faire? Corydon a de mauvaises mœurs. Sur ce point je ne peux ni ne veux rien entendre. J'ai l'esprit large, on le sait; on m'a vu serrer la main et parler à d'avérés filous; il en est d'amusants et qui ne font pas tache dans le monde; avec ceux-ci je peux encore m'entendre; avec les pédérastes, point; il n'y a plus auprès d'eux estime ou amitié qui tienne; à la première insinuation que le monde hasarda contre Corydon, je ne cherchai pas à le défendre: je rompis.

Je rompis très ouvertement, franchement. Vu l'ancienneté de nos relations et l'affection qu'on savait que je portais à Corydon, cette brusque rupture, dont le bruit, de salon en salon, se répandit, ne laissa pas que de me faire honneur. L'exemple vertueux que je donnais fut suivi, et devant Corydon beaucoup de portes se fermèrent; tant il est vrai que le geste courageux d'un seul suffit parfois pour rappeler la société au sentiment de la vertu.

Depuis ma rupture avec lui, je n'ai pas été sans rencontrer Corydon plusieurs fois; je lui tourne le dos résolument devant le monde; quand je sais que l'on ne peut nous voir, je l'aborde assez volontiers; Corydon est bon garçon; il interprète comme il veut mon attitude officielle et cela ne nous empêche pas de causer.

Pourtant, je vous l'ai dit, j'évitais de monter chez Corydon; on a vite fait de jaser; sur ce sujet un seul sourire me désoblige. La fermeté de mes

---

* In this and the following appendices obvious misprints have been corrected.

principes est connue; il fallait, dis-je, le désœuvrement de l'été pour me pousser à passer outre. Du reste tous mes amis étaient absents, une visite à Corydon ne tirait pas à conséquence; telle démarche, aventureuse et compromettante en hiver, se présente au mois d'août sous un aspect moins ténébreux.

Corydon, à la porte de qui je me risquai donc à frapper, vint m'ouvrir lui-même; il fut surpris de ma visite, mais ne consentit pas à le montrer. Corydon est subtil parleur; je cause moi-même volontiers; si je rapporte ici les propos que nous échangeâmes ce n'est certes pas que les siens m'aient convaincu; c'est au contraire pour mettre en garde contre tels pernicieux sophismes, que je pense avoir démasqués, les esprits moins solides que le mien et moins habiles à se défendre. Néanmoins la pratique de l'impartialité me force de rapporter intégralement ses paroles, je veux dire avec cette sorte d'éloquence passionnée qu'il sut y mettre par instants et qui, je l'avoue, m'a parfois presque démonté; mais elle ne saurait résister à la critique; et, si je n'ai pas toujours mené celle-ci aussi loin que j'aurais pu, c'est pour laisser à mon lecteur le plaisir de réfuter lui-même, plaisir des plus flatteurs que je sache.

Mon impartialité me force également à reconnaître que je n'eus point en pénétrant dans l'appartement de Corydon la fâcheuse impression que j'en espérais; il est vrai que Corydon ne la donne pas non plus par sa mise, qui reste correcte, avec même une certaine affectation de sévérité. Mes yeux cherchaient en vain, dans la pièce où il m'introduisit, ces marques d'efféminement que les spécialistes retrouvent à tout ce qui touche les invertis, et à quoi ils prétendent ne s'être jamais trompés. Pourtant on pouvait remarquer, au-dessus de son bureau américain, une grande photographie d'après Michel-Ange: celle de la formation de l'homme – où l'on voit, obéissant au doigt créateur, la créature Adam, nue, étendue sur le limon plastique, tourner vers Dieu son regard ébloui de reconnaissance. Corydon professe un certain goût pour l'œuvre d'art, derrière lequel il eût pu s'abriter si j'avais été critiquer le choix de ce sujet bizarre.

Sur sa table de travail, dans un cadre de marqueterie, l'image d'un vieillard à grande barbe blanche, que je reconnus aussitôt pour l'Américain Walt Whitman, à cause que son portrait est reproduit en tête d'un gros livre que mon ami Léon Bazalgette vient de publier sur son œuvre. C'est au sujet de cette photographie que la conversation s'engagea:

I

– Après lecture [*and so on*]

Corydon; Introduction to Dialogue II (Proof Copy, 1920)

Avertissement

Avant d'aller se faire tuer sur le chemin des Dames, mon ami D. m'a remis un singulier petit livre, que je me doutais un peu qu'il avait écrit; que je ne savais pas qu'il avait fait imprimer; qu'il n'avait fait imprimer qu'à 20 exemplaires lesquels il avait mis sous clef.

Il m'a chargé de rééditer ce volume. Et malgré son désir nettement exprimé j'ai longtemps hésité. Non point que je craignisse de nuire à sa mémoire – ne donnant point son nom je sais bien que ce faisant je ne nuis qu'à moi. Mais, de l'autre côté du tombeau, s'il allait ne plus penser de même? De son vivant, il tenait à ceci. Il me l'a dit de reste. Bien plus: les pensées que sous une forme parfois inutilement ironique il exprime lui paraissaient des plus importantes; il tenait pour nécessaire de les présenter. Mais je le savais d'autre part très soucieux du bien public et prêt à cacher sa pensée dès qu'il pensait qu'elle pût troubler l'ordre; c'est bien aussi pourquoi, plutôt que par prudence personnelle, il serra ce livre dans ses tiroirs et l'y étouffa si longtemps. Dans les derniers temps de sa vie néanmoins il se prit à regretter ce silence; il tenta de me persuader que sa théorie, pour subversive qu'elle fût en apparence, ne combattait après tout que le mensonge et que rien n'était plus malsain au contraire, pour l'individu et pour la société que le mensonge accrédité.

– Ma théorie, me disait-il, ne fait pas que *cela* soit. Cela *est*. Je tâche d'expliquer ce qui est. Et puisque l'on ne veut point, à l'ordinaire, admettre que *cela est*, j'examine, je tâche d'examiner, s'il est vraiment aussi déplorable qu'on le dit – que cela soit.

Je dois avouer qu'après avoir pris connaissance de ce petit livre, je ne laissai pas d'être assez sensible à la force de certains arguments. Je n'ai pas qualité pour juger du plus ou moins de valeur de ses dissertations zootechniques et ne sais trop ce qu'il sied d'en penser. De plus érudits que moi les jugeront plus tard et diront si peut-être elles ne doivent qu'à leur fausseté même leur apparence de nouveauté; car pour constatés que soient les faits qu'il rappelle, il ne me paraît point qu'on les ait encore jamais fait servir aux conclusions qu'il en prétend tirer. Il n'en reste pas moins, et quand il aurait trois fois raison, que le ton de ce petit livre m'irrite; et je juge qu'il irritera plus d'un. Je le lui dis tout aussitôt: – ce n'est pas un livre de bonne foi et vous n'y jouez pas franc jeu. Le lecteur se prêtera mal à ce jeu de dialogue où vous épousez la sottise, et laissez au fictif adversaire toujours les meilleurs arguments.

Il fallait, ou les mieux combattre, ou les endosser hardiment. En feignant de les mettre au compte d'autrui vous ne dupez personne et de plus vous passerez pour déloyal.

– Vous avez peut-être raison, me répondit-il. Aujourd'hui, si je devais récrire ce livre, sans doute le récrirais-je différemment. Pourtant je ne puis pas le récrire. Il est sorti de moi comme cela. Mais tenez: puisque avec lui je vous livre les pages qui devaient me servir à le compléter, je vous laisse libre de traiter celles-ci de la manière qui vous paraîtra la plus probante.

C'est ce travail que je présente à la suite de *Corydon*. Et puisqu'il ne s'agit point ici d'une œuvre d'art, il m'a paru plus honnête de rompre parfois le ton moqueur et de faire trêve à l'ironie, malgré le désaccord inévitable qui en résulte, par quoi le persiflage du début risque de paraître d'autant plus irritant.

L'an 189. un scandaleux procès remit sur le tapis une fois encore l'irritante question de l'uranisme [*and so on*]

Corydon: Introduction to Dialogue III (1911)

Le lendemain, quand je m'en vins chez Corydon, ce fut sans grand espoir de l'amener à composition, mais plutôt avec la curiosité de savoir jusqu'où l'entraînerait sa folie; si ses raisonnements m'avaient quelque peu ébranlé, la veille, je m'étais ressaisi durant la nuit; néanmoins, désireux de le laisser pousser sa pointe, je pris le parti de ne pas me servir des nouveaux arguments que m'avait fournis mon sommeil, contre sa vulnérable théorie; donc nous ne revînmes d'abord sur la conversation de la veille, que pour en préciser les quelques points qu'il estimait avoir acquis. La zoologie n'est pas mon fort; et j'étais heureux de le voir arriver à l'homme. Sur ce nouveau terrain il serait d'autant plus gêné que je me sentirais plus à l'aise; je le pressai donc de fournir quelques explications d'une phrase que je n'avais eu garde de laisser échapper: 'L'amour est une invention tout humaine.' Je réservais mon attaque pour des affirmations plus subversives et commençai tout doucement:

– Sauf le mot: *invention*, qui me chiffonne, j'avoue que votre aphorisme n'est pas pour me déplaire. J'ai toujours trouvé fort désobligeante toute assimilation de l'homme aux bêtes; contre de telles dépréciations de l'idéal protesteront toujours les natures délicates et poétiques . . .

Corydon m'interrompit en souriant:

– Je ne cultive point le séraphisme et laisse à la littérature l'agrément de planer au-dessus du réel. Oui, je vous ai parlé de l'amour comme d'une invention humaine . . . mais laissez-moi rejoindre ce point lentement; aussi bien, quittant la zoologie arrivons-nous aujourd'hui tout naturellement à l'amour.

Il m'avait invité à m'asseoir mais continuait à arpenter la pièce; durant quelques instants de silence, je le vis repousser de la main plusieurs phrases qui se présentaient à son esprit; visiblement il cherchait un biais par où entrer en matière. Brusquement s'arrêtant de marcher:

I

Nous avons pu considérer hier [*and so on*]

Corydon: Appendix (1911)

Péril, ou difficulté du coït – ou rareté des postulants. Y a-t-il témérité à rapporter à ces suppositions un petit fait que signale Fabre sans y attacher l'importance qu'il me semble mériter:

Fabre entre en possession d'une femelle de minime à bandes (bombyx du chêne). Deux jours après la sortie du cocon, l'émanation de la femelle attire quantité prodigieuse de mâles (une soixantaine en un jour, évalue le naturaliste).

Or ce papillon est rare dans la contrée; si rare que Fabre, qui habite le pays depuis vingt ans, n'a pu encore le rencontrer, et le gamin qui lui apporta le cocon, berceau de celui-ci, n'a pu lui en procurer un second malgré promesses de récompense; les mâles sont certainement venus de fort loin.

Or ce papillon est rare partout, car comment expliquer sinon que seraient accourus de si loin tant de mâles s'ils avaient pu trouver plus près d'eux une femelle,[1] eux que leur courte vie n'invite qu'une fois à l'amour?

Les expériences de Fabre sur l'insecte au prodigieux flair, qui l'avertit, des lieues à la ronde, de la présence de cette rarissime femelle, sont racontées de manière fort intéressante.

Sans l'extraordinaire acuité de ce flair avertisseur, la femelle courrait grand risque de demeurer infécondée.

Le flair semble, par contre, faire à peu près complètement défaut à un autre minime (bombyx du trèfle) aussi commun que l'autre est rare, (et

---

1 'Née dans la matinée, la femelle du grand paon de nuit a des visiteurs parfois le soir même, plus souvent le lendemain, après une quarantaine d'heures de préparatifs. Celle du minime diffère davantage les convocations; ses bans de mariage ne sont publiés qu'après deux ou trois jours d'attente.' VII, p. 373. Ne serait-ce pas aussi que les mâles de la minime, beaucoup plus rares, viennent de beaucoup plus loin?

Il est bien regrettable que Fabre ne nous renseigne en rien sur ce point très important: la femelle de ces paons de nuit et de ces minimes à bande continuerait-elle d'attirer les mâles même après fécondation?

sans doute précisément en raison de cela): 'Il est fréquent autour de ma demeure; jusque dans mon enclos, je trouve son cocon, si facile à confondre avec celui du bombyx du chêne. Je suis tout d'abord dupe de la ressemblance. De six cocons, d'où j'attendais la minime à bande, il m'éclôt sur la fin d'août six femelles de l'autre espèce. Eh bien, autour de ces six mères, nées chez moi, jamais un mâle n'apparaît, bien que les empanachés soient présents, à n'en pas douter, dans les environs.' VII, p. 374.

Les mâles sont abondants; tout proches; le coït est facile: le flair* tout aussitôt se relâche.

* le flair] l'instinct *manuscript correction*.

Concordance to the Editions and English Translations of *Corydon* (by page number)

1911	1920	1924	1930	Œuvres complètes IX	1947	1950 USA	1956 UK	1985 USA UK	
—	—	—	—	—	—	—	—	—	Preliminary leaves
						v	5	v	Contents
						vii			Publisher's note
							7		Publisher's note (new)
								vii	Translator's note
						xi	9		Preface to the first English edition
							11		Extract from the *Journal* 19.x.1942
		9	9	177	7	xv	13	xix	Preface dated 1922
	6	13	13	181	11	xix	15	xxiii	Preface to second edition
7	7	15	15	183	13	1	17	1	Dialogue I
13	11	17	17	187	17	6	20	4	I(i)
21	19	25	25	193	25	13	25	10	(ii)
31	29	35	35	201	35	22	31	17	(iii)
39	37	43	43	207	43	29	37	23	Dialogue II
43	39	44	44	210	47	33	40	26	II(i)
51	47	53	53	217	55	41	45	32	(ii)
59	55	61	61	223	63	48	49	37	(iii)
67	63	68	68	228	70	55	53	43	(iv)
75	71	76	76	234	77	62	57	48	(v)
83	79	85	85	241	86	69	61	54	(vi)
97	93	100	100	253	102	81	69	65	(vii)
105	103	111	111	261	113	89	75	73	Dialogue III
109	105	113	113	265	117	93	78	76	III(i)
115	111	118	118	269	122	98	81	80	(ii)
	121	128	128	276	131	106	86	86	(iii)
	127	133	133	280	136	111	89	90	(iv)
	139	145	145	289	148	121	95	98	(v)
	143	149	149	291	151	125	97	101	Dialogue IV
121									Appendix (Fabre)
			185	319	187	153	117	127	Appendix
			187	321	189	155	119	129	Letter to Porché
			198	328	199	163	124		Letter from Porché
			208	335	209	171			Crémieux and Kochnitzky
							129		Crémieux (only)
				342					Lettre d'un jeune homme
		185	219		219				Contents
						179			Comment by F. Beach
						191	131		Gide's footnotes separately printed

Notes

ABBREVIATIONS

BAAG	= *Bulletin de l'Association des Amis d'A. Gide*
JFM	= *Journal des Faux-Monnayeurs*
Journal, I	= *Journal 1889–1939*
Journal, II	= *Journal 1939–1949*
NRF	= *Nouvelle Revue Française*
Pléiade	= *Romans; Récits et Soties; Œuvres lyriques.*
'Subjectif'	= 'Le "Subjectif" d'A. Gide . . . (1889–1893)'
Correspondance	= The particular correspondence to which reference is made in the text (see Bibliography for full details).

PREFACE

1. First mentioned in Gide's *Journal*, 21 June 1910; the final stages of composition coincide with those of *Corydon* (*Journal*, 14 January 1918). First published in a private limited edition 1920–1; first public edition 1926.

2. See Appendix A.

3. Gide made regular contributions to the *Revue Blanche* round about 1900 (see 'La Revue Blanche' in *Feuillets d'automne*, pp. 135–8 – the article is dated 1 October 1946); he published frequently in *L'Ermitage* (founded in 1890 by Henri Mazel and edited from 1896 onwards by Édouard Ducoté), and his name featured prominently in the advertising copy for 1 January 1899 – another contributor was Gide's 'comrade' Henri Ghéon. Gide published in the *Mercure de France* in 1894, 1895, 1897, was on reasonably good terms with its director Alfred Vallette, but seldom attended the literary *salon* held by his wife Rachilde. Even so, he clearly read the regular 'Revue de la quinzaine' which took up a large space in each issue of the *Mercure* where Rachilde reviewed recent novels and other contributors discussed the latest books and ideas (topics which reappear in Gide's arguments: depopulation, the emancipation of women and the reform of the divorce laws, moral freedom and homosexuality). Gide's brief reminiscences are published in 'Le Mercure de France' in *Feuillets d'automne*, pp. 135–8 – article dated 1 October 1946. Many of Gide's books bear the imprint of the Mercure.

CHAPTER 1: THE CHRONOLOGY OF *CORYDON*

1. Delay, II p. 553 'January–March 1895'. Similarly, a continuity of interest is shown, for example, by the statement that 'we lack martyrs' (cf. *Corydon*, p. 22) and a reference to the need for scandal (Matthew 18:7) in Gide's confessional letter to Ruyters of 4 March 1905, referring to Gide's love for Maurice Schlumberger.

2. *Correspondance*, p. 26.

3. Gide–Ghéon Correspondance, p. 756.

4. Twenty-two copies were printed, according to Naville, *Bibliographie*; twelve according to Gide's 1920 preface; twenty according to the 1920 *Avertissement*.

5. *Journal*, 1911, p. 334.

6. 13 or 14 September 1911, p. 53.

7. 17 January 1914, p. 108.

8. Her translation of *Le Prométhée mal enchaîné* (*Prometheus Illbound*) was published by Chatto & Windus in 1919. Gide had corresponded with her (*Journal*, 21 September 1917), and recorded lunching with her on 22 May 1919.

9. *Bulletin du Bibliophile*, I 1971, pp. 1–9.

10. *Colpach*, p. 99. Gide invariably wrote Verbeke's name thus.

11. Chapon, letter ? 2 August 1920, p. 9.

12. *Journal*, 13 August 1922.

13. *Journal*, I p. 746.

14. *Journal, loc. cit.*

15. Naville, *Bibliographie*, LXXIII. A letter from Gide to Martin du Gard mentioning the possible first printing of *Corydon* ('It cannot come out before the 20th') should probably not be dated 13 June 1924 as given in the current edition of the *Correspondance*, but somewhat earlier.

16. Naville, *Bibliographie*, CXX.

17. See Martin du Gard's comment in his letter of 9 January 1928 (*Correspondance*, pp. 321–5).

18. These date from 1906 (Dora Forster in *Ère nouvelle*, February–March 1906, pp. 42–5: ms. Doucet γ 885.54) to 25 September 1910 (*Le Temps*: γ 885.39), and again from 23 October 1913 (*Le Matin*: γ 885.40) to 3 December 1917 (*Débats*: γ 885.37).

19. *Journal*, 16 June 1907.

20. For what it is worth he sent a copy of it to Jean Schlumberger, who thanked him warmly (8 March 1919), which may well indicate that he had acquired the book on his recent trip to Cambridge. (Extract from a letter kindly communicated by Pascal Mercier.)

CHAPTER 2: *CORYDON*: A SUMMARY

1. Gide appended a citation in Latin from Aquinas, with incomplete reference, to *Corydon* in *Œuvres complètes*, IX p. 205: the sexual act in marriage is a mortal sin when performed for lustful reasons (*Summa theologica*, III Supplement, XLIX 6). There is no attempt to provide an analysis of Aquinas' views, and the note was probably supplied by a friend since Gide gives no sign of knowing Aquinas' hostile comments elsewhere on lust and 'unnatural vice' (see in particular *Summa* 1a 2ae 31.7; 1a 2ae 94.3 ad 2; 2a

2ae 154.11–12. For a discussion of Aquinas' views on homosexuality, see Boswell, pp. 318–32).

2. 'Fifteen' as the lower limit (1920 edn) was presumably corrected to thirteen to conform with La Bruyère's cited definition of adolescence.

3. On an undated slip of paper, loosely inserted into the *Journal* for 1910 (ms. Doucet γ 1581.21), there is a draft covering this point, but couched in dialogue form: '– You have not persuaded me that pederasty should exist, nor do I see it naturally flowing by deduction or induction . . . – I have not sought to prove that it should exist; but you must understand that we must start from here, from this fact: it does exist [*elle est*]. There are many representatives of the human race who are completely frigid, or nearly so, when they are faced with women, but who are capable of desires which are more or less powerful, and sometimes ungovernable when faced with . . .'. The latter part of the argument was not retained.

4. See Appendix C.

CHAPTER 3: CHARACTERISATION AND IRONY

1. See Appendix B.

2. 1911: at the beginning of the second Dialogue he resolves 'to put an end to Corydon's raillery'. This is overtly hostile.

3. Page 49. Also p. 95, the example of La Fontaine's pigeons.

4. See above, p. 5.

CHAPTER 4: LANGUAGE AND IDEOLOGY:
A LEXIS FOR *CORYDON*

1. The word's earliest recorded appearance in French seems to be 1891 (Courouve, *s.v.*).

2. Page 671. Some related 'Feuillets' are also printed at the end of the 1911 *Journal*.

3. As a note to 'déshonoré' p. 22. See above, p. 195.

4. Gide changed this word in the translation he used. See above, p. 51.

5. Corydon asks us to see the veil as an ornament of women in an artistic (not a puritanical) light (p. 130).

6. Pierron's translation, I p. 118.

7. Gide added a somewhat similar thought concerning pederasty and chastity to his *Journal* on 12 March 1938: 'It is easy for a pederast to appear chaste in the eyes of a heterosexual. On the other hand, a person who is really chaste is easily thought of by a homosexual as being a homosexual who is not aware of himself or who is repressed. It must be admitted that these suspicions frequently have some foundation. Chastity is less often occasioned by fear or a decision or a vow, than by simple lack of desire – or sometimes even by disgust.'

8. See above, p. 66.

9. Lilja, p. 129.

10. Ms. Doucet γ 885.44. See Chapter 9.

11. See also Diderot, above, p. 204.

CHAPTER 5: IDEOLOGIES

1. 'Subjectif', p. 89, 29 October 1890.

2. There is another ms. reference to 'some interesting articles to be read later in the small volumes "Médecine" (10 vols) in the Bibliothèque Cardinale' in 1890 (ms. Doucet γ 1563), but I have not been able to identify the work in question, unless Gide's source of information was unreliable and the Panckoucke edition is meant.

3. I have inserted a comma here.

4. Similarly in the article 'Prisons', the unacceptable moral attitudes and the gross behaviour of the inmates are mentioned (vol. 45 p. 240).

5. *Journal*, II pp. 390–1.

6. With a reference to Caelius Rhodiginus, *Lectiones antiquae* XV 9. See also Herodotus, I 135.

7. One may also refer to the article on 'Marriage'. Marriage is presented as a healthy institution from which persons abstain at their own risk; married persons live longer than celibates; 'Reason' invented marriage to counter and control the excessive demands of sexual appetite. (See Malthus' arguments above, pp. 66–8.) In the article on 'Copulation' we are told that Augustus legislated in favour of marriage by taxes on celibacy, when unnatural debauchery had reached an extreme degree; Constantine decreed the death penalty for pederasts. Similarly, in the article on 'Célibat', we read that Nature did not intend sexual energy to be entirely repressed, hence the institution of marriage to avoid onanism and other disorders.

8. 'Subjectif', p. 89. See also Schopenhauer, above, p. 46.

9. A. Schopenhauer, *Le Monde comme volonté et comme représentation*, traduit... pour la première fois par J.A. Cantacuzène.

10. Schopenhauer, II p. 850.

11. Cf. J.M. Gesner, *Socrate et l'amour grec: Socrates sanctus paiderastes*. Traduit... texte latin... par A. Bonneau (Paris, 1877). Schopenhauer praises Socrates for rejecting Alcibiades in Plato's *Symposium*.

12. Conclusion, II p. 967.

13. I p. 98.

14. Gide stated that he owed his philosophical initiation to Schopenhauer and 'to him alone' (*Si le grain ne meurt*, p. 519). Notes of reading Schopenhauer: Book I, 11 April 1890 (ms. Doucet γ 1552); parts, especially Book II, July 1890 and 14 September 1891 ('Subjectif', pp. 35, 37, 41). In two letters to Valéry (28 August and 3 November 1891) he admitted that he was tiring of this exercise; he expressed his annoyance with what he called the empirical moral system of Schopenhauer ('Fondement de la morale') in the *Journal*, 8 August 1891. After indicating further reading of the 'Métaphysique de l'amour' in the 'Subjectif', (p. 93: 7 January 1892), the only further note is of reading 'some' to his wife in July 1898 (ms. Doucet γ 1567). Even the fictional hero of *Les Cahiers d'André Walter* leaves his reading of Book IV unfinished.

15. '"A mundo jejunantes" Clément d'Alex. (Strom. III 15). Cité par Schopenhauer. t.I. p. 526' (ms. Catherine Gide. 'Those who have castrated themselves from all sin for the sake of the Kingdom of Heaven are blessed, *for they renounce the World*').

16. See above, p. 301.

17. Pléiade, p. 6.

18. *Journal*, I p. 98.

19. *Journal*, I p. 98: 'Feuillets' (undated).

20. *Ibid.*

21. Ms. Doucet γ 1562.30 (verso).

22. Schopenhauer, II p. 845.

23. LXXVIII April and May 1909, pp. 193–215, 428–442. See above, pp. 133–5.

24. *Corydon*, pp. 121–2.

25. Gide first read the *Ethica* with some application at the time when he was composing *Les Cahiers d'André Walter* (*circa* 1886), which contains several references, particularly to Book IV. He used the translation by either E. Saisset (Paris: Charpentier,

1842), or J.G. Prat (Paris: Hachette, 1880–3). André Walter copies out the text 'neglecting the scholia', in order to understand 'the sequence of the propositions'; he also derives his awareness of the individuality of each soul's view of the world from Spinoza (A. *Walter* (1986), p. 99). There is, however, an interesting point to be noted when the text of the translation Gide used in his *Journal* in 1909 is checked: Gide's word 'volupté' is a substitute for the editor's 'épanouissement' (which might be rendered 'joy' or 'joyfulness'). The Latin is 'gaudium' – Gide has in fact cited this, too, in his text (*Corydon*, p. 122). And in Part 3, Definition xvi, there is an explanation of this word: 'gaudium est laetitia concomitante idea rei praeteritae, quae praeter spem evenit' (which Appuhn translates: 'Joy [*épanouissement*] is a happiness [*joie*] accompanied by the idea of a past thing which has happened against hope'). Here we are even further from Gide's 'volupté'. *Ethique* . . . texte latin soigneusement revu, traduction nouvelle, notice et notes par C. Appuhn (Paris: Garnier frères, 1908). One other reference (*Journal*, 11 July 1909) relates to 'the last words of the *Ethica*: "In all things, excellence is as difficult as it is rare."' Ruyters brought to Gide's attention on 31 May 1907 the recent translation by Comte Henri de Boulainvilliers (Paris: Armand Colin, 1907).

26.   See above, p. 290.
27.   Gide used the translation by H. Albert, *La Volonté de puissance* (1903).
28.   There is also a possibility that Gide read the extracts from Nietzsche published in various French literary periodicals at the turn of the century, and, in particular, 'Nietzsche contre Wagner' (*Revue Blanche*, XIII August 1897, pp. 167–78) in which Nietzsche explains how he distanced himself from Wagner, having perceived in him a tendency to spiritualise sensuality. It is also clear that Gide was reading some Nietzsche in German in early 1900 (ms. Doucet γ 1567), but we unfortunately know nothing more precise about this.
29.   The standard second augmented edition first appeared in Paris in 1808.
30.   *Œuvres choisies* (Maximes, § 6).
31.   'Feuillets', I p. 354.
32.   'Subjectif', p. 62. Gide recommended Bourget's *Essais* (1883) to his mother (letter of 5 July 1894). It is amusing to note the conversation on *L'Immoraliste* which occurred when Gide first met Bourget in 1915 (see above, p. 363).
33.   *Correspondance*, p. 118.
34.   *Histoire romaine*, II p. 162: 'Feuillets' (*circa* 1911), I p. 355.
35.   Ms. Doucet γ 1567 (July 1898: the first 130 pages; October 1899: Chapter 5).
36.   See above, on Sulla, p. 348.
37.   *Corydon*, p. 159; Herder (trans. Quinet), vol. II Book 13, Chapter 4, pp. 465–6. He knew Quinet's translation by about 1887 (ms. Doucet γ 1556.7), and his note to read it was subsequently crossed through.
38.   *Ioläus*, pp. 208–9: 'Herder on Greek Friendship' (neither Carpenter nor Gide gives the title in full).
39.   *Corydon*, p. 159; proofs, 1920.
40.   See above, on Sulla, p. 347.
41.   Ms. Doucet γ 1572.10; *L'Esprit des lois*, ed. Laboulaye, vol. 3 p. 317.
42.   *Corydon*, p. 175.
43.   B. Constant, Commentaire sur Filangieri, IV i, cited by Laboulaye.
44.   *Corydon*, p. 142. See above, p. 31.
45.   II p. 306.
46.   II p. 322.
47.   *Corydon*, p. 182.
48.   *Journal*, I p. 682 (May–October 1920, but perhaps to be dated June 1922 – ms. Doucet γ 1597.64 (a loose leaf)). Montesquieu, *Correspondance*, publiée par F. Gebelin avec la collaboration de M.A. Morize (1914).

49. Cited in Goulet, p. 593.

50. *Journal*, 16 March 1943 (= ed. Bury, vol. 1 p. 76 and note). Gide's citation is in English.

51. Ed. Bury, vol. 3 p. 106 and note; Ammianus Marcellinus, XXXI 9.

52. Ed. Bury, vol. 4 p. 504 and notes.

53. *Corydon*, p. 159 (on Herder: *Ioläus*, pp. 208–9); p. 160 (a note on the *Iliad*: *Ioläus*, pp. 68–9); p. 161 (on Aeschylus and Sophocles, and the *Myrmidons*: *Ioläus*, pp. 73–4); p. 162 (a note on heroes: *Ioläus*, p. 85 (and, in the 1920 proofs, a general reference to *Ioläus*, pp. 67–74)); p. 168 ((1920 proofs) on Khartoum and Tacitus: *Ioläus*, p. 12); p. 169 (on Aristotle: *Ioläus*, p. 23); p. 170 (an added footnote, in the 1920 edition, to J.A. Symonds: *Ioläus*, p. 16); p. 181 (the example of St Augustine (*Confessions*, IV 6): *Ioläus*, pp. 99–102); p. 183 (an addition to the note on *Amelia*, in the 1920 edition, referring to stories in *Ioläus*, pp. 115–8).

54. See *Corydon* (1947), p. 129.

55. Quoted in *Ioläus*, pp. 221–2.

56. See *Corydon* (1947), p. 183.

57. See *Corydon*, p. 168 (a note appended to the words: 'aux yeux de leurs amants'); *Ioläus*, p. 12.

58. Tacitus, *Germania* XIII–XIV (also referred to in the deleted footnote). Ammianus
Marcellinus, XVI 13.

59. *Corydon*, p. 160; *Ioläus*, pp. 15–16.

60. II iv, vi, viii.

61. *Intermediate Types*, p. 106. Penelope and Nausicaa occur, of course, in the *Odyssey* – not in the *Iliad*.

62. *Intermediate Types*, p. 111; J.A. Symonds, *In the Key of Blue* (London, 1893), p. 64.

63. *Intermediate Types*, p. 111.

CHAPTER 6: SOCIAL THEORY

1. Martin, p. 433.

2. *La Plume* (1901), p. 445.

3. ' "Je serais inconsolable de dire quoi que ce soit directement qui peut être interprété dans un sens contraire à la vertu. Mais je ne pense pas que les fautes dont il s'agit (*actes contraires à la chasteté*) doivent dans les questions morales être envisagées seules, ou même qu'elles soient les plus graves qu'on puisse concevoir." Malthus p. 489.' The translation Gide used is by G. Prévost, with notes by J. Garnier, and is not always faithful: 'I should be extremely sorry to say anything, which could either directly or remotely be construed unfavourably to the cause of virtue; but I certainly cannot think that *the vices which relate to the sex* [that is, to women] are the only vices which are to be considered in a moral question; or that they are even the greatest and most degrading to the human character' (Book IV Chapter 4). The phrase I have italicised has a more general application in the French.

4. Page 476. Gide quotes in French and has not retained the opening phrase, printed here in square brackets. Except where indicated, the translation follows Malthus quite closely.

5. *Corydon* simply has 'une vertu forcée' – the French translation has the whole phrase.

6. French translation: 'légitime' (lawful, reasonable).

7. This whole sentence reads (in French): 'Prostitution, which is harmful to society, obviously tends to weaken the most noble affections of the heart and degrade the character. . . . All other unlawful intercourse [*commerce illicite*] tends as much as marriage to increase the population' – to which the translator adds a note to the effect that infanticide and other illegal means of controlling the number of births are obviously out of the question. Gide's quotation follows at this point.

8. See above, p. 87.

9. Book I Chapter 2: 'Of the general checks to population, and the mode of their operation' (see esp. p. 8 (French translation, p. 14)). See also in the *Mercure de France*, LXXX August 1909, pp. 722–6: 'Questions juridiques: Le Néo-malthusianisme devant les tribunaux' (on birth control) by José Théry; and *ibid.*, CXXVIII August 1918, pp. 526–9: 'Lettres anglaises: Marie Stopes, *Married Love* (London, Fifield)' – a review by H.-D. Davray. Cf. *Corydon*, p. 70 (ms. Doucet γ 885.62 and .64 attack Neo-Malthusianism).

10. French: 'the disruption [*dérèglement*] of morals'.

11. French: 'le libertinage'.

12. French: 'artifices'.

13. French: 'criminal or irregular liaisons'.

14. Ms. Doucet γ 1573.

15. *Corydon*, pp. 91–2.

16. Cf. *ibid.*, p. 129.

17. Chapters 8 to 14 are concerned with the sexual organs in insects and other animals together with a discussion of the several methods of achieving copulation. Chapter 15 is on courtship behaviour; 16 is on polygamy and monogamy among animals as diverse as antelopes ('Le harem de l'antilope'), pigeons and carnivores (both groups are monogamous), and insects (who are incorrigibly polygamous). Chapter 17 continues this subject with a discussion of the behaviour of 'social' animals (ants, bees, beavers).

18. *Physique de l'amour*, pp. 228–41.

19. *Physique de l'amour*, p. 272.

20. *Arts et idées*, April 1938. Ed. Louis Combelle. Two further letters from Gide to Gourmont (unpublished) feature in the catalogue of the Librairie Les Argonautes, Paris (19 May 1988, item 1090): June 1891, thanking Gourmont for his remarks on *André Walter* ('When, as you say, he realises how powerless his thought is to control events, and his lack of social usefulness, then he will become indignant . . . and he will awake, armed with irony. . . . How true. . . . The world often makes the most delicate souls turn hostile [*méchantes*]'); and November 1896 ('I am happy to see that you think that the predictions which you made about me in 1891 have come true'). Five from Gourmont (9 August 1896 to 7 May 1904) and one from Gide (March 1902) are recorded in *La Correspondance générale*, I–VI.

21. Rees, p. 167. Gide seems not to have collaborated, but did he read Hirschfeld's 'Les Types sexuels intermédiaires', 7 1910, pp. 401–17?'

22. *Journal*, '17 March (?)' 1904.

23. In an effort to revitalise the almost defunct periodical *L'Ermitage* a new editorial committee was announced in XV December 1904, consisting principally of Gide and Gourmont. It was set up in January 1905. Anglès, who characterises this as an 'improbable tandem' (I p. 23: see also pp. 69–70 and 94–6), records Gide's 'mistrust', and further narrates how the new periodical *Antée* took over from *L'Ermitage* with some of the same contributors (including Gide and Gourmont), and the same animosities. Both Gide and Gourmont contributed to the *Mercure de France*, which had been refounded in 1889 largely under the patronage and influence of Gourmont.

24. 'L'Amateur de M. Rémy de Gourmont' in NRF, 1 April 1910, pp. 425–37, reprinted in *Nouveaux Prétextes*, pp. 102–11.

25. Cf. a similar remark in *Si le grain ne meurt*, p. 596.

26. *Promenades philosophiques*, 3ᵉ série, pp. 192–8, 'Les Livres sur l'amour'.

27. *La Culture des idées*, 3ᵉ éd., pp. 205–33, 'La Morale de l'amour'.

28. *Épilogues*, série I pp. 102–5, 'Problèmes d'alcôve' (1897).
29. There already existed a law of 2 August 1882 'Ayant pour object la répression des outrages aux bonnes mœurs' (amended 16 March 1898 and 7 April 1908) which dealt with the distribution and public display of books, pamphlets, pictures and songs alleged to be obscene. A hostile article by José Théry on the later amendment appeared in the section 'Questions juridiques' in the *Mercure de France*, LXXIII May 1908, pp. 117–20.
30. *Épilogues*, série III pp. 132–41, 'L'Obscénité'. See Gide: 'La Licence, la dépravation et les déclarations de M. le sénateur Bérenger', in *L'Ermitage*, XVII April 1906, pp. 252–5, reprinted in *Nouveaux Prétextes*, pp. 85–9. There were at this time in Paris two vociferous purity leagues – La Ligue de la licence des rues, and La Ligue pour le relèvement de la moralité publique – who had found a spokesman in the person of Albert Eyquem in 1905 (*De la répression des outrages à la morale publique . . . ou de la pornographie au point de vue historique, législatif et social, avec une étude complète de droit comparé* (Paris: Marchal et Billard, 1905). Cited in Barbedette and Carassou, p. 145). His main concern was with the publication and display of pornographic and obscene material, but he also complained that certain districts of Paris had become such dens of iniquity that 'civilised' persons dared no longer frequent them. This was a reference to places where young male and female prostitutes plied their trade.
31. Published in 1926, pp. 157–62, 'La Bestialité'.
32. Georges Duviquet, *Héliogabale raconté par les historiens grecs et latins . . .*, 2ᵉ éd. (Paris: Mercure de France, 1903) (in *Promenades littéraires*, 6ᵉ série 1926, pp. 225–38). See above, p. 171.
33. *Épilogues*, série I pp. 312–18, 'Sur le sadisme' [1898].
34. *Ibid.*, série II pp. 318–27.
35. See also *ibid.*, série IV pp. 264–71 'Morale de théâtre' [1906]: 'It will soon be necessary to show feminine beauty naked on our stages, as was the custom in the Roman Atellanae [low vulgar farces].'
36. *Ibid.*, série II pp. 242–5 [1901].
37. *Ibid.*, pp. 159–65, 'La Liberté de mœurs' [1900].
38. *Lettres à l'Amazone*, pp. 197–205, 'Tirésias'.
39. See above, p. 53; *Promenades littéraires*, 3ᵉ éd., pp. 89–95, 'Nietzsche et l'amour'.
40. *Épilogues*, série III pp. 277–9, 'Internats d'adultes' [1904].
41. Pages 98–100 (reproduced in *Épilogues*).
42. *Dialogues des amateurs sur les choses du temps*, 1905–7, pp. 202–3 [= *Épilogues*, série IV]. Ms. Doucet γ 885.60 refers to this by page number, adding: 'Quote the text quoted by Gourmont.'
43. *Épilogues*, série V pp. 41–8, 'L'Amour à l'envers' [1907].
44. Cf. *Corydon*, p. 35.
45. Cf. *ibid.*, p. 55.
46. Cf. *ibid.*, p. 78 ff.
47. Cf. *ibid.*, p. 54.
48. Cf. *ibid.*, p. 22: 'We have had many victims, but no martyrs.'
49. *Nouveaux Prétextes*, p. 108.
50. P.E. Jacob, p. 124.
51. *Physique de l'amour*, p. 106.
52. Ward (1903), p. 325.
53. *Corydon*, p. 75.
54. *Ibid.*, p. 118
55. Ms. Doucet γ 885.10; Ward (1906), II p. 71.
56. γ 885.17; Ward (1906), II pp. 100–1.
57. γ 885.18; Ward (1906), II p. 78.
58. γ 885.19; Ward (1906), II p. 78.

59. ɣ 885.20; Ward (1906), II pp. 104–5.

60. ɣ 885.21; Ward (1906), II p. 56.

61. ɣ 885.22 and .23; Ward (1906), II p. 67.

62. Ward (1906), II p. 111. This chapter on phylogenetic love is the source for several more extracts copied by Gide (vol. II pp. 3–175 of the French translation (Chapter 14): *Corydon*, p. 63 (Ward (1906), II p. 36); p. 64 (Ward (1906), II p. 30); ms. Doucet ɣ 885.50 (Ward (1906), II pp. 103–4); and others.

63. *Corydon*, pp. 63, 71–2.

64. *Journal*, 28 July 1908: 'Read some Bergson (*L'Évolution créatrice*), but didn't get very far. Splendid importance of this book which will allow philosophy a new development.' On 1 March 1924 Gide wrote in his *Journal* that he knew virtually nothing of Bergson, and on 18 July 1927 that he had difficulty in completing the *Essai sur les données immédiates de la conscience*.

65. *Corydon*, pp. 71–2.

66. My italics, to show the phrase quoted *ibid.*, p. 72. We may note the following misprints: 'pour', 'organique' (Gide) for 'par', 'inorganique' (Bergson).

67. *Corydon*, p. 63, with a reference to Bergson, 'p. 130'.

68. My italics: this phrase is quoted in *Corydon*.

69. *Corydon*, p. 63.

70. Geneslay cites the Flammarion edition, p. 173.

71. Geneslay refers to Élie Metchnikoff, *Études sur la nature humaine*, 3ᵉ éd. (Paris: Masson, 1905). Gide may also have known the following: P. Geddes and J.A. Thomson, *The Evolution of Sex* (French translation by Henry de Varigny, Paris, 1892) which contains three propositions – (1) anabolic processes preponderate in the female, and catabolic in the male (this accounts for differentiation which is itself a variable); (2) environmental conditions influence the determination of sex; (3) sexual dimorphism has an adaptive significance. Among the books 'to be read' in 1905, and subsequently crossed through as having been dealt with, is Paul Jacoby, *Études sur la sélection chez l'homme* (ms. Doucet ɣ 1573 – referring probably to the second edition, 1904) – a severely positivist book detailing the physical determinants of madness and crime; it has nothing to say on homosexuality.

72. The French population returns for 1901 showed 857,000 births (as against 827,000 in 1900) and 784,000 deaths (853,000 in 1900). For the preceding ten years 1891–1900 the yearly average birthrate had been 853,000, and the figure for deaths 829,000. In 1901 there were 303,000 marriages (299,000 in 1900) and 7,741 divorces (7,157 in 1900) (*Times* report, 12 November 1902, p. 5e. See *Annuaire statistique de la France, Résumé rétrospectif*, vol. 72 (nouvelle série, 14)). There was a gradual decline in live births from about 1886 onwards, although the natural growth of the population as a whole remained fairly steady from 1886 to 1913, amounting to a total of 4 per cent over the whole period. The excess of births over deaths fell from a high level in 1874 (+4.8, for every 1,000 persons) to low points in 1900 (−0.6) and 1911 (−0.9).

73. Ms. Doucet ɣ 885.46. See above pp. 33 and 112–3.

74. Oysters also feature in the citation from Thomson, discussed above, p. 113 (ms. Doucet ɣ 885.7).

75. Ms. Doucet ɣ 885.5.

76. Ms. Doucet ɣ 885.6.

CHAPTER 7: MEDICO-LEGAL ATTITUDES

1. For a detailed account, see H.C. Kennedy, 'The "Third Sex" Theory of K.H. Ulrichs', in S.J. Licata and R.P. Petersen (eds), *The Gay Past* (New York: Harrington

Park Press, 1985), pp. 103–11 (= *Journal of Homosexuality*, 6 (1/2), Fall/Winter 1980/1).

2. It was later to be mentioned by Albert Prieur in his column 'Sciences' in the *Mercure de France*, XXXI September 1899, pp. 803–11, together with Moll (*Les Perversions de l'instinct sexuel*) and Schrenck-Notzing.

3. *Correspondance*, 6 December 1895 (p. 252). There is a passing remark to 'Moll. K. Ebbing [sic] and others' in ms. Doucet γ 1571.4 (August 1903).

4. Delay, II p. 522.

5. *Correspondance*, I p. 245. See above, p. 407.

6. Raffalovich also published several articles in *Archives d'anthropologie criminelle, de criminologie et de psychologie normale et pathologique*: XIX 1904, pp. 926–36; XX 1905, pp. 283–6; XXII 1907, pp. 267–8; and esp. XXII 1907, pp. 606–32 and 767–86, and XXIV 1909, pp. 353–91 (= 'Chronique de l'unisexualité'). Cf. also his presentation of a translation of Chapter XLIII of E. Westermarck, *The Origin and Development of the Moral Ideas* (London: Macmillan, 1908), *ibid.*, XXV 1910, pp. 295–305 and 353–75.

7. *Mercure de France*, LXXXIII January 1910, pp. 328–9. (Another volume, *La Pudeur, la périodicité sexuelle, l'auto-érotisme* (Paris: Mercure de France, 1909), had already been reviewed by Danville (*ibid.*, LXXVIII March 1909, pp. 330–1). There are a number of differences between the French and English texts (the content of the English edition was itself altered in subsequent printings); these include some extra footnotes in the French, minor textual variations and deletions, and the omission of both Appendix B (a summary of Ulrich's views) and Appendix D (the case of Countess Sarolta V.). An account of the 1898 prosecution of Ellis' book (the so-called 'Bedborough Trial') written by Laurence Jerrold was published in *La Revue Blanche*, XVII October 1898, pp. 238–9 (fuller details can be found in P. Grosskurth, *Havelock Ellis*, pp. 191–204).

8. Weeks, p. 61; see also Grosskurth, *Havelock Ellis*, Chapter 12. The first edition of Ellis' work dated 1897 was published in England, but not put on general sale. It was prosecuted and most copies were destroyed. A second edition, with the same date but omitting J.A. Symonds' essay on homosexuality, appeared shortly afterwards.

9. Ellis (2nd edn, 1897), p. 4.

10. *Ibid.*

11. *Ibid.*

12. *Ibid.*, p. 12.

13. *Ibid.*, p. 13.

14. *Ibid.*, p. 24.

15. *Ibid.*, p. 42.

16. *Ibid.*, p. 146.

17. *Ibid.*, p. 147.

18. *Ibid.*

19. *Ibid.*, p. 155.

20. See also above, p. 274.

21. 'Vorläutige Mitteilungen über die Darstellung eines Schemas der Geschlechts-differenzierungen' (pp. 327–56).

22. *Mercure de France*, LXV January 1907, pp. 168–9.

23. Vol. VII pt 1, pp. 153–288.

24. *Mercure de France*, LXIX October–November 1907, pp. 545, 563.

25. *Ibid.*, LXXIX June 1909, p. 548.

26. *Ibid.*, LXXII April 1908, p. 551.

27. *Ibid.*, LXXII April 1908, p. 745.

28. *Ibid.*, LXXVI December 1908, p. 742.

29. *Ibid.*, LII October 1904, pp. 258–9.

30. *Weltbühne*, XXIV 1928 no. 35, pp. 322–7.

31. *Der Amethyst*, his second venture which combined libertinism and erudition, was announced in the *Mercure de France* in early 1906, and was briefly reviewed in the April issue (LX April 1906, p. 452); its demise was reported in February 1907 (LXV February 1907, pp. 735–6), a victim of censorship. It was replaced in 1908 by another periodical, *Hyperion*, issued by Blei and C. Sternheim. No. 4 of *Hyperion* contained Blei's translation of Gide's *Bethsabé*, which thus had the privilege of being printed here before the French original appeared in *Vers et Prose*. Gide's unpublished *Journal* for 1905 contains notes of several addresses, including Franz Blei's (ms. Doucet γ 1573.32. See Chapter 15 note 26).

32. Among the material in *Archives d'anthropologie criminelle, de criminologie et de psychologie normale et pathologique* there appeared an overview which Gide might have read: P.L. Ladame, 'Chronique allemande. Les travaux récents des auteurs allemands sur l'homosexualité', XXVIII 1913, pp. 827–61.

33. X January–June 1896. See also Chapter 17 note 31.

34. *Ibid.*, pp. 253–5.

35. *Ibid.*, pp. 304–6.

36. *Ibid.*, pp. 277–8.

37. *Ibid.*, pp. 278–9.

38. *Ibid.*, pp. 289–93.

39. Cf. *Corydon*, p. 95.

40. Chevalier, p. 13.

41. *Ibid.*, pp. 167–8. See also E. Laurent, *Les Bisexués gynécomastes et hermaphrodites* (Paris: Georges Carré, 1894) (which has a short section on 'pédérastes', that is sodomites) – Chapter xiv is about 'uranistes' and 'hermaphrodisme artificiel'.

42. A brief review of the book, by Albert Prieur, appeared in the *Mercure de France*, XXXIV April 1900, p. 217.

43. Féré (1904), p. 2.

44. *Ibid.*, p. 56.

45. *Mercure de France*, L April 1904, pp. 202–6. The book had first appeared in Russian in 1885, but the French translation is from the English, itself a translation from the German.

46. The second edition was reviewed by Gaston Danville in the *Mercure de France*, LXXXIX January 1911, pp. 154–7, together with Anton Nyström's *La Vie sexuelle et ses lois* (Paris: Vigot, 1910: this has little to say about homosexuality, but it does distinguish the sexual drive from the procreative need – compare *Corydon*'s argument).

47. 'Laupts' (1910), p. 187.

48. 'Laupts' (1896), p. 367.

49. Authorised translation by C.G. Chaddock (1895: reissued, New York: Julian Press, 1956).

50. See above, p. 96.

51. Again in the *Mercure de France* (LXXVI November 1908, p. 122), but this time in the column 'Questions juridiques' written by José Théry, there appeared an account of a review of the book in the *Journal de droit international privé* (1908, nos. vii–x), where it was reported on at the same time as 'another study by Dr J. Crocq on the same subject'. (I have been unable to identify Crocq's book.) In giving a lengthy quotation from Hirschfeld's work describing the Berlin homosexual bars frequented by soldiers, Théry commented that nothing like the questionnaire circulated by Hirschfeld's *Komitee*, with the resultant percentage figures, had ever been attempted in France – and perhaps it should be. His tone, however, is somewhat ironic.

52. Rysselberghe, II p. 413 (24 October 1934). See Chapter 15 note 26.

53. J. Fryer, *Isherwood. A Biography of Christopher Isherwood* (London: New English

Library, 1977), p. 118. A letter from Gide to Hirschfeld was published in *Die literarische Welt*, 13 July 1928; two letters from Hirschfeld to Gide (31 January 1927, 24 September 1934) are recorded in *La Correspondance générale* I–VI. The Institute was burned by the Nazis in May 1933, and Hirschfeld died two years later.

54. N. Kostyleff, *Le Mécanisme cérébral de la pensée* (Paris: F. Alcan, 1914), characterised as owing something to Pavlov, was described as a study of objective psychology, and especially of the Russian school. It followed, said the reviewer, the formula developed by Ribot in *La Vie inconsciente et les mouvements*. E. Régis and A. Hesnard, *La Psychanalyse* (Paris: F. Alcan, 1914), 'a remarkable exposition of Freud's theories'.

55. Colpach, p. 103.

56. 'Gide et Freud' in *Revue d'histoire littéraire de la France*, January–February 1977, pp. 48–74.

57. A translation by Yves Le Lay, 'Cinq leçons sur la psychanalyse (1909)', according to the editor: See *Über Psychoanalyse. Fünf Vorlesungen gehalten zur 20jährigen Gründungsfeier der Clark University . . .* (Leipzig, 1910).

58. 'Eugénie Sokolnicka, pionnier de la psychanalyse et inspiratrice d'A. Gide', in *Médecine de France*, 219 February 1971, pp. 17–22. She had moved from Poland, and held meetings in her Paris flat which were attended by Gide, Roger Martin du Gard, Jean Schlumberger and other friends (see Rysselberghe, I pp. 110–11, 114, 121; II p. 273). According to Gourévitch, the details Gide used for the description of the course of analysis undergone by Boris derive directly from an article by Sokolnicka on obsessional neurosis which she lent Gide – 'Analyse einer infantilen Zwangsneurose' (*Internazionale Zeitschrift für Psychanalyse*, VI 1920, pp. 228–41). Because of her belief in mysticism (in real life and in the novel), Steel thinks that she is more Jungian than Freudian, and he may well be right.

59. *Correspondance*, I p. 253.

60. *Ibid.*, 7 May 1921.

61. See *Journal*, 29 December 1932. The German original first appeared in 1908.

62. *Conditions of Nervous Anxiety and their Treatment . . .* translation by R. Gabler (London: Kegan Paul, 1923; this English translation is slightly abridged).

63. Other relevant works by Stekel include *Onanie und Homosexualität (die homosexuelle Parapathie* (English translation: *The Homosexual Neurosis*, trans. J.S. van Teslaar (Boston: R.G. Badger, 1922); see esp. part 2), first published in Vienna in 1917 and reissued in an augmented third edition in 1923. Gide could have read this work, in German, during the time when he was composing the final version of *Corydon*. In the section on masturbation, Stekel gives voice to an opinion which seems almost like a direct comment on one of Corydon's propositions: 'The rebellion against the notion of purposiveness in love may drive the individual also into homosexuality. In such a case the imperative of reproduction is not brought in between instinct and gratification: love has no other purpose than the acquisition of pleasure' (translation by van Teslaar).

64. *Le Comportement sexuel de l'homme* (Paris: Éd. du Pavois, 1948).

CHAPTER 8: NATURAL HISTORY AND ANTHROPOLOGY

1. Gide considered himself, with some degree of truth, to be a more practical entomologist than Gourmont.

2. Volume X was reviewed by Georges Bohn in the *Mercure de France*, LXXXV June 1910, pp. 519–20.

3. *Journal*, 19 June 1910; 10 January 1925. However, on 18 August 1908 Gide wrote to Ruyters that he had only read one volume so far – vol. IX, he thought – the others were waiting to be ordered, and he was too busy to read them immediately.

4. *Journal*, I p. 156.

5. *Corydon*, p. 98; Fabre, I pp. 39–70.

6. Fabre, III pp. 337–61, and III xviii, 'Répartition des sexes', p. 376; *Corydon*, p. 81.

7. *Corydon*, pp. 106, 108. The second part of note p. 106 (after the phrase 'chez la *mantis religiosa*') was added in ms. to the 1911 proof copy.

8. *Ibid.*, p. 85.

9. Cited *ibid.*, note p. 85.

10. Fabre, V p. 265.

11. *Descent of Man*, Chapters 9–11.

12. Pléiade, p. 234.

13. *Corydon*, p. 91; Fabre, VII xxiii, 'Le Grand Paon'; xxiv, 'Le Minime à bande'; and xxv, 'L'Odorat'.

14. *Corydon*, p. 96; Fabre, III p. 272.

15. Fabre, II p. 273.

16. *Ibid.*, p. 307.

17. *Meloe* is also mentioned in the *Journal*, 19 June 1910, but on 23 August 1908 Ruyters had already drawn Gide's attention to the 'stupendous' account of the *meloe*.

18. *Corydon*, pp. 73–6.

19. *Ibid.*, p. 124.

20. Ms. Doucet γ 885.45.

21. *Corydon*, p. 127. See plate 10.

22. *Revue hebdomadaire*, 15 June 1912, pp. 295–324.

23. Ms. Doucet γ 885.49.

24. *Corydon*, p. 79, note 1.

25. *Ibid.*, pp. 81–2.

26. See above, p. 33.

27. Ms. Doucet γ 885.7 (unused in *Corydon*). In the *Mercure de France*, LXXV October 1908, pp. 499–500, there appeared a review by Georges Bohn of J.A. Thomson's *Heredity*, which Gide probably saw. The chapter of *Study of Animal Life* from which Gide made his note is called, appropriately enough, 'The Struggle for Life' (Part 1: The everyday life of animals. Chapter 3). He probably read this book destined for the educated layman with great interest. Thomson does not mention what he would doubtless have considered 'aberrant' sexual behaviour.

28. 3rd edn, 1882–6. 'Samson' is an incorrect form of the author's name.

29. *Corydon*, pp. 87–8; *Zootechnie*, V p. 181 (wrong reference in *Corydon*).

30. *Corydon*, p. 89; *Zootechnie* II p. 87.

31. *Corydon*, p. 89; *Zootechnie*, V pp. 181–2; cf. Fabre's reports on the greater peacock moth (above).

32. *Corydon*, p. 102; *Zootechnie*, III pp. 214–23.

33. *Corydon*, p. 73.

34. *Corydon*, p. 81; Claus, p. 636.

35. Reviewed by Gaston Danville in the *Mercure de France*, XCI June 1911, pp. 612–13. This was probably where Gide first noticed it.

36. Namely: (c) the search for food (pp. 101–4), and (f) on instinct in the new psychology (p. 121). On pp. 101–4 (cited in *Corydon*, p. 58), Bohn discusses the feeding habits of insects, expounding as he does so the theories of Marchal, with whom he agrees in denouncing the misuse of the word 'instinct'. Gide's reference to 'Bohn, loc. cit., p. 121' (*Corydon*, p. 58) was added to the 1911 proofs, together with: ' "In fact, [your] Bohn very wisely says [in a little book fresh off the press that I've just read] the danger does not lie in using the word "instinct" but in not knowing what might lie behind this word and in using it like an explanation" [I agree.] Place as a note.' ([   ] indicates words deleted subsequently by Gide in handwriting.)

37. *Corydon*, p. 58 (where the name is wrongly reproduced as 'Max Weiler' following the additional ms. note in Gide's hand in the 1911 proofs); 'La Modification des instincts et particulièrement des instincts sociaux' (1907) (a study of comparative and animal psychology, presenting the work of Georges Bohn, Jacques Loeb and Alfred Giard). See further, H.H. Frost, *The Functional Sociology of Émile Waxweiler and the Institut de Sociologie Solvay* (Brussels: Académie royale de Belgique, 1960: Mémoires LIII, fasc. 5: Classe de lettres et sciences morales et politiques). Goulet's suggestion (p. 127) is thus confirmed, and he does right to notice that Anthime, in *Les Caves du Vatican*, is a correspondent of 'Loeb, Bohn and Max Weiler' (a ms. draft, with the same collocation of names as in *Corydon*, which also cites Robert Mearns Yerkes, *The Dancing Mouse, A Study in Animal Behavior* (New York: Macmillan, 1907; on experimental animal psychology)). See above, p. 371.

38. *Corydon*, p. 66.

39. *Correspondance*, p. 194: 'Je m'amuse avec Darwin.' See also the letters to his mother on 4 December 1893 and 5 January 1894.

40. *Journal*, I p. 220. The month is not certain.

41. *Corydon*, p. 77; *Voyage*, p. 216. The remark is from a section on lower marine animals in the Falkland Islands (Chapter IX).

42. *Corydon*, p. 78.

43. *Voyage*, pp. 433–4; *Corydon*, pp. 128–9 (both the footnote and the remarks in the text).

44. *Voyage*, p. 438.

45. *Corydon*, p. 129; cf. p. 134.

46. Stevenson's *Correspondence*, edited by S. Colvin, is mentioned in a letter from Gide to Edmund Gosse 8 October 1911. Gosse's *Critical Kit-Kats* (London: Heinemann, 1896), which contains essays on Whitman, Pater and Stevenson, was also known to Gide (*Correspondence*, p. 117). *In the South Seas* was first mentioned to Gide by Ruyters in his letter of 3 October 1905 and cited again on 21 November 1905 ('"This is the rule in Polynesia, with few exceptions; the higher the family, the better the man – better in sense, better in manners, and usually taller and stronger in body." Stevenson, *In the South Seas*, p. 72').

47. *In the South Seas*, p. 39.

48. *Ibid.*, pp. 39–40.

49. It is worth mentioning here a note Gide made concerning kinship patterns in non-European societies. A quotation (ms. Doucet γ 885.8), in English, from Tagore's *Hungry Stones* (p. 193, 'Living or Dead') is preceded by the observation: 'Family. To be included with the story of the children who have escaped from their natural family, who have been adopted, etc. See Darwin *Tahiti*, Stevenson, etc.' The Tagore extract reads as follows: 'If a woman fosters another's child, her love for him is all the stronger because she has no claim upon him – no claim of kinship that is, but simply the claim of love. Love cannot prove its claim by any document which society accepts, and does not wish to prove it; it merely worships with double passion its life's uncertain treasure.' Although this is not directly focused on the question of homosexuality and was not retained in *Corydon*, it shows Gide's concern for nonconformity in a wider context. It is possible that he also read a review article in the *Mercure de France*, CXXXIII June 1919, pp. 712–14, of A.D. Rebreyrend, *Les Amours marocaines* (Paris: La Maison française d'art et d'édition, 1919): this book concentrates on the family and the position of women, and only alludes briefly to homosexuality. It does however recount an amusing anecdote of a man who married his daughter to his own Ganymede, thus keeping him in the family.

50. *Corydon*, p. 79 (already included in the 1911 edition). The translation Gide used was *La Descendance de l'homme et la sélection naturelle*, traduit par E. Barbier (see *Corydon*, p. 130).

51. We may note, by way of parenthesis, the inclusion of an extract in English on polygamy in the *Corydon* archive taken from *The Autobiography of Mark Rutherford*: 'Polyg. "After a time, the thought of Mary occurred to me. I was distressed to find that, in the very height of my love for Theresa, my love for Mary continued unabated. Had it been otherwise, had my affection for Mary grown dim, I should not have been so much perplexed, but it did not. It may be ignominious to confess it, but so it was; I simply record the fact." p. 244' (ms. Doucet γ 885.90).

52. *Corydon*, p. 130.

53. 'Feuillets' (*circa* 1911), *Journal*, I p. 341. Much earlier, *The Origin of Species* featured among those works Gide thought he would take to Iceland (where, in the event, he never travelled) – ms. Doucet γ 1562, 2 January 1892.

54. *Corydon*, p. 66.

55. *The Cambridge Natural History* (London: Macmillan, 1909), vol. IV pp. 100–7.

56. *Monograph*, II pp. 23–30.

57. *Ibid.*, II p. 29.

58. *Ibid.*, II p. 15.

59. *Ibid.*, I p. 291.

60. *Ibid.*, II p. 23.

61. *Corydon*, p. 67.

62. *Ibid.*, p. 116. Here, Quinton's name is added in ms. to the 1911 proofs.

63. Hugo de Vries published between 1889 and 1912 a series of works including studies on mutation theory and the origin of species in the vegetable kingdom (*Opera e periodicis collata* (Utrecht: A. Oosthoek, 1918–27)). Of particular interest here is *Espèces et variétés, leur naissance par mutation*... traduit de l'anglais par L. Blaringhem (Paris: F. Alcan, 1909).

64. Deville on segregated male animals: Ellis (trans. van Gennep), II p. 14; *Corydon*, p. 99 without attribution of source.

65. *Corydon*, p. 94.

66. *Ibid.*, pp. 96–8.

67. Ms. Doucet γ 885.27; cf. *Corydon*, p. 92. The periodical from which it comes is unidentified. The *Archives d'anthropologie criminelle, de criminologie et de psychologie normale et pathologique* contain several reports of this type, unrecorded by Gide, though he might have come across this journal from time to time (a dog with a complaisant and eager chicken, a masochistic horse, and so on).

CHAPTER 9: VICTIMS, MARTYRS AND A SOCIAL CONSCIENCE

1. 'Subjectif', p. 80. Gide visited Bluebeard's castle during a holiday in Brittany (letter to his mother 31 August 1892).

2. Ms. Doucet γ 1563.

3. There is no other evidence that Gide was interested in de Sade, nor that he was acquainted with any of his licentious writings.

4. F. Mouret, 'La Première Rencontre d'A. Gide et d'O. Wilde' in *French Studies*, XXII 1 January 1968, pp. 37–40.

5. Delay, II pp. 447–64. See also F. Mouret, 'Quatorze Lettres et billets inédits de Lord Alfred Douglas à A. Gide 1895–1929' in *Revue de littérature comparée*, 3

July–September 1975, pp. 483–502. It may be added that the St Catherine Press in Bruges (which published *Corydon*) printed Douglas' *Poems* in 1908.

6. Gide's letter to his mother 28 January 1895 (see Delay, II p. 448). Gide compares Wilde to Elagabalus (letter to his mother 30 January 1895, p. 590), a description which his mother takes up: 'A Roman Emperor of the most decadent period' (*ibid.* 23 February 1895, p. 614).

7. Delay, II p. 451.

8. Cf. also the later article: Claude Cahun, 'La *Salomé* d'Oscar Wilde, le procès Billing et les 47,000 pervertis du *Livre Noir*' in the *Mercure de France*, CXXVIII July 1918, pp. 69–80. This is an account of the trial in London on 29 May 1918 in which the dancer Miss Maud Allan brought a case against Mr Pemberton Billing MP for an allegedly slanderous and obscene article on her in the *Vigilante*, a paper for which he was responsible. Douglas was a witness, and the nature of his relationship with Wilde was raised. The trial had political overtones, there being a question of blackmail and the involvement of German agents. Billing was acquitted. It is a reasonable inference from the mention of the trial in Ruyters' letter to Gide of 11 June 1918 that Gide was following the affair. A similar interest is behind Gide's request to Larbaud (letter of 14 June 1913) to procure him the first edition of Arthur Ransome's *Oscar Wilde, A Critical Study* (1912), since the second edition which he had just acquired omitted 'all the passages which gave rise to the trial' (Douglas had sued Ransome unsuccessfully for insinuating that Douglas had caused Wilde's downfall and had abandoned him in his hour of need).

9. 'Subjectif', p. 107.

10. Ms. Doucet γ 1567 and γ 1573.

11. Delay, II p. 477 (*Correspondance*, p. 639: Gide's mother regularly sent him press cuttings which she thought might interest him).

12. See the full account of the proceedings in H. Montgomery Hyde, *Oscar Wilde* (London: Eyre Methuen, 1976), Chapters 5, 6 and 7. See also above, p. 103.

13. Gide–Valéry *Correspondance*. Letter to Valéry 9 July 1891 pp. 108–9: 'Paul Adam a des invoûtements et de je ne sais quelles magies' (he casts spells and magic charms).

14. Ms. Doucet γ 885.88.

15. Hugues Rebell, 'Défense d'Oscar Wilde', XV August 1895, pp. 182–90; later the same month Camille Mauclair printed a one-page review of *The Picture of Dorian Gray* in which he spoke warmly in praise of the author (pp. 237–8). A translation by H.-D. Davray of the *Ballad of Reading Gaol* was published in XXVI May 1898, pp. 356–70, and the same critic's article 'Oscar Wilde posthume' featured in LV June 1905, pp. 481–91, giving rise to further notes on this and on a partial publication of *De Profundis*, in LVI August 1905, pp. 633–8. In CXXVIII July 1918, pp. 59–68, Rachilde, referring most probably to *Oscar Wilde and Myself* (first published in 1914), spoke of Lord Alfred Douglas' recently published 'cold but correctly written' book. Mentioning the incomplete publication of *De Profundis*, she concluded that the manuscript should be burned 'for the sake of the descendants of Wilde and Douglas', thus demonstrating the limits of her libertarianism. 'Imagine what will happen in 1960,' she exclaimed, when the full manuscript is revealed.'

16. See above, pp. 170–71.

17. My translation from Davray.

18. Pages 401–29; reprinted in *Prétextes* (1947), pp. 221–52. Both articles are to be found in the English translation, *Oscar Wilde* (London: William Kimber, 1951). Gide was disinclined to write a preface for *Salomé* when invited to do so in 1916 (see Gide's letter to X, 30 May 1916, in BAAG, 62 April 1984, p. 310).

19. My translation of Gide's French: 'The Disciple', a prose poem, has a somewhat different text in O. Wilde, *The Works*, ed. G.F. Maine (London: Collins, 1948), p. 844.

20. Ms. Doucet γ 1564. See also above, p. 103.

21. Ms. Doucet γ 1567.32. *De Profundis. Aufzeichnungen und Briefe aus dem Zuchthaus in Reading*. Herausgegeben und eingeleitet von Max Meyerfield (Berlin, 1905). *De Profundis, précédé de lettres écrites... à Robert Ross, suivi de la Ballade de la geôle de Reading*. Traduits par Henry-D. Davray (Paris: Mercure de France, 1905). (The first complete edition, in English, did not appear until 1962: see *The Letters of Oscar Wilde*, ed. Rupert Hart-Davis (London: Hart-Davis, 1962), pp. 423–511.)

22. Cited in *BAAG*, 62 April 1984, p. 163.

23. *Correspondance*, p. 483.

24. See *Jahrbuch für sexuelle Zwischenstufen*, V (2) 1903, pp. 1304 ff.

25. See *Corydon*, p. 37.

26. See T. Royle, *Death before Dishonour: The True Story of Fighting Mac* (Edinburgh: Mainstream, 1982); and *Jahrbuch für sexuelle Zwischenstufen*, V (2) 1903, pp. 1322 ff. There is a reference to Macdonald's suicide in a letter to Gide from Ghéon in April 1903 (*Correspondance*, I p. 510), together with an allusion to 'the Versailles affair' (the discovery of the corpses of the director of a Belgian casino and his young chauffeur) which Gide did not understand (*ibid.*, 7 April 1903, I p. 512) and which Ghéon explained later (April, I p. 513).

27. See above, p. 96.

28. Cf. *Corydon*, p. 175. *Die Zukunft* is represented as publicly thanking the Freemason Anthime in *Les Caves du Vatican* (Pléiade, p. 705. Written between 1911 and 1914). Ruyters drew Gide's attention to the suspension of *Die Zukunft* (*Correspondance*, 15 July 1917).

29. See *Corydon*, p. 37 (a description from *Le Journal*).

30. CXXV January 1918, p. 189 ('Échos' – 'Le Droit pénal allemand dans l'avenir').

31. *Code pénal, annoté par E. Garçon*, where a full commentary is available, especially on Articles 330–5.

32. Under the Penal Code the relevant articles are the following:

Article 330 (loi du 13 mai 1863) 'Outrage public à la pudeur'. The punishment ranged from three months' to two years' imprisonment and a fine of 16 to 200 Frs. A further penalty was enacted on 21 March 1905 (modified on 6 December 1912) for those with a (specified) previous criminal record, who could be sentenced to join the light infantry in Algeria. The essence of the crime was that it had to be committed in public. 'In public' was defined as a place to which a third party had access and where he/she would be an *unintentional* witness. Certain persons (young children, or participants in an orgy) did not count as 'public'.

Article 331 (loi du 13 mai 1863) 'Attentat à la pudeur'. If such an act had been attempted, successfully or unsuccessfully – but without violence – on a child of either sex under the age of thirteen, the penalty was imprisonment. The same punishment was awarded on conviction to persons who had authority over the child so long as the child was under twenty-one and unmarried.

Article 332 (loi du 28 avril 1832) stipulated the penalty for rape (sexual intercourse with violence). If the victim was under fifteen, then the maximum penalty (forced labour for a term of years) was to be exacted.

Article 333 (loi du 13 mai 1863) stipulated the punishment for rape committed by a person who was in a position of authority over the victim.

Article 334 (loi du 3 avril 1903). This law against procuring set out the penalties (imprisonment from six months to three years and a fine of 50–5,000 Frs) for several categories of offenders. Section 1 concerned 'anyone who commits an offence against public decency by persistently inciting, encouraging or abetting the commission of vice

or the corruption of young people of either sex under 21 years of age' ('Quiconque aura
attenté aux mœurs en excitant, favorisant ou facilitant habituellement la débauche ou
la corruption de la jeunesse de l'un ou de l'autre sexe au-dessous de l'âge de 21 ans').
One notes the emphasis on 'encouragement', the need for the act to be 'habitual', and
the age of the young person – under twenty-one. Sections 2–4 dealt with procuring
women and with the white slave traffic. (The details are recorded in *Code d'instruction
criminelle et code pénal*, 15ᵉ édition (Paris: Dalloz, 1915). The substance of the enactments remains largely unchanged in a later edition of 1939.)

Two further points are of interest. The loi du 11 avril 1908 ('Concernant la
prostitution des mineurs') provided a range of penalties for minors under the age of
eighteen who habitually prostituted themselves. By far the largest number of prosecu-
tions under this law were of young girls. Articles 354–7 of the Code pénal dealt with
seduction and kidnapping of minors, but the enactments concerned girls under the age
of sixteen.

33. Page 37: Count Hohenau (from *Le Journal*).

34. Ms. Doucet γ 885.58.

35. Also: 'Les Jurés par eux-mêmes' in *L'Opinion*, 18 and 25 October 1912. Published
in volume form Paris, NRF, 1914.

36. See further A. Cullerre and L. Desclaux, 'L'Affaire Redureau – assassinat de sept
personnes par un enfant de quinze ans. Examen mental', in *Archives d'anthropologie
criminelle, de criminologie et de psychologie normale et pathologique*, XXIX 1914,
pp. 629–45 (with photograph). Gide would not have been indifferent to the age of the
youth.

37. Source: *Jahrbuch für sexuelle Zwischenstufen*, Supplt I (1910) Heft 2 pp. 173–93:
Numa Praetorius – 'Homosexuelle Ereignisse in Frankreich und in Italien'.

38. Extract given in T. d'Arch Smith, *Love in Earnest* (London: Routledge, 1970),
p. 48.

39. Ms. Doucet γ 885.42.

40. Ms. Doucet γ 885.44 and .112.

41. Ms. Doucet γ 885.41.

42. Ms. Doucet γ 885.39.

43. Ms. Doucet γ 885.40.

44. Ms. Doucet γ 885.37.

45. Ms. Doucet γ 885.38.

46. There is, for example, no reason to believe that Gide had read a report in the
Mémoires of the nineteenth-century chief of the Paris Sûreté, Louis Canler, where a
male brothel is linked with the trafficking of false coins (*Mémoires* (Paris: F. Roy,
1882), Chapter LXV 'Les Antiphysitiques et les chanteurs').

47. In the *Mercure de France*, LXIX October 1907, pp. 699–700, Rachilde reviewed
Fersen's *Une Jeunesse*, a novel which featured boy-love among other sentimental
attachments. She disliked the book.

48. Peyrefitte, p. 238.

49. Anglès, I p. 154. For the forensic evidence, see A. Bertillon, 'Affaire Renard et
Courtois (Assassinat du financier Y), document de technique policière', in *Archives
d'anthropologie criminelle, de criminologie et de psychologie normale et pathologique*, XXIV
1909, pp. 753–82.

50. Quoted above, p. 65.

51. Rouveyre, pp. 203 and 205. There is a comment in Gide's *Journal*, 11 November
1924.

52. *Œdipe* was probably begun in 1927, and first published and performed in 1931.

53. *Corydon*, p. 178.

54. '[?]' added by Gide.

55. Balzac, quoted in *Corydon*: 'Morals are a nation's hypocrisy' (p. 179). This material is in *Journal* 'Feuillets' (*circa* 1911) (vol. I p. 354), adding Diderot (see above, p. 203).

56. LXXX 'Juges', pp. 115–17.

57. This article was reviewed at length by C.H. Hirsch in the *Mercure de France*, XXXVIII May 1901, p. 497. Dubois-Desaulle also published in XLII May 1902, pp. 382–412, an article on homosexuality in early eighteenth-century France: 'Les Mignons du Marquis de Liembrune'. Gide has left no comment.

58. Ms. Doucet γ 885.28. André Raffalovich had written about the activities of homosexuals in Les Halles in Paris (Gide was probably well aware of what went on there, for the place was notorious): 'Les Groupes uranistes à Paris et à Berlin', in *Archives d'anthropologie criminelle, de criminologie et de psychologie normale et pathologique*, XIX 1904, pp. 926–36. The article was referred to in passing by Rachilde in the *Mercure de France*, LIII February 1905, p. 595.

59. *Corydon*, pp. 30–4.

60. Gide–Ghéon *Correspondance*, Préface pp. 38 and 69–72.

61. Cf. the analysis of themes in *Corydon*, above, p. 30.

62. There has been some speculation that Alexis B. may be connected with 'Armand Bavretel', who is mentioned in *Si le grain ne meurt* – see Goulet, pp. 452–6.

63. *Corydon*, pp. 34–5.

CHAPTER 10:   THE ANCIENT WORLD

1. Gide knew little or no Greek, though in an early letter to his mother (17 October 1894) he says that he managed to read Plato's *Crito*, which he had probably had to study at school, 'more or less fluently'. Despite his claims to the contrary, he read virtually no Latin apart from Vergil – and then with difficulty.

2. Reviewed in the *Mercure de France*, CXX March 1917, p. 301 by Georges Palante. The second edition (1914) dissociates friendship from Greek love; the first edition is more open on the matter.

3. There is an ms. note in German (not in Gide's hand) among the archive material, referring to Plutarch, *Amatorius* 5, Athenaeus XIII, and Lucian, *Amores* 54 (on Achilles and Patroclus, with a citation from Aeschylus' *Myrmidons* (fragment 135 Radt) in Greek): ms. Doucet γ 885.66. See also above, p. 341.

4. 'Subjectif', p. 97. Taine's text is to be found in *Essais de critique et d'histoire*, pp. 215–51.

5. 'Feuillets', p. 102; *Paradise Lost*, III 472; *Phaedo* 59 c. Gide's reference here to Cleombrotus, the disciple of Socrates who committed suicide by drowning, probably derives from an annotated edition of *Paradise Lost* (for example, *The Poetical Works*, ed. H.J. Todd (London: 1852): the punctuation of Gide's citation agrees with this text). The drowning is not mentioned in Plato, but can be found in Cicero, *Tusc.* I 84 and Montaigne, *Essais*, II 3. Gide obtained some of his knowledge of Plato from Montaigne (see 'Suivant Montaigne' in *Œuvres complètes*, XV pp. 41, 46: citing *Essais*, I 56 and III 12), and many of his references to Socrates are taken from there, too (see *Œuvres complètes*, XV p. 4 (*Essais*, III 12); p. 9 (II 6); p. 25 (III 13); p. 26 (I 11); p. 28 (III 12); p. 47 (III 12); p. 66 (III 13)). Another possible source of information is a review by Georges Palante in the *Mercure de France*, CXX March 1917, pp. 299–301 of Plato's *Le Banquet . . . traduction intégrale . . . suivie des commentaires de Plotin sur l'amour, avec . . . notes par Mario Meunier* (Paris: Payot, 1914), and of Camille Spiess' *Pédérastie et homosexualité* (Paris: L. Vanier, 1915).

6. The *Gorgias* is mentioned incidentally in a footnote to '*Au service de l'Allemagne par Maurice Barrès*' which Gide first published in *L'Ermitage*, XVI July 1905, pp. 41–5 (reprinted in *Œuvres complètes*, IV pp. 435–40). Another reference appears in a lecture, 'De l'importance du public', which Gide delivered in Weimar on 5 August 1903 (in *Nouveaux Prétextes*, pp. 28–41, see esp. p. 38): this is garbled, for an allusion to the *Gorgias*, recalling how Socrates was made angry by flattery, is coupled with a remark about how Plato forbids poets to be in his Republic, reminding us that Orpheus was a 'coward' – 'just like the musician he was' (from Phaedrus' speech at the opening of the *Symposium*).

7. Gide's extract appears in vol. II pp. 327–9 (Book VIII Chapter 1: 'Lutte de Socrate contre les sophistes'). The Gorgias in question is the real-life Gorgias (not the character in Plato's dialogue), whose ideas are discussed in a footnote on pp. 337–9. We find the remarks about Orpheus, in virtually the same words which Gide used, in Volume II p. 218, in the section entitled 'Théorie de l'amour' (Book VI Chapter 3: vol. II pp. 202–36).

8. There are references here to Aristophanes, *Knights* 876, Scholia to Aeschines, *Contra Timarchum* p. 175 a, and Gesner's *Socrates sanctus paederasta*.

9. A simple reference to Aeschines' *Against Timarchus* also occurs in a passage quoted from the French translation of Curtius (*Histoire grecque*) which was deleted from the 1920 proofs (*Corydon*, p. 172. See above, p. 172). Gide's reference, however, is to §137 (against prostitution), whereas the context obviously requires §138 (slaves prohibited from the gymnasia). There is an excellent assessment of Aeschines' speech in K.J. Dover, *Greek Homosexuality*.

10. Vol. I: Book VII Chapter 1.

11. Another section of Fouillée (vol. II: Book I) covers non-Platonic ideas on love (the Pre-Socratics; Aristotle; the Neo-Platonists).

12. *Correspondance*, p. 116.

13. Letter to his mother 17 October 1894 (*Correspondance*, p. 497).

14. Rysselberghe, I p. 113 (31 March–7 May 1921).

15. Ms. Doucet γ 885.1 and .2.

16. Ms. Doucet γ 885.72.

17. *Corydon*, p. 161.

18. *Ibid.*, p. 142.

19. *Ioläus*, p. 23, citing Plutarch, *Vit. Pelopidae* (quoted in *Corydon*, p. 169).

20. *Corydon*, p. 185 ('ami' 1920; 'amant' later editions).

21. See the Oriental chapter for a similar image, above, p. 178.

22. *Laws* 838 e and 837 b–d, quoted by Guthrie, IV p. 394.

23. 'Feuillets' (*circa* 1918), p. 671.

24. 'Ouranios', as distinct from 'Pandemos' (Vulgar, or Earthly) – the subject of Pausanias' speech in the *Symposium*.

25. §49 (Lucian, with an English translation by M.D. Macleod. Loeb Classical Library (London: Heinemann, 1921–67), vol. VIII).

26. P. Louÿs, *Journal intime* (Paris: Éditions Montaigne, 1929), 26 January 1885.

27. Dialogue 5 (trans. M.D. Macleod, Loeb Classical Library).

28. 751 a (trans. W.C. Helmbold: Plutarch's *Moralia*, Loeb Classical Library (London: Heinemann, 1927–76), vol. IX).

29. Gide does not cite this part among his remarks on Epaminondas.

30. This was probably the new edition of William Burton's sixteenth-century English version, published by the Shakespeare Head Press in 1923. There are several early translations of the novel into French. Before 1924 the most recent were by C. Zévort (1856), and A. Pons (1880).

31. 36 (trans. S. Gaselee, Loeb Classical Library (London: Heinemann, 1917)).

32. *The Loves of Cleitophon and Leucippe, Literally and Completely Translated from the Greek* (Athens: Privately printed for the Athenian Society, 1897).

33. *Vies des hommes illustres*, traduction nouvelle par Alexis Pierron 6ᵉ éd. (1882). It is an ordinary octavo edition – not 'a huge volume for pressing ecclesiastical bands' (Corydon's description, p. 167 – this would apply more appropriately to Amyot's translation, a folio copy of which Gide acquired on 1 December 1905 (*Journal*)).

34. Misspelt 'Pammenis' in *Corydon*, p. 168.

35. See the material from P. Paris cited in Appendix A.

36. *Corydon*, pp. 177, 184.

37. See above, p. 60.

38. Ms. Doucet γ 885.73, .74, .75–6.

39. Ms. Doucet γ 885.78: Pascal, VI 353 (pp. 490–1).

40. Ms. Doucet γ 885.84, .84 bis: *Vit. Ages.* xx 5.

41. Ms. Doucet γ 885.81: *Vit. Ages.* xi 7.

42. Ms. Doucet γ 885.84 bis: *Vit. Ages.* xxv 1–3.

43. *Vit. Ages.* xxxiv 6.

44. Ms. Doucet γ 885.83 and .83 bis.

45. *Corydon*, p. 171 (included after the words: 'à votre disposition', but replaced by a line of dots in later editions): *Vit. Ages.* xxxiv 6–8.

46. Ms. Doucet γ 885.63 and .80: *Vit. Lys.* xxii 3.

47. Ms. Doucet γ 885.63: *Vit. Ages.* ii 1–2.

48. Ms. Doucet γ 885.63: *Vit. Lys.* i 1–2, ii 1.

49. *Corydon*, p. 171 (included after the words: 'la chasteté, il n'y prétendait pas').

50. A short quotation from *Vit. Pelop.* xxviii 5.

51. References made by Gide by page number to Pierron's translation of *Vit. Ages.* xi 5–7 (the story of Megabates and Agesilaus); xiii 3 (Agesilaus and a young athlete); xiii 4 (Agesilaus' conduct with a sick youth whom he loved); xx 5–6 (how Agesilaus helped Agesipolis in his pursuit of handsome boys); xxv 1–3 (Agesilaus loves the handsome young Cleonymus); xxviii 6 (the noble death of Cleonymus).

52. *Corydon*, p. 162 (included after the words: 'crible expurgateur').

53. Ms. Doucet γ 885.3 and .4: *Vit. Demetr.* xix 5, xxiv 2.

54. Ms. Doucet γ 885.80: *Vit. Ag. et Cleom.* xxxvii 7.

55. *Corydon*, p. 163 (included after the words: 'tient à coeur').

56. *Biographie universelle*, art. 'Aspasie': Plutarch, *Vit. Per.* xxiv and xxxii.

57. Ms. Doucet γ 885.52: *Moralia* t. III p. 511 (*Quaest. conviv.* IV 5, 671 b):

> Montivagus cernens divinum Bacchus Adonin,
> Cyprum perlustrans egregiam, rapuit.

58. Ms. Doucet γ 885.31: *Parallela Graeca et Romana* 33.

59. *Correspondance* [? March 1933], I p. 553.

60. The footnote in Meier's book gives the reference, Plato, *Laws* VIII p. 836, not included in Martin du Gard's letter.

61. *Corydon*, p. 162 (appended to the words: 'crible expurgateur').

62. *Ioläus*, pp. 68–9. Gide later noted an entry from the index of Giguet's translation of the *Iliad*: ' "Love: a feeling much less keen than friendship", and "The god of love does not appear in the *Iliad*, but only in Vergil's *Aeneid*" ' (*Journal*, 1 September 1937, and letter to Martin du Gard 4 September 1937). Under the entry 'Friendship' Giguet writes: 'Heroic friendship is founded upon a relationship of feelings, age and, especially, a noble sharing in bold deeds and danger' (not cited by Gide).

63. Page 161: *Ioläus*, p. 73.

64. Carpenter is mistaken: Homer clearly regarded Patroclus as the elder (*Iliad*, XI 787).

65. Page 158; ed. 1924, p. 170.

66. Privately printed in 1883 and 1908, and published in the true first edition of Havelock Ellis' *Sexual Inversion* (London: Wilson & Macmillan, 1897). If, after 1918, Gide's English friends told him of this book and its companion, *A Problem in Modern Ethics*, there is no trace in his writings of any knowledge of them.

67. Above, p. 62.

68. Ms. Doucet γ 1563.31.

69. A. *Walter* (1986), p. 70.

70. *Ibid.*, p. 103; the ms. version (ms. Doucet γ 1559) is recorded *ibid.*, p. 203.

71. Ms. Doucet γ 1558.

72. Ms. Doucet γ 1560.24: 'Mais mon mal est si noir que je ne puis le dire.' The line is an alexandrine which Gide may have modelled on a tragic original (as for example Racine's *Phèdre*: 'Mon mal vient de plus loin . . . une flamme si noire' (lines 269, 310)).

73. Ms. Doucet γ 1560.

74. *Divers*, p. 42; *Dionysiaca* XI, note 15.

75. See Epaminondas and Aspasia in *Corydon*, and 'Héliodore' in *Journal*, 20 March 1905 (with inaccurate title).

76. See p. 551, *Le Traité du Narcisse*.

77. Ovid, *Metamorphoses* X 83–5 (Orpheus the founder of pederasty).

78. Ms. Doucet γ 885.70.

79. See above, p. 264.

80. Ms. Doucet γ 885.96. A frequently used symbol of boy-love, this story was retold by Rachilde in an article in the *Mercure de France*, XXVII September 1898, pp. 638–46, 'La Mort d'Antinoüs'.

81. Ms. Doucet γ 885.96. See *Poetae Melici Graeci*, ed. D. Page (Oxford, 1962), fragment 471. See above, p. 231.

82. Ms. Doucet γ 885.95.

83. Ms. Doucet γ 885.56. See further, above, pp. 235–6.

84. Delay, II p. 96. Gide asked Marcel Drouin to send him a Theocritus in April/May 1897 (see Martin, p. 189).

85. *L'Immoraliste*, pp. 398, 462; *Corydon*, p. 143; letter from Gide to M. Schwob 17 November 1928 in *NRF*, XXXII January–June 1929, p. 57.

86. Paul Desjardins, an intimate of Gide's circle, published a limited luxury edition of Theocritus: *Œuvres*, traduction nouvelle de P. Desjardins, eaux-fortes par Armand Berton (Paris: Société des Cent Bibliophiles, 1910). Gide refers to a project to publish this translation in the *NRF* in a letter to Larbaud (27 June 1911).

87. Ms. Doucet γ 1562.22.

88. *Renoncement au voyage*, III, in *Œuvres complètes*, IV p. 265 (he never quoted from it).

89. *The Poems of Virgil*, translated into English prose by J. Conington (London: Longmans, 1882). For an account of homosexuality in Vergil, see Lilja, pp. 62–70.

90. Menalcas, in Vergil, is a person on the move; he loves Amyntas (*Ecl.* III 66), the rival in singing of Mopsus (*Ecl.* IV). Mopsus, however, is not entirely homosexual (cf. *Ecl.* III 78, 'I love Phyllis above all other girls'). The song contests (on love and other themes) in *Les Nourritures terrestres* replicate the structure of these bucolic poems.

91. Cf. *Ecl.* X 35, a phrase often quoted by Gide.

92. Letter to A.R., Ravello 20 April 1897, printed in *Œuvres complètes*, II p. 480.

93. 'La Marche turque' (1914) in *Incidences*, p. 105. Cf. also as early as *Les Cahiers d'André Walter* (1986), p. 145; letter from Gide to Christian Beck 12 October 1908 in *Mercure de France*, CCCVI June 1949, p. 627; *Journal*, April 1923 (p. 756), and 7 April 1932.

94. Similarly, in *Mopsus* XII (*Œuvres complètes*, III p. 11): 'If Damon still weeps for

Daphnis [*], and Gallus for Lycoris [*Ecl.* X], let them come hither; I will guide their steps towards forgetfulness,' says Mopsus to Ménalque, (*Gide has misunderstood: in *Eclogue* VIII Damon weeps for Nysa, who has been betrothed to Mopsus, while Alphesiboeus successfully casts a spell to win the boy Daphnis for himself.)

95. The folio copy of the *Greek Anthology* in Gide's father's library (*Si le grain ne meurt*, p. 491) would have remained a closed book to him, for he could not read Greek. The pederastic love poems (including Strato's) appear in Book 12. In the standard nineteenth-century French translation by Félix Dehèque (1863) the whole of Book 12 is in Latin – which Gide might have found very difficult to translate.

96. Herodotus, I 135; *Le Livre d'amour*, p. 94.

97. *Le Livre d'amour*, p. 95; *Deipnosophistae* XIII 79.

98. 'Book XIII 81' (that is, 603 e); *Corydon*, p. 172 (Gide's references are a little garbled). *Le Livre d'amour* p. 89. Another part of the *Corydon* note refers to 'section 82'.

99. There was an ancient tradition, of which Gide was clearly unaware, to the effect that Euripides was a misogynist either because he disliked intercourse with women or because he had two wives simultaneously (Gellius, XV 20).

100. Apart from the early French translations by Marolles (1680) and Lefebvre de Villebrune (1789–92), there is a version of Book XIII by T. Sandre, which was not published until 1924 (Paris: Malfère). We have no reason to think that Gide read any of these.

101. *Nouveaux prétextes*, p. 88.

102. See above: Huysmans, *À rebours*. Laurent Tailhade's translation of Petronius appeared in 1902, and was reviewed by A.F. Hérold (a friend of Gide's) in the *Mercure de France*, XLIV October 1902, pp. 223–6 (in this number appeared Gide's response to the 'Enquête sur l'influence allemande' (pp. 835–6)).

103. A. *Walter* (1986), pp. 62–3. Martin comments *ad loc.* that Gide wrote to Roger Martin du Gard on 18 August 1947 saying that he was reading the book (in Latin) for the first time. Had Gide forgotten? or was André Walter pretending to knowledge which his creator did not possess? A third possibility is that he had previously read it in translation.

104. Book VIII 26 and 29.

105. Suetonius, *Vit. Tib.* XLIII–XLIV.

106. *Journal*, p. 217.

107. *Ibid.*, 17 March 1904.

108. *Ibid.*, p. 662.

109. Ms. Doucet γ 885.35.

110. *Mercure de France*, CVII January 1914, pp. 89–132. The same issue contained (p. 181) a review of Maurice Caullery, *Les Problèmes de la sexualité* (Paris: Flammarion, 1913), which discusses the effects of hormones, hermaphroditism and sexual polymorphism in animals.

111. See, for a fuller discussion: J.N. Adams, *The Latin Sexual Vocabulary* (London: Duckworth, 1982); and D'A. W. Thompson, *A Glossary of Greek Birds* (Oxford: OUP 1936).

112. Gide made no specific reference to G. Duviquet's *Héliogabale*, with a preface by Gourmont (see above, p. 75), which was reviewed by Ghéon in *L'Ermitage*, XIV August 1903, p. 303 ('A curious compilation of contradictory texts'), nor to Émile Sicard's tragedy *Héliogabale*, with music by Déodat de Séverac, performed in Béziers in 1910 and in Paris in 1911 (see the *Mercure de France*, LXXXVIII September 1910, pp. 356–8, and XC April 1911, p. 642: the Emperor's favourite, Claudian, becomes a Christian and falls in love with Coelia).

113. *Corydon*, pp. 139–40: Diodorus Siculus, V 32; Aristotle, *Politica* 5–6 (the ms.

445

reads 'II 6 (7)', the printed text has 'II 6–7'). Private collection.
114. Gide's reference is garbled, but the words he quotes come from J. Barthélemy St Hilaire's bilingual edition of the *Politics* (Paris, 1837).
115. Ms. Doucet γ 885.73: *Histoire grecque* (1883), II p. 567.
116. Pierre Quillard had published in the *Mercure de France*, XXXIV April 1900, pp. 149–56, a translation of this anecdote (preserved in Athenaeus, XIII 603–4), together with other extracts from Athenaeus (VIII 360 and XIII 575) and Plutarch, under the general title 'Hellenica'.
117. *Corydon*, p. 165 (included after the words: 'quelque infirmité'); Curtius, I p. 172 (Book 2 Chapter 1). Since they did not possess the imagination of the Achaeans, Curtius avers, and, unlike them, did not record the history of their race, they were 'less able to embroider the incidents of their existence as the Ionians would have done. They devoted their thoughts and their strength to the practical aspects of life – to the accomplishment of serious and useful duties.'
118. *Corydon*, p. 172 (as a footnote to the words: 'entendre par là'). Curtius, V p. 113 (Book 7 Chapter 2).
119. See above, pp. 59–60.
120. Ms. Doucet γ 885.91.
121. Becker (1854), II p. 207. (There are many references and quotations in Greek in this 'Excursus' which Gide did not use.)
122. The phrase between square brackets was added as an afterthought to the ms.
123. *Thésée*, p. 1441.
124. See W. Poole, 'Male Homosexuality in Euripides', in A. Powell (ed.), *Euripides, Women, and Sexuality* (London: Routledge, 1990), pp. 108–50.
125. Euripides, *Hippolytus* 615 ff.
126. 'Pentheus refuses to acknowledge Bacchus through a lack of understanding [*défaut d'intelligence*]', *Incidences*, p. 126. See above, pp. 309–10.

CHAPTER 11:   THE ORIENT

1. *Correspondance*, I p. 185. The scene and song are repeated in 'Amyntas. Nouvelles feuilles de route', November–December 1903 (*L'Ermitage*, XVI February 1905, pp. 65–83).
2. *Prétextes*, p. 126.
3. Ms. Doucet γ 885.85.
4. Gide describes his first meeting with J.C. Mardrus in Marseilles in a letter to Valéry 7 January 1898, saying (*ibid.* 12 January) that he was to have dined with him; on 24 July 1899 Valéry wrote to Gide asking for Mardrus' address (see Martin, pp. 253–4).
5. Reviewed in *L'Ermitage*, 1899, reprinted in *Prétextes*, pp. 126–33 and 175–85.
6. *Prétextes*, p. 128.
7. *Ibid.*, p. 130.
8. IV, pp. 214–7.
9. VI, pp. 65–75.
10. *Prétextes*, p. 181.
11. Ruyters' letters to Gide 12 and 16 July 1918, with Gide's reply 14 July (a copy of the Benares edition in sixteen vols).
12. Martin, p. 100.
13. Ms. Doucet γ 1567.
14. *Prétextes*, pp. 131–3. Gide recommended Hammer's translation, which he 'constantly re-read . . . the one referred to by Goethe', to Ruyters on 25 July 1898.

On 12 June 1902 Ruyters wrote and asked Gide if he knew Groulleau's translation (published in Paris by Charles Carrington (see *Prétextes*, p. 131)). In this connection we should notice that on 12 September 1902 Ruyters sent Gide Carrington's catalogue which included many libertine 'anthropological' and 'medical' books in French and English, as, for example, *The Ethnology of the Sixth Sense. Its Anomalies, Perversions and Follies*, [*circa* 1900], and J. Rosenbaum, *The Plague of Lust* (1901). On 30 October 1908 Gide wrote to Larbaud, congratulating him on his review of James Blyth's book on Fitzgerald and 'Posh', Fitzgerald's fisherman companion (in *La Phalange*, 15 October 1908).

15. *Corydon*, p. 173.

16. Cited in Martin, p. 353.

17. Ms. Doucet γ 885.67.

18. Translated into French in its entirety and commented upon by Jules Mohl in seven volumes in 1876-8. An extensive preface deals with the life of the poet and the historical background to the events narrated. There is a separate translation of part of the work: *Histoire de Minoutchehr selon le Livre des Rois* (Paris; Piazza, 1919).

19. *L'Ermitage*, IX July 1898, p. 58. There is a review of Franz Toussaint's translation by Edmond Pilon in *NRF*, IX March 1913, pp. 503-5.

20. I have used here *The Gulistan or Rose Garden*, trans. E. Rehatsek (London: Allen & Unwin, 1964), pp. 182-204.

21. It was briefly reviewed by Ghéon in *L'Ermitage*, XIV March 1903, p. 222.

22. Gide uses the image of the sleeping cup-bearer, but represents him as watched over by Hafiz, in *Les Nourritures terrestres* (Pléiade, p. 225).

23. XLVIII December 1903, pp. 658-65 (poems); pp. 767-9 (novel).

24. *Journal*, I pp. 543, 551.

25. It was briefly reviewed in the *Mercure de France*, CXII November 1915, p. 723, and is in the same series as *Hungry Stones and Other Stories by Sir Rabindranath Tagore* (see above, Chapter 8, note 49).

26. There is a reference to Nerval's *Voyage en Orient* in a book list written by Gide in about 1887 (ms. Doucet γ 1556.57).

27. The principal texts are the following: Genesis 19 (the story of Sodom); Leviticus 18:22 (Mosaic prohibition), 20:13 (capital punishment inflicted for homosexual behaviour); Judges 19:22-5 (the incident at Gibeah – a parallel to the Sodom story); 1 Samuel 20:41 (David and Jonathan: 'they kissed one another, and wept one with another, until David exceeded'); 2 Samuel 1:26 (David and Jonathan; 'thy love to me was wonderful, passing the love of women'); Romans 1:26-7 (homosexuality as a punishment for rejecting God); 1 Corinthians 6:9-10 (Pauline condemnation of homosexuality); 1 Timothy 1:9-10 (Pauline condemnation of homosexuality); Jude 7 (the punishment of Sodom). To this list we should add Genesis 38:9 (Onan spilling his seed).

28. 1887-90. Ms. Doucet γ 1559, reproduced in A. *Walter* (1986), p. 206.

29. *Correspondance*, p. 18 (letter XXIII). Lot's wife is presented as a symbol of the need to look forward in *Journal*, 'Feuillets' (1911), p. 347, and *ibid.*, 8 November 1931. See also above, p. 319 (*Les Nouvelles Nourritures*).

CHAPTER 12:   SIXTEENTH AND SEVENTEENTH
CENTURIES

1. *Journal*, I p. 21, and 'Subjectif', p. 97 (15 June 1891).

2. Gide published two articles on Montaigne: 'Essai sur Montaigne' (*Commerce*, XVIII

Winter 1928, pp. 7–48), and 'Suivant Montaigne' (*NRF*, XXXII June 1929, pp. 745–66). Both are conveniently printed in *Œuvres complètes*, XV pp. 1–68, and in the authorised English translation by Stephen Guest and Trevor Blewitt in 1929. In 1939, Gide published *Les Pages immortelles de Montaigne* consisting of a new preface largely derived from the 'Essai' together with extracts from Montaigne including material on his friendship with La Boétie (pp. 66–7: *Essais*, I 27), on marriage (p. 132; *Essais*, III 5), and on the laws of nature (pp. 198–9; *Essais*, III 13).

3. 'Subjectif', p. 71 (ms. Doucet γ 1552).

4. *Corydon*, p. 47: 'De la Coutume' (*Essais*, I 23).

5. *Montaigne* (trans. Guest), p. 65. In this chapter, the authorised translation by Guest and Blewitt is used where indicated.

6. *Montaigne*, p. 90: *Essais*, III 316.

7. (Trans. Guest), p. 34.

8. Gide does not distinguish here between the first, second and third editions of the *Essais*, only between material in the earlier and later sections.

9. (Trans. Guest, using Florio's translation of the *Essais*), pp. 43–4.

10. (Trans. Guest), pp. 46–7.

11. *Journal*, 21 March 1906, and 'Feuillets' (*circa* 1911) in *Journal*, I pp. 353–4.

12. The passage between angle brackets is cited in *Montaigne* (trans. Guest), pp. 93–4. The sophist in question is Bion of Borysthenes, a hedonist Scythian philosopher (*circa* 325–255 BC) – see Plutarch, *Amatorius* 220 b (= fragment 15 Mullach = F56 Kindstrand, who comments 'as the two heroes killed the tyrant, so the beard puts an end to the tyranny of love').

13. *Montaigne* (trans. Guest), pp. 31–2. We may observe (and Gide seems not to have been aware of this) that la Boétie contributed notes and critical suggestions on Plutarch's *Dialogue on Love* to Ferron for his Latin translation published by J. de Tournes (Lyon, 1557). He also wrote a poem 'Hermaphroditus' in answer to one by Auratus entitled 'De Androgyno et Senatu semestri'. See R. Dezeimeris, *Remarques et corrections d'É. de la Boétie sur le traité de Plutarque intitulé ΕΡΩΤΙΚΟΣ . . .* (Bordeaux: G. Gounouilhou, 1867).

14. 'Étienne de la Boétie, l'ami de Montaigne' *Causeries du lundi* (1882–5), vol. IX pp. 140–61.

15. Ms. Doucet γ 1552.

16. *Les Pages immortelles . . .* , preface, p. 27.

17. This is a possible source for the illustrations from La Fontaine and La Bruyère in *Corydon*, pp. 95 and 185.

18. Ed. Ristelhuber, I p. 178.

19. I 15: 'Que notre désir s'accroit par la malaisance'. *Corydon*, p. 127.

20. II 8: 'De l'affection des pères aux enfants'. For homosexual activity among the Celts, see above, p. 171.

21. *Montaigne* (trans. Guest), p. 56.

22. I 30: 'De la modération' (Cicero, *De officiis* I 40). This *Essai* is not the source for the remarks about Sophocles in *Corydon*. See above p. 168.

23. Ms. Doucet γ 885.57 and .59. This edition was brought to Gide's attention by Ruyters on 22 June 1907.

24. Gide cites this, beginning at 'certain Portuguese', and ending at 'd'Ancona', indicating the ellipsis after 'lived together'. Alessandro d'Ancona's edition of the *Journal de voyage* was published in 1889.

25. *Voyage*, p. 239.

26. Gide could also have remembered the brief account of Muret in the preface to Havelock Ellis' *Sexual Inversion* (trans. van Gennep).

27. *Mercure de France*, XIX September 1896, pp. 533–5; reprinted in Gourmont's

Épilogues, série I pp. 70–3.
28. I p. 140 (Chapter 10).
29. *Œuvres* (1875): Dialogue IV, with the text reading 'ou bien peu'.
30. Ms. Doucet γ 885.65.
31. Gide recorded reading some Calderón (but not this play) in his 'Subjectif', p. 64, in 1893. There is also a request to Valéry in a letter dated September 1893 (*Correspondance*, p. 186) to verify a quotation from *La Vida es sueño* (trans. Damas Hinard, p. 368).
32. *Journal*, I p. 98: 'Méditation II' (*circa* 1896).
33. *Journal* (1906), I p. 200.
34. *Journal*, 27 June 1908.
35. *Ibid.*, 9 and 14 February 1916. Cf. also 16 October 1918 (I p. 659).
36. Cf. also *Numquid et tu . . . ?* in *Journal*, I p. 601.
37. *Corydon*, pp. 47, 48, 53.
38. Referred to in *Journal*, I p. 97 (*circa* 1896) (Gide's quotation is marked with angle brackets), and I p. 723 ('Feuillets', *circa* 1921). See further above, pp. 348–9.
39. Ms. Doucet γ 885.87.
40. Ms. Doucet γ 1563.14. The *Histoire amoureuse des Gaules* chronicles the period *circa* 1634–59. Gide's reference ('Chap. II' – the work is not so divided) suggests an imperfectly remembered verbal recommendation. The text may be found in R. de Bussy-Rabutin, *Histoire amoureuse des Gaules* (1856–76), III pp. 345–509.
41. Bussy-Rabutin, *Histoire amoureuse des Gaules*, III p. 360.
42. The 1920 edition of *Corydon*, when referring to this quotation two pages later, erroneously puts 'quinze' (fifteen), subsequently corrected in order to maintain textual consistency. The lower limit of 'treize' (thirteen) may well be a slip – or a sign of Corydon's preferences.

CHAPTER 13:   THE ENLIGHTENMENT AND AFTER IN FRANCE

1. Contrast the quotation in *Corydon*, p. 50: 'If with all that you don't fall in love [with a woman] then you've been badly brought up' (A. Dumas *fils*, Preface to *La Question d'argent*).
2. (1865) I p. 222; the work is also cited in Gide's *Journal*, 17 December 1916. The supposititious *Mémoires de Mademoiselle Quinault aînée* (Paris: C. Allardin, 1836), a farrago of sentimental tittle-tattle actually written by Baron E.L. La Mothe-Houdancourt, are not relevant, despite the coincidence that Mlle Quinault fell in love with a heterosexual youth named Alexis (called Mademoiselle Alexis by his rivals at the Comédie Française) whose graceful charms she describes (Chapters 12–13). There is no reason to believe that Gide knew the book.
3. See above, Chapter 9 note 57, for the Marquis de Liembrune.
4. *Corydon*, p. 29.
5. *Correspondance*, nouvelle édition par L. Perey et G. Maugras (Paris: C. Lévy, 1881). (There is another edition of this date edited by E. Asse.)
6. For example he wrote to her on 15 September 1770: 'Man is made for enjoyment or suffering; let us enjoy life and let us try not to suffer. It is our fate.' And again, he wrote on 9 November 1776: 'After much reflection, I believe that the most colourless person would be the greatest man of our age, for he would let all evils [*maux*] continue to exist (and that is necessary), while giving the impression that he wished to cure them (and that is also necessary). Turgot, who seriously wished to cure things, fell from power;

Terray, who openly said he wanted to cure nothing, was execrated; a colourless man would say what Turgot said, and would do what Terray did, and everything would work splendidly.' On 22 November 1777, he wrote to her daughter, the Vicomtesse de Belsunce, on Mme d'Épinay's poor state of health: 'And I hope that even if she is not in a hurry to become well she will live and will eventually be cured of everything – except old age.'

7. *Lord Jim*, Chapter 20. Gide wrote to Ruyters on 23 March 1912 that he was reading the novel 'very slowly'.

8. *Journal*, I p. 354, with reference to the *Supplément* 'Part IV, p. 205. Édition du Centenaire'.

9. See above, p. 59.

10. See above, p. 115.

11. Édition du Centenaire, p. 208.

12. See Diderot, *Œuvres philosophiques* (1956), pp. 328–9.

13. Page 376. Contrast the strictures of Tardieu and the medical encyclopaedias mentioned above.

14. Ms. Doucet γ 1563.14.

15. *Corydon*, p. 40.

16. See Lilja, pp. 112–21 (the scope of the *Lex Scantinia* is obscure). For a brief summary of the views of Voltaire see J. Stockinger, 'Homosexuality and the French Enlightenment' (who argues that Voltaire was more tolerant), in Stambolian, *Homosexualities*, pp. 161–85.

17. Ms. Doucet γ 885.71.

18. *NRF*, 1 April 1913, pp. 533–41.

19. Gide's note of purchase, May 1891; and a quotation of the same date: '"I want not to be good" – Stendhal in the Supplement to *De l'amour*' (ms. Doucet γ 1563).

20. Published, Paris: Édouard Champion, 1925. Gide finished writing the preface on 16 June 1921, that is between the private and public editions of *Corydon* (*Journal des Faux-Monnayeurs*, p. 46).

21. *Journal*, 8 December 1907.

22. Ms. Doucet γ 1561.28.

23. The case of Octave is a very particular one indeed, since, as is well known, the book was composed largely as a literary joke at the expense of Stendhal's contemporary the Duchesse de Duras, who was reputed to specialise in describing situations which were considered grotesque. Hence we should be cautious about taking Octave's 'problem' too seriously.

24. Ms. Doucet γ 1559.41, cited in A. *Walter* (1986), p. 209.

25. Ms. Doucet γ 1563.4 (post-1889), referring to Gautier's short biography of Balzac (ed. 1859, pp. 154–7) in which there is no mention of the possible homosexual content of the play, but of the political scandal.

26. Hunt calls him 'a kindly nanny' and a 'diabolic gangster' (p. 425).

27. 'Balzac du côté de Sodome', *L'Année balzacienne* (1979), pp. 147–77. See also Marguerite Drevon and Jeannine Guichardet, 'Fameux sexorama', *ibid.* (1972), pp. 257–74 (examples of true and alleged male friendships in Balzac, together with an analysis of the relationship of Vautrin and Lucien de Rubempré).

28. Berthier (p. 150) also cites *Le Père Goriot*: Vautrin deliberately takes the beautiful young man's crime upon himself – 'a gesture of chivalrous pederasty [*pédérastie chevaleresque*]' (éd. Pléiade, p. 189). Proust, in *Contre Sainte-Beuve* (éd. Pléiade, pp. 273–4), and Charlus, in *À la recherche du temps perdu* (II p. 1050), see in episodes from *Illusions perdues* and *Le Père Goriot* examples of Vautrin's homosexuality.

29. Cited by Hunt, p. 365. See Berthier, pp. 160–4.

30. See also M. Delcourt, 'Deux Interprétations romanesques du mythe de

l'androgyne' (1972). It is further to be noted that a novel by Hyacinthe de Latouche, *Fragoletta* (1829), in a similar vein, features a hermaphrodite loved by a man and a woman.

31. A. *Walter* (1986), pp. 43, 118.

32. Ms. Doucet γ 1560.45.

33. 'Subjectif', p. 71.

34. *Journal*, 9 April 1908: M. Pézard, '*Salammbô* et l'archéologie punique', *Mercure de France*, LXXI February 1908, pp. 622–38.

35. Gide made several notes of Flaubert's sources in his 'Objectif' (ms. Doucet γ 1563.12), but included nothing explicitly homosexual.

36. Gide further reports reading *Albertus, ou l'âme et le péché* aloud, and being stopped by his mother at a particularly sensual (heterosexual) passage (*Si le grain ne meurt*, p. 489).

37. 'Subjectif', p. 73. The supplement (in square brackets) is in ms. Doucet γ 1552.

38. *Corydon*, p. 141 (where 'Xanthé' is a misprint for 'Ianthé' and the italics are Gide's). The edition used is the first (Paris: F. Renduel, 1835–6).

39. 'Subjectif', p. 94.

40. Cf. Foucault, p. 59.

41. *Mademoiselle de Maupin*, ed. A. Boschot (Paris: Garnier, 1966).

42. 'Subjectif', p. 86 (12 May 1891) – there is a confused reference to *À cœur perdu* and *Cœur en peine*. *À cœur perdu* is illustrated with a lascivious engraving by Félicien Rops, showing a nude woman bound to the tree of knowledge by a serpent (reproduced in Bory (1977), p. 59): see above, p. 411. Cf. Gide's reference to his mother's visit to the Peladan exhibition (*Correspondance*, 25 March 1892, p. 134), and her warning to him not to be trapped by Rosicrucianism (24 May 1894, p. 379).

43. A short but enthusiastic review of *L'Androgyne* appeared next to a notice of *Les Cahiers d'André Walter* in the *Mercure de France*, II June 1891, pp. 368–9.

44. Similar material by Peladan appeared in *Akadémos* in 1909 (see above, p. 251) and in the *Mercure de France*, LXXXIV April 1910, pp. 634–51, 'Théorie plastique de l'androgyne'.

45. Paris: Éd. GLM, 1938.

46. 'Péd. Maldoror – p. 254 à 261' – ms. Doucet γ 885.53, probably to be dated to the time of composition of *Corydon* and his discovery of the sixth *Chant*. The edition he used was issued in 1874. Gide wrote to Ruyters on 23 November 1905: 'Like me, you probably know the work imperfectly. I have opened it many times, read a few pages haphazardly and shut it up again, bored by its monotonous tone and put off by its lack of psychology – although quite strongly affected by its lyricism.'

47. Ms. Doucet γ 1563. Gide sold this copy in 1925 (*Catalogue de vente*, Hôtel Drouot 27–28 April 1925, item 197).

48. O'Brien (Lautréamont), pp. 54–8; Steel (Lautréamont), p. 283. *Les Nourritures terrestres*, p. 186 (first published in 'Le Récit de Ménalque', *L'Ermitage*, VII January, 1896, pp. 1–8); *Maldoror, Chant* 1.

49. From a doorway, Maldoror watches a quiet candle-lit family scene composed of mother, father and young son; the son is sent into the next room to fetch the scissors. In Gide's narrative, Ménalque watches through a window; the father sits by the lamp, the mother is sewing, and the child is seated, studying, near his father. Gide made no comment on O'Brien's ideas when he was sent a copy of his article, although he commended his book, *The Novel of Adolescence in France* (1937), in warm but somewhat conventional terms (see Gide–O'Brien *Correspondance*, pp. 3–6). Steel's other suggested parallels are less convincing: Éric, the swan-slayer in *Le Voyage d'Urien*, is not, I feel, sufficiently close to Maldoror dislodging the nests of sea birds, even though both occur in a polar seascape (see above, p. 307). The scissors referred to in

Lautréamont's family scene may have suggested Moktir's theft in *L'Immoraliste*, but this, too, is problematic.

50. Gide was especially amused by the fact that only his wife and Larbaud had spotted the 'similarity in tone' between *Les Caves* (the rescue from the fire) and *Maldoror* (letter to Larbaud, 22 January 1914).

51. 'Subjectif', p. 103; 'extravagant praise' (ms. Doucet γ 1552). The other poets about whom Verlaine wrote were Mallarmé, Marceline Desbordes-Valmore, Villiers de l'Isle-Adam and himself ('Pauvre Lélian'); he also discussed *Les Amours jaunes* of Tristan Corbière, whom he characterised as 'that child of the heather and the shore', a Breton with a ferocious love of the sea. Corbière's brutal charm is well illustrated by a moving extract on the death of a friend which Verlaine quotes.

52. Ms. Doucet γ 1563. He read Rimbaud intensively during August 1894 (letter to Valéry, 3 September 1894, *Correspondance*, pp. 213–4: 'the copy of *Les Illuminations* which you gave me').

53. Ms. Doucet γ 1564.54.

54. Probable date: letter reported in BAAG, 62 April 1984, p. 303.

55. Plutarch, *Vit. Lycurgi* viii 1 (the boy died, having had his bowels torn out by the animal's teeth).

56. See *Journal, ad loc.*

57. Ms. Doucet γ 885.92–6.

58. *Paul Verlaine* (1907). The book was reviewed, together with E. Delahaye, *Rimbaud*, by Jean de Gourmont in the *Mercure de France*, LXVII June 1907, pp. 498–501: the critic speaks of their 'strange fellowship' ('leur singulière amitié') but does not mention homosexuality.

59. Anglès, I p. 110. The date given there (1908) cannot however be correct.

60. LXXXIV March 1910, pp. 236–44.

61. CV September 1913, pp. 449–82.

62. CXXIX September 1918, pp. 5–35.

63. Ms. Doucet γ 885.96 verso.

64. Gourmont, *Le Livre des masques*, I pp. 161–4 (referred to in *Journal*, 23 November 1905).

65. Another parallel with the theme of 'vagabondage' in Gide.

66. 'We retorted with courage, joy and potatoes.'

67. 'For our passions insolently and immoderately satisfied, bringing jubilation to our minds, brought everything – youth and friendship – to our senses which were entirely reassured. And our hearts, ah! now free from women who are pitied and seduced, free from the ultimate prejudice, leaving misgivings and fear of orgies to the good hermit, since, once the boundary is crossed, Ponsard recognises no more limits.'

68. These are possibly echoes from *Ioläus*.

69. 'The happiness of two men living together, better than the model married couple that we're not, each contributing sums of strong and faithful feelings to the common store.'

70. After Verlaine's divorce, his son eventually became employed in the Métro; his father never saw him agin.

71. These accusations were possibly even of a straightforwardly political nature, designed to rid the extreme democratic party in Athens of a difficult opponent.

72. An interesting reference is to be found in Stendhal's *Lucien Leuwen*, where Lucien's father sends him to the Opéra accompanied by a bevy of girls to allay suspicions that 'he might be a Saint-Simonien'.

73. 'There is nothing in modern and ancient legend more noble and more fine than two friends', *Bonheur* XV.

74. 'Émile Verhaeren', Conférence, 1920, in *Œuvres complètes*, X p. 4.

75. *Journal*, I pp. 13, 671.
76. *Journal sans dates* (*circa* 1909) in *Œuvres complètes*, VI p. 40.
77. Pléiade, p. 1150.
78. 'Verlaine et Mallarmé', Conférence, 22 November 1913, in *Œuvres complètes*, VII pp. 409–43; see *ibid.*, p. 430.
79. Republished with a detailed preface by J.-P. Corsetti and J.-P. Giusto (Paris: Le Livre à venir, 1985). Gide never mentions Rimbaud's *Les Stupra*, a collection of three obscene sonnets first published in 1923.
80. 'Subjectif", p. 103.
81. See above, p. 164.
82. Iseler, p. 99.
83. X pp. 233–42, 324–32; XI pp. 56–66, 145–53, 262–9; XII pp. 41–56, 163–76, 234–48.
84. *Les Scandales de Londres dévoilés par la 'Pall-Mall Gazette'. Traduction littérale des articles de ce journal* (Paris: E. Dentu, 1885).
85. XIII January 1895, pp. 94–8.
86. 'Subjectif', p. 93.
87. *Ibid.*, p. 79.
88. 1893: *Journal*, I p. 40.
89. *Nouveaux prétextes*, p. 102 (originally published in *NRF*, III April 1910, pp. 425–37); Gide refers to Gourmont's article of 1903.
90. Ms. Doucet γ 885.82 (recto and verso): akin to the debate on Perrier's ideas (*Corydon*, pp. 124–5).
91. On Gide's connections with Louÿs, see: H.P. Clive, *Pierre Louÿs* (1978); Martin, esp. pp. 56–7; P. Iseler, *Les Débuts d'A. Gide vus par P. Louÿs* (1937). To these can be added a curious ms. note (ms. Doucet γ 1560.58), probably to be dated 28 March 1889, in which Gide replied to Louÿs' dream of going to the Opéra dressed as a woman, by saying that he would prefer them to go to Venice together – himself as Harlequin, 'light and graceful', and Louÿs as Columbine, 'as pretty and as feminine as possible'. The fantasy includes gondolas, serenades, and the two friends walking arm in arm: it features on another ms. page (γ 1558.31, probably to be dated between March and July 1889), where the transvestite element is omitted. Gide wrote to Louÿs in somewhat similar terms on 18 September 1891: 'We are like two girlfriends, for we are so little like men really. You go with me in my aesthetic dreams. We are like Alcaeus and Sappho' (cited in Delay, II p. 61).
92. Reprinted in Louÿs, *Œuvres complètes*, XI pp. 21–32 (where it is dated 27 December 1905).
93. We read with interest in the *Mercure de France*, XXVII September 1898, p. 835 of a mixed nudist colony at Veldes on the then Austrian coast of the Adriatic where, presumably, ideals similar to those advocated by Louÿs were practised. Later still (*ibid.*, LXXVI November 1908, p. 122), a review by Henri Mazel appeared of Louis Fiaux, *Un Nouveau Régime de mœurs* (Paris: F. Alcan, 1908) (proposing properly supervised public *voluptuaria*), and of Alfred Naquet, *Vers l'union libre* (Paris: Juven, 1908) (on free divorce).
94. Reprinted in Louÿs, *Œuvres complètes*, XI pp. 101–37.
95. Stora-Lamarre, p. 90.
96. Louÿs, *Œuvres complètes*, VIII p. 45.
97. *Journal*, I p. 232.
98. Iseler, p. 28. (Emmanuèle, shortened to 'Em', was also the affectionate name which Gide gave to his wife Madeleine.)
99. See 'Autour de M. Barrès' in *Prétextes*, pp. 45–66 (articles dated 1897–1902).
100. Ms. Doucet γ 1560 (together with a reading of Maurice Rollinat, *Les Névroses*

(Paris: Charpentier, 1883; often reissued) – a volume of decadent poetry in the style of Baudelaire).

101. Gide refers to Zola himself almost uniquely in the context of the Dreyfus Affair; other allusions are perfunctory. Homosexuality is presented in some of Zola's novels, notably *Nana* and *La Curée*, as yet another form of degeneracy (see P. Pollard, 'Variations on the Myth of the Androgyne: Scientism in Zola', in H. Cockerham and E. Ehrman (eds), *Ideology and Religion in French Literature. Essays in honour of Brian Juden* (Camberley: Porphyrogenitus, 1989), pp. 305–19).

102. Ms. Doucet γ 885.43.

103. In the *Mercure de France*, I July 1890, p. 251, there appeared a short notice of a novel, *Sébastien Roch* by Octave Mirbeau: 'The adventures of a boy spoiled by onanistic manoeuvres caused by his Jesuit teachers' – the hero grows up to become a (hetero-sexual) soldier. Similarly, in II May 1891, p. 315, Michel Réallès' *Puberté* was briefly reviewed: 'Poems where the author performs distasteful [*pénibles*] variations on the theme of masculine or feminine prostitution'.

104. A very early example of the use of the word 'homosexualité' in French.

105. Eekhoud was also the author of *Le Cycle patibulaire*. Gide was in contact with him on 30 April 1900, thanking him for having an article published for him in *La Réforme* (Bibl. royale Albert 1er, *Présence d'A. Gide* (1970), p. 44). See also Gide–Douglas *Correspondance*, p. 497 note 79; and above, p. 263. Gide first met Eekhoud when staying with Ruyters in Brussels (see Gide's letter to Ruyters, 18 January 1897), and Eekhoud was one of the first to receive a signed copy of *Saül* (letter to Ruyters, mid-January 1904, *Correspondance*, I p. 178. See also *ibid.*, I pp. 18, 152).

106. XXXVI December 1900, pp. 837–43 (see in addition XXXIV June 1900, p. 814; XXXVII January 1901, pp. 235–44; XXXVII March 1901, pp. 835–44). He also described a recent performance of Gluck's *Iphigénie en Tauride*, analysing at length the noble love of Oreste and Pylade, which, in his opinion, dominates the opera (XXXIV June 1900, p. 814).

107. XXXV–XXXVI September–November 1900.

108. Note should also be taken of several books about adolescents published at this date: Ferri-Pisani, *Les Pervertis, roman d'un potache* (Paris: Librairie Universelle, 1905), set in a lay boarding school, reviewed by Rachilde in *Mercure de France*, LIII February 1905, p. 595; Achille Essebac, *Dédé* (Paris: Ambert, 1901); Jean Rodez, *Adolescents*, the story of a young man in a Jesuit college who resists all temptations, reviewed by Rachilde, *ibid.*, XLIX March 1904, pp. 738–9; Jean Bosc, *Le Vice marin*, includes a fourteen-year-old's diary of life on board ship: 'The famous nautical vice is just what you think – only with more of a sway' - Rachilde's review, *ibid.*, LIV March 1905, pp. 105–6; Jacques Adelsward-Fersen, *Lord Lyllian*, not explicitly homosexual, but very decadent, reviewed *ibid.*, LIV April 1905, p. 575 (see above, p. 133); Henry Mirande, *Élagabal*, reviewed *ibid.*, LXXXIII February 1910, p. 692; L.B., *Pédérastie passive, ou mémoires d'un enculé* [Paris, 1911], a pornographic description of an adolescent's experiences in boarding school, leading to an enjoyable life of vice with a rich admirer when he reaches his twenties.

109. Anglès, I pp. 67–8, records that it was finished in 1905.

110. *Ibid.*, I p. 159.

111. Ms. Doucet γ 885.36.

112. Ms. Doucet γ 1581.

113. *Mercure de France*, LXXVII February 1909 pp. 575–6 (NRF) and pp. 712–15 (Akadémos).

114. LXXVIII March 1909, pp. 354–5; LXXIX May 1909, pp. 160, 345; LXXX August 1909, p. 730; LXXXI September 1909, pp. 327–8; LXXXII November 1909, p. 354.

115. I April 1909, pp. 229–40.

116. Printed in the contents as 'Debrouze'.

117. See above, p. 134.

118. Anglès, I p. 140.

119. After the publication of *Corydon* another short-lived homophile periodical, *Inversions*, appeared in late 1924. Barbedette and Carrassou (p. 165) plausibly suggest that this is the work referred to by Gide in a letter to Valéry, 11 January 1925 (the issue for 1 January 1925 contains a favourable article on *Corydon*).

120. Painter, II pp. 106–7.

121. Actually Chapter 13 in both the Gallimard edition (1954: the date of first publication) and the English translation by S. Townsend Warner (London: Chatto & Windus, 1958). It was deliberately excluded by the editors of the Pléiade edition of *Contre Sainte-Beuve* (1971).

122. *Journal*, I p. 543.

123. Fragments of *À la recherche* began to appear in the *NRF*, XI June 1914. Negotiations for publishing the book by the NRF had started in November 1911 through approaches to Copeau and Gallimard (Painter, II pp. 185–6; *Correspondance* (ed. Kolb), XI, letters 142–4, 146, 160). Gide wrote to Proust on 20 March 1914 to suggest that the rest of the book should be published by the NRF since Proust was under no contractual obligation to Bernard Grasset, the publisher of the early volumes.

124. Letter from Antoine Bibesco to Proust, July 1912 (according to Painter). See the letter from Proust to Reynaldo Hahn [17/18 August 1912]: 'I learned before I left Paris that Gide and Ghéon, separately, were not just satisfied with a vague form of Platonism. And the details I learned made Ghéon's hypocrisy in his articles on *Saint Sébastien* in the *N.R.F.* [H. Ghéon, 'M. D'Annunzio et l'art. À propos du Martyre de St. Sébastien', VI July 1911, pp. 5–16] all the more revolting' (*Correspondance* (ed. Kolb), XI, and note *ad loc.*).

125. The *salons* of Joseph de Heredia and Mary Finaly: see Painter, I p. 140. According to Delay (II p. 128), Gide first met Proust at the house of Gabriel Trarieux on 1 May 1891. Proust refers to not having seen Gide 'for twenty years' in a letter to Jacques Copeau [15 November 1913] (*Correspondance* (ed. Kolb), XII, and note *ad loc.*).

126. Cf. Baudelaire's cynical maxim: 'We love women in proportion to their difference from us. To love intelligent women is a pleasure known to pederasts. So bestiality excludes pederasty' (*Fusées*, ed. A. Guyaux (Paris: Gallimard, 1986), no. 6, p. 69).

127. *NRF*, XI June 1914, pp. 921–69. Letter of 6 June 1914, with Kolb's note *ad. loc.* (= À *l'ombre des jeunes filles en fleurs* (éd. Pléiade), I pp. 658–61 and 751–67).

128. *Correspondance* (ed. Kolb), XIII, letter 141: Kolb notes that Gide is referring to Baron Doäzan, who died in Paris on 10 April 1907.

129. Substantially the same points are made in the earlier 'La Race maudite' (éd. Pléiade, II pp. 601–32).

130. But note the satirical portrait of M. de Vaugoubert, a homosexual who espoused chastity when he entered the diplomatic service (éd. Pléiade, II p. 664).

131. As we read in *Contre Sainte-Beuve*: 'The sin of homosexuality dates its historical origin from when, having lost its good name, it did not conform.'

132. Gide–Proust *Correspondance*, p. 9; *Correspondance* (ed. Kolb), XIII (dated 10/11 January 1914: the letter is printed in two versions).

133. Reported in Gide–Ghéon *Correspondance*, preface pp. 88–90. Gide's cavils about Proust's syntax can be found in *Interviews imaginaires*, pp. 34–6, and, more fully, in ms. Doucet γ 890 J 55–60.

134. An allusion to *Du côté de chez Swann*, I p. 141 (note Kolb).

135. Cited in Painter, II p. 186.

136. *Journal*, May 1921, pp. 691–4.

137. Nor, unfortunately, do we know which (if any) of these poems with homosexual themes were read to Gide by Cavafy's translator in Athens in 1938 (*Journal*, 9 September 1940).

138. *Correspondance*, letters dated 17 March 1931, 31 July 1931, 3 August 1931.

139. A reference to the libertarian attitudes which generated the 'dispute concerning the five-legged calf' ('la querelle du veau à cinq pattes') between them, namely a debate on the nature of deviancy. See below, Chapter 24 note 19.

140. *Correspondance*, I p. 704 (entry dated 18 August 1931). There is also a long description of the performance here. *Ibid.*, pp. 705–8 (entry dated 30 November 1931).

141. There is also an interesting homosexual episode (composed in 1944) in Martin du Gard's *Mémoires du Lieutenant-Colonel de Maumort* (éd. Pléiade, 1983): a soldier and a village boy become involved in a relationship which ends tragically ('La Noyade', Pt II Chapter 13, pp. 423–91).

142. *Mercure de France*, LXXXV June 1910, p. 662. The date of Gide's first meeting with Cocteau is stated to be October 1913 in J.Cocteau–Anna de Noailles, *Correspondance* (Paris: Gallimard, 1989), p. 153.

143. *Journal*, 14 January 1918.

CHAPTER 14:   BRITISH AND AMERICAN LITERATURE

1. Gide dedicated a copy of *Le Voyage d'Urien et Paludes* (1897) to Davray (Sotheby, 15 April 1986, lot 80), and there are several letters extant written by Davray to Gide in 1899 (*La Correspondance générale*, I). Davray organised Gosse's visit to Paris in February 1904, which was the prelude to Gide's long friendship with the English writer.

2. Ms. Doucet γ 1563. This was most probably the seventh edition (1890–1); but possibly the sixth (1885–7). There is no significant difference between them, both being virtual reprints of the third (1873–4).

3. *Journal*, 18 June 1914. Also referred to in *La Porte étroite*, pp. 564–5.

4. Ms. Doucet γ 1563; *The Tempest*, A4 scene 1, lines 48–9. The translation used was by François-Victor Hugo, vol. II p. 250.

5. Above, p. 310.

6. A heterosexual portrait of Shakespeare, based on the Sonnets and the plays, was published by André Fontainas, 'L'Œuvre et la passion de William Shakespeare' (*Mercure de France*, LXXXIV March 1910, pp. 586–600); a short discussion 'Shakespeare, sixième comte de Derby, M. W.H. et Oscar Wilde' (*ibid.*, CXXXI February 1919, pp. 761–2) mentions with approval Wide's identification of the dedicatee of the Sonnets as Willie Hughes in *The Portrait of Mr W.H.* Several French translations of the Sonnets had appeared by 1923, notably: *Les Sonnets . . . traduits . . . par* F.V. Hugo (Paris: Michel-Lévy frères, 1857) (French only); *Les Sonnets*, traduction de Charles-Marie Garnier (Paris: J.M. Dent, 1922) (bilingual edition – the date of Gide's *Journal* entry may well indicate that he used this edition. The translation was first published in the *Cahiers de la quinzaine*, December 1906 and March 1907, and, in book form (French only), by the *Cahiers* in 1906).

7. D.A. Steel, 'J. Raverat et A. Gide. Une amitié', in P. Pollard (ed.), *A. Gide et l'Angleterre*, p. 81.

8. Page 79. *Marlowe*, ed. Havelock Ellis, with an introduction by J.A. Symonds (London, 1887), p. xx.

9. Announced in the *Mercure de France*, XX November 1896, p. 400. Martin (p. 242) records a visit Eekhoud paid Gide in December 1897 (see above, p. 246). In 1900 the

Belgian writer had quoted widely from Gide's speech on influence in literature (*La Réforme*, 1 April 1900. Gide's text is in *Prétextes*, pp. 9–30. See Martin, p. 443 note 29). Gide lent him the manuscript itself (*Présence d'A. Gide* (Brussels, 1970), nos 110–11), and wrote and thanked Eekhoud on 3 April 1900.

10. Ms. Doucet γ 885.70. The information most probably came from the small annotated school edition of Spenser which Gide acquired in the market in Toulouse on 10 November 1912 (*Journal*, *ad loc.*).

11. See above, p. 164.

12. *Hero and Leander*, I 143–4 and 154–6.

13. For example, *Faerie Queene*, III xii 7f. (references to Zeus and Ganymede, Hercules and Hylas, and others); *The Shepherd's Calendar*, 'April' (Hobbinoll, who greatly loved Colin, tells of the boy's misadventure in love). A mention of Bacon in *Corydon* (p. 90) is of no relevance to our subject.

14. The whole of this note first appeared in the 1924 edition. *Spectator*, no. 265; *Corydon*, p. 126.

15. Book III Chapters 3 and 4.

16. *Enlevé!* (Paris: P.V. Stock, 1905) (ms Doucet γ 1574.48); *Journal*, 13 August and 2 September 1905. Gide first read *Robinson Crusoe* – 'with trembling admiration' – in 1911 (letter to Ruyters 6 January 1911).

17. *Journal*. Later, his 'Notes en manière de préface à *Tom Jones*' were first printed separately in his *Œuvres complètes*, XIII, pp. 412–16, the year before they appeared as a foreword to the novel published by Gallimard in 1938. They are first referred to in a letter to Dorothy Bussy written on 13 February [1924].

18. Ruyters had originally brought the volumes to Gide's attention on 12 November 1916 (*Correspondance*).

19. The effete and foppish sea-captain Whiffle, who appears in Chapters 34 and 35, constitutes a satire on the type of person who prefers scent to tobacco and handsome young men to coarse sailors.

20. Gide may also have come across Cleland's *Memoirs of a Woman of Pleasure* (cf. *Mémoires de Fanny Hill*, entièrement traduits de l'anglais pour la première fois par Isidore Lisieux (Paris; I. Lisieux, 1887), limited to 165 copies. There are many other earlier but incomplete versions in French). It contains two noteworthy episodes: (1) At a masked ball, Emily, disguised as a shepherd, is seduced by a handsome man who exclaims mournfully on discovering her true sex. His attempts to sodomise her are deftly 'corrected', and the heroine survives to tell the tale to a censorious Mrs Cole. (2) Emily spies on two young men, aged about seventeen and nineteen, at an inn, whose love making is described in detail. Mrs Cole comments on the depraved viciousness of these despicable 'unsex'd male-misses'. (See the edition by Peter Sabor (Oxford: OUP, 1985), pp. 154–60.) Not unexpectedly perhaps, in these examples from Smollett and Cleland some opprobrium is shown while the reader's salacity is indulged.

21. Ms. Doucet γ 1560.7. Cited by J. Cotnam, 'Premières lectures anglaises de Gide', in P. Pollard (ed.), *André Gide et l'Angleterre*, p. 11; he identifies the translation Gide used as *Le Corsaire suivi de Lara*, traduit par M. Laurencin, 3ᵉ éd. (Paris: Librairie de la Bibliothèque nationale, 1871).

22. *Op. cit.*, p. 12.

23. *Correspondance*, p. 120 (and note). *The Poems of Digby Mackworth Dolben*, edited with a Memoir by Robert Bridges (London: OUP, 1911). The latest edition, edited by Martin Cohen (Avebury Publishing Co., 1981), prints all known surviving poems and restores the text which was cut and altered by Bridges. Larbaud's article on Dolben appeared in *La Phalange*, 20 October 1912. See also T. d'Arch Smith, *Love in Earnest* (London: Routledge, 1970), pp. 188–91.

24. *Journal*, 10 January 1925. He read part of *Sesame and Lilies* on 20 August 1914 (*Journal*).

25. A curious coincidence with Corydon's later dismissal of this artist.

26. *Journal*, 2 October 1915. See the Bibliography below for details of selected translations of Whitman.

27. Gide–Ghéon *Correspondance*, I p. 246 (September 1899).

28. *Journal*, 28 March 1914.

29. *Ibid.*, 29, 24, 27 June 1914.

30. Claudel–Gide *Correspondance*, 9 March 1914.

31. *Journal*, 12 November 1917.

32. Gide–Valéry *Correspondance*, 1 November 1917.

33. *Journal*, 12 October 1918.

34. Line 30; Pléiade, p. 858.

35. H. Traubel, *With Walt Whitman in Camden* (28 March–14 July 1888) [= ed. Boston, 1906, pp. 74–6]. The Symonds letter is dated 7 February 1872.

36. See further P. Grosskurth, *J.A. Symonds*, pp. 151–5, 271–4; J.A. Symonds, *Walt Whitman. A Study* (London: J.C. Nimmo, 1893), esp. Chapters IV and V; J.A. Symonds, *The Letters* (III: 1885–93), ed. H.M. Schueller and R.L. Peters (Detroit: Wayne State University Press, 1969), letter of 3 August 1890; Whitman's reply is 19 August 1890. Cf. Ernest Raynaud, 'L'Expression de l'amour chez les poètes symbolistes', *Mercure de France*, CXXXV October 1919, pp. 385–407 (on androgynes, and on the distinction between Platonic Eros and carnal desire; with particular mention of Whitman and Nietzsche).

37. Ms. Doucet γ 885.11–16.

38. See above, p. 228.

39. When Fabulet asked Gide for advice about translating Whitman, Gide replied on 27 April 1918: 'Keep the word *amant*. "Love[r]" = *amant*, and *bien aimé* = "well beloved". There's no getting away from that. And it's just too bad for anyone who is offended by it' (cited in *BAAG*, 60 October 1983, p. 572).

40. Ms. Doucet γ 885.96.

41. 'Pédéraste': not 'lover of boys' but an example of Gide using the word in its common acceptation: 'homosexual'.

42. Presumably Gide here means 'lover of boys'.

43. Although neither Bazalgette nor Gide knew this, there is manuscript evidence that the original gender of the companion in 'Once I Pass'd' was male (*The Uncollected Poetry and Prose of Walt Whitman*, ed. Emory Holloway (Garden City, NY, 1921), cited in Kaplan, p. 143). Kaplan provides general documentation on Whitman's homoerotic relationships.

CHAPTER 15: GERMAN, SCANDINAVIAN AND DUTCH LITERATURE

1. *Journal*, 17 June 1924.

2. *Journal*, 'Feuillets' (*circa* 1937), I p. 1282.

3. *Journal*, 'Feuillets' (*circa* 1896). I p. 99.

4. *Journal*, 9 April 1906.

5. Müller, p. 231 (Wednesday, 7 April 1830).

6. *Journal*, 27 February 1928.

7. 20 August 1892, September 1892, 10 October 1892 'read vol. 2'; 'Les Confessions d'une belle âme', September 1892.

8. *Wilhelm Meister* traduit par M. T. Gautier fils (Paris: G. Charpentier, 1874).

9. Book III, Chapter xviii (vol. 2, pp. 613–15 in Gautier's translation).

10. For Gide's view of Castor and Pollux, see above, pp. 309–10.

11. It is not always obvious whether Gide read these poems in the original (though he sometimes speaks of 'penetrating their meaning with difficulty'). If not, he would have had to rely on de Wolffer's translation, *Élégies romaines* (1837) and Schropp's version *Épigrammes* (1889). The *Römische Elegien* are first mentioned in the 'Subjectif' in September 1892 ('*Élégies latines*: the greatest influence on me this year'). In 1893 he was 'overwhelmed' by reading them, and wrote on 18 March to his brother-in-law Marcel Drouin, to whom he was very close, that they were a revelation of happiness (Delay, II pp. 215–16). On one visit to Munich he acquired a fine press edition of the *Elegien* published by the Janus Presse, Leipzig, 1907 (limited to 150 copies) [private collection]. Both groups of poems were re-read on 17 June 1924 and the fact was noted in the *Journal*. They provided, as he again admitted on 20 September 1940 (*Journal*), an invitation to enter a sensual paradise.

12. Ross, p. 211.

13. Cf. *Journal*, I pp. 1058–9 (July 1931).

14. 'Subjectif', p. 74. The keen-eyed watchman Lynceus makes an appearance in *Les Nourritures terrestres* and features in *Faust* Part 2 (Act 5, scene 3).

15. We do not know how familiar Gide was with Winckelmann's writings, though we may surmise that he read his *Histoire de l'art chez les anciens* (1802 translation). In early April 1900 he wrote to Eekhoud that he was enjoying reading Winckelmann's *Correspondence* (*Présence d'A. Gide*, item 110). Lambert, p. 122.

16. See above, p. 62.

17. Gide here omits, probably as inappropriate (he is talking of Verhaeren's death in a railway accident), the words 'in reward for his devotion to them'.

18. Page 167. Gide referred to the book again after reading it 'with great enjoyment' (*Journal*, 8 May 1920). The details of Winckelmann's death at the hands of his (presumed) lover could also have been read by Gide in the preface to the translation of Ellis' *Sexual Inversion* which he consulted (see above, p. 92).

19. This book also contains essays on 'The Poetry of Michel Angelo' (pp. 63–90. Translated in the *Mercure de France*, XXXI September 1899, pp. 577–606), and on 'Leonardo da Vinci', in which he touches delicately on Leonardo's attraction to male beauty (pp. 91–122). Gide's earliest reading of Pater in English seems to date from 1912, when he attempted *Marius the Epicurean* (*Journal*, 29 July 1912 and 29 June 1913). See above, pp. 290–92.

20. See the sympathetic article by Ludwig Frey, 'Aus dem Seelenleben des Grafen Platen', in *Jahrbuch für sexuelle Zwischenstufen*, I 1899, pp. 150–214; VI 1904, pp. 357–447.

21. *Ioläus*, p. 152.

22. Ms. Doucet γ 1552.

23. See above, p. 97.

24. Gide first met Mann on 13 May 1931 (*Journal*), but their contacts went back to at least January 1922 (*Correspondance générale*, IV). A review by Félix Bertaux of *Der Tod in Venedig* appeared in the *NRF*, XII August 1914, pp. 338–42: 'The ideal which Aschenbach has formed imprisons him; he begins to stifle, and travels without a fixed goal; he falls in love with the beauty of a fair Polish fifteen-year-old boy . . .'

25. Ms. Doucet γ 1571.

26. There is a passing reference to Gide, who at the International Congress of Writers in Paris in 1935 attempted to talk to Heinrich Mann about Robert Musil (author of *Der Jung Törless*) but then swiftly changed the subject, in A. Gide – Thea Sternheim. *Correspondance*, édition établie par C. Foucart (Lyon: Centre d'Études Gidiennes, 1986), p. lxv, with note. In the same place, there are references to Gide meeting Hirschfeld in Berlin in 1928 (pp. xli, xliv), and to Gide's probable discussions of a production on 31 March 1925 of Carl Sternheim's *Oscar Wilde*, which dramatised

Hirschfeld's theory of an intermediate sex (pp. xxxvi–xxxvii).
27. *Corydon*, p. 183, and noted among the books Gide read in 1905 (ms. Doucet ɣ 1573).
28. See Gide–Last *Correspondance*, 'Préface'.

CHAPTER 16: ITALIAN LITERATURE

1. Journal, 26 August 1938. There is an early reference to reading the *Inferno* in the unpublished *Journal* for 7 February 1888 (ms. Doucet ɣ 1560).
2. The allusion in a footnote (*Corydon*, p. 160) to Dante's reference to Achilles is drawn from Carpenter's *Ioläus* (p. 69), where an extract from J.A. Symonds' *The Greek Poets* is cited.
3. *Corydon*, p. 192. See a hostile commentary on the style and approach of this open letter, by Gide's friend Roger Martin du Gard (in his letter to Gide dated 9 January 1928) after its publication in *Les Nouvelles littéraires*, January 1928.
4. *Inferno* XV. This is also quoted in Havelock Ellis (trans. van Gennep), preface p. 38, making the point that great men are often fond of this vice. The idea (and the quotation) have in fact become commonplace. Ellis of course realised that homosexuality is widespread in all levels of society.
5. Lamennais' translation and notes are used by Gide.
6. Suetonius, *Jul.* 49.
7. There is a quotation from Leonardo's *Treatise on Painting* in the *Journal*, 17 March 1904, but this has no bearing on our present discussion.
8. (Trans. van Gennep), p. 40. In his third edition (Philadelphia: F.A. Davis, 1919), p. 32, Ellis gives more details about the case: the charges were made in 1476 but do not appear to have been substantiated. 'Throughout his life,' Ellis writes, 'he loved to surround himself with beautiful youths and his pupils were more remarkable for their attractive appearance than for their skill; to one at least of them he was strongly attached, while there is no record of any attachment to a woman. Freud, who has studied Leonardo with his usual subtlety, considers that his temperament was marked by "ideal homosexuality" (S. Freud, *Ein Kindheitserinnerung des Leonardo da Vinci*, 1910).' Freud's interpretation is, however, open to dispute, and it is unlikely that Gide read this third English-language edition.
9. (Trans. van Gennep), p. 41.
10. Bibliographical references in van Gennep to C. Parlagrecco, 1888; L. von Scheffer, 1892; J.A. Symonds, 1893; Numa Praetorius in *Jahrbuch für sexuelle Zwischenstufen*, II 1908, pp. 254–67.
11. Ed. 3 1919, p. 32.
12. Grimm, II pp. 353 and 359. Ms. Doucet ɣ 885.68 and .69.
13. Ms. Doucet ɣ 885.48 and .24.
14. We note that 'Quelques lettres de Michel-Ange', translated by M.C. Martin, appeared in the *Mercure de France*, CXXIII October 1917, pp. 437–59, and included letters to Cavalieri and Riccio.
15. The Greek is Aphrodite Ourania (heavenly), namely the opposite of sensual, earthbound love (Pandemos: literally 'of all the people'). It is from this name that the term uranist for homosexual was coined.
16. Ms. Doucet ɣ 1563.16 ('princeps': see the Bibliography, below).
17. Book VI Chapter xxx (pp. 426–9 Leclanché).
18. Book VII Chapter lxi (pp. 498–500 Leclanché).
19. Book VII Chapter lxxi (pp. 520–1 Leclanché). *Perseus* was singled out by Gide as one of the sights of Florence which he found especially fine (letter to his mother, 28 May 1894).

CHAPTER 17:   EARLY PROSE WORKS: ASCETICISM

1. Delay, I pp. 520–39.
2. See above, p. 411.
3. Illustrated in *L'Œuvre graphique complète* (ed. Bory), p. 455 (and also p. 524 in a slightly different state). The only other picture by Rops which features a woman with a monkey is *Gamiani, IV: Le Singe* (*ibid.*, p. 599) in which a caged monkey sodomises a nude girl who is backing into the bars of his cage from the outside; two smaller monkeys look on, one with curiosity, the other with amusement.
4. *Eclogue* X 35.
5. Chopin's Scherzo in C sharp minor, op. 39.
6. Ms. Doucet 1561: 'Voyage en Bretagne'. During this trip Gide met Paul Gauguin quite by chance at an inn (*Si le grain ne meurt*, p. 520–1) and stole a glance at some of his canvases – among these was doubtless 'A Breton Boy', painted that same year (see plate 11).
7. *La Wallonie*, June–August 1891, pp. 229–38 (=*Œuvres complètes*, I pp. 7–22).
8. These are of young sailors. Two other similar descriptions appeared in *Floréal*, 3, March 1892, pp. 65–7 (cited by C. Martin in *A. Walter* (1986), pp. 284–5).
9. Ms. Doucet ɣ 1559 (reproduced in *A. Walter* (1986), p. 217).
10. It is interesting to note a similar expression of concern in the 1922 preface to *Corydon* (p. 8).
11. Delay, I p. 498.
12. *Ibid.*, I p. 520.
13. *Journal*, p. 33.
14. See above, pp. 161 and 409; cf. also on the Bible, p. 185.
15. Ms. Doucet ɣ 1558.
16. Delay, II p. 44.
17. See Michaud, IV pp. 28–31: 'Le Symbole idéaliste'.
18. Mondor, p. 8.
19. See *Hommages*, NRF 1951, p. 407 (*Correspondance*, p. 54), and Mondor, pp. 122–5.
20. See above, p. 122. It seems unlikely that Gide knew of the exclusively homosexual versions of the legend of Narcissus recorded by the Greek writer Conon (*Narrationes* 24), either directly or through the pages of a mythological handbook. In Ovid (*Met.* III 341 ff.) the legend appears in its most familiar form: the youth is mainly the object of heterosexual love, and is transformed at length into the flower which bears his name, having rejected the attentions of admirers of both sexes. He is the archetypal image of self-love. Gide found Ovid in general too decadent and sentimental (letter from Valéry to Gide, 15 April 1891).
21. Reproduced in Pléiade, pp. 1464–5.
22. Labuda, I p. 175.
23. Apollonius Rhodius, *Argonautica* I 609–910 (cf. Aeschylus, *Choephori* 631–8). Additionally, Hercules and his small band of companions refrain – like Urien and his ascetic friends – from sexual encounters at the court (Ap. Rhod., I 855–6).
24. *Chant* 2. But see above, p. 225.
25. Delay, II pp. 193–211.
26. Note the symbolic character Angaire, who only likes women who are veiled (p. 27) – without their veil he fears they will become wanton and immodest (cf. *Corydon*, above p. 32). Angaire also features in *Les Nourritures terrestres* (Gide wrote to Valéry in October 1896 that Valéry was Angaire, 'unless you object').
27. Delay, II p. 201.
28. *Ibid.*

29. Cf. Origen's self-mutilation, discussed above, p. 301.

30. Delay, II p. 207.

31. Erik, the hunter, also features in *The Flying Dutchman*, which Gide saw in Munich, in May 1892 (ms. Doucet γ 1552). The inspiration for the ghostly crew is possibly also derived from the same source. The twelve just men can be thought of as Knights of the Grail (*Parsifal*).

32. See above, p. 49.

33. A fragment of the *Traité* on which Gide was working on 2 July 1914 (*Journal*) was published in the NRF in 1919 (reprinted in *Incidences* (1924), pp. 125–30). Another version appeared as part III of 'Un Esprit non prévenu' (*Divers* (1931), pp. 81–9, with some additional fragments pp. 90–3). A third variant extract forms part of the letter to Rouveyre (11 April 1928, published in NRF, XXX June 1928, p. 729, reprinted in *Divers*, pp. 182–6).

34. See the auction catalogue cited in BAAG, 69 January 1986, p. 97. For Theseus, see above, p. 396.

35. Pindar, *Nem*. X.

36. Ms. Doucet γ 1556.

37. A. *Walter* (1986), p. 70. Gide, who generally disliked opera, nevertheless wrote to J. E. Blanche on 24 February 1918, 'I would like to go with you to hear Rameau's *Castor et Pollux*' – but we do not know what was the outcome of this suggestion.

CHAPTER 18:   EARLY PROSE WORKS: ECSTASY

1. 'Gide's "Nourritures terrestres" and Vergil's "Bucolics"', *Romanic Review*, XLIII (2) 1952, pp. 117–25. See also D. Walker, 'The Dual Composition of *Les Nourritures terrestres*: autour du "Récit de Ménalque"', *French Studies*, XXIX October 1975, p. 421–433.

2. II Kings 4:34.

3. See above, p. 167.

4. Pléiade, p. 193. Cf. also p. 200.

5. *Ibid.*, p. 186; cf. pp. 207 and 236.

6. One instinctively remembers the episode of Bernardino the handicapped boy so amorously described in 'Acquasanta' (*Journal*, II pp. 1106–12 (late summer 1912)).

7. Mélibée is the Vergilian name Gide chose for the handsome naked youth with a flute, who, in *Le Prométhée mal enchaîné*, seduces Angèle and runs off with her to Rome (*Prométhée*, begun *circa* 1896, published 1899).

8. Pléiade, p. 198: an echo of Ecclesiastes 3:5–6.

9. Pléiade, p. 227; cf. p. 188.

10. Brée cogently writes: 'It is certain that behind this gospel of liberation and realisation is the need Gide felt to justify his own sexual experience; by insisting on the infinite diversity of forms created by Nature–God and on their uniform value he affirms that there is no other law than to exist in full harmony with oneself and, in consequence, that there is neither norm nor exception' (p. 85).

11. In both his reworkings of the myth of Persephone (*Proserpine*, before 1912, and *Perséphone*, 1934) Gide presents two facets of the symbol of the Mother: first, Demeter, the goddess, mother of Persephone, is shown as the inspirational force which sets humanity on its future noble independent course (*Perséphone*, and the preface to the *Retour de l'U.R.S.S.*, 1936). Secondly, Metaneira, the mortal mother of Persephone's betrothed Demophoon, symbolises unimaginativeness and moral constraint, as by a timorous act she prevents her son from attaining immortality (cf. Creusa and other women, above, pp. 61 and 397). Gide also wrote (*Les Nouvelles Nourritures*, p. 298) that even if a goddess is involved the example of Achilles, who was vulnerable only in that spot where his mother's fingers had gripped his ankle, should remind us to beware of women's protective urges.

12. Pléiade, p. 299; Genesis 19:26–38.

13. Cf. Pléiade, p. 285.

14. Gide also published travel notes containing material similar to that on which he drew for descriptions in *Les Nourritures terrestres* and elsewhere. The collection entitled *Amyntas* first appeared in 1906 and included 'Mopsus' (dated April 1899, and first published in *L'Ermitage*, X April 1899, pp. 339–48), 'Feuilles de route' (March–April 1896, first published 1899), 'De Biskra à Touggourt' (December 1900, first published in *L'Ermitage*, XV November 1904, pp. 161–71), and 'Renoncement au voyage' (1903–4, parts of which were published in 1905 in *L'Ermitage* and *Vers et Prose*). 'Feuilles de route' is less poetical in its descriptions but contains some arresting pictures: the negroes with their 'langueur voluptueuse', the children at the performances of the obscene puppet show Karagöz ('One boy who is strangely beautiful plays the bagpipes: others gather round him, they are his admirers. . . . This shop is not a den of vice – it is more a court of love', *Amyntas* (1925), p. 35). 'Renoncement au voyage' has a tone of sadness (in a market crowd only Ali and Saïd appear handsome, but Ali is now married, and Saïd, whose feet were once so delicate, has changed with time).

15. Literally: 'The Pilgrim'. Gide uses the name indifferently to signify the person addressed by the narrator, and the title bestowed on the poet–narrator by the Prince.

16. p. 1508, alluding to the Oriental character of the *récit*, and adding: 'without self-compromise'.

17. Ms. Doucet γ 1560.21.

18. *Proserpine* (1977), p. 115.

19. 1887–8: cited in A. *Walter* (1986), pp. 217–18. A somewhat similar passage (but without Oriental echoes) occurs in the text of A. *Walter* (1986), pp. 137–8.

20. 'S'altère': 'grows thirsty', or 'becomes corrupt'.

21. From a slightly different point of view, Brée reaches a similar conclusion: 'El Hadj therefore seems to symbolise that ambiguous and occult vital strength which allows a man to live within the conflicting and absurd elements of his condition' (p. 103).

CHAPTER 19: *PHILOCTÈTE*

1. Delay, I p. 364; ms. Doucet γ 1563.

2. Ms. Doucet γ 1567 (two short extracts appeared in the *Revue sentimentale*, August–December 1897).

3. *Œuvres complètes*, III p. viii. An idea now resurrected by Martin, p. 268.

4. Gide to Eugène Rouart, 24 January 1898 (cited by Y. Louria, 'Le Contenu latent du "Philoctète" gidien', *French Review*, April 1952, p. 350). Cf. a similar thought in a letter to the same correspondent, 28 January 1898 (advertised for sale by A. Rosenthal Ltd, Oxford, in *Catalogue* of the 30th London Book Fair, June 1989, p. 111): 'what one respects in a republic is men or the *law*. The feeling that the law has been violated is abominable. . . .' See *Œuvres complètes*, II, pp. 485–93.

5. Delay, II p. 505.

6. Watson-Williams, pp. 59, 66.

7. Gide to Drouin, 9 November 1895, quoted by Delay, II p. 564.

8. Delay, II p. 245 (cf. also Gide's letter to Drouin cited *ibid.*, pp. 215–16).

9. Gide read Sophocles' *Philoctetes* in French on 11 August 1892 ('Subjectif', p. 95): he would only have known of the versions by Aeschylus and Euripides (neither play survives) through Eckermann, and not directly from Dio Chrysostom (*Orat.* 52). We

know that Gide returned to Paris on 28 October 1896, and then went to Brussels on 8 November (Martin, pp. 171–2) – but we do not know if he attended the performance of Pierre Quillard's translation at the Odéon on 1 November. He could certainly have read the review (*Mercure de France*, XXI January 1897, pp. 212–13) commenting on Mme Segond-Weber's appearance as Neoptolemus in the production. (Gide published a letter and his 'Notes de voyage' in the *Mercure*, XXI February 1897, pp. 225–46, 428–9.)

10. *Hommages*, NRF 1951, p. 389.
11. *Journal*, I p. 98 (*circa* 1896).
12. For example, O'Brien, *Portrait of A. Gide*, p. 262.
13. Ireland, p. 155.

CHAPTER 20: *SAÜL*

1. Ms. Doucet γ 1563.
2. I Samuel 17–20; 24; 28; 31. I Chronicles 10:13–14.
3. Cf. 'Quid tum si fuscus Amyntas', see above, p. 166.
4. Cf. Gide's sexual encounter with the boy in the sand dune recounted in *Si le grain ne meurt*, p. 560.
5. Pages 56–7, 74–8, 104–5, 125–8, 131.
6. Pages 101–6 (a pastiche of a Biblical psalm).
7. We must keep quite distinct the David of this play and the heterosexual David of Gide's *Bethsabé*.
8. There is a parallel in Gide's shaving of his own face.
9. Jean Vilar, 'Notes et documents sur A. Gide', *Revue de la Société d'Histoire du Théâtre*, III 1951 p. 267.
10. I Samuel 18:1–4.
11. In a letter to François Porché in January 1928, Gide drew attention to this element in *Saül*. The play, he maintained, provided a more important example than *L'Immoraliste*, which Porché had mentioned (*Corydon*, p. 191). In a conversation reported by Pierre-Quint (*A. Gide*: 'Entretiens. [January 1930]', p. 489), Gide regretted that in Copeau's performance one of the demons was played by 'a fat woman who climbed on to Saül's lap' – nimble boys would have served the author's purpose (and tastes) far more suitably.
12. See above, p. 167.
13. *Corydon*, p. 36.
14. *Interviews imaginaires*, p. 207.
15. Page 137. An echo of Ecclesiastes 3:1–8.
16. The same point is made in Gide's letter to Valéry 22 October 1898.
17. NRF, XXXI July 1928, p. 41.
18. *Ibid.*, p. 46.
19. *La Table ronde*, January 1953, p. 92.
20. Delay's suggested date, II p. 656.
21. Letter to Christian Beck, 27 February 1907.
22. *Nouveaux Prétextes*, pp. 28–41.
23. A similar idea occurs in the critique of Passavant's work in *Les Faux-Monnayeurs* (see above, p. 382).

CHAPTER 21: *LE ROI CANDAULE*

1. For Gide this gestation period is unusually short. The play appeared in book form (Paris: La Revue Blanche) in 1901, and was produced by Lugné-Poë at the Nouveau

Théâtre on 9 May 1901. The acting version is preserved in the Bibliothèque Doucet, ms. y 884 A1–4, B5–67. All versions present textual variants.

2. We should pay particular attention to his informed criticism of the play (*L'Ermitage*, XII July–December 1901, pp. 107–19: 'Notes sur une renaissance dramatique (4e article): *Le Roi Candaule*'). Gide regretted having adopted Ghéon's suggested cuts in the first act (ms. Doucet y 1567.18, August 1899). Much of the erudition in the play is clearly due to Ghéon. Gide sent three deleted pages to Ruyters on 20 August 1899.

3. Herodotus, I 8 (Gide quotes Larcher's translation with a few minor alterations); Plato, *Republic* II 359 d. Gide may also have had in mind the story of Polycrates, the tyrant of Samos, who, fearful lest the gods should punish him for his uninterrupted good fortune, cast away his signet ring only to have it returned to him by a fisherman (Herodotus, III 40–2): 'You know the tale,' Ruyters wrote to Gide on 22 October 1901.

4. *Le Roi Candaule* (Paris: Ferroud, 1893). Ghéon wrote to Gide 20 July 1899, giving him some information about the ancient sources taken from the preface to this edition by Anatole France. Apart from the differences in detail, in both Gautier and Gide Gygès rushes off, after witnessing the Queen's nakedness, to wash his hands in cold water – a symbolic act to escape pollution; and the Queen abandons her veil once she has been the object of *lèse-pudicité*. Baudelaire ('Théophile Gautier', *L'Artiste*, 13 iii 1859; republished in *L'Art romantique*) commented on Gautier's story: 'Modesty – a vulgar, threadbare emotion common to all women', but which was here elevated to something akin to religion. 'To contemplate is to possess.' Gide also asked Ruyters for the Queen's name (see Ruyters' reply, 14 January 1899).

5. *Incidences*, p. 127.

6. *Journal*, summer 1911, p. 336.

7. 'Lettre à Angèle', *L'Ermitage*, X November 1899, p. 412. Similarly, Gide wrote to Ruyters of the 'anarchic and dangerous character of my hero [Candaule]' on 1 February 1906.

8. *L'Évolution du théâtre* (Brussels, 25 March 1904).

9. L. Pierre-Quint (conversation, December 1927), p. 391. It is noteworthy that Candaule feels the stirrings of jealousy when he learns that the Queen especially enjoyed her night of love with Gygès (*Théâtre*, p. 238).

10. *Correspondance*, [July 1899] p. 226.

11. One recalls the phrase 'androgyne qui se dédouble' in *Le Traité du Narcisse* (Pléiade, p. 6 – an expression of the dualism of being and appearance), but this is not conclusive proof that Gide was already interested in the Gyges legend in 1890.

12. *Divers*, p. 87

13. Aelian, *Varia Historia* VIII.9, and Plato, *II Alcib.* 141 d.

14. *Essais*, II 12 (éd. Motheau et Jouaust, vol. IV p. 79). Diogenes Laertius, II 19.

15. Athenaeus, XIII 602 e; Plutarch, *Amatorius* 751 c.

16. Appian, *Bellum civile* II 91, and Caesar, *Bellum Alexandrinum* 70.

17. A detail shown in the seating plan in the Revue Blanche edition, 1901, p. 16.

18. September–December 1899, p. 366.

19. On the difficulty of finding true friends see also Montaigne, *Essais*, I 27, and Louis de Sacy, *De l'amitié*, Book II p. 263 (the tyrant of Syracuse who was poor because he had no friends). It is probable that Gide knew both these texts.

20. Page 244, underlined in the acting version (Doucet copy).

21. *Revue hebdomadaire*, 16 January 1932, p. 278.

22. As suggested by C. Delorme, '*Le Roi Candaule* ou les dangers de l'amour', *Cahiers A. Gide*, I p. 316.

23. This phrase, which became a favourite of Gide's, comes originally from Montaigne. Brée (p. 152) has noted that Gygès can be likened to David in *Saül*: he is

not 'généreux', and does have his idiosyncratic notion of 'pudeur'. Ireland (p. 170) is quite wrong to suggest that Candaule's gesture 'constitutes a moral breakthrough which may well be thought to elevate him above Gygès'.

24. Pléiade, p. 12. Cf. also *Corydon*, p. 130.

25. Rachel in *La Tentative amoureuse*; Angaire in *Le Voyage d'Urien*, and elsewhere. See R. Bastide, 'Thèmes gidiens', *Cahiers du Sud*, 328 1955.

26. Gide–Ghéon *Correspondance*, p. 185.

27. 'Le Roi Candaule ou les dangers de l'amour', *Cahiers A. Gide*, I pp. 299–318.

28. See above, p. 202.

29. McLaren (p. 26), while insisting on the need to interpret the play in a moral light, suggests that it is concerned with the defeat of abstraction and illusion (Candaule) by reality (Gygès). This is too sophisticated an interpretation.

30. As, for example, Watson-Williams (p. 85), who remains undecided between the two possibilities.

31. 'Journal sans dates' (*circa* 1909), *Nouveaux Prétextes*, p. 164; *Journal*, 16 January 1916; *Incidences*, p. 32 (1923: 'L'Avenir de l'Europe'). See also Verhaeren's enthusiastic rejoinder to Gide, dated November–December 1915, in *Rilke, Gide et Verhaeren, Correspondance*, ed. C. Bronne. Gide recommended Montesquieu's *Dialogue de Sylla et d'Eucrate* to Ruyters after re-reading it on 18 April 1901 (the editors of the correspondence note that he had probably first read it in June/July 1899).

32. Michelet, *Histoire romaine*, 2ᵉ édition, revue et augmentée (Paris: Hachette, 1833), vol. 2 p. 162. Quoted by Gide, except for the bracketed portion, in 'Feuillets' (1910–11), *Journal*, I p. 355.

33. *Histoire romaine*, Book III Chapter 3 (vol. 2 p. 212 ff.). Plutarch, to whose *Life of Sulla* Michelet refers, tells the story of Sulla's dictatorship, his excesses and his wars. There is no doubt that Gide could also have read this *Life* in the same way in which he consulted the *Lives* of Pelopidas and Lycurgus for the portrait of Epaminondas in *Corydon*.

34. *Vit. Alex.* lxxii 1–3.

35. *Ibid.*, lxvii 4.

36. *Ibid.*, xxi 3.

37. *Ibid.*, xxii 3.

38. *Journal*, I p. 97. See above, pp. 197–8. Furthermore, this is reminiscent of Eucrates' judgement on Sulla.

39. I p. 723.

40. I p. 358.

41. *Journal*, January 1912.

42. *Ibid.*, 28 February 1912: a contrast between Ajax and Thésée – the former has no inner firmness. Gide also started an *Ajax*, but abandoned the project (*Journal*, 22 April 1907). The probable date of composition is 1901 (see *Œuvres d'A. Gide . . . Bibliothèque M. Bolloré* (Sale, Hôtel Drouot 11 February 1954, lot 23)).

43. *Journal*, January 1912, I p. 358.

CHAPTER 22: *L'IMMORALISTE*

1. *Complete Works*, ed. O. Levy (Edinburgh: Foulis, 1911), vols 6 and 7: Aphorism 19. See above p. 53.

2. *Correspondance*, p. 44. See above, p. 136.

3. *Correspondance*, p. 22. Ghéon also began writing a novel using this material as its base – *L'Adolescent*. See further Gide–Ghéon *Correspondance*, notes by the editors to letters 154, 517, 740.

4. *Mercure de France*, XLIII July 1902, pp. 182–4.

5. Pléiade, pp. 367–8.

6. Some links with Oscar Wilde are well brought out by F. Mouret, 'À la recherche d'Oscar Wilde dans la vie et l'œuvre d'A. Gide', in *Cahiers A. Gide*, I pp. 167–84. Brée (p. 166) is right to observe that he owes some, but not all, elements of his character to Wilde.

7. Pléiade, pp. 425–9, 430–3, 435–7.

8. Interesting extra details (later suppressed) which clarify this point are recorded in the notes to the Pléiade edition, p. 1527.

9. There is a deleted passage from the manuscript, reproduced in the notes to the Pléiade edition (p. 1527), which refers to the preceding few days. The standard text reads: 'I found I was not yet strong [*robuste*], but could well become so – harmonious, sensual and almost handsome' (p. 402). Michel has been sunbathing in order to acquire the robust health of the handsome peasants he admires. The continuation of the text was: 'However, a desire, not new but one whose strength was previously unknown to me, swelled and made my flesh erect. It was like an overbrimming of life and joy, ready . . . to fertilise another being with my seed.' Michel runs back to Marceline, but when he reaches her, the moment has passed: 'I put everything off again until the following day.' It is tempting to conjecture that this episode provides another example of documents based on an event in Gide's life being incorporated into the *récit*.

10. p. 405. An echo of Dante, *Inferno*, V 118 ff. (Paolo and Francesca).

11. A description of a child near the irrigation system also features in *Amyntas* (Pléiade, notes p. 1522: ms. variants reproduced here record extra details on diseases of the eyes – these were deleted, presumably so as not to emphasise the misery of Arab life at this point in the narrative).

12. The reference to Theocritean shepherd-boys seen in Syracuse is reminiscent of Biskra, p. 398.

13. It may also be observed that in a short ms. passage (reproduced in the Pléiade notes, p. 1524) there is a description of Jamina, a young girl 'whose grace and beauty I cannot find words to tell'. In the same place, descriptions of the other boys ('Agib, elegant as a Faun', and others) which originally featured in the ms. may also be found. Guérard (p. 255), in a brief account of the ms. variants, records a 'full realistic evocation of the twenty-year-old Sadek'.

14. These details from real life are documented elsewhere in *Les Nouvelles Nourritures*, and in *Amyntas* (p. 162 and elsewhere).

15. Cf. the description of drunken labourers in *Amyntas*.

16. See above, p. 171.

17. Cf. a similar theme in *Paludes*.

18. Meyer, p. 168.

19. Oliver speaks of Michel's 'moral paralysis', but then – more questionably – sees the hero as a 'palimpsest' who is unaware of the multiplicity of meanings he bears.

20. Brée (p. 158) rightly describes Michel as another Saül or Candaule, but she is not correct to add the name of Philoctète, who, as we have seen, showed he could attain an ideal purity.

21. *L'Ermitage*, XIII August 1902, pp. 155–7. Letter from Gide to Ghéon, 14 August 1902.

CHAPTER 23: *LES CAVES DU VATICAN*

1. There is a brief discussion of the chronology in the Pléiade edition, p. 1565.

2. *Sic* – an anatomical inaccuracy: Gide means the sacrum.

3. Letter to Gide, [6/7 April 1914].

4. However, see above, p. 272.

5. For a note on Gide's visit to Covigliaio and a notice forbidding *la bestemmia* ('blasphemy': he had at first misunderstood this to mean 'bestiality'), see 'Chronique bibliographique', by Claude Martin (and Daniel Moutote), *BAAG*, 72 October 1986, pp. 45–7. Gide transcribed the text in his *Journal* (unpublished: ms. Doucet γ 1566 [1895]).

6. The source of this description is Fabre, VII p. 361, where a wide-awake, unwashed seven-year-old boy, who brings the naturalist his vegetables, offers him an insect and is given 2 sous against a promise to provide a regular supply of specimens. Fabre proceeds to experiment on his insects by removing their antennae and other parts. Beppo earns 10 sous for helping with the shopping and the household chores, and regularly brings Anthime 'rats, mice, sparrows, frogs – this Moloch welcomed everything'. Less convincingly, Steel (*Enfance*, p. 305 and note) suggests as a source the boys who steal pigeons in Venice (Gide's letter to Marcel Drouin, 18 April 1898, in *Hommage à André Gide* (1951), p. 392), or Gide's photographic models in Rome (*Et nunc manet in te*, p. 1133). As we have seen above (pp. 114–5), Anthime, with his knowledge of natural history similar to Gide's, seems to be a 'negative' of his creator.

7. Pages 744, 813, 816–17, 822–3.

8. *Heautontimoroumenos* 77: a well-known adage.

CHAPTER 24: *LES FAUX-MONNAYEURS*

1. *Journal de Rouen*, September 1906, and press reports for 7/8 August 1907.

2. *Journal des Faux-Monnayeurs* (JFM), p. 33.

3. JFM, p. 87

4. Martin du Gard disapproved of 'too clear' a description of Édouard's homosexuality, fearing that it might invite comparison with 'real life' (letter to Gide, 16 December 1921).

5. JFM, p. 12.

6. *Ibid.*, p. 28.

7. Brée (p. 287) draws our attention to the limited world of Gide's novel: 'It is too evident that for Gide "prostitution, shame and crime" – which after all furnish the subject matter of his novel – are not at all the same among the unknown masses [shown to Bernard by his Angel] as they are in his own bourgeois milieu where they are variations of a game. . . .'

8. JFM, p. 75

9. See this example used in 'Considérations sur la mythologie grecque' (1919), in *Incidences*, p. 130.

10. Grieve (pp. 175–7) asserts that this love seems the only happy one in *Les Faux-Monnayeurs* but 'appears on closer inspection to be so similar to other loves in Gide that one wonders how this experience, which has nothing but ill-effects on others, can possibly do Olivier any good. . . . Each is trying to imitate an insincere image of himself: himself as he would like the other to see him.' This is a superficial interpretation: Grieve is wrong to assimilate pederasty to heterosexuality by relating all these expressions of love to the model of Jérôme and Alissa in *La Porte étroite*, where love is not redemptive but destroys the hero's purposiveness.

11. There is a reference to the Argonauts in JFM, p. 50 (August 1921), where Gide remarks that all groups have their dissenters. As early as 1906, he intended to use the Argonauts as the focus of a treatise on heroism (alternative title: *Considérations sur la mythologie grecque*) – letter to Paul Fort, 8 December 1906, cited in *BAAG*, 69 January 1986, p. 97. See above, p. 309.

12. Page 1202: cf. Acts 17:28.

13. Page 1110; cf. JFM, p. 78 – Bernard does give up his place to him.

14. Contrast Gide's apparent approval of similar traits in Uncle de Gesvres in *Les Caves du Vatican*.

15. 'Know one, know them all', Vergil, *Aeneid* II 65–6. (Correct reading: 'Ab uno . . .', but the phrase is proverbial.)

16. Goulet (pp. 452–62), appealing to evidence from *Corydon* and *Si le grain ne meurt*, analyses this character and emphasises Gide's homosexual attraction towards Armand Bavretel which, he asserts, lies behind its creation. I do not agree with his psychoanalytical remarks, which I find modish and superficial.

17. JFM, pp. 134–6.

18. See also Pléiade, p. 1231.

19. This is very close to the motif of incest present in *Œdipe* (begun in 1927 and published in 1931). There, in addition to Œdipe' incest, one of his sons, Étéocle, wants to find an authorisation for sleeping with his sister, Ismène. This is an echo device (*mise en abyme*) of the main Oedipus-motif. Polynice, the other son, is composing an ode which is distinctly reminiscent of Armand's poem. The whole presentation of the idea is best considered in the light of a discussion between Gide, Dorothy Bussy and Roger Martin du Gard, which centred on the symbolic figure of 'the five-legged calf': was such an animal interesting *because* of its anomaly (thus Gide and Bussy), or *in spite of* its unnaturalness (Martin du Gard)? In other words, was 'the child of sin' necessarily weak and deformed – as Martin du Gard maintained? (Gide-Martin du Gard, *Correspondance*, I pp. 452, 699–704).

20. See also *Geneviève* (1936), which focuses on female liberation and features an adolescent girl on the dangerous threshold of 'special relationships'.

21. Laura's predicament is described in her letter, p. 984.

22. *Corydon*, p. 178.

23. Similarly, we read in Gide's *Journal*, 22 October 1928, remarks on solitary pleasures 'which invite dreaming to supersede reality so that one comes to prefer an imaginary world to actual possession'. This in turn is not unconnected with the motifs of desire and possession set out in Gide's early works, particularly in *Les Cahiers d'André Walter* (see above, p. 300).

24. See a discussion of these chronological problems in Goulet, pp. 105–13.

25. See above, p. 106. Several details from her article on a case of obsessional neurosis were used in the novel, including even the wording of Boris' talisman. Sexual repression also features as a theme in *Œdipe* and *Le Treizième Arbre* (1935).

26. Cf. Goulet (pp. 464–72), who makes the point that 'virile love' would have saved Boris from suicide (as happened in Olivier's case).

27. Cf. above, p. 348 (*Alexandre aux Indes*).

28. See Gide's preface to *Armance*, in *Incidences*, pp. 167–81 (and above, p. 211).

29. There are also remarks on this in the *Journal des Faux-Monnayeurs*, pp. 37–8: a character is described who expresses 'pure' love, but he is misunderstood by his wife (who is misled by 'infidelities of the flesh').

30. A. Gide, 'Entretiens, Noël 1927'. Cf. the example cited in JFM, p. 38: when deprived of his wife's love, the male character is 'jealous of God', who has stolen her from him.

CHAPTER 25: *THÉSÉE*: A HOMOSEXUAL CODICIL

1. The American edition contains an extra chapter (9), featuring a poem by Ariane. Gide intended to compose a *Thésée* of some sort as early as 1911 (*Journal*, 'Feuillets', I

p. 347). 'Considérations sur la mythologie grecque' (1919), an article on mythology (1929) and the 'Monologue de Thésée' (probably composed 1924–5) are three closely related works exploring the 'psychological reality' of a hero (*Divers*, p. 83; *Romans* (Pléiade), 'Notices' p. 1607 (= *Œuvres complètes*, XIII p. 405)). Work on the *Thésée* which we know probably began in 1931 (*Journal*, 18 January 1931: a suggestion by Malraux that Gide should write a sequel to *Œdipe* – a reinvention of the meeting between Theseus and Oedipus in Sophocles' *Oedipus at Colonus*; and *Journal*, 16 September 1931: a reworking of the story of Daedalus and Icarus, to be incorporated into Thésée's Cretan adventure). In what follows, the French form of Greek names has been retained to differentiate Gide's characters from their mythological originals.

2. See further my article 'The Sources of André Gide's *Thésée*', *Modern Language Review*, 65 (2) April 1970, pp. 290–7. The chief source is Plutarch's *Life of Theseus*.

3. *Divers*, p. 84. 'Fate' is 'internal necessity' (*Incidences*, p. 127).

4. *Incidences*, p. 127

5. *Ibid.*

6. In *Divers* (pp. 84–5) this text is enlarged to emphasise the ideal of a hero who has the ultimate Nietzschean strength born of his own convictions: 'In Thésée I can only perceive heroism. I let others show their annoyance at his cynicism. If he goes to Hades with Pirithous, his faithful friend, it is to rape Proserpine.'

7. *Les Nourritures terrestres*, IV p. 198 (written *circa* 1895).

8. Wife of Aeneas, cf. Vergil, *Aeneid* II 673 ff., 736 ff.

9. *Journal*, 12 May 1927. This is a frequent image of woman in Gide, and is not restricted to Ariadne: *Journal*, 8 November 1931, 26 November 1931. Also: *Les Nourritures terrestres*, IV p. 185; *Journal*, 'Feuillets' (1911), p. 347: *Incidences*, p. 130 (in *NRF*, XIII September 1919). The interpretation is altogether very hard on Ariadne, who was usually portrayed in legend as cruelly deserted by Theseus through no fault of her own. See Plutarch, *Vit. Thes.* xx, for the variants of Ariadne's plight; and Homer, *Odyssey* XI 321 ff., for an unsympathetic view of her.

10. *Corydon*, p. 159 (citing Halévy, p. 97). *La Vie de Nietzsche* was reviewed by Henri Albert in the *Mercure de France*, LXXXII November 1909, pp. 170–1, and by Gide's close friend Jean Schlumberger in the *NRF* II December 1909, pp. 420–3.

11. Contrast Gide's earlier reflection on this myth (unpublished *Journal*, 13 January 1896): 'I want to write the start of a poem where I shall make Pasiphaë's love for the bull out of this greed, this desire to be penetrated, brutalised and filled with Nature' (see Delay, II pp. 575–6, who believes that he can discern the influence of d'Annunzio, whom Gide then knew and admired). This violent expression of savagery is unusual for Gide, but it does have parallels in some of his early interests – in, for example, Gilles de Rais.

12. These characteristics are mentioned by Plutarch, who also tells how when they first met during a raid by Pirithous against Theseus each was deeply impressed by the beauty and daring of the other (*Vit. Thes.* xxx 1–2). When Theseus, aged fifty, raped the child Helen (the first recorded instance of contraceptive sodomy – cf. Dover, p. 188), Pirithous was at his side to help him (*Vit. Thes.*, *ibid.*), and both went down to Hades impiously to rape the goddess Persephone (also referred to by Gide, Pléiade, pp. 1444–5). These and other sexual adventures of theirs are not very edifying.

13. Xenophon, *Symp.* viii 31.

14. We may note in passing the story told in antiquity of a homoerotic relationship between Minos and Theseus, recorded in Athenaeus, XIII 601 f. Gide does not capitalise on this, being probably unaware of it since his only knowledge of Athenaeus was derived indirectly via Carpenter and *Le Livre d'amour des anciens*.

15. See above, p. 174.

16. *Vit. Thes.* xxiii 1–2.

EPILOGUE

1. A. *Walter* (1986), pp. 123–4.

APPENDIX A PEDERASTY AND ART

1. *Amyntas* (1925), p. 125 (the first edition is 1906). See also: 'Les Limites de l'art' (1901) in *Prétextes*, p. 37; letter to G.F. Le Grix, 10 March 1923, 'I maintain that without sensuality, sexuality and pride no work of art can exist' (Lalou, p. 7).

2. Gide–Ghéon *Correspondance*, September 1899, I p. 245.

3. Idrac's marble *Mercure inventant le caducée* was acquired for the Luxembourg museum on 21 November 1879. Gide could not therefore have seen it before his tenth birthday.

4. *Journal*, 8 July 1930.

5. Ms. Doucet γ 1567.

6. Collignon, I pp. 485–516 (L'Époque des grands maîtres – Polyclète. See esp. p. 498). Pliny, *Nat. Hist.* XXXIV 56: 'Polycletus . . . Diadumenum fecit molliter iuvenem . . . Doryphorum viriliter puerum fecit.' As for the relative ages, Collignon misrepresents Pliny, who has used the word 'boy' for the *Doryphorus* (though it must be admitted that the statue is of an adolescent). Plato, *Protagoras* 309 a. See above, p. 142. In 1894 Gide passed through Naples without seeing the erotic collections in the Museo Nazionale (letter to his mother 13 April 1894, and from her on 15 April 1894). Annoyed by what he saw in the Vatican Museum (letters to his mother of 6 and 12 May 1894), and generally bored with Rome, he reacted in a hostile manner to the insipid and inept restorations which had been carried out on ancient statues. Apollo had been given arms more suitable for Antinous, he said: honestly displayed fragments would have been preferable.

7. Ms. Doucet γ 885.86. Paris, p. 179. Contrast the point made in connection with Castor and Pollux (above, p. 310).

8. Page 70. See above, pp. 161–2.

9. *Journal*, 1896 (I p. 65).

10. *Journal*, 18 January 1902. This is reminiscent of Lafcadio's 'milk hair': see above, p. 366.

11. *Journal*, I pp. 235–6. This statue, only doubtfully attributed to Michelangelo at the date of Gide's visit (although he does not say so), is not now considered to be his. Reproduction in J.A. Symonds, *The Life of Michelangelo Buonarotti*, 3rd edn (London: J.C. Nimmo, 1899), II p. 48.

12. Ms. Doucet γ 1550.47: this is a rewording of an entry of the previous year concerning the same picture (γ 1558.24 (5 March 1888) – 'il déconcerte, il désoriente').

13. *Verve*, I 1 January 1938, pp. 7–8.

14. *Corydon*, p. 136 – cf. p. 127 where for similar reasons Bouguereau's tasteless nudes are condemned for their artificiality (see Plate 10).

15. It is now generally considered that the *Pastoral Concert* was left unfinished at Giorgione's death, and was probably completed by Titian. Corydon's comment is absurd.

16. See Gide's own reaction to this painting: 'The head of the young man on the left . . . is of a marvellous quality [*substance*]. All the tones are melted and fused together to achieve a new unique unknown colour everywhere on the canvas – and so intimately bound together that nothing can be removed nor any touch added; one's glance follows the forehead, the temple, the soft edge of hair, without noticing any joins; it is like melted enamel which has been poured still liquid over the canvas. Standing before it one can think of nothing else' ('Feuilles de route', *Journal*, 16 December 1895, p. 58).

17. The Council was held 1545–63; the painting is now not attributed to Titian. Details, with a reproduction, in *Catalogue sommaire illustré des peintures du Musée du Louvre*, II (Italie, and elsewhere) (Paris: Éd. de la Réunion des Musées Nationaux, 1981), p. 260 (Inv. 751). Gide has nothing to say of Caravaggio (1573–1610), or his imitators, whose paintings might reasonably be thought to have appealed to him.

18. A fuller and more precise account of sexuality in Venice than Gide had access to, covering the period 1326–1500, is available in G. Ruggiero, *The Boundaries of Eros* (1985).

19. Ms. Doucet γ 1563.19 and .20: The others are: *L'Amour à travers les âges* (a nude woman on top of a hill up which numerous small naked, half-naked and lame persons are hurrying), *Juillet* (a young girl, naked except for her hat and her small lifebelt, steps into a boat), *La Messe de Gnide* (a man and a woman in transparent drapery approach the couch on which Aphrodite lies naked), *La Fleur lascive orientale* (around a bouquet of huge arum lilies, six semi-naked Oriental women climb and suggestively disport themselves), *Isis* (probably to be identified as *Jamais assez – Jamais trop*: Isis, with her twelve breasts, labelled front view 'Never enough' and rear view 'Never too much'). The engravings are reproduced in Bory, pp. 462, 435, 68, 76 and 425, 539. Gide also purchased Ramiro's *Catalogue descriptif* (1887) in 1891 (ms. Doucet γ 1563.20). See above, p. 298, and P. Pollard, 'Gide amateur de Félicien Rops' in P. Delaveau (ed.), *Écrire la peinture* (Paris: Editions universitaires, 1991) pp. 117–124.

20. *Nouveaux Prétextes*, pp. 85–9. See above, p. 74.

SELECT BIBLIOGRAPHY

Details of works not mentioned here will be found in the relevant footnotes. References in the text to works and correspondences by Gide are made to the following collected editions and separate publications. In the case of a work known to have been consulted by Gide, or where there are good grounds for believing this:

* indicates the edition he used, or one not differing materially from it.
† indicates an edition other than or not identifiable as the one used by him.

Texts and translations of standard authors (for example, Plato, Vergil, Shakespeare, Goethe) have not been included unless attention needs to be drawn to a particular edition.

Works by Gide

Œuvres complètes. Paris: NRF, [n.d.] – 1939.
Journal 1889–1939. Paris: Bibliothèque de la Pléiade, 1951.
Journal 1939–1949; Souvenirs. Paris: Bibliothèque de la Pléiade, 1954.
Romans; Récits et Soties; Œuvres lyriques. Paris: Bibliothèque de la Pléiade, 1958.
Théâtre. Paris: Gallimard, 1947 (for *Saül, Le Roi Candaule, Œdipe*).
Théâtre complet. Neuchâtel: Ides et Calendes, 1947–9 (for *Philoctète*).

Amyntas. Paris: Gallimard, 1925.
Les Cahiers et les poésies d'André Walter avec des fragments inédits du Journal. Édition établie . . . par C. Martin. Paris: Gallimard, 1986.
Divers. Paris: Gallimard, 1931.
Feuillets d'automne. Paris: Mercure de France, 1949.
Incidences. Paris: Gallimard, 1924.
Interviews imaginaires. Paris: Gallimard, 1942.
Journal des Faux-Monnayeurs. Paris: Gallimard, 1927.
Montaigne. An Essay in Two Parts by A. Gide, trans. S.H. Guest and T.E. Blewitt. London: Blackamore Press, 1929.
Nouveaux Prétextes. Paris: Mercure de France, 1951.
Œdipe. See *Théâtre*, 1947.

473

Les Pages immortelles de Montaigne choisies et expliquées par A. Gide. Paris: Corrêa, 1939.

Philoctète. See *Théâtre complet*, 1947 (vol. I).

Préfaces. Neuchâtel: Ides et Calendes, 1948.

Prétextes. Paris: Mercure de France, 1947.

Proserpine. Perséphone. Édition critique établie et présentée par P. Pollard. Lyon: Centre d'Études Gidiennes, 1977.

Le Roi Candaule. See *Théâtre*, 1947.

Saül. See *Théâtre*, 1947.

Si le grain ne meurt. See *Journal 1939–1949.*

Souvenirs de la Cour d'Assises. Paris: Gallimard, 1924.

'Le "Subjectif" d'A. Gide . . . (1889–1893)', éd. par J. Cotnam, *Cahiers d'André Gide* I. Paris: Gallimard, 1969 (pp. 15–113).

Principal Editions of *Corydon*

C.R.D.N. [Bruges: The St Catherine Press Ltd], 1911. (Anonymous.)

Corydon (nouvelle édition). [Bruges: L'Imprimerie Sainte Catherine], 1920. (Anonymous.)

André Gide. *Corydon.* Nouvelle édition. Paris: NRF, [1924]. (The 'achevé d'imprimer' is 7 January 1924 for copies on 'hollande', and 9 January for ordinary copies; the copyright dates are 1923 and 1924 respectively.)

André Gide. *Corydon.* Édition augmentée. Paris: NRF–Gallimard, [1929].

Corydon, in *Œuvres complètes*, IX pp. 173–347, [1935].

André Gide. *Corydon.* Paris: NRF–Gallimard, [1947].

Corydon. Préface de Élisabeth Porquerol. [Lausanne: La Guilde du Livre, 1971].

English Translations

Corydon. With a Comment on the Second Dialogue . . . by F. Beach. New York: Farrar, Straus & Company, 1950.

Corydon. Four Socratic Dialogues [trans. P.B.]. London: Secker & Warburg, 1952.

Corydon. Trans. and introduced by R. Howard. New York: Farrar, Straus & Giroux, Inc. (London: Gay Men's Press), 1983.

Manuscript Material

C.R.D.N. [Bruges: The St Catherine Press Ltd], 1911. Proofs (or rather a corrected copy, with additional ms. annotations). Bibliothèque nationale (Réserve): Rés. pY^2.2566

Corydon (nouvelle édition). [Bruges: L'Imprimerie Sainte Catherine], 1920. Proofs (private collection).

Material connected with *Corydon* and its composition: Bibliothèque littéraire Jacques Doucet. Fonds Gide y 885.

SELECT BIBLIOGRAPHY

Correspondences

A. Gide–F.P. Alibert. *Correspondance 1907–1950*. Éd. établie... par C. Martin. Lyon: Presses universitaires de Lyon, 1982.

'Lettres à C. Beck', *Mercure de France*, CCCVI June 1949, pp. 385–402, 616–37.

Correspondance A. Gide–J.E. Blanche 1892–1939. Éd. établie... par G.P. Collet. Paris: Gallimard, 1979.

Correspondance A. Gide–D. Bussy. Éd. établie... par Jean Lambert; notes de R. Tedeschi. Paris: Gallimard, 1979–82.

P. Claudel et A. Gide. Correspondance 1899–1926. Préface et notes par R. Mallet. Paris: Gallimard, 1949.

Deutsch-französische Gespräche 1920–1950: La Correspondance de E.R. Curtius avec A. Gide, C. du Bos et Valery Larbaud. Éd. par H. et J.M. Dieckmann. Frankfurt am Main: V. Klostermann, 1980.

'Quatorze lettres et billets inédits de Lord Alfred Douglas à A. Gide 1895–1929', éd. F. Mouret, *Revue de littérature comparée*, 3, July–September 1975, pp. 483–502.

H. Ghéon–A. Gide. Correspondance 1897–1944. Texte établi par J. Tipy... notes d'A.M. Moulènes et J. Tipy. Paris: Gallimard, 1976.

The Correspondence of A. Gide and E. Gosse 1904–1928. Ed. L.F. Brugmans. London: Peter Owen, 1960.

F. Jammes et A. Gide. Correspondance 1893–1938. Préface et notes par R. Mallet. Paris: Gallimard, 1948.

Correspondance A. Gide–V. Larbaud 1905–1938. Éd. établie... par F. Lioure. Paris: Gallimard, 1989.

A. Gide–J. Last. *Correspondance 1934–1950*. Éd. établie... par C.J. Greshoff. Lyon: Presses universitaires de Lyon, 1985.

P. Iseler. *Les Débuts d'A. Gide vus par P. Louÿs*. Paris: Éd. du Sagittaire, 1937.

A. Gide–R. Martin du Gard. *Correspondance 1913–51*. Introduction par J. Delay. Paris: Gallimard, 1968. (Index, par S.M. Stout. Paris: Gallimard, 1971.)

'Lettres d'A. Gide à Madame Mayrisch', in *Colpach* [Luxembourg: V. Buck, 1957], pp. 93–105.

A. Gide. *Correspondance avec sa mère 1880–1895*. Éd. établie... par C. Martin. Paris: Gallimard, 1988.

A. Gide et. A. Mockel. *Correspondance (1891–1938)*. Éd. établie... par G. Vanwelkenhuyzen. Geneva: Droz, 1975.

A. Gide–J. O'Brien. *Correspondance 1937–1951*. Éd. établie par J. Morton. Lyon: Centre d'Études Gidiennes, 1979.

M. Proust. *Lettres à A. Gide*. Neuchâtel: Ides et Calendes, 1949. (See also below, Proust, M. *Correspondance*.)

Rilke, Gide et Verhaeren. Correspondance inédite recueillie et présentée par C. Bronne. [n.p.], 1955.

A. Gide–A. Ruyters. *Correspondance 1895–1950*. Éd. établie... par C. Martin et V. Martin-Schmets avec la collaboration... de P. Masson. Lyon: Presses universitaires de Lyon, 1990.

A. Gide–P. Valéry. *Correspondance 1890–1942*. Préface et notes par R. Mallet. Paris: Gallimard, 1955.

A. Gide: *Correspondance avec Francis Vielé-Griffin 1891–1931*. Édition établie, présentée et annotée par H. de Paysac. Lyon: Presses universitaires de Lyon, 1986.

Bibliothèque nationale. *André Gide*. Paris, 1970. (Exhibition.)

Bibliothèque royale Albert Ier. *Présence d'André Gide*. Brussels, 1970. (Exhibition.)

SELECT BIBLIOGRAPHY

General

Catalogue du fonds Lacassagne, rédigé par M.C. Roux. Lyon: Impr. nouvelle Lyonnaise, 1922. (Bibliothèque de la ville de Lyon.)

Catalogue général de la librairie française . . . rédigé par D. Jordell [s.v. Instinct sexuel; Médecine légale]. Especially the following volumes:
- Tome XVI[–XVII] (table des matières des tomes XIV et XV, 1891–9). Paris: Librairie Nilsson, 1905–6.
- Tome XX (table des matières des tomes XVIII et XIX, 1900–5). Paris: D. Jordell, 1910.
- Tome XXIII (table des matières des tomes XXI et XXII, 1906–9). Paris: D. Jordell, 1912.

Dynes, W.R. *Homosexuality: A Research Guide*. New York and London: Garland Publishing, 1987.

Herzer, M. *Bibliographie zur Homosexualität*. Berlin: Verlag rosa Winkel, 1982.

Periodicals

Akadémos. Revue mensuelle d'art libre et de critique. Paris, 1909. (All published.)

Archives d'anthropologie criminelle, de criminologie et de psychologie normale et pathologique. Paris, 1886–1914.

Bulletin de l'Association des Amis d'André Gide. Lyon [Montpellier and Paris]: Centre d'Études Gidiennes, 1968→

L'Ermitage. Paris, 1890–1906.

Inversions. Paris, 1924. (All published.)

Jahrbuch für sexuelle Zwischenstufen unter besonderer Berücksichtigung der Homosexualität. Hrsg. von Dr. med. M. Hirschfeld. Leipzig: Max Spohr, 1899–1923.

Mercure de France. Paris, 1890→

La Nouvelle Revue Française. Paris, 1908→

La Revue Blanche. Paris, 1891–1903.

Monographs and Other Works

Achilles Tatius. *The Loves of Clitophon and Leucippe*, translated . . . by William Burton. Oxford: The Shakespeare Head Press, 1923.

Adam, P. 'L'Assaut malicieux', *Revue Blanche*, 15 May 1895, pp. 458–62.

Anglès, A. A. *Gide et le premier groupe de la N.R.F.* [1890–1914]. Paris: Gallimard, 1978–86.

Anthologie de l'amour arabe, par F. de Martino et Abdel Khalek bey Saroit. Introduction de Pierre Louÿs, 3ᵉ éd. Paris: Mercure de France, 1902.

Anthologie grecque, [traduite par Félix Dehèque]. Paris: Hachette, 1863.

Arabian Nights. A Plain and Literal Translation of . . . The Book of the Thousand Nights and a Night with introduction, explanatory notes on the manners and customs of Moslem men and a terminal essay upon the history of The Nights. By Richard F. Burton. Benares [i.e. London]: Kamashastra Society, 1885–8. (The unillustrated 'Benares' edition, in 16 vols.)

Arabian Nights. Le Livre des mille nuits et une nuit. Traduction littérale . . . par le Dr

J.C. Mardrus. Paris: Éd. de la Revue Blanche, 1899–1904.

*Arabian Nights. Die Erzählungen aus den tausend und ein Nächten. Vollständige deutsche Ausgabe in zwölf Bänden auf Grund der Burton'schen englischen Ausgabe besorgt von Felix Paul Greve. Leipzig: Insel Verlag, 1907–8.

*Aristophanes. Traduction nouvelle, avec une introduction et des notes, par C. Poyard. Paris: Hachette, 1860.

Barbedette, G. and Carassou, M. Paris Gay 1925. Paris: Presses de la Renaissance, 1981.

Bataille, G. Le Procès de Gilles de Rais. Paris: Pauvert, 1965.

*Bayle, P. Dictionnaire historique et critique. Nouvelle édition augmentée de notes. Paris: Desoer, 1820.

*Bazalgette, L. Walt Whitman. L'homme et son œuvre. Paris: Mercure de France, 1908.

†Becker, W.A. Charikles... in zweiter Auflage berichtigt... von K.F. Hermann. Leipzig: F. Fleischer, 1854.

†Belèze, G.L.G. Dictionnaire universel de la vie pratique à la ville et à la campagne. Paris: Hachette, 1859.

*Bergson, H. L'Évolution créatrice. Paris: F. Alcan, 1907.

*Bersot, E. Un Moraliste. Études et pensées d'Ernest Bersot. Paris: Hachette, 1882.

Berthier, P. 'Balzac du côté de Sodome', L'Année balzacienne, 1979, pp. 147–77.

*Binet-Valmer, G. Lucien. 3ᵉ éd. Paris: P. Ollendorff, 1910.

*Biographie universelle ancienne et moderne... ouvrage rédigé par une société de gens de lettres et de savants. Paris: Michaud frères, 1811–55.

*Blum, L. Du mariage. Paris: P. Ollendorff, 1907.

*Bohn, G. La Nouvelle Psychologie animale. Paris: F. Alcan, 1911.

Bonnetain, P. Charlot s'amuse... Édition augmentée d'une pièce relative au procès jugé par la Cour d'Assises de Paris, le 27 décembre 1884. Paris: A. Charles, [1885].

Bory, J.F. L'Œuvre graphique complète: Félicien Rops. Ouvrage établi et présenté par J.F. Bory. Paris: A. Hubschmid, 1977.

Boswell, J. Christianity, Social Tolerance, and Homosexuality. Chicago: University of Chicago Press, 1980.

*Bourget, P. Physiologie de l'amour moderne. Fragments posthumes d'un ouvrage de Claude Larcher recueillis et publiés par Paul Bourget. Paris: A. Lemerre, 1891.

Braak, S. A. Gide et l'âme moderne. Amsterdam, 1923.

Brée, G. A. Gide. L'Insaisissable Protée. Paris: Les Belles Lettres, 1953.

Buffière, F. Éros adolescent. La pédérastie dans la Grèce antique. Paris: Les Belles Lettres, 1980.

Busst, A.J.L. 'The Image of the Androgyne in the Nineteenth Century', in I. Fletcher (ed.), Romantic Mythologies. London: Routledge & Kegan Paul, 1967, pp. 1–96.

†Bussy, D. Olivia. London: Hogarth Press, 1949.

†Bussy-Rabutin, R. de. Histoire amoureuse des Gaules. Paris: P. Jannet, 1856–76.

*Calderón. Drames religieux... Traduits pour la première fois en français avec des notices... par Léo Rouanet. Paris: A. Charles, 1898.

Carpenter, E. Intermediate Types among Primitive Folk. A Study in Social Evolution. London: G. Allen & Co., 1914.

*Carpenter, E. Ioläus, an Anthology of Friendship. 2nd edn, enlarged. London: Swan Sonnenschein, 1906.

*Cellini, B. La Vie de Benvenuto Cellini écrite par lui-même. Traduction L. Leclanché. Illustrée de neuf eaux-fortes par F. Laguillermie. Paris: A. Quantin, 1881.

Chapon, F. 'Note sur l'édition du second Corydon', Bulletin du bibliophile, I 1971, pp. 1–9.

Chevalier, J. *De l'inversion de l'instinct sexuel au point de vue médico-légal*. Paris: O. Doin, 1885.

*Claus, C. *Éléments de zoologie* . . . traduit sur la 4e éd. allemande par G. Moquin-Tandon. Paris: F. Savy, 1889.

Clive, H.P. *Pierre Louÿs. A Biography*. Oxford: Clarendon Press, 1978.

†Cocteau, J. *Le Livre blanc*. [Paris: Les Quatre Chemins, 1928].

Code d'instruction criminelle et Code pénal. 15e éd. Paris: Dalloz, 1915.

Code pénal, annoté par E. Garçon. Paris: Librairie de la Société du recueil général des lois et des arrêts, 1901–6.

Coffignon, A. *Paris vivant. La Corruption à Paris*. Paris: La Librairie Illustrée, [*circa* 1888].

*Collignon, M. *Histoire de la sculpture grecque*. Paris: Firmin-Didot, 1892–7.

Colpach. See 'Lettres d'A. Gide à Madame Mayrisch'.

Copley, A. *Sexual Moralities in France 1780–1980. New Ideas on the Family, Divorce and Homosexuality*. London: Routledge, 1989.

Courouve, C. *Vocabulaire de l'homosexualité masculine*. Paris: Payot, 1985.

*Curtius, E. *Histoire grecque* . . . traduite . . . sous la direction de A. Bouché-Leclerq. Paris: E. Leroux, 1883.

*Dante Alighieri. *L'Enfer*. (In F. Lamennais: *Oeuvres posthumes* publiées par E.D. Forgues. I. Paris: Paulin et le Chevalier, 1856.)

*Dante Alighieri. *La Divine Comédie. L'Enfer*, traduction nouvelle . . . de L'Espinasse-Mongenet. Préface de Charles Maurras. Paris: Nouvelle Librairie Nationale, 1912.

†Darwin, C. *La Descendance de l'homme et la sélection naturelle*, traduit par E. Barbier. Paris: C. Reinwald, 1881.

*Darwin, C. *A Monograph on the Sub-class Cirripedia, with figures of all the species*. London: Ray Society, 1851–4.

*Darwin, C. *L'Origine des espèces au moyen de la sélection naturelle* . . . traduit sur l'édition anglaise définitive par E. Barbier. Paris: C. Reinwald, 1880.

*Darwin, C. *Voyage d'un naturaliste autour du monde fait au bord du navire le Beagle de 1831 à 1836* . . . traduit . . . par M.E. Barbier. Paris: C. Reinwald, 1875.

Davies, J.C. *Gide: L'Immoraliste and La Porte étroite*. London: Arnold, 1968.

Delay, J. *La Jeunesse d'A. Gide*. Paris: Gallimard, 1956–7.

Delcourt, M. 'Deux interprétations romanesques du mythe de l'androgyne: Mignon et Séraphita', *Revue des langues vivantes*, XXXVIII (4) 1972, pp. 228–40, 340–7.

*D'Épinay, Mme Louise de la Live. *Mémoires* . . . avec des additions, des notes . . . par M. Paul Boiteau. Paris: G. Charpentier, 1865.

Descaves, L. *Sous-Offs*. Paris: Tresse et Stock, 1890.

Dictionnaire des sciences médicales par une société de médecins et de chirurgiens. Paris: C.L.F. Panckoucke, 1812–22.

*Diderot, D. *Oeuvres choisies*. Édition du centenaire. Paris: G. Reinwald, 1884.

Diderot, D. *Oeuvres philosophiques*. Textes établis, avec introductions, bibliographies et notes, par Paul Vernière. Paris: Garnier frères, 1956.

Dover, K.J. *Greek Homosexuality*. London: Duckworth, 1978.

Drain, H. *Nietzsche et Gide*. Paris: Éd. de la Madeleine, 1932.

Dubois-Dessaule, G. 'Le Bagne militaire', *Revue Blanche*, 1 April 1901, p. 481.

Dugas, L. *L'Amitié antique d'après les mœurs populaires et les théories des philosophes*. Paris: F. Alcan, 1894.

†Eekhoud, G. *Escal-Vigor*. Paris: Mercure de France, 1899.

Ellis, H. *Studies in the Psychology of Sex*. Vol. 1: *Sexual Inversion*. [2nd, i.e. 1st public, edition]. London: The University Press, Watford, 1897.

*Ellis, H. *Études de psychologie sexuelle II: L'inversion sexuelle*. Édition française, revue et augmentée par l'auteur. Traduite par A. van Gennep. Paris: Mercure de France, 1909.

Estienne, H. *Apologie pour Hérodote*, avec introduction et notes par P. Ristelhuber. Paris: Lisieux, 1879.

*Fabre, J.H. *Souvenirs entomologiques. Études sur l'instinct et les mœurs des insectes*. Paris: C. Delagrave, 1879–1910.

Féré, C. *L'Instinct sexuel, évolution et dissolution*. Paris: F. Alcan, 1899.

Féré, C. *The Evolution and Dissolution of the Sexual Instinct*. Complete authorised translation of the revised 2nd edn. Paris: C. Carrington, 1904.

†Fielding, H. *The History of Amelia*. London: Hutchinson, 1905.

Foucault, M. *La Volonté de savoir*. Paris: Gallimard, 1976.

Fouillée, A. *La Philosophie de Platon*. 2ᵉ éd. augmentée. Paris: Hachette, 1888–9.

*Fouillée, A. *La Philosophie de Socrate*. Paris: Ladrange, 1874.

*Freud, S. 'Origine et développement de la psychanalyse', *Revue de Genève*, no. 6–8, December 1920–February 1921 (pp. 865–75; 80–7; 195–220. Preceded by: E. Claparède, 'Freud et la psychanalyse', no. 6, pp. 846–64).

*Freud, S. *Trois Essais sur la théorie de la sexualité*. Tr. Dr Reverchon. Paris: NRF, 1923.

†Galiani, F., l'abbé. *Lettres de l'abbé Galiani à Madame d'Épinay . . . publiées . . . avec notice biographique par E. Asse. Paris: G. Charpentier, 1881.

†Galiani, F., l'abbé. *Correspondance . . . Nouvelle édition . . . par L. Perey et G. Maugras. Paris: C. Lévy, 1881.

*Gautier, T. *Mademoiselle de Maupin*. Paris: E. Renduel, 1835–6.

*Gautier, T. *Le Roi Candaule*. Préface par Anatole France, illustré de vingt-et-une compositions par Paul Avril. Paris: A. Ferroud, 1893.

†Gibbon, E. *The History of the Decline and Fall of the Roman Empire*. Ed. . . . J.B. Bury. London: Methuen, 1896–1900.

†Gibbon, E. *Histoire de la décadence et de la chute de l'Empire romain*, traduite . . . nouvelle édition . . . précédée d'une notice . . . et accompagnée de notes . . . par M.F. Guizot. Paris: Maradan, 1812.

Giffen, L.A. *Theory of Profane Love among the Arabs: The Development of the Genre*. New York: New York University Press, 1971.

Goethe, J.W. von. *Élégies romaines de Goethe, suivies de ses Épigrammes, Ballades et Épîtres . . . traduites par M. de Wolffers. Paris: Veuve Dondey-Dupré, 1837.

Goethe, J.W. von. *Épigrammes (Venise 1790)*, seule traduction complète par Ralph Schropp. Paris: A. Ghio, 1889.

*Goethe, J.W. von. *Wilhelm Meister*, traduit par M.T. Gautier fils. Paris: G. Charpentier, 1874.

*Gosse, E. *Critical Kit-Kats*. London: Heinemann, 1896.

Gould, T. *Platonic Love*. London: Routledge, 1963.

Goulet, A. *Fiction et vie sociale dans l'œuvre d'A. Gide*. Paris: Minard, 1985.

Gourmont, R. de. *La Culture des idées*. 3ᵉ éd. Paris: Mercure de France, 1900.

*Gourmont, R. de. *Dialogues des amateurs sur les choses du temps 1905–7*. [Épilogues IV série.] 2ᵉ éd. Paris: Mercure de France, 1907.

Gourmont, R. de. *Épilogues I–V*. Paris: Mercure de France, 1903–10.

Gourmont, R. de. *Épilogues* [1912]. (Volume complémentaire.) Paris: Mercure de France, 1913.

Gourmont, R. de. *Lettres à l'Amazone*. Paris: G. Crès, 1914.

Gourmont, R. de. *Le Livre des masques*. Paris: Mercure de France, 1896–8.

SELECT BIBLIOGRAPHY

*Gourmont, R. de. *Physique de l'amour. Essai sur l'instinct sexuel*. Paris: Mercure de France, 1903.

Gourmont, R. de. *Promenades littéraires*. 6e série. Paris: Mercure de France. 1926.

Gourmont, R. de. *Promenades philosophiques*. 3e série. Paris: Mercure de France, 1909.

Grand-Carteret, J. *Derrière 'Lui' (L'Homosexualité en Allemagne)*. Paris: E. Bernard, [1908].

Grieve, J. 'Love in the Work of A. Gide', *Australian Journal of French Studies*, III 1966, pp. 162–79.

*Grimm, H. *Leben Michelangelos*. Hanover: C. Rümpler, 1860–3.

Grosskurth, P. *Havelock Ellis. A Biography*. London: A. Lane, 1980.

Grosskurth, P. *J.A. Symonds*. London: Longmans, 1964.

Guérard, A.J. *A. Gide*, 2nd edn. Cambridge, Mass.: Harvard University Press, 1969.

Guérin, D. *Shakespeare et Gide en correctionnelle?* Paris: Les Éditions du Scorpion (Collection Alternance), 1959.

Guthrie, W.K.C. *A History of Greek Philosophy*. Cambridge: CUP, 1967–81.

Hacquard, G. *Histoire d'une institution française: l'École Alsacienne. Naissance d'une école libre 1871–1891*. Paris: Garnier, 1982.

*Hafiz. *Quelques odes*, traduites pour la première fois en français par A.L.M. Nicolas. Paris: E. Leroux, 1898.

Hafiz. *Les Poèmes érotiques ou Ghazels de Chems ed Dîn Mohammed Hâfiz . . . notes . . . par Arthur Guy*. (Les Joyaux de l'Orient, II.) Paris: P. Geuthner, 1927.

*Hafiz. *Der Diwan* . . . übersetzt von J. von Hammer. Stuttgart and Tübingen: J.G. Cotta, 1812–13.

*Halévy, D. *La Vie de F. Nietzsche*. Paris: C. Lévy, [1909].

*Herder, J.G. von. *Ideen zur Philosophie der Geschichte der Menschheit*, mit Einleitung und Anmerkungen herausgegeben von J. Schmidt. Leipzig: F.A. Brockhaus, 1869.

*Herder, J.G. von. *Idées sur la philosophie de l'histoire de l'humanité*, traduit . . . par E. Quinet. Paris: F.G. Levrault, 1827–8.

Hirschfeld, M. *Le Troisième Sexe. Les homosexuels de Berlin*. Paris: Jules Rousset, 1908.

Hunt, H.J. *Balzac's 'Comédie humaine'*. London: Athlone Press, 1959.

*Huysmans, K.J. *À rebours*. Paris: G. Charpentier, 1884.

Hyde, H.M. *Oscar Wilde*. London: Eyre Methuen, 1976.

Ireland, G.W. *André Gide: A Study of his Creative Writings*. Oxford: Clarendon Press, 1970.

Iseler, P. See correspondence with P. Louÿs.

Jacob, P.E. *R. de Gourmont*. Urbana: University of Illinois Press, 1931. (= University of Illinois Studies in Language and Literature, vol. 16 (2).)

*Jacob, P.L. [pseudonym of Paul Lacroix]. *Curiosités de l'histoire de France. Deuxième série. Procès célèbres. Le Maréchal de Rays. Gutemberg. La Comtesse de Chateaubriant. La Veuve de Molière. Le Marquis de Sade. Gamain. Marat. André Chénier*. Paris: A. Delahays, 1858.

*Jacobsen, J.P. *Entre la vie et le rêve. Niels Lyhne*. Traduit du danois par Madame R. Rémusat. Paris: C. Lévy, 1898.

†Jacoby, P. *Études sur la sélection chez l'homme*. Avant propos par M. Gabriel Tarde. 2e éd., revue et augmentée. Paris: F. Alcan, 1904. (1st edn: Paris: Germer Baillière, 1881.)

*Kabir. *One Hundred Poems of Kabir*, trans. Rabindranath Tagore, assisted by E. Underhill. London: Macmillan, 1915.

Kaplan, J. *Walt Whitman. A Life*. New York: Simon & Schuster, 1980.

Krafft-Ebing, R. von. *Psychopathia sexualis, avec recherches spéciales sur l'inversion sexuelle*. Traduit sur la huitième éd. allemande par Émile Laurent et Sigismond

Csapo. Paris: Georges Carré, 1895.

†Labé, Louise. *Œuvres*, publiées avec une étude et des notes par Prosper Blanchemain. Paris: Librairie des Bibliophiles, 1875.

Labuda, A. *Les Thèmes de l'adolescence dans l'œuvre d'A. Gide*. Poznań, 1968–9.

Lacroix, Paul. See Jacob, P.L.

Lalou, R. *A. Gide*. Strasbourg: J. Heissler, 1928.

Lambert, J. *Gide familier*. Paris: Julliard, 1958.

Lang, R. *A. Gide et la pensée allemande*. Paris: Plon, 1955.

*Last, J. *Zuydersée*. Paris: Gallimard, 1938.

Laupts, Dr [pseudonym of G. Saint-Paul]. *L'Homosexualité et les types homosexuels*. Nouvelle édition de 'Perversions et perversité sexuelles'. Préface d'É. Zola. Paris: Vigot frères, 1910. (1st edn: Paris: Georges Carré, 1896.)

*Lautréamont [pseudonym of Isidore Ducasse]. *Les Chants de Maldoror*. Paris and Brussels: en vente chez tous les libraires, 1874.

*Leonardo da Vinci. *Textes choisis: pensées, théories, préceptes, fables et facéties*, traduits . . . avec une introduction par Peladan. Paris: Mercure de France, 1907.

*Lepelletier, E. *Paul Verlaine. Sa vie – son œuvre*. Paris: Mercure de France, 1907.

Lerner, A.L. *Passing the Love of Women: A Study of Gide's* Saül *and its Biblical Roots*. Lanham, Md: University Press of America, 1980.

Lilja, S. *Homosexuality in Republican and Augustan Rome*. Helsinki: Societas Scientiarum Fennica, 1983 (= Commentationes Humanarum Litterarum, 74).

*Le Livre d'amour des anciens, éd. par B. de Villeneuve. Paris: Bibliothèque des curieux, 1912.

Louÿs, P. *Œuvres complètes*. Paris: Éditions Montaigne, 1929–30.

Lucian. *Les Dissertations amoureuses de Lucien*. Introduction, notes et appendice par B. de Villeneuve. Paris: Bibliothèque des curieux, 1909.

*Lucian. *Scènes de la vie des courtisanes*, [trans. P. Louÿs]. Paris: à la Sphinx, 1894.

McLaren, J.C. *The Theater of A. Gide*. Baltimore: The Johns Hopkins University Press, 1953.

*Malthus, T.R. *Essai sur le principe de population*, traduit . . . par Mm. Pierre et Guillaume Prévost . . . notes par M. Joseph Garnier. Paris: Guillaumin, 1845. (2nd edn: 1852.)

Mantegazza, P. *L'Amour dans l'humanité. Essai d'une ethnologie de l'amour*. Traduit par E. Chesneau. Paris: Fetscherin et Chuit, 1886.

Marchand, M. *Le Complexe pédagogique et didactique d'A. Gide*. [Oran], 1954.

Marlowe, C. *Édouard II* . . . adaptation de G. Eekhoud. Brussels: Éd. de la Société Nouvelle, 1896.

Martin, C. *La Maturité d'A. Gide*. Paris: Klincksieck, 1977.

†Martin du Gard, R. *Un Taciturne*. Paris: Gallimard, 1948.

*Meier, M.H.F. *Histoire de l'amour grec dans l'antiquité*, augmentée . . . par L.R. de Pogey-Castries. Paris: Stendhal et Cie., 1930.

Méténier, O. *Vertus et vices allemands. Les Berlinois chez eux*. Paris: Albin Michel, 1904.

Meyer, J. *Homosexuality and Literature 1890–1930*. London: Athlone Press, 1977.

†Michelet, J. *L'Amour*. 5e éd. Paris: Hachette, 1861.

*Michelet, J. *Histoire romaine*. 2e éd. revue et augmentée. Paris: Hachette, 1833.

Minuchihri. Texte, traduction et notes . . . par A. de Biberstein Kazimirski. Paris: Klincksieck, 1886.

Moll, A. *Les Perversions de l'instinct génital. Étude sur l'inversion sexuelle basée sur des documents officiels* . . . Traduit . . . par le Dr Pactet et le Dr Romme. Paris: G. Carré, 1893.

Mondor, H. *Les Premiers Temps d'une amitié*. Monaco: Éditions du Rocher, 1947.

SELECT BIBLIOGRAPHY

*Montaigne, M. de. *Les Essais*, publiés d'après l'édition de 1588 avec les variantes de 1595 . . . par H. Motheau et D. Jouaust. Paris: Librairie des Bibliophiles, 1886–9.

*Montaigne, M. de. *Journal de voyage*, publié avec une introduction . . . par L. Lautrey. Paris: Hachette, 1906.

*Montesquieu, Baron de. *Œuvres complètes*, avec les variantes . . . et des notes nouvelles par E. Laboulaye. Paris: Garnier frères, 1875–9.

*Montesquieu, Baron de. *Correspondance*, publiée par François Gebelin, avec la collaboration de M. André Morize. Bordeaux: Impr. Gounouilhou, 1914.

*Montesquieu, Baron de. *Voyages*. Bordeaux: G. Gounouilhou, 1894–6.

Mouret, F. 'La Première Rencontre d'A. Gide et d'Oscar Wilde', *French Studies*, XXII 1 January 1968, pp. 37–40.

*Müller, F. von. *Goethes Unterhaltungen mit dem Kanzler Friedrich von Müller*. Herausgegeben von C.A.H. Burkhardt. 2e Aufl. Stuttgart: J.G. Cotta, 1898.

Naville, A. *Bibliographie des écrits d'André Gide. Depuis 1891 jusqu'en 1952*. Paris. Guy Le Prat, [1952].

*Nerval, G. de. *Voyage en Orient*.6e éd. Paris: G. Charpentier, 1862.

†Nietzsche, F.W. *Humain, trop humain*. (Première partie.) Traduit par A.M. Desrousseaux. 4e éd. Paris: Mercure de France, 1899.

Nietzsche, F. *Le Voyageur et son ombre. Opinions et sentences mêlées*. (*Humain, trop humain*, deuxième partie.) Traduits par H. Albert. Paris: Mercure de France, 1902.

*Nietzsche, F.W. *La Volonté de puissance* . . . traduit par H. Albert. Paris: Mercure de France, 1903.

O'Brien, J. *The Novel of Adolescence in France*. New York: Columbia University Press, 1937.

O'Brien, J. *Portrait of A. Gide*. London: Secker & Warburg, 1953.

O'Brien, J. 'A Rapprochement: Monsieur André Gide and Lautréamont', *Romanic Review*, XXVIII February 1937, pp. 54–8.

Oliver, A. 'Michel, Job, Pierre, Paul: intertextualité de la lecture dans *L'Immoraliste* d'A. Gide', *Archives A. Gide* 4. Paris: Lettres Modernes, 1979.

*Omar Khayyam. *Les Quatrains*, traduits du persan par J.B. Nicolas. Paris: L'Imprimerie Impériale, 1867.

Omar Khayyam. *Les Quatrains*, traduits . . . avec une introduction et des notes, par C. Grolleau. Paris: C. Carrington, 1902.

O'Neill, K. 'Gide lecteur de Schopenhauer', *Cahiers André Gide I*. Paris: Gallimard, 1969. (pp. 115–22.)

Painter, G. *Marcel Proust. A Biography*. London: Chatto & Windus, 1959–65.

*Paris, P. *La Sculpture antique*. Paris: Quantin, [1889].

*Pascal, B. *Pensées* . . . avec une introduction et des notes par Léon Brunschvicg. Paris: Hachette, 1904.

*Pater, W. *Studies in the History of the Renaissance*. London: Macmillan, 1873.

*Peladan, J. *À cœur perdu*. Paris: G. Edinger, 1888.

*Peladan, J. *Cœur en peine*. Paris: E. Dentu, 1890.

Peyrefitte, R. *L'Exilé de Capri*. Paris: Flammarion, 1959.

Pierre-Quint, L. *André Gide*. Paris: Stock, 1952.

†Plutarch. *Les Vies des hommes illustres, grecs et romains* . . . translatées de grec en françois, par maistre J. Amyot . . . et depuis en ceste seconde édition reveuës et corrigées. Paris: M. de Vascosan, 1565.

*Plutarch. *Vies des hommes illustres*, traduction nouvelle par A. Pierron. 6e éd., entièrement revue et corrigée. Paris: G. Charpentier, [1882].

Plutarch. *Dialogue sur l'amour (Eroticos)*. Texte et traduction avec une introduction et notes par R. Flacelière. Paris: Les Belles Lettres, 1952.

Pollard, P. [ed.] *André Gide et l'Angleterre*. Actes du Colloque de Londres 22–24 novembre 1985. London: Birkbeck College, 1986.

Polti, G. 'Les 36 Situations dramatiques (suite): XXVIe situation. Crimes d'amour. (L'Épris–l'Aimé)', *Mercure de France*, XII September 1894, pp. 51–4.

†Proust, M. *À la recherche du temps perdu*. Texte établi et présenté par P. Clarac et A. Ferré. Paris: Bibliothèque de la Pléiade, 1954.

Proust, M. *Contre Sainte-Beuve, suivi de Nouveaux Mélanges*. Préface de Bernard de Fallois. Paris: Gallimard, 1954.

Proust, M. *Correspondance*. Texte établi, présenté et annoté par P. Kolb. XIII, 1914. Paris: Plon, 1985. (Contains correspondence with H. Ghéon and A. Gide.)

Rachilde [pseudonym of Marguerite Eymery, afterwards Vallette]. *Les Hors-Nature*. Paris: Mercure de France, 1897.

Raffalovich, A. 'Les Groupes uranistes à Paris et à Berlin', *Archives d'anthropologie criminelle, de criminologie et de psychologie normale et pathologique*, XIX 1904, pp. 926–36.

Raffalovich, A. *Uranisme et unisexualité. Étude sur différentes manifestations de l'instinct sexuel*. Lyon and Paris: Storck et Masson, 1896.

*Ramiro, E. *Catalogue descriptif et analytique de l'œuvre gravé de Félicien Rops*. Paris: Librairie Conquêt, 1887. (2nd edn: Brussels: Deman, 1893; *Supplément*: Paris: Floury, 1895.)

Rees, G. *Rémy de Gourmont. Essai de biographie intellectuelle*. Paris: Boivin, 1940.

Rey, E. 'Métaphysique de l'amour', *Mercure de France*, LXXVIII April and May 1909, pp. 193–215, 428–42.

Ribbing, S. *L'Hygiène sexuelle et ses conséquences morales . . . traduit du suédois*. Paris: F. Alcan, 1895.

*Ribot, T. *Les Maladies de la personnalité*. Paris: F. Alcan, 1885.

*Ribot, T. *La Philosophie de Schopenhauer*. Paris: Librairie Germer-Baillière, 1874.

*Rimbaud, A. *Oeuvres*: préface de Paul Claudel. Paris: Mercure de France, 1912.

Rivers, J.E. *Proust and the Art of Love*. New York: Columbia University Press, 1980.

Rops, F. See Bory and Ramiro.

Ross, F.E. *Goethe in Modern France. With Special Reference to Maurice Barrès, Paul Bourget, and André Gide*. Urbana: University of Illinois Press, 1937. (= University of Illinois Studies in Language and Literature, vol. 21 (3/4).)

*Rouveyre, A. *Le Reclus et le retors: Gourmont et Gide*. Paris: G. Crès, 1927.

Royle, T. *Death before Dishonour: The True Story of Fighting Mac*. Edinburgh: Mainstream, 1982.

Ruggiero, G. *The Boundaries of Eros. Sex Crime and Sexuality in Renaissance Venice*. Oxford: OUP, 1985.

*Ruskin, J. *Sésame et les lys . . . traduction, notes et préface par Marcel Proust*. Paris: Mercure de France, 1906.

*Rutherford, M. *The Autobiography of Mark Rutherford*, edited by his friend Reuben Shapcott. London: Hodder & Stoughton, [1913].

Rysselberghe, M. van. *Les Cahiers de la Petite Dame (1918–1951)*. Paris: Gallimard, 1973–7. (= Cahiers A. Gide, 4–7.)

Sa'di. *Gulistan, ou le Parterre-de-fleurs . . . traduit . . . par N. Semelet*. Paris: Imprimerie Royale, 1834.

Sa'di. *The Gulistan or Rose Garden of Sa'di*, trans. E. Rehatsek. London: G. Allen & Unwin, 1964.

*Sainte-Beuve, C.A. *Causeries du lundi*. 3e éd. Paris: Garnier frères, 1882–5.

Saint-Paul, G. See Laupts.

*Sanson, A. *Traité de zootechnie*. 3ᵉ éd. Paris: Librairie agricole de la maison rustique, 1882–6.

*Schlumberger, J. *Heureux qui comme Ulysse*... Paris: Cahiers de la Quinzaine, 1906.

*Schopenhauer, A. *Le Monde comme volonté et comme représentation*, traduit... pour la première fois par J.A. Cantacuzène. Leipzig and Paris: F.A. Brockhaus, 1886.

Schrenck-Notzing, A. von. *Ein Beitrag zur Aetiologie der conträren Sexualempfindung*. Vienna: Hölder, 1895.

Senancour, E.P. de. *De l'amour selon les lois primordiales et selon les convenances des sociétés modernes*. [Éd. par C.A.V. de Boisjolin]. Paris: Mercure de France, 1911.

*Shakespeare, W. *Œuvres complètes*. Traduites par F.-V. Hugo. Paris: Pagnerre, 1859.

*Spinoza, B. *Éthique*... text latin soigneusement revu, traduction nouvelle, notice et notes par C. Appuhn. Paris: Garnier frères, [1908]. (= *Œuvres*, vol. IV.)

Stambolian, G. and Marks, E. [eds.] *Homosexualities and French Literature. Cultural Contexts/Critical Texts*... Preface by Richard Howard. Ithaca and London: Cornell University Press, 1979.

Steel, D.A. 'Les Débuts de la psychanalyse dans les lettres françaises: 1914–1922. Apollinaire, Cendrars, "Le Mercure de France", "La Revue de l'Époque", Morand, Bourget, Lenormand', *Revue d'histoire littéraire de la France*, January–February 1979, pp. 62–89.

Steel, D.A. 'Gide et Freud', *Revue d'histoire littéraire de la France*, January–February 1977, pp. 48–74.

Steel, D.A. 'Gide et Lautréamont', *Revue des sciences humaines*, XXXIII (130) April–June 1968, pp. 279–94.

Steel, D.A. 'Le Thème de l'enfance dans l'œuvre d'A. Gide'. Thèse: Université de Paris VII, 12 janvier 1974. (Mimeograph.)

Stekel, W. *Les États d'angoisse nerveux et leur traitement*... traduction française du Dr Lucien Hahn. Paris: Payot, 1930.

Stekel, W. *Onanie und Homosexualität (Die homosexuelle Parapathie)*. Vienna: Urban & Schwarzenberg, 1917.

*Stevenson, R.L. *In the South Seas, being an account of experiences and observations in the Marquesas, Paumotus and Gilbert Islands in the course of two cruises, on the yacht 'Casco' (1888) and the schooner 'Equator' (1889)*. London: Chatto & Windus, 1900.

*Stevenson, R.L. *The Letters*... selected and edited with notes... by S. Colvin. London: Methuen, 1899.

Stora-Lamarre, A. *L'Enfer de la IIIᵉ République. Censeurs et pornographes (1881–1914)*. Paris: Éditions Imago, 1990.

Storzer, G.H. 'The Homosexual Paradigm in Balzac, Gide and Genet', in G. Stambolian and E. Marks (q.v.), pp. 186–209.

*Strabo. *Géographie*, traduite par A. Tardieu. Paris: Hachette, 1867–90.

Symonds, J.A. *The Letters*, ed. H.M. Schueller and R.L. Peters. Detroit: Wayne State University Press, 1969.

Symonds, J.A. *Walt Whitman. A Study*. London: J.C. Nimmo, 1893.

*Tagore, R. *Hungry Stones and Other Stories*. London: Macmillan, 1916.

*Taine, H. *Essais de critique et d'histoire*. Paris: Hachette, 1858.

†Taine, H. *Histoire de la littérature anglaise*. 3ᵉ éd. Paris: Hachette, 1873–4.

*Taine, H. *Philosophie de l'art en Grèce*. 2ᵉ éd. Paris: Librairie Germer Baillière et Cie., 1883.

Tardieu, A. *Étude médico-légale sur les attentats aux mœurs*. 7ᵉ éd. [augmentée]. Paris: J.B. Baillière et fils, 1878.

Tarnovsky, V.M. *L'Instinct sexuel et ses manifestations morbides au double point de vue *de la jurisprudence et de la psychiatrie.* Traduction française, suivie d'une bibliographie des ouvrages traitant de l'inversion sexuelle. Préface par le professeur Lacassagne. Paris: C. Carrington, 1904.

Thomson, J.A. *Heredity.* London: Bliss, Sands & Co., 1908. (2nd augmented edn: 1912.)

*Thomson, J.A. *Study of Animal Life.* London: J. Murray, 1892.

Thomson, J.A. and Geddes, P. *L'Évolution du sexe,* traduit par Henry de Varigny. Paris: Veuve Babé, 1892. (= Bibliothèque évolutionniste III.)

Thornhill, R. and Alcock, J. *The Evolution of Insect Mating Systems.* Cambridge, Mass.: Harvard University Press, 1984.

*Traubel, H. *With Walt Whitman in Camden (March 28–July 14 1888).* New York: M. Kennerley, 1915.

*Verlaine, P. *Femmes.* [Brussels], '1891'.

Verlaine, P. *Femmes; Hombres.* Édition établie, présentée et annotée par Jean-Paul Corsetti et Jean-Pierre Giusto. Paris: Le Livre à venir, 1985.

Villeneuve, B. de. See *Le Livre d'amour des anciens.*

†Voltaire. *Dictionnaire philosophique* . . . avec introduction, variantes et notes par J. Benda. Texte établi par R. Naves. Paris: Garnier, 1954.

Walker, D.H. 'L'Inspiration orientale des *Nourritures terrestres*', *Comparative Literature,* XXVI (3) 1974, pp. 203–19.

*Ward, L.F. *Sociologie pure* . . . traduite . . . par Fernand Weil. Paris: V. Giard et E. Brière, 1906.

Watson-Williams, H. A. *Gide and the Greek Myth.* Oxford: Clarendon Press, 1967.

*Waxweiler, É. 'La Modification des instincts et particulièrement des instincts sociaux à propos des variations expérimentales de F. Houssay', *Bulletin et Mémoire de la Société d'Anthropologie de Bruxelles,* 26 1907, pp. clxxxii–cxciii.

Weeks, G. *Coming Out. Homosexual Politics in Britain, from the Nineteenth Century to the Present.* London: Quartet Books, 1977.

Weindel, H. de and Fischer, F.P. *L'Homosexualité en Allemagne.* Paris: F. Juven, 1908.

*Whitman, W. *Feuilles d'herbe.* Traduction intégrale d'après l'édition définitive par Léon Bazalgette. Paris: Mercure de France, 1909.

Whitman, W. *Poèmes choisis,* traduits et précédés d'une introduction nouvelle par Léon Bazalgette. Poitiers: 1912.

Whitman, W. *Poèmes.* Version française de Léon Bazalgette. Paris: F. Rieder, 1914.

*Whitman, W. *Œuvres choisies,* poèmes et proses traduits par Jules Laforgue . . . A. Gide [and others]. Paris: NRF, 1918.

Whitman, W. *Calamus, poèmes.* Version nouvelle de L. Bazalgette. Geneva: Éd. du Sablier, 1919.

Whitman, W. *Six poèmes* . . . version nouvelle de L. Bazalgette. Paris: A.J. Gonon, 1919.

Wilde, O. *The Works,* ed. G.F. Maine. London: Collins, 1948.

*Wilde, O. *De Profundis. Aufzeichnungen und Briefe aus dem Zuchthaus in Reading.* Herausgegeben und eingeleitet von Max Meyerfield. Berlin: S. Fischer, 1905.

†Winckelmann, J.J. *Histoire de l'art chez les anciens,* [trans. Huber and Jansen]. Paris: Jansen et Gide, 1790–1803.

Wolff, C. *Magnus Hirschfeld. A Portrait of a Pioneer in Sexology.* London: Quartet Books, 1986.

Worms, R. *La Sexualité dans les naissances françaises.* Paris: M. Giard et E. Brière, 1912.

*Yourcenar, M. *Alexis, ou le traité du vain combat.* Paris: Au sans pareil, 1929.

INDEX

Items which occur very frequently have been indexed selectively.

Mythological and historical persons and imaginative representations of them are generally included together under the same main heading.

INDEX

INDEX

INDEX

INDEX

INDEX